BUSINESS MATHEMATICS TODAY

Arthur H. Boisselle
PIKE'S PEAK COMMUNITY COLLEGE

Donald M. Freeman
PIKE'S PEAK COMMUNITY COLLEGE

Lyle V. Brenna
LATE PROFESSOR OF MANAGEMENT
PIKE'S PEAK COMMUNITY COLLEGE

McGraw-Hill Publishing Company
New York   St. Louis   San Francisco   Auckland   Bogotá   Caracas   Hamburg
Lisbon   London   Madrid   Mexico   Milan   Montreal   New Delhi
Oklahoma City   Paris   San Juan   São Paulo   Singapore   Sydney   Tokyo   Toronto

BUSINESS MATHEMATICS TODAY

Copyright © 1990 by McGraw-Hill, Inc. All rights reserved. Printed in the United States of America. Except as permitted under the United States Copyright Act of 1976, no part of this publication may be reproduced or distributed in any form or by any means, or stored in a data base or retrieval system, without the prior written permission of the publisher.

2 3 4 5 6 7 8 9 SEM SEM   9 4 3 2 1 0

ISBN {STUDENT EDITION} 0-07-557061-0
ISBN {TEACHER'S EDITION} 0-07-006440-7

This book was set in Palatino by Ruttle, Shaw & Wetherill, Inc.
The editors were Robert A. Weinstein, Anne B. Wightman, and Jack Maisel;
the designer was Nancy Blodget;
the production supervisor was Michael Weinstein.
Project supervision was done by Carnes Publication Services, Inc.
Semline, Inc., was printer and binder.

Library of Congress Cataloging-in-Publication Data

Boisselle, Arthur H., (date).
    Business mathematics today / Arthur H. Boisselle, Donald M. Freeman, Lyle V. Brenna.
        p.   cm.
    Includes index.
    1. Business mathematics.   I. Freeman, Donald M., (date).
II. Brenna, Lyle V., (date).   III. Title.
HF5691.B668 1990
    650'.01'513—dc20   89-2659
ISBN (SE) 0-07-557061-0
ISBN (TE) 0-07-006440-7

Dedication

This book is dedicated to the very special people in our lives: Ruth Brenna and the Brenna family, Gary, Linda, Janice, and Jim; to Dorla Boisselle and the Boisselle family, Rene Ann, Dale, and Cheryl; to Marilyn Freeman and the Freeman family, Peggy, Deborah, and Mark.

A Special Memorial

Lyle V. Brenna
(1919–1986)

During the development of this text, we were saddened by the death of our colleague Lyle Brenna. We wish to remember him as he was—a man of excellence, a foremost educator, a loving husband and father, and a dear friend. His sense of humor and his ability to cut through the fog to deal with realism were special. He was a person who was able to create new ideas, mold solutions, and leave a mark of friendship on all who knew him.

Contents

Preface ... xi

PART I BASIC MATHEMATICS AND PROBLEM SOLVING ... 1

CHAPTER 1 Whole Number Mathematics ... 3

1.1 The Decimal Number System ... 4
1.2 Addition ... 8
1.3 Subtraction ... 11
1.4 Multiplication ... 14
1.5 Division ... 17
1.6 Approximating and Estimating ... 21
1.7 The Calculator ... 24
Key Terms ... 30
Looking Back ... 30
Let's Review ... 31
Chapter Test ... 31

CHAPTER 2 Fractions ... 34

2.1 Fractions in Use ... 35
2.2 Improper Fractions and Mixed Numbers ... 39
2.3 The Common Denominator ... 42
2.4 Multiplication and Division of Fractions and Mixed Numbers ... 48
Key Terms ... 53
Looking Back ... 53
Let's Review ... 53
Chapter Test ... 54

CHAPTER 3 Decimals and Percents — 56

- 3.1 The Decimal Point — 57
- 3.2 Converting Fractions to Decimals — 59
- 3.3 Changing Fractions and Decimals to Percents — 64
- *Key Terms* — 69
- *Looking Back* — 69
- *Let's Review* — 70
- *Chapter Test* — 70

CHAPTER 4 Problem Solving — 72

- 4.1 Problem Solving Strategies — 73
- 4.2 Number Progressions — 73
- 4.3 Stating Problem Variables — 77
- 4.4 Identifying Problem Variables — 80
- 4.5 Problem Solving Techniques — 83
- 4.6 Solving Problems with Formulas — 84
- 4.7 Solving Problems for Changing Values — 92
- *Key Terms* — 98
- *Looking Back* — 98
- *Let's Review* — 99
- *Chapter Test* — 100

PART II MATHEMATICS FOR OFFICE TRANSACTIONS — 101

CHAPTER 5 Bank Records — 102

- 5.1 Checking Accounts — 103
- 5.2 Checks — 108
- 5.3 The Check Register — 111
- 5.4 Bank Statement Reconciliation — 115
- *Key Terms* — 123
- *Looking Back* — 123
- *Let's Review* — 123
- *Chapter Test* — 126

CHAPTER 6 Payroll — 129

- 6.1 Computing Gross Earnings — 130
- 6.2 Deductions — 140
- 6.3 Forms and Records — 146
- *Key Terms* — 153
- *Looking Back* — 153
- *Let's Review* — 153
- *Chapter Test* — 156

CHAPTER 7 Customer Invoicing and Statements — 158

- 7.1 Purchasing Supplies and Merchandise — 159
- 7.2 Calculating and Preparing the Monthly Statement — 166
- 7.3 Quantity Discounts — 172
- 7.4 Trade Discounts — 175
- 7.5 Cash Discounts — 182
- *Key Terms* — 191
- *Looking Back* — 191

		Let's Review	192
		Chapter Test	193

PART III INTEREST AND PERSONAL FINANCE 197

CHAPTER 8 Simple Interest 199

8.1	Simple Interest	200
8.2	The Time Fraction	203
8.3	Solving for Other Factors in the Simple Interest Formula	211
8.4	Discounting Negotiable Instruments	216
	Key Terms	224
	Looking Back	224
	Let's Review	224
	Chapter Test	225

CHAPTER 9 Personal Finance 227

9.1	Credit Cards and Revolving Charge Accounts	228
9.2	Installment Loans and Purchases	236
9.3	Loan Payoff	250
	Key Terms	255
	Looking Back	256
	Let's Review	256
	Chapter Test	257

CHAPTER 10 Mortgages, Taxes, and Insurance 259

10.1	Home Mortgages	260
10.2	Property Taxes	268
10.3	Insurance	273
	Key Terms	290
	Looking Back	290
	Let's Review	290
	Chapter Test	293

PART IV FINANCIAL APPLICATIONS 295

CHAPTER 11 Depreciation and Inventory Valuation 297

11.1	Depreciation	298
11.2	Accelerated Cost Recovery System (ACRS) Method	319
11.3	Inventory Valuation	325
	Key Terms	333
	Looking Back	334
	Let's Review	334
	Chapter Test	336

CHAPTER 12 Investments 338

12.1	Compound Interest	339
12.2	Annuities	347
12.3	Present Value	353

12.4	Stocks	357
12.5	Bonds	365
	Key Terms	368
	Looking Back	369
	Let's Review	369
	Chapter Test	370

PART V RETAIL PRICING AND PROFIT 373

CHAPTER 13 Pricing the Product 375

13.1	Markup (Pricing on Cost)	376
13.2	Margin (Pricing on Retail)	380
13.3	Markdown	385
13.4	Converting Markup to Margin	388
13.5	Converting Margin to Markup	392
	Key Terms	395
	Looking Back	395
	Let's Review	395
	Chapter Test	396

CHAPTER 14 Retail Operations 398

14.1	Inventory Turnover	399
14.2	Open to Buy	404
14.3	Average Margin and Maintained Margin	408
	Key Terms	413
	Looking Back	413
	Let's Review	414
	Chapter Test	415

CHAPTER 15 Determining Profit 417

15.1	Types of Cost	418
15.2	Production Price and Markup	424
15.3	Gross and Net Profit	429
	Key Terms	434
	Looking Back	434
	Let's Review	435
	Chapter Test	437

PART VI MATHEMATICS FOR BUSINESS DECISIONS 439

CHAPTER 16 Financial Statements and Ratios 441

16.1	Vertical Analysis	442
16.2	Horizontal Analysis	451
16.3	Ratios	458
	Key Terms	464
	Looking Back	464
	Let's Review	465
	Chapter Test	467

CHAPTER 17 Business Statistics and Graphs — 471

- 17.1 Statistical Measures — 472
- 17.2 Statistical Tables and Charts — 479
- 17.3 Presentation of Tables and Charts — 483
- 17.4 The Standard Deviation—Statistical Dispersion — 486
  - *Key Terms* — 492
  - *Looking Back* — 492
  - *Let's Review* — 492
  - *Chapter Test* — 493

APPENDIX A An Introduction to MICROPAK Software for Business Mathematics — A-1

- Useful Terms — A-1
- Loan Payment Schedule — A-2
- Descriptive Statistics — A-3
- Open to Buy — A-4
- Average Margin — A-6
- Breakeven Analysis — A-7
- Annuity Value — A-8
- Inventory Turnover — A-9
- Depreciation Schedule — A-9
- Determine Interest Rate — A-10
- Financial Ratios — A-11

APPENDIX B Breakeven Analysis — A-15

- Breakeven Graphical Method — A-15
- Breakeven Formula Method — A-18
- Let's Review — A-21

APPENDIX C Symbols, Weights, and Measures — A-23

- U.S. Symbols — A-23
- U.S. Weights and Measures — A-25
- Metric Conversions — A-29

APPENDIX D Reference Tables — A-33

- Social Security Employee Tax Table for 1988 — A-34
- Federal Income Tax Withholding Table, Weekly Payroll — A-36
- Federal Reserve Table for Computing Annual Percentage Rates for Monthly Payment Plans — A-40
- Compound Interest, Present Value, and Annuity Table — A-48

GLOSSARY — A-57

ANSWERS TO EVEN-NUMBERED PROBLEMS — A-65

PHOTO CREDITS — A-77

INDEX — I-1

Preface

Business Mathematics Today is designed to be a useful and flexible teaching tool to maximize the learning potential of the majority of students pursuing a business career. It will help instructors teach efficiently and effectively the business mathematics students need to succeed in such fields as accounting, management, sales, marketing, secretarial science, and office information technology.

After many years of teaching business mathematics, we found that the available textbooks presented mathematics without nurturing an understanding of business procedures. Using a nonalgebraic approach, this text-workbook reviews basic arithmetic skills, then progresses gradually to more advanced business topics including mortgages and taxes, depreciation, investments, financial statements, and business statistics and graphs. The focus on applications places mathematical skills in the context of business procedures and illustrates the need for these skills in the business world.

The topics are organized in a logical sequence with each new topic presented in a direct, conversational style using clear, step-by-step explanations. Check for Understanding exercises provide the instant feedback that students need to evaluate their own progress; Skill Exercises provide the practice necessary to reinforce learned skills; and Applications provide motivating, real-world problems.

Business Mathematics Today is divided into 17 chapters grouped in six parts. Each part provides ample drill of skills and applications. This makes *Business Mathematics Today* a flexible text that can be adapted to many teaching styles ranging from lecture classes to independent study.

Features That Show Real-World Applications

In *Business Mathematics Today* we provide students with a real sense of how they can apply their mathematical skills effectively in the business world. We use business terminology and real-world documents to motivate students and help them to feel comfortable with the many forms they are likely to encounter on the job. We show students how to approach new problems successfully by using techniques they already know.

Coming Up A brief introduction explaining the connection between material in the chapter and its application to the business world establishes a clear starting point for each chapter and motivation for what follows.

Business Documents We use the most up-to-date examples available of working documents, including checks, invoices, tax forms, insurance tables, and more. These documents can be used for in class reference and to reinforce the connection between the classroom and real on-the-job experiences students will encounter.

Calculator Tips The calculator has become a standard tool for anyone who deals with numbers on a daily basis. In addition to an instructional section on the use of the calculator in Chapter 1, we include 32 Calculator Tip boxes that illustrate correct and efficient use of the calculator in solving problems.

Applications Nearly 700 word problems teach students to apply the skills they are learning to realistic situations and to extract the necessary information from a word problem and set it up for solution. Selected applications are visually linked to business situations through carefully chosen photographs. Answers to the even-numbered problems are provided in the back of the text.

Features That Develop Skills and Understanding of Concepts

Learning Objectives Each chapter begins with a list of learning objectives. These help the instructor and student to focus on the most important skills in each chapter.

Concept Development Each new concept is explained thoroughly before the student is asked to apply it to a practical example.

Detailed Worked Examples Over 300 examples with special annotated solutions illustrate important skills and concepts. Each solution is displayed with parallel commentary that explains every step. This annotation anticipates students' questions and enhances their understanding of the concepts. Color is used carefully to highlight key procedures.

Check for Understanding After each set of worked examples, students are presented with two or three questions to check their understanding of the concept and mathematical skill just presented. The answers at the bottom of the page provide immediate feedback.

Skill Exercises Over 1000 skill exercises in 90 exercise sets provide ample drill for isolated mathematical skills. These exercise sets cover small "chunks" of material (there is often more than one set per section). They are presented using new terminology, but without the clutter associated with word problems. The student performs calculations as explained in the examples. This isolation and repetition of mathematical skills gives students a chance to master one set of skills before they apply it to more comprehensive word problems. Answers to the even-numbered exercises are provided in the back of the text.

Highlight Boxes Important ideas and formulas are displayed in color-screened boxes. This helps students to locate important information and facilitates review.

Problem Solving Strategy Throughout the book, 46 special boxes give students extra insight by providing shortcuts, practical hints, and alternative methods for solving problems.

End-of-Chapter Features

Key Terms A list of key terms with page references provides a checklist to help students review material found within each chapter.

Looking Back A comprehensive summary restates the important issues and concepts from each chapter. This capsule review helps put the material into perspective.

Let's Review At the end of each chapter is a set of review exercises covering the whole chapter. With nearly 300 additional exercises, these sets help to pull together the concepts and skills of each chapter. Answers to the even-numbered exercises are provided in the back of the text.

Chapter Test Each chapter concludes with a Chapter Test. Answers are *not* provided in the back of the book (the answers are in the Instructor's Edition), allowing instructors to assign the Chapter Test as a real test or as a review exercise set.

Additional Features

Appendixes Four appendixes provide additional detail on breakeven analysis; a review of symbols, weights, and measures; and complete tables for federal taxes, annual percentage rates, compound interest, present value, and annuity. Also included are special exercises designed for use with MICROPAK software, which is available as part of the teaching/learning package.

Glossary A glossary gives short definitions for all the important terms from the text.

The Accompanying Teaching/Learning Package

Instructor's Edition A separate teacher's edition includes answers to all exercises.

Instructor's Resource Manual This manual includes suggestions for five different syllabi, chapter outlines (with approximate time to cover), 100 transparency masters of skill exercises with answers, selected tables and forms, and answers to the printed tests.

Printed Tests A test manual, complimentary to adopters, provides 101 printed tests for use in the classroom: five per chapter, one of which is a multiple-choice test; two pretests and post-tests for Chapters 1–4; two midterms, and ten final exams, two for each of the syllabi recommended in the Instructor's Resource Manual.

Overhead Transparencies A packet of 50 two-color overhead transparencies specifically designed to help classroom presentation of key concepts is available free to adopters.

Computerized Test Bank A unique computer testing system for IBM and compatible microcomputers is available free to adopters. The testing system enables instructors to select from a data bank of over 1500 questions by selection, topic, question type, level of difficulty, and other criteria. In addition, instructors may add their own questions. A printed listing of the questions in the Computerized Test Bank is also available.

MICROPAK This computer disk contains utility software for solving ten different types of business problems covered in *Business Mathematics Today*. The programs, which run on IBM and compatible computers, can be used to solve any problem in the text. In addition, special exercises designed to be used with the software are provided in an appendix to the text.

Acknowledgments

Business Mathematics Today was created with the support of many people. Our sincerest thanks to the many friends, acquaintances, and business associates who shared their ideas with us.

We thank the many instructors of business mathematics who reviewed the manuscript during the development stages. Their encouragement, criticisms, and suggestions helped shape the book.

    James Burke, *Cuyahoga Community College*
    Dick Clark, *Portland Community College*
    James W. Cox, *Lane Community College*
    Ree Erickson, *Utah Technical College, Salt Lake*
    Carlton S. Everett, *Des Moines Area Community College*
    Arlen Gastineau, *Valencia Community College*
    Martha Griggs, *State Fair Community College*
    William Harwood, *Dutchess Community College*
    Patricia Hirschy, *Delaware Technical and Community College*
    Frederick Janke, *Tompkins-Cortland Community College*
    James Moore, *Mid-State Technical Institute*
    Gary Phillips, *Oakton College*
    Mary Robertson, *Midlands Technical College*
    Vicki Schell, *Pensacola Junior College*
    Ned Schillow, *Lehigh County Community College*
    John Snyder, *Sinclair Community College*
    Margene Sunderland, *Fayetteville Technical Community College*
    David Wheaton, *Terra Technical College*

Additional thanks to James Cox, Carlton S. Everett, and William Harwood for checking the accuracy of all the examples and exercises in the book, and to Carl Sonntag for checking the accuracy of the printed tests.

Our special recognition to Carl Sonntag and Robert Prall of Pike's Peak Community College, Mr. David Nord of Farmers Insurance, Steve Covalt and Gary Mosely of Covalt Reeves and Associates, P.C., Gene Dover of Century Bank, and Marie Nakayama and Paul Masar of Valley Bank for their helpful contributions. We are particularly grateful for the help of Dale Arthur Boisselle, who developed the software that accompanies the text.

Our deepest thanks to our editor Wayne Yuhasz for his patience, perception, and personal support throughout the evolution of this book. Seldom in our lives have we experienced the mutual sharing of ideas and ideals that brought this project to fruition. And a special thanks to developmental editors Robert Fiske and Anne Wightman for their exceptionally insightful suggestions, which helped to mold this project into one of excellence.

We wish to thank Robert Weinstein for making the transition of this project painless for the authors. He came into the project late, but showed dedication and offered the support needed to see it through to completion.

Without the skillful efforts of Ed Huddleston at Carnes Publication Services, this project would never have made it from manuscript to bound book. We are deeply indebted to him for the care and professional dedication with which he guided the project through production. Special thanks also to Geri Davis for her help with photo research.

We extend our warmest appreciation to Rene Ann Boisselle, Cheryl Jean Wood, and Linda Ahmuty for their help in typing the initial manuscript, and a special thanks to Marilyn Freeman and Dorla Boisselle for proofreading.

                                                            Arthur H. Boisselle
                                                            Donald M. Freeman

PART I

Basic Mathematics and Problem Solving

Whole Number Mathematics

1

OBJECTIVES

When you complete this chapter you will be able to:

- *Understand the whole number decimal system. (1.1)*
- *Add columns of numbers quickly and accurately. (1.2)*
- *Subtract positive and negative numbers. (1.3)*
- *Find solutions using multiplication. (1.4)*
- *Divide using short and long division. (1.5)*
- *Estimate products and quotients. (1.6)*
- *Use a hand calculator to solve problems in addition, subtraction, multiplication, and division. (1.7)*

COMING UP

Taxes have increased $500.... Profits are down 20 percent.... Price these items at $275 each.... Mark up this cost by 45 percent.... As you can see, a large part of the language of business is mathematics. A study of this subject starts with a review of the fundamentals of basic arithmetic. Think of how important it is to be able to quickly evaluate changes in production costs or to show a customer the advantages of buying your product instead of a competitor's. On an annual basis it could be worth thousands of dollars! Make the effort! Give it the time it deserves. We feel that this review will provide a positive payoff as you challenge the balance of the text.

The Decimal Number System

1.1 Number Values

The numbers used in business are based on the **decimal system.** The value of a number in this system depends on two important elements: the integers, which include the ten digits 0, 1, 2, 3, 4, 5, 6, 7, 8, and 9; and the place value the digit holds within the number. Each place is assigned a value based on its position relative to the decimal point. Review these concepts:

- The decimal point is the reference dot (.).
- Each place in a number has a value ten times the value of the place to its right.
- The value of the units position (directly to the left of the decimal point) is one.
- For whole numbers (no decimal point shown), the decimal point holds an implied location to the immediate right of the units position.

Figure 1.1 identifies the names and the number expressions for all positions in the decimal system up to the billions position. Position names can be used to express a whole number. A whole number is an expression of digits written in a particular place. The value represented by a place digit is the value of that digit multiplied by the place value. The value of a whole number is the sum of the digit values multiplied by the place values. For instance, examine the number 573:

The value is: $573 = 5 \times 100 + 7 \times 10 + 3 \times 1$
The name is: Five hundred seventy-three

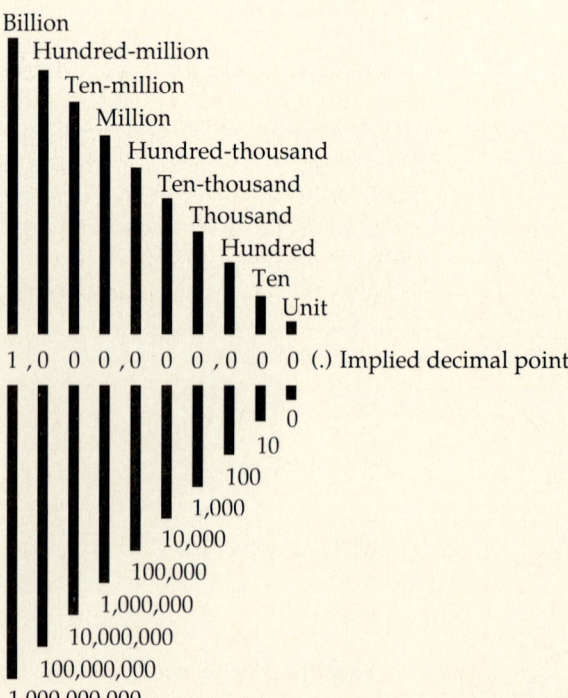

FIGURE 1.1
Decimal system whole number structure

EXAMPLE 1   Identify the name of the following number: 164,028. (implied decimal position)

Solution: One hundred sixty-four thousand, twenty-eight.

EXAMPLE 2   Express a number that has three tens and eight units. What is its common name?

Solution:

$$\rightarrow 38 \leftarrow$$

Tens   Units

Thirty-eight

EXAMPLE 3   Break down the following number and give its common name: 9,476,008,405.

Solution:

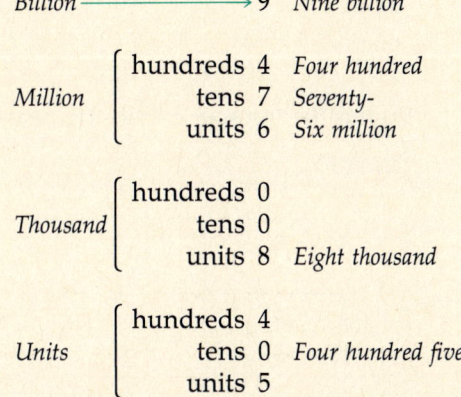

ANSWER: Nine billion, four hundred seventy-six million, eight thousand, four hundred five.

PROBLEM SOLVING STRATEGY

For each place in the number, identify the digit representing the place. The digit name is used with the place name to create the number expression. For instance, 312,251,641 is read three hundred twelve million, two hundred fifty-one thousand, six hundred forty-one. This shows the pattern of how numbers are expressed. Notice that, as you move from hundreds to thousands to millions, a comma is inserted between the different-named groups.

✔ **CHECK FOR UNDERSTANDING**

1. Write the following numerically: Two hundred sixty-eight thousand, forty-four.

2. What is the numerical representation for Nineteen billion, eight million, forty thousand?

Answers to ✔ Check for Understanding
1. 268,044.   2. 19,008,040,000.

Section 1.1   The Decimal Number System

Rounding Whole Numbers

Business does not always require the exact value of a number. Very often, a procedure called **rounding** is used to find quick approximations for estimating values and decision making. **Approximations** can be used to express such things as revenue, cost, operating expense, and general profitability, and they require whole number rounding.

To round whole numbers, identify the name and place to be used for decision making. If, for example, we know that a business is selling for $86,284, we could identify the significant place in the price as ten thousands, or thousands. The sale value could be approximated as $90,000 or $86,000. Follow these steps:

1. Identify the number place that is significant for the business decision.
2. Read the single digit of the number place immediately to the right of the significant place:
    a. If that digit is less than 5, change it and all digits to its right (up to the implied decimal point) to zero.
    b. If that digit is equal to or greater than 5, increase the digit in the significant place by one. All digits to the right become zero.

EXAMPLE 4 Round the number 546 to the nearest hundred.

Solution:

5 4 6	• Significant place is hundreds.
5 4 6	• Reference digit 4 is less than 5.
5 0 0	• That digit and digits to right change to zero.

EXAMPLE 5 Round the number 3,847 to the significant thousands position.

Solution:

3, 8 4 7	• Significant place is thousands.
3, 8 4 7	• Reference digit 8 is more than 5.
4, 8 4 7	• Significant place is increased by one.
4, 0 0 0	• Reference digit and digits to right change to zero.

✓ CHECK FOR UNDERSTANDING

1. Write the number sixteen million, eight hundred fifty-six thousand, two hundred seventy-three. Round it to the significant ten millions place.

2. Write the number twenty-eight thousand, nine hundred eleven. Round it to the significant thousands place.

3. To what significant place would the number 349,746 be rounded in order to arrive at a rounded value of 350,000?

SKILL EXERCISES

Round off the following whole numbers as indicated:

	Tens	Hundreds	Thousands
1. 89 _____	654 _____	8,621 _____
2. 46 _____	592 _____	5,430 _____
3. 58 _____	841 _____	3,642 _____
4. 21 _____	912 _____	7,560 _____
5. 73 _____	486 _____	6,827 _____

Write the following whole numbers in numerical form:

6. Twenty-seven thousand, one hundred, twelve _____

7. One hundred sixty-nine thousand, fifty-four _____

8. Nine hundred fifty-eight _____

9. Eight thousand, eight _____

10. Twenty-six thousand, four hundred, nine _____

11. One million, thirty thousand, five hundred _____

12. Eighty-six thousand, four hundred, ten _____

13. One billion, two hundred million, six thousand _____

14. Eight hundred, twelve _____

15. Three hundred twenty-eight thousand, six hundred _____

Identify the position name for the underlined digit in each of the following numbers:

16.   3 6, 9 4 2, 1 <u>3</u> 8   _____

17.   <u>2</u> 1, 4 4 4   _____

Answers to ✓ Check for Understanding
1. 16,856,273   20,000,000.   2. 28,911   29,000.   3. Ten thousands.

Section 1.1   The Decimal Number System   **7**

18.   7 9, 8 6 5   _____

19.   1, 3 8 4, 7 1 2   _____

20.   6 5 1, 8 3 0   _____

Addition

1.2

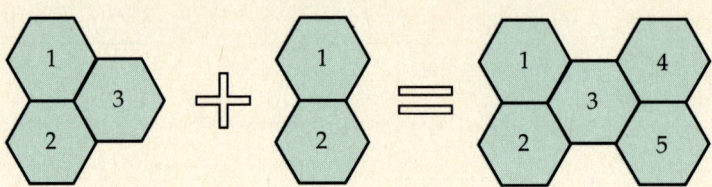

Addition is typically the first mathematical operation we learn. The numbers we add are called **addends,** and the total is called the **sum.**

Adding is performed within vertical columns of numbers. The most effective way is to group the numbers by tens. To illustrate, if we add 3, 7, 6, 1, 2, 9, 4, and 8, by the usual process of 3 + 7 = 10, 10 + 6 = 16, 16 + 1 = 17, etc., until the sum becomes 40, we are using a slower process. We could instead look for groups of 10. Note that 3 + 7 = 10, 6 + 4 = 10, 9 + 1 = 10, and 8 + 2 = 10. Then by adding the four tens we get the sum 40.

Grouping the digits into clusters of tens allows for a quick sum of most of the addends. The remaining addends are put with the sums of ten to complete the addition.

EXAMPLE 6   Add 32, 46, 27, 59, and 2.

Solution:

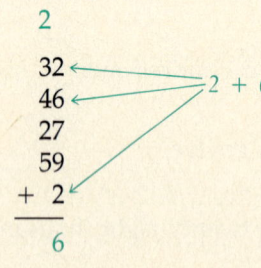

- Find groups of ten in the units position.
  2 + 6 + 2 = 10
- Add remaining digits (those not used in groups of tens): 7 + 9 = 16.
- Add the tens to the sum of the remaining digits: 10 + 16 = 26.
- Write 6 in the units position and carry the 2 to the tens position. Then find groups of ten in the tens position.

2 + 3 + 5 = 10

- Add the remaining digits: 4 + 2 = 6.
- Add the tens to the sum of the remaining digits: 10 + 6 = 16.
- Write the number with the 6 in the tens position and the 1 in the hundreds position.   □

8   Chapter 1   Whole Number Mathematics

> **PROBLEM SOLVING STRATEGY**
>
> Always move from right to left one column at a time. The units digit of the column sum is placed in the column being added. The remaining values are moved to the column to its left and added to its total. When the last column on the left is added, the sum is shown below it.

EXAMPLE 7   **Addition Can Also Be Expressed as a Word Problem**   John went to the grocery store and bought the following items for the month: meat, $79; cereal, $18; vegetables, $71; flour, $12. How much did he spend?

Solution:

$$\begin{array}{r} 1\;2 \\ 79 \\ 18 \\ 71 \\ +12 \\ \hline 180 \end{array}$$

$2 + 7 + 1 = 10$

$10 + 8 = 18$

- Two tens groups exist. The sum of these is (20).
- The sum is 180.

> **PROBLEM SOLVING STRATEGY**
>
> Problems can also be expressed in narrative form. They are called *word problems*. The basic steps for solving a word problem include the following:
> **a.** Identify the problem elements and their number values.
> **b.** Establish the relationships stated for the numbers.
> **c.** Identify the appropriate mathematical operation.
> **d.** Apply the needed mathematical operation.

✓ CHECK FOR UNDERSTANDING

1. Rita checked in the following shipment at the warehouse: detergent, 379 cases; meat, 562 cases; milk, 139 cases; eggs, 186 cases; and ice cream, 279 cases. How many cases were included in the total shipment?

2. Add 1,276 + 342 + 71 + 389,653.

3. Add 469,735 + 27,863 + 186 + 197,257 + 1,272,142.

SKILL EXERCISES

Complete the following problems using addition:

1.	2.	3.	4.
326	546	227	175
287	285	193	227
+192	+733	+865	+929

Answers to ✓ Check for Understanding
1. 1,545.   **2.** 391,342.   **3.** 1,967,183.

5.	427	6.	4,629	7.	1,539	8.	3,625
	128		62,533		265		7,954
	+ 32		+22,712		+1,177		+ 365

9.	99	10.	14,523	11.	3,207
	87		3,467		4,306
	+76		+45,698		3,256
					+ 276

12. 23,476 + 65,907 + 24,796 + 7,598 = _____.

13. 89,708 + 43,776 + 53,798 + 795,007 = _____.

14. 67,507 + 34,980 + 78,403 + 378 = _____.

15. 3,207 + 4,306 + 3,256 + 276 = _____.

APPLICATIONS

Complete the following problems using addition:

1. When Jim bought lumber to build tool chests, he paid $3,685 for plywood, $1,368 for hinges, $963 for locks, and $1,795 for lacquer. What was the total bill for materials?

2. Rhonda's annual property taxes were county, $89; city, $96; school district, $485; and irrigation, $77. What was the total amount of property tax she paid?

3. Jen's lot cost $19,900 with an additional $2,700 for landscaping and $5,628 for concrete work. If her house will cost $82,600 to build, how much will her total cost be for the house and property?

4. An interior decorator quoted the following prices to Mrs. Goldrolling to remodel her living room: wallpaper, $680; carpet, $4,652; three occasional chairs, $1,250 each; two end tables, $987 each; miscellaneous pictures and knickknacks, $1,875; and labor for installation, $790. What will the remodeling cost Mrs. Goldrolling?

5. When the Downtown Garage checked their equipment they needed a new grease gun for $245, a high pressure hose for $125, and a floor jack for $325. What did the new equipment cost the company?

6. When an American tourist returned from Canada he had items that cost him the following duty: glassware, $34; woolens, $55; and silverware, $124. How much total duty did he pay?

7. The pro shop at the City Tennis Club bought 10 rackets for $480; 20 dozen balls for $340, and 30 pairs of shoes for $1,257. What did the order cost the club?

8. If an invoice contains charges of $765 for generators, $4,875 for starters, $1,565 for batteries, and $2,350 for tires, what is the total amount of the invoice?

9. A manufacturing firm produced 5,675 belts on Tuesday; 4,985 on Wednesday; 6,800 on Thursday; and 5,842 on Friday. What was the total production for the four days?

10. The log for a diesel tractor showed 3,800 miles traveled in June; 2,700 miles in July; 4,200 miles in August; and 3,450 miles in September. How many miles were traveled in the four-month period?

Subtraction

1.3

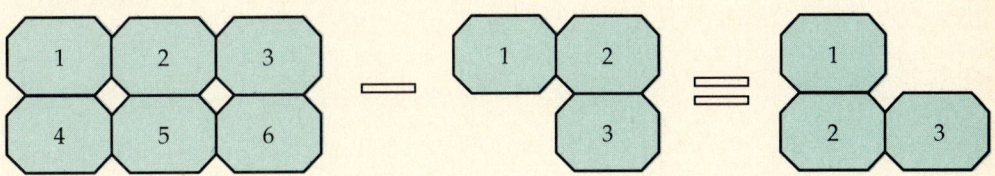

Subtraction is used to reduce a number by a stated value. The number from which another number is subtracted is called the **minuend**. Normally the minuend is the larger number. (Sometimes in the case of a business loss situation, the minuend could be a value smaller than the number being subtracted.) The number being subtracted is the **subtrahend**, and the answer is known as the **difference**. To subtract, move column by column from right to left reducing the minuend digit by the value of the subtrahend to find the difference.

PROBLEM SOLVING STRATEGY

When a digit in the subtrahend is larger than the minuend digit in the same column, a procedure called **borrowing** is used. Each digit position in a number is a power of ten; that means it is ten times larger than the number immediately to its right. The "1" being borrowed from the digit on the left becomes "10" when it is moved right one column. The digit in the "borrowed" column is reduced by one. Ten is added to the minuend digit. Now the minuend is larger than the subtrahend and subtraction can continue.

EXAMPLE 8   Subtract 2,462 from 3,769.

Solution:

```
  3,769    minuend
- 2,462    subtrahend
  -----
  1,307    difference
```

- In this case the minuend values are larger than the subtrahend values (no borrowing is necessary).
- Reduce the minuend by the value of the subtrahend. The value below is the difference.

Section 1.3   Subtraction   11

EXAMPLE 9   Subtract 1,687 from 2,786.

Solution:

$$\begin{array}{r} 2\,7\,\overset{7}{\cancel{8}}\,\overset{16}{\cancel{6}} \\ -1\,6\,8\,7 \\ \hline 9 \end{array}$$

- This operation requires borrowing.
- To subtract 7 from 6, borrow 10 from the tens position.
- The tens position changes from 8 to 7.
- Ten is added to units $10 + 6 = 16$.
- Subtract $16 - 7 = 9$.
- Place the 9 in the units position.

$$\begin{array}{r} 2\,\overset{6}{\cancel{7}}\,\overset{17}{\cancel{8}}\,6 \\ -1\,6\,8\,7 \\ \hline 9\,9 \end{array}$$

- To subtract 8 from 7 in the tens position borrow 10 from the hundreds position.
- The hundreds position is reduced to 6.
- Ten is added to the tens: $7 + 10 = 17$.
- Subtract $17 - 8 = 9$.
- Place the 9 in the tens position.

$$\begin{array}{r} 2\,\overset{6}{\cancel{7}}\,\overset{7}{\cancel{8}}\,6 \\ -1\,6\,8\,7 \\ \hline 1\,0\,9\,9 \end{array}$$

- Subtract the hundreds position: $6 - 6 = 0$.
- Place a 0 in the hundreds position.
- Subtract the thousands position: $2 - 1 = 1$.
- Place the 1 in the thousands position. □

PROBLEM SOLVING STRATEGY

You can quickly verify your subtraction answer by calculating a check. The check is completed by adding the difference to the subtrahend. It should equal the minuend if the subtraction was done correctly.

EXAMPLE 10   If the invoice for goods purchased was $467,550 and the customer paid $498,640, by how much did the customer overpay?

Solution:

$$\begin{array}{r} \$498{,}640 \\ -\ 467{,}550 \end{array} \qquad \begin{array}{r} 4\,9\,8\,\overset{5}{\cancel{6}}\,\overset{14}{\cancel{4}}\,0 \\ -\ 4\,6\,7\,5\,5\,0 \\ \hline 3\,1\,0\,9\,0 \end{array} \qquad \text{Check:} \quad \begin{array}{r} 31{,}090 \\ +467{,}550 \\ \hline 498{,}640 \end{array}$$

□

EXAMPLE 11   Subtract 93,456 from 80,234.

Solution:

$$\begin{array}{r} 80{,}234 \\ -\ 93{,}456 \\ \hline (80{,}234) \\ (-\ 13{,}222) \end{array}$$

- Note: This subtraction is a loss.
- When the minuend is smaller than the subtrahend, subtract the minuend from the subtrahend.
- Because 93,456 is larger than 80,234, the difference of 13,222 is given a minus sign. □

EXAMPLE 12 Use subtraction and check: $5,643 from $3,212.

Solution:

```
  3,212         Check:   5,643      · This is a loss.
 -5,643                 -2,431
 (3,212)                ------
 -2,431                  3,212
```

✔ CHECK FOR UNDERSTANDING

1. When Missy checked her cash register slip, she found the items added up to $362 and the clerk had charged her $429. How much was she overcharged?

2. When balancing his checkbook against his bank statement, Leo found he had made an error on a check by entering $396 instead of $369. By how much was his checkbook in error?

3. Joe checked an invoice that listed the following items: jacks, $6,750; tires, $1,694; chains, $2,268; and batteries, $6,975, for a total of $18,846. Was this total correct? If not, by how much was it off?

SKILL EXERCISES

Complete the following subtraction exercises:

1. 287 − 154 = _____
2. 1,369 − 1,257 = _____
3. 79,682 − 584 = _____
4. 119,253 − 7,426 = _____
5. 12,903 − 865 = _____
6. 345 − 34 = _____
7. 452 − 376 = _____
8. 23 − 12 = _____
9. 347 − 236 = _____
10. 65 − 42 = _____
11. 120 − 76 = _____
12. 1,993 − 196 = _____
13. 3,542 − 67 = _____
14. 27 − 19,635 = _____
15. 1,792 − 791 = _____
16. 34 − 457 = _____
17. 128 − 145 = _____
18. 3,568 − 1,246 = _____
19. 4,597 − 4,675 = _____
20. 17,632 − 8,765 = _____

Answers to ✔ Check for Understanding
1. $67.   2. $27.   3. No; $1,159.

APPLICATIONS

Use subtraction for the following problem sets:

1. 72,635
   −   62

2. 1,386
   − 989

3. 10,063
   −10,005

4. 97,238
   − 7,992

5. If an invoice amount was $4,567 and the accountant inadvertently sent in $4,657, by how much did she overpay?

6. If 435 loads of sand were needed to fill a hole in the street and 267 loads were delivered, how much more is needed?

7. An engine piston in Maud's car needed to be ground down by 30 units. When it was checked, it was only ground down by 21 units. How much more grinding was needed?

8. The power company needed to buy 40,000 circuit breakers. If 27,800 were already on order, how many additional breakers must be ordered?

9. If a restaurant banquet check was $4,266 and the customer left $5,020, how much was left for the tip?

10. The total revenue from parts sales for an equipment manufacturer was $5,785, including sales tax. If sales tax was $353, how much were sales alone?

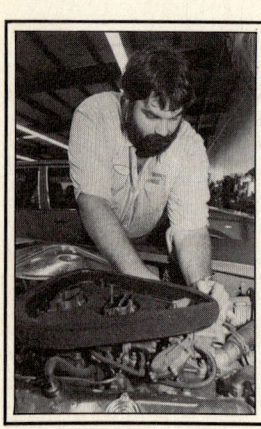

Multiplication

1.4

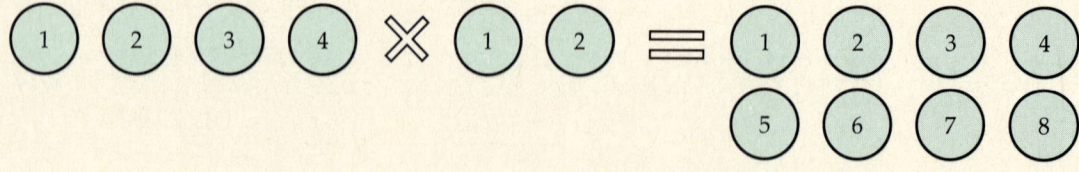

Multiplication is a rapid form of addition. If you bought 4 yards of cloth at $3 per yard what would it cost you? There are two ways to reach an answer. We can add 3 + 3 + 3 + 3 = 12. Or, if we note there are 4 threes, the solution could be found by multiplying 3 by 4 to find 12 (3 × 4 = 12). The number being multiplied is called a **multiplicand**; the **multiplier** identifies the number of additions necessary for the multiplicand; and the answer is called the **product**. The multiplicand and multiplier are sometimes referred to as **factors**.

14 Chapter 1 Whole Number Mathematics

Multiplication of numbers larger than single digits requires that we use position to bring about the proper answers.

EXAMPLE 13 Multiply 35 by 27.

Solution:

$$\begin{array}{r} 35 \\ \times\ 27 \\ \hline 245 \end{array}$$ *Multiplicand*   *Multiplier*

• Multiply each digit of the multiplier beginning from the right to get a partial product 7 × 35 = 245.

$$\begin{array}{r} 35 \\ \times\ 27 \\ \hline 245 \\ 70 \end{array}$$

• 2 × 35 = 70 (Notice that 70 is one place to the left.)

$$\begin{array}{r} 35 \\ \times 27 \\ \hline 245 \\ 70 \\ \hline 945 \end{array}$$

• Add the partial products to get the final product.

PROBLEM SOLVING STRATEGY

Use each digit in the multiplier one at a time from right to left. The partial product for each multiplier is written below, vertically aligned with its respective multiplier. This provides place position for their sum, which becomes the product. To check your answer, divide the product by the multiplier.

EXAMPLE 14 Multiply 362 × 487.

Solution:

$$\begin{array}{r} 362 \\ \times\ 487 \\ \hline 2534 \\ 2896 \\ 1448 \\ \hline 176{,}294 \end{array}$$ *Multiplicand*   *Multiplier*

• Partial product from 7 × 362 = 2534.
• Partial product from 8 × 362 = 2896 (one place to the left).
• Partial product from 4 × 362 = 1448 (two places to the left).
• Sum of the partial products.
• Check: 176,294 ÷ 487 = 362.

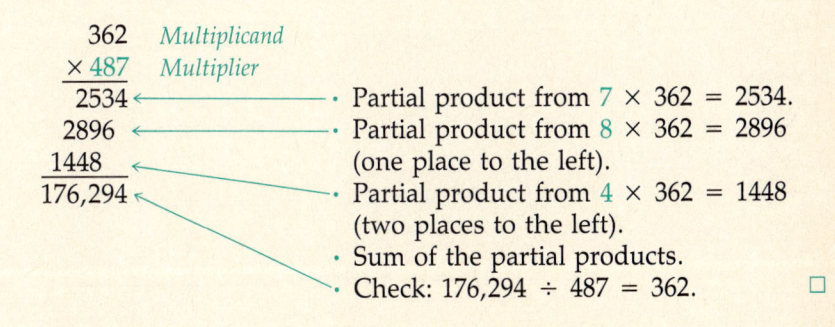

Use this practical short cut when the multiplier or multiplicand has zeros on its right side: Remove the zeros, perform the multiplication, and replace all of the removed zeros to the right of the product.

EXAMPLE 15 Multiply 2,300 × 40.

Solution:

$$\begin{array}{r} 23 \\ \times\ 4 \\ \hline 92 \end{array}$$

• 23 → 00 2 zeros
• 4 → 0 1 zero (total 3 zeros)
• Product 92 ← 000 results in 92,000

Section 1.4 Multiplication

EXAMPLE 16 Multiply 25,000 × 4,000.
Solution:

$$\begin{array}{r} 25 \\ \times\ 4 \\ \hline 100 \end{array}$$

- 25 → 000 3 zeros
- 4 → 000 3 zeros (total 6 zeros)
- 100 ← 000000 results in 100,000,000 □

PROBLEM SOLVING STRATEGY

Find square measurements by multiplying the length × width. Problems requiring cubic measures are found by multiplying the length × width × height. See Appendix C for measures.

✔ **CHECK FOR UNDERSTANDING**

1. The X-TRON Company plans to build a new warehouse that will measure 187 feet × 296 feet and be 32 feet high. How many cubic feet will be available?

2. Multiply 8,632 × 2,641.

3. Multiply 4,000 × 26.

SKILL EXERCISES

Complete the following multiplications:

1. 29 × 9   = _____   2. 472 × 36   = _____

3. 1,285 × 27 = _____   4. 1,700 × 4,200 = _____

5. 269 × 7   = _____   6. 729 × 54   = _____

7. 125 × 198   = _____   8. 3 × 407   = _____

9. 14 × 78   = _____   10. 98 × 45   = _____

11. 6 × 10,087 = _____   12. 95 × 106   = _____

13. 1,273 × 77 = _____   14. 56 × 49   = _____

15. 23 × 1,007 = _____   16. 1,606 × 353 = _____

17. 632 × 76   = _____   18. 005 × 07   = _____

19. 659 × 453 = _____   20. 47 × 378   = _____

Answers to ✔ Check for Understanding
1. 1,771,264.   2. 22,797,112.   3. 104,000.

Chapter 1 Whole Number Mathematics

APPLICATIONS

Refer to Appendix C for square and cubic measure solutions if needed.

1. If a building is 186 feet long and 39 feet wide, how many square feet does it contain?

2. If Sam sold 15 cars at an average of $9,287 each, how much were his total sales?

3. The Mosley Dairy has 150 milk cows. If the average cow needs 2 gallons of water per hour, how much water will they use in a 12-hour day?

4. How much space will be needed in a school building if the projected enrollment is 1,275 students and the estimated space per student is 46 square feet?

5. How many cubic feet are there in a warehouse that is 170 feet long, 52 feet wide, and 38 feet high?

6. How many square feet are in a lot that is 87 feet wide and 135 feet long?

7. How many square inches in a table that is 4 feet long and 3 feet wide?

8. How many spectators can view a football game if the stadium has 525 rows of seats, each of which can hold an average of 132 people?

9. How many square feet of sod will be needed to cover the playing field and sidelines if the total space to be covered is 134 feet long and 78 feet wide?

10. How many cubic feet of fill will be needed to level the street if there is a hole 7 feet deep and 38 feet square?

Division

1.5

As we considered multiplication a process of repeated addition, division is often viewed as repeated subtraction. Division is also considered an operation that is reverse multiplication. If we were to divide 9 by 3, the repeated subtraction solution would involve $9 - 3 = 6$; $6 - 3 = 3$; $3 - 3 = 0$. The three is subtracted 3 times, so we have divided by 3 with no remainder in our answer. Reviewing division as an operation that is reverse multiplication, our solution would consider that $3 \times 3 = 9$; therefore $9 \div 3 = 3$.

The number to be divided is the **dividend,** and the number used to divide by is the **divisor.** The answer to a division problem is the **quotient.** If, as often happens, one number does not divide exactly into another, the amount left over is called the **remainder.** To check an answer, multiply the quotient times the divisor to equal the dividend. Add the remainder if appropriate.

EXAMPLE 17 Divide 6,895 by 7.

Solution:

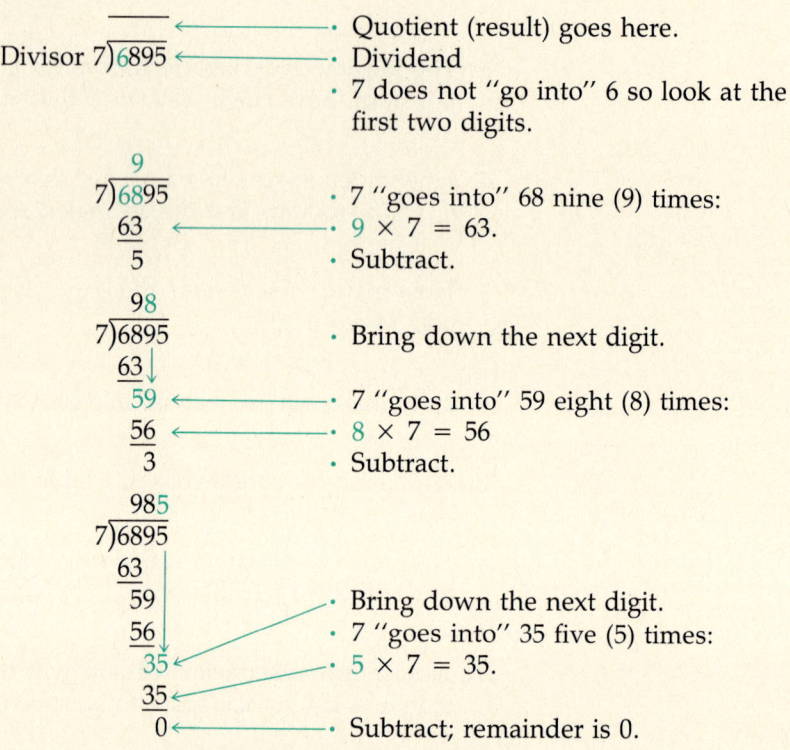

PROBLEM SOLVING STRATEGY

Write the problem with the divisor to the left and the dividend to the right. Start from the left digit of the dividend. Find the first group of digits that become larger than the divisor. In Example 17, that group was 68. Divide that number by the divisor and write the quotient above the line. Write the product of this partial quotient and the divisor below the dividend. Subtract. Bring down the next digit in the dividend. If a number is brought down that does not make the remainder larger than the divisor, represent it by a zero position in the quotient and bring down another number. Divide the result by the divisor. Repeat until all digits in the dividend have been used.

EXAMPLE 18 Divide 978 by 6.

Solution: Partial Quotients

$$\begin{array}{r} 163 \\ 6\overline{)978} \\ \underline{6}\downarrow \\ 37 \\ \underline{36}\downarrow \\ 18 \\ \underline{18} \\ 0 \end{array}$$

- Final quotient is 163.
- Product of **1** × 6 = 6.
- Subtract, bring down the 7.
- Product of **6** × 6 = 36.
- Subtract, bring down the 8.
- Product of **3** × 6 = 18.
- Subtract; remainder is 0.

Division that involves a multiple-digit divisor is more complex. The process is the same, however. You can check the accuracy of the quotient by multiplying it by the divisor.

EXAMPLE 19 Divide 12,692 by 38.

Solution:

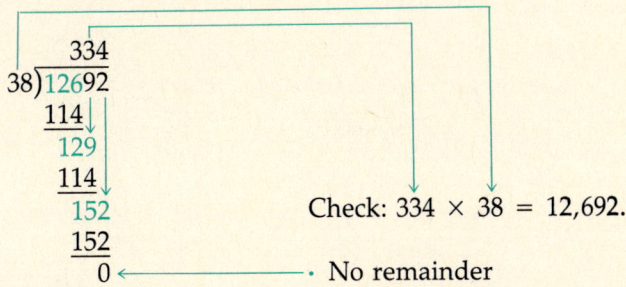

EXAMPLE 20 Divide 43,948 by 76.

Solution:

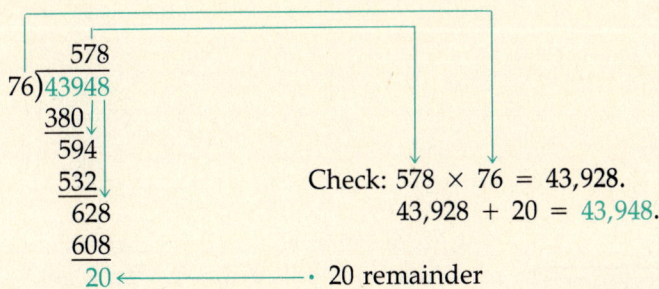

✔ CHECK FOR UNDERSTANDING

1. Divide 4,639 by 43.

2. Divide 37,895 by 5.

3. If 8,940 tires were to be divided equally among 6 stores, how many tires would each store receive?

SKILL EXERCISES

Complete the following division problems:

1. $36 \div 6$ = _____   2. $95 \div 5$ = _____

3. $147 \div 7$ = _____   4. $2,642 \div 2$ = _____

5. $9,648 \div 8$ = _____   6. $786 \div 35$ = _____

7. $7,697 \div 42$ = _____   8. $927 \div 9$ = _____

Answers to ✔ Check for Understanding
1. 107 and 38 remainder.   2. 7,579.   3. 1,490.

9. 82,468 ÷ 4 = _____ 10. 7,281 ÷ 3 = _____

11. 143,528 ÷ 7 = _____ 12. 46,134 ÷ 9 = _____

13. 1,295 ÷ 52 = _____ 14. 2,820 ÷ 60 = _____

15. 35)78,600 16. 42)7,896

17. 423)7,191 18. 52)1,248

19. 598)2,392 20. 296)37,027

APPLICATIONS

1. A diesel truck was driven 45,500 miles and used 9,100 gallons of fuel. How many miles per gallon did the truck get?

2. A computer manufacturer had $3,345,024 to spend for new construction. If the cost of construction is $93 per square foot, how many square feet can be built?

3. With 850 shares of stock worth $35,700, how much is each share worth?

4. A company's direct mail advertising costs are $150,000. The cost per bulk mailing is 12 cents. How many clients were reached?

5. How many oil changes can be made from 36, 24-quart cases, if each change requires 6 quarts of oil?

6. If an average annual utility bill is $852, and the power company bills equal payments per month, how much is each payment?

7. A major league baseball player has come to bat 1,236 times in a season. He got a hit on the average of once every three times at bat. How many hits did he get in his total times at bat?

8. If 42 workers produce 3,234 parts in one week, what is the average production per person?

9. Nationwide there were 17,577 total accidents in July. How many accidents occurred per day in that month?

10. A student has 63 honor points in 18 hours of college subjects. Find the grade point average.

Approximating and Estimating

1.6

In business, you are accountable for a calculated answer. Think how embarrassing it would be to explain why you billed a customer $155 instead of $1,550! When you get an answer, review it to see if it is reasonable. One method for doing this is **estimating.** The examples show how you can estimate products and quotients using the approximate values previously discussed in Section 1.1.

To estimate products:
- Add the total zeros removed from the number being multiplied (**multiplicand**) and the number used to multiply (**multiplier**).
- Perform the multiplication using the remaining integers and replace the zeros.

EXAMPLE 21   Use approximation to estimate the result of this multiplication (**product**). Marchland Kids Shop purchased 48 baby cribs for resale. The cribs cost $87 each wholesale. Calculate an estimated answer using approximate values. Compare it with the actual amount. Is it reasonable?

Solution:

48 rounds to 50	• Choose the significant tens place to approximate.
$87 rounds to $90	• Choose the significant tens.
5 ⟶ 0	• Remove the zeros.
9 ⟶ 0	
5 × 9 = 45	• Multiply remaining integers.
0 from 5, 0 from 9 (00)	• For product estimating, collect the removed zeros.
45 ⟵ 00 4500	• Return the zeros to the product.
$4,500	• This results in the estimated value.
48 × $87 = $4176	• The actual answer.
Pretty close.	• Based on the estimated product, the actual answer looks reasonable.

To estimate quotients:
- Remove the zeros from the rounded digits.
- Remember to leave a larger number of digits in the dividend than in the divisor.
- Subtract the number of zeros removed from the **divisor** from the zeros of the **dividend.**
- Divide and replace the remaining zeros to the **quotient.**

EXAMPLE 22 Use approximation to obtain the result of this division problem **(quotient).** A shopping mall manager was planning an area of 276,000 square feet. She believed approximately 47 businesses could fit into the area with an average of 6,000 square feet per store. Is she correct?

Solution:

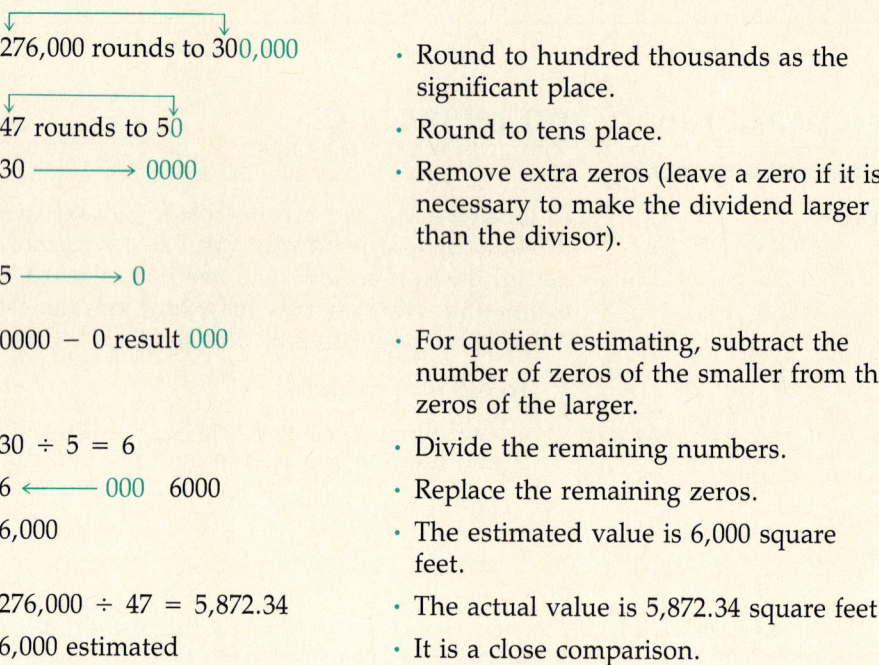

- 276,000 rounds to 300,000 • Round to hundred thousands as the significant place.
- 47 rounds to 50 • Round to tens place.
- 30 ⟶ 0000 • Remove extra zeros (leave a zero if it is necessary to make the dividend larger than the divisor).
- 5 ⟶ 0
- 0000 − 0 result 000 • For quotient estimating, subtract the number of zeros of the smaller from the zeros of the larger.
- 30 ÷ 5 = 6 • Divide the remaining numbers.
- 6 ⟵ 000 6000 • Replace the remaining zeros.
- 6,000 • The estimated value is 6,000 square feet.
- 276,000 ÷ 47 = 5,872.34 • The actual value is 5,872.34 square feet.
- 6,000 estimated • It is a close comparison.
- 5,872.34 actual • She is correct.

PROBLEM SOLVING STRATEGY

To estimate, focus on the use of zeros. Use approximation and round the whole number to the desired significant digit. Then remove the zeros from the rounded digits. Follow the steps for multiplication and division. Although not used frequently, estimating is also possible with addition and subtraction.

✓ **CHECK FOR UNDERSTANDING**

1. Approximate and find the estimated products for these factors. What are the actual products?
   (a) 4,654 × 221
   (b) 98,516 × 32
   (c) 114 × 869

2. Approximate and estimate these quotients. What are the actual results?
   (a) 165,260 ÷ 1,590
   (b) 54,000 ÷ 75
   (c) 734,860 ÷ 1,876

Answers to ✓ Check for Understanding
1. (a) Estimated: 1,000,000; Actual: 1,028,534. (b) Estimated: 3,000,000; Actual: 3,152,512. (c) Estimated: 90,000; Actual: 99,066. 2. (a) Estimated: 100; Actual: 103.9. (b) Estimated: 625; Actual: 720. (c) Estimated: 350; Actual: 391.7.

SKILL EXERCISES

Approximate and estimate the following products and quotients:

1. 86,360 × 421   Estimate _____   Actual _____

2. 192 × 709   Estimate _____   Actual _____

3. 1,663 × 57   Estimate _____   Actual _____

4. 2,865 × 2,642   Estimate _____   Actual _____

5. 11,389 × 8,432   Estimate _____   Actual _____

6. 26,497 ÷ 174   Estimate _____   Actual _____

7. 899 ÷ 32   Estimate _____   Actual _____

8. 745,123 ÷ 538   Estimate _____   Actual _____

9. 28,435 ÷ 1,962   Estimate _____   Actual _____

10. 789 ÷ 54   Estimate _____   Actual _____

APPLICATIONS

1. The typical compact car costs the dealer $6,823. If there are 823 cars in inventory, what is the estimated value of the inventory to the closest thousand?

2. A production sequence takes 185 minutes to complete one part. Estimate to the closest hundred thousand how many minutes of production would be required for an order of 2,489 parts.

3. The typical wage for a semi-professional football player is $34,200 per year. If there were 889 players in the football league, estimate the total payroll for a year to the closest million.

4. A new roadway was completed at a cost of $35,467,900. The total distance of the new section was 69 miles. Estimate the cost per mile to the closest hundred thousand.

5. 20,000 miles.

5. Ding-Dong delivery service recorded a total of 762,356 miles traveled on its vehicles in one year. For a fleet of 38 trucks, estimate the miles traveled per vehicle to the closest thousand miles.

The Calculator

1.7

The hand calculator is an excellent tool for business. It is manufactured by many companies and is widely available. So far, this chapter has discussed whole number math to be performed manually. From this point on—and throughout the text—you are encouraged to use a hand calculator to work out the problems. Obtain a calculator, read the instructions, and spend some time doing various types of problems. The instruction book for the calculator will explain procedures for its operation as well as for using memory and constants. Feature sections in each chapter will show how to solve different problems with a calculator. Use Example 23 to illustrate the Calculator Tip feature.

EXAMPLE 23 Add 45 + 67 + 38 and multiply the sum by 8.

CALCULATOR TIP

This problem requires you to add and find a **sum**. The sum is then used in a continuous math sequence of multiplication to find a **product**.

45 [+] 67 [+] 38	Add these numbers.
[=] 150	Use the total (equal key) for answer.
[×] 8	Use the multiply key and 8 on the answer.
[=] 1200	Use the equal key to find the product.

EXAMPLE 24 Add 78 + 87 and multiply the sum by 12.

Solution:

78 [+] 87 [=] 165   • Enter each number and sum [=].
165 [×] 12 [=] 1980 • Enter the [×] key then 12 to multiply. The [=] calculates the product.

PROBLEM SOLVING STRATEGY

The calculator has the capability to do operations in sequence to solve more complex problems. For sequence operation problems, calculators sometimes require you to use the total key [=] as you complete an addition or subtraction sequence. The [=] key prepares a total so you can proceed with a multiplication or division operation. Going from multiplication or division to addition, most calculators do not require you to total with the equal key. The operations can be performed simply by pressing either the [+] or [−] key.

---

24 Chapter 1 Whole Number Mathematics

EXAMPLE 25 Perform these instructions in a continuous sequence. Add 37 to 86, then subtract 23, multiply by 7, and then divide by 4.

Solution:

37 [+] 86	• Add then subtract. The [=] key is needed on some calculators before multiplication or division. Try yours and see.
37 [+] 86 [−] 23	
37 [+] 86 [−] 23 [×] 7	• Continuous multiplication and division are possible by using the next operation key.
37 [+] 86 [−] 23 [×] 7 [÷] 4	
[=] 175	• Hit the [=] key for the answer. □

EXAMPLE 26 Use a continuous sequence and solve 75 ÷ 5 × 46 + 37 − 12.

Solution: Follow the sequence above from left to right.

75 [÷] 5 [×] 46 [+] 37 [−] 12 [=] 715   • Enter each number and operation in sequence. Do not stop until the problem is complete. □

PROBLEM SOLVING STRATEGY

Calculators also use decimal numbers. Insert the decimal where it appears in the number. The mathematics operation is not changed.

Example: 43.5 [×] 7.8 [=] 339.3
         123.9 [÷] 4.3 [=] 28.813953

For problems not directed to be performed in left-to-right sequence, solve with the mathematics **order of operations** and **memory**. The order of operations follows three steps:

Step 1. Calculate any expression within parentheses or brackets.
Step 2. Calculate multiplications and divisions as encountered in order from left to right.
Step 3. Calculate additions and subtractions as encountered in order from left to right.

Most calculators have a "constant" feature, which permits continuous multiplication or division by a given number, without re-entering the constant. For example, you could find the sales tax on three items with different prices more easily using a constant percentage. Research how your calculator uses its constant feature. It may require the constant to be entered as the first or the second number in the series, or it may use a "k" constant key.

EXAMPLE 27 Use the constant feature of your calculator to multiply 300, 400, and 500 by .75. (Note: Enter the decimal point as it appears in the number using the decimal point key.)

Solution: **Four-function calculator**   **k-Key calculator**

.75 [×] 300 [=] 225   ← Enter the →   .75 [×] [k] 300 [=] 225
                               multiplier
                               first.   Note: k-key after
                                                                   multiplier.

Section 1.7   The Calculator   **25**

Complete the sequence in either calculator without entering the multiplier again.

Four-function calculator			k-Key calculator	
Enter	400		Enter	400
Depress	=		Depress	=
Result	300		Result	300
Enter	500		Enter	500
Depress	=		Depress	=
Result	375		Result	375

☐

EXAMPLE 28 Divide using the constant feature of your calculator. Divide 80, 90, and 70 by 10.

Solution: **Four-function calculator**   **k-Key calculator**

80 ÷ 10 = 8   ← Enter the →   10 ÷ k 80 = 8
                       divisor.

Note: divisor   Note: k-key after
entered second.   (10 entered first).

Complete the sequence without the divisor again.

Four-function calculator   **k-Key calculator**

90 = 9   90 = 9
70 = 7   70 = 7   ☐

Today's calculators have memory banks, which allow you to store numbers and recall them for successive calculations. Most calculators have one of two common types of memory key sets. For a four-function calculator, memory keys are identified as:

M+ and M−	· Enter as + or − data for summation.
MR	· Recall the memory total.
MC	· Clear memory.

A common alternate type of memory key set includes the following functions:

STO	· Allows for holding one number to be re-entered later.
RCL	· Calls the number out of the STO register to use.
SUM	· Enters data as a + or − for summation.
EXC	· Recalls the memory total.

Practice the use of memory in problem solving with these examples. If a problem contains elements within parentheses, solve the parenthetical operations first. Use memory to store the results.

26 Chapter 1 Whole Number Mathematics

Two types of calculator: k-key (left) and four-function.

EXAMPLE 29 Solve (42 × 54) + (34 × 24).

Solution:

Enter 42 $\boxed{\times}$ 54 $\boxed{=}$ (2268) $\boxed{M+}$ (or $\boxed{STO}$).
Enter 34 $\boxed{\times}$ 24 $\boxed{=}$ (816) $\boxed{+}$ $\boxed{MR}$ (or $\boxed{RCL}$) $\boxed{=}$ 3084. □

EXAMPLE 30 Solve the following problem, adding each column and totaling each of the subtotals.

16	37	42
18	29	57
35	115	18
17	36	36
Subtotal $\boxed{M+}$	Subtotal $\boxed{M+}$	Subtotal $\boxed{M+}$	Total $\boxed{MR}$

Solution: This type of problem asks you to add each column separately and to retain the sums in memory. The memory is recalled to obtain the total of the sums.

16 $\boxed{+}$ 18 $\boxed{+}$ 35 $\boxed{+}$ 17	• Add these numbers.
$\boxed{=}$ 86	• Total.
$\boxed{M+}$ or $\boxed{SUM}$	• Place in memory.
37 $\boxed{+}$ 29 $\boxed{+}$ 115 $\boxed{+}$ 36	• Add these numbers.
$\boxed{=}$ 217	• Total.
$\boxed{M+}$ or $\boxed{SUM}$	• Place in memory.
42 $\boxed{+}$ 57 $\boxed{+}$ 18 $\boxed{+}$ 36	• Add these numbers.
$\boxed{=}$ 153	• Total.
$\boxed{MR}$ or $\boxed{EXEC}$	• Recall from memory.
456	• Result. □

EXAMPLE 31 Solve (65 × 78) + (45 ÷ 9).

Solution: 65 $\boxed{\times}$ 78 $\boxed{=}$ (5070) $\boxed{M+}$ 45 $\boxed{\div}$ 9 $\boxed{=}$ (5) $\boxed{+}$ $\boxed{MR}$ $\boxed{=}$ 5075. □

✔ CHECK FOR UNDERSTANDING

Use your calculator and perform the indicated operations. If a number contains a decimal, enter it using the decimal point key on your calculator.

1. Solve this problem using left-to-right sequence: 45 × 6 × 8 ÷ 27

2. (45 × 12) + (76 ÷ 2)

3. An invoice included charges of $35, $24, $67, and $78. How much would the total cost be if there was a $40 discount?

4. Use the constant multiplication feature and calculator memory to multiply 320, 450, and 790 by 5 and find the total.

SKILL EXERCISES

Use the features of your calculator to solve the following problems:

1. 12 + 25 + 38 + 27 = _____

2. 24 + 19 + 18 + 27 = _____

3. 27 × 6 × 87 ÷ 360 = _____

4. (14 × 6) + (18 ÷ 9) = _____

5. $\dfrac{12 \times 7 \times 6}{32 \times 5}$ = _____

6. $\dfrac{63 \times 72 \times 84}{38 \times 7}$ = _____

Add

7.   64,375
     72,286
   596,875
+733,536

8.   1,275
   23,627
       876
+17,421

Subtract

9.   685,976
− 32,682

10. 7,239
−1,585

Answers to ✔ Check for Understanding
1. 80.   2. 578.   3. $164.   4. 7,800.

28   Chapter 1   Whole Number Mathematics

Use Constant to multiply

11. 385 × 62 = _____

12. 627 × 62 = _____

13. 326 × 62 = _____

14. 276 × 62 = _____

15. 1,865 × 62 = _____

Use Constant to divide

16. 1,240 ÷ 15,493 = _____

17. 2,631 ÷ 15,493 = _____

18. 4,587 ÷ 15,493 = _____

19. 3,912 ÷ 15,493 = _____

20. 1,812 ÷ 15,493 = _____

Combined operations

21. (32 × 16 ÷ 9) + 16 = _____

22. (16 + 37 + 28) ÷ 17 = _____

23. (127 + 8,965 + 23 − 65) × 65 = _____

24. (43 × 22) + (17 ÷ 4) = _____

25. (7 × 89) − (5 × 34) = _____

Use memory

26. (15 ÷ 17) × (22 ÷ 16) = _____

27. (26 × 18) × (15 × 22) = _____

28. 76 + 35 + 127 subtotal _____, 18 × 12 subtotal _____,
    15 ÷ 12   subtotal _____   = Total _____

29. (26 × 16) + (15 × 12) = _____

30. (14 × 6) − (23 × 2) = _____

APPLICATIONS

Complete the following problems using your hand calculator:

1. How much would 24 dozen eggs cost if the price for each dozen was 69 cents?

2. How far can you travel on 75 gallons of gasoline if you can go 27 miles on each gallon?

3. How many cubic feet are there in a building that is 85 feet wide, 165 feet long, and 18 feet high?

4. How much would 7,656 oranges cost if they were $3 a dozen?

5. If a 40-pound bag of fertilizer covers 2,500 square feet of lawn, how many pounds would be needed to cover a lawn that is 86 feet wide and 385 feet long?

6. One of the major cost factors for a self-service laundry is water. If 42 machines use an average of 380 gallons each daily, how much water would be saved if each machine used 15 fewer gallons? What would the new total be?

7. Find the total production for the week if the daily production was Monday, 876 tons; Tuesday, 956 tons; Wednesday, 875 tons; Thursday, 764 tons; and Friday, 850 tons.

8. How many people need to pledge in a charity drive if the average pledge is $16 and the goal is $564,800?

9. How much money would be left to finance if the cost of a new car was $8,765 and you put $1,550 down?

10. If one pair of pants costs $35, how much will 7 pairs cost?

Key Terms

Addend (8)
Approximation (6)
Borrowing (11)
Decimal system (4)
Difference (11)
Dividend (18)
Divisor (18)
Estimating (21)
Factor (14)

Minuend (11)
Multiplicand (14)
Multiplier (14)
Product (14)
Quotient (18)
Remainder (18)
Rounding (6)
Subtrahend (11)
Sum (8)

Looking Back

The operations of addition, subtraction, multiplication, and division can be performed manually or with a hand calculator. Although the primary review of these four operations is to refresh your memory regarding some of the fundamentals, you will more than likely use a hand calculator for most of the course.

A four-function calculator will serve most of your needs. However, it is important that you become knowledgeable about the features of any calculator you use. You are now ready to take the next step in our fundamental review of mathematics.

Let's Review

Addition

1. 26
    +94

2. 24
    +95

3. 90
    +26

4. 13
    +72

5. 72
    +71

6. 425,138
    +505,336

7. 2,564
    +1,606

8. 5,800
    +9,367

9. 9,216
    +9,017

10. 1,474
    +2,589

Subtraction

11. 96
    −67

12. 91
    −85

13. 93
    −52

14. 86
    −43

15. 35
    −16

16. 805
    −560

17. 560
    − 97

18. 602
    −160

19. 512
    −397

20. 452
    − 98

Multiplication

21. 342
    × 47

22. 734
    × 63

23. 236
    × 75

24. 104
    × 17

25. 628
    × 43

Division

26. 2)76

27. 4)6,756

28. 33)26,928

29. 88)3,960

30. 624)24,960

Chapter Test

1. What is the sum of 35 + 56 + 97 + 217?

2. The sum of $3,786, $12,309, and $6,788 is _____.

3. Find the sum of the following numbers: 3489, 237, 76, 132.

4. Find the difference between $35,676 and $87,545.

5. If a laborer worked 36 hours at a rate of $7 an hour and received a check for $237 after deductions, how much was withheld for deductions?

6. What is the difference between 389 and 243?

7. What were the labor costs for the week if 32 hours were worked at an average of $11 an hour?

8. Find the product of 468 × 547.

9. How many total square feet of space are needed for production if each worker must have 37 square feet and there are 2,368 workers?

10. What is the quotient of 462 divided by 33?

11. If 699,992 tons of sand are needed to construct a building and each truckload weighs 17 tons, how many truckloads will be needed?

12. A school has 1,920,000 square feet of space. How many students can it serve if each student needs 40 square feet of space?

For Problems 13 through 18, perform the operations within the parentheses first, then complete the remaining operation.

13. (25 ÷ 7) × (15 ÷ 2) = _____

14. 12 + 5 + 16 + 92 ÷ (13 + 6) = _____

15. (12 × 7) + 15 + 9 = _____

16. 12 + 16 + 92 _____ subtotal, + 17 + 15 + 9 _____ subtotal, + 12 + 18 + 86 = _____ Total _____

17. (16 × 95) ÷ (15 × 3) = _____

18. (17 × 12) × (15 × 7) = _____

19. 75 × 362 _____
    75 × 580 _____
    75 × 695 _____
    75 × 890 _____
    75 × 422 _____   Grand total = _____

20. 2)176
21. 3)1,638
22. 4)6,756
23. 9)8,262

24. 5)5,690
25. 60)3,960
26. 84)21,084

27. (45 ÷ 9) × (80 ÷ 20) = _____

32 Chapter 1 Whole Number Mathematics

28. 12 + 5 + 11 + 92 ÷ (14 + 6) = _____

29. (12 × 7) + 15 + 9 + 12   = _____

30. 12 + 46 + 92 = _____ subtotal
    47 + 15 + 9 = _____ subtotal
    12 + 26 + 86 = _____ total _____

Fractions

2

OBJECTIVES

When you complete this chapter you will be able to:

- *Identify common fractional forms and convert fractions to higher terms and reduce them to lower terms. (2.1)*
- *Use improper fractions and mixed numbers in problem solving. (2.2)*
- *Calculate common denominators for addition and subtraction. (2.3)*
- *Solve problems using multiplication and division of fractions and mixed numbers. (2.4)*

COMING UP

One-half off ... one-third down.... Yes, it's true the business environment is not simply a block of whole numbers. Fractions are alive and well! Although different methods may be used to solve business problems, many involve fractional relationships. The majority of the fractional forms used for business transactions are simple. When a fraction consists of large numbers $\left(\frac{23}{276}\right)$, it might be easier to convert to decimal form prior to solving. This chapter provides a review of the basic mathematical rules that apply to fractions. You will find these rules useful in helping to solve some of the problems in later chapters.

Fractions in Use

2.1

A common fraction is a simple expression of a numerical relationship. It is expressed with two general terms: the **numerator** (number above the line), which shows the number of representative parts existing in the relationship; and the **denominator** (number below the line), which is the number representing the whole unit. Figure 2.1 illustrates a fractional relationship.

$$\frac{5}{6}$$

5 Is the number of representative parts in this relationship

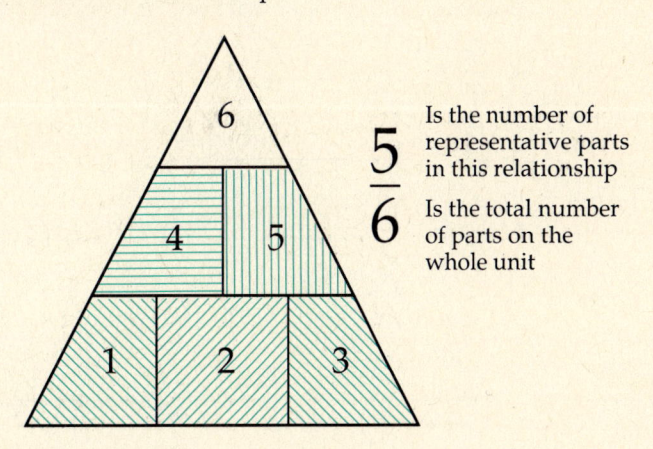

6 Is the total number of parts on the whole unit

FIGURE 2.1
A fractional relationship

Each common **proper fraction** is an expression whose value is less than one. Therefore, in a proper fraction, the numerator is smaller than the denominator.

EXAMPLE 1 Proper Fractions

$$\frac{5}{8} \quad \frac{1}{2} \quad \frac{3}{8} \quad \text{Numerators} \atop \text{Denominators}$$

Fractions whose numerators are equal to or larger than the denominators are called **improper fractions.** Mixed numbers are changed to improper fractions prior to multiplication and division.

EXAMPLE 2 Improper Fractions

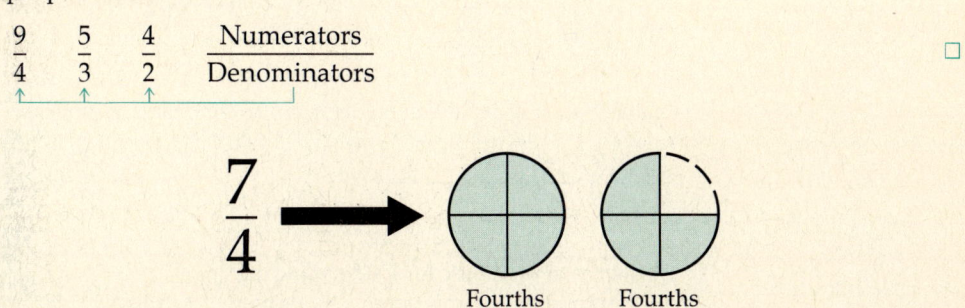

$$\frac{9}{4} \quad \frac{5}{3} \quad \frac{4}{2} \quad \text{Numerators} \atop \text{Denominators}$$

$$\frac{7}{4} \rightarrow$$

Fourths   Fourths

FIGURE 2.2
An improper fraction

Mixed numbers consist of a whole number and a fraction.

EXAMPLE 3   Mixed Numbers

$3\frac{2}{3}$ $5\frac{6}{8}$ $7\frac{1}{4}$

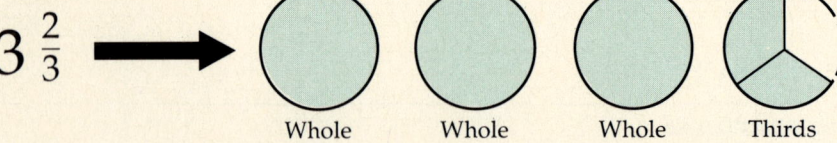

$3\frac{2}{3}$ → ◯ ◯ ◯ ◷
      Whole Whole Whole Thirds

FIGURE 2.3
A mixed number

✔ CHECK FOR UNDERSTANDING

Indicate in the space provided whether the following fractions represent a proper fraction, an improper fraction, or a mixed number:

1. $\frac{58}{26} = $ _____
2. $\frac{19}{16} = $ _____
3. $\frac{12}{25} = $ _____
4. $4\frac{2}{9} = $ _____
5. $\frac{7}{7} = $ _____

SKILL EXERCISES

Identify the proper fractions in each of the following groups:

1. $\frac{6}{7}$ $\frac{9}{5}$ $\frac{4}{7}$ $\frac{10}{9}$ _____
2. $\frac{12}{10}$ $\frac{30}{34}$ $\frac{29}{16}$ $\frac{81}{85}$ _____
3. $\frac{3}{21}$ $\frac{47}{38}$ $\frac{39}{30}$ $\frac{75}{78}$ _____
4. $\frac{4}{3}$ $\frac{1}{2}$ $\frac{5}{4}$ $\frac{15}{16}$ _____
5. $\frac{25}{35}$ $\frac{15}{25}$ $\frac{38}{43}$ $\frac{22}{17}$ _____

Identify the improper fractions in each of the following groups:

6. $\frac{3}{9}$ $\frac{4}{3}$ $\frac{3}{4}$ $\frac{5}{2}$ _____
7. $\frac{6}{5}$ $\frac{3}{8}$ $\frac{6}{11}$ $\frac{17}{12}$ _____
8. $\frac{8}{7}$ $\frac{5}{16}$ $\frac{3}{4}$ $\frac{17}{16}$ _____
9. $\frac{9}{4}$ $\frac{5}{7}$ $\frac{3}{3}$ $\frac{9}{10}$ _____
10. $\frac{7}{8}$ $\frac{13}{12}$ $\frac{15}{9}$ $\frac{8}{15}$ _____

Identify each of the following as a proper fraction, an improper fraction, or a mixed number:

11. $1\frac{7}{8}$ _____
12. $\frac{9}{5}$ _____

Answers to ✔ Check for Understanding
1. Improper.   2. Improper.   3. Proper.   4. Mixed.   5. Improper.

Chapter 2   Fractions

13. $\frac{3}{4}$ _____   14. $2\frac{1}{2}$ _____

15. $\frac{12}{11}$ _____   16. $\frac{1}{9}$ _____

17. $3\frac{2}{3}$ _____   18. $4\frac{1}{2}$ _____

19. $\frac{3}{5}$ _____   20. $\frac{4}{9}$ _____

Converting Fractions to Higher or Lower Terms

> To raise a fraction to higher terms, we *multiply* both the numerator and the denominator by the same number. When we reduce fractions to lowest terms, we *divide* the numerator and denominator by the same number.

Multiplying or dividing the numerator and the denominator by the same number changes only the *form* of the fraction, not its *value*. Changing fractions to higher terms may be necessary in order to have a common denominator when adding or subtracting fractions.

EXAMPLE 4 Wayne has a $\frac{5}{8}$ measuring device. How many 40ths would that be?

Solution:

$$40 \div 8 = 5$$

- Determine the number of times 8 divides into 40.

$$\frac{5 \times 5}{8 \times 5} = \frac{25}{40}$$

- Multiply the numerator and denominator by the answer in Step 1.
- $\frac{5}{8}$ has been raised to $\frac{25}{40}$ without changing the value.

ANSWER: $\frac{25}{40}$

EXAMPLE 5 Reduce $\frac{24}{36}$ to lowest terms.

Solution:

$$\frac{24 \div 12}{36 \div 12} = \frac{2}{3}$$

- Divide the numerator and the denominator by the largest number you can think of that will go into both exactly.
- Determine if the new fraction $\frac{2}{3}$ can be reduced further.
- $\frac{24}{36}$ has been reduced to lowest terms $\left(\frac{2}{3}\right)$ without changing the value.

ANSWER: $\frac{2}{3}$

EXAMPLE 6 Reduce the fraction $\frac{45}{60}$ to lowest terms.

Solution:

$$\frac{45 \div 5}{60 \div 5} = \frac{9}{12}$$

$$\frac{9 \div 3}{12 \div 3} = \frac{3}{4}$$

- Divide the numerator and the denominator by the largest number you can think of that will go into both exactly.
- Can the new fraction $\frac{9}{12}$ be reduced further? Yes, then divide the new fraction by the largest number you can think of that will go into both exactly.
- Even though we didn't use the greatest common denominator (GCD), which is 15, dividing by 5 and then by 3 worked well.

ANSWER: $\frac{3}{4}$

✔ CHECK FOR UNDERSTANDING

1. Raise the following fractions to those with denominators of 16:
   (a) $\frac{7}{8}$ _____   (b) $\frac{3}{4}$ _____

2. Reduce the following fractions to lowest terms:
   (a) $\frac{15}{20}$ _____   (b) $\frac{9}{36}$ _____

SKILL EXERCISES

Change the following to fractions with higher denominators:

1. $\frac{2}{3} = \frac{}{27}$ 2. $\frac{5}{6} = \frac{}{18}$ 3. $\frac{11}{12} = \frac{}{36}$ 4. $\frac{7}{8} = \frac{}{16}$ 5. $\frac{5}{18} = \frac{}{72}$

6. $\frac{4}{9} = \frac{}{36}$ 7. $\frac{1}{2} = \frac{}{12}$ 8. $\frac{7}{16} = \frac{}{32}$ 9. $\frac{3}{4} = \frac{}{20}$ 10. $\frac{4}{7} = \frac{}{28}$

Reduce the following fractions to their lowest terms:

11. $\frac{25}{30} = \frac{}{6}$ 12. $\frac{28}{35} = \frac{}{5}$ 13. $\frac{108}{144} = \frac{}{4}$ 14. $\frac{54}{72} = \frac{}{4}$ 15. $\frac{34}{85} = \frac{}{5}$

16. $\frac{18}{54} = \frac{}{3}$

APPLICATIONS

Apply the skills learned to the following word problems:

1. If the stock market went up $\frac{3}{4}$ points, how many eighths did it rise?

2. If you walked $\frac{25}{10}$ miles, how far did you walk? Express your answer in units of half miles.

Answers to ✔ Check for Understanding
1. (a) $\frac{14}{16}$. (b) $\frac{12}{16}$. 2. (a) $\frac{3}{4}$. (b) $\frac{1}{4}$.

38   Chapter 2 Fractions

3. If the temperature dropped $\frac{24}{36}$ degrees, how far did it drop expressed as thirds?

4. Shortening a trouser belt $\frac{14}{16}$ of an inch would be the same as shortening the belt how many eighths of an inch?

5. The local speed drag strip measured $\frac{3}{5}$ of a mile. How long was the track measured in tenths of a mile?

Change the following to fractions with the modified denominators:

6. $\frac{2}{3} = \frac{}{15}$
7. $\frac{3}{4} = \frac{}{16}$
8. $\frac{7}{8} = \frac{}{24}$
9. $\frac{6}{12} = \frac{}{2}$
10. $\frac{10}{40} = \frac{}{20}$

11. $\frac{5}{25} = \frac{}{5}$
12. $\frac{3}{8} = \frac{}{32}$
13. $\frac{4}{5} = \frac{}{35}$
14. $\frac{7}{28} = \frac{}{4}$
15. $\frac{12}{27} = \frac{}{9}$

Improper Fractions and Mixed Numbers

2.2

> An **improper fraction** may be converted to a mixed number by dividing the numerator by the denominator.

If the answer is not a whole number, the **remainder** becomes the numerator of the remaining fraction.

EXAMPLE 7 Convert $\frac{65}{7}$ to a whole or mixed number.

Solution:

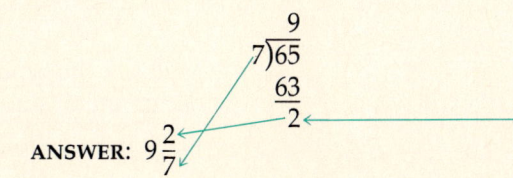

$$\begin{array}{r} 9 \\ 7\overline{)65} \\ \underline{63} \\ 2 \end{array}$$

- Divide the numerator by the denominator.
- The remainder becomes the numerator of the fraction in the mixed number.

ANSWER: $9\frac{2}{7}$

Section 2.2 Improper Fractions and Mixed Numbers

EXAMPLE 8 Convert $\frac{337}{8}$ to a whole or mixed number.

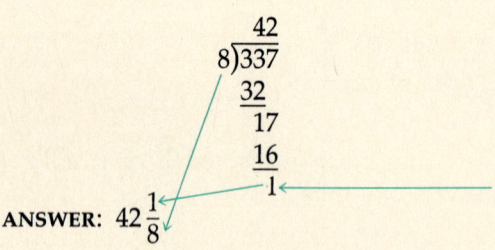

Solution:

$$\begin{array}{r} 42 \\ 8\overline{)337} \\ \underline{32} \\ 17 \\ \underline{16} \\ 1 \end{array}$$

- Divide the numerator by the denominator.
- The remainder becomes the numerator of the fraction in the mixed number.

ANSWER: $42\frac{1}{8}$

EXAMPLE 9 Convert $\frac{32}{10}$ to a whole or mixed number.

Solution:

$$\begin{array}{r} 3 \\ 10\overline{)32} \\ \underline{30} \\ 2 \end{array}$$

- Divide the numerator by the denominator.
- The remainder becomes the numerator of the fraction in the mixed number.

$3\frac{2}{10}$

$\frac{2 \div 2}{10 \div 2} = \frac{1}{5}$

- Reduce the remaining fraction.

ANSWER: $3\frac{1}{5}$

> A **mixed number** can be converted to an improper fraction by multiplying the denominator of the fraction by the whole number and adding the numerator, then placing the total over the denominator.

EXAMPLE 10 Convert $3\frac{3}{4}$ to an improper fraction.

Solution:

$3\frac{3}{4} = 15$

- Multiply the whole number times the denominator and add the numerator.

ANSWER: $\frac{15}{4}$

- Place the total over the denominator.

EXAMPLE 11 Betty was working with a piece of elastic for her dress that measured $4\frac{7}{8}$ inches. How many eighths are there in her measurement?

Solution:

$4\frac{7}{8} = 39$

- Multiply the whole number times the denominator and add the numerator.

ANSWER: $\frac{39}{8}$

- Place the total over the denominator.

Chapter 2 Fractions

EXAMPLE 12 There are $6\frac{2}{3}$ pies on the table. If each pie is to be cut into 3 pieces, how many thirds will there be?

Solution:

$$6\frac{2}{3} = 20$$

- Multiply the whole number by the denominator and add the numerator.
- Place the total over the denominator.

ANSWER: $\frac{20}{3}$

CALCULATOR TIP

When converting a large improper fraction to a whole or mixed number, use your calculator.

Problem: Convert $\frac{612}{25}$ to an improper fraction.

- Enter 612 ÷ 25 = 24.48 (Ignore the .48.) 24 is the largest whole number that divides into 612.
- Enter 24 × 25 = 600. Note how close we are to 612.
- Enter 612 − 600 = 12 (The remainder)

ANSWER: $24\frac{12}{25}$ (A combination of the whole number from Step 1 and the remainder from Step 3.) Reduce the fraction if appropriate.

✔ **CHECK FOR UNDERSTANDING**

1. Convert $\frac{47}{8}$ to a whole or mixed number.

2. Convert $\frac{472}{12}$ to a mixed number and reduce the fraction to lowest terms.

3. Convert $17\frac{5}{6}$ to an improper fraction.

SKILL EXERCISES

Change the following improper fractions to whole or mixed numbers:

1. $\frac{509}{21} =$ _____   2. $\frac{806}{13} =$ _____   3. $\frac{73}{12} =$ _____

4. $\frac{127}{9} =$ _____   5. $\frac{245}{8} =$ _____   6. $\frac{311}{16} =$ _____

7. $\frac{77}{11} =$ _____   8. $\frac{365}{19} =$ _____   9. $\frac{286}{14} =$ _____

10. $\frac{73}{7} =$ _____

Answers to ✔ Check for Understanding

1. $5\frac{7}{8}$.   2. $39\frac{1}{3}$.   3. $\frac{107}{6}$.

Section 2.2   Improper Fractions and Mixed Numbers

Change the following mixed numbers to improper fractions:

11. $3\frac{7}{8}$ = _____ 12. $5\frac{6}{7}$ = _____ 13. $9\frac{4}{9}$ = _____

14. $17\frac{2}{3}$ = _____ 15. $12\frac{1}{2}$ = _____ 16. $22\frac{1}{8}$ = _____

17. $6\frac{5}{8}$ = _____ 18. $7\frac{4}{5}$ = _____ 19. $4\frac{9}{15}$ = _____

20. $33\frac{1}{3}$ = _____

The Common Denominator

2.3   A common denominator of a set of fractions is a whole number that can be divided exactly by the denominators of all the fractions in the set. The **lowest common denominator (LCD)** is the smallest such whole number. Adding and subtracting fractions requires that the denominators be alike or have a common denominator.

The common denominator can often be found through observation. For instance, if the fractions $\frac{1}{2}$ and $\frac{3}{4}$ were used, it can be seen that each would divide evenly into 4. This would make 4 the common denominator. A common denominator can also be found by multiplying the denominators together.

A common denominator need not be the lowest possible one, however. It is best to use the lowest common denominator initially to eliminate the need to reduce later. If you can't determine the LCD through observation, there is a simple **prime number** method that works well. A prime number is any whole number greater than one that is divisible only by itself and 1. The prime numbers you will use most commonly in this text will be 2, 3, 5, and 7. Once the LCD is found, change each fraction to the new common denominator to allow addition or subtraction.

EXAMPLE 13   Find the lowest common denominator for $\frac{2}{6}, \frac{3}{4}, \frac{4}{7},$ and $\frac{8}{15}$.

Solution:

Prime Number Divisors   Denominators

Divisor				
3	6	4	7	15
2	2	4	7	5
2	1	2	7	5
7	1	1	7	5
5	1	1	1	5
	1	1	1	1

$\boxed{3 \times 2 \times 2 \times 7 \times 5 = 420}$

- List the denominators horizontally. Find a prime number that will divide into more than one denominator, if possible.
- Divide that prime number and list the quotients beneath the dividends. Bring down any dividend not divided.
- Continue the process until all dividends are reduced to one.
- Multiply the prime numbers together to determine the LCD.

ANSWER: 420

> **PROBLEM SOLVING STRATEGY**
>
> When determining the LCD, the order in which you select your prime numbers doesn't matter. In Example 13, we could have used 7, 2, 3, 5, 2, or any other order.

EXAMPLE 14 In working with 4 different recipes, you discovered the following requirement for cups of milk: $\frac{2}{3}, \frac{4}{5}, \frac{4}{9},$ and $\frac{3}{15}$. Using the LCD, determine how many total cups of milk are needed.

Solution:

Divisors   *Denominators*

Divisors				
	3	5	9	15
3				
	1	5	3	5
5				
	1	1	3	1
3				
	1	1	1	1

$\boxed{3 \times 5 \times 3 = 45}$

- List the denominators. Divide them by prime numbers until no two have a common prime divisor or until all are reduced to one.

- Multiply the prime numbers to obtain the LCD.

Converts to

$\frac{2}{3} \quad \substack{\times 15 \\ \times 15} \quad \frac{30}{45}$

$\frac{4}{5} \quad \substack{\times 9 \\ \times 9} \quad \frac{36}{45}$

$\frac{4}{9} \quad \substack{\times 5 \\ \times 5} \quad \frac{20}{45}$

$\frac{3}{15} \quad \substack{\times 3 \\ \times 3} \quad \frac{9}{45}$

$\frac{95}{45}$

- Using the technique of raising fractions to higher terms, change each fraction to 45ths.

- Remember, when *adding* fractions, add only the *numerators* and place over 45.

$\frac{95}{45} = \frac{19}{9} \text{ or } 2\frac{1}{9}$

- Reduce to lowest terms.

ANSWER: $2\frac{1}{9}$ cups

EXAMPLE 15 Find the LCD and then add the following fractions: $\frac{5}{12} + \frac{1}{10} + \frac{4}{15} + \frac{5}{6}$.

Solution:

Divisors   *Denominators*

Divisors				
	12	10	15	6
5				
	12	2	3	6
3				
	4	2	1	2
2				
	2	1	1	1
2				
	1	1	1	1

$\boxed{5 \times 3 \times 2 \times 2 = 60}$

- List the denominators. Divide them by prime numbers until no two have a common prime divisor or until all are reduced to one.

- Multiply prime numbers to get the LCD.

Section 2.3 The Common Denominator

$$\frac{5}{12} \quad \overset{\text{Converts to}}{\underset{\times 5}{\times 5}} \quad \frac{25}{60}$$

$$\frac{1}{10} \quad \underset{\times 6}{\times 6} \quad \frac{6}{60}$$

$$\frac{4}{15} \quad \underset{\times 4}{\times 4} \quad \frac{16}{60}$$

$$\frac{5}{6} \quad \underset{\times 10}{\times 10} \quad \frac{50}{60}$$

$$\frac{97}{60}$$

- Using the technique of raising fractions to higher terms, change each fraction to 60ths.
- Add the four numerators and place over 60.

$$\frac{97}{60} = 1\frac{37}{60}$$

- Change the improper faction to a mixed number; reduce the fraction if necessary.

ANSWER: $1\frac{37}{60}$

EXAMPLE 16 Find the lowest common denominator and subtract $\frac{5}{8}$ from $\frac{11}{12}$.

Solution:

$$\frac{11}{12} \quad \overset{\text{Converts to}}{\underset{\times 2}{\times 2}} \quad \frac{22}{24}$$

$$\frac{5}{8} \quad \underset{\times 3}{\times 3} \quad \frac{15}{24}$$

$$\frac{7}{24}$$

- By observation, the LCD of denominators 8 and 12 is 24.
- Raise the denominators to 24's.
- Remember, when *subtracting* fractions, subtract the *numerators* and place over 24.
- Check to see if $\frac{7}{24}$ can be reduced.

ANSWER: $\frac{7}{24}$

EXAMPLE 17 Subtract the following mixed numbers: $8\frac{5}{6} - 3\frac{3}{4}$.

Solution:

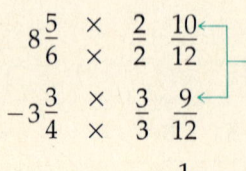

$$8\frac{5}{6} \quad \underset{\times 2}{\times 2} \quad \frac{10}{12}$$

$$-3\frac{3}{4} \quad \underset{\times 3}{\times 3} \quad \frac{9}{12}$$

$$\frac{1}{12}$$

$$\begin{array}{r} 8 \\ -3 \\ \hline 5 \end{array}$$

- Subtract the fractions first.
- By observation, the LCD of denominators 6 and 4 is 12.
- Raise the denominators to 12's.
- Subtract the numerators and place over 12. Check to see if $\frac{1}{12}$ can be reduced.
- Subtract whole numbers.
- Combine the results of both steps to get the final answer.

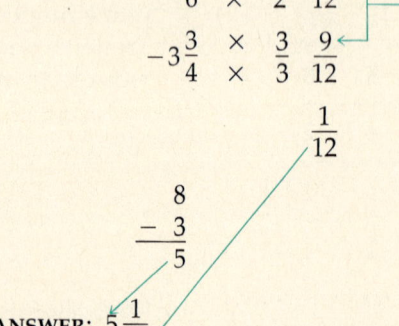

ANSWER: $5\frac{1}{12}$

44 Chapter 2 Fractions

EXAMPLE 18 The bank is currently using an interest rate of $7\frac{5}{8}$. If they lower it to $7\frac{1}{3}$, how much did it drop?

Solution:

$$7\frac{5}{8} \times \frac{3}{3} = \frac{15}{24}$$
$$-7\frac{1}{3} \times \frac{8}{8} = \frac{8}{24}$$
$$\frac{7}{24}$$

- Subtract the fractions first.
- By observation the LCD of 8 and 3 is 24.
- Raise the denominators to 24's.
- Subtract the numerators and place over 24. Check to see if $\frac{7}{24}$ can be reduced.
- Subtract the whole numbers.
- Combine the results of whole number and fraction subtraction for final answer.

$$\begin{array}{r}7\\-7\\\hline 0\end{array}$$

ANSWER: $\frac{7}{24}$

✔ CHECK FOR UNDERSTANDING

1. Find the lowest common denominator of $\frac{3}{8}, \frac{2}{5}, \frac{4}{6},$ and $\frac{2}{3}$.

2. Add these fractions: $\frac{3}{7} + \frac{6}{14} + \frac{14}{21}$.

3. Subtract $\frac{3}{4}$ from $\frac{5}{6}$.

4. The door for a cabinet is $24\frac{3}{4}$ inches wide and needs to be narrowed by $\frac{3}{8}$ inch on each side. How wide will the door be when it is finished?

SKILL EXERCISES

Add the following fractions using the LCD. Record the LCD and your answer in the spaces provided.

Fractions	LCD	Answer
1. $\frac{4}{5} + \frac{5}{9} + \frac{14}{15}$	_____	_____
2. $\frac{3}{4} + \frac{5}{6} + \frac{7}{9}$	_____	_____
3. $\frac{4}{7} + \frac{7}{9} + \frac{5}{6} + \frac{3}{4}$	_____	_____
4. $4\frac{3}{4} + 7\frac{5}{12} + 2\frac{6}{10}$	_____	_____
5. $\frac{7}{8} + \frac{2}{3} + \frac{3}{7} + \frac{4}{5}$	_____	_____

Answers to ✔ Check for Understanding
1. 120.   2. $1\frac{11}{21}$.   3. $\frac{1}{12}$.   4. 24 inches.

Section 2.3 The Common Denominator

6. $\frac{1}{2} + \frac{3}{4} + \frac{5}{8}$ _____ _____

7. $2\frac{3}{4} + 4\frac{5}{6} + 3\frac{7}{8}$ _____ _____

8. $32\frac{5}{8} + 17\frac{2}{9}$ _____ _____

9. $\frac{4}{5} + \frac{2}{3} + \frac{1}{6} + \frac{3}{8}$ _____ _____

10. $\frac{9}{16} + \frac{3}{32} + \frac{3}{4}$ _____ _____

Subtract the following fractions or mixed numbers using the LCD. Record the LCD and your answer in the spaces provided.

                                    LCD   **Answer**

11. $\frac{11}{12} - \frac{6}{7}$ _____ _____

12. $\frac{3}{4} - \frac{3}{8}$ _____ _____

13. $\frac{5}{8} - \frac{1}{3}$ _____ _____

14. $6\frac{7}{8} - 3\frac{3}{5}$ _____ _____

15. $\frac{19}{24} - \frac{3}{24}$ _____ _____

16. $\frac{1}{2} - \frac{1}{8}$ _____ _____

17. $12\frac{7}{16} - 7\frac{1}{3}$ _____ _____

18. $\frac{3}{5} - \frac{1}{3}$ _____ _____

19. $\frac{5}{6} - \frac{5}{7}$ _____ _____

20. $101\frac{3}{4} - 56\frac{1}{5}$ _____ _____

APPLICATIONS

Apply the skills learned to the following word problems:

1. A 4-foot sheet of plywood is cut 4 times. If each saw width is $\frac{1}{32}$ inch, what is the combined width of the pieces?

2. Maida had $7\frac{3}{4}$ cans of paint. She needed $12\frac{1}{2}$ cans. How many was she short?

3. Four men worked on the ballfield last week. Their individual hours were $37\frac{2}{3}$, $42\frac{1}{2}$, 40, and $43\frac{3}{5}$. How many total hours were worked?

4. With a total of $875\frac{6}{7}$ miles to drive, George traveled $432\frac{2}{7}$ miles. How far did he have yet to travel?

5. Stock held by Bounder Inc. rose from a price of $37\frac{3}{8}$ per share to $51\frac{7}{8}$ per share. How much did it increase in value?

6. What is the combined value of stocks that list for $45\frac{3}{8}$, $37\frac{5}{8}$, $23\frac{5}{8}$, and $167\frac{7}{8}$?

7. What is the combined thickness of boards that are $\frac{3}{4}$ inch, $\frac{5}{8}$ inch, $\frac{3}{16}$ inch, and $1\frac{3}{8}$ inches thick?

8. If a space is $36\frac{3}{8}$ inches wide and a board is $42\frac{5}{16}$ inches wide, how much do you need to cut off to make the board fit the space?

9. An office atrium space needs to be planted. Three different types of plants require $7\frac{1}{3}$ square yards, $8\frac{3}{4}$ square yards, and $15\frac{5}{9}$ square yards of growing space. What is the total square yards of space needed?

10. A manufacturing space is a rectangle that measures $87\frac{5}{8}$ feet long and $34\frac{3}{5}$ feet wide. What is the total distance around the edge of the area?

11. The city passed an ordinance requiring all streets to be $27\frac{7}{8}$ feet wide. If the street containing your business was $16\frac{4}{5}$ feet wide, how much must it be widened?

12. The flood stage on the local river is $19\frac{3}{4}$ feet. The depth of the river is currently $14\frac{3}{8}$ feet. How much farther can it rise before it threatens to flood?

13. Before you can open your ski area, you will need $49\frac{1}{2}$ inches of snow. There is currently $37\frac{2}{7}$ inches on the ground. How much more is needed?

14. A restaurant recipe called for $\frac{1}{8}$ cup orange juice, $\frac{1}{8}$ cup water, $\frac{1}{5}$ cup milk, and $\frac{1}{6}$ cup pineapple juice. How many total cups of liquid were needed for the recipe?

15. A rock mixture had $\frac{3}{4}$ ton of red rock, $\frac{4}{5}$ ton of Colorado gold ore rock, and $6\frac{2}{3}$ tons of white river rock. How many total tons were in the mixture?

Multiplication and Division of Fractions and Mixed Numbers

2.4

Both multiplication and division of fractions involve the process of multiplication.

> **Multiplication**
> To multiply fractions, multiply numerator times numerator (straight across), and denominator times denominator (straight across). The result will be a fraction that perhaps can then be reduced to lowest terms.

EXAMPLE 19 Multiply the following fractions: $\frac{3}{8} \times \frac{5}{6}$.

Solution:

$\frac{3}{8} \times \frac{5}{6} = \frac{15}{48}$ · Multiply the numerators.
· Multiply the denominators.

$\frac{15}{48} = \frac{5}{16}$ · Reduce the fraction to lowest terms.

ANSWER: $\frac{5}{16}$

EXAMPLE 20 With three-quarters of a load of sand available, calculations show that only one-third of the available sand is needed. How much of the total load of sand is needed?

Solution:

$\frac{3}{4} \times \frac{1}{3} = \frac{3}{12}$ · Multiply numerators; multiply denominators.

$\frac{3}{12} = \frac{1}{4}$ · Reduce to lowest terms.

ANSWER: $\frac{1}{4}$

> **Mixed Numbers**
> To multiply or divide mixed numbers, convert them to improper fractions, multiply or divide, then change the result to whole or mixed number form.

Chapter 2 Fractions

EXAMPLE 21 Multiply the following mixed numbers: $3\frac{4}{5} \times 2\frac{5}{8}$.

Solution:

$$3\frac{4}{5} = \frac{19}{5}$$

$$2\frac{5}{8} = \frac{21}{8}$$

- Change each mixed number to an improper fraction.

$$\frac{19}{5} \times \frac{21}{8} = \frac{399}{40}$$

- Multiply the numerators; multiply the denominators.

$$\frac{399}{40} = 9\frac{39}{40}$$

- Change the improper fraction to a mixed number.

ANSWER: $9\frac{39}{40}$

EXAMPLE 22 Each wheelbarrow load holds $2\frac{1}{4}$ cubic feet of top soil. If the pile contains enough for only $4\frac{1}{2}$ trips, how much top soil was transferred?

Solution:

$$2\frac{1}{4} = \frac{9}{4}$$

$$4\frac{1}{2} = \frac{9}{2}$$

- Change each mixed number to an improper fraction.

$$\frac{9}{4} \times \frac{9}{2} = \frac{81}{8}$$

- Multiply the numerators; multiply the denominators.

$$\frac{81}{8} = 10\frac{1}{8}$$

- Change the improper fraction to a mixed number.

ANSWER: $10\frac{1}{8}$

PROBLEM SOLVING STRATEGY

It is acceptable to cancel the fractions in a problem before you multiply the numerators together and the denominators together. A factor of any numerator may cancel with a like factor of any denominator. To cancel means to divide the same number into a numerator and denominator. For example:

$$\frac{1}{\cancel{2}} \times \frac{\cancel{2}}{3} = \frac{1}{3}$$

$$\frac{\cancel{9}^3}{\cancel{3}_1} \times \frac{\cancel{4}^1}{\cancel{8}_2} = \frac{3}{2} = 1\frac{1}{2}$$

- Divide 2 into numerator 2 and denominator 2 (cancel 2's).
- Multiply numerators together and denominators together.
- Answer is $\frac{1}{3}$.

- Divide 3 into numerator 9 and denominator 3.
- Divide 4 into numerator 4 and denominator 8.
- Multiply numerators together and denominators together.
- Change improper fraction to a mixed number.
- Answer is $1\frac{1}{2}$.

The canceling process cuts down the time-consuming task of reducing the final answer.

Section 2.4 Multiplication and Division of Fractions and Mixed Numbers

> **Division**
>
> To divide fractions, invert the divisor and multiply. The divisor is always the number following the divide symbol. Inverting a fraction means: $\frac{3}{8} \rightarrow \frac{8}{3}$.

EXAMPLE 23   Divide the following fractions: $\frac{7}{8} \div \frac{5}{6}$.

Solution:

$$\frac{7}{8} \div \frac{5}{6} = \frac{7}{8} \times \frac{6}{5}$$ • Invert the divisor.

$$\frac{7 \times 6}{8 \times 5} = \frac{42}{40}$$ • Multiply numerators and denominators straight across.

$$\frac{42}{40} = 1\frac{2}{40} \text{ or } 1\frac{1}{20}$$ • Convert the improper fraction to a mixed number and reduce to lowest terms.

ANSWER: $1\frac{1}{20}$

EXAMPLE 24   Divide $\frac{5}{7}$ by $2\frac{3}{8}$.

Solution:

$$\frac{5}{7} \div \frac{19}{8}$$ • Rewrite the problem, changing the mixed number to an improper fraction.

$$\frac{5}{7} \times \frac{8}{19}$$ • Invert the divisor.

$$\frac{*5}{7} \times \frac{8}{19} = \frac{40}{133}$$ • Multiply the numerators; multiply the denominators.
   • Reduce the fraction if necessary.

ANSWER: $\frac{40}{133}$

✓ CHECK FOR UNDERSTANDING

1. Find the quotient of $\frac{3}{7} \div \frac{4}{5}$.

2. Find the product of $\frac{6}{15} \times \frac{3}{8}$.

* Cancellation may also be used in this step before multiplication.

Chapter 2   Fractions

3. If a recipe calls for $\frac{3}{4}$ cup of sugar, and only one-half the recipe is needed, how much sugar will be required? (Hint: $\frac{1}{2}$ of $\frac{3}{4}$ is the same as writing $\frac{1}{2} \times \frac{3}{4}$. The "of" means multiply.)

SKILL EXERCISES

Multiply, and reduce the products to lowest terms:

1. $\frac{2}{3} \times \frac{4}{5} =$ _____
2. $\frac{7}{8} \times \frac{3}{5} =$ _____
3. $\frac{5}{9} \times \frac{2}{3} =$ _____
4. $\frac{5}{6} \times \frac{8}{9} =$ _____
5. $\frac{4}{7} \times \frac{5}{6} =$ _____
6. $2\frac{1}{2} \times \frac{2}{3} =$ _____
7. $3\frac{3}{4} \times \frac{7}{8} =$ _____
8. $7\frac{1}{4} \times \frac{5}{9} =$ _____
9. $\frac{9}{16} \times 4\frac{3}{8} =$ _____
10. $\frac{7}{8} \times \frac{9}{32} =$ _____

Divide, and express the quotients as fractions or mixed numbers:

11. $\frac{3}{4} \div \frac{7}{8} =$ _____
12. $\frac{2}{3} \div \frac{5}{6} =$ _____
13. $\frac{1}{2} \div \frac{5}{8} =$ _____
14. $\frac{7}{8} \div \frac{3}{5} =$ _____
15. $\frac{5}{6} \div \frac{9}{10} =$ _____
16. $3\frac{1}{4} \div \frac{2}{3} =$ _____
17. $\frac{4}{5} \div 2\frac{1}{2} =$ _____
18. $4 \div \frac{3}{4} =$ _____
19. $\frac{5}{8} \div 2 =$ _____
20. $\frac{3}{5} \div \frac{2}{3} =$ _____

APPLICATIONS

Apply the skills learned to the following word problems:

1. An office kitchen area needs a new cabinet. The cabinet door opening is 3 feet wide and 4 feet 6 inches long. If the door needs a $\frac{1}{4}$ inch overlap on all sides of the door, to what dimension should the sheet of material be cut?

Answers to ✓ Check for Understanding
1. $\frac{15}{28}$.   2. $\frac{3}{20}$.   3. $\frac{3}{8}$ cup.

Section 2.4 Multiplication and Division of Fractions and Mixed Numbers

2. A new paint formula calls for $2\frac{1}{5}$ ounces of resin. The quantity being produced requires $3\frac{1}{2}$ times that amount. How much resin is needed?

3. A racetrack is $\frac{7}{8}$ miles long on the inside rail. If the outside of the track is $\frac{1}{9}$ mile longer, what is the outside length of the track?

4. If a patio is $15\frac{3}{4}$ feet wide, and the owners decide to double the width, what will the new dimension be?

5. There are 3,500 pipe fittings in inventory. The manager told Rodney to reduce the inventory by $\frac{2}{7}$. How many will be left in inventory?

6. A par 5 golf hole is 436 yards long. If a golfer hits the ball an average of $145\frac{1}{3}$ yards, how many strokes will it take to get to the green?

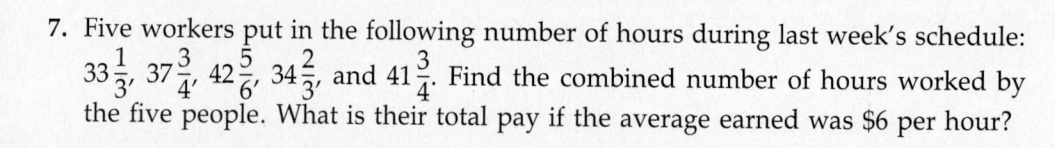

7. Five workers put in the following number of hours during last week's schedule: $33\frac{1}{3}$, $37\frac{3}{4}$, $42\frac{5}{6}$, $34\frac{2}{3}$, and $41\frac{3}{4}$. Find the combined number of hours worked by the five people. What is their total pay if the average earned was $6 per hour?

8. If you need 3 gallons of gasoline for the garden tractor and you have only a $\frac{1}{3}$ gallon container, how many times would you need to fill the container to transfer the gasoline?

9. A construction crew is working on a new ditch area. It will take 256 yards of concrete to pour the ditch. If each truckload contains $6\frac{2}{3}$ yards, how many truckloads will it take to finish the job?

10. Each truckload contains $3\frac{3}{7}$ cubic yards of sand. How much sand will be hauled in a day when $6\frac{1}{2}$ truck loads were delivered?

11. How wide must a sheet of paper be to be cut into 4 equal pieces each measuring $3\frac{7}{8}$ inches?

12. If the thickness of a board is $\frac{5}{6}$ inch, how many can be stacked in an inventory bin that is 14 feet high?

13. The price of gasoline is $1.04 a gallon, and Jon's car gets $32\frac{1}{2}$ miles to a gallon. How much will it cost Jon to drive 750 miles?

14. Water costs $$12\frac{1}{2}$ for 1,000 gallons. If Susan needs 42,300 gallons to water the new landscape, how much will the water cost?

15. What will be the combined weight of 55 radios if the average weight is $1\frac{3}{4}$ pounds each?

Chapter 2 Fractions

Key Terms

Denominator (35)
Improper fraction (35)
Lowest common denominator (42)
Mixed number (36)
Numerator (35)
Prime number (42)
Proper fraction (35)
Remainder (39)

Looking Back

The lowest common denominator is easiest to work with when adding or subtracting fractions. However, it is acceptable to solve these problems with any common denominator.

Remember that the denominator of any whole number is 1. When using fractions and whole numbers, it is sometimes easier to remember that 1 is the denominator of a whole number. If the whole number were inverted, the 1 would then become the numerator.

Obtaining answers to fraction problems may provide many alternative responses. The desired method is to find the answer with the fractions expressed in lowest terms.

Let's Review

Indicate whether each of the following numbers is a proper fraction, an improper fraction, or a mixed number:

1. $6\frac{2}{3} =$ _____
2. $\frac{9}{5} =$ _____
3. $\frac{4}{7} =$ _____
4. $\frac{19}{17} =$ _____
5. $\frac{3}{5} =$ _____
6. $4\frac{3}{7} =$ _____

Find the sums:

7. $\frac{3}{4} + \frac{4}{5} + \frac{2}{15} + \frac{1}{8} =$ _____
8. $\frac{2}{3} + \frac{1}{4} + \frac{1}{6} + \frac{3}{8} =$ _____
9. $\frac{7}{8} + \frac{2}{2} + \frac{4}{5} + \frac{1}{7} =$ _____
10. $\frac{9}{16} + \frac{7}{8} + \frac{1}{3} + \frac{1}{6} + \frac{7}{12} =$ _____

Find the differences:

11. $\frac{4}{5} - \frac{3}{9} =$ _____
12. $\frac{7}{7} - \frac{3}{8} =$ _____
13. $\frac{1}{2} - \frac{3}{8} =$ _____
14. $\frac{2}{3} - \frac{1}{6} =$ _____

Find the products:

15. $2\frac{1}{2} \times 7\frac{3}{4}$ = _____

16. $\frac{7}{8} \times \frac{4}{5}$ = _____

17. $\frac{9}{10} \times \frac{8}{15}$ = _____

18. $1\frac{1}{2} \times 3$ = _____

Find the quotients:

19. $\frac{3}{4} \div \frac{1}{2}$ = _____

20. $\frac{7}{8} \div \frac{2}{3}$ = _____

21. $11\frac{3}{4} \div 7\frac{1}{2}$ = _____

22. When Jan planned a party for 16 office members she figured $3\frac{1}{2}$ cupcakes per person. How many cupcakes did she need?

23. If a stock is selling for $67\frac{1}{4}$, and it drops to $64\frac{1}{8}$, how much change was there?

24. If the current road is 16 miles long and it is to be increased in length by $\frac{1}{8}$, what will its new length be?

25. When the stadium was remodeled, seating capacity was increased by $\frac{1}{7}$. If the old seating capacity was 56,000, how many seats will the stadium now hold?

Chapter Test

1. A cabinet maker was working on frames for his windows, which had openings of $36\frac{1}{2}$ inches by 18 inches. If the outside of the frames needed to be $\frac{7}{8}$ inches greater than the opening on all 4 sides, what would be the outside dimension of the frames?

2. The Chicken Ranch Restaurant buys chickens for 48 cents a pound. If the chickens average $3\frac{1}{4}$ pounds, and they can serve 4 people from each chicken, what is the cost of chicken per serving?

3. How many square feet are there in a warehouse floor that is $87\frac{1}{3}$ feet long and $56\frac{3}{4}$ feet wide?

4. The sporting goods department was remodeled. The manager anticipates a $\frac{1}{7}$ increase in sales during the year. If this year's sales are $560,000, what sales increase is expected for next year?

5. A storage tank contains 6,300 gallons of water. If it were filled one more inch, it would increase the amount of water by $\frac{1}{9}$. How much water would be in the tank after the increase?

6. How many cubic inches are there in a box that is $16\frac{1}{2}$ inches wide, $24\frac{2}{3}$ inches long, and $9\frac{1}{4}$ inches deep?

7. Employee training grades on a new production system were calculated. Margie had 45 points for $17\frac{1}{2}$ training hours. How many points did she average for each training hour?

8. The average hourly earning rate was $6\frac{2}{3}$ dollars an hour. Bill was working for $4\frac{1}{8}$ dollars per hour. How much below average pay was he receiving?

9. The job required a total of $42\frac{3}{4}$ hours. With $15\frac{1}{5}$ hours needed to finish it, how many hours had been worked?

10. The jewelry department's sales decreased sales by $\frac{1}{10}$ from last year. Last year's sales were $345,000. What was the amount of decrease?

11. The catalog department reduced the square footage it occupied by $\frac{1}{5}$. If they originally occupied 600 square feet, how many square feet will they have after the reduction?

12. A salesperson worked $9\frac{2}{3}$ hours in a day. If $3\frac{1}{2}$ hours were spent driving and the rest of the time meeting customers, how many hours did she have for customer contact?

13. The distance from the nearest shipping dock was 1,675 miles. If the driver covered $\frac{3}{5}$ of the distance the first two days, how many miles did he have left?

14. The city has $4,560,000 from tax revenues. If it collects $\frac{1}{3}$ of the total, how much has been collected?

15. A tire has total mileage expectancy of 56,000 miles. If $\frac{5}{8}$ of its life has been used up, how many miles are left?

Decimals and Percents

3

OBJECTIVES

When you complete this chapter you will be able to:
- *Understand the decimal point system and rounding. (3.1)*
- *Make fraction to decimal conversions. (3.2)*
- *Convert fractions and decimals to percents. (3.3)*

COMING UP

Business calculations have been accelerated extensively by the use of automated equipment. Calculators, computers' digital readouts, and bar-coding have all modernized transaction processing. We even see people walking down the aisles of the supermarket with hand calculators figuring their purchases.

This trend toward automation has also affected the type of mathematics we use. Today's trend reduces our use of fractions and moves us closer to using the more adaptable decimal. As you perform business calculations, the process will almost always involve the decimal system and percents. This chapter provides some needed review of the rules of decimals and percents.

The Decimal Point

3.1

The decimal point (.) is a position of reference. Numbers to the left of the decimal point indicate whole numbers; numbers to the right of the decimal point indicate numbers with values less than one. Figure 3.1 shows decimal positions and appropriate names through the billionths place. When no decimal point is included in a whole number, it is assumed to be after the whole number; for example, 32 becomes 32.0.

```
                                                    Billionths
                                        Hundred-millionths
                                        Ten-millionths
                                    Millionths
                        Hundred-thousandths
                        Ten-thousandths
                    Thousandths
                Hundredths
            Tenths

Decimal point  (.)  0  0  0  0  0  0  0  0  1
                   .1
                       .01
                           .001
                               .0001
                                   .00001
                                       .000001
                                           .0000001
                                               .00000001
                                                   .000000001
```

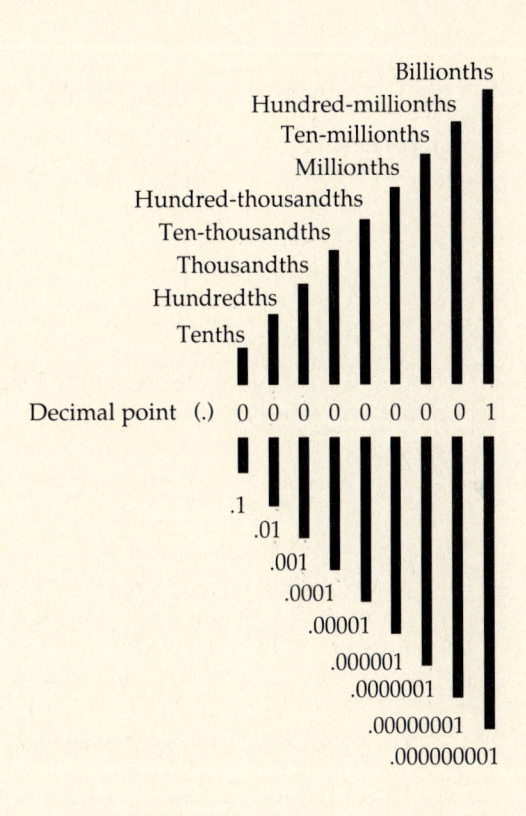

FIGURE 3.1
Decimal positions

To read a decimal, identify the name of the position represented by the number of digits to the right of the decimal. Thus, in the number .1234, the 4 is in the ten-thousandths position. The number is read in normal fashion (1,234)—one thousand, two hundred thirty-four, then add ten thousandths. If you familiarize yourself with the names of the numerical placements, you will be able to express numbers with accuracy and confidence. Decimals may also be read using the word "point." Therefore, the number .657 can be read as point 657 or as six hundred fifty-seven thousandths.

There is a direct relationship between fractions and decimals. Each decimal can be expressed as a fraction and each fraction can be converted to a decimal. The most commonly used form in business is the decimal because it lends itself to calculators and data systems.

Rounding of Decimal Places

When we use decimals in mathematic calculations, the answers do not always come out as whole numbers. Some decimal answers, especially if they are a continuing decimal, may need to be **rounded off.** There are **rules of rounding** that will help you. The number of decimal positions to use is an arbitrary decision based upon need and accuracy desired.

> When the number of desired decimal positions is determined, observe the digit to the right of that significant place. If that number is less than 5, leave the significant place digit the same. If the digit to the right is 5 or greater, raise the significant place digit by one and drop all digits to the right of that place. Thus, .342573 would become .342<u>6</u> if the number were rounded to 10,000ths, or four places. It would be .3<u>4</u> if rounded to 100ths.

EXAMPLE 1 Round 0.19375 to 10,000ths, or four decimal places.

Solution:

$$0.19375$$
$$0.1938$$

- The significant place is the 7.
- The number to the right is 5 or larger.
- The 7 must be raised to an 8.

EXAMPLE 2 Round the following decimal to the significant place required in each of the following situations: 0.364291734

Solution:

0.364	=	0.36	• Rounded to two places.
0.36429	=	0.3643	• Rounded to four places.
0.364291	=	0.36429	• Rounded to five places.
0.3642917	=	0.364292	• Rounded to six places.

✔ CHECK FOR UNDERSTANDING

1. Using the decimal value 0.47836942, complete the indicated roundings:

    The nearest hundredth _____
    The nearest ten-thousandth _____
    The nearest hundred-thousandth _____
    The nearest thousandth _____

2. Review the decimal value and round 23.143876509 to the thousandths position.

Answers to ✔ Check for Understanding
1. 0.48; 0.4784; 0.47837; 0.478.   2. 23.144.

Chapter 3 Decimals and Percents

SKILL EXERCISES

Round the following decimals to the nearest hundredth:

1. 0.98376 = _____
2. 0.481 = _____
3. 0.49983 = _____
4. 0.0274 = _____
5. 0.1119 = _____
6. 0.44999 = _____
7. 0.6731 = _____
8. 0.2156 = _____
9. 0.7335 = _____
10. 0.8891 = _____

Round the following decimals to the nearest thousandth:

11. 0.00064 = _____
12. 0.13911 = _____
13. 0.81182 = _____
14. 0.91496 = _____
15. 0.0842 = _____
16. 0.11399 = _____
17. 0.3464 = _____
18. 0.39772 = _____
19. 0.7149 = _____
20. 0.50001 = _____

APPLICATIONS

Apply the skills learned above to round each of the following numbers by eliminating the last digit and rounding either up or down using the rounding rule:

1. .79684 = _____
2. .865 = _____
3. .436274 = _____
4. .279897 = _____
5. .12344 = _____
6. .78765 = _____
7. .8643 = _____
8. .279621 = _____
9. .576354 = _____
10. .39652 = _____

Converting Fractions to Decimals

3.2

Converting, changing a fraction to a decimal, makes the number easier to work with on the calculator. Although fractions are easier to work with when reduced to lowest terms, the use of the calculator eliminates this step and reduces the potential for error. Table 3.1 shows some common fractions and their decimal equivalents.

TABLE 3.1
Fraction and Decimal Equivalents

Fraction		Decimal	Fraction		Decimal
$\frac{1}{2}$	=	.5	$\frac{3}{5}$	=	.6
$\frac{1}{4}$	=	.25	$\frac{4}{5}$	=	.8
$\frac{3}{4}$	=	.75	$\frac{3}{8}$	=	.375
$\frac{1}{8}$	=	.125	$\frac{5}{8}$	=	.625
$\frac{1}{5}$	=	.2	$\frac{7}{8}$	=	.875
$\frac{2}{5}$	=	.4	$\frac{1}{10}$	=	.1
$\frac{1}{3}$	=	.3333*	$\frac{2}{3}$	=	.6667*

* A continuing decimal rounded to ten-thousandths place.

> To find the decimal value of any fraction, divide the numerator by the denominator. If it is an improper fraction, the quotient will contain a whole number followed by a decimal.

EXAMPLE 3 Convert $\frac{3}{8}$ to a decimal.

Solution:

$\frac{3}{8}$ Numerator $\frac{3}{8} = 0.375$ · Divide the numerator by the denominator.

EXAMPLE 4 Convert $5\frac{2}{5}$ to decimal form.

Solution:

$\frac{2}{5} = 0.4$ · $5\frac{2}{5}$ really means $5 + \frac{2}{5}$; change the fraction to a decimal.

$5.0 + .4 = 5.4$ · Add 5.0 to the decimal from Step 1.

EXAMPLE 5 Convert $\frac{7}{6}$ to decimal form and round to four places.

Solution:

$\frac{7}{6} = 1.1666666$ · Convert to decimal; divide numerator by denominator.

$1.1666666 = 1.1667$ · Round to four places.

CALCULATOR TIP

In working Example 5, some calculators will automatically round the last displayed digit to 1.1666667.

Chapter 3 Decimals and Percents

✔ CHECK FOR UNDERSTANDING

Round all of the following continuing decimals to four places:

1. Convert $\frac{13}{54}$ to decimal form.

2. Convert $12\frac{3}{8}$ to decimal form.

3. Convert $\frac{9}{5}$ to decimal form.

SKILL EXERCISES

Convert the following fractions to decimal form and round all continuing decimals to three places.

1. $\frac{6}{8}$ = _____   2. $\frac{4}{32}$ = _____

3. $\frac{3}{5}$ = _____   4. $\frac{28}{64}$ = _____

5. $\frac{9}{7}$ = _____   6. $\frac{1}{9}$ = _____

7. $\frac{8}{3}$ = _____   8. $\frac{11}{5}$ = _____

9. $5\frac{6}{7}$ = _____   10. $\frac{13}{5}$ = _____

11. $\frac{6}{23}$ = _____   12. $\frac{9}{15}$ = _____

13. $\frac{2}{9}$ = _____   14. $\frac{14}{3}$ = _____

15. $\frac{3}{7}$ = _____   16. $5\frac{3}{23}$ = _____

17. $\frac{85}{7}$ = _____   18. $\frac{7}{9}$ = _____

19. $3\frac{5}{9}$ = _____   20. $4\frac{1}{2}$ = _____

APPLICATIONS

Express all answers in decimal form to the thousandths place if applicable.

1. A local company's stock was listed as $58\frac{1}{8}$ yesterday. Today, it dropped to $32\frac{1}{4}$. How far did it drop?

Answers to ✔ Check for Understanding
1. 0.2407.   2. 12.375.   3. 1.8.

Section 3.2 Converting Fractions to Decimals

2. Peggy bought 4 pieces of material measuring $\frac{1}{3}$ yard; $\frac{5}{8}$ yard; $3\frac{2}{5}$ yards; and $2\frac{1}{2}$ yards. How many total yards were purchased? (Change each to a decimal first.)

3. If there are 6 delivery trucks on the road and it takes $\frac{3}{4}$ of an hour for each delivery, how many total hours are used in making the first delivery?

4. If coffee costs $3\frac{3}{4}$ dollars a pound, how much would 25 pounds cost?

5. On a recent trip, Marsha drove 964 miles. If she used $30\frac{1}{3}$ gallons of gasoline, how many miles per gallon did her car get?

6. Betty counted $7\frac{3}{8}$ truckloads of wheat and Sara counted $5\frac{1}{3}$ truckloads. What is the total number of truckloads?

7. If $15\frac{5}{8}$ feet is needed in the underpass to clear trucks, and the current height is $13\frac{4}{8}$ feet, how much more is needed?

8. If each cow gives $8\frac{2}{5}$ quarts of milk at each milking, how much milk would you get from 25 cows?

9. If Dana has $3,770, how many shares of stock can she purchase if the cost per share is $47\frac{1}{8}$ dollars?

10. Marilyn purchased $7\frac{5}{6}$ yards of material. If she makes a skirt requiring $4\frac{1}{8}$ yards of material, how much is left?

11. A fruit stand has the following baskets of produce: melons, $4\frac{2}{3}$; apples, $12\frac{3}{4}$; onions, $5\frac{2}{5}$; squash, $1\frac{3}{8}$; and peaches, 4. How many total baskets of produce are there?

12. What is the grade point if $19\frac{1}{2}$ credit hours have $63\frac{3}{4}$ honor points?

Converting Decimals to Fractions

The procedure for conversion of decimals to fractions is a two-step process.

1. Determine the number of decimal places in the number and identify the name of the last decimal place used. The number of positions used in the decimal will determine the denominator of the fraction.
2. The numbers in the decimal become the numerator.

62   Chapter 3   Decimals and Percents

EXAMPLE 6 Convert .3200 to a fraction and reduce to lowest terms.

Solution:

$$\frac{3,200}{10,000}$$

- .3200 is read three thousand two hundred ten-thousandths. Place 3200 over 10,000.

$$\frac{3,200}{10,000} = \frac{8}{25}$$

- Reduce if possible.

EXAMPLE 7 Convert 6.33 to a mixed number.

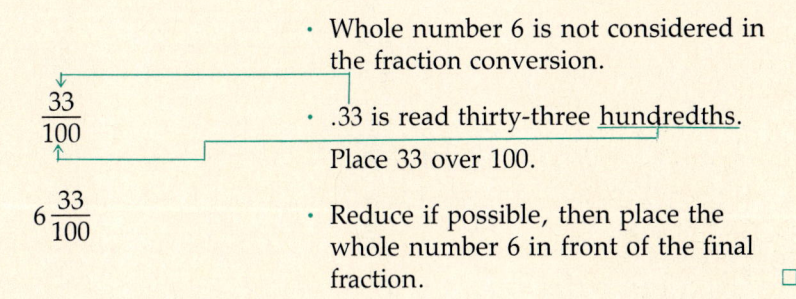

Solution:

- Whole number 6 is not considered in the fraction conversion.

$$\frac{33}{100}$$

- .33 is read thirty-three hundredths. Place 33 over 100.

$$6\frac{33}{100}$$

- Reduce if possible, then place the whole number 6 in front of the final fraction.

✔ **CHECK FOR UNDERSTANDING**

1. Convert 0.532 to a fraction.

2. Convert 0.787 to a fraction.

3. Convert 5.44 to a mixed number.

SKILL EXERCISES

Express the following decimals in fraction form. Do not reduce to lowest terms.

1. 0.834 = _____   2. 0.948 = _____

3. 0.13   = _____   4. 0.0001 = _____

5. 0.9   = _____   6. 0.48   = _____

7. 0.9372 = _____   8. 0.161 = _____

9. 0.32   = _____   10. 0.625 = _____

Answers to ✔ Check for Understanding
1. $\frac{133}{250}$.   2. $\frac{787}{1000}$.   3. $5\frac{11}{25}$.

Section 3.2 Converting Fractions to Decimals

APPLICATIONS

Convert fractions and mixed numbers to decimals. Use your calculator to perform the functions indicated and round continuing decimals to four places.

1. $3\frac{7}{8} \times 425 =$ _____

2. $4\frac{1}{5} \times .875 =$ _____

3. $4\frac{1}{4} \times 3\frac{1}{8} =$ _____

4. $67 \times 15\frac{4}{15} =$ _____

5. $76 \times 22\frac{3}{8} =$ _____

6. $42 \div \frac{3}{4} =$ _____

7. $\frac{2}{3} \div 18 =$ _____

8. $12 + \frac{7}{12} =$ _____

9. $\frac{5}{6} + \frac{4}{5} =$ _____

10. $78\frac{1}{2} + 3\frac{4}{5} =$ _____

11. $6\frac{3}{4} - \frac{7}{8} =$ _____

12. $85\frac{2}{3} - 35\frac{5}{6} =$ _____

13. $7\frac{8}{9} - \frac{7}{8} =$ _____

14. $123\frac{1}{2} + \frac{2}{5} =$ _____

15. $\frac{2}{7} - \frac{1}{5} =$ _____

Changing Fractions and Decimals to Percents

3.3

Percent is used extensively in business. Like a fraction, a percent shows a relationship to a whole. Since the whole unit is 100%, any percent less than 100% is a part of the whole unit—just as the fraction $\frac{3}{4}$ is a part of the whole. Any number larger than 100%, such as 250%, contains more than one whole unit. Your calculator is decimal oriented and in some cases has a % key. If used when calculating, this key converts a percent to a decimal. However, examples and calculator solutions in the text are presented without the use of the % key.

Converting Decimals to Percents

> To change a decimal to a percent, move the decimal point (or implied decimal to the right of a whole number) two places to the right and add the percent sign.

If a fraction or mixed number is involved, it must be changed to a decimal before the point is moved. Mathematically, we are multiplying the number by 100 when we move the decimal two places to the right.

EXAMPLE 8 Convert .63 to a percent.

Solution:

.63   • Move the decimal point two places to the right.

63%   • Add the percent sign.

Chapter 3 Decimals and Percents

EXAMPLE 9 Convert 2 to a percent.

Solution:

$$2.00$$ • Move the decimal point two places to the right. The implied decimal point is after the whole number.

$$200\%$$ • Add the percent sign.

EXAMPLE 10 If $\frac{1}{4}$ of the class are males, what percent of the class is male?

Solution:

$$\frac{1}{4} = .25$$ • Change the fraction to a decimal. (Note: *no % sign* has been added.)

$$.25 = 25\%$$ • Move the decimal point two places right and add % sign.

EXAMPLE 11 Convert $2\frac{2}{3}$ to a percent and round to ten-thousandths.

Solution:

$$\frac{2}{3} = 0.6666666$$ • Convert $\frac{2}{3}$ to a decimal and add the whole number.

$$2.0 + .6666666 = 2.6666666$$

$$2.6666666 = 266.6667\%$$ • Move the decimal two places right, *round to 4 places*, and add the % sign.

✔ CHECK FOR UNDERSTANDING

1. Convert 0.53926 to a percent and round to the nearest hundredth of one percent.

2. Convert $\frac{4}{7}$ to a percent and round to the nearest tenth of one percent.

3. Convert 2.786 to a percent and round to the nearest hundredth of one percent.

4. Convert $4\frac{1}{6}$ to a percent and round to the nearest hundredth of one percent.

SKILL EXERCISES

Change the following decimals, fractions, and mixed numbers to percents and round continuing decimals to hundredths place:

1. 0.196 = _____
2. 1.324 = _____
3. 0.004 = _____
4. 0.19 = _____
5. 0.03 = _____
6. $\frac{3}{4}$ = _____

Answers to ✔ Check for Understanding
1. 53.93%.   2. 57.1%.   3. 278.60%.   4. 416.67%.

Section 3.3 Changing Fractions and Decimals to Percents

7. $\frac{7}{8}$ = _____   8. $1\frac{2}{3}$ = _____

9. $2\frac{1}{2}$ = _____   10. $\frac{5}{16}$ = _____

11. 0.0032 = _____   12. 0.49 = _____

13. 0.327 = _____   14. 3.16 = _____

15. 1.001 = _____   16. $\frac{2}{5}$ = _____

17. .4762 = _____   18. 90 = _____

19. 34.2 = _____   20. .08 = _____

APPLICATIONS

1. By rearranging the office, there is $3\frac{1}{2}$ times more working space. What percent increase is that?

2. What percent does .3475 represent?

3. If you multiply by .32, what percent are you using?

4. Express 2.55 as a percent.

5. Express $\frac{5}{6}$ as a percent.

6. Convert $\frac{25}{237}$ to a percent.

7. Convert .0007 to a percent.

8. Express $\frac{1}{6}$ as a percent and round to ten-thousandths place.

9. When converted to a percent, which is larger—$\frac{3}{8}$ or $\frac{5}{16}$—and by how much?

10. Convert 2.863 to a percent.

Converting Percents to Decimals

Percent is expressed as a number followed by either the word percent or the percent sign (%).

> When converting from a percent to a decimal, move the decimal point, or implied decimal point if after a whole number, two places to the left and remove the percent sign (%).

66   Chapter 3   Decimals and Percents

If there is a fraction or mixed number involved, it should be converted to a decimal before any changes are made. If there are not enough digits to the left of the decimal point or assumed decimal point, add zeros as needed. Mathematically, we are dividing by 100 when we move the decimal point two places to the left.

EXAMPLE 12 Convert 35% to a decimal.

Solution:

.35%   • Move the decimal point or implied decimal point two places left.

.35   • Remove the % sign.

EXAMPLE 13 Mark saw that interest rates were being raised $\frac{1}{2}$%. How would that be expressed as a decimal?

Solution:

$\frac{1}{2}\% = .5\%$ • Change fraction to decimal. Percent sign has *not* been removed.

.00.5% = .005   • Remove the % sign and move the decimal point two places left.

EXAMPLE 14 Change 575% to decimal form.

Solution:

5.75%   • Move implied decimal point two places left.

5.75   • Remove the % sign.

EXAMPLE 15 Change $8\frac{5}{8}$% to a decimal.

Solution:

$\frac{5}{8}\% = 0.625\%$ • Convert $\frac{5}{8}$ to a decimal and add the whole number 8.0.

8.0% + .625% = 8.625%   • Retain the % sign.

.08.625% = .08625   • Drop the % sign and move the decimal point two places left.

✔ **CHECK FOR UNDERSTANDING**

1. Convert 37.37% to a decimal and round to the nearest thousandth.

2. Convert $6\frac{3}{8}$% to a decimal and round to the nearest ten-thousandth.

3. Convert $\frac{1}{4}$% to a decimal.

4. Convert 335% to a decimal.

Answers to ✔ Check for Understanding
1. 0.374.   2. 0.0638.   3. 0.0025.   4. 3.35.

SKILL EXERCISES

Change the following percents to decimals:

1. 12.6% = _____

2. $\frac{3}{5}$% = _____

3. 472.7% = _____

4. 96% = _____

5. 82.4% = _____

6. $5\frac{1}{2}$% = _____

7. $6\frac{1}{6}$% = _____

8. $\frac{1}{7}$% = _____

9. 62% = _____

10. 29.9% = _____

11. 16% = _____

12. 3% = _____

13. 1% = _____

14. 122% = _____

15. 0.2% = _____

16. 235% = _____

17. 2% = _____

18. .0003% = _____

19. 13% = _____

20. $\frac{5}{8}$% = _____

APPLICATIONS

Apply the procedures for converting fractions, mixed numbers, and percents to decimals in the following word problems:

1. Unemployment in the nation moved up $\frac{1}{2}$% last quarter. Express that in decimal form.

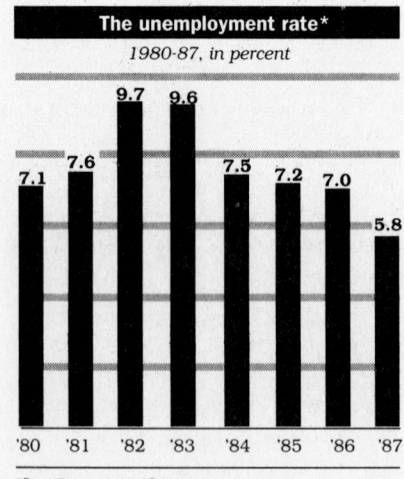

The unemployment rate*
1980-87, in percent

'80: 7.1
'81: 7.6
'82: 9.7
'83: 9.6
'84: 7.5
'85: 7.2
'86: 7.0
'87: 5.8

*For civilian population 16 and over.
Source: Statistical Abstract of the United States, 1988
Globe staff chart

Chapter 3 Decimals and Percents

2. What decimal would you use to find 54.87% of a number?

3. If you have 40% of the needed fruit in the warehouse and 25% more has just been unloaded, express the total now available in decimal form.

4. The power company rates are $9\frac{1}{26}$ cents a kilowatt. If the power company gets a 12% increase, how will the increase be expressed in decimal form?

5. If there are 6,785 employees in the factory and $17\frac{1}{2}$% are laid off, express the reduction in a decimal.

6. What is 346% expressed as a decimal?

7. If attendance at the racetrack increased 7.46% this year, what is the increase in decimal form?

8. Express $\frac{1}{5}$% as a decimal.

9. The cost of living increased 114% since 1980. How is that stated in decimal form?

10. Convert 875% to decimal form.

Key Terms

Converting (59)
Percent (64)
Rounding (58)
Rules of rounding (58)

Looking Back

The conversions of fractions to decimals and percents to decimals are the cornerstones of this text. Each problem you encounter will usually have a conversion or a rounding at its conclusion to put the ansers in final form. You will need to be able to apply the concepts introduced in this chapter with a 99.9 percent reliability.

There is a significant difference between a fraction and a fractional percent. $\frac{1}{2}$ converts to .50 decimal. $\frac{1}{2}$% converts to .005 decimal. It is sometimes better to use a two-step conversion: convert the fraction to a decimal, then change it to the percent form.

If you are using a calculator with a decimal set for output, let the calculator round to the desired number of places automatically. Hand calculators usually perform with a floating-point logic, which will require you to round to the correct decimal place as needed.

The key to rounding a decimal is to read the value of the number immediately to the right of the significant place. You do not need to go any further than one decimal position to the right in making that decision.

Let's Review

Round the following to thousandths:

1. .783456 = _____
2. .32879 = _____
3. .4322998 = _____
4. .76453 = _____
5. .22231 = _____
6. .5543666 = _____

Convert to decimals, round to hundredths:

7. $\frac{3}{4}$ = _____
8. $\frac{5}{6}$ = _____
9. $\frac{33}{15}$ = _____
10. $\frac{12}{27}$ = _____
11. $\frac{17}{14}$ = _____
12. $\frac{4}{9}$ = _____

Convert to fractions, reduce to lowest terms:

13. .346 = _____
14. .76 = _____
15. .875 = _____
16. .9724 = _____
17. .355 = _____
18. .7505 = _____

Convert to percents:

19. .4547 = _____
20. $7\frac{1}{8}$ = _____
21. .43 = _____
22. 3.75 = _____
23. $\frac{1}{5}$ = _____
24. .0075 = _____

Convert to decimals and round continuing decimals to four places:

25. 34% = _____
26. $\frac{1}{4}$% = _____
27. 235% = _____
28. 87.5% = _____
29. $\frac{3}{7}$% = _____
30. $2\frac{1}{5}$% = _____

Chapter Test

Work the following problems and round all continuing decimals to four places:

1. If the price of gas goes down $10\frac{5}{8}$%, what is the decimal equivalent of the decrease?

70   Chapter 3   Decimals and Percents

2. The inventory in the sporting goods department increased by $\frac{1}{8}$. Express this as a percent.

3. If the cost of living increased by .07, what percent does this represent?

4. When the decrease in tax revenue was .125, what was the fractional reduction?

5. An increase in taxes of $\frac{1}{3}$ is the same as what percent?

6. What percent more water flow is needed if $\frac{1}{4}$ more is required?

7. When working with percent problems, what action needs to be taken before problems can be solved?

8. The Candy Shop increased its volume of busines $2\frac{1}{4}$ times. What percent does this represent?

9. If the car is $\frac{3}{4}$ full of gasoline, what percent is left to fill?

10. When $\frac{2}{3}$ of total sales have been reached, what percent does this represent?

11. When the figure .3467 is used, what percent does it represent?

12. To calculate a loss of 32%, what decimal would you need to use?

13. If you have traveled $\frac{4}{7}$ of your trip, what percent do you have left to go?

14. What is the decimal conversion of 23.78%?

15. An increase of .625 is an increase of what percent?

Chapter Test

Problem Solving

4

OBJECTIVES

When you complete this chapter you will be able to:

- *Understand problem solving strategies. (4.1)*
- *Solve for missing progression numbers. (4.2)*
- *Develop problem statements for variables. (4.3)*
- *Identify word problem variables. (4.4)*
- *Understand problem solving techniques. (4.5)*
- *Solve word problems with formulas. (4.6)*
- *Solve word problems for changing values. (4.7)*

COMING UP

The automobile industry is an excellent illustration of the need to change in business. The competitive products being produced today are the results of problem solving to make a better product. Problem solving is a continuous process in business. Whether for setting prices, determining costs, comparing investments, or evaluating information, it is all part of keeping competitive. The problem solving challenge is not usually in performing mathematics calculations but in analyzing and stating the problem correctly. This chapter reviews some basic problem solving methods. Use them to strengthen your confidence; they will appear extensively throughout the text.

Problem Solving Strategies

4.1 The hardest task in any mathematics course is mastering the ability to solve problems. Dealing with problems that involve a set of circumstances and an unknown requires the understanding of problem solving strategies. Consider these four important steps in evaluating information for problem solution.

> 1. **Identify the problem.**
>   What type of business is it?
>   What type of transaction is occurring?
>   What unit of measurement is being used?
>   What math operation is implied in its terms?
> 2. **Look for number change patterns.**
>   Look for sequences of number changes.
>   Determine whether change is an increase or a decrease.
>   Identify the amount of change taking place.
> 3. **Create expressions for problem components.**
>   Express and label problem components.
>   Show the relationships with other components.
> 4. **Isolate the unknown.**
>   Identify the total number of problem components.
>   Match given problem data with known component.
>   Identify the unknown component.

Number Progressions

4.2 When the information in a problem is identified and organized, the relationships between the information can be stated. The associations established by the numbers in a problem typically represent business activity. The pattern formed by the numbers may represent situations that can be used to evaluate the problem, predict the next occurrence, or assist in establishing the solution.

A first step in gaining problem solving confidence is to evaluate numbers and determine patterns. Start with this exercise to evaluate simple number sequences for change.

Step 1. Examine the number values in the pattern.
Step 2. Determine by how much each number in the sequence changes.
Step 3. Observe whether the number has increased or decreased.
Step 4. Find which of the math operations—addition, subtraction, multiplication, or division—could cause the change.

Step 5. State all the possibilities of how that number could have changed. For instance, a change from 2 to 6 could have been a +4 or a ×3 change.

Step 6. Evaluate all possible change(s) for each series number.

Step 7. Write down and evaluate the pattern of change values.

Step 8. Select the pattern that is most logical to you.

Step 9. Use this same pattern to establish the value of the next missing variable in the sequence.

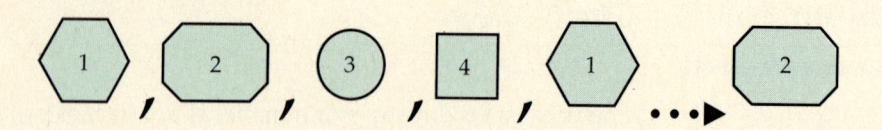

1, 2, 3, 4, 1, ... 2

EXAMPLE 1 For the series 4, 5, 6, 7, 8, n, . . . , establish the change pattern and find the value of n (the missing number).

Solution: Evaluate the number pattern.

4 to 5	(add 1)	• First number change.
5 to 6	(add 1)	• Second number change.
6 to 7	(add 1)	• Third number change.
7 to 8	(add 1)	• Fourth number change.
Addition used for all		• The pattern is addition
Number change is 1		• 1 is the constant change.
Addition with 1		• The change sequence.
8 + 1 = 9		• Add 1 to last number.
9		• Next number in sequence. □

PROBLEM SOLVING STRATEGY

Sometimes a numerical relationship is not established for each number in the sequence, but for alternate numbers instead. Look for this type of change as well. Along with the number change pattern, look for patterns in the mathematic operations to repeat. For example the procedure may go from +, −, ×, and ÷ and repeat +, −, ×, . . . n. The next operation is probably division (÷), since it completes the previous sequence.

EXAMPLE 2 For an alternate series, find the change pattern:
7, 8, 6, 9, 5, 10, n, . . .

Solution: Evaluate the number pattern.

7 to 8	(add 1)	• First number change.
8 to 6	(subtract 2)	• Second number change.
6 to 9	(add 3)	• Third number change.
9 to 5	(subtract 4)	• Fourth number change.
5 to 10	(add 5) (multiply by 2)	• Two possible changes.
Alternate addition and subtraction		• The pattern of change (multiply does not fit).
Numbers increase 1		• The value of the change.

74   Chapter 4   Problem Solving

+1, −2, +3, −4, + 5	· Complete change sequence.
6	· Next number in sequence.
Subtract	· Next sequence operation.
10 − 6 = 4	· Subtract 6 from sequence.
4	· Next number is 4.

Multiplication and division may also be involved in the series relationship.

EXAMPLE 3 Find the value n for the series
10, 5, 8, 4, 8, 4, n, . . .

Solution: Evaluate the change in numbers, watch for patterns.

10 to 5	(divide by 2 or subtract 5)	· First change.
5 to 8	(add 3)	· Second change.
8 to 4	(divide by 2 or subtract 4)	· Third change.
4 to 8	(add 4 or multiply by 2)	· Fourth change.
8 to 4	(divide by 2 or subtract 4)	· Fifth change.
Divide 2		· Repeats in alternate step.
Subtract		· Repeats but not a pattern.
Add		· Alternate step pattern.
Addition increases by 1		· Value change for addition.
Divide by 2, add 1		· Sequence change pattern.
8 ÷ 2 = 4		· Last change in pattern.
4 + 1 = 5		· Next change is add 5.
4 + 5 = 9		· Add 5 to last number.
9		· Next number in sequence.

EXAMPLE 4 Find the value of n for the series
2, 4, 8, 16, 32, n, . . .

Solution: Evaluate the number change pattern.

2 to 4	(multiply 2 or add 2)	· First change.
4 to 8	(multiply 2 or add 4)	· Second change.
8 to 16	(multiply 2 or add 8)	· Third change.
16 to 32	(multiply 2 or add 16)	· Fourth change.
Multiply 2 is consistent		· Pattern identified.
Addition not consistent		· Disregard addition.
2, ×2, ×2, ×2,		· Pattern math sequence.
32 × 2 = 64		· Next step in sequence.
n = 64		· Next number in sequence.

✓ CHECK FOR UNDERSTANDING

Evaluate the following series and find the next number in sequence:

1. 7, 9, 11, 14, 17, 21, 25, n . . . _____

2. 21, 19, 16, 12, 7, n . . . _____

Section 4.2 Number Progressions

3. 12, 9, 6, 3, 9, 15, n . . . _____

4. 12, 10, 8, 10, 8, 6, n . . . _____

5. 15, 20, 4, 20, 15, 20, n . . . _____

SKILL EXERCISES

Review the number changes in the following integers. Identify the possible math operations (+, −, ×, or ÷) and results for the change taking place. See Problem 1 for illustration.

Number series	Possible change Operation/value	Possible change Operation/value
1. 12, 6	− 6	÷ 2
2. 28, 7	_____	_____
3. 15, 75	_____	_____
4. 9, 21	_____	_____
5. 74, 37	_____	_____

Identify the values and math operations that could have caused the following number series to change. Problem 6 is worked as an illustration.

Number series	Operation/value	Operation/value
6. 15, 8, 16 a.	− 7	none
b.	+ 8	× 2
7. 11, 21, 7 a.	_____	_____
b.	_____	_____
8. 32, 12, 72 a.	_____	_____
b.	_____	_____
9. 27, 24, 12 a.	_____	_____
b.	_____	_____
10. 26, 16, 6 a.	_____	_____
b.	_____	_____

Answers to ✓ Check for Understanding
1. Sequence: +2, +2, +3, +3, +4, +4 (+5) = 30.   **2.** Sequence: −2, −3, −4, −5 (−6) = 1.   **3.** Sequence: −3, −3, −3, +6, +6 (+6) = 21.   **4.** Sequence: −2, −2, +2, −2, −2 (+2) = 8.   **5.** Sequence: +5, ÷5, ×5, −5, +5 (÷5) = 4.

76   Chapter 4   Problem Solving

Stating Problem Variables

4.3

Known and unknown values can be represented by numbers, letters, or symbols. Usually letters are selected for unknowns. A letter can also be used to represent a number. It is not intended to represent a specific number but a **variable** quantity. Variables are problem quantities or functions that may assume any given value or symbol. Letters may also be used with numbers to represent relationships to other information in the problem. They may also be used to express relationships with other variables; for example, $x-7$, $3b$, $y-x$, $a+2$. If two math expressions are set equal to each other, the result is an **equation.** The words "equal" and "is" identify the values that are equal. $2a$ is 12 means $2a = 12$ or $(x - 2)$ equals $(a + b)$ means $x - 2 = a + b$. Remember, the word "of" means "multiply."

To illustrate how these expressions are formed:

> Let x represent the unknown:
> $6x$ means 6 of x, or 6 times x.
> Let m represent an unknown:
> $m + 8$ means the variable m plus 8.
> Let t represent the unknown:
> $3t - 4$ means three times variable t minus 4.
> Let b represent a value:
> $45 - b$ means number 45 minus the value b.
> Let p represent an unknown:
> $p \div 6$ means the variable p divided by 6.

If no numeral is expressed with the variable (for example, x, y, b), it is to be understood that there is only one.

EXAMPLE 5   What is the math expression for this statement?
Eight more than the unknown y.

Solution:

y	· Represents the unknown value.
$+8$	· Eight in addition to the unknown.
$y + 8$	· Problem statement completed. □

EXAMPLE 6   Determine the expression for the situation: the sum of five times b plus b divided by six.

Solution:

b	· Represents the unknown variable.
$5b$	· 5 times b
$b \div 6$	· b divided by six
$5b + b \div 6$	· The expressions are combined. □

Section 4.3   Stating Problem Variables   77

EXAMPLE 7   Express a term that could represent 50% of the profits.
Solution: Let p represent profits.

.50	• Expresses percent as a decimal.
.50 of p	• Sets the math relationship.
$.50p$	• Is the term.

EXAMPLE 8   Create an expression or equation to represent a 26% increase in sales from last year.
Solution: Let y equal last year's sales.

.26	• Express the percent as a decimal.
$.26y$	• Is the percent increase of y.
$y + .26y$	• Last year's sales plus increase.
$y + .26y$	• Is the expression.

✔ CHECK FOR UNDERSTANDING

Write the expression or equation for the following problems:

1. A number that remains after the unknown (m) has been reduced by 9.

2. One fifth of twice an unknown (y) reduced by 12.

3. The number of minutes in (h) hours.

4. 28 multiplied by twelve times the unknown (q).

5. An unknown (r) is 15 less than three times the unknown.

SKILL EXERCISES

Evaluate the following problem statements and write the expression. Use x for all variables.

Statement	Problem expression
1. Fifty percent of a number.	_____
2. Three times a number plus 5.	_____
3. 15 reduced by a variable.	_____

Answers to ✔ Check for Understanding
1. $m - 9$.   2. $2y \div 5 - 12$.   3. $h \times 60$.   4. $28 \times 12q$.   5. $r = 3r - 15$.

78   Chapter 4   Problem Solving

4. 12 less than six times a number. _____

5. A number times the number. _____

6. A number less 12% of the number. _____

7. Six times a number plus seven. _____

8. Ten reduced by a number. _____

9. One half of four equals 6 times a number. _____

10. Two times a number minus 3 equals thirty. _____

APPLICATIONS

Find the missing number in the following sequences, or write the mathematical expression directed by the problem. Use y for all unknown symbols.

1. 4, 12, 6, 18, 9.

   ____ ____ ____ ____ . . . $n =$ _____

2. 28, 7, 21, 19, 20, 5.

   ____ ____ ____ ____ ____ . . . $n =$ _____

3. 18, 17, 16, 15, 17, 19.

   ____ ____ ____ ____ ____ . . . $n =$ _____

4. Six times a certain number minus three is equal to three times the same number plus eighteen.

5. A sales agent sold on a commission basis. Her commission was 32 dollars per unit sold. What is the expression to show the number of units sold if total sales were $4,460?

6. Stock was sold for $101 per share. This amount was $2\frac{1}{2}$ times what was paid for it.

7. Sixty is twice an unknown plus 8.

8. Five drinks cost $3.20 more than the $8.00 a person offered.

9. One hundred is twelve less than a given number.

10. This year's total profit was $15,000 less than twice last year's profit.

Identifying Problem Variables

4.4

Once you can identify problem variables quickly and accurately, you can begin the problem solving process. This section introduces some short exercises to sharpen your skill in identifying variables and assigning their values. If the value of a problem quantity is unknown, identify it as "U." Applications of these concepts will be found throughout the text.

Distance, Rate, and Time Expressions

In problems involving speed and distance, use these variables:

D = Distance traveled.
R = Rate of speed while traveling.
T = Time of travel (usually expressed in hours).

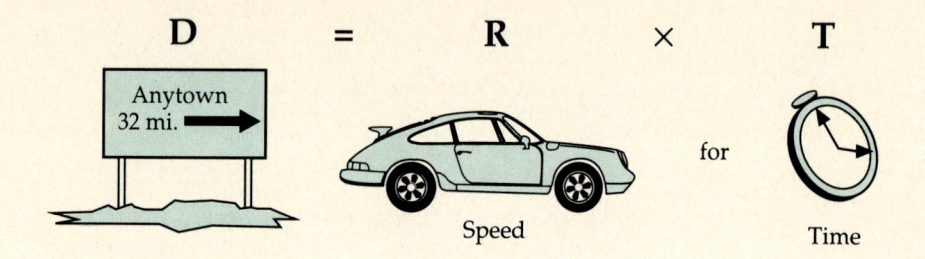

$$D = R \times T$$

for Speed, Time

EXAMPLE 9 If a rate of 55 mph was sustained for four hours, what are the variable values?

Solution:

Variables

- Distance   Rate   Time
- $D =$ __U__ $R =$ __55 mph__ $T =$ __4 hours__

EXAMPLE 10 Dorla jogged at the rate of $3\frac{1}{2}$ miles per hour for 1 hour and 2 miles per hour for the remaining half-hour. Identify the variable values.

Solution:

Variables

- Distance   Rate   Time
- $D =$ __U__ $R_1 =$ __3.5 mph__ $T_1 =$ __1 hour__
                    $R_2 =$ __2 mph__ $T_2 =$ __.5 hours__

EXAMPLE 11 If Rene Ann traveled 35 miles on her moped in a period of 1 hour and 45 minutes, what are the variable values?

Solution:

Variables

- Distance   Rate   Time
- $D =$ __35 miles__ $R =$ __U__ $T =$ __1.75 hours__

EXAMPLE 12 If you were required to calculate how much time it would take to travel 928 miles at an average speed of 58 miles per hour, what would the variable values be?

Solution:

Variables

- Distance   Rate   Time
- D = __928 miles__   R = __58 mph__   T = __U__

Base, Rate, and Part Expressions

For problems using base, rate, and a part, use these variables:

B = The original whole value in units.
P = A piece or component of the whole unit.
R = The percent of the part to the base.

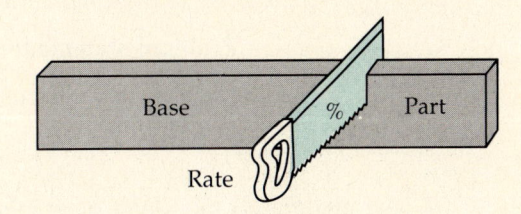

EXAMPLE 13 David borrowed 20% of what he needed to buy a new basketball. If he borrowed $6.00, what are the variable values?

Variables

- Base   Rate   Part
- B = __U__   R = __20%__   P = __$6.00__

EXAMPLE 14 To pass a new club resolution the by-laws required 50.1% of the membership. With 1,200 members in the club, what would the problem variables be?

Solution:

Variables

- Base   Rate   Part
- B = __1,200 membership__ R = __50.1%__   P = __U__

EXAMPLE 15 19,200 miles of a 60,000 mile warranty had already been driven. If the percent of the warranty used was asked for, what would the variable values be?

Solution:

Variables

- Base   Rate   Part
- B = __60,000 mi__   R = __U__   P = __19,200 mi__

Section 4.4 Identifying Problem Variables

✔ CHECK FOR UNDERSTANDING

1. The Concorde traveled 5,897 miles in 4.75 hours. What is the value of the speed variable for this problem?

2. $28,000 of a $237,000 building budget will be spent for plumbing supplies. What is the value of the base?

SKILL EXERCISES

Identify the value of the variable indicated in the following statements:

Problem statement	Variable	Value
1. Thirty percent of the 300 students had difficulty.	Part	_____
2. Approximately 825 parts from a batch of 15,000 were defective.	Base	_____
3. Eighty percent of the total amounted to 222 people.	Part	_____
4. Speeding at 85 mph he went 40% of the distance.	Rate	_____
5. Twenty-five percent of the total cost amounted to $37.50.	Base	_____
6. Traveling at 70 mph it took 9.5 hours to travel the distance.	Time	_____
7. It cost $9.26 to borrow $1,200 at 9%.	Part	_____
8. What rate of speed will it take to travel 855 miles in 7.25 hours?	Distance	_____
9. The evening shift completed 89 percent of their work. They finished 112 jobs.	Base	_____
10. The company reached $40,000 of its $160,000 sales target. They only achieved 25% of their goal.	Part	_____

Answers to ✔ Check for Understanding
1. U— unknown.   2. $237,000.

APPLICATIONS

Identify the unknown variable in the following problems. What is the formula name for the variable?

1. A large cargo van traveled 1,784 miles in 26.5 hours. What speed did it average?

2. Interest rates of 12.5% earned the company $1,500,000 this year. How much did the company loan to its customers?

3. Twenty-eight percent of the total 640 acres was under water. How many acres have water damage?

4. Each subway travels at an average speed of 39 mph. How long would it take to move between stations 4.7 miles apart?

5. Sixteen of the 290 students will graduate with honors. What percent of the class will receive honors?

Problem Solving Techniques

4.5

The task of solving **word problems** is made easier if you use a systematic approach. Review these five problem solving techniques to assist you.

1. **Read the problem.**
   Re-read the problem.
   Clarify what type of data is given.
   Focus on what type of solution is needed.
   Identify the type of units used for the unknown.

2. **Look for key words in the problem.**
   "What is $\frac{1}{4}$ of 12?" A number on either side of the word "of" implies multiplication is needed.
   The words "is" and "are" frequently mean equal or equal to. "The total budget is $125,000" means the budget = $125,000.

3. **Focus on the missing problem element.**
   Check the goals of the problem.
   Collect terms and isolate variables.
   Establish the missing variable.
   Set the variables into an equation if appropriate.
   Use a solution formula if possible.

4. **Complete the mathematics.**
   Perform the math functions identified either in the equation or the solution formula.
   Watch for the sequence of steps to be followed.
   Evaluate the sequence of operations to be used.

5. **Check the results.**
   If possible, check your answer exactly.
   Use approximation and estimating to support the logic of your answer.
   "$50 is too much sales tax to pay on a $120 purchase."

Solving Problems with Formulas

4.6

Two common formulas are used to solve many business problems. This section introduces these formulas and the wording used to apply them to problem solving. Identify the known variables and place their values into the proper formula. Solve for the unknown variable.

Base, Rate, and Part Problems

These problems involve variables that refer to some whole unit, or a referenced value. We identified the letters of these variables in the previous section as B, R, and P. A more detailed study is needed to solve for unknowns.

The **base** *(B)* is the unit of reference, which represents the whole amount or total. It is also the focus for a particular problem and always equals 100%.

The **part** *(P)* is any amount that is not the base. Its value can be larger or smaller than the base. In a problem, it is a representative amount of the base. It must have the same type of units as the base. (One could not select a part from a production batch of new toasters and refer to the part as radios.)

The **rate** *(R)* is an expression, in percent, that reflects the ratio of the value of the part compared to the value of the base.

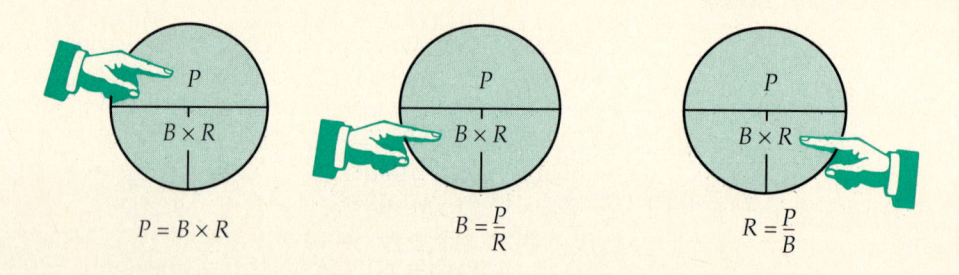

$$P = B \times R \qquad B = \frac{P}{R} \qquad R = \frac{P}{B}$$

The above graphic represents the relationship of these three variables. It is not a formula; however, if you identify or cover the unknown variable, the arrangement of the remaining variables shows the mathematical relationship between them. The formulas illustrated by the graphic are shown below:

$$
\begin{aligned}
B &= \text{Part} \div \text{Rate} &\text{or}& & B &= P \div R \\
R &= \text{Part} \div \text{Base} &\text{or}& & R &= P \div B \\
P &= \text{Base} \times \text{Rate} &\text{or}& & P &= B \times R
\end{aligned}
$$

EXAMPLE 16 When a company manufactures a product, some of the materials are wasted, which affects the cost of the product. If the total cost of the materials is $150, and the waste factor is typically 4.5%, what is the cost of the waste?

Solution: The missing variable is cost of waste, a part:

$P = B \times R$	• Formula for the part.
$P = 150 \times .045$	• Place variables in formula.
	• 4.5 percent is .045 the rate.
	• Total cost $150 is the base.
$P = 150 \times .045 = 6.75$	• Calculate the price.
$6.75	• The amount of waste.

84 Chapter 4 Problem Solving

EXAMPLE 17 At a nearby college, 29% of the students do not favor a recommended change from quarters to semesters. How many of its 10,000 students are unhappy?

Solution: The missing variable, the opposed students, is a part:

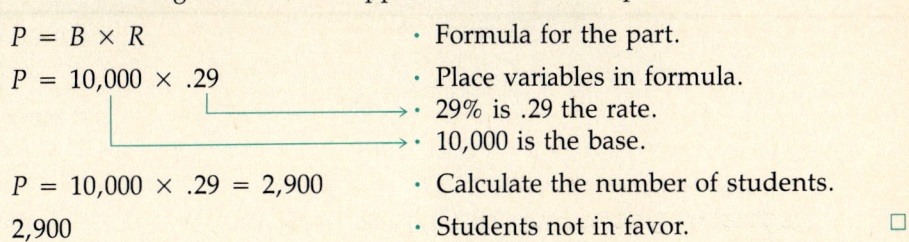

$P = B \times R$ · Formula for the part.
$P = 10,000 \times .29$ · Place variables in formula.
· 29% is .29 the rate.
· 10,000 is the base.
$P = 10,000 \times .29 = 2,900$ · Calculate the number of students.
2,900 · Students not in favor.

EXAMPLE 18 A small component of goods shipped is damaged and must be replaced. If the shipment of 1,786 units included 47 damaged units, what percent had to be replaced?

Solution: The missing variable, percent replaced, is a rate:

$R = \dfrac{P}{B}$ · Formula for the rate.
$R = \dfrac{47}{1,786}$ · Place variables in formula.
· 47 damaged units is a part.
· 1,786 units is the base.
$R = 47 \div 1,786 = .0263$ · Calculate the rate.
$.0263 = 2.63\%$ · Percent replaced.

EXAMPLE 19 If 10,108 seats of a stadium with 72,200 seats are not sold for season tickets, what percent is available for public sale?

Solution: The missing variable is a rate:

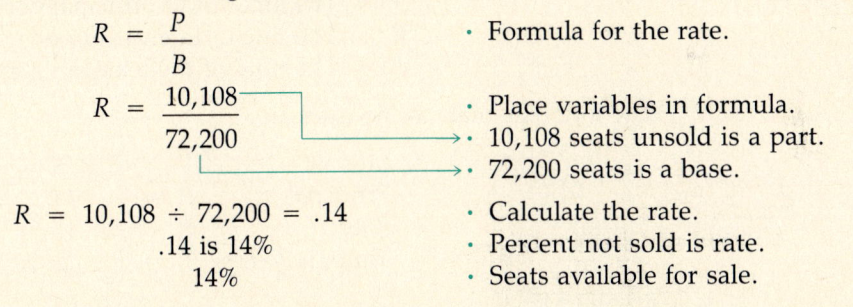

$R = \dfrac{P}{B}$ · Formula for the rate.
$R = \dfrac{10,108}{72,200}$ · Place variables in formula.
· 10,108 seats unsold is a part.
· 72,200 seats is a base.
$R = 10,108 \div 72,200 = .14$ · Calculate the rate.
.14 is 14% · Percent not sold is rate.
14% · Seats available for sale.

EXAMPLE 20 The evening computer operations shift is credited with completion of 40% of the daily workload. If the evening shift completed 128 job runs, how many total jobs were performed that day?

Solution: The missing variable, total jobs, is a base:

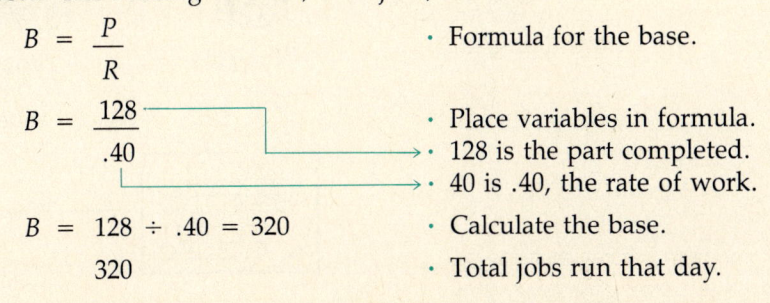

$B = \dfrac{P}{R}$ · Formula for the base.
$B = \dfrac{128}{.40}$ · Place variables in formula.
· 128 is the part completed.
· 40 is .40, the rate of work.
$B = 128 \div .40 = 320$ · Calculate the base.
320 · Total jobs run that day.

Section 4.6 Solving Problems with Formulas

EXAMPLE 21 Total profits for a small company were $21,000. If this represented a 6% return on investment, what was the original investment?

Solution: The missing variable, original investment, is a base:

$B = \dfrac{P}{R}$ · Formula for the base.

$B = \dfrac{21,000}{.06}$
· Place variables in formula.
· 21,000 part of investment.
· 6% is .06, the rate.

$21,000 \div .06 = 350,000$ · Calculate the base.

$350,000 · Original investment, the base. □

Interest, Principal, Rate, and Time Problems

Another common formula that uses business variables is one for lending money with simple **interest**. This section introduces interest variables; Chapter 8 will show interest problems for time periods other than years. The components of this formula are:

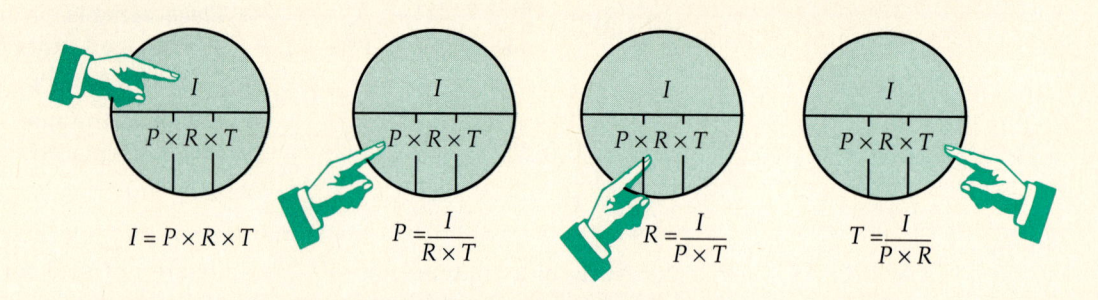

$$I = P \times R \times T \qquad P = \dfrac{I}{R \times T} \qquad R = \dfrac{I}{P \times T} \qquad T = \dfrac{I}{P \times R}$$

I = The amount of interest in dollars.
P = The amount of principal borrowed.
R = The rate of interest in percent.
T = The time of the loan in years.

The formulas that can be used are:

Interest $I = P \times R \times T.$
Principal $P = I \div (R \times T).$
Rate $R = I \div (P \times T).$
Time (in years) $T = I \div (P \times R).$

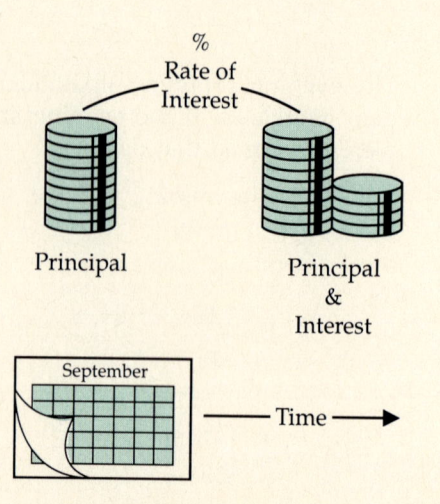

86 Chapter 4 Problem Solving

> **CALCULATOR TIP**
>
> The calculator can be easily applied to the use of the base, rate, and part formula solution. For speed in problem solving, a calculator procedure exists that allows for a quick chain calculation without the use of calculator memory. The standard procedure involves calculating the product of the two numbers in the denominator. The numbers are stored in memory and used as a divisor into the numerator value. The recommended calculator procedure is to divide the numerator by each factor of the denominator in succession. Follow this example:
>
> | | |
> |---|---|
> | $2,000 | • The principal or P value is the base. |
> | 2 years | • Value for time (T) is 2. |
> | $454 | • The interest to be used as the numerator. |
> | $R = I \div (P \times T)$ | • Standard formula requires multiplication $(P \times T)$ before division. |
> | $R = I \div P \div T$ | • Calculator method recommended (Divide the interest by the principal and the time in sequence). |
>
> $454 \boxed{\div} 2,000 \boxed{\div} 2 \boxed{=} .1135$ or 11.35%.

EXAMPLE 22 Red Rocks Concrete Company needs to earn $1,800 in the next year. If they invest in a fund that earns 6% interest, how much would they have to place on deposit for the year?

Solution: The missing variable is the principal:

$$P = \frac{I}{(R \times T)}$$ • Formula for the principal.

$$P = \frac{1,800}{.06 \times 1}$$
• Place variables in formula.
• 1,800 amount is a part.
• 1 year is the time.
• 6% is .06, the rate.

$(.06 \times 1) = .06$ • Calculate the denominator.
$P = 1,800 \div .06 = 30,000$ • Calculate the base.
$P = 1,800 \div .06 \div 1 = 30,000$ • Calculator method.
$30,000 • To be deposited is principal.

EXAMPLE 23 If a loan earned $6,750 in interest for the bank over a 2-year period and was originated with a $12\frac{1}{2}\%$ simple interest rate, what was the original amount of the loan?

Solution: The missing variable is the principal:

$$P = \frac{I}{(R \times T)}$$ • Formula for the principal.

$$P = \frac{6,750}{.125 \times 2}$$
• Place variables in formula.
• 6,750 is the interest.
• 2 total years is the time.
• $12\frac{1}{2}\%$ is .125, the rate.

$(.125 \times 2) = .250$ • Calculate the denominator.
$P = 6,750 \div .250 = 27,000$ • Calculate the base.
$P = 6,750 \div .125 \div 2 = 27,000$ • Calculator method.
$27,000 • Amount borrowed is principal.

EXAMPLE 24 What interest is earned if $32,500 is placed at $11\frac{3}{4}$% simple interest for four and a half years?

Solution: The missing variable is interest:

$I = P \times R \times T$ · Formula for the interest.
$I = 32,500 \times .1175 \times 4.5$ · Set variables in formula.
 · 4.5 years is the time.
 · $11\frac{3}{4}$ is .1175 the rate.
 · 32,500 invested principal.
$I = 32,500 \times .1175 \times 4.5 = 17,184.38$ · Calculate the interest.
$17,184.38 · Interest earned for 4.5 years. ☐

EXAMPLE 25 If the Moody Company borrows $2,400 at a local bank, with a rate of $10\frac{1}{2}$% simple interest for 18 months (1.5 years), what interest will they pay?

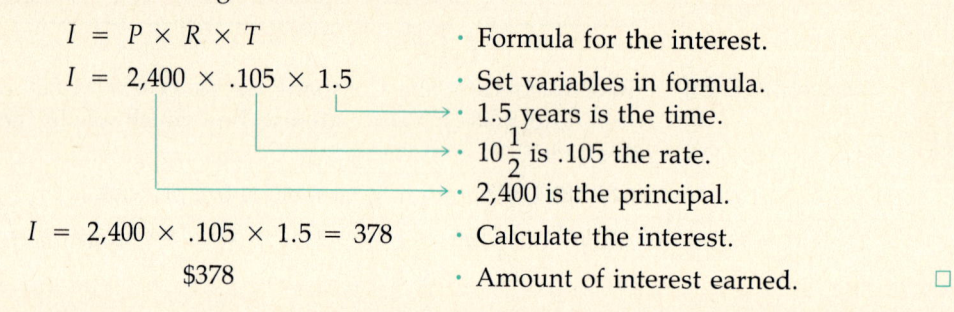

Solution: The missing variable is interest:

$I = P \times R \times T$ · Formula for the interest.
$I = 2,400 \times .105 \times 1.5$ · Set variables in formula.
 · 1.5 years is the time.
 · $10\frac{1}{2}$ is .105 the rate.
 · 2,400 is the principal.
$I = 2,400 \times .105 \times 1.5 = 378$ · Calculate the interest.
$378 · Amount of interest earned. ☐

EXAMPLE 26 What rate of interest was used on a simple interest loan taken for one year if the interest paid was $1,650 and the amount borrowed was $12,500?

Solution: The missing variable is the rate:

$R = \dfrac{I}{(P \times T)}$ · Formula for the rate.

$R = \dfrac{1,650}{12,500 \times 1}$ · Place variables in formula.
 · 1,650 interest paid.
 · 1 year is the time.
 · 12,500 is the principal.
$(12,500 \times 1) = 12,500$ · Calculate the denominator.
$R = 1,650 \div 12,500 = .132$ · Calculate the rate.
$R = 1,650 \div 12,500 \div 1 = .132$ · Calculator method.
.132 or 13.2% · Interest rate used. ☐

EXAMPLE 27 What rate of simple interest was paid on a note for $8,000 if $1,050 interest was paid and the loan was for 1.5 years?

88 Chapter 4 Problem Solving

Solution: The missing variable is the rate:

$$R = \frac{I}{(P \times T)}$$ • Formula for the rate.

$$R = \frac{1{,}050}{8{,}000 \times 1.5}$$
• Set variables in formula.
→ • 1,050 is interest earned.
→ • 1.5 years is time.
→ • 8,000 is the principal.

$(8{,}000 \times 1.5) = 12{,}000$ • Solve for the denominator.
$R = 1{,}050 \div 12{,}000 = .0875$ • Calculate the rate.
$R = 1{,}050 \div 12{,}000 \div 1.5 = .0875$ • Calculator method.
.0875 or 8.75% • Interest rate used. ☐

EXAMPLE 28 If a simple interest loan carried an interest charge of $456 on an amount of $2,400 at $9\frac{1}{2}\%$, how long was the loan taken for?

Solution: The missing variable is time:

$$T = \frac{I}{(P \times R)}$$ • Formula for the time.

$$T = \frac{456}{2{,}400 \times .095}$$
• Place variables in formula.
→ • 456 is the interest charge.
→ • $9\frac{1}{2}$ is .095, the rate.
→ • 2,400 is the principal.

$(2{,}400 \times .095) = 228$ • Solve for the denominator.
$T = 456 \div 228 = 2$ • Solve for time.
$T = 456 \div 2{,}400 \div .092 = 2$ • Calculator method.
2 years • Time period of the loan. ☐

EXAMPLE 29 A loan for $9,600 taken at 11% interest carried an interest charge of $2,640. What was the length of the loan?

Solution: The missing variable is time:

$$T = \frac{I}{(P \times R)}$$ • Formula for the time.

$$T = \frac{2{,}640}{9{,}600 \times .11}$$
• Set variables in formula.
→ • 2,640 is the interest.
→ • 11% is .11, the rate.
→ • 9,600 is the principal.

$(9{,}600 \times .11) = 1{,}056$ • Solve for the denominator.
$T = 2{,}640 \div 1{,}056 = 2.5$ • Solve for time.
$T = 2{,}640 \div 9{,}600 \div .11 = 2.5$ • Calculator method.
2.5 years • Time period of loan. ☐

✓ **CHECK FOR UNDERSTANDING**

1. Sandra borrowed 26% of what she needed to buy a new pair of skis. If she borrowed $143, what was the price of the skis?

Section 4.6 Solving Problems with Formulas 89

2. Marion planned to be a candidate for a local county office. Plans called for getting 50.1% of the votes in order to win the district. If the county had 126,000 registered voters, how many votes does Marion need to meet her goal?

3. The travel expense budget for a summer vacation was planned to be $2,800. The travelers had already spent $1,420. What percent of the travel budget was remaining to cover the rest of the trip?

4. Thirty-two percent of the total cost of a college course was $54. What was the total cost of the course?

5. If 12,500 miles of a 40,000 mile tire warranty had been driven, what percent of the warranty had been used?

6. Hi-Peak Corporation borrowed $6,000 for $2\frac{1}{2}$ years, simple interest. What is the total interest charge if the rate quoted was 9% per year?

7. Panke Inc. borrowed $4,500 in short-term funds at 10% simple interest to assist in its seasonal cash flow needs. What is the annual interest charge on the loan?

8. It cost $1,860 in interest to borrow $8,500 for two years, simple interest. What was the interest rate? (Accurate to two decimal places.)

9. What amount was borrowed if the interest charges quoted at 15% simple interest for a year amounted to $540?

10. The No-Toe Boot Company needed to borrow $16,000 for two years. If the maximum interest they could pay was $4,800, what was the largest interest rate they could pay?

SKILL EXERCISES

Use the following variable sets and identify the equation needed to find the variables: Base, Rate, Part (B, R, P); Interest, Principal, Rate, Time (I, P, R, T).

Variable set		Variable equation solution
1. Interest	T	_____
2. Base	P	_____
3. Base	R	_____
4. Interest	I	_____
5. Interest	P	_____

Answers to ✔ Check for Understanding
1. $550.   2. 63,126.   3. 49.3%.   4. $168.75.   5. 31.25%.   6. $1,350.   7. $450.
8. 10.94%.   9. $3,600.   10. 15%.

6. Base   B   _____

7. Interest   R   _____

APPLICATIONS

Identify the missing value and solve the following problems:

1. A construction company needs to earn an additional $3,000 on its invested money during the next year. If it has $25,000 to invest, what is the minimum interest rate that would allow them to reach their goal?

2. Total costs for manufacturing a new kitchen cleaner item was $368,000. Variable costs for this product were $156,400. What percent of the total costs were comprised of variable costs?

3. An $8,790 vehicle is expected to be $4\frac{1}{2}$% higher next year. What will the increase be?

4. If a $2,800 loan cost a borrower $210 interest for one year, what interest rate was charged?

5. Sandy invested $5,800 to purchase $14\frac{1}{2}$% of a business. What was the total value of the business?

6. An invoice that showed $365 as the total charges showed a 3% discount if paid within 10 days. What was the amount of the discount being offered?

7. An $11,500 two-year simple interest note carried a $2,185 interest charge. What was the interest rate?

8. Of the 3,600 students who took a standard test, only 18 made an error on problem 30. What percent of the students had difficulty with the problem?

9. If there are 31 male students in a class of 68, what percent of the class is female?

10. The total payroll for the month, which amounted to $2,800, was 35% of total monthly expenses. What were the total expenses for the month?

11. A simple interest note for $3,500 at 11% carried an interest charge of $1,925. What was the time length of the note?

12. If the lumber for a construction project was quoted to a buyer at 26.3% of the total costs of the $126,000 contract, what was the cost of the lumber?

13. A test contains 90 questions. If each is graded with an equal weight, how many can you miss and still achieve a 70% accuracy score for the test?

Section 4.7 Solving Problems for Changing Values

14. Pastor John invested $4,300 of his savings for a new cross-country motorcycle. The amount represented 42% of his savings. What are his total savings?

15. Eighty members of a youth group decided to attend the spring festival. If there were 125 total members in the group, what percent attended the festival?

Solving Problems for Changing Values

4.7

Problems involving change use a percent "more than" or "less than" some original value. The number being changed (the original value) is always the base. As a base, it assumes the value of 1 or a rate of 100% for reference. If, for instance, profits for one year were 20% more than in a prior year (the base), they are the original amount (base = 100%) plus the increase (20% additional), or 120% of the original value. If they were 20% less, they would be 80% of the original value. There are four things to remember involving change:

1. Problems can be solved with the base, rate, or part logic.
2. Change involves activity over a period of time. The earliest time period, or the one from which the change has occurred, is the base of reference and it assumes the value of a "base" or the 100% rate value.
3. The change can be expressed either as an amount or type of "unit" or in percent; see Figure 4.1.
4. Identify the variables given. Use them to solve with the base, rate, or part logic.

Figures 4.1 to 4.4 illustrate how change relates to a base value. Visualize the change with the use of percent. Once the unknown percent value is stated, the solution involves either simple addition or subtraction, multiplying the rate times the base to find a part, or dividing the respective part value by its rate to find the base. Figure 4.5 summarizes the calculation alternatives for finding the various change components:

1. To find the new condition in units, solve for a part using the rate of new condition.
2. To find the change in units, solve for a part using the rate of change.
3. To find the percent value for change, solve for a rate, using the units of change.
4. To find the percent value for new condition, solve for a rate using the units of new condition.
5. To find the original value (base), use the respective values of units of change and rate of change or units of new condition and rate of new condition.

Five Relevant Terms

Original Condition	(Base), B
Change Condition	(Part), P_1
New Condition	(Part), P_2
Rate of Change	(Rate), R_1
Rate of New Condition	(Rate), R_2

FIGURE 4.1
Change relationship logic

Uses the base, rate, and part formulas.

FIGURE 4.2
Statement: 30% increase (no units indicated)

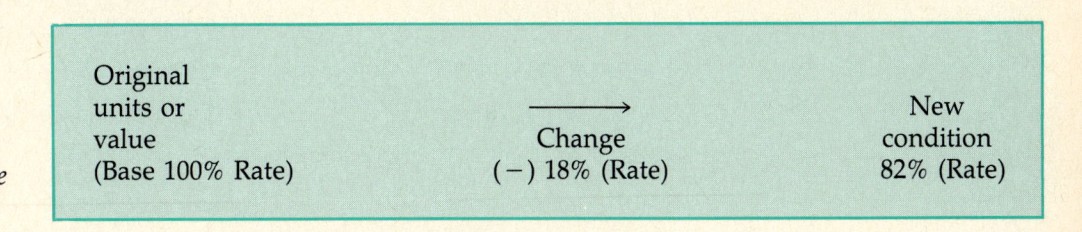

| Original units or value (Base 100% Rate) | ⟶ Change (+) 30% (Rate) | New condition 130% (Rate) |

FIGURE 4.3
Statement: 18% decrease (no units indicated)

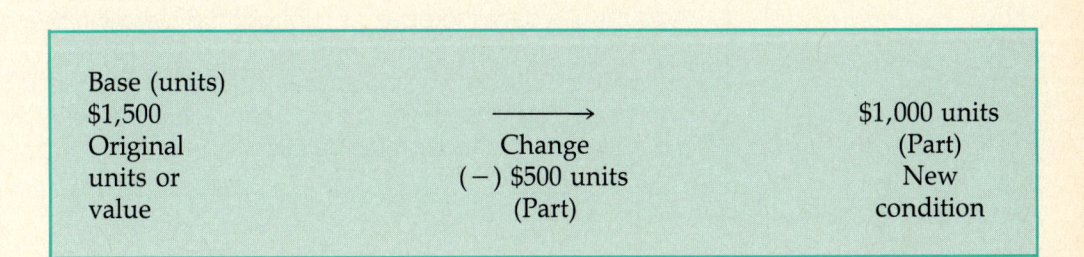

| Original units or value (Base 100% Rate) | ⟶ Change (−) 18% (Rate) | New condition 82% (Rate) |

FIGURE 4.4
Statement: $500 loss (units dollars)

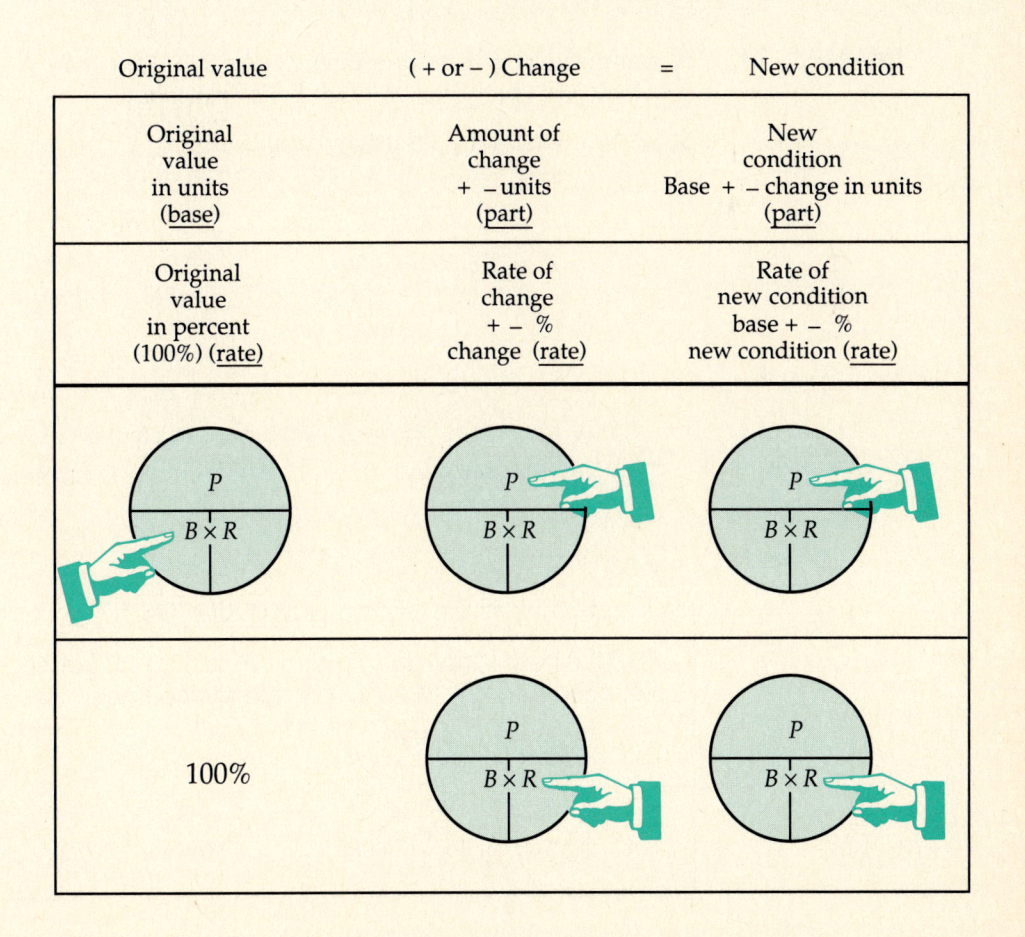

| Base (units) $1,500 Original units or value | ⟶ Change (−) $500 units (Part) | $1,000 units (Part) New condition |

FIGURE 4.5
Mathematical change relationships

| Original value | (+ or −) Change | = | New condition |

| Original value in units (base) | Amount of change + − units (part) | New condition Base + − change in units (part) |
| Original value in percent (100%) (rate) | Rate of change + − % change (rate) | Rate of new condition base + − % new condition (rate) |

(Circles showing P over B × R for each cell, with pointing hands)

100%

Section 4.7 Solving Problems for Changing Values

EXAMPLE 30 Last year company workers totaled 9,520 hours in overtime. This year's total will be 15% greater. How many hours of overtime will be worked this year?

Solution: Solve for a more-than condition. (Note that in a time sequence the earliest period receives the change and is therefore the base.) The missing variable is new condition, a part:

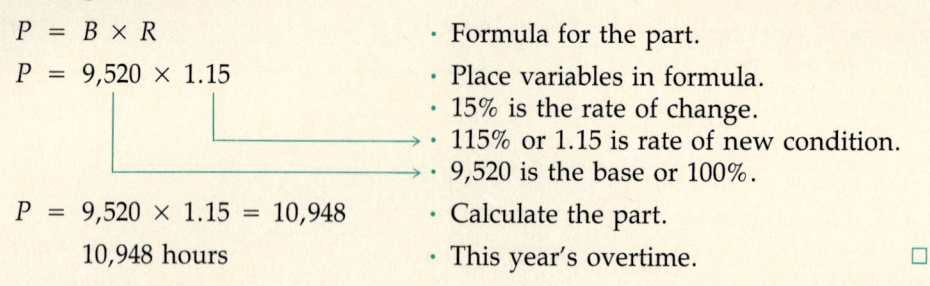

$P = B \times R$ · Formula for the part.
$P = 9{,}520 \times 1.15$ · Place variables in formula.
· 15% is the rate of change.
· 115% or 1.15 is rate of new condition.
· 9,520 is the base or 100%.

$P = 9{,}520 \times 1.15 = 10{,}948$ · Calculate the part.
10,948 hours · This year's overtime.

CALCULATOR TIP

Add the percent increase or subtract the percent decrease from the base 100%. This provides a rate that can be easily entered into the calculator to obtain the solution. For the above solution, the base 9,520 is multiplied by 1.15 to get the answer. In this procedure, the percent change is included in the rate used for the formula solution.

EXAMPLE 31 A manufacturing test component costs 14% less than it did two years ago. If the previous cost was $28,000, what is its cost today?

Solution: Solve for a less-than condition.
The missing variable is a new condition, a part:

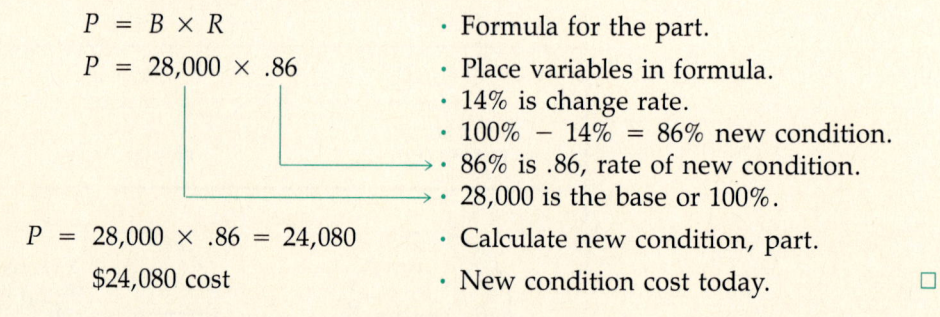

$P = B \times R$ · Formula for the part.
$P = 28{,}000 \times .86$ · Place variables in formula.
· 14% is change rate.
· 100% − 14% = 86% new condition.
· 86% is .86, rate of new condition.
· 28,000 is the base or 100%.

$P = 28{,}000 \times .86 = 24{,}080$ · Calculate new condition, part.
$24,080 cost · New condition cost today.

CALCULATOR TIP

Find the new condition rate and amount by subtracting the change rate from the base percent. Multiply this rate by the base.

Base value = 100%
100% − 14% = 86%   · New condition.
(B)28,000 × (R).86   · Formula values needed.
28,000 × .86 = 24,080   · New condition.

---

94 Chapter 4 Problem Solving

EXAMPLE 32 This year's production of 108,000 units compares favorably with the 96,000 of last year. What was the rate of increase?

Solution: Solve for the missing increase, rate of change:

$R = \dfrac{P}{B}$ • Formula for the rate.

$R = \dfrac{108,000}{96,000}$
• Place variables in formula.
• 108,000 is new condition units.
• 96,000 is base in units.

$108,000 \div 96,000 = 1.125$ • Calculate the rate.

$1.125 = 112.5\%$ • Rate of new condition.

New Condition % − Base % • Find the change percent.

$112.5\% - 100\% = 12.5\%$ • Calculate the change rate.

12.5% • Rate production change.

✓ CHECK FOR UNDERSTANDING

1. Next year's cost for housing will be 12% higher. If this year's costs are $7,800, what will next year's be?

2. Our production of Product M will be 34% less this year than last. If last year's production was 62,394 units, what will this year's production be?

3. A house lot increased in value 28% since purchased. If the purchase price was $15,000, what is its present value?

4. A weekly production run of 375 units was 25% less than the previous week's run. How many were produced last week?

5. After purchasing a new drill press for $6,800, the company's owner discovered that installation would cost an additional 22%. What was the total cost of the press?

SKILL EXERCISES

Express the percent of the new condition relative to the base after the following statements are applied:

Statement of change	New condition (%)
1. 30% more than last year	_____
2. 20% discount	_____

Answers to ✓ Check for Understanding
1. $8,736.   2. 41,180 units.   3. $19,200.   4. 500 units.   5. $8,296.

Section 4.7 Solving Problems for Changing Values

3. 45% loss   _____

4. 29% additional cost _____

5. 51% less than last year _____

6. 13% higher   _____

7. 38% profit   _____

8. 8% decrease   _____

9. 12% increase   _____

10. 46% reduction   _____

Find the missing change value:

	Original value (Base)	Change (Part)	New condition (Part)
11.	_____	$2,600	116%
12.	$4,200	(+) $756	_____
13.	100%	_____	67%
14.	$1,800	(+) 55%	_____
15.	100%	(+) 28%	_____
16.	$2,800	(−) $700	_____
17.	_____	(−) 14%	$124.70
18.	$1,680	(−) 42%	_____
19.	$782	_____	$179.86
20.	$654	_____	81%

APPLICATIONS

Use base, rate, part, and change logic to find the missing values in the following problems:

1. A construction framer's average monthly income during the two-year period before he was injured was $940. When he retired he received an income from a savings plan of $319.60 per month. What was the rate of decrease in income from his previous monthly average?

96 Chapter 4 Problem Solving

2. A computer science department shows a current enrollment of 1,126 students. Last year's enrollment was 943. What was the percent of enrollment increase?

3. TAYCO T-Shirts, Inc., manufactured 36,288 t-shirts last year. This was 12% greater production than for the previous year. What was the previous year's production?

4. If a $32,000 cash income per month is 20% less than a company needs, what is the required cash income?

5. The total price of a carpet steamer was $253.12. This price included a 5% city tax plus 8% of the retail price for a service contract. What was the original price of the carpet steamer?

6. A purchase of $12,224 was settled by a cash payment of $10,268.16. What percent less than the original purchase price was the payment?

7. Last year's utilities for the company totaled $3,870. If an 8.7% increase is expected, what would the budgeted amount be for this year?

8. Koolbreze Fan Company sells its products for 42.5% more than it costs to manufacture them. If a large window fan costs the company $62, what would it sell for?

9. An investment had gained 26% over the past year. If the investment plan showed a balance of $2,501.10, what was the amount of the original investment?

10. Last year's labor costs were $118,400. If this year's labor cost was $134,000, and labor expense was typically 15.6% of total sales, how much did sales increase?

11. Bad check expenses for a small company rose from $628 last year to $658.15 this year. What was the rate of increase in bad check expense?

12. Typically, invoices are reduced $2\frac{1}{2}$% for prompt payment. If $3.65 was the amount reduced under this company policy, what was the amount actually paid on the invoice after the discount?

13. For a purchase invoice of $782, 10% was allowed for a return of unwanted goods. Another 5% was authorized as a discount for prompt payment. If both of these actions were taken, how much would it take to settle the account?

14. Last year a house had a $50,000 replacement cost in case of total destruction. The household goods were valued at $1\frac{1}{2}$ times the house replacement cost. This year's increase for both categories was 6%. If insurance was charged at $2.50 per $1,000 value, for each category what is the total for this year?

15. The price of a dozen golf balls increased $18\frac{1}{2}$% over last year. If you just paid $16.59 for a dozen, what was last year's price?

16. Thirty-four percent of a ski-lift ticket is profit. If this year's ski-lift ticket cost $24 and included a 6.1% increase over last year, what was the amount of profit per ticket last year?

17. Auto parts are sold for $52\frac{1}{2}$% more than they cost. If a part costs $16.42, what is the selling price?

18. Ten years ago the stock of HRCZ Company was selling at $82 per share. As of today it has decreased $26 per share. What percent of the original price is it currently selling for?

19. Philippa earns $12\frac{1}{4}$% more than Marcia. If she earns $22,000 per year, what are Marcia's annual earnings?

20. Julie recently purchased stock at $80 per share. If the stock increased 30% one month and dropped 12% the next month, what was its price per share after the two changes?

Key Terms

Base (84)

Equation (77)

Interest (86)

Part (84)

Rate (84)

Variable (77)

Word problem (83)

Looking Back

Number sequences provide an exercise to illustrate how values can change. Look for this change and how the pattern of change repeats. You will be able to use this pattern to project the next number in a sequence.

Before struggling with a word problem, explain to yourself what is happening in the problem. Your explanation will usually reveal the math pattern the problem is establishing and ultimately the steps needed to find the solution. The rules for working with word problems may be the most important ingredient in getting comfortable with your mathematics success level. They are worth reviewing again.

Using a formula for problem solving (instead of a "best guess technique") is as important to your development as a good business math student as your calculator. Focus on selecting the problem elements that are available to substitute in the formula.

Change is an everyday element of business. Remember that the element that is changing is always the base. If there are multiple changes taking place in the problem, there is more than one base being indicated. Solve for each element individually and in sequence.

Let's Review

1. Five hundred twenty-five components failed the production tolerance inspection test. If 46,000 components had been manufactured, what percent of the batch did not pass inspection?

2. A simple interest loan for two years cost a borrower $532 interest at $9\frac{1}{2}$% interest. How much was borrowed?

3. Twenty-four percent of the total 26,400 student population were majoring either in business or in economics. How many students did that percentage include?

4. What was the original investment if the interest rate of 11.5% earned $4,312.50?

5. What would be the amount of interest on a simple interest $600 loan taken at $13\frac{1}{4}$% for three years?

6. Thirty-five percent of a company's profits were made by Department A. If Department A profits were $87,500, what were the total profits of the company?

7. If a $1,200 simple interest loan taken at 12% interest was charged $360 interest, how long had the loan been in effect?

8. Fifteen percent of the total cost of a dinner for eight amounted to $18. What was the cost of the dinner?

9. The total payback amount on a loan was $8,577.03. This amount included $15\frac{1}{2}$% more than the original amount borrowed. What was the original amount of the loan?

10. Lightflower earns 14% more than Marion. If Lightflower's earnings are $189 per week, what does Marion earn per week?

11. The sales tax rose from 5% to $6\frac{1}{4}$%. How much more would a $12,000 vehicle cost a consumer because of the raise in taxes?

12. If Mr. Cortez's piano, which cost $264, is 22% more expensive than his guitar, what did the guitar cost?

13. A charity campaign collected $85,420 more than last year. If the current year's campaign totaled $562,920, what percent increase from the previous year did they experience?

14. A total of $285 of a loan taken for a full year was the 12% interest on the amount borrowed. What is the total amount (principal and interest) that must be repaid?

15. Sixty percent of a salesperson's 3,828 customers renew their accounts. If the 3,828 customers represent 80% of the total customer accounts, what number of the salesperson's customers renew their accounts? How many total customers does the company have?

Chapter Test

1. A candidate for election was 100 votes short of the 50% he needed. If he actually received 380 votes, how many votes were cast?

2. A simple interest loan was charged $248 on a principal of $1,984. If the loan was for one year, what was the interest rate?

3. A speed walker traveled 25.5 miles in six hours. What was her average walking speed?

4. Fifteen percent of an agent's customers are women. If he has 330 female customers, how many total customers does the agent have?

5. Only 148 of the group tested liked the new toothpaste product. If 3,700 were tested, what percent liked the product?

6. Rent for an apartment was 28% of a couple's monthly total income. If the rent was $392 per month, what was the couple's income?

7. How long would it take to travel 150 miles if one-third of the trip was driven at 55 miles per hour, and the speed for the remaining two-thirds of the trip averaged 50 miles per hour?

8. Our $240,000 profit represented an increase of 6% over last year. What were last year's profits?

9. Raenelle purchased a new condo and paid $15,000 down. If her remaining balance on her condo was $47,000, what percent of her purchase does she still have to finance?

10. Absenteeism during the flu season results in a 17% increase in the rate of production hours lost over the normal rate. If 204 additional lost hours due to absenteeism are experienced during the flu season, what is the normal rate of hours lost for the company?

PART II
Mathematics for Office Transactions

Bank Records

5

OBJECTIVES

When you complete this chapter you will be able to:

- *Understand procedures for opening an account, using checking services, and the legal requirements regarding check endorsements. (5.1)*
- *Correctly prepare a check to support business transactions. (5.2)*
- *Understand transaction codes and the procedures to maintain a check register. (5.3)*
- *Validate checking account balances through bank reconciliation. (5.4)*

COMING UP

Banks are important to business because they perform an important service. With service, however, usually come procedures. In one way or another, you will be involved in bank transactions throughout your lifetime. It's important to find out just how they work.

Opening and maintaining a checking account will likely be your most common exposure to banking. Business banking and accounting also impose a fundamental rule: as you write checks and make deposits, so must you periodically reconcile the process. Verifying cash balances is vital for cash flow planning.

Because of our involvement with banking, we should also recognize and understand the use of common banking forms. They represent some important procedures to be followed for check writing and depositing money. Records and forms that are properly maintained improve the accountability of a business with its auditors, investors, and creditors.

Checking Accounts

5.1

Most businesses and individuals pay routine bills by check in order to reduce the amount of cash they need. **Cancelled checks,** checks processed and returned by a bank, are a customer's receipt should a question arise over payment. Figure 5.1 shows typical cancellation marks on the back of a check.

FIGURE 5.1
Cancelled check

To open a checking account, an individual must complete a signature card and make a deposit. As you will notice in Figure 5.2, the typical signature card requires the following information:

1. The account number.
2. Owners of the account.
3. Type of account.
4. Authorized signature.
5. Complete personal information on each owner/authorized user.
6. Date opened.
7. Initial deposit.

Once a signature card has been completed, a deposit must be made. Figure 5.3 shows a typical deposit slip. If only a few checks are deposited at once, the front side of the deposit slip with limited room for checks as well as currency and coin should be adequate. Banks ask that the **American Banking Association (ABA) numbers** be used when checks are listed for deposit. These numbers are printed in the upper right-hand corner of most checks and are assigned by the ABA. To see an example of these numbers, see the check illustrated in Figure 5.5 on page 108.

Before checks are deposited, transferred, or cashed, they need to be endorsed. This endorsement transfers ownership from the holder to a bank or to another business or person. Four types of endorsements are illustrated in Figure 5.4.

FIGURE 5.2
Signature card

FIGURE 5.3
Deposit slip showing use of ABA numbers

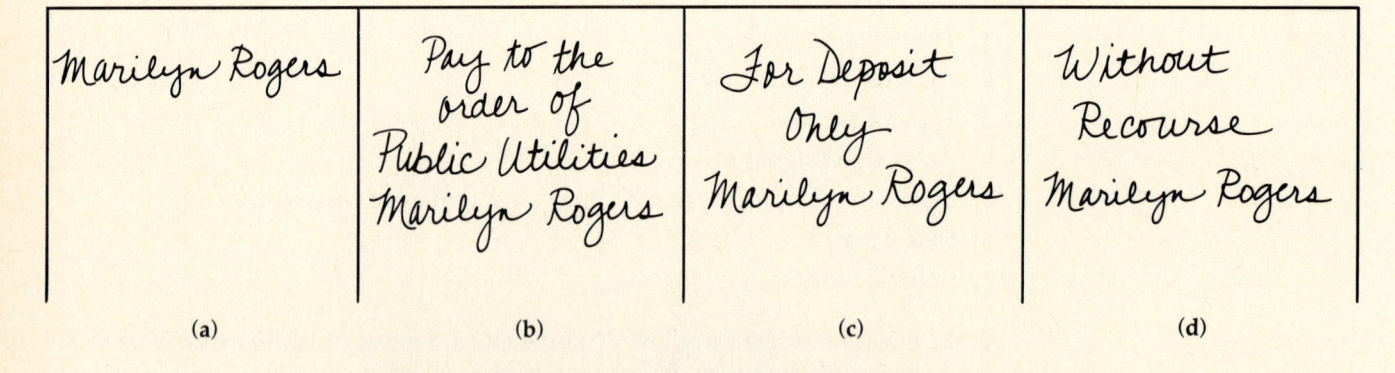

FIGURE 5.4
Types of endorsements

(a) **Blank endorsement:** *Only a signature is required. A check endorsed in this manner can be cashed by anyone who possesses it.*
(b) **Special endorsement:** *This type limits who can cash or deposit the check to the person or business named in the endorsement.*
(c) **Restrictive endorsement:** *The endorsement limits the use of the check. This type should be used if you are mailing your deposit or sending it to the bank with a third person.*
(d) **Qualified endorsement:** *This type relieves the endorsee of all responsibilities in the event that the original drawer of the check does not pay.*

104   Chapter 5   Bank Records

EXAMPLE 1 Using the following information, calculate the amount of the deposit by category and indicate the total deposit: 3 $20 bills; 2 $10 bills; 8 $1 bills; 10 quarters; 6 dimes; and 3 checks: #81–104 for $151.15; #92–86 for $23.47, and #19–402 for $87.50.

Solution:

Currency: $88.00
- Calculate the total of the currency: Includes three $20 bills ($60) plus two $10 bills ($20) plus eight $1 bills ($8).

Coin: $3.10
- Calculate the total in coins: Includes ten quarters (2.50) plus six dimes (.60).

Checks:
81–104 $151.15
92–86 $23.47
19–402 $87.50
        $353.22
- List three checks.
- Total the deposit: Add all three categories.

PROBLEM SOLVING STRATEGY

The number of checks that can be listed on the front of a deposit slip is limited. If need be, list checks on the back side of the deposit slip and bring the total to the appropriate line on the front side of the slip.

CALCULATOR TIP

In Example 1, both the currency and the coins require a subtotal. Use the calculator's memory function to accumulate answers to several parts:

3 × 20 = 60 M+   • Value of $20 bills in memory.
2 × 10 = 20 M+   • Value of $10 bills added to memory.
8 × 1 = 8 M+   • Value of $1 bills added to memory.
MR = 88   • Total of currency recalled from memory.

Do the coins in the same manner.

✔ **CHECK FOR UNDERSTANDING**

1. Tom Hughes used several different cash items to start his new checking account at Rockford National Bank. If Tom brought 10 quarters; 5 dimes; two $5 bills; and three checks: #81–110 for $25.80; #75–86 for $35.20; and #69–42 for $126.75, calculate his deposit by category and the total deposit.

2. The Rocket Plastic Corporation shows the following cash summation for Friday, January 10: 8 $20 bills; 5 $10 bills; 4 $5 bills; 24 $1 bills; one 50-cent piece; 9 quarters; 14 dimes; 9 nickels; 18 pennies; check #15–101 for $42.16; #24–101 for $72.13; #18–10 for $184.15; and #21–75 for $518.36. Prepare the deposit by category and calculate the total. **[Answers on page 106.]**

SKILL EXERCISES

Working down the columns, calculate the amount of the deposit by category and record it at the bottom of the drill. Then calculate the total deposit for each column.

Item	Column A Quantity	Column B Quantity	Column C Quantity	Column D Quantity	Column E Quantity
$20 bill	5	4	1	7	6
$10 bill	2	8	7	5	14
$5 bill	1	12	9	4	3
$1 bill	13	21	10	32	19
Half dollars	3	0	5	1	0
Quarters	9	18	15	28	20
Dimes	0	50	6	25	50
Nickels	3	0	11	13	25
Pennies	0	100	50	0	28
Check amounts	$152	$187	$215	$118	$315
CURRENCY					
COIN					
CHECKS					
TOTAL					

APPLICATIONS

Complete the deposit slips in the following problems:

1. Using the following information, calculate the deposit by each category and then calculate the total deposit: 3 $10 bills; 3 $5 bills; 3 $1 bills; 20 quarters; 50 dimes; and four checks: $18.50; $32.15; $450.00; and $127.35.

2. Each payday Bill took his paycheck to the bank but also tried to bring along loose change that he kept adding to a jar each day at home. Calculate the total deposit from the following information: three 50-cent pieces; 13 quarters; 36 dimes; 18 nickels; and his paycheck, #14–181 for $835.32.

3. Use a deposit slip to record the following deposit by category and calculate the total deposit: 3 $20 bills; 4 $5 bills; five 50-cent pieces; 20 quarters; 100 dimes; and four checks: #72–14 for $87.19; #18–90 for $300.00; #15–62 for $176.49; and 9–48 for $52.55.

Answers to ✓ Check for Understanding on page 105
1. Currency: $10.00; coin: $3.00; checks: $187.75. Total = $200.75. 2. Currency: $254.00; coin: $4.78; checks: $816.80. Total = $1,075.58.

4. Record the following deposit on the deposit slip, breaking it down into the appropriate category, listing each check separately, and calculating the total: 5 $10 bills; 17 $1 bills; 15 quarters; 8 dimes; 12 pennies; and two checks: #8–24 for $515.45 and #6–46 for $82.50.

5. Mark had the following items he planned to deposit. Make out the deposit slip by category and calculate the total: 1 $50 bill; 3 $20 bills; 4 $10 bills; 12 quarters; 19 dimes; and three checks: #31–105 for $72.35; #25–87 for $15.85; and #25–87 for $37.20.

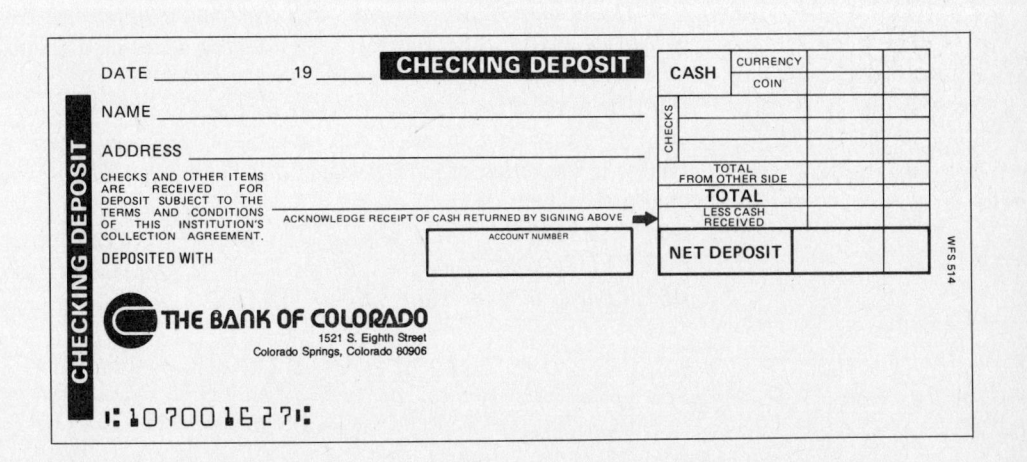

Section 5.1 Checking Accounts 107

Checks

5.2

It is essential that checks be written properly and clearly. Although each person may have a different style of check writing, there are several key points that must be watched for:

- The amount written in figures and words must agree.
- The legibility of all parts is essential.
- The amount must be carefully and completely filled in using figures and words so that the amounts cannot be altered or added to.

Figure 5.5 illustrates a typical personal check.

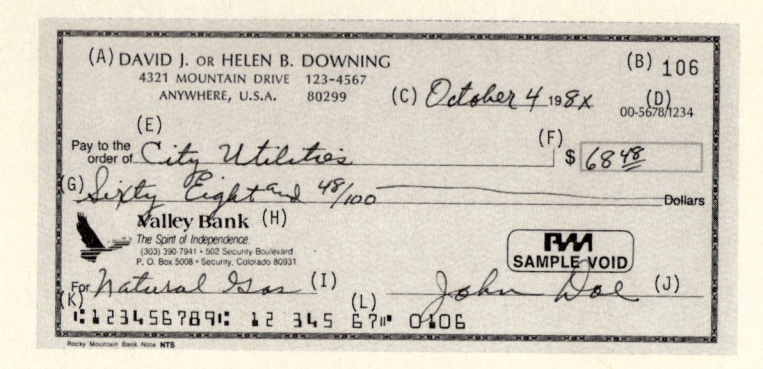

FIGURE 5.5
Personal check

(A) Name and address of account holder(s), which are normally preprinted when checks are purchased.
(B) The check number, which can be preprinted in consecutive order.
(C) The date on which the check is written must be entered.
(D) The American Banking Association (ABA) Number. The first set (82) identifies the city, state, or territory where the bank is located. The second set (162) identifies the specific bank. The first two digits of the third set (10) identify the federal reserve district in which the bank is located. The last digit or digits in the third set indicate the type of collection arrangements the bank uses. Only the first two sets are used to identify the check on deposit slip.
(E) The payee: the name of the person or business to whom the check is written.
(F) The dollar amount of the check in figures. The cent figures should be written as a fraction of one dollar $\left(\frac{00}{100}\right)$ or as a raised figure for clarity and to make it difficult to alter.
(G) The amount of the check written in words. This must agree with the amount in figures. If there is a discrepancy, the bank will use the amount in words. Start at the very beginning of the line and fill it in completely by drawing a line after the words all the way to "dollars."
(H) The bank where the account is located, called the drawee.
(I) The type of item or expense for which the check was written.
(J) Signature of the account holder called the drawer. This signature must agree with the one on the signature card.
(K) The identification numbers in "D" that are repeated here in Magnetic Ink Characters (MICR) to be read by machine and assist the federal reserve system in processing checks.
(L) The depositor's account number in MICR numbers.

EXAMPLE 2 Write a check using the following information: Date—October 13, 198X; Payee—Triple A Car Financing; Amount—$132.48; For—car payment.

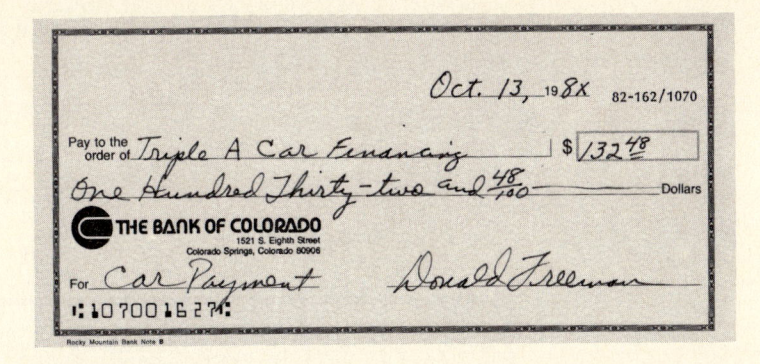

Check filled out: Oct. 13, 198X; Pay to the order of Triple A Car Financing $132.48; One Hundred Thirty-two and 48/100 Dollars; The Bank of Colorado; For Car Payment; Signed Donald Freeman

✓ CHECK FOR UNDERSTANDING

1. Write a personal check for $26.38 to Adams Furniture Company for an installment payment on a couch. Use the current date and your signature.

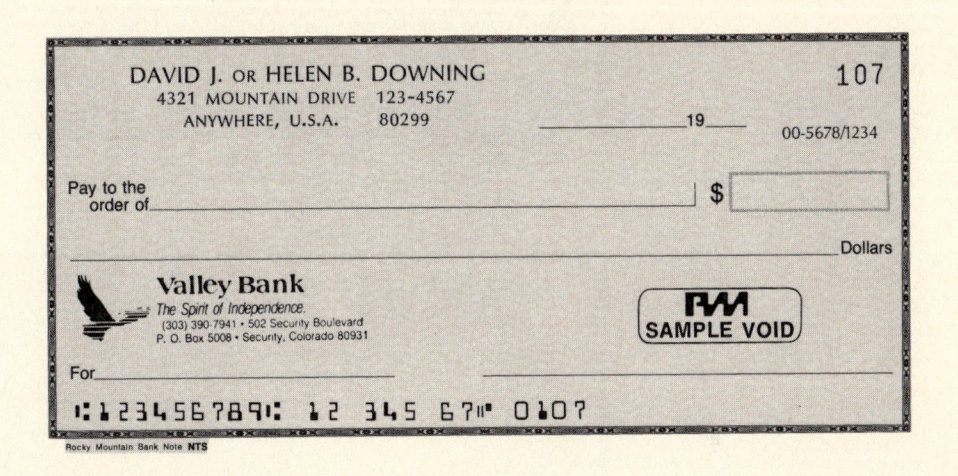

Blank check: David J. or Helen B. Downing, 4321 Mountain Drive 123-4567, Anywhere, U.S.A. 80299; Check No. 107; Valley Bank; SAMPLE VOID

2. Write a business check for $305.44 to ABC Concrete for 5 yards of concrete. Use the current date and sign your name as the check writer for your company. (Note: Business checks are usually larger in size. The signature on a business check can be done by a check-writing machine.)

Blank business check: The Bank of Colorado, Colorado Springs, Colorado 80906; VOID VOID

Section 5.2 Checks

APPLICATIONS

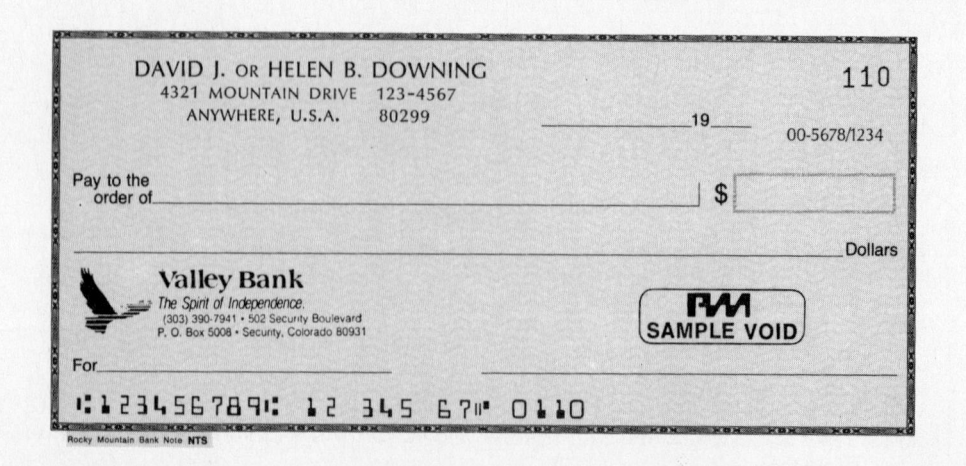

1. Write three personal checks. Use the current date and sign your name.

Payee	For	Amount
A. Water Department	Water	$42.50
B. Neat Insurance Company	Life Insurance	$61.92
C. David Frank	Car Part	$15.50

110   Chapter 5   Bank Records

2. Write two business checks. Use the current date and sign your name.

	Payee	For	Amount
A.	Appliance Wholesale	Merchandise	$632.62
B.	Mountain Floral	Potted Plants	$124.75

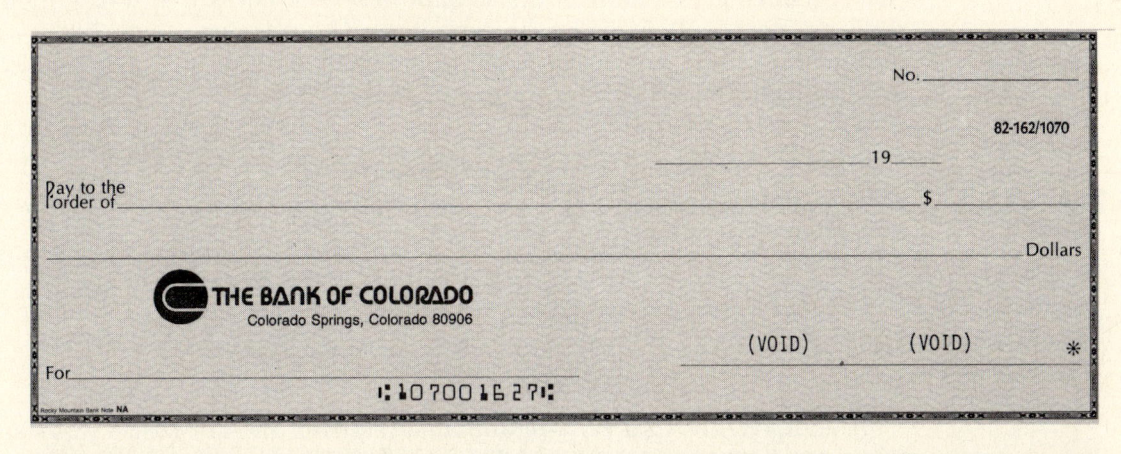

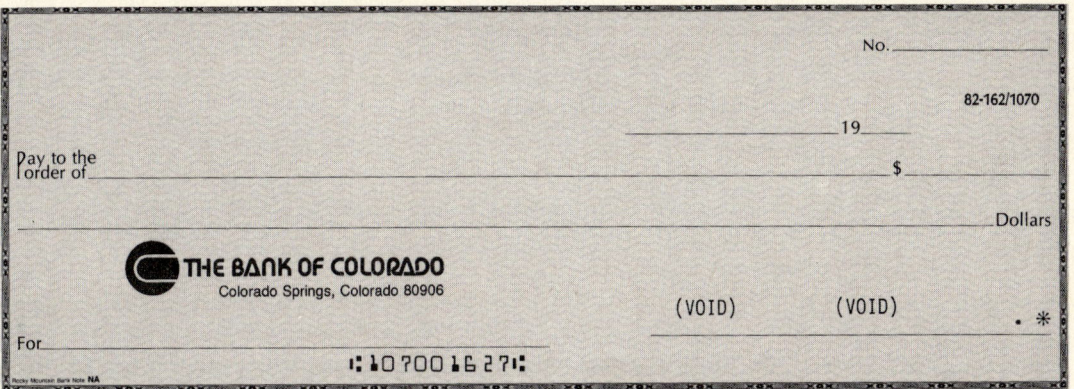

The Check Register

5.3

Once the original deposit is made, record the amount in the check register or on the check stub as the beginning balance. Each additional deposit and any subsequent checks that are written must be entered and a running balance maintained. Figure 5.6 illustrates a partial page of a typical check register.

FIGURE 5.6
The check register

(A) Date of the transaction.
(B) Check number.
(C) Description of the transaction.
(D) Amounts other than typical deposits or check amounts. Examples: service charges, overdraft charges, error corrections.
(E) Column to note tax deductible items (T).
(F) Deposits (added).
(G) Check or withdrawal amounts (subtracted).
(H) Continuous (running) balance.
(I) Reminders to assist in staying current and in balance.

Other Check Register Adjustments

Bank statements must be checked carefully for other deductions to be entered on the check register. The most common charge will be a **service charge** (fees charged by the bank for various services). Some other charges are for new checks, an **overdraft** charge (not enough money in the account to cover a check that was written), automatic payments authorized by the depositor, and a safe deposit box fee. If money is being deposited by some type of electronic funds transfer, that amount also needs to be verified.

EXAMPLE 3 Marilyn had an opening deposit of $375. During the remainder of the month she wrote four checks:

> #101 April 18 Gasoline $8.75
> #102 April 22 Telephone $47.80
> #103 April 23 Groceries $15.95
> #104 April 24 Utilities $117.65

In addition, on April 27, a refund on a returned dress of $68.75 was deposited. When her bank statement arrived on April 30, she noted the following charges: service charge, $5.25; new check charge, $7; and bank loan payment automatically deducted, $47.80. Make the appropriate entries in the check register and maintain a running balance after each entry.

Solution: Use the check register below:

- Record the beginning balance on the top line of the balance column.
- Record check number, date, amount of check, and subtract each from the previous balance.
- Record date and amount of deposit and add to previous balance.
- Record last date of month, label each charge from the bank statement, and subtract each amount from the previous balance.

19 _8X_   BE SURE TO DEDUCT ANY PER ITEM CHARGES, SERVICE CHARGES, OR FEES THAT MAY APPLY.

DATE	NUMBER	TRANSACTION DESCRIPTION	(+OR−) OTHER	✓T	(+) AMOUNT OF DEPOSIT	(−) AMOUNT OF PAYMENT OR WITHDRAWAL	BALANCE
							375 00
4/18	101	GASOLINE				8 75	366 25
22	102	TELEPHONE				47 80	318 45
23	103	GROCERIES				15 95	302 50
24	104	UTILITIES				117 65	184 85
27		RETURNED DRESS			68 75		253 60
30		SERVICE CHARGE	5 25				248 35
30		NEW CHECKS	7 00				241 35
30		LOAN PAYMENT				47 80	193 55

REMEMBER TO RECORD ALL DEPOSITS AND WITHDRAWALS AS WELL AS PRE-AUTHORIZED TRANSACTIONS.

> ### CALCULATOR TIP
>
> Keep a running total in your calculator as you enter the subtractions and additions in Example 3.
>
> | ENTER | ENTER | DISPLAY | |
> |---|---|---|---|
> | 375 | − | 375 | • Opening balance. |
> | 8.75 | − | 366.25 | • Subtract check; new balance. |
> | 47.8* | − | 318.45 | • New balance. |
> | 15.95 | − | 302.50 | • New balance. |
> | 117.65 | + | 184.85 | • Use plus; next entry is a deposit. |
> | 68.75 | − | 253.60 | • Use minus; next entry is subtracted. |
>
> Continue in like fashion to obtain a final balance.
>
> ---
>
> * Trailing zero or zeros need not be entered: (47.80 = 47.8).

✔ CHECK FOR UNDERSTANDING

1. Using the following summary, calculate the ending check register balance: opening deposit, $325.00; checks written, $82.96, $115.35, $26.55, $42.11; additional deposit, $65.50. The bank statement summary shows the following: service charge, $5.25; new checks, $12; overdraft, $8.00.

2. Calculate the check register balance using the following information: beginning balance, $2,400.75; checks for $245.60, $72.95, $427.45, $12.36, $19.57, $19.85; deposits, $325.64, $1,145.10; bank statement summary, service charge, $7.15; automatic loan payment, $81.75.

APPLICATIONS

Apply your new skill to the following check register problems:

1. Peggy was having trouble making her check register agree with the bank balance. She decided to recalculate the past several entries. What is her correct check register balance? Balance on top of page, $615.49; deposits of $1,100.35 and $62.85; checks of $82.20, $15.10, $36.70, $620.00, and $24.15. She had also recorded a service charge of $3.25.

2. In reviewing her check register, Robin found the following items:

Balance at the top	$760.55	Deposit	$900.00
New check charge	$8.50	Service charge	$4.75
Check	$77.45	Check	$12.40
Check	$5.64	Check	$133.62
Check	$91.83		

   Calculate the entries to determine her check register balance.

Answers to ✔ Check for Understanding
1. $98.28.   2. $2,984.81.

Section 5.3   The Check Register

3. Dave's check register balance at the end of August was $2,294.51. Use the following information either to verify or change his check register balance: beginning balance, $1,341.78; check, $339.14; check, $7.39; check, $66.00; check, $64.89; check, $76.24; check, $98.62; deposit, $1,525.30; deposit, $85.00; service charge, $4.75.

4. The following information is a typical listing of the types of entries that could be found in a page of a check register. Using the register page, fill in all information including dates and check numbers. Be sure to keep a running balance after each entry. Balance to begin page—$938.50.

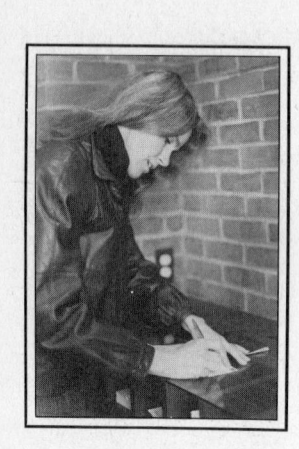

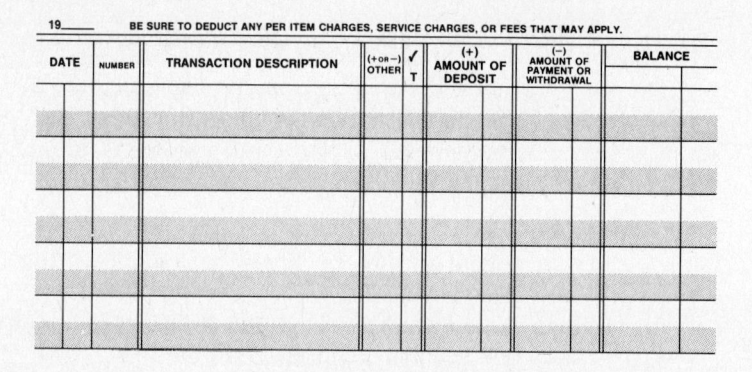

Date	Check #	Description	Amount
November 16	Check #489	Groceries	$62.20
November 18	Check #490	Gasoline	$13.65
November 22	Deposit		$375.00
November 22	Check #491	Eye exam	$54.00
November 25	Check #492	Rent	$425.00
November 28	Check #493	Safe deposit rental	$15.00
Bank statement entries:		Service charge	$3.50
		Automatic payment	$37.25

5. The final page of the check register for the month of January is listed below. Using your calculator and what you know about the entries, please verify each balance figure and the ending balance for January.

Date	Number	Transaction Description	(+ or −) Other	✓ T	(+) Amount of Deposit	(−) Amount of Payment or Withdrawal	Balance
							1850 62
Jan 25	1106	Groceries				118 92	1731 70
27	1107	Gas				11 50	1760 16
28		Paycheck			380 60		2097 20
31		Service Charge	6 00				2091 20
31		Overdraft Charge	8 00				2083 20
31		Paycheck			400 00		2483 20
31		Auto Loan Pay.				132 50	2350 70

114 Chapter 5 Bank Records

Bank Statement Reconciliation

5.4

Once each month, the bank sends a **bank statement** to each business, person, or organization that has a checking account. With the statement, the bank includes all checks it has processed since the last statement (cancelled checks) and verification of all deposits during the month. In addition, the bank may include several other papers showing (a) transfer of money from a savings account to checking; (b) notes on **nonsufficient funds (NSF)**, checks you have written that have been returned because the account balance at the time the check was submitted was less than the amount of the check; and (c) other types of miscellaneous transactions. Most banks do not include a transaction paper for any prearranged payment from or deposit to the account.

As you will notice on the bank statement in Figure 5.7, like transactions are grouped together. Some bank statements will not group like transactions but will list them in date order. Notice the summary of activity line, which includes the beginning balance, the amount of debits (subtractions), the amount of credits (additions), and the ending balance.

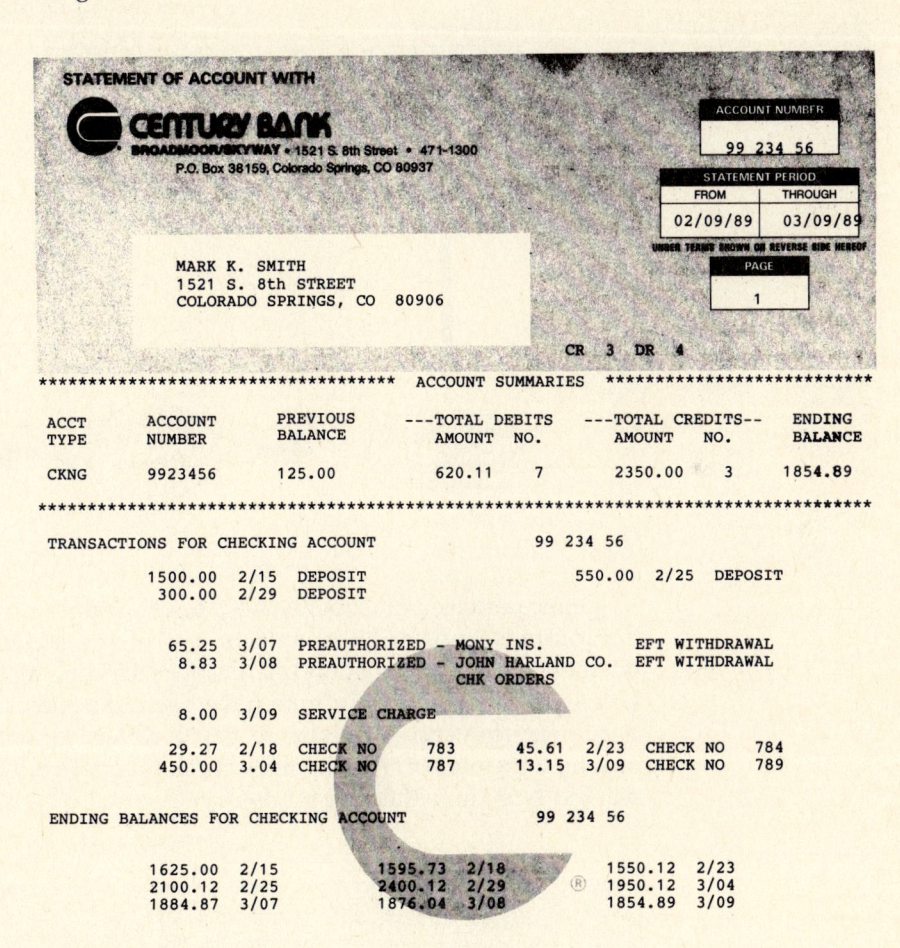

```
STATEMENT OF ACCOUNT WITH
CENTURY BANK
BROADMOOR/SKYWAY • 1521 S. 8th Street • 471-1300
P.O. Box 38159, Colorado Springs, CO 80937

ACCOUNT NUMBER
99 234 56

STATEMENT PERIOD
FROM        THROUGH
02/09/89    03/09/89

MARK K. SMITH
1521 S. 8th STREET
COLORADO SPRINGS, CO  80906

                                             PAGE
                                              1

                                        CR  3  DR  4

*********************************  ACCOUNT SUMMARIES  *********************************

ACCT     ACCOUNT       PREVIOUS      ---TOTAL DEBITS    ---TOTAL CREDITS--    ENDING
TYPE     NUMBER        BALANCE       AMOUNT      NO.    AMOUNT       NO.      BALANCE

CKNG     9923456       125.00        620.11      7      2350.00      3        1854.89

****************************************************************************************

TRANSACTIONS FOR CHECKING ACCOUNT              99 234 56

         1500.00  2/15  DEPOSIT                    550.00  2/25  DEPOSIT
          300.00  2/29  DEPOSIT

           65.25  3/07  PREAUTHORIZED - MONY INS.          EFT WITHDRAWAL
            8.83  3/08  PREAUTHORIZED - JOHN HARLAND CO.   EFT WITHDRAWAL
                                       CHK ORDERS

            8.00  3/09  SERVICE CHARGE

           29.27  2/18  CHECK NO    783     45.61  2/23  CHECK NO    784
          450.00  3.04  CHECK NO    787     13.15  3/09  CHECK NO    789

ENDING BALANCES FOR CHECKING ACCOUNT           99 234 56

         1625.00  2/15        1595.73  2/18        1550.12  2/23
         2100.12  2/25        2400.12  2/29        1950.12  3/04
         1884.87  3/07        1876.04  3/08        1854.89  3/09
```

FIGURE 5.7
Bank statement

Section 5.4 Bank Statement Reconciliation   115

When the bank statement arrives, compare the ending balance on the statement with the balance in the check register. If there is a difference, it can probably be attributed to a time difference in processing transactions rather than an error. The illustration that follows lists the steps involved in the reconciliation process. The three most common reasons adjustments are necessary are as follows:

- **Service charges** (A fee charged for a variety of services).
- **Outstanding checks** (Checks that have not yet been processed by the bank's accounting department).
- **Outstanding deposits** (Deposits not yet processed by the bank's accounting department).

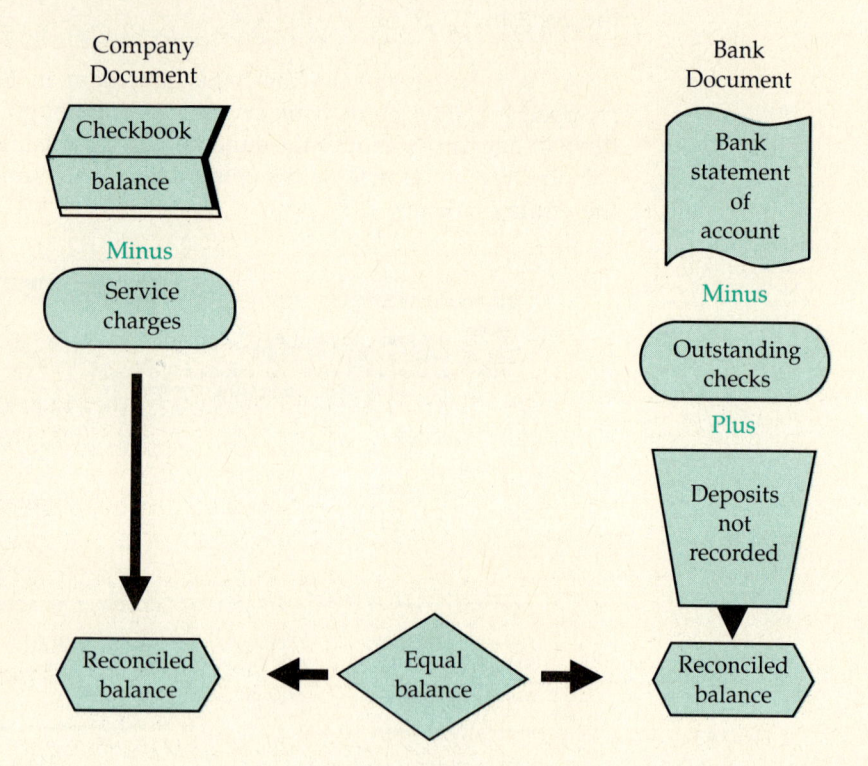

```
Company Document                              Bank Document
    Checkbook                                   Bank statement
     balance                                      of account
      Minus                                         Minus
    Service                                      Outstanding
    charges                                        checks
                                                    Plus
                                                  Deposits
                                                    not
                                                  recorded
    Reconciled        ←  Equal   →              Reconciled
     balance              balance                  balance
```

Other possible adjustments are interest charges on a check guarantee plan, electronic funds transfer either into or out of the account, and cost of new checks. Business accounts may show charges for collecting a promissory note or an addition because the proceeds of a note have been deposited. A **promissory note** is a legal document showing a promise to pay a certain amount of money at a future date usually with interest. A customer's check that does not clear the bank will be returned marked NSF (nonsufficient funds).

Procedures for Reconciliation

1. Put the cancelled checks in numerical order and check them off in the check register as being returned.
2. List by number and amount all checks which have not been returned. These are outstanding checks and need to be subtracted from the bank statement.

of Lockhart's records showed that 38 checks had been written with the following four outstanding: #4210, $86.50; #4216, $2,000; #4217, $108.62; and #4218, $24.58. There was also an outstanding deposit of $1,536.70.

Solution:

			$14,423.12	• List bank statement balance.
#4210		86.50		• List total and *subtract* outstanding checks.
#4216	+	2,000.00		
#4217	+	108.62		
#4218	+	24.58		
	−	2,219.70		
		12,203.42		• Subtotal.
	+	1,536.70		• List and *add* outstanding deposits.
		$13,740.12		• Adjusted bank balance.

$11,258.37 • List check register balance.

• List, total, and *subtract* bank charges.

Note collect. fee   15.00
Service charge   + 3.25
                  − 18.25

11,240.12   • Subtotal.
+ 2,500.00   • List and *add* deposits from bank statement.
$13,740.12   • Adjusted check register balance.

Make sure adjusted balances agree: $13,740.12 = $13,740.12. □

EXAMPLE 6 Hughes Contractors Inc. showed a cash balance of $3,115.36 on September 30. After checking the bank statement, it found a service charge of $5.15; a new check charge of $11.15; and a NSF check for $65.69. The comparison also showed a bank statement balance of $3,459.98; an outstanding deposit of $375; and outstanding checks #1015, $315.87; #1021, $36.15; and #1022, $562.43. Reconcile the bank balance.

Solution:

Check register			*Bank statement*	
Balance		$3,115.36	Balance	$3,459.98
Service charge	5.15		Outstanding checks	−914.45
New checks	+ 11.15			$2,545.53
NSF check	+ 65.69			
		− 81.99	Outstanding deposits	+375.00
Adjusted balance		$3,033.37	Adjusted balance	$2,920.53

Check register	3,033.37	• Subtract balances to determine difference.
Bank statement	−2,920.53	
(See Tip 5 on page 117.)	112.84	

112.84 ÷ 9 = 12.5377777   • Divide difference by 9 to check for transposition error.

12.5377777   • Doesn't divide exactly; no transposition error. □

Look for the difference (112.84) on the list of checks on the bank statement to see if a check for that amount wasn't subtracted from the check register. This is the most logical search because the adjusted check register figure is larger than the adjusted bank statement figure. (See Tip 6 on page 117.)

Section 5.4 Bank Statement Reconciliation

If you do not find the exact amount on the bank statement, look on the check register for the amount. If you find that amount, it wasn't listed as an outstanding check. This error would be more logical if the adjusted bank balance were larger than the adjusted check register balance. (See Tip 7 on page 117.)

The error was an outstanding check not subtracted from the check register. Now make the adjustment:

	$3,033.37	• Adj. check register balance.
	−112.84	• Subtract Check #994.
Adjusted balance	$2,920.53	= $2,920.53

PROBLEM SOLVING STRATEGY

On the back of most bank statements, a format for reconciling is printed. These formats and their logic vary by bank and the format changes frequently. The reconciliation system presented in the text is a standard system that works and provides the information necessary for making entries in the accounting records.

✔ **CHECK FOR UNDERSTANDING**

1. Bill Gardner's checkbook balance was $460 on March 31. After verifying the cancelled checks returned with his bank statement, Bill had the following outstanding checks: #713 for $67; #714 for $35; and #716 for $13. The bank statement showed a balance of $453; a service charge of $4; and an overdraft charge of $8. He also noticed that a deposit he made on March 31 for $110 was not listed on the bank statement. Reconcile the two balances.

2. Hi Class Bowling Lanes' bookkeeper compared her checkbook with the bank statement on June 29. She found three outstanding checks totaling $112.82 and a check written for $42 incorrectly entered in the check register as $24. Other comparisons showed that a deposit made on June 28 for $350.82 did not appear on the bank statement; the bank returned an NSF check for $15.25; and a service charge of $2.95 was listed on the bank statement. Prepare the bank reconciliation assuming a check register balance of $5,296.50 and a bank statement balance of $5,022.30.

3. Faye Cromwell's checkbook balance on July 31 was $817.75. The bank statement balance was $897.35. There were four outstanding checks totaling $115.65; service charge of $5; and check guarantee interest of $2.15. The bank statement also showed an insurance payment of $32.50 sent electronically. After being unable to reconcile the bank statement balance of $781.10 and the checkbook balance of $778.10, Faye determined that Check #813 was entered in the check register for $25.16, but the correct amount should have been $21.56. Reconcile the bank balance.

Answers to ✔ **Check for Understanding**
1. $448.   2. $5,260.30.   3. $781.70.

Note: The difference between the two adjusted balances ($781.70 − $778.10) is $3.60, which divides evenly by 9. Therefore, there is a strong possibility that a transposition error was made. Checking back through the check register verified a transposition error on Check #813.

SKILL EXERCISES

Analyze the factors in Problems 1 through 8 that are involved in bank reconciliation. Place each item under the affected balance and indicate whether it is to be added or subtracted. Item 1 is given as an example.

		Check register	Bank statement
1.	Service charge	Subtract	
2.	Outstanding checks		
3.	Outstanding deposit		
4.	Overdraft		
5.	Automatic loan payment		
6.	New check charge		
7.	NSF check		
8.	Interest on check guarantee plan		

In Problems 9 through 18, use the information in each horizontal problem to calculate the reconciled balance and record it in the last column of each row.

	Check Register Balance	Bank Statement Balance	Outstanding Checks	Outstanding Deposit	Service Charge	Interest	NSF Check	Overdraft Charge	Balance
9.	$500	$618	$125		$5	$2			$
10.	$375	$275	$75	$150	$2		$15	$8	$
11.	$425	$186	$40	$230	$4	$3	$35	$7	$
12.	$135	$438	$315		$3	$1		$8	$
13.	$2,700	$1,815	$240	$1,100			$25		$
14.	$3,630	$3,007	$815	$1,305	$2	$4	$115	$12	$
15.	$412	$424	$27		$5	$3		$7	$
16.	$4,185	$4,343	$672	$150	$4		$350	$10	$
17.	$1,643	$1,436	$214	$363		$2	$50	$6	$
18.	$1,229	$972	$138	$250	$5		$140		$

Section 5.4 Bank Statement Reconciliation

APPLICATIONS

1. The bank statement for the Hoyle Furniture Company on May 31 shows the following:

   Balance $3,359.33

   | Automatic loan payment | $155.00 | Overdraft | $22.50 |
   | NSF check returned | $327.82 | Service charge | $12.45 |

   Information gathered from the company's check register comparisons shows:

   | Outstanding Check #5242 | $1,832.90 | Check #5261 | $216.16 |
   | Check #5262 | $36.00 | Outstanding deposit | $2,424.48 |

   Hoyle's cash records showed a balance of $4,216.52. Reconcile the cash balances.

2. The accountant at Juggle, Jiggle, and Break Pottery Company has made the normal adjustments to both the bank statement balance and the check register balance but still finds the cash balance not agreeing after the adjustments have been made. The adjusted check register balance is $1,489.62 and the adjusted bank balance is $1,401.50.
   (a) What is the difference in the two balances?
   (b) Has a transposition error been made?
   (c) If not, what type of error will you look for?
   (d) In what record will you look?

3. After comparing his personal cash records to the bank statement, Paul Ballard listed the following information:

Bank statement balance	$992.05
Personal cash balance	$1,073.35
Service charge	–0–
Interest on check guarantee plan	$1.25
Two electronic payments totaling	$192.80
Bank loan payment subtracted at bank	$63.00
Four outstanding checks totaling	$315.90
Outstanding deposit	$140.15

   Reconcile the bank balance for the month.

4. The March bank statement for Debby Peterson's checking account revealed the following information: balance, $827.37; service charge, $4.50; and interest on a check guarantee plan, 87 cents. After comparing the cancelled checks to her check register, she found two outstanding checks that totaled $92.36. She also discovered that she didn't subtract Check #2406 for $33.90 from her check register. Her current balance is $774.28. Reconcile the cash balance.

5. The We Sell Advertising Agency showed an ending cash balance of $776.88 on May 31. The bank statement indicated several adjustments had been made by the bank that will affect the ending balance: deposit of $1,100 from a promissory note collection; an automatic loan payment of $72.95; a service charge of $8.35; and an overdraft charge of $13.50. The bank balance on the statement was $2,225.80. There were five outstanding checks that totaled $443.72. Reconcile the cash balances.

6. Mike's comparison of his check register with the bank statement for October revealed the following:

Check register balance	$1,526.15
Bank statement balance	$763.84
Check guarantee interest	$2.12
Outstanding deposit	$817.00
NSF check	$28.75
Automatic payment	$81.57
Safe deposit box charge	$15.00
Outstanding checks totaling	$182.13

Prepare the bank reconciliation.

Key Terms

ABA numbers (103, 108)
Bank statement (115)
Blank endorsement (105)
Cancelled checks (103)
Nonsufficient funds (NSF) check (115)
Outstanding check (116)
Outstanding deposit (116)

Overdraft (112)
Promissory note (116)
Qualified endorsement (105)
Reconciliation (116)
Restrictive endorsement (105)
Service charge (112, 116)
Special endorsement (105)

Looking Back

Accuracy in completing the deposit slip and the check is essential. Because accurate home or business records are based on properly maintaining your check register (check stub), complete the register entry before you write the check. Because the endorsement affects the legal status of the check and your personal liability, review the four principal types of endorsement. Know when to use each type.

Reconciliation must be done faithfully because (1) the bank reconciliation may show adjustments to cash records are necessary and, if not made, are not included in either the financial statements or the cash flow predictions; (2) not reconciling could cause an overdraft; and (3) proving that business cash records agree with an outside agency (bank) shows proper checks and balances are in place within the cash management system.

Let's Review

1. Ever-Ready Security Systems show a cash balance of $986.32 on September 30. The bank statement comparison shows bank statement balance, $1,042.49; automatic payment, $71.61; service charge, $8.30; NSF check, $122.84; and promissory note collection and deposit, $215. The check register comparison shows four outstanding checks totaling $255.42; outstanding deposit of $185; and Check #7215 for $26.50 was never entered in the check register. Prepare the reconciliation.

2. The bank statement balance on a personal checking account shows a November 30 balance of $403.27. It also shows an overdraft charge of $11.25; a service charge of $4.75; and a new check charge of $6.35. A check register comparison shows two outstanding checks: #426 for $15.82 and #430 for $44.92. If the check register balance is $364.88, what is the reconciled balance?

3. Using the following information, open a new page of the check register; write business checks as indicated, signing your name for the business; and make appropriate entries in the check register, keeping a running balance after each entry. Beginning cash balance $862.55.

Check no.	Date	Payee	For	Amount
1645	Oct. 26, 198X	Noram Products	Supplies	$26.84
1646	Oct. 28, 198X	Morton Equipment	Equip. rent	$82.43
1647	Oct. 28, 198X	Second National Bank	Loan	$426.82
Deposit	Oct. 30, 198X			$852.42

Bank statement deductions, Oct. 30: service, $3.85; automatic loan payment for inventory, $73.38.

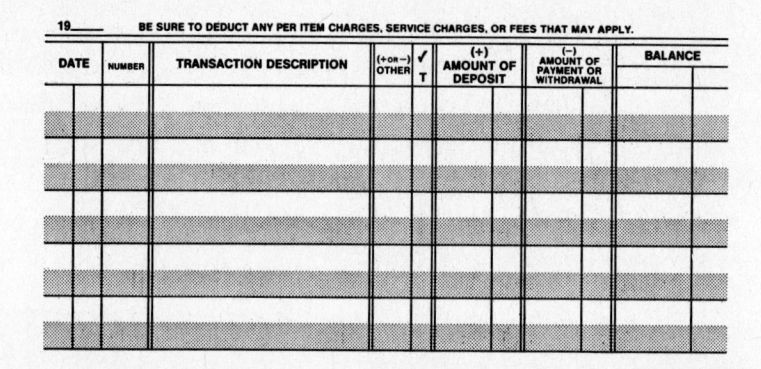

124 Chapter 5 Bank Records

4. The final cash tally for the day at Over-the-Road Car Rental showed 4 $20 bills; 6 $10 bills; 2 $5 bills; 31 $1 bills; six 50-cent pieces; 25 quarters; 50 dimes; 15 nickels; and 6 checks totaling $336.82. Calculate the deposit by category and then calculate the total deposit.

5. Page 4 of Che's check register shows an opening balance of $522.63 on January 16. Use the following list of entries to calculate an ending balance.

January 16 Deposit	$350.00	January 29 Check #2364	$107.61
16 Check #2361	$88.45	30 Deposit	$350.00
19 Check #2362	$22.61	31 Bank statement info	
23 Deposit	$350.00	Interest	$1.25
27 Check #2363	$50.49	Service charge	$6.30
		Automatic payment	$77.50

6. Use the deposit slip to make the following deposit and calculate the total.

Currency	$141.00	Date: February 6, 198X
Coin	$8.53	Account No. 70–1645
Checks: #15–40	$15.82	
#15–38	$27.85	
#13–105	$126.00	

7. Don's end of the month information from the check register and the bank statement include

Bank statement balance	$723.83	Outstanding checks	$315.62
Check register balance	$1,052.87	Automatic payment	$82.17
Service charge	$4.15	Outstanding deposit	$550.34
Overdraft charge	$8.00		

Determine the reconciled balance.

Let's Review 125

8. Holloways Candy Shop had an ending check register balance of $2,351.72 on August 31. Outstanding checks included #8164, $115.54; #8165, $20.89; #8174, $329.87; and #8175, $7.96; outstanding deposit of $1,482.16; NSF check of $21.75; service charge of $7.45; note collection fee of $12; promissory note deposit at the bank of $815. The bank statement balance was $2,081.62.
   (a) What is the adjusted check register balance?
   (b) What is the adjusted bank statement balance?
   (c) What type of error was probably made?
   (d) What would you look for the error?

Chapter Test

1. Using the following information, write the first two checks and make the necessary entries in the check register. Be sure to keep a running total after each entry.

Check no.	Date	Payee	For	Amount
Balance				1,506.42
505	March 24, 198X	City Water Dept.	Water	$36.50
506	March 24, 198X	Mountain Side Telephone	Phone	$27.83
507	March 25, 198X	Second National Bank	Mortgage	$642.34
508	March 27, 198X	Lots of Service	Gas	$13.25
Deposit	March 28, 198X			$2,120.66
509	March 30, 198X	City Electric	Electricity	$28.90

Bank statement deductions: new checks $7.42; service charge $5.30.

126   Chapter 5   Bank Records

2. Brad's check register balance was $382.64 on July 31. Two adjustments, a service charge of $6.40, and an overdraft charge of $10, had not been entered on the check register. There were two outstanding checks totaling $73.53 and an outstanding deposit of $150. The bank statement showed a balance of $289.77. Prepare the reconciliation.

3. The Big Muddy Car Wash's cash tally for Friday, November 16, was as follows: 3 $50 bills; 5 $20 bills; 6 $10 bills; 14 $5 bills; 65 $1 bills; 22 quarters; 75 dimes; 12 nickels; and 50 pennies. There were eight checks totaling $122.50. (Please enter these as if they were listed on the back of the deposit slip.) If its account number is 82–1652, make the deposit by category; calculate an accurate total.

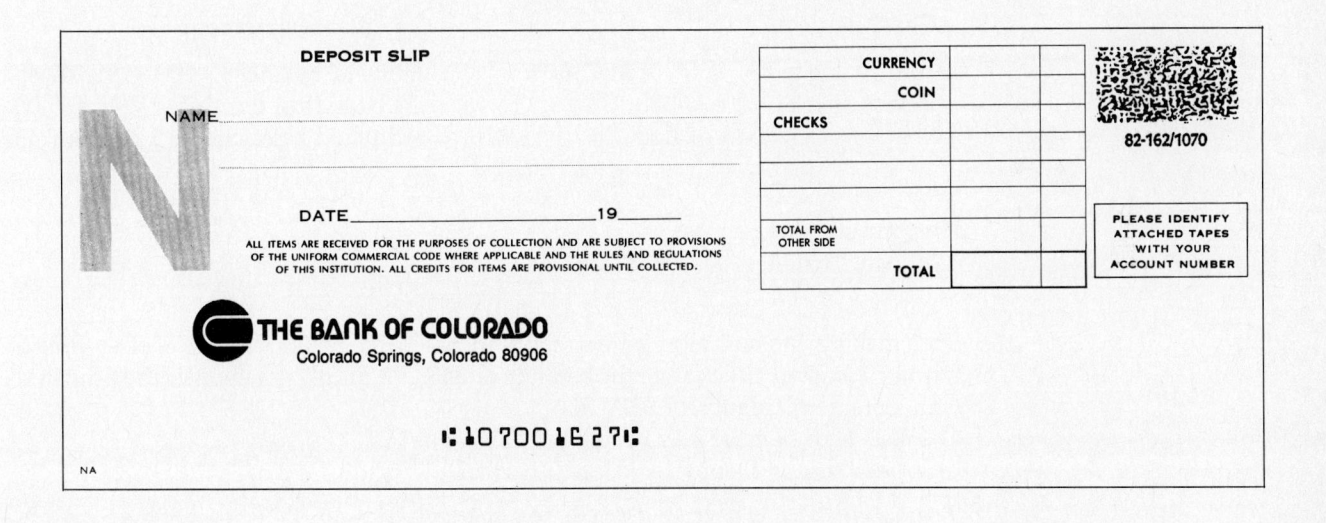

4. The bank statement and check register for the Bradley Farm Equipment Company listed the following information:

Bank statement balance	$8,721.08	Collection fee	$28.00
Electronic transfer payment	$210.80	Check register balance	$6,216.36
Overdraft charge	$16.85	Outstanding checks	$1,488.65
2 promissory notes deposited at bank	$1,542.62		

Error on check #9265 entered in check register as $1,147.84 should have been $1,418.74. Prepare the bank reconciliation.

5. Part of Betty's check register for March is illustrated below. Check entries and the running balance and make any necessary changes.

NUMBER	DATE	CHECKS ISSUED TO OR DESCRIPTION OF DEPOSIT	(−) AMOUNT OF CHECK	✓ T	(−) CHECK FEE (IF ANY)	(+) AMOUNT OF DEPOSIT	BALANCE
							815 68
	5/31	SERVICE CHARGE			8.00		8 00
							807 68
	31	BANK AUTO LOAN PAYMENT	85 65				85 65
							722 03
1506	6/1	ESSEX APARTMENTS RENT	475 00				475 00
							247 03
1507	1	CITY OF LEXINGTON UTILITIES	110 00				110 00
							137 03
1508	5	Void					
1509	5	CONOCO, INC GAS	14 35				14 35
							122 68
	7	SALARY				975 00	975 00
							1097 68
1510	10	GMAC CAR PAYMENT	187 62				187 62
							1285 30
1511	15	GROCERIES	72 75				72 75
							1212 55

6. The bookkeeper for Always-Kleen Window Service completed the bank reconciliation for March. It balanced, but there was some question as to whether it was correct. Review the procedure and make corrections if necessary.

Check register

Current balance	$1,759.16
Service charge	4.00
NSF	+ 21.50
	− 25.50
	1,733.66
Outstanding checks	+ 133.79
Adjusted balance	$1,867.45

Bank statement

Current balance	$1,702.45
Outstanding deposit	+ 165.00
Adjusted balance	$1,867.45

7. After making the common adjustments in her bank reconciliation, Debby found that her adjusted check register balance of $433.92 didn't agree with the adjusted bank statement balance of $379.92.
   (a) What type of error has probably been made?
   (b) Where should Debby look for the error?

8. A comparison of the bank statement and the cash records at the Top-of-the-Heap Landfill showed the following:

Check register balance	$4,867.54	Outstanding deposit	$1,150.00
Bank statement balance	4,322.51	Service charge	8.25
Seven outstanding checks	769.42	New check charge	9.50
Automatic transfer payment	146.70		

Prepare the bank reconciliation.

Payroll

6

OBJECTIVES

When you complete this chapter you will be able to:

- *Compute employee gross earnings for salaried, hourly, piece-rate, and commissioned employees. (6.1)*
- *Compute income tax, social security tax, and net (take home) pay. (6.2)*
- *Calculate employer contributions to social security and unemployment taxes. (6.2)*
- *Complete common payroll forms and understand their use. (6.3)*

COMING UP

PAYDAY!... Have you ever thought about the complexities of the activities and transactions necessary to make a payday happen? Earnings, deductions, taxes, checks, cash.... How do companies do it repeatedly without making errors?

    Whether payroll is completed using a hand calculator or with some type of automated assistance, it takes a lot of information. The information must be accurate and prepared in proper reporting format to meet state and federal requirements. This type of activity and information falls into four general categories: calculation of earnings, deductions, maintaining records, and employer liabilities. This chapter presents an introduction to the details of payroll and what it takes to make that payday happen.

Computing Gross Earnings

6.1

Earnings are normally divided into two categories—salaries and wages. Salaried employees have agreed to an annual rate of pay and also to work as many hours as necessary to get the work completed (i.e., not paid for overtime).

Wage earners have also agreed to a rate of pay; however, their paychecks depend on other factors, such as number of hours worked, number of items produced, or amount of sales made.

Salaried Employees

To find an amount of pay for a salaried employee, we divide the annual salary by the number of pay periods in a year. Thus if a company pays monthly, we divide by 12; semi-monthly, by 24; bi-weekly, by 26; and weekly, by 52.

EXAMPLE 1   The Burns Radiator Corporation pays its executives semi-monthly. If the annual salaries for four of its executives are $34,000, $32,000, $30,000, and $25,000, what are the semi-monthly gross earnings for each executive and what is the total payroll each pay period?

Solution:

$34,000 ÷ 24 = $1,416.67	• Divide each salary by 24 (number of pay periods per year).
$32,000 ÷ 24 = $1,333.33	
$30,000 ÷ 24 = $1,250.00	
$25,000 ÷ 24 = $1,041.67	
$5,041.67	• Total of the salaries.

CALCULATOR TIP

Use the constant divide function and memory to cut down on steps in Example 1:

34000 ÷ 24 = 1416.67 M+   • Place divisor in constant position and answer in memory.

32000 = 1333.33 M+   • Divide by constant (24); add answer to memory.
30000 = 1250.00 M+
25000 = 1041.67 M+

MR   5041.67   • Total of the salaries.

---

130   Chapter 6   Payroll

EXAMPLE 2 Store Front Warehouse pays its managers bi-weekly. Its three loading dock supervisors earn salaries of $26,500, $27,300, and $28,100. What are the gross earnings per pay period for each supervisor?

Solution:

$26,500 ÷ 26 = $1,019.23
$27,300 ÷ 26 = $1,050.00
$28,100 ÷ 26 = $1,080.77

• Divide each gross salary by 26 (the total pay periods per year).

✔ CHECK FOR UNDERSTANDING

1. R & D Development pays its salaried employees monthly. If Sara Benson's annual salary is $31,800, what are her monthly gross earnings?

2. A manager at a local construction company earns $35,400 annually. If the company pays all of its employees weekly, how much will the manager earn each week in gross pay?

SKILL EXERCISES

Using the following salaries and pay periods, calculate the amount of gross earnings for each situation:

Salary	Pay period	Amount of pay
1. $22,500	Monthly	$ _____
2. $19,850	Weekly	$ _____
3. $38,600	Semi-monthly	$ _____
4. $14,450	Bi-weekly	$ _____
5. $42,440	Semi-monthly	$ _____

Hourly Wage Earners

To calculate hourly earnings, total the hours worked and then multiply the hours by the rate per hour.

EXAMPLE 3 During the week of July 11, Clarence Snow worked the following hours: Monday, 8; Tuesday, 10; Wednesday, 8; Thursday, 5; and Friday, 8. Calculate his total pay if he is paid $3.85 per hour.

Solution:

8 + 10 + 8 + 5 + 8 = 39   • Calculate total hours worked.
39 × $3.85 = $150.15   • Calculate total pay: hours worked × rate of pay.

Answers to ✔ Check for Understanding
1. $2,650.00.   2. $680.77.

Section 6.1 Computing Gross Earnings   **131**

EXAMPLE 4 Greg Smith's time card for the week ending July 10 showed the following hours: Monday, 9; Tuesday, 7; Wednesday, 6; Thursday, 7; and Friday, 7. If he is paid $6.75 per hour, what are his gross earnings?

Solution:

$9 + 7 + 6 + 7 + 7 = 36$ · Calculate total hours.

$36 \times \$6.75 = \$243$ · Calculate gross earnings: total hours × rate of pay.

✔ CHECK FOR UNDERSTANDING

1. Micro Media Inc. pays its beginning stock clerks $4.10 per hour. Barbara Henderson's time card this week shows: Monday, 6 hrs; Tuesday, 8 hrs; Wednesday, 5 hrs; Thursday, 8 hrs; and Friday, 3 hrs. What are her gross earnings?

2. Peter James worked $36\frac{1}{2}$ hours during the week ending August 25. What are his gross earnings if he is paid $5.95 per hour?

SKILL EXERCISES

Complete the following drill by totaling the number of hours worked and multiplying by the rate to get total earnings. Put the total earnings of each employee into calculator memory. Total the daily hours, the employee hours, and the earnings columns.

	Name	M	T	W	T	F	Total hours	Rate	Total earnings
1.	Archibald	6	8	9	8	7	_____	$3.90	$ _____
2.	Carlson	8	8	8	8	8	_____	$4.65	$ _____
3.	Montgomery	9	4	7	9	8	_____	$3.75	$ _____
4.	Stewart	10	8	5	8	8	_____	$3.95	$ _____
5.	Covalt	7	6	8	8	9	_____	$4.15	$ _____
	Totals	—	—	—	—	—	_____ *		$ _____

* Daily totals in hours must equal the total hours worked by all employees.

Overtime Pay

Federal legislation may affect wages. Legislation sets a minimum wage and under certain instances a pay rate of $1\frac{1}{2}$ times **(time and a half)** the normal rate of pay. The Fair Labor Standards Act of 1938 generally requires a rate of time and a half to be paid on any full-time hours worked over 40 in any week if the business is involved

Answers to ✔ Check for Understanding
1. $123.   2. $217.18.

in interstate commerce. Many wage contracts require **double time** be paid for work on Sundays and holidays.

In order to figure overtime pay, multiply the regular hourly rate by 1.5 or 2 then multiply the rate times the number of overtime hours. Overtime pay is then added to regular pay to complete the total earnings.

EXAMPLE 5 Hal Stone worked the following hours during the week ending January 17: Monday, 9; Tuesday, 8; Wednesday, 10; Thursday, 7; and Friday, 8. If the company pays time and a half for all hours over 40, and his rate of pay was $5.75 per hour, what were Hal's gross earnings?

Solution:

$9 + 8 + 10 + 7 + 8 =$	42	· Calculate total hours.
$40 \times \$5.75 =$	$230.00	· Calculate regular earnings.
*$5.75 \times 1.5 = 8.625 \times 2 =$	17.25	· Calculate overtime earnings.
	$247.25	· Add to get total earnings.

CALCULATOR TIP

Unless the overtime rate needs to be recorded, the overtime pay process in Example 5 can be shortened. Enter 5.75 × 1.5 × 2 = 17.25. Put both 230 and 17.25 into memory for an easy MR total, $247.25.

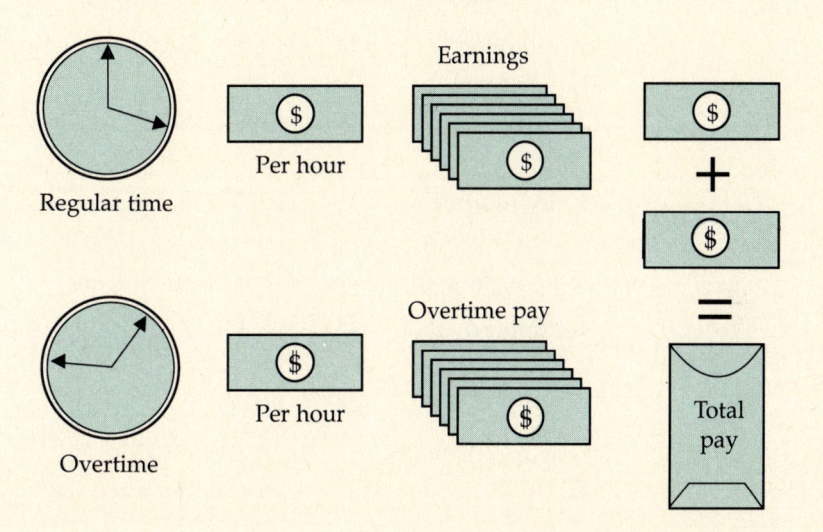

FIGURE 6.1
Overtime pay

EXAMPLE 6 Murray Brown worked a total of 50 hours for the week ending May 6. Of the 50 hours, 4 were worked on Saturday and 6 on Sunday. If the company pays time and a half for hours over 40 and double time for Sundays and holidays, how much did Murray earn if his regular hourly rate is $5.50?

Solution:

$40 \times \$5.50 =$	$220.00	· Calculate regular earnings.
$5.50 \times 1.5 \times 4 =$	33.00	· Calculate Saturday pay (1.5 rate).
$5.50 \times 2 \times 6 =$	66.00	· Calculate Sunday earnings (double).
	$319.00	· Add to get total earnings.

---

* In this text, the overtime rate (8.625 here) is *not* rounded (to 8.63). Leave all half cent rates in three decimal places, such as .625.

✔ CHECK FOR UNDERSTANDING

1. Brooke worked a total of 49 hours for the week ending January 21. If her company pays time and a half for all hours worked over 40, and she earns $4.80 per hour, what are her gross earnings?

2. Morgan Realty pays time and a half for all hours worked over 40 in a week. Mike earns $5.10 per hour and turned in 45 hours for the pay period ending November 14. What are Mike's gross earnings?

3. Betty Valdez turned in the following hours on her weekly time card: Monday, 8; Tuesday, 10; Wednesday, 11; Thursday (Thanksgiving), 8; and Friday, 7. If her rate of pay is $4.65 per hour and the company pays time and a half for all hours worked over 40 and double time on Sundays and holidays, what is her gross pay?

SKILL EXERCISES

Using the total hours and the rate of pay, complete the following drill by calculating the overtime rate; regular pay; overtime pay; and total earnings. Calculate the totals for all six employees and record them on the totals line.

Name	Hours	Regular rate	Overtime rate	Regular pay	Overtime pay	Total earnings
1. Archibald	43	$3.90	$_____	$_____	$_____	$_____
2. Carlson	49	$4.65	$_____	$_____	$_____	$_____
3. Montgomery	41	$3.75	$_____	$_____	$_____	$_____

In Problems 4–6, use double time as the overtime rate.

4. Romero	44	$5.35	$ 10.70	$_____	$_____	$_____
5. White	45	$6.10	$_____	$_____	$_____	$_____
6. Hoyle	50	$4.80	$_____	$_____	$_____	$_____
Totals	_____			$_____	$_____	$_____

APPLICATIONS

Calculate the gross earnings in each of the following situations:

1. A concrete batch plant pays its workers time and a half for all hours worked over 40 per week. Larry Shirley's rate of pay is $5.85 per hour. Calculate Larry's total earnings if he worked the following hours: Monday, 9; Tuesday, 11; Wednesday, 6; Thursday, 8; Friday, 9; and Saturday, 5.

Answers to ✔ Check for Understanding
1. $256.80. **2.** $242.25. **3.** $241.80.

2. Vegetable Truck Farms Inc. has 50 employees who are paid time and a half for all hours worked over 40 per week and double time for Sundays and holidays. Jesse Sands turned in the following hours on his weekly time card: Sunday, 6; Monday, 6; Tuesday, 10; Wednesday, 9; Thursday, 8; and Friday, 10. If his regular pay is $4.40 per hour, what are his gross earnings?

3. Determine the total weekly earnings for Betty Trujillo, whose company pays time and a half for all hours worked over 40 per week. She worked $44\frac{1}{2}$ hours during the week and is paid $5.15 per hour.

4. Calculate the total earnings for each employee. The company's overtime policy is time and a half over 40 hours per week and double time on Sunday.

Employee	S	M	T	W	T	F	S	Total hours	Hourly rate	Total earnings
1. Malper	4	6	9	8	8	7	0	_____	$3.95	$_____
2. Nunn	0	8	8	10	8	9	2	_____	$3.80	$_____
3. Persky	6	10	7	8	8	8	0	_____	$4.65	$_____
4. Rader	0	8	8	8	8	8	8	_____	$4.00	$_____
5. Suggs	0	9	7	8	8	6	4	_____	$4.15	$_____
Totals	—	—	—	—	—	—	—	_____		$_____

5. Power Search Inc. pays its salaried employees semi-monthly. Annual salaries for four executives are Pat, $39,000; Bob, $21,500; Larry, $27,300; and Peter, $33,600. Calculate the gross earnings for each employee per pay period.

6. Speed Dry Concrete uses a semi-monthly pay period and pays time and a half for all hours worked over 40 in any week. For the pay period ending February 28, the following information was available:

   Employee No. 1   Salary of $26,250.
   Employee No. 2   Salary of $18,950.
   Employee No. 3   Hours of 40 and 43 and a rate of $6.75.
   Employee No. 4   Hours of 40 and 38 and a rate of $7.25.
   Employee No. 5   Hours of 42 and 43 and a rate of $8.50.

   Calculate the gross earnings for each employee and the company total for salaries and wages.

7. Members of the Mid-Continent Bulls professional basketball team are paid monthly. Calculate the monthly gross earnings using the following information: Player No. 1, $350,000; Player No. 2, $395,000; Player No. 3, $475,000; Player No. 4, $785,000; and Player No. 5, $810,000.

Section 6.1 Computing Gross Earnings

8. The following wage earners all worked 44 hours for the week ending May 9:

Name	Pay rate	Earnings
1. Mannerly	$4.00	$ _____
2. Nelson	$5.80	$ _____
3. Valdez	$6.15	$ _____
4. Reynolds	$3.80	$ _____

Calculate gross earnings with time and a half for any hours worked over 40.

9. Ann worked 46 hours during the week and has an hourly rate of $5.15. Her supervisor has an annual salary of $19,800. What are their gross weekly earnings if the company pays time and a half?

10. Howard turned in the following hours for the week ending October 14: Monday, 10; Tuesday, 8; Wednesday, 8; Thursday (Thanksgiving), 9; Friday, 9; and Saturday, 4. If his company pays time and a half over 40 hours and double time on holidays, and his regular rate is $6.30 per hour, what are his gross earnings?

Earnings Using Straight Piece Rate

Earnings can also be based on a **piece-rate system.** This is the same as the hourly system, except that the rate is per piece or unit produced, not a rate per hour worked. This system is used to calculate earnings of production-line workers, such as those making electronic components or computer chips.

EXAMPLE 7 Bob King worked on the electronics assembly line and his piece-rate time card for the week ending November 8 showed: Monday, 46; Tuesday, 53; Wednesday, 51; Thursday, 47; and Friday, 49. If he is paid $.85 per piece, what are his total earnings?

Solution:

$46 + 53 + 51 + 47 + 49 = 246$ · Calculate total pieces.

$246 \times \$.85 = \$209.10$ · Calculate total earnings.

✓ CHECK FOR UNDERSTANDING

1. Hans Whitehead turned in the following number of parts passing his work station during the week ending April 16: Mon., 382; Tues., 394; Wed., 368; Thur., 386; and Fri., 390. If he is paid 18 cents per part, what are his weekly earnings?

2. Carol is paid 22 cents for each calculator part she molds. On Wednesday she molded 329 pieces. What were her gross earnings for Wednesday?

SKILL EXERCISES

Calculate the total earnings for each of the following employees and the total earnings for all employees:

Number	Name	Units produced	Rate per unit	Earnings
1.	Foster, L.C.	1,280	$.14\frac{1}{2}$	$ _____

Answers to ✓ Check for Understanding
1. $345.60.   2. $72.38.

136   Chapter 6   Payroll

2.	Garver, M.	750	$.27$\frac{1}{2}$	$ _____
3.	Hahn, F.	687	$.26	$ _____
4.	Muniz, B.	1,302	$.13$\frac{3}{4}$	$ _____
5.	Luger, L.	1,400	$.18	$ _____
			Total	$ _____

Earnings Using a Rate of Commission

Earnings based on a **commission** are common for people who sell large items—real estate, autos, large appliances, and others. To calculate earnings, multiply total sales in dollars times the commission rate.

EXAMPLE 8   Pat Hanson sells printing equipment for Sullivan Graphics Inc. During September she sold $25,000 worth of equipment. What are Pat's earnings if she receives a commission rate of 6%?

Solution:

$25,000 × .06 = $1,500   • Calculate earnings: total sales × commission rate.

EXAMPLE 9   The used car salespeople at Westside Auto earn a commission rate of 5% on total sales. Ray Sanchez sold 10 cars totaling $36,000 during the month of May. What was his commission?

Solution:

$36,000 × .05 = $1,800   • Calculate earnings.

Graduated Commissions on the Incentive Plan

In a **graduated commissions system,** earnings are figured in a stair-step fashion. An employee selling $18,000 of merchandise under the incentive pay scale in Example 10 would not receive a commission of 4% on the entire $18,000. He would earn $2\frac{1}{2}$% on the first $5,000; 3% on the next $5,000 and 4% on the last $8,000. Under this system, a salesperson is encouraged to sell more because the greater the volume, the higher the commission rate.

EXAMPLE 10   An appliance dealer pays salespeople under the following incentive scale:

Sales volume	Rate
$ 0 – $ 5,000	$2\frac{1}{2}$%
$ 5,001 – $10,000	3%
$10,001 +	4%

What would Marge Decker's total earnings be if she sold $12,185 in appliances?

Solution:

$5,000 × .025 = $125.00	·	Calculate level one earnings.
$5,000 × .03 = 150.00	·	Calculate level two earnings.
$2,185 × .04 = 87.40	·	Calculate base for level three (12,185 − 10,000 = 2,185); then multiply by rate for level three.
Total earnings $362.40	·	Add the three levels.

✔ CHECK FOR UNDERSTANDING

1. Salespeople at Gates Auto Sales receive different commission rates based on seniority and whether they sell new or used autos. Using the following list of employees and their sales and rates, calculate their gross earnings.

	Name	Rate	Sales	Earnings
1.	Mossberg	5%	$28,500	$ _____
2.	Ross	6%	$24,750	$ _____
3.	Stearns	5%	$20,250	$ _____
4.	Taylor	$4\frac{1}{2}$%	$24,000	$ _____
5.	Weinberg	$6\frac{1}{4}$%	$21,600	$ _____

2. Calculate the gross earnings for Felix Martinez if his total sales for the week were $6,540 and the graduated commission rates are:

$$\begin{aligned} \$\ \ \ \ 1 - \$1,000 &= 5\% \\ \$1,001 - \$4,000 &= 6\% \\ \$4,001 + \ \ \ \ \ \ \ \ \ \ &= 8\% \end{aligned}$$

SKILL EXERCISES

Calculate the gross earnings in the following drill on commissions. Calculate total earnings for the first five employees. Use calculator memory.

	Sales	Rate	Gross earnings
1.	$45,000	$4\frac{1}{2}$%	$ _____
2.	$19,250	$7\frac{1}{4}$%	$ _____
3.	$15,235	5%	$ _____
4.	$30,300	$3\frac{3}{4}$%	$ _____
5.	$11,750	$5\frac{1}{2}$%	$ _____
		Total	$ _____

Answers to ✔ Check for Understanding
1. $1,425; $1,485; $1,012.50; $1,080; $1,350.   2. $433.20.

Using the following incentive commission rate scale, calculate the earnings in Problems 6–10.

Sales	Rate
$ 0 – $1,500	$1\frac{1}{2}\%$
$1,501 – $3,500	$2\frac{1}{2}\%$
$3,501 – $8,000	3%
$8,001+	4%

6. $9,855 $ _____

7. $7,535 $ _____

8. $11,150 $ _____

9. $5,285 $ _____

10. $6,390 $ _____

APPLICATIONS

Calculate the following gross earnings using either piece rate or rate of commission:

1. Marty Thompson works on a production sewing line, putting collars on blouses. On August 5 she turned in the following totals: Monday, 30; Tuesday, 36; Wednesday, 42; Thursday, 34; and Friday, 38. If she is paid $77\frac{1}{2}$ cents per collar, what are her gross earnings?

2. During May, Marie Trujillo sold two houses for $82,500. The agency's commission scale is:

    $ 1 – $ 50,000 = 4%
    $ 50,001 – $200,000 = 6%
    $200,001+ = 7%

    What was her commission for the month?

3. The top salesperson for the week at Always-Here Auto sold four cars totaling $32,850. The graduated commission scale is:

    $ 1 – $10,000 = 3%
    $10,001 – $25,000 = 4%
    $25,001+ = 6%

    What is her commission?

4. Paul sold two houses totaling $115,475 during the past month. If his commission rate is $6\frac{1}{4}\%$, what are his gross earnings?

5. Western Fit Inc. pays 15 cents per pocket sewn on jeans or shirts. If Rose sews 1,500 pockets, what are her gross earnings?

6. Burger Packers Ltd. packs 12 frozen hamburgers per carton. If Lucey is paid 8 cents per hamburger packed, and on Tuesday she packed 100 cartons, what are her total earnings for that day?

7. Part of the closing costs on the sale of Henry Nelson's house was a commission to his real estate agent. Henry sold his home for $72,500 and his agent's commission rate was $5\frac{3}{4}\%$. What amount did Henry pay in commission?

8. Downtown Developers Inc. specializes in selling office buildings. If it sells a large building in Colorado Springs for $8.5 million and its commission rate is 6%, what are its commissions on the sale?

9. Pete helps small vegetable farms each spring by setting out bell pepper plants at the rate of 3 cents per plant. If the pepper plants come 20 plants per flat and he sets out 40 flats on Friday, how much did he earn?

10. A large computer chip manufacturer estimates that it has 6.5 million microfilm frames to be processed. If its micrographics technician is paid $\frac{1}{4}$ cent per frame, what will he be paid when the project is finished?

Deductions

6.2

Deductions can be divided into two types: mandatory and voluntary. The **mandatory deductions** are for taxes—federal and state income taxes and the social security tax (FICA). **Voluntary deductions** can be for a variety of things—group insurance plans (hospitalization, life, disability); savings bonds; credit union deposits; charitable contributions; union dues, and others. Voluntary deductions will not be covered in this text.

The amount withheld each pay period for mandatory deductions is set by legislation, and these rates and limits have been incorporated into tables and charts in this book.

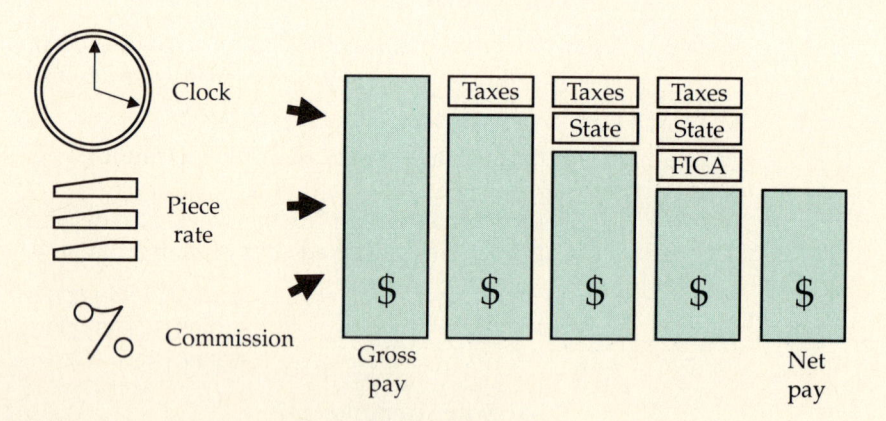

FICA (Social Security Tax) Deductions

The **Federal Insurance Contribution Act (FICA)** established the social security tax to provide assistance to individuals in planning for retirement, possible disability, medical assistance, and death. All of these benefits are combined into one tax rate. Congress is responsible for not only setting the tax rate but also establishing the maximum amount of earnings that the tax is based on each calendar year. The act also provided that employers must match, dollar for dollar, the contributions made by each employee. Table 6.1 shows a 12-year history and projection of FICA rates, their base, and the maximum amount of tax in any calendar year.

TABLE 6.1
FICA Rates, Bases, and Maximum Taxes

Year	Percent	Base	Maximum Tax
1978	6.05%	$17,700	$1,070.85
1979	6.13%	$22,900	$1,403.77
1980	6.13%	$25,900	$1,587.67
1981	6.65%	$29,700	$1,975.05
1982	6.70%	$32,400	$2,170.80
1983	6.70%	$35,700	$2,391.90
1984	6.70%	$37,800	$2,532.60
1985	7.05%	$39,600	$2,791.80
1986	7.15%	$42,000	$3,003.00
1987	7.15%	$43,800	$3,131.70
1988***	7.51%	$45,000	$3,379.50
1989	7.51%	$48,000	$3,604.80
1990*	7.65%	$50,700	**

* Estimated.
** Cannot be calculated until maximum is set by Congress.
*** This text uses 1988 rates and maximums.

The tax rate we will be using is 7.51% on maximum earnings of $45,000 per calendar year.

EXAMPLE 11 Jay Frank earned $86.22 for the pay period, and Freda Gorman earned $238.95. Using the social security employee tax table on page A–35 of Appendix D, calculate their deductions.

Solution: From the social security employee tax table:

WAGES

At least	But less than	Tax is
86.09	86.22	6.47
86.22	86.36	6.48

- For Jay.
- Locate in the wages column Jay's earnings of $86.22.
- Note that the *correct row* indicates that he earned at least $86.22 but less than $86.36. The row just above is *incorrect* because it states that he earned at least $86.09 *but less than* $86.22.
- The social security tax is $6.48.
- For Freda use the lower right-hand corner of the table where the deductions per hundred are listed.

$15.02

- Locate $200 in the lower right-hand corner and enter the tax into the calculator.
- Locate the balance of Freda's salary in the table ($38.95) and enter the tax into the calculator.

+ 2.93
$17.95

- Total the entries.

CHECK FOR UNDERSTANDING

1. Frankie has weekly earnings of $215.32. Using the social security tax table, compute her tax.

2. John earned $352. Using the social security tax table, calculate his tax.

SKILL EXERCISES

Using the social security tax table, calculate the amount of tax to be withheld. Check your answers by using 7.51% in your calculator.

	Earnings	Tax		Earnings	Tax
1.	$ 496.21	$ _____	6.	$687.02	$ _____
2.	$ 162.42	$ _____	7.	$399.80	$ _____
3.	$ 852.38	$ _____	8.	$450.00	$ _____
4.	$1,435.89	$ _____	9.	$360.00	$ _____
5.	$ 148.12	$ _____	10.	$380.23	$ _____

Maximum Earnings under Social Security

The amount of earnings that may be taxed for social security during any calendar year is limited. We must use a system to ensure that we do not withhold taxes on any employee's earnings that exceed $45,000.

EXAMPLE 12 During the week of November 19, Pete Horn had earnings of $750. His total accumulated earnings as of last week were $44,452. Using the rate of 7.51%, calculate Pete's deduction for social security.

Solution: Our first job is to determine how much, if any, of the current earnings ($750) are to be taxed for social security. If we subtract the accumulated earnings as of the last pay period from the maximum ($45,000), we get the amount yet to be taxed. If current earnings are more than that difference (amount yet to be taxed), we tax the difference. If current earnings are less than that difference (amount yet to be taxed), we tax current earnings.

$45,000 − $44,452 = $548
- Subtract accumulated earnings from maximum taxable earnings to determine amount yet to be taxed.
- Check to see if employee has made at least $548 in this current pay period. If he has, tax him on $548. If his current earnings are less than $548, tax him only on the current earnings.

$548 × .0751 = $41.15
- Multiply the number obtained in the previous step by .0751 or use the tax table.

ANSWER: $41.15

Answers to ✔ Check for Understanding
1. $16.17.   2. $26.44.

EXAMPLE 13   Fred has accumulated earnings of $44,730 as of December 15. If he earns $230 this pay period, what will his FICA tax be?

Solution:

$45,000 − $44,730 = $270
- Subtract accumulated earnings from maximum earnings to determine amount in this calendar year yet to be taxed.
- Check to see if employee has made at least $270. If he has, tax him on $270. If current earnings are less than $270, tax only on the current earnings.

$230 × .0751 = $17.27
- Calculate the tax or use tax table based on his *current earnings* only.

ANSWER: $17.27

✔ CHECK FOR UNDERSTANDING

1. Jane's earnings at the end of last week were $43,674. If she earns $268 this week, how much should be withheld from her pay for FICA tax?

2. Fred Knutson is paid $3,750 per month. At the end of November he had earned $41,250. How much if any will be withheld from his check in December for social security?

SKILL EXERCISES

Calculate the amount of social security tax, considering the accumulated earnings from the last pay period and a rate of 7.51%.

	Accum. earnings last pay period	Current earnings	Amount of tax		Accum. earnings last pay period	Current earnings	Amount of tax
1.	$44,200	$825.00	$_____	6.	$43,480	$305.00	$_____
2.	$42,815	$2,280.00	$_____	7.	$42,900	$815.00	$_____
3.	$43,565	$185.00	$_____	8.	$43,700	$1,335.00	$_____
4.	$44,719	$690.00	$_____	9.	$43,950	$715.00	$_____
5.	$44,112	$718.50	$_____	10.	$43,514	$1,486.00	$_____

Federal Income Tax

The amount of federal income tax to be withheld is governed by the number of withholding allowances claimed by an employee. Each employee is required to have on file with the employer a current **W-4 (Employee's Withholding Allowance Cer-**

Answers to ✔ Check for Understanding
1. $20.13.   2. $281.63.

tificate), which shows the number of allowances claimed. The number of allowances, the amount of earnings, type of pay period, and whether the employee is single or married are all factors considered in figuring the tax. See Figure 6.2, which illustrates the W-4 form.

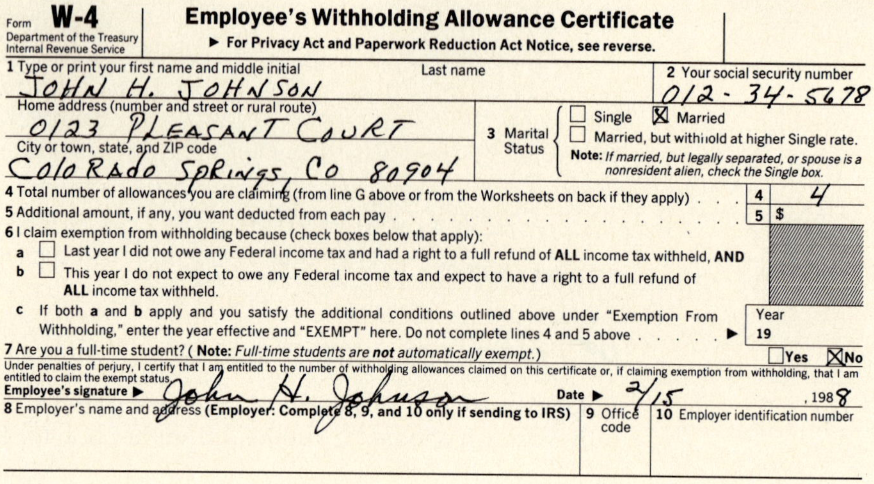
Form **W-4** Department of the Treasury Internal Revenue Service

Employee's Withholding Allowance Certificate

▶ For Privacy Act and Paperwork Reduction Act Notice, see reverse.

1 Type or print your first name and middle initial — JOHN H. — Last name — JOHNSON

2 Your social security number — 012-34-5678

Home address (number and street or rural route) — 0123 PLEASANT COURT

City or town, state, and ZIP code — COLORADO SPRINGS, CO 80904

3 Marital Status — ☐ Single ☒ Married ☐ Married, but withhold at higher Single rate.
Note: *If married, but legally separated, or spouse is a nonresident alien, check the Single box.*

4 Total number of allowances you are claiming (from line G above or from the Worksheets on back if they apply) . . . 4 — 4

5 Additional amount, if any, you want deducted from each pay . . . 5 — $

6 I claim exemption from withholding because (check boxes below that apply):

a ☐ Last year I did not owe any Federal income tax and had a right to a full refund of **ALL** income tax withheld, **AND**

b ☐ This year I do not expect to owe any Federal income tax and expect to have a right to a full refund of **ALL** income tax withheld.

c If both **a** and **b** apply and you satisfy the additional conditions outlined above under "Exemption From Withholding," enter the year effective and "EXEMPT" here. Do not complete lines 4 and 5 above . . . . . ▶ Year 19

7 Are you a full-time student? (**Note:** *Full-time students are **not** automatically exempt.*) ☐ Yes ☒ No

Under penalties of perjury, I certify that I am entitled to the number of withholding allowances claimed on this certificate or, if claiming exemption from withholding, that I am entitled to claim the exempt status.

Employee's signature ▶ John H. Johnson **Date** ▶ 2/15, 1988

8 Employer's name and address **(Employer: Complete 8, 9, and 10 only if sending to IRS)** | 9 Office code | 10 Employer identification number

FIGURE 6.2
W-4 form

EXAMPLE 14 Shirley Moore is paid weekly, is married, and claims two withholding allowances. Her total earnings for the week are $350.

Solution: Calculate using wage bracket method: the married persons weekly payroll period on page A–36 of Appendix D has the same design as the social security tax table used earlier.

- Come down the "Wages at Least" column to the horizontal row that reads "$350 but less than $360."
- Locate the column headed "2" (withholding allowances).
- Match the earnings row with the column headed 2.
- Tax is $33. □

EXAMPLE 15 Charles is single, is paid weekly, and claims no allowances on his W-4. If his current earnings are $315, what is his federal income tax deduction?

Solution: Calculate using wage bracket methods: use single persons—weekly payroll period on page A–38 of Appendix D.

- Locate the horizontal row reading "310 but less than 320."
- Move across to the column headed "0" allowances.
- Tax is $44. □

PROBLEM SOLVING STRATEGY

When using tables, it is important to note that there is a different table for each type of pay period. In addition to different tables for married or single tax payers, there are tables for each type of common pay period. In deciding which pay-period table to use, remember that *bi-* means twice or two, and *semi-* means half. Therefore, "bi-weekly table" refers to a pay period of every two weeks, but a "semi-monthly table" refers to a pay period of twice a month. The type of pay period is irrelevant in figuring social security tax but is extremely important in calculating income tax. See Table 6.2.

TABLE 6.2
Federal Income Tax Tables by Pay Periods

Type of Tax Table	Pay Period	Number of Pay Periods per Year
Weekly	Once each week	52
Bi-weekly	Every two weeks	26
Semi-monthly	Twice per month	24
Monthly	Once each month	12
Daily or miscellaneous	Varies	Varies

SKILL EXERCISES

Using the appropriate tax tables in Appendix D and the following information, calculate the amount of tax. All employees are paid weekly.

	Employee	Marital status	Allowances	Earnings	Tax
1.	Myra Abbot	S	2	$200	$ _____
2.	K.T. Darling	S	0	$380	$ _____
3.	Ray Frank	M	6	$820	$ _____
4.	Paul Garcia	M	1	$505	$ _____
5.	Lynn Hayes	M	0	$495	$ _____
6.	Ray Long	S	3	$240	$ _____

APPLICATIONS

Calculate the amount of gross earnings, federal income tax, social security tax, and net pay as required in the following problems:

1. Calculate Gary's federal income tax, his social security tax, and his net pay if he earns $275 weekly, is married, and has 2 allowances.

2. Sara had total yearly earnings of $43,950 as of her last pay period. Her gross earnings for the week were $850 and she is married, claiming no allowances. Calculate her federal income tax, social security tax, total deductions, and net pay.

3. Using the following information, calculate the net pay for Lois for the weekly pay period ending September 20: total hours worked, 46; hourly rate of $6.50 with time and a half over 40 hours; married, claiming one allowance.

Section 6.2 Deductions

4. Calculate the federal income tax and social security tax deduction for the following employees:
   Ramon: earnings of $310 weekly; single; two allowances
   Jessie: earnings of $280 weekly; single; one allowance

5. Ray's gross earnings every week are $463. If he is single with one allowance, calculate his federal income tax, his social security tax, and his net pay.

6. Herb worked $45\frac{1}{2}$ hours for the week ending February 12. Four of those hours were on a holiday. If his rate of pay is $14.25 per hour and the company pays time and a half for all hours worked over 40 per week and double time for holidays, what are his total earnings and social security tax deduction?

7. Dennis earned $44,495 as of last pay period. If his current gross earnings are $644, how much, if any, is his social security tax deduction?

8. Joyce worked 50 hours, 8 of which were holiday hours, during the week ending November 28. If she makes $11.75 per hour, is paid time and a half for hours over 40, and double time for holiday hours, what are her gross earnings? If she has already earned $43,315 during this calendar year, what is her social security tax deduction for the week?

Forms and Records

6.3

Federal and state law requires that companies issuing payrolls maintain employee documentation to substantiate the tax requirements. This section covers the principles for preparing employee documentation.

Employee Earnings Record

The **employee earnings record** is a *summary* of payroll information for each employee. It summarizes information from the W-4 and from each pay period's payroll register. Additional information from the employee's personnel file may also be included.

The employee earnings record may also be a source document for preparing reports such as Form 941 (Employer's Quarterly Federal Tax Return); quarterly returns to the state revenue service; and the W-2 form (Wage and Tax Statement). See Figure 6.3, which illustrates the relationship of payroll forms.

Payroll Register

Whether prepared by computer or by hand using a calculator, the **payroll register** is a very important form, which collects all earnings and deductions for each employee for each payroll period. It is the source for writing payroll checks, making entries in the employee earnings record, and making accounting entries for both employee and employer payroll expenses. See Figure 6.3.

W-4: Employee's Withholding Allowance Certificate

This form is completed by employees at the time they are hired or any other time that they have changes in their claimed allowances. It provides the bases for calculating an employee's state and federal income tax withholding.

W-2: Wage and Tax Statement

This form is prepared for each employee within 30 days after the end of the calendar year or within 30 days of an employee's termination. The form, prepared in six parts (see Figure 6.3), summarizes the employee's wages, deductions of federal and state income tax, FICA tax, and any local tax. The W-2 serves as the base for employees filing their individual income tax returns.

Form 941: Employer's Quarterly Federal Tax Return

This form is filed no later than the end of the month following the close of each quarter. It summarizes the total earnings of the employees, the amount of federal income tax withheld, the amount of FICA tax withheld from employees and matched by the employer, and the gross earnings by pay period. There are penalties for not filing the form on time. Figure 6.3 shows an example of the form.

The Payroll Check

One of the final steps is the preparation of the payroll check. Most companies provide not only the check but also a summary of the total earnings and the amounts withheld for various taxes and voluntary deductions. This type of check has two stubs—one for the checkbook record and one for the employee showing earnings and deductions. See Figure 6.3 for an example.

Employer Payroll Tax Expense

The company is liable for two additional payroll-related expenses. The company must match dollar for dollar the amount of FICA tax withheld for each employee. It is also responsible for paying an unemployment tax. The tax can vary both in rate and maximum amount taxable among the different states. This text uses a rate of 6.2% on the first $7,000 paid each employee in any calendar year. Of the maximum of 6.2% for unemployment, the federal government receives .8% for **Federal Unemployment Tax (FUTA)** and the state receives a maximum of 5.4%. The amount the company pays in **statement unemployment contributions** is based on a history of employee layoffs.

One of the most common methods of calculating a company's base for unemployment and social security tax liability is to put two earnings columns in the payroll register (see Figure 6.3). If any of the current earnings are still subject to unemployment or social security tax or both, the amount of those earnings is entered into the appropriate column or columns.

FIGURE 6.3

The interrelationship of payroll forms

1. Employee's earnings record (A) *receives* information from:
   (B) W-4 employee's withholding allowance certificate
   (C) Payroll register

2. Employee's earnings record is the *source* of information for:
   (D) Employer's quarterly federal tax return
   (E) W-2 wage and tax statement

3. Payroll register is the *source* of information for:
   (F) Payroll check

(A) Employee's Earnings Record

WEEK NO.	DATE	EARNINGS	ACCUM. EARNINGS	FICA TAX	FEDERAL INC. TAX	STATE INC. TAX	CREDIT UNION	HOSP.	TOTAL DEDUC.	NET EARNINGS
13	Sept. 30	846.15	32,999.85	60.50	147.00	31.51	35.00	23.27	297.28	548.87
TOTAL 3rd Qt.		32,999.85		235.95	5733.00	1228.89	1365.00	907.53	11593.92	21405.93
1	Oct. 7	846.15	33,846.00	60.50	147.00	31.51	35.00	23.27	297.28	548.87
10	Dec. 2	846.15	41,461.35	60.50	147.00	31.51	35.00	23.27	297.28	548.87
11	Dec. 9	846.15	42,307.50	38.51	147.00	31.51	35.00	23.27	275.29	570.86
12	Dec. 16	846.15	43,153.65	-0-	147.00	31.51	35.00	23.27	236.78	609.37
13	Dec. 23	846.35	44,000.00	-0-	147.00	31.51	35.00	23.27	236.78	609.57
TOTAL 4th Qt.		11,000.15		643.51	1911.00	409.63	455.00	302.51	3721.65	7278.50
YEAR TOTAL		44,000.00	44,000.00	3003.00	7644.00	1638.52	1820.00	1210.04	15315.52	28684.48

NAME	S.S. NO.	MARITAL STATUS	PAY CLASS	DEDUCTIONS			
Johnson, John H.	012-34-5678	M	S-6	CREDIT UNION $35	UNION DUES -0-	HOSPITAL $23.27	BONDS -0-
ADDRESS	BIRTHDATE		RATE OF PAY				
0123 Pleasant Court Colo. Spgs. 80904	4/4/38		$44,000 Ann Pd. Weekly $846.15				
HIRE DATE	WITHHOLD. ALLOW.		OVERTIME RATE				
1/2/76	4		-0-				

Summarized here.

(B) Form W-4 — Employee's Withholding Allowance Certificate

- Name: JOHN H. JOHNSON
- SSN: 012-34-5678
- Address: 0123 PLEASANT COURT, COLORADO SPRINGS, CO 80904
- Marital Status: Married
- Total allowances: 4
- Additional amount: $-0-
- Signature: John H. Johnson   Date: 2/15, 1988

Week of Dec. 9 summarized on earnings record.

(C) PAYROLL REGISTER

FOR WEEK ENDED: DECEMBER 9, 198X

NAME	MARITAL STATUS	WITH. ALLOW.	TOTAL HOURS	RATE	EARNINGS	ACCUM. EARNINGS CURRENT	TAXABLE WAGES FOR UNEMPLOY. $0-7,000	TAXABLE WAGES FOR FICA $0-42,000	FICA TAX	FED. TAX	STATE TAX	CREDIT UNION	HOSP. INSUR.	SAVINGS BONDS	TOTAL DEDUCTIONS	NET PAY	CHECK NO.
Anderson	S	0	40	$5.50	$260.00	$18,425.00	$ -0-	$260.00	$18.59	$36.00	$18.20	$	$ 7.15	$	$ 79.94	$180.06	#1001
Bagley	S	2	39.5	6.25	246.88	17,339.00	-0-	246.88	17.65	25.00	17.28	10.00	6.79	5.00	81.72	165.15	#1002
Ferguson	M	2	36	5.15	185.40	15,675.00	-0-	185.40	13.26	11.00	12.98		5.10		42.33	143.07	#1003
Johnson, J.	M	4			846.15	42,307.00	-0-	450.15	38.51	147.00	31.51	35.00	23.27		275.29	570.86	#1004
Stearns	S	1	40	7.10	284.00	6,355.00	284.00	284.00	20.31	36.00	19.88		7.81		84.00	200.00	#1005
TOTALS			155.5		$1822.43	$100,190.00	$284.00	$1426.43	$108.32	$255.00	$99.85	$45.00	$50.12	$5.00	$563.28	$1259.14	

148 Chapter 6 Payroll

(D) — Total of all employees for third quarter summarized on Form 941.

Form 941 (Rev. January 1986)
Department of the Treasury
Internal Revenue Service

Employer's Quarterly Federal Tax Return
► For Paperwork Reduction Act Notice, see page 2.
Please type or print

4141

Your name, address, employer identification number, and calendar quarter of return. (If not correct, please change.)

Name (as distinguished from trade name): PLASTIC MOLDS, INC.
Date quarter ended: September 30, 198X
Trade name, if any:
Employer identification number: 84-0000000
Address and ZIP code: 1682 Industrial Parkway, Security, CO 80911-5432

OMB No. 1545-0029
Expires: 8-31-88

If address is different from prior return, check here ▶ ☐

If you are not liable for returns in the future, check here ▶ ☐   Date final wages paid ▶

Complete for First Quarter Only
1a Number of employees (except household) employed in the pay period that includes March 12th ▶ | 1a
b If you are a subsidiary corporation AND your parent corporation files a consolidated Form 1120, enter parent corporation employer identification number (EIN) ▶ | 1b

Line	Description	Amount
2	Total wages and tips subject to withholding, plus other compensation	23,700 00
3	Total income tax withheld from wages, tips, pensions, annuities, sick pay, gambling, etc.	3,315 00
4	Adjustment of withheld income tax for preceding quarters of calendar year (see instructions)	-0-
5	Adjusted total of income tax withheld	3,315 00
6	Taxable social security wages paid . . . $ 23,700 00 X 14.3% (.143)	3,389 10
7a	Taxable tips reported . . . . $ _____ X 7.15% (.0715)	
b	Tips deemed to be wages (see instructions) $ _____ X 7.15% (.0715)	
c	Taxable hospital insurance wages paid . . $ _____ X 2.9% (.029)	
8	Total social security taxes (add lines 6, 7a, 7b, and 7c)	3,389 10
9	Adjustment of social security taxes (see instructions for required explanation)	-0-
10	Adjusted total of social security taxes (see instructions)	3,389 10
11	Backup withholding	-0-
12	Adjustment of backup withholding tax for preceding quarters of calendar year	
13	Adjusted total of backup withholding	
14	Total taxes (add lines 5, 10, and 13)	6,704 10
15	Advance earned income credit (EIC) payments, if any (see instructions)	-0-
16	Net taxes (subtract line 15 from line 14). This must equal line IV below (plus line IV of Schedule A (Form 941) if you have treated backup withholding as a separate liability).	6,704 10
17	Total deposits for quarter, including overpayment applied from a prior quarter, from your records	6,704 10
18	Balance due (subtract line 17 from line 16). This should be less than $500. Pay to IRS	-0-
19	If line 17 is more than line 16, enter overpayment here ▶ $ _____ and check if to be: ☐ Applied to next return or ☐ Refunded.	

Record of Federal Tax Liability (Complete if line 16 is $500 or more) See the instructions under rule 4 for details before checking these boxes.
Check only if you made eighth-monthly deposits using the 95% rule ▶ ☐   Check only if you are a first time 3-banking-day depositor ▶ ☐

Tax liability (Do not show Federal tax deposits here.)

Date wages paid	First month of quarter	Second month of quarter	Third month of quarter
1st through 3rd	A	I	Q
4th through 7th	B 515.70	J 515.70	R 515.70
8th through 11th	C 515.70	K	S
12th through 15th	D	L 515.70	T 515.70
16th through 19th	E 515.70	M	U
20th through 22nd	F	N 515.70	V 515.70
23rd through 25th	G 515.70	O	W
26th through the last	H 515.70	P 515.70	X 515.70
Total liability for month	I 2,578.50	II 2,062.80	III 2,062.80

IV Total for quarter (add lines I, II, and III) ▶ 6,704.10

Under penalties of perjury, I declare that I have examined this return, including accompanying schedules and statements, and to the best of my knowledge and belief it is true, correct, and complete.

Signature ▶ *Clarence Dixon*   Title ▶ Manager   Date ▶ 10/15/8X

(E) — Year's totals summarized on W-2.

1 Control number: 22222   OMB No. 1545-0008
2 Employer's name, address, and ZIP code:
PLASTIC MOLDS, INC.
1682 INDUSTRIAL PARKWAY
SECURITY, CO 80911-5432

3 Employer's identification number: 84-0000000
4 Employer's state I.D. number: 16-00000
5 Statutory employee ☐ Deceased ☐ Pension plan ☐ Legal rep. ☐ 942 emp. ☐ Subtotal ☐ Deferred compensation ☐ Void ☐
6 Allocated tips
7 Advance EIC payment

8 Employee's social security number: 012-34-5678
9 Federal income tax withheld: 7,844
10 Wages, tips, other compensation: 47,000.00
11 Social security tax withheld: 3,379.50
12 Employee's name, address, and ZIP code:
JOHN H. JOHNSON
0123 PLEASANT COURT
COLORADO SPRINGS, CO 80904
13 Social security wages: 45,000.00
14 Social security tips
16 | 16a Fringe benefits incl. in Box 10

17 State income tax: 1,724.52
18 State wages, tips, etc.: 47,000.00
19 Name of state: COLO.
20 Local income tax
21 Local wages, tips, etc.
22 Name of locality

Form W-2 Wage and Tax Statement
Employee's and employer's copy compared ☐

Check #1004 prepared from payroll register.

1004
DATE December 9, 19 8X
FOR WAGES TO AND INCLUDING ABOVE DATE
ISSUED TO: Johnson, J. H.

BAL. FOR'D	1413 00
REG. PAY	
OVER-TIME	
TOTAL EARN.	846 15
F.I.C.A.	38 51
FED. WITH. TAX	147 00
STATE WITH. TAX	31 51
Cr.Un	35 00
Hosp.	23 27
TOTAL DED.	275 29
THIS CHECK	570 86
BALANCE	842 14

PLASTIC MOLDS, INC.
DATE December 9, 19 8X
FOR WAGES TO AND INCLUDING ABOVE DATE
ISSUED TO: Johnson, J. H.

REGULAR HOURS 56	
OVERTIME HOURS 66	
TOTAL EARNINGS	846 15
F.I.C.A.	38 51
FED. WITH. TAX	147 00
STATE WITH. TAX	31 51
Cr.Un	35 00
Hosp.	23 27
TOTAL DEDUCTIONS	275 29
NET PAY	570 86

STATEMENT OF WAGES AND DEDUCTIONS FOR EMPLOYEE'S RECORD.
DETACH BEFORE CASHING

PLASTIC MOLDS, INC.   1004
1682 Industrial Parkway
Security, CO 80911-5432   82-162/1070

                              December 9, 19 8X

Pay to the
order of John H. Johnson $ 570.86

Five Hundred-Seventy and 86/100----------------------- Dollars

THE BANK OF COLORADO
1521 S. Eighth Street
Colorado Springs, Colorado 80906   SAMPLE VOID

For Payroll Ended December 9, 198X

⑈00 1004⑈ ⑆1070 0 1627⑆: 12 34567⑈

(F)

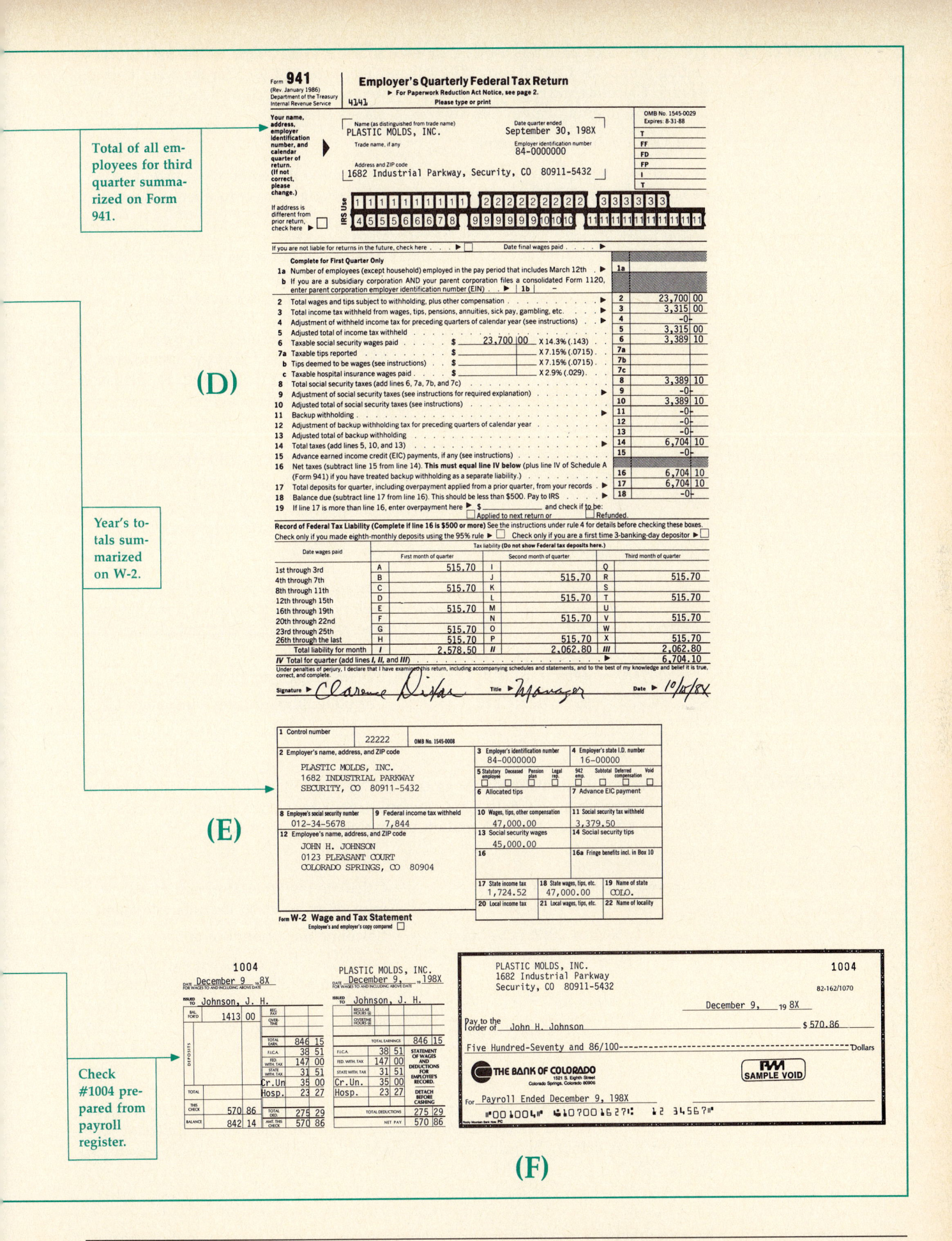

Section 6.3 Forms and Records   149

EXAMPLE 16 The accumulated earnings for Coghill were $5,850 and for Trapp $7,050 for the week ending March 29. Coghill earned $1,450 and Trapp earned $465 for the week ending April 5. Calculate the *employer's* unemployment tax and matching social security tax. Use a 6.2% unemployment rate and 7.51% for social security.

Solution: *Coghill unemployment*

Max. to be taxed	−	Accum. earnings	=	Amount yet to be taxed
$7,000	−	$5,850	=	$1,150

- Determine the amount of current *earnings*, if any, subject to unemployment tax.
- The rule is to tax the smaller amount—the amount calculated in the previous step or his earnings for the week.
- Coghill's base is $1,150 because it is less than his earnings this week ($1,450). The $1,150 is the amount yet to be taxed to bring him up to the maximum of $7,000.

Trapp unemployment

Base	Trapp
$7,000	$7,050

- Since his accumulated earnings *exceeded* the maximum, none of his wages are subject to tax.

$1,150 × .062 = $71.30

- Calculate total unemployment tax.

Coghill and Trapp: Social Security

- Since both have accumulated earnings well below the maximum, it is obvious that all current earnings should be taxed.

$1,450 + $465 = $1,915

- Calculate the base of the tax.

$1,915 × .0751 = $143.82

- Calculate the employer's matching tax.

EXAMPLE 17 Loretta Brent's accumulated earnings as of last pay period were $6,345. Calculate her employer's matching FICA tax and unemployment tax if her current earnings are $955. Use a FICA rate of 7.51% and an unemployment rate of 6.2%.

Solution:

$7,000 − $6,345 = $655

- Calculate the amount of current earnings yet to be taxed for unemployment.

$655 × .062 = $40.61

- Calculate the amount of tax.

$955 × .0751 = $71.72

- Determine if accumulated earnings are less than $45,000. If obvious, calculate FICA tax using current earnings as the base.

EXAMPLE 18 Using the following schedule of employees: 1. Calculate the amount of wages subject to unemployment and social security taxes. 2. Total the columns. 3. Calculate the company's tax liability by using an unemployment rate of 6.2% and a social security rate of 7.51%.

150 Chapter 6 Payroll

Employee	Accum. earnings last pay period	Current earnings	Taxable wages for Unemployment $ 0–7000	FICA tax $ 0–45,000
1. Grover	$43,715	$1,450	$ –0–	$ 1,285.00
2. King	$ 6,850	$ 560	$ 150.00	$ 560.00
3. Little	$ 6,050	$ 700	$ 700.00	$ 700.00
4. Rankin	$24,490	$ 735	$ –0–	$ 735.00
		Totals	$ 850.00	$ 3,280.00

Solution:

Grover: No current earnings are less than $7,000; enter zero in unemployment column. $45,000 − $43,715 = $1,285. Only $1,285 of the current earnings are entered in the FICA tax column.

King: $7,000 minus $6,850 = $150. Since he earned at least this much, $150 is entered in the unemployment column. All of King's earnings are subject to FICA tax.

Little: $7,000 − $6,050 = $950. Since he didn't earn this much, only his current earnings of $700 are entered in the unemployment column. All of his earnings are taxable for FICA.

Rankin: None of his earnings are subject to unemployment. Enter zero in the unemployment column. $45,000 − $24,490 = $20,510. Since he didn't earn that much, only his current earnings are entered in the FICA column.

$150 + $700 = $850 · Calculate the base of unemployment.
$850 × .062 = $52.70 · Calculate the tax.
$1,285 + $560 + $700 + $735 = $3,280 · Calculate the base of FICA tax.
$3,280 × .0751 = $246.33 · Calculate the tax.

✔ CHECK FOR UNDERSTANDING

1. Morgan James had accumulated earnings last week of $6,745. If she earns $372 this week, how much of her earnings are taxable for unemployment? How much is the unemployment tax using a rate of 6.2%?

2. At the end of November, Dennis had earned $42,560. If he earns $3,852 in December, how much if any is the employer's matching social security tax?

SKILL EXERCISES

1. Calculate the amount of earnings during the week ending December 22 that would be included in the "Taxable Wages" columns for the employer's unemployment and matching social security tax. There is a large difference in salaries because several employees weren't hired until August.

Answers to ✔ Check for Understanding
1. $255; $15.81.   2. $183.24.

2. Determine the total earnings subject to unemployment tax of 6.2% and social security tax of 7.51%.

3. Calculate the unemployment and social security tax.

Employee	Accum. earnings December 15	Current earnings December 22	Taxable wages for Unemployment 0–$7000	Soc. security 0–$45,000
1	$44,675	$525	$ _____	$ _____
2	$ 5,805	$325	$ _____	$ _____
3	$ 5,915	$405	$ _____	$ _____
4	$44,635	$320	$ _____	$ _____
5	$44,615	$535	$ _____	$ _____
6	$ 6,450	$542	$ _____	$ _____
		Totals	$ _____	$ _____
		Taxes	$ _____	$ _____

Wage Payments—Check

The most common method of paying wages is by check. The payroll register is the source of information for writing the check and informing the employee of the amount of each deduction.

EXAMPLE 19 Using the following partial payroll register, complete the check stub, the employee portion, and write the check.

PAYROLL REGISTER

FOR WEEK ENDED: DECEMBER 9, 198X

NAME	MARITAL STATUS	WITH. ALLOW.	TOTAL HOURS	RATE	EARNINGS	ACCUM. EARNINGS CURRENT	TAXABLE WAGES FOR UNEMPLOY. $0-7,000	FICA $0-42,000	FICA TAX	FED. TAX	STATE TAX	CREDIT UNION	HOSP. INSUR.	SAVINGS BONDS	TOTAL DEDUCTIONS	NET PAY	CHECK NO.
Anderson	S	0	40	$5.50	$260.00	$18,425.00	$ -0-	$260.00	$18.59	$36.00	$18.20	$	$ 7.15	$	$ 79.94	$180.06	#1001
Bagley	S	2	39.5	6.25	246.88	17,339.00	-0-	246.88	17.65	25.00	17.28	10.00	6.79	5.00	81.72	165.15	#1002
Ferguson	M	2	36	5.15	185.40	15,675.00	-0-	185.40	13.26	11.00	12.98		5.10		42.33	143.07	#1003
Johnson, J.	M	4			846.15	42,307.00	-0-	450.15	38.51	147.00	31.51	35.00	23.27		275.29	570.86	#1004
Stearns	S	1	40	7.10	284.00	6,355.00	284.00	284.00	20.31	36.00	19.38		7.81		84.00	200.00	#1005
TOTALS			155.5		$1822.43	$100,190.00		$284.00	$1426.43	$108.32	$255.00	$99.85	$45.00	$50.12	$5.00	$563.28	$1259.14

Solution: The solution is a matter of transferring the information correctly from the payroll register to the check, check stub, and the employee's stub. Lastly, subtract the amount of the check from the previous balance to keep the checkbook current.

See Figure 6.3 for a complete relationship of the payroll register to the payroll check.

Key Terms

Commission (137)
Double time (133)
Earnings (130)
Employee earnings record (146, 148)
Employer's Quarterly Federal Tax Return (Form 941) (147, 149)
FICA tax (140)
FUTA tax (147)
Graduated commissions system (137)

Mandatory deductions (140)
Payroll register (146, 148)
Piece-rate system (136)
State unemployment contributions (147)
Time and a half (132, 133)
Voluntary deductions (140)
W-4 Employee's Withholding Allowance Certificate (3, 147, 148)
W-2 Wage and Tax Statement (147, 149)

Looking Back

There is a significant difference between gross and net earnings. The calculation for tax withholdings as well as the figures for the reports are always based on gross earnings.

Calculating payroll correctly, completing the required payroll forms and records, and filing withholdings and reports with state and federal agencies on time are a must. Payroll deals with *employee* earnings, their tax withholdings, and retirement contributions. Payroll records and the money that must be deposited with state and federal governments are checked very carefully. If assigned deadlines are not met, interest and penalties will be assessed to the company. Maximum penalties involve closing the business and jail sentences.

The amount of the income base, the income tax rates, the social security tax rates, and the unemployment rates are all subject to change by the legislature. Concentrate on the present procedures of how to calculate the taxes using present rates. Check frequently for any state or federal changes in your area.

Let's Review

1. Hans Yowell sold a house for his client. If this week's commissions were $1,265, and he is married with four allowances, calculate his federal income tax, his social security tax, and his net pay.

2. Using the current date and checkbook balance of $1,514.80, and the information in Problem 1, write payroll check number 1405 to handle Hans' net pay. Be sure to complete his informational stub as well as the company check stub.

3. A local arts and crafts dealer uses the following incentive commission rate plan for all salespeople:

$$\begin{aligned} \$\ \ \ 1 - \$2{,}250 &= 3\% \\ \$2{,}251 - \$4{,}500 &= 3\tfrac{1}{2}\% \\ \$4{,}501 - \$7{,}000 &= 5\% \\ \$7{,}001 + \ \ \ \ \ \ \ \ \ &= 7\% \end{aligned}$$

If Rita Hastings sells $7,200 worth of merchandise, what is her commission?

4. Using the tables in Appendix D, complete the following weekly payroll register, being sure to total columns and prove column totals across where appropriate. Information for Employee 1 has been completed as an example.

Employee	Marital Status	Accum. earnings	Wages	Allowances	S.S. tax	Federal tax	Credit union	Total deductions	Net pay
1	M	$12,380	268	4	20.13	8	25	53.13	214.87
2	M	$44,710	436.40	5	____	____	–0–	____	____
3	S	$18,110	295	2	____	____	35	____	____
4	M	$ 9,725	690	0	____	____	10	____	____
5	S	$17,335	350	6	____	____	15	____	____
	Totals		$_____		____	____	85	____	____

5. The chef at a local steak house had earned $42,800 by the end of November. His salary for the month of December was $3,580. What is the amount of the FICA deduction?

6. At the end of September, Deborah Darcy had accumulated earnings of $6,345, and her salary for October was $850. Calculate the amount of the employer's liability for unemployment and matching social security tax.

7. Carl is being paid 63 cents for each item he quality checks through his work station. Calculate his weekly pay if his item count is Monday, 147; Tuesday, 191; Wednesday, 158; Thursday, 106; and Friday, 216.

8. Employees at Electrical Engineers receive time and a half for any hours over 40 per week and double time for holidays and Sundays. Morris Parker, married and with three allowances, turned in the following weekly time card: Monday, $9\frac{1}{2}$ hrs; Tuesday, 8 hrs; Wednesday, 10 hrs; Thursday, 9 hrs; Friday, 6 hrs; and Sunday, 6 hrs. Figure his earnings, social security tax, federal income tax, and net pay if he receives $6.20 per hour.

9. Mark James had earnings of $1,350 in November, and his earnings record showed accumulated earnings on October 31 of $14,250. Calculate his employer's tax liability for unemployment and matching social security tax.

10. Marge Weaver's hourly rate is $16 per hour, with time and a half paid after 40 hours in any week. As of December 14, Marge had earned $44,505. If, during the week of December 21, she worked 41 hours, what is the amount of earnings and social security tax?

Chapter Test

1. Complete the following payroll register. Verify column totals by adding and subtracting across where appropriate.

Employee	Marital status	Allowances	Accum. earnings	Earnings	FICA tax	Federal tax	Other	Total deductions	Net pay
1. Martin	M	2	$17,000	$282.75	$____	$____	$ 5.00	$____	$____
2. Peters	S	1	$11,250	$205.80	$____	$____	$15.00	$____	$____
3. Ritter	M	2	$13,535	$595.65	$____	$____	$ 0	$____	$____
4. Stevens	S	2	$ 9,425	$163.50	$____	$____	$18.50	$____	$____
5. Tyler	M	4	$43,472	$628.00	$____	$____	$22.50	$____	$____
6. Wynn	M	5	$43,111	$590.00	$____	$____	$37.50	$____	$____
			Totals	$____	$____	$____	$____	$____	$____

2. At the end of November a salaried employee had accumulated $43,465.80. Using the rate of 7.51%, figure the social security tax on the December salary of $1,855.50.

3. Craig Lown has accumulated $6,892.68 in earnings. His current weekly earnings are $226.15. What amount of his earnings is taxable for unemployment? What is the unemployment tax?

4. Myra worked $46\frac{1}{2}$ hours, 4 on a holiday, during the week ending May 28. If she earns $6.25 per hour, is paid double time for holiday work and time and a half for hours over 40, what are her gross earnings? What are the deductions for income tax and social security if she is single with 3 allowances?

5. Production workers at a brick cleaning company cleaned the following number of bricks: Glass, 525; Hahn, 580; Manzanares, 615; and Tucker, 498. If they are paid at the rate of 28 cents per brick, how much did each earn?

6. Paul sold two used cars this week for a total of $10,375. If his commission rate is 5%, what are his gross earnings?

7. Marty Thompson sells furniture on an incentive commission plan. On August 5, she turned in a total sales figure of $38,285. Using the following scale, calculate her gross earnings:

$$\begin{aligned} \$\ \ \ \ \ 1 - \$\ 5,000 &= 2\% \\ \$\ 5,001 - \$15,000 &= 3\% \\ \$15,001 - \$35,000 &= 5\% \\ \$35,001 + \ \ \ \ \ \ \ \ \ \ &= 7\% \end{aligned}$$

8. Using the total hours and the rate of pay given for each employee, calculate the regular earnings, overtime earnings (assuming time and a half for hours over 40 per week), and total earnings for each employee. Total the columns if appropriate.

Employee	Hours	Regular rate	Regular earnings	Overtime earnings	Gross earnings
1. Archibald	45	$3.90	$ _____	$ _____	$ _____
2. Carlson	49	$6.65	$ _____	$ _____	$ _____
3. Montgomery	51	$3.75	$ _____	$ _____	$ _____
4. Stewart	46	$5.95	$ _____	$ _____	$ _____
Totals	_____		$ _____	$ _____	$ _____

9. The Fox Company uses an incentive commission plan to encourage a higher sales base each week. Using the following scale, calculate Byron's weekly earnings if he sold $9,575.

Sales	Commission rate
$ 1 – $ 2,500	4%
$ 2,501 – $ 6,000	5%
$ 6,001 – $10,000	$5\frac{1}{2}$%
$10,001 +	7%

10. Wade worked 44 hours during the week ending May 15, including 6 on Sunday. His hourly rate of pay is $7.75 with time and a half over 40 hours and double time for Sundays and holidays. Calculate his gross earnings.

11. Marlene has accumulated earnings of $43,895. Calculate the deduction for FICA tax if her current earnings were $1,090.

12. Ray Blinde sold four cars during the week for a total of $41,750. If he has a $5\frac{1}{4}$% commission rate, how much is his commission? How much is his social security tax deduction?

Chapter Test

Customer Invoicing and Statements

7

OBJECTIVES

When you finish this chapter you will be able to:

- *Extend purchase orders and verify invoice extensions and totals. (7.1)*
- *Understand the common shipping terms and be able to calculate invoice totals involving shipping, returns, and allowances. (7.2)*
- *Determine item costs using quantity discount schedules. (7.3)*
- *Use the list price–trade discount systems for establishing purchasing costs. (7.4)*
- *Calculate payment requirements for invoices using the date of purchase, end of month, and receipt of goods cash discount systems. (7.5)*

COMING UP

The lifeblood of any business is its customers. A company receives an order from a customer, fills and ships it, records the transaction for billing, and follows up at the end of the month by sending a statement of account for any amount still owed.

The process is then reversed. In order to do business, a company usually becomes the customer of some other company; the other company is the supplier. Merchandise and materials are ordered from the supplier, the order is received and the customer billed, and the bill is paid within a suitable period of time. The supplier issues a monthly statement for any outstanding balance. This flow of bills and payments provides much of the workload of the accounting office of a business.

The process of buying and selling also involves a rather complex structure of discounts. The effectiveness of the discount process depends on adherence to the rules of calculating discount amounts. The agreements and terms offered and accepted vary from company to company, yet they are an important part of the flow of commerce.

This chapter focuses on the flow of business transactions. As you begin to grasp the sequence and timing of these procedures, you will see that, although the procedures are complex, they make sense for business.

Purchasing Supplies and Merchandise

7.1

Purchasing is the first step in the transaction cycle. If a need for supplies or inventory exists, a **purchase requisition** is prepared and sent to the purchasing department. See Figure 7.1.

Once the requisition is received, a **purchase order** is prepared from catalog descriptions or by phone consultation and is then mailed to the **supplier.**

```
                    PURCHASE REQUISITION
                                              REQUISITION NO.
                                                  B1141

    DATE      May 19, 198X      DEPARTMENT    B
    DATE WANTED  June 12, 198X

    QUANTITY   STOCK NO.            DESCRIPTION

    10 boxes              Microcomputer printer paper, 20#, white
       5                  Ribbons, Model RT4 Phoenix Printer, black



    REQUISITIONED BY  Thompson       APPROVED BY
```

FIGURE 7.1
Purchase requisition

EXAMPLE 1 Department B just sent a purchase requisition for 10 boxes of microcomputer printer paper with tractor feed and 5 cartridge ribbons for a Model RT4 Phoenix printer. Prepare the purchase order. See Figure 7.2.

Solution:

- Complete the top half of the purchase order with standard information from the supplier's catalog.
    - **(A)** Purchase Order Number—An assigned consecutive number: #1168.
    - **(B)** Date—Current.
    - **(C)** Terms—n/30. Time of payment; net (total) amount due in 30 days.
    - **(D) FOB (Free on Board)**—Enter the point of origin or the point of destination by city.
- Complete the bottom half of the purchase order:
    - **(E)** Quantity, 10; Catalog No. P200; Description, #20 paper with tractor feed; Unit Price, $28.50; Total, 28.50 × 10 = $285.00.
    - **(F)** Quantity, 5; Catalog No. C104ph; Description, printer ribbons, black; Unit Price, $5.70; Total, 5.70 × 5 = $28.50.
    - **(G)** Add the total price extensions together, $313.50.
    - **(H)** Prepaid shipping added, $13.00.
    - **(I)** Add total supplies plus shipping to get the grand total of $326.50.

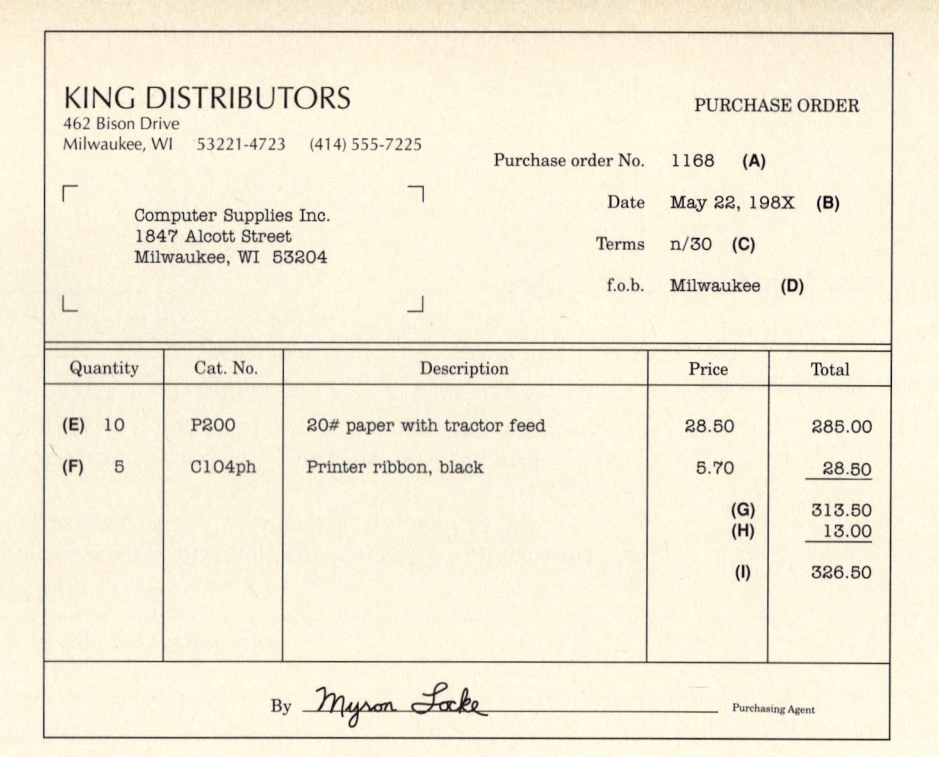

```
        KING DISTRIBUTORS                              PURCHASE ORDER
        462 Bison Drive
        Milwaukee, WI  53221-4723   (414) 555-7225
                                              Purchase order No.   1168    (A)
              Computer Supplies Inc.          Date        May 22, 198X   (B)
              1847 Alcott Street
              Milwaukee, WI  53204            Terms       n/30    (C)

                                              f.o.b.      Milwaukee   (D)
```

Quantity	Cat. No.	Description	Price	Total
(E) 10	P200	20# paper with tractor feed	28.50	285.00
(F) 5	C104ph	Printer ribbon, black	5.70	28.50
			(G)	313.50
			(H)	13.00
			(I)	326.50

By _Myron Locke_ Purchasing Agent

FIGURE 7.2
Purchase order

CALCULATOR TIP

When extending purchase orders, invoices, and statements, enter your extended figures into memory so that a grand total can be calculated:

- 10 × 28.50 = 285   M+   • Item one figured, added to memory.
- 5 × 5.70 = 28.50   M+   • Item two figured, added to memory.
- MR 313.50   • Total entered into add function.
- + 13 = 326.50   • Shipping added, grand total displayed.

EXAMPLE 2 The following items of merchandise have reached their reorder points:

   3-ring binder, cloth   3-ring binder, plastic
   felt tip pen, black   felt tip pen, blue
   3-hole notebook paper, wideline, white

Prepare the purchase order, ordering the normal quantities that we typically buy, and add $37.85 prepaid shipping.

Solution:

- Complete the top half using standard information from the supplier.
- **(A)** Enter:

Quantity	Stock no.	Description
50	68425	3-ring binder, cloth

Unit price	Total
$2.35	$117.50 (50 × 2.35)

- **(B)** Enter each item in like manner and multiply the quantity times the unit price to get the total.
- **(C)** Calculate the merchandise total.
- **(D)** Add prepaid shipping.

---

160   Chapter 7   Customer Invoicing and Statements

```
         ┌─────────────────────────────────────────────────────────────────┐
         │                                                                 │
         │   KING DISTRIBUTORS                          PURCHASE ORDER     │
         │   462 Bison Drive                                               │
         │   Milwaukee, WI   53221-4723   (414) 555-7225                   │
         │                                                                 │
         │                                       Purchase order No.  1170  │
         │   ┌─                            ─┐                              │
         │    Office Supply Warehouse            Date      April 1, 198X   │
         │    8568 Mississippi Blvd.                                       │
         │    Salt Lake City, UT  84209          Terms     3/10, n/30 EOM  │
         │                                                                 │
         │                                       f.o.b.    Salt Lake City  │
         │   └─                            ─┘                              │
         ├─────────────────────────────────────────────────────────────────┤
```

Quantity	Stock No.	Description	Price	Total
50	68425	3-ring binder, cloth, blue	2.35	117.50
50	78450	3-ring binder, plastic, red	2.15	107.50
1	50625	Felt tip pen, black	36.00 gr.	36.00
1	50630	Felt tip pen, blue	36.00 gr.	36.00
10	40150	3-hole notebook paper, wide, white	27.75 ctn.	277.50
				574.50
			Prepaid shipping	37.85
				612.35

By _Myron Lake_ _____ Purchasing Agent

✓ CHECK FOR UNDERSTANDING

1. Extend the following items on the partial purchase order and then take a grand total of all items. Use your calculator memory.

Quantity	Catalog no.	Description	Unit cost	Total
8 cartons	3232	$\frac{3}{4}$-inch tape, 12 per carton	$7.50/ctn.	$ _____
2 gross	8748	No. 2 lead pencil	$17.30/gr.	$ _____
4 cartons	7256	Red eraser, 12 per carton	$4.48/ctn.	$ _____
18 boxes	6054	No. 4 staple, 5,000 per box	$2.15/box	$ _____
			Total	$ _____

SKILL EXERCISES

Extend the following items on each of the partial purchase orders and then record the grand total of each purchase order. Use the memory feature on your calculator.

	Quantity	Catalog no.	Description	Unit cost	Total
1.	18	43652	Men's pullover, white, small	$2.16	$ _____
	18	43655	Men's pullover, white, medium	$2.16	$ _____
	24	53652	Women's pullover, white, small	$2.42	$ _____
	24	53655	Women's pullover, white, medium	$2.42	$ _____
	36	20425	Men's walking short, blue, medium	$3.40	$ _____
				Total	$ _____

Answer to ✓ Check for Understanding
Grand total = $151.22.

Section 7.1   Purchasing Supplies and Merchandise

2. | 48 | 16548 | 3-inch garden tool | $1.40 | $ _____
   | 30 | 16642 | 1½-inch garden tool | $1.55 | $ _____
   | 6 | 48255 | Long-handled spade | $4.60 | $ _____
   | 50 bags | 10250 | Kentucky blue grass seed, #10 | $5.10 | $ _____
   | | | | Total | $ _____

Preparing Sales Invoices

Once the purchase order is received by the supplier, the order must be filled. As soon as it is determined that the items are in stock, the **invoice** is prepared. The invoice (Figure 7.3) is really the bill that is mailed to the ordering company. If it resembles the purchase order, it is because the information on the purchase order is verified, corrected if necessary, and used to prepare the invoice.

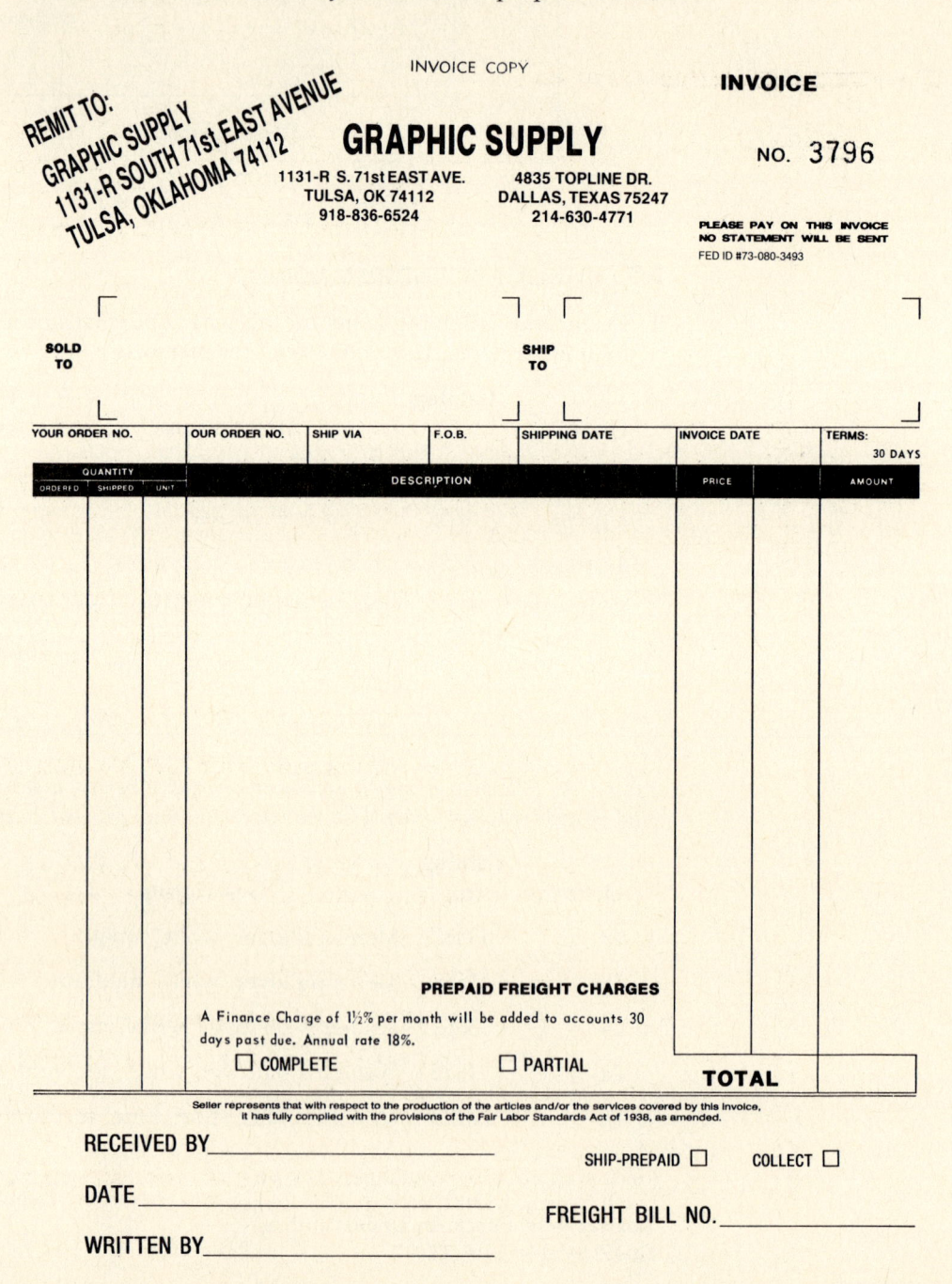

FIGURE 7.3
Invoice

162 Chapter 7 Customer Invoicing and Statements

EXAMPLE 3 Using the following verified purchase order, prepare the invoice.

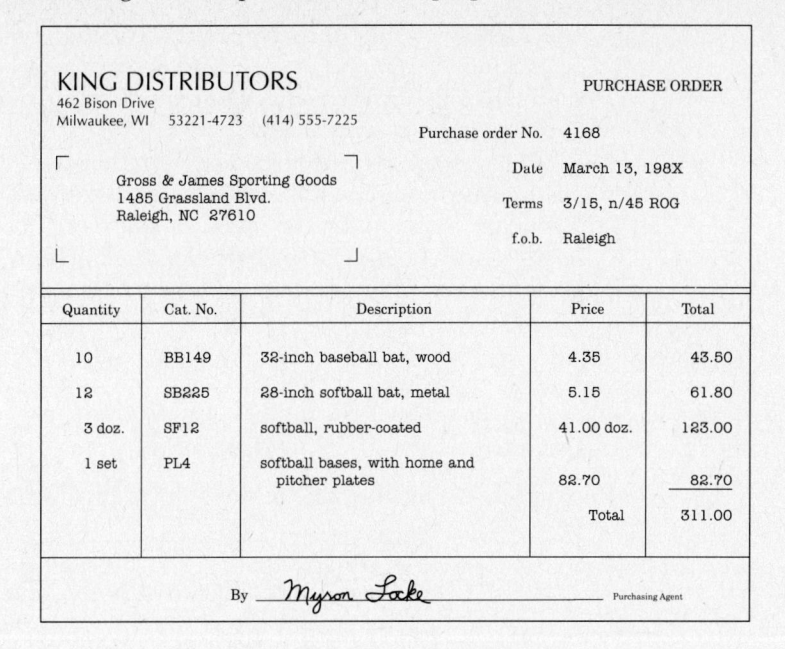

```
┌─────────────────────────────────────────────────────────────┐
│  KING DISTRIBUTORS                        PURCHASE ORDER    │
│  462 Bison Drive                                            │
│  Milwaukee, WI  53221-4723  (414) 555-7225                  │
│                                    Purchase order No.  4168 │
│  ┌─                          ─┐                             │
│     Gross & James Sporting Goods   Date    March 13, 198X   │
│     1485 Grassland Blvd.                                    │
│     Raleigh, NC  27610             Terms   3/15, n/45 ROG   │
│                                    f.o.b.  Raleigh          │
│  └─                          ─┘                             │
└─────────────────────────────────────────────────────────────┘
```

Quantity	Cat. No.	Description	Price	Total
10	BB149	32-inch baseball bat, wood	4.35	43.50
12	SB225	28-inch softball bat, metal	5.15	61.80
3 doz.	SF12	softball, rubber-coated	41.00 doz.	123.00
1 set	PL4	softball bases, with home and pitcher plates	82.70	82.70
			Total	311.00

By _Myron Locke_ _____ Purchasing Agent

Solution:

(A) Complete mailing address (inside the brackets) using the heading on the purchase order.

(B) Terms: enter 3/15, n/45 ROG. Terms are listed in the supplier's catalog.

(C) Date: use current date.

(D) P.O. Number: use #4168 from the purchase order. This gives a definite tie between the two forms.

(E) FOB: Raleigh

(F) Our number (invoice): invoices are usually bought in prenumbered, consecutive sets. If not, enter the next available number from your records.

(G) Complete the bottom half in the same manner as the purchase order.

(H) Enter **"prepaid shipping"** on the bottom and add it to the merchandise total. This charge is normal if shipping terms are FOB point of origin.

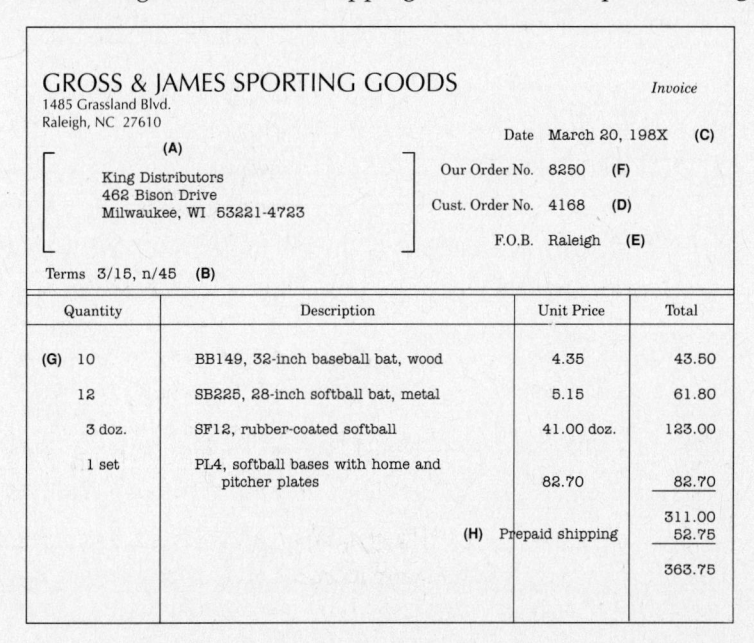

```
┌─────────────────────────────────────────────────────────────┐
│  GROSS & JAMES SPORTING GOODS                    Invoice    │
│  1485 Grassland Blvd.                                       │
│  Raleigh, NC  27610                                         │
│              (A)              Date   March 20, 198X   (C)   │
│  ┌─                         ─┐                              │
│     King Distributors           Our Order No.  8250   (F)   │
│     462 Bison Drive                                         │
│     Milwaukee, WI  53221-4723   Cust. Order No. 4168  (D)   │
│                                 F.O.B.  Raleigh      (E)    │
│  └─                         ─┘                              │
│  Terms  3/15, n/45   (B)                                    │
└─────────────────────────────────────────────────────────────┘
```

Quantity	Description	Unit Price	Total
(G) 10	BB149, 32-inch baseball bat, wood	4.35	43.50
12	SB225, 28-inch softball bat, metal	5.15	61.80
3 doz.	SF12, rubber-coated softball	41.00 doz.	123.00
1 set	PL4, softball bases with home and pitcher plates	82.70	82.70
			311.00
	(H) Prepaid shipping		52.75
			363.75

Handling Additional Invoice Items

There are two additional invoice charges that a business might use: a special carton or packing charge and an expedite delivery charge. The **expedite delivery charge** is used when the buyer wants a shipment before a normal delivery date and is willing to pay extra to receive it early.

The amount of the invoice may be reduced, or an allowance given, if the customer has to return merchandise because an order was incorrectly filled or items arrived damaged. Since invoicing involves shipments between manufacturers and wholesalers, and wholesalers and retailers, retail sales tax is not normally a factor. Sales tax is charged only by the business dealing with the final customer.

EXAMPLE 4 Complete the bottom portion of an invoice using the following information:

Quantity	Description	Unit price	
6 sets	Stock #428; ceramic duck, greenware	$4.85	$ _____
10 ea	Stock #713; ceramic clown, greenware	$3.40	$ _____
22 ea	Stock #415; ceramic frog, greenware	$1.70	$ _____
14 sets	Stock #605; 3-apple set, greenware	$5.20	$ _____

Prepaid shipping $12.25 and special packaging charge of 5% of total merchandise.

Solution:

- List each item on a separate line and extend the prices.
- Calculate the total of all the merchandise.
- List and add the prepaid shipping charge.
- List, calculate, and add the special packaging charge:
  Total merchandise 173.30 × .05 = $8.67.
- Add merchandise, shipping, and packaging to calculate the invoice total.

Quantity	Stock No.	Description	Unit Price	Amount
6 sets	428	ceramic duck, greenware	4.85	29.10
10	713	ceramic clown, greenware	3.40	34.00
22	415	ceramic frog, greenware	1.70	37.40
14	605	ceramic 3-apple set, greenware	5.20	72.80
				173.30
			Prepaid shipping	12.25
			Special packaging	8.67
				194.22

EXAMPLE 5 If, in Example 4, the customer returned 3 clowns and 4 frogs because they were damaged, what is the total amount owed?

Solution:

$3 \times 3.40 = 10.20$ • Multiply quantity returned times price per unit.

$4 \times 1.70 = \underline{6.80}$

17.00 • Total the returns.

$194.22 - 17 = 177.22$ • Subtract returns from total invoice.

Note: A portion of the shipping and the packaging might also be refunded by the seller.

> **CALCULATOR TIP**
>
> In Example 5 after storing the total of each return in memory, enter the total invoice and press the minus key to set up the subtraction without having to re-enter the merchandise total.
>
> 3 × 3.40 = M+   10.20   • Total of return one.
> 4 × 1.70 = M+   6.80   • Total of return two.
> 194.22 − MR = 177.22   • Invoice total entered and total of returned merchandise in memory is subtracted.

✓ CHECK FOR UNDERSTANDING

1. Baker Wholesaler's invoice shows total merchandise of $865.70, prepaid shipping of $62.85, and a special packing charge of $21. What is the grand total?

2. The total amount of merchandise on Invoice No. 3980 is $4,250. If the expedite delivery charge is 5% of the total merchandise, what is the delivery charge?

3. The special carton charge is 6% of the total merchandise on Invoice No. 825. If the merchandise total is $1,604.25 and there is prepaid shipping of $115, what is the grand total?

4. The extra charges on the bottom of Invoice No. 715 were for expedite delivery (5% of total merchandise) and special shipping cartons (8% of total merchandise). If the merchandise total is $923.75, what is the grand total?

SKILL EXERCISES

Using the following partial invoice listings, extend the amounts, calculate the total amount of merchandise, add any additional charges, and calculate the grand total:

1.

Quantity	Catalog no.	Description	Unit cost	Total
16 cartons	1638	16K-memory expansion board, 12 per carton	$465/ctn.	$ _____
12 cartons	3216	Disk-drive interface cards, 24 per carton	$2,040/ctn.	$ _____
48	8016	Parallel printer cable	$21.45	$ _____
4	6112	Monochrome, 12-inch monitor	$135.85	$ _____
18 boxes	7218	$5\frac{1}{4}$-inch single sided, double density disks, 10 per box	$13.50/box	$ _____

Total merchandise $ _____
Prepaid shipping $ 37.80
Special carton, 15% of Total merchandise $ _____
Grand total $ _____

Answers to ✓ Check for Understanding
1. $949.55.   2. $212.50.   3. $1,815.51.   4. $1,043.84.

Section 7.1 Purchasing Supplies and Merchandise

2.

Quantity	Stock no.	Description	Unit cost	Total
4 boxes	115	Duplicator paper, 24#, white, 10 per	$21.30	$ _____
5 boxes	108	Micro printer paper, 12", white with tractor feed	$17.30	$ _____
5 reams	85	Bond letterhead, 20#, white	$ 8.15	$ _____
2 boxes	202	Index cards, 3 × 5, white, 50 point	$14.75	$ _____
10 boxes	72	Envelopes, No. 10, white with return	$13.80	$ _____

Total merchandise $ _____
Prepaid shipping $ 28.70
Grand total $ _____

3. Using the invoice in Exercise 2, calculate the expedite delivery charge of 18% based on the total merchandise. Calculate the new grand total.

4. Using the invoice in Exercise 2, calculate a new grand total if 1 box of #108 paper, 1 ream of #85 letterhead, and 1 box of #72 envelopes were returned and an allowance of $50 was given for envelope printing being the wrong color.

5. Calculate the grand total of the following invoice:

Quantity	No.	Description	Cost	Total
18	K462	Corn popper, 12"	$14.75	$ _____
12	K350	Blender	$21.00	$ _____
32	L235	Steam iron	$11.75	$ _____
8	K110	Food processor	$39.80	$ _____

Shipping, $51.70, special packaging 10% of merchandise total.

Calculating and Preparing the Monthly Statement

7.2

The statement of account is prepared monthly by the seller (supplier) for each customer's account that has an outstanding balance. It is a summation of the month's activity showing purchases (debits), payments (credits), and the ending balance. See Figure 7.4.

As a recipient of a **monthly statement,** a business must verify the accuracy of the statement before any payments are made. This includes verifying the correct invoice, the correct amount of each invoice, and the correct addition and subtraction of the statement.

STATEMENT OF ACCOUNT

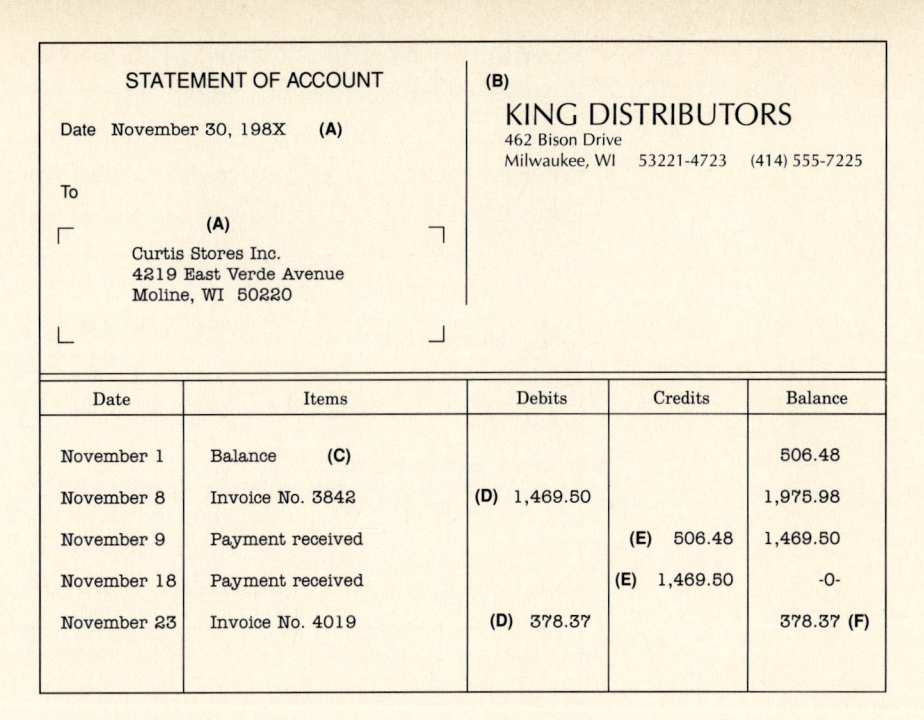

Date November 30, 198X (A)

(B) KING DISTRIBUTORS
462 Bison Drive
Milwaukee, WI 53221-4723 (414) 555-7225

To

(A)
Curtis Stores Inc.
4219 East Verde Avenue
Moline, WI 50220

Date	Items	Debits	Credits	Balance
November 1	Balance (C)			506.48
November 8	Invoice No. 3842	(D) 1,469.50		1,975.98
November 9	Payment received		(E) 506.48	1,469.50
November 18	Payment received		(E) 1,469.50	-0-
November 23	Invoice No. 4019	(D) 378.37		378.37 (F)

FIGURE 7.4
Statement of account

(A) *Heading, including date and mailing address.*
(B) *Seller's name and address.*
(C) *Opening balance; the month began with carryover charges from October.*
(D) *An invoice listed as a debit adds to the balance.*
(E) *A payment listed as a credit reduces the balance.*
(F) *Amount still owed at the end of the month.*

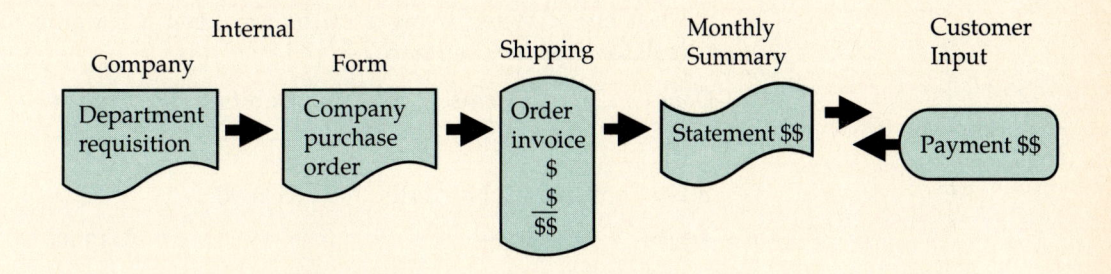

Normal flow of forms

Company — Department requisition → Internal Form — Company purchase order → Shipping — Order invoice $ $ $$ → Monthly Summary — Statement $$ ← Customer Input — Payment $$

EXAMPLE 6 Using the following information, prepare the statement of account.

TO: Bar X Tack & Saddle Shop; 1586 East Verde, Pueblo, CO 81004

Date	Invoice no.	Invoice amount	Payment received
6/10	516	$ 356.00	
6/19	572	$ 852.50	
6/20			$356.00
6/26	915	$ 618.75	
6/29			$852.50
6/29	962	$1,050.00	

Solution:

- Complete To: and Date: sections using information given.
- Keep the entries in date order and keep a running balance after each entry.
- Enter Invoice No. 516 as a debit; carry to balance column.

Section 7.2 Calculating and Preparing the Monthly Statement

- Enter Invoice No. 572 as a debit; *add* to previous balance.
- Enter payment received as a credit; *subtract* from previous balance.
- Enter Invoice No. 915 as a debit; *add* to previous balance.
- Enter payment received as a credit; *subtract* from previous balance.
- Enter Invoice No. 962 as a debit; *add* to previous balance.

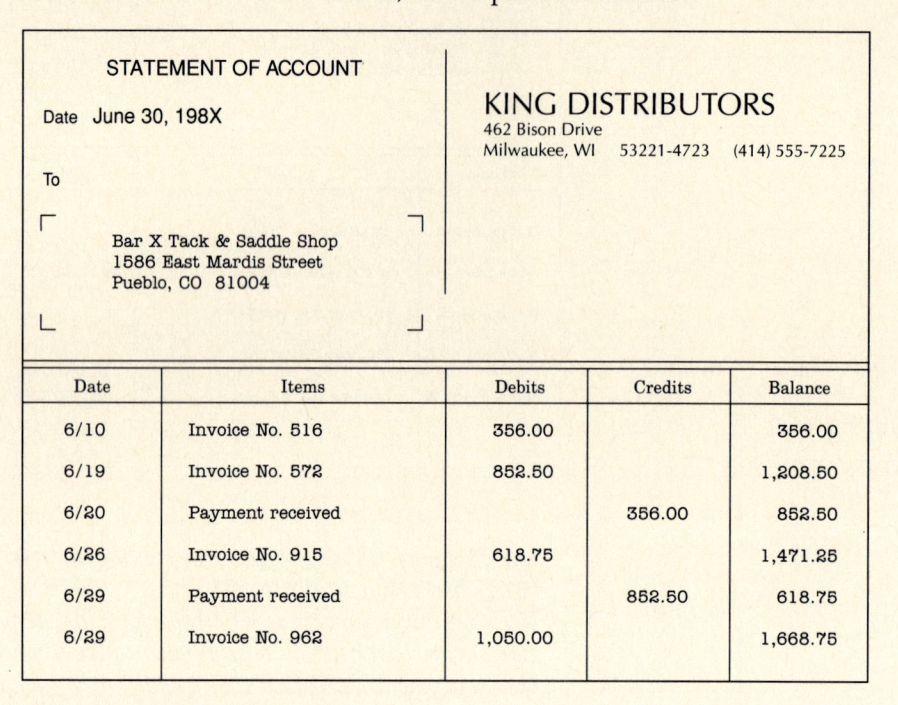

STATEMENT OF ACCOUNT

Date June 30, 198X

To

Bar X Tack & Saddle Shop
1586 East Mardis Street
Pueblo, CO 81004

KING DISTRIBUTORS
462 Bison Drive
Milwaukee, WI 53221-4723 (414) 555-7225

Date	Items	Debits	Credits	Balance
6/10	Invoice No. 516	356.00		356.00
6/19	Invoice No. 572	852.50		1,208.50
6/20	Payment received		356.00	852.50
6/26	Invoice No. 915	618.75		1,471.25
6/29	Payment received		852.50	618.75
6/29	Invoice No. 962	1,050.00		1,668.75

✔ **CHECK FOR UNDERSTANDING**

1. Complete the following statement of account by filling in the balance column after the last entry. When using a calculator, keep a running total in memory. (See Calculator Tips in Chapter 5.)

Date	Items	Debits	Credits	Balance
5/12	Invoice No. 9346	$715.85		$ 715.85
5/19	Invoice No. 9410	$336.90		$1052.75
5/21	Payment		$415.85	$ 636.90
5/27	Invoice No. 9550	$915.15		$1552.05
5/29	Payment		$636.90	$ _____

2. Verify the computations on the following statement of account, making corrections if necessary:

Date	Items	Debits	Credits	Balance
2/1	Balance			$1,977.69
2/9	Invoice No. 6690	$482.36		$2,460.05
2/9	Payment		$ 432.69	$2,027.36
2/10	Payment		$1,405.00	$3,432.36
2/19	Payment		$ 482.36	$2,950,00

Answers to ✔ Check for Understanding
1. Final balance = $915.15. 2. Corrected balance = $140.00.

168 Chapter 7 Customer Invoicing and Statements

SKILL EXERCISES

Complete the following statement of account by filling in the balance column after each entry:

1.

Date	Items	Debits	Credits	Balance
8/1	Balance			$ 640.50
8/6	Invoice No. 1218	$472.75		$ _____
8/9	Payment		$340.50	$ _____
8/11	Invoice No. 1257	$319.60		$ _____
8/11	Payment		$300.00	$ _____
8/16	Payment		$472.75	$ _____
8/19	Invoice No. 1390	$117.15		$ _____
8/21	Payment		$319.60	$ _____
8/28	Invoice No. 1505	$610.00		$ _____
8/29	Payment		$117.15	$ _____

2. Verify the computations on the following statement of account, making corrections if necessary:

Date	Items	Debits	Credits	Balance
12/1	Balance			$1,586.50
12/6	Payment		$ 530.25	1,506.25
12/9	Invoice No. 4318	$ 708.36		1,764.61
12/10	Payment		$1,056.25	703.86
12/17	Invoice No. 4605	$ 318.32		1,022.18
12/19	Payment		$ 708.36	313.82
12/26	Invoice No. 4691	$1,530.95		1,844.77
12/27	Payment		$ 318.32	1,526.45

APPLICATIONS

1. Calculate the ending balance using the following statement of account information: Beginning balance, $1,408.65.

Debit	Credit
$918.52	$816.35
$605.38	$592.30

Section 7.2 Calculating and Preparing the Monthly Statement

2. Calculate the total amount of merchandise ordered using the following partial purchase order:

Quantity	Stock no.	Description	Unit cost	Total
18	482	Talking doll	$18.15	$ _____
10	685	Teddy bear	$26.30	$ _____
15	670	Walking clown	$11.70	$ _____
24	365	Alligator	$ 7.65	$ _____
			Total	$ _____

3. Complete the invoice and calculate the grand total using the following information: Date: current; To: Easy-On T-Shirt Company, 4185 Atlantic Drive, Bangor, ME 04401; Terms: n/30; Invoice No.: 4415; Customer Order No.: 1633; Shipped Via: Union Pacific.

Quantity shipped	Unit	Description	Unit price
6	Box	Red fabric paint, 12 cans each	$82.80
9	Each	Green mosaic paint	$16.50
4	Each	Silk screen rolls	$ 8.45

Shipping: $63.75.

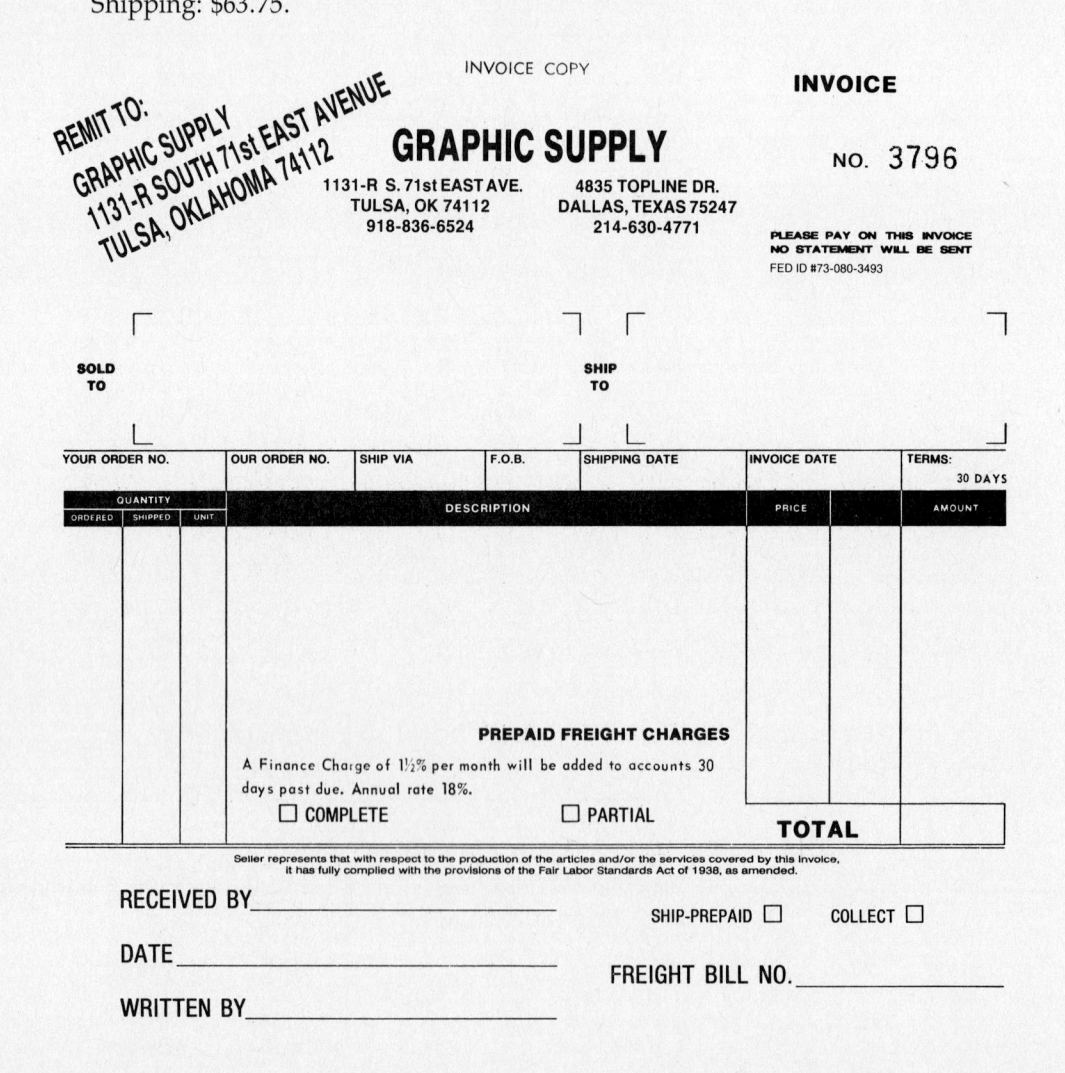

4. The total amount of merchandise on the invoice was $1,630.75. If the expedite delivery charge was 12% of the merchandise total, what was the grand total?

5. Verify the price extensions and the totals on the partial invoice. Make any necessary corrections.

Quantity	No.	Description	Price	Total
4	A7259	Microcomputer	$612.80	$2,451.20
6	T9230	Electronic typewriter	$562.25	$3,733.50
2	P1655	Printer	$315.55	$ 631.10
4	S3056	VDT, 16"	$204.90	$ 819.60
			Total merchandise	$7,635.40
			Expedite delivery, 5%	$ 381.77
			Grand total	$7,253.23

6. Prepare a statement of account for the month of November using the following information: 11/1 Balance, $816.80.

Date	Invoice no.	Invoice amount	Payment amount
11/11			$304.40
11/20	8804	$505.15	
11/24			$512.40
11/29	8880	$330.80	

Date	Items	Debits	Credits	Balance

7. The Hartsel Beef Company ordered pharmaceuticals totaling $1,482.75. If special packing was 6% of the total merchandise and shipping was $45, what was the total invoice?

8. Verify the price extensions on the following purchase order received from Always-Green Sod Farm. Make corrections as needed.

Quantity	Stock no.	Description	Unit cost	Total
6	S114	8" staple gun	$16.25	$ 97.50
16 boxes	St005	Staples, 8 boxes per carton	$14.00/ctn.	$ 28.00
8 cartons	T100	Adhesive tape, $1\frac{1}{2}$", 16 rolls per carton	$9.50/ctn.	$ 19.00
4 pairs	B404	Overboots, size 12	$9.25/pr.	$ 37.00
			Total	$181.50

9. Before the following monthly statement can be paid, it needs to be verified. Check to see if the amounts are in their proper columns and correctly added and subtracted in the balance column.

Date	Items	Debit	Credit	Balance
7/1	Balance			$ 570.90
7/8	Invoice No. 694	$390.35		$ 961.25
7/10	Payment		$570.90	$ 390.35
7/18	Invoice No. 726	$705.20		$1,095.55
7/19	Payment	$390.35		$1,485.90
7/28	Payment		$705.20	$ 780.70

10. Ceramic Wholesalers prepared an invoice showing these extended totals for items purchased: $118.30, $416.05, $82.90, and $109.29. If the shipping charge is $52.90 and there is a 3% special carton charge based on the total merchandise, what is the grand total?

Quantity Discounts

7.3

When a buyer selects merchandise and determines the amount needed, consideration must be given to cost per item. One common way to reduce costs is to buy in larger quantities. Suppliers frequently issue **quantity discounts** based on the dollar value of the order or the number of units purchased.

Quantity discounts are an application of the $P = B \times R$ formula presented in Chapter 4. The base is the **list price,** which can be called the catalog price or the suggested retail price. The rate is the percent of quantity discount and the part we are solving for is the amount of the discount or the net amount.

EXAMPLE 7 The Oil Rite Company quoted the following prices on oil filters:

$$1 \text{ to } 50 = 40\% \text{ discount}$$
$$51 \text{ to } 100 = 43\% \text{ discount}$$
$$101 \text{ to } 250 = 46\% \text{ discount}$$

If the list price is $4.50 and the Back-up Garage ordered 125 filters, how much did it pay?

Solution 1: Unknown is the total list price (base):

$125 \times 4.50 = 562.50$ · Calculate total list price.

Unknown is the quantity discount (part):

$P = B \times R$ · Formula for part.
$P = 562.50 \times .46$ · Enter variables into the formula.
· 562.50 is the base.
· .46 is the rate.

$562.50 \times .46 = 258.75$ · Calculate the part, the discount.
List 562.50 · Subtract discount from list to get net.
Discount -258.75
Net 303.75 · The net amount.

Solution 2: Unknown is the net amount rate:

$$\begin{aligned} \text{List} &= 100\% \\ \text{Discount} &= -46\% \\ \text{Net} &= 54\% \end{aligned}$$

- Use the *less-than logic* developed in Chapter 4. The net amount is 46% less than the list price.
- The 54% is the **complement** of 46%. (A complement is either of two numbers that makes a whole. The complement of 65% is 35%, for example.)

Unknown is the total list price (base):

$125 \times 4.50 = 562.50$ • Calculate total list price.

Unknown is the net amount (part):

$P = B \times R$ • Formula for part.
$P = 562.50 \times .54$ • Enter variables into formula.
- 562.50 is the base.
- .54 is the net amount rate.

$562.50 \times .54 = 303.75$ • Calculate the part.
$\$303.75$ • The net amount. ☐

EXAMPLE 8   The following office supplies were ordered from Aspen Office Supplies:

6 cartons	Microcomputer paper	$16.50 per ctn.	$ 99.00
10	XL 43 printer ribbons	$ 7.00 each	$ 70.00
12	Staple removers	$ 4.50 each	$ 54.00
12	Interface boards	$62.75 each	$753.00

If the supply company uses the following quantity discount schedule, what is the net amount of the invoice?

$$\begin{aligned} \$1 - \$150 &= 3\% \\ \$151 - \$500 &= 5\% \\ \$501 - \$2,000 &= 7\% \end{aligned}$$

Solution: Unknown is total list price (base):

$99 + 70 + 54 + 753 = 976 \text{ total}$ • Determine total list price; add.

Unknown is the net amount rate:

$100\% - 7\% = 93\%$ • Determine the correct discount rate; subtract to determine net amount rate.

Unknown is the net amount (part):

$P = 976 \times .93$ • Enter variables into the formula.
$976 \times .93 = 907.68$ • Calculate the part.
$\$907.68$ • The net amount. ☐

✔ **CHECK FOR UNDERSTANDING**

1. The OK Company ordered the following equipment:

Item	Quantity	Unit cost	Total cost
Golf balls	25 dozen	$18.00	$ 450.00
Golf tees	5600	$ 4.00 per hundred	$ 224.00
Spikes	135 sets	$ 3.85	$ 519.75
Gloves	85 pairs	$ 6.25	$ 531.25
		Total	$1,725.00

Section 7.3   Quantity Discounts   **173**

Verify the invoice extensions and the grand total. Using the following discount schedule, calculate the net amount:

$$\begin{aligned} \$1 - \$250 &= \text{none} \\ \$251 - \$750 &= 4\% \\ \$751 - \$1{,}500 &= 6\% \\ \$1{,}501 - \$3{,}000 &= 9\% \\ \$3{,}001+ &= 13\% \end{aligned}$$

SKILL EXERCISES

Figure the quantity discount and the net amount of the following items:

	Quantity	List price	Discount rate	Quantity discount	Net amount
1.	25	$52.50	3%	$ _____	$ _____
2.	18	$12.75	2%	$ _____	$ _____
3.	40	$35.50	4%	$ _____	$ _____
4.	96	$12.08	1.5%	$ _____	$ _____
5.	70	$16.40	2%	$ _____	$ _____

APPLICATIONS

1. What is the total quantity discount for the following invoice?

Quantity	Description	Unit price	Discount
72 barrels	Light beer	$51.36	11%
150 cases	2–12 pack	$ 4.56	14%
55 cases	Wine cooler/12-bottle case	$ 8.65	12%

2. The following price list for the Give and Go Parts House is set up in columns indicating the discounts for different quantities:

Name	Part no.	List price	Quantity	Discount
Spark plug	45-C	$ .79	over 50	10%
Filter	17-Y	$ 2.57	over 50	12%
Brake fluid	26-B	$ 3.45	over 25	8%
Points	15-P	$17.50	over 25	10%
Valves	78-V	$12.54	over 30	10%

Find the total cost to the Ringmaster Garage for:

Quantity	Number	Item	Net price
45	45-C	Plugs	$ _____
90	17-Y	Filters	$ _____
55	15-P	Points	$ _____
80	78-V	Valves	$ _____
		Total	$ _____

Answer to ✔ Check for Understanding
1. $1,569.75.

3. The Superior Wholesale Grocery Company prices its case lots and then gives a quantity discount for total items bought in one order. The price list is as follows:

Item	Description	Package	Price
Peas	12 oz. cans	case of 24	$ 7.56
Oatmeal	16 oz. boxes	case of 12	$13.07
Coffee	26 oz. cans	case of 6	$27.00
Beans	16 oz. cans	case of 24	$ 8.94

A notation is made in the price list that purchases of 20 to 40 units will receive a 3% discount and purchases of 41 or more units will receive an 8% discount. What is the amount billed on the following order?

        10 cases of peas   36 cases of coffee
        12 cases of oatmeal   25 cases of beans

4. How many cases would you need to buy to get the quantity discount if peaches sold for $8.65 per case and the cannery offered a quantity discount on purchases over $750 at one time?

5. The Gary Company ordered the following:

        500 board feet, mahogany; 87 cents per board foot
        800 board feet, pine; $1.18 per board foot
        400 squares of shingles; $18.50 per square
        50 pounds of nails; 29 cents per pound

What is the total invoice price if the quantity discount allows a 5% discount on purchases of $100 to $1,500, or a 7% discount if the purchase is over $1,500?

Trade Discounts

7.4

The **trade discount** is the amount that the **list price** or **suggested retail price** is reduced before the invoice is prepared. The trade discount may be quoted as a percent or as a dollar figure; generally it is expressed as a percent.

If the seller wishes to change prices, the trade discount can be adjusted rather than publishing a new catalog. The $\frac{P}{B \times R}$ formula also applies to trade discount calculations.

EXAMPLE 9   The Bryan Wholesale Co. listed chairs at $375 with a 40% trade discount. If the Exton Furniture Store ordered 12 chairs, what is their cost?

Solution 1: Unknown is the total list price (base):

    375 × 12 = 4,500   • Calculate total list price (base).

Unknown is the trade discount (part):

    P = B × R   • Formula for calculating the part.
    P = 4,500 × .40   • Enter variables into the formula.
                                    • 4500 is the list price, the base.
                                    • .40 is the discount rate.
    4,500 × .40 = 1,800   • Calculate the discount.

Unknown is the net amount:

    4,500 − 1,800 = 2,700   • Subtract to get net amount.

Solution 2: Unknown is the total list price (base):

$$375 \times 12 = 4{,}500$$ • Calculate total list price (base).

Unknown is the net amount rate:

$$100\% - 40\% = 60\%$$ • Calculate the net amount rate, the complement of 40%.

Unknown is the net amount (part):

$$P = B \times R$$ • The formula for part.
$$4{,}500 \times .60 = \$2{,}700$$ • Enter variables into the formula and calculate the part.
$$\$2{,}700$$ • The net amount. ☐

EXAMPLE 10 A stereo receiver lists at $329. If the retailer pays $214 net, what is the trade discount? What is the rate of discount?

Solution: Unknown is the trade discount?

$$\text{List price} - \text{Net price} = \text{Trade discount}$$

$$\$329 - \$214 = \$115$$ • Calculate the trade discount.

Unknown is the trade discount rate (rate):

$$R = \frac{P}{B}$$ • Formula for rate.

$$R = \frac{115}{329}$$ • Enter variables into formula.
• 115 is trade discount, the part.
• 329 is list price, the base.

$$\frac{115}{329} = .3495$$ • Calculate trade discount rate.

$$.3495 = 34.95\%$$ • Change decimal to percent. ☐

EXAMPLE 11 The trade discount on the auto parts order was 40%. If the net amount paid was $360, what was the list price?

Solution: Unknown is the net amount rate:

$$\text{List price rate} - \text{Trade discount rate} = \text{Net amount rate}$$

$$100\% - 40\% = 60\%$$ • Determine the net amount rate.

Unknown is the list price (base):

$$B = \frac{P}{R}$$ • Formula for unknown base.

$$B = \frac{360}{.60}$$ • Enter variables into formulas.

$$\frac{360}{.60} = 600$$ • Calculate the base.

$$\$600$$ • The list price. ☐

✔ **CHECK FOR UNDERSTANDING**

1. A catalog lists an item at $268.50. If the item carries a 26% trade discount, what is the net price?

176   Chapter 7   Customer Invoicing and Statements

2. Wheelbarrows listed at $76.80 are net priced at $52.10 to the retailer. What is the rate of discount?

3. The net amount paid by Collier's Men Clothing on a shipment is $3,485. If the trade discount is 20%, what is the list price?

SKILL EXERCISES

Calculate the unknown values using the part, base, rate formula and the information given for each of the following problems.

	List price	Trade discount percent	Trade discount	Net amount percent	Net amount
1.	$127.50	32%	$ _____	_____%	$ _____
2.	$827.60	40%	$ _____	_____%	$ _____
3.	$ 62.80	_____%	$ 9.42	_____%	$ _____
4.	$ 38.00	_____%	$ 7.60	_____%	$ _____
5.	$422.00	_____%	$ _____	_____%	$ 316.50
6.	$ 14.95	_____%	$ _____	_____%	$ 10.02
7.	$955.75	_____%	$ _____	72%	$ _____
8.	$127.35	_____%	$ _____	81%	$ _____
9.	$ _____	30%	$ _____	_____%	$ 12.36
10.	$ _____	25%	$ _____	_____%	$ 5.06

APPLICATIONS

1. An invoice was received at Joe's Carving Shop for the following:

Item	Quantity	List price	Discount
Knife	18	$7.50	35%
Block maple	15	$9.00	15%
Block pine	25	$6.50	17%
Oil, lemon	18	$2.40	30%

What is the total invoice price if there is also an additional 3% discount if over 50 items are ordered and billed on the same invoice?

2. Leo bought shoes for resale that had a net price of $56.59 and a trade discount of 48%. What was the list price per pair?

3. Shawna was purchasing police uniforms for the Right Stuff Shop. If the uniforms listed at $235 each and she had to stock 25 to cover the sizes, how much did they cost if the trade discount was 32%?

4. Furniture Discount Wholesalers advertise a couch at a list price of $525. If a retailer pays $383.25, what is the amount of the discount and the rate of the discount?

5. What is the list price of a car carrying a net price of $7,875 if the trade discount is 16%?

Answers to ✓ Check for Understanding
1. $198.69.   2. 32.16%.   3. $4,356.25.

6. If a pro shop pays $207 for golf equipment that lists for $375, what is the rate of the trade discount?

7. Bruce's Appliance Store buys refrigerators at a trade discount of 33%. What is the list price if a refrigerator's net price is $875?

8. What is the net price of an item that lists for $550 and has a trade discount of 42%? What is the net price rate?

9. What is the rate of discount if the list price is $476 and the net price is $287?

10. What is the list price of an item that has a net price of $986 if the trade discount is 38%?

Using Series Trade Discounts

The supplier may express the trade discount as a series of percents. They are used to provide for special-category customers, promotional pricing, or volume buying. The **series trade discounts** are expressed by listing sequential percents separated by a slash (/). For example, 30/15/10 means the list price less 30%, less 15%, less 10%. This discount is not the same as a 55% discount because series discounts use a reducing base concept. We still use our formula, base × rate, but the base changes before each multiplication.

EXAMPLE 12 Merchandise is listed at $520, with 40/15/5 trade discounts. What is the net price?

Solution: Unknown is first discount (part) and new base:

$P = B \times R$ · Formula for part.
$P = 520 \times .40$ · Enter variables into formula.
· 520 is the list price, the base.
· 40% is .40, the first rate.

Base = $520.00   · Calculate first discount; subtract to de-
520 × .40 = (−)208.00   termine new base.
         $312.00   · New base.

Unknown is second discount (part) and new base:

312 × .15 = (−)46.80   · Calculate second discount; subtract to
         $265.20   determine new base.

Unknown is third discount (part) and new base:

265.20 × .05 = (−)13.26   · Calculate third discount; subtract.
          $251.94   · Net amount paid.

PROBLEM SOLVING STRATEGY

The most common procedure used to figure the amount paid is to first change the discount percents into net price percents. To convert a series of discount percents into net price percents, subtract each discount percent from 100 percent. The answer, or *complement*, is the net price percent. Example 12 would be:

List price percent	100%	100%	100%
Discount percent	− 40%	− 15%	− 5%
Net price (complement) percent	60%	85%	95%

See Example 13 for its application.

178   Chapter 7   Customer Invoicing and Statements

EXAMPLE 13 What is the net price of merchandise listed at $125 with 30/20/5 trade discounts?

Solution: Unknown are the net price rates (rate):

List price	100%	100%	100%	• Calculate the rate of net price.
Discount	− 30%	− 20%	− 5%	
Net price	70%	80%	95%	

Unknown is the net price (part):

$125 × .70 × .80 × .95 = $66.50 • Convert the net percents to decimals and sequentially multiply times list price.

ANSWER: $66.50

✔ CHECK FOR UNDERSTANDING

1. A two-door refrigerator lists at $729, less 25/15/10 trade discounts. If the retailer wanted to stock 12 of them what would the total net price be?

2. Merchandise lists at $385.50. If a trade discount of 40/15 is offered, what amount will be saved from the list price?

SKILL EXERCISES

Determine the discount and the net price of the following:

	List price	Trade discount series	Discount	Net price
1.	$400	20/10/5	$ _____	$ _____
2.	$300	25/10/10	$ _____	$ _____
3.	$480	30/15	$ _____	$ _____
4.	$37.50	20/12.5/10	$ _____	$ _____
5.	$250	10/10/10	$ _____	$ _____
6.	$175	25/15/10	$ _____	$ _____
7.	$790	8/5/5	$ _____	$ _____
8.	$105	25/5	$ _____	$ _____
9.	$860	15/5/2	$ _____	$ _____
10.	$180	25/10/2	$ _____	$ _____

Answers to ✔ Check for Understanding
1. $5,019.17.   2. $188.90.

APPLICATIONS

1. The manager of Lincoln's Garage ordered 54 tires with an average list of $64.50. If the discount was 30/20/10 what did the 54 tires cost?

2. If a refrigerator lists at $976 and carries discounts of 25/15/12, what is the net price?

3. Bruce's Wood Products Co. bought hardwood chairs with a list price of $156. If the discounts were 40/20/10, what was their cost?

4. The Jeremy House ordered 40 soccer balls that had a list price of $4.56 with discounts of 30/20/10. What did the 40 balls cost?

5. The Jan Shoe Store ordered 160 pairs of shoes at an average list price of $55. If they carried discounts of 35/15/6, what was the store's total cost?

Calculating and Using Single Equivalent Discounts

The series discount may be expressed as a **single equivalent discount,** one rate representing the entire discount series. The single equivalent rate is used for comparison purposes when making purchasing decisions, or in calculating the net price. Let's look at the way to determine the net price again:

List price rates	100%	100%	100%
Trade discount rates	− 25%	− 15%	− 5%
Net price rates	75%	85%	95%

> The retailer will actually pay list price × .75, × .85, × .95. If we do not include the list price but multiply the net percents .75 × .85 × .95, we get the **single equivalent net rate** of .6056. Therefore, the net price is 60.56% of list.

To determine the single equivalent *discount* rate, we subtract:

List price rate	100.00%
(Subtract) Single equivalent net rate	− 60.56%
Single equivalent discount rate	39.44%

EXAMPLE 14 A trade discount of 20/10/5 is offered. What is the equivalent net percent and the equivalent discount percent?

Solution:

- Determine the net price rates:

List price rate in decimals 1.00 1.00 1.00
Discount rates in decimals − .20 − .10 − .05
Net price rates in decimals .80 .90 .95

.80 × .90 × .95 = .684 or 68.4%
1.00 − .684 = .316 or 31.6%

- Calculate the equivalent *net rate*.
- Calculate the equivalent *discount rate*.

EXAMPLE 15   The list price of a rotary lawn mower is $205 with a trade discount series of 15/10/5 if purchased in quantities over 25. Using the equivalent rates, calculate the net price and the discount.

Solution:

	List price
	Discount rates
	Net rates

- Determine the net price rates:

```
 1.00     1.00     1.00
- .15    - .10    - .05
 ----    -----    -----
  .85      .90      .95
```

.85 × .90 × .95 = .72675
1.00 − .72675 = .27325

- Calculate the equivalent net rate.
- Calculate the equivalent discount rate.

$$B \times R = P$$
$$\$205 \times .72675 = \$148.98$$

- Calculate net price; list price × net rate.

$$B \times R = P$$
$$\$205 \times .27325 = \$56.02$$

- Calculate discount; list price × discount rate.

✔ CHECK FOR UNDERSTANDING

1. A trade discount of 30/18/10 was quoted to a retailer. What is the equivalent discount rate?

2. What is the net price of a catalog item listed at $167.90 with a 15/20/8 trade discount? Use the equivalent net rate to solve this problem.

SKILL EXERCISES

Calculate the single equivalent net and discount rates for each of the following problems:

Trade discount	Single equivalent net rate	Single equivalent discount rate
1. 30/10/2	_____	_____
2. 20/10/6	_____	_____
3. 35/20/5	_____	_____
4. 40/20/2	_____	_____
5. 10/10/10	_____	_____
6. 40/25	_____	_____
7. 30/5/2	_____	_____

Answers to ✔ Check for Understanding
1. 48.34%.   2. $105.04.

8. 25/8/4   _____   _____

9. 20/10/5   _____   _____

10. 30/10/5   _____   _____

APPLICATIONS

1. What is the discount equivalent of a 30/20/10 series of discounts?

2. What is the equivalent net rate if a series of 25/15/10 discounts is applied?

3. Calculate the equivalent discount rate for a series of 35/25 discounts and use it to calculate the discount on an item with a list price of $646.80.

4. What is the equivalent net rate if the series discounts are 20/18/12? Using that rate and a list price of $1,246, figure the net price.

5. What is the equivalent discount rate if the series of discounts is 35/15/12?

Cash Discounts

7.5

While most companies offer 30-day open accounts (n/30) to their customers, the seller may wish to stimulate an earlier payment by offering an optional **cash discount.** These terms, 2/10, n/30, give the buyer the option of paying within 10 days and earning a 2% discount or waiting and paying the entire invoice within 30 days. If taken, the cash discount reduces the cost of merchandise to the retailer and the wholesaler receives most of the invoice amount 20 days sooner. All cash discounts are base × rate problems and vary only in some facets of their application.

Cash discount terms are included in the invoice and are in code. Three very common time frames on which cash discounts are based are: date of invoice, end of month (EOM), and receipt of goods (ROG).

> Cash discounts are allowed only on the goods purchased and not on any other charges on the invoice such as shipping charges, packing charges, and damaged or returned goods.

Cash Discount—Date of Invoice (Regular Dating)

> **The notation 2/10, n/30 means:**
>
> 2% cash discount *may be taken* if paid 10 days from *date of the invoice*.
>
> Net (total) amount *must be* paid within 30 days of the *date of the invoice*.

EXAMPLE 16   Appliance Repair received a shipment of parts that totaled $125.42, with terms 3/10, n/30. The invoice was dated June 6. What amount was sent if paid on June 14?

Solution 1:

    June 14 − June 6 = 8 days   • Determine the number of days it took to pay. Qualify? *Yes!*

Unknown is the discount (part):

$P = B \times R$ • Formula for part.
$P = \$125.42 \times .03$ • Enter variables into the formula.
    • 125.42 is invoice price, the base.
    • 3% is .03, the cash discount rate.

$\$125.42 \times .03 = \$3.76$ • Calculate the part, the discount.
$\$125.42 - \$3.76 = \$121.66$ • Calculate amount due (Invoice − discount).

Solution 2:

    June 14 − June 6 = 8 days   • Determine the number of days it took to pay. Qualify? *Yes!*

Unknown is the net amount rate:

$100\% - 3\% = 97\%$ • Calculate the amount paid *rate*.
$P = B \times R$ • Formula for part, the amount paid.
$B \times R = P$
$\$125.42 \times .97 = \$121.66$ • Calculate amount paid.

PROBLEM SOLVING STRATEGY

In working with time in business, both the beginning date and ending date cannot be counted. Common practice is not to count the beginning date but to count the ending date. In Example 15, we don't count June 6 but we count June 14. If you counted the 6th through the 14th on a calendar, you would get 9 days. When you subtract 14 − 6 you get only 8, the correct answer.

EXAMPLE 17   Colorado Pacific received an invoice for $648.60. It included a freight charge of $14.25 and merchandise to be returned of $146 and had terms of 4/10, n/60. If it is paid within the discount period, what is the total amount due?

Solution:

Total invoice	$648.60	• Determine the base of the discount.
	− 14.25	• Less freight.
	− 146.00	• Less merchandise returned.
	$488.35	• Merchandise only, the base.
$B \times R =$	P	
$\$488.35 \times .96 =$	$468.82	• Calculate net amount of *merchandise*.
	+ 14.25	• Add freight.
	$483.07	• Calculate total amount due.

✓ CHECK FOR UNDERSTANDING

1. On September 20, Harwick Wholesale sold material to Randolph Retail and sent an invoice for $1,262.80. Terms of the invoice were 2/10, n/30. If the invoice was paid September 29, how much should the payment be?

2. Charles Wholesale, whose invoice terms are 3/10, n/45, received a check for $234.56 from a customer who paid within the discount period. What is the amount of the invoice?

SKILL EXERCISES

Using the part, base, rate formula, compute the missing values. If necessary, review Example 11 on page 176 to solve for invoice amount, the unknown base in Problems 3 and 4.

	Invoice amount	Terms	Discount	Payment
1.	$625.00	2/10, n/30	$ _____	$ _____
2.	$952.80	3/10, n/30	$ _____	$ _____
3.	$ _____	2/10, n/60	$ _____	$150.00
4.	$ _____	3/10, n/45	$ _____	$369.64

Calculate the end date of the discount period.

	Date of invoice	Terms	Date goods received	Discount period
5.	Feb. 12	2/10, n/30	Feb. 14	_____
6.	Oct. 31	3/10, 2/20, n/30	Nov. 8	_____

APPLICATIONS

1. If the terms of an invoice are 3/10, n/30, and the amount of the check after the discount is $1,432, what is the amount of the original invoice?

2. The total invoice is for $865 and includes $42 freight and $22 in damaged goods. If the terms are 3/10, n/30, and it is paid within the discount period, what will the total payment be?

3. If an invoice dated July 7 has terms of 3/10, n/30, and the total invoice is $456, what will be the last date a cash discount can be taken? What will the payment be if paid within the discount period?

4. The Kelly Jean Shoppe received an invoice with terms of 3/10, n/60. If the invoice was for $1,245 including freight of $65 and damaged goods of $24, what is the cash discount the shop can take if paid within the discount period?

Answers to ✔ Check for Understanding
1. $1,237.54.   2. 241.81.

5. Rita's Boutique receives an invoice that includes merchandise for $1,180, packing and handling of $45, and freight of $46. The terms are 3/10, n/30, and the invoice is dated June 16. If Rita pays the bill on June 24, what should the total amount of the check be?

Cash Discount—End of Month (EOM)

The beginning date for figuring the discount period is the **end of the month (EOM)** in which the invoice is dated. This includes goods billed on or before the 25th of the month. However, goods billed after the 25th of any month are considered part of the following month's purchases. The mathematics of calculating the discount, the net amount, the original invoice, or their respective rates is identical to the math used in the previous section.

EXAMPLE 18 An invoice is dated October 23 with terms 2/10, n/30 EOM. What is the last date the invoice can be paid and still qualify for the discount?

Solution:
- Was the invoice dated on or before the 25th? *Yes!*
- The discount period begins the last day of the month in which it is dated—October 31.
- The discount is valid through November 10 because of the terms 2/10. *Do not count the 31st but count the 10th.*

EXAMPLE 19 If an invoice is dated September 27, with terms of 3/15, n/30 EOM, what is the last date it can be paid and still receive the discount?

Solution:
- Was it billed after the 25th of the month? *Yes!*
- Treat it as having been billed the next month.
- Beginning date is October 31. Last day of discount is November 15 because of terms, 3/15.

✔ CHECK FOR UNDERSTANDING

1. An invoice dated March 26 for $1,625 carried terms of 3/10, n/30 EOM. What amount should be paid on April 6? What amount should be paid on May 10?

2. An invoice dated July 4 for $1,776 had terms of 2/10, n/30 EOM. If the invoice included $1,700 for goods and $76 for shipping, what amount would be due if paid August 10?

SKILL EXERCISES

Each of the following examples is paid within the discount period. Using the part, base, rate formula, compute the missing values.

	Invoice amount	Terms	Discount	Payment
1.	$ 727.80	3/10, n/30 EOM	$ _____	$ _____
2.	$1,464.00	2/10, n/30 EOM	$ _____	$ _____

Answers to ✔ Check for Understanding
1. Pay $1,576.25 on both dates.   2. $1,742.

3. $ _____   4/10, n/60 EOM $ _____ $388.40

4. $ _____   2/10, n/30 EOM $12.50 $ _____

Calculate the end date of the following discount periods:

Date of invoice	Terms	End date of discount period
5. Nov. 29	2/10, n/30 EOM	_____
6. Sep. 16	3/15, n/30 EOM	_____
7. Jul. 6	2/10, n/30 EOM	_____
8. May 27	3/15, n/30 EOM	_____
9. Aug. 12	2/10, n/60 EOM	_____
10. Feb. 28	3/10, n/30 EOM	_____

APPLICATIONS

1. An invoice lists terms of 3/10, n/30 EOM. If the total invoice is $654, how much is the discount and what will be the latest allowable discount date if the invoice is dated August 16?

2. An invoice includes goods for sale, $875; freight charges, $45; and special handling, $135. The terms are 2/10, n/30 EOM, and the invoice is dated May 27. What is the total amount to be paid if paid within the discount period? What is the latest date the discount could be taken?

3. If the following invoice is paid on August 8, what is the amount of the check?

James Market Company

Terms: 3/10, n/30 EOM   Date: July 18

5 cases of peas	$4.25 each	$21.25
6 cases of asparagus	$7.98 each	$47.88
10 cases of beans	$9.60 each	$96.00
10 cases of corn	$5.60 each	$56.00

Prepaid freight: $17.25.

4. An invoice is for $1,234 with terms of 3/10, n/30 EOM dated November 16. What is the latest date the discount may be taken? If the discount is taken, what is the amount of the check?

5. A check for $2,400 is sent on December 9 by the Missy Company to cover an invoice billed with terms of 2/10, n/30 EOM. What was the amount of the original invoice if the cash discount was allowed?

6. The OK Company took a cash discount on an invoice with terms of 3/10, n/30 EOM. If the amount of the discount is $64.50, and the invoice is dated July 17, what is the amount of the invoice before the discount is applied?

Cash Discount—Receipt of Goods (ROG)

Certain types of merchandise are shipped by means which take an indeterminate time to be delivered. Such shipments might include appliances in carload lots, truckload shipments, and shipments by water. A **bill of lading,** which is a shipping document listing the merchandise, is noted when the goods are received. The discount period begins as of the **receipt of goods (ROG)** date. The math for calculating the discount, net amount, and rates is the same as that used in the previous two sections.

EXAMPLE 20 The terms on an invoice were 2/10, n/30 ROG. The invoice was dated January 12; goods were received on January 24. If the bill was to be paid on February 2, would a cash discount be valid?

Solution:

ROG date = Jan. 24	• Determine the beginning discount date.
Feb. 2 − Jan. 24 = 9 days	• Determine number of days it took to pay. Qualify for discount? *Yes!* □

EXAMPLE 21 An invoice dated May 16, with terms of 3/10, 2/20, n/30 ROG, for $1,262.50 was paid on May 29. If the goods were received on May 18, what was the check amount?

Solution:

May 29 − May 18 = 11 days	• Determine the number of days to pay.
11 days = 2% discount	• Determine the discount rate.
1.00 − .02 = .98	• Calculate the net amount, rate.
B × R = P	
$1,262.50 × .98 = $1,237.25	• Calculate amount due. □

✔ CHECK FOR UNDERSTANDING

1. Terms 2/10, 1/20, n/30 ROG are offered on an invoice dated February 6. Goods are received on February 17. The total of the invoice, including freight, is $622.40. Returned goods are $68.50, and freight is $15.49. If the goods are paid for on February 28, what is the amount due?

2. Goods on an invoice dated October 12 with terms 3/10, n/30 ROG were delivered on October 27. If the price of the goods was $682, with an additional $32 shipping charge, what was the payment if made on November 6?

Answers to ✔ Check for Understanding
1. $548.52.   **2.** $693.54.

SKILL EXERCISES

Using the part, base, rate formula, compute the following missing values:

	Invoice amount	Terms	Discount	Payment
1.	$2,748	4/10, n/30 ROG	$ _____	$ _____
2.	$ 482	2/10, n/60 ROG	$ _____	$ _____
3.	$ _____	3/10, n/30 ROG	$26.40	$ _____
4.	$ _____	2/10, n/30 ROG	$ _____	$1,587.40

Calculate the end date of the following discount periods:

	Date of invoice	Terms	Date goods received	Discount period
5.	Jun. 6	3/10, n/30 ROG	Jun. 12	_____
6.	Dec. 1	4/10, n/30 ROG	Dec. 8	_____
7.	Jun. 6	3/10, n/30 ROG	Jun. 23	_____
8.	May 16	2/15, n/30 ROG	Jun. 6	_____
9.	Aug. 10	4/20, n/60 ROG	Aug. 27	_____
10.	Mar. 6	3/10, n/30 ROG	May 6	_____

APPLICATIONS

1. What is the total amount due on an invoice for $580 with terms of 3/10, n/30 ROG if the goods are received on May 27 and the invoice is paid on June 7?

2. **Bright Furniture Manufacturer**

   Terms: 3/10, n/30 ROG

60	Chairs	$69.50 each
10	Tables	$99.00 each
15	Desks	$87.00 each

   Special packing: 3%

   Please extend the invoice and determine a merchandise total. If the invoice was paid on July 6 and the goods were received on June 29, what was the total paid?

3. An invoice with terms of 3/10, n/30 ROG was dated February 10. The goods were received on February 19. If the invoice was paid on February 27 with a check for $460, what was the amount of the original invoice?

4. Equipment billed on an invoice dated June 10 was delivered June 12. Terms were 2/10, n/30 ROG. The invoice, totaling $772.80, included $62.50 for shipping charges. If the invoice was paid on June 21, what was the amount of the remittance?

5. The Linda Travel Shoppe got an invoice for $28,000 dated May 16 with terms of 5/15, n/30 ROG. The merchandise was delivered June 6. What is the last date the cash discount can be taken and how much is it?

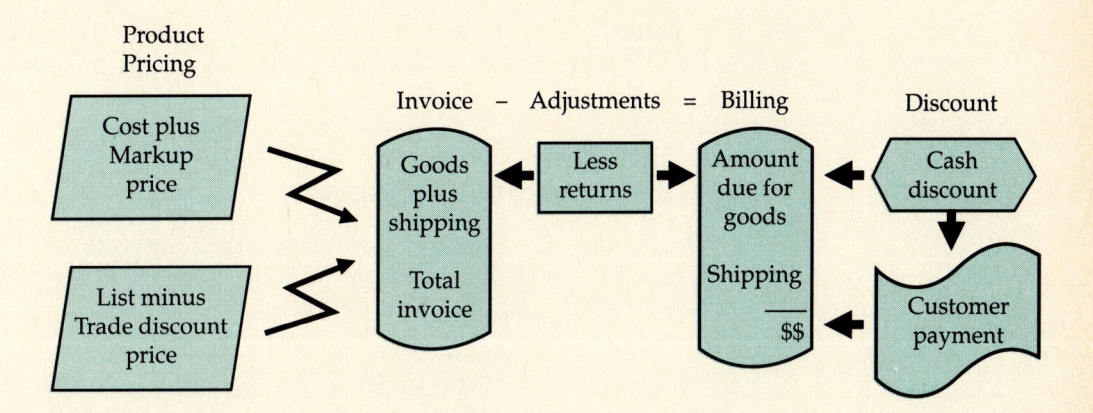

Invoice transmission sequence

Handling Partial Payments

Sometimes customers will not be able to pay an entire invoice during the cash discount period. They can take advantage of some of the discount by making a **partial payment** during the discount period. The customer determines an amount to pay. When the payment is received, the customer's account is credited for the amount of the check plus the discount. Since the partial payment is a part in the $\frac{P}{B \times R}$ formula, we have to divide the payment by its rate in order to determine the total amount of credit. The partial payment rate is 100% minus the discount rate. Not all 30-day accounts provide for partial payments. When they are authorized, however, the percent of discount is the same as that stated in the invoice terms.

EXAMPLE 22

A partial payment of $300 is made within the discount period on a $493 invoice with terms of 2/10, n/30. What amount will be due at the end of the net period?

Solution: Unknown is the net rate:

Original invoice rate	Discount rate	Payment rate
100%	− 2%	= 98%

· Determine the *rate* of payment.

Unknown is the amount of credit (base):

$$B = \frac{P}{R}$$

· Formula for base.
· Enter variables into the formula.

$$B = \frac{\$300}{.98}$$

· $300 is the part, the partial payment.
· 98% is .98, the net amount rate.

$$\frac{\$300}{.98} = \$306.12$$

· Calculate the amount of credit.

	Invoice	Amount of credit		Amount due	
	$493	− $306.12	=	$186.88	• Calculate the amount due.

EXAMPLE 23 An invoice for goods of $1,265 has terms of 3/10, n/30. If a partial payment of $1,000 is made, what is the amount of discount?

Solution:

100%	−	3%	=	97%	• Calculate the payment rate.
P	÷	R	=	B	
$1000	÷	.97	=	$1030.93	• Calculate the amount of credit.
$1030.93	−	$1000	=	$30.93	• Calculate the discount.

✔ CHECK FOR UNDERSTANDING

1. On January 12, Harrison Company sold Faldworth $875 worth of goods with terms 2/10, n/30. If a payment of $500 is made on January 17, how much will be due at the end of the net period?

2. An invoice dated October 30 with terms 3/10, n/30 ROG for $1,580.65 includes $38 for shipping. If $420 worth of goods were returned, and a partial payment of $800 was made on December 5, what amount was due at the end of the period?

SKILL EXERCISES

Complete the following partial payment problems. Payment within the discount period is assumed. Calculate the missing values.

	Terms	Invoice amount	Partial payment	Balance due
1.	4/10, n/45	$1,640.00	$1,000	$ _____
2.	2/10, n/30	$1,240.00	$ 840	$ _____
3.	3/10, n/30	$ 965.00	$ 565	$ _____
4.	3/10, n/30	$3,478.50	$2,000	$ _____
5.	2/10, n/30	$ _____	$ 250	$106.00
6.	4/10, n/60	$ _____	$1,500	$421.70
7.	3/10, n/45	$ _____	$ 500	$126.80
8.	2/10, n/30	$ _____	$ 800	$238.50

Answers to ✔ Check for Understanding
1. $364.80.   2. $335.91.

APPLICATIONS

Solve the following problems using the partial payment logic developed earlier:

1. A partial payment of $450 is submitted within the discount period on an invoice with cash terms of 4/10, n/30. How much will be credited for this payment?

2. An invoice for $1,620 carries terms of 3/10, n/30 EOM. How much is due at the end of the net period if a partial payment of $750 is made within the discount period?

3. Prichard Wholesale received a $3,000 partial payment on April 26. The $5,800 invoice contained cash discount terms of 2/10, n/30 ROG. The goods were delivered on April 18. What amount will be due at the end of the net billing period? What date is the remaining balance due?

Key Terms

Bill of lading (187)
Cash discount (182)
Complement (173, 176, 178)
Date of invoice (182)
EOM (end of month) (185)
Expedite delivery charge (164)
FOB (free on board) (159)
Invoice (162)
List price (172, 175)
Monthly statement (167)
Partial payment (189)

Prepaid shipping (163)
Purchase order (159)
Purchase requisition (159)
Quantity discount (172)
ROG (receipt of goods) (187)
Series trade discount (178)
Single equivalent discount (180)
Single equivalent net rate (180)
Suggested retail price (175)
Supplier (159)
Trade discount (175)

Looking Back

Invoices and statements are a very important part of the business paperwork system. They serve as the basis for cash expenditures and the appropriate accounting journal entries.

Review the invoices carefully for quantity discounts, cash discounts, and special charges. Remember only the total merchandise is the base for cash discounts. Do not include shipping charges, damaged goods, or special handling or packing charges in your cash discount calculation.

Trade discounts are based on the list price. The list price in many industries is the suggested retail price. The difference between the suggested retail price and the net price after the trade discounts are subtracted is the business markup. In the trade discount series, each discount is taken separately.

The real difference in the cash discount systems is simply establishing the date when the cash discount period begins.

Let's Review

1. If a couch lists for $786 and carries a 38% trade discount, what is the amount a retailer must pay for it?

2. What is the net cost of a refrigerator that lists for $850 if the trade discounts are 30/20/10?

3. You received the following purchase order from the Young Realty Company for office supplies. Please verify the extended items and check the total before typing the invoice. All items are in stock.

Quantity	Stock no.	Description	Unit price	Total
8 boxes	S154	Staples, 5,000 count	$ 5.20	$ 41.60
6 bundles	P172	Yellow pad, 20 per bundle	$11.25	$ 56.25
22	C125	Calendar refills	$ 3.18	$ 69.96
12 gross	E615	Disposable pens	$ 6.10	$ 73.20
			Total merchandise	$314.21
			Expedite delivery, 10%	31.42
			Grand total	$345.63

4. An invoice of $4,780 was dated August 26 and had terms of 3/15, n/30 EOM. If it is paid on October 13, what will be the amount of the check?

5. If an invoice for $650 has terms of 2/10, n/30 and is dated August 25, what is the latest date the cash discount can be taken? What is the total amount paid if remitted September 4?

6. An invoice for $4,560 was dated September 1. With goods received September 17 and terms of 3/10, n/30 ROG, how much will be due if paid in full on September 25?

7. Using the following information contained on a purchase order, extend the prices and calculate the grand total of the invoice.

Quantity	Catalog no.	Description	Unit price	Total
16	1462M	Jogging suit	$58.75	$ _____
16	1482W	Jogging suit	$63.25	$ _____
24	1624M	Jogging shoe	$48.15	$ _____
24	1534W	Jogging shoe	$44.60	$ _____
			Prepaid shipping	$ 26.75
			Grand total	$ _____

8. If the trade discount is 40%, what is the rate of the net amount?

9. Prepare a statement of account for Wadsworth Sports, 987 Peach Street, Kansas City, MO 64108 for the month of April using the following information:
4/1, Balance $842.57; 4/20, Payment received, $516.27; 4/15, Invoice No. 6306, $419.86; 4/17, Payment received, $326.30; 4/23, Invoice No. 6410, $212.15; 4/25, Payment received, $419.86.

```
Date                                    KING DISTRIBUTORS
                                        462 Bison Drive
To                                      Milwaukee, WI   53221-4723   (414) 555-7225
```

Date	Items	Debits	Credits	Balance

10. An invoice is dated April 7 with terms of 2/10, n/30 ROG, and goods are received April 26. If a check for $496.50 is received on May 5, what was the amount of the original invoice?

11. What is the equivalent discount of a series of 25/15/5 discounts?

12. How much would be credited to an account if a partial payment of $750 was received on an invoice with terms of 3/15, n/45 EOM paid within the discount period?

13. A partial payment of $1,200 was made in the discount period on an invoice. The cash discount terms were 2/10, n/30. If the amount still owed is $225.51, how much was the original invoice?

14. If a series of 30/20/10 discounts is quoted, what is the net rate equivalent?

Chapter Test

1. The following items were purchased with terms of 2/10, n/30:

    75 cases   24 cans per case   38 cents per can
    100 gallons $3.65 per gallon
    35 cartons $6.95 per carton

    If the shipping charges are $12.60 and 15 cases are returned, what would be the amount of the check if paid within the discount period?

2. A December 1 invoice for goods totaling $1,242.80 had terms of 3/10, 2/15, n/30. What would be the amount of the check if paid on December 14?

3. Terms of 4/10, n/45 ROG were offered on a $112.60 invoice dated March 11. The goods were delivered on March 24. If the payment was submitted on April 4, what amount of discount should be taken?

4. A barrel manufacturer was ready to pay an invoice dated April 16 for $1,642.80 with terms 3/10, 2/15, n/30 EOM. The payment date was May 16. What amount of discount can be deducted from the total?

5. Shoes with a list price of $38.80 were bought with a trade discount of 22%. What is the net price?

6. What is the equivalent net amount rate if the discount series is 20/10/5?

7. Prepare an invoice for Oceanside Sporting Goods, 5005 Beach Drive, San Diego, CA 92101. Use the current date; Invoice No. 3256; Customer Order No. 1508; FOB San Diego; Terms: 3/15, n/45. The following items were shipped: Qty. 4 dozen No. B149 baseballs, horsehide cover, unit price $38.30 per dozen; Qty. 1 case (48 dozen) No. G692 golf balls, orange, unit price $8.75 per dozen; Qty. 18 No. G146 canvas golf bags, unit price $7.75; shipping $21.45.

GROSS & JAMES SPORTING GOODS
1485 Grassland Blvd.
Raleigh, NC 27610

Invoice

Date

Our Order No.

Cust. Order No.

F.O.B.

Terms

Quantity	Description	Unit Price	Total

8. How much discount can be taken from an item listed at $67.20 with 12/9/5 trade discounts?

194 Chapter 7 Customer Invoicing and Statements

9. Verify the following purchase order by checking the extended prices and the totals. Make any necessary changes.

Quantity	No.	Description	Unit price	Total
6	J42L	Sports jacket, blue	$72.50	$435.00
8 pairs	S36	Slacks, gray, 36" × 30"	$22.90	$183.20
10	S34	Slacks, white, 15" × 34"	$12.00	$210.00
12	B32	Briefs, white, 32–34, 3 per	$ 2.70	$ 32.40
			Grand total	$860.60

10. Complete the body of the statement of account using the following information. Be sure and keep a running balance. 8/1, Balance: $1,546.90; 8/8, Payment Invoice #6250, $890.15; 8/9, Invoice #6406, $1,050.40; 8/10, Payment Invoice #6306, $656.75; 8/16, Payment Invoice #6406, $1,050.40; 8/26, Invoice #6542, $915.45.

Date	Items	Debits	Credits	Balance

11. What is the equivalent discount rate of the series 25/15/8?

12. An invoice of $6,840 contained cash discount terms of 3/10, n/45. If a partial payment was made during the discount period for $4,000, what amount would be due at the end of the net period?

PART III

Interest and Personal Finance

Simple Interest

8

OBJECTIVES

When you complete this chapter you will be able to:

- *Calculate simple interest using different values for principal, rate, and time. (8.1)*
- *Calculate the number of days in the interest calculation using various available methods. (8.2)*
- *Calculate the principal, the rate, or the time when the other values in the interest formula are known. (8.3)*
- *Calculate the bank charge and the proceeds when discounting promissory notes and drafts. (8.4)*

COMING UP

Is there interest about interest? You bet there is! Whether you are an individual or a business, borrowing money or investing extra cash requires an understanding of interest—the charge for using money or the reward for investing it.

There are several factors that must be known before you can calculate interest. The amount of interest you pay or earn is affected by the amount you borrow or invest. The amount of time the loan or deposit is in effect and the interest rate are other prime considerations.

Business also uses promissory notes. Because you may choose to discount a note at the bank, it is important to know how the process works. This chapter shows you how to calculate interest and how the discounting process works.

Simple Interest

8.1

Simple interest is the charge for the use of money when the charges are based only on any balance owed. You are familiar with the interest formula, $\frac{I}{P \times R \times T}$, from your work in Chapter 4. Until now, we assumed that all loans were for one year. To solve for interest (I) we multiplied **principal** (P) times rate (R) and really ignored the time element (T).

The interest formula is the Part = Base × Rate formula we used earlier but modified to accommodate the special terminology of finance. When we multiply $1,300 times 9% ($B \times R$) we get $117, the interest for one year.

> Adding time to the formula means we are going to adjust the full year by multiplying it by a fraction for time less than a year or by a whole number or mixed number when the time is greater than a year: $1300 \times .09 \times 1$ (full year) $= 117$; $1300 \times .09 \times \frac{1}{2}$ (half year) $= 58.50$; or $1300 \times .09 \times 3$ (3 years) $= 351$.

The fraction we use to express the time involved in a loan can vary with how the terms are stated. Or, it may be affected by your preference as to how it should be entered into a calculator. For example, a loan of *three months* could be shown as a fraction of a year in months $\frac{3}{12}$; in days $\frac{90}{360}$; as a reduced fraction $\frac{1}{4}$; or as a decimal (.25). Because the majority of loans in business are for less than or more than one year, we need to work with the time fraction.

EXAMPLE 1

An individual borrows $800 at 8% for 1 year. How much is the interest? Would the answer be different if it were borrowed for only one-half year?

Solution A:

$I = P \times R \times T$ · Unknown is the interest.
$P \times R \times T$ · Formula for interest.
$800 \times .08 \times 1$ · Enter variables into formula.
$800 \times .08 \times 1 = 64$ · Calculate one year's interest.

ANSWER: $64 · The interest.

Solution B:

$I = P \times R \times T$ · Unknown is the interest.
$P \times R \times T$ · Formula for interest.
$800 \times .08 \times \frac{1}{2}$ · Enter variables into the formula.
$800 \times .08 \times \frac{1}{2} = 32$ · Calculate one-half year's interest.

ANSWER: $32 · The interest.

EXAMPLE 2 Cora borrowed $1,200 at 9% for 3 years. How much interest did she pay?

Solution: Unknown is 3 years' interest:

$P \times R \times T = I$
$1200 \times .09 \times 3 = 324$

- Enter variables into the formula and calculate 3 years' interest.

CALCULATOR TIP

There are several ways to figure interest using your calculator. The most efficient way is to multiply the numerators across and divide by the denominators. Using Example 1, visualize its setup:

$\dfrac{800 \boxed{\times} .08 \boxed{\times} 1}{1 \quad 1 \quad 2}$;

Multiply $800 \boxed{\times} .08 \boxed{\times} 1$, then $\boxed{\div} 1 \boxed{\div} 2 \boxed{=} 32$.

Because multiplying a number by one or dividing a number by one doesn't change the answer, we can shorten our calculation to:

$800 \boxed{\times} .08 \boxed{\div} 2 \boxed{=} 32$.

✔ **CHECK FOR UNDERSTANDING**

1. The James Corporation borrowed $3,000 for one-fourth of a year at a rate of 9%. What is the interest charge?

2. Stude Corporation borrowed money at 10% to assist its cash flow. If it borrowed $800 for one-eighth of a year, what is the amount of interest?

3. If the Moody Company borrows $2,400 at a local bank at a rate of $11\frac{1}{2}\%$, what is the amount of interest if the money is borrowed for 4 years?

SKILL EXERCISES

Calculate the following amounts of interest using $I = P \times R \times T$:

	Principal	Rate	Time	Interest
1.	$ 900	9%	3 yrs.	$ _____
2.	$1,500	11%	$\frac{1}{3}$ yr.	$ _____
3.	$2,400	10%	$\frac{3}{4}$ yr.	$ _____
4.	$1,800	$11\frac{1}{2}\%$	4 yrs.	$ _____
5.	$ 250	$10\frac{3}{4}\%$	$\frac{1}{4}$ yr.	$ _____
6.	$ 850	14%	2 yrs.	$ _____
7.	$3,000	8%	$\frac{1}{6}$ yr.	$ _____

Answers to ✔ Check for Understanding
1. $67.50.   2. $10.   3. $1,104.

8.	$1,250	7%	$\frac{1}{4}$ yr.	$ _____
9.	$1,000	$8\frac{1}{2}$%	$\frac{1}{8}$ yr.	$ _____
10.	$2,100	$9\frac{1}{4}$%	$\frac{1}{2}$ yr.	$ _____

APPLICATIONS

1. The Pick-Em-Up Potato Company borrowed $725 for three-quarters of a year. If the finance company charged a 12% interest rate, how much interest did the company pay?

2. The Atlas Corporation needs to borrow money for 1 year. If it borrows $2,500 at a rate of $9\frac{1}{4}$%, what amount of interest must be repaid?

3. Fresh Vegetable Produce must borrow $800 for one-half year. If National Finance Company charges 11% and Edgewater Bank and Trust charges $10\frac{1}{2}$%, how much would the firm save by borrowing from the bank?

4. If a deposit of $500 is made in a simple interest account at $6\frac{1}{4}$%, what is the total in the account at the end of one-fourth of a year?

5. The Learning Corporation borrowed $2,800 at 11%. If they pay the money back in 3 years, how much interest will they pay?

6. The All-Hours Service Center needs to borrow $20,000 for a period of 4 years. If the best interest rate available is $7\frac{3}{4}$% annually, how much interest will it pay over the 4-year period?

7. A construction company plans to borrow $15,000 for three-fourths of a year at 10%. If it could pay the loan off in 6 months, how much interest would the company save?

8. The Clearview First Bank advertises an interest rate of 9% on loans of $5,000 for 1 year. If, however, you borrow only $4,000, the rate jumps to $10\frac{1}{2}$%. Would the Clearview Lawn Service save any money by borrowing $5,000 rather than the $4,000 they need? If so, how much?

9. Farr Farms Inc. borrowed $8,500 for one-third of a year at $11\frac{1}{4}$%. How much interest will be due when the loan is repaid?

10. A home improvement loan for $3,750 carries an interest rate of 13%. If the loan is not repaid for 5 years, how much total interest will be paid?

The Time Fraction

8.2

In previous problems you were given time as a fraction, such as $\frac{1}{4}$, $\frac{3}{4}$, or $\frac{1}{3}$ year. In business, the time is normally given in either years or months, or transaction dates are given and you develop your own time fraction. The number of days we use to represent the calendar year also varies.

The Numerator of the Time Fraction

The numerator is calculated in one of two ways. If the problem specifies a **30-day month,** we calculate the time between two dates, assuming that all months have 30 days. Or, if the problem asks us to use **exact time,** we use the exact number of days in each month including using 29 days if February is involved in a leap year calculation. See Table 8.1.

TABLE 8.1
Number of Days in Each Month

Month	No. of Days	Month	No. of Days
January	31	July	31
February*	28	August	31
March	31	September	30
April	30	October	31
May	31	November	30
June	30	December	31

* In a leap year, February has 29 days. Any year other than a century year that divides evenly by 4 is a leap year. In a century year (1900, 2000, etc.) the year must divide evenly by 400 in order to be a leap year. Leap year affects *only exact-time* calculations.

EXAMPLE 3 Calculate the number of days between the following dates, using both the 30-day method and the exact-time method: January 28 and March 26, 1991.

Solution:

30-day method

```
  30 days in January
 -28 = date of note
   2 days left in January
 +30 days in February
 +26 days used in March
  58 total days
```

- Determine the number of days left in opening month. Subtract the transaction date.
- Add full-month days.
- Add days in ending month.
- Total all days

Exact-time method

```
  31 days in January
 -28 = date of note
   3 days in January
 +28 days in February
 +26 days in March
  57 total days
```

- Determine the number of days left in opening month.
- Add full-month days.
- Add days in ending month.
- Total all days.

There is another way to figure the time in the 30-day-month method. *The key is remembering that there are 30 days between the same dates one month apart.* Thus, there are 30 days between May 18 and June 18.

EXAMPLE 4 Using the 30-day-month method, calculate the number of days between July 16 and September 24. Then calculate the number of days between May 30 and August 12.

Solution A:

$$\underbrace{1 \quad + \quad 1}_{} = 2 \text{ months}$$

Jul. 16   Aug. 16   Sep. 16

$$2 \times 30 = 60 \text{ days}$$
$$\text{Sep. 24} - \text{Sep. 16} = +8 \text{ days}$$
$$\text{Total days} = 68 \text{ days}$$

- Determine the number of full months; change to days.
- Calculate number of days from ending date in the first step and ending date in problem.
- Add to get total days.

Solution B:

$$\underbrace{1 \quad + \quad 1 \quad + \quad 1}_{} = 3 \text{ months}$$

May 30   Jun. 30   Jul. 30   Aug. 30

$$3 \times 30 = 90 \text{ days}$$
$$\text{Aug. 30} - \text{Aug. 12} = -18 \text{ days}$$
$$\text{Total days} = 72 \text{ days}$$

- Determine number of full months and calculate the days.
- Calculate number of days from ending date in first step and ending date in problem.
- Subtract to get total days. □

✔ CHECK FOR UNDERSTANDING

1. Using 30-day months, calculate the number of days between July 18 and November 11.

2. If we use 30-day months, how many days are there between January 18, 1992, and May 5, 1992?

3. Calculate the number of days between April 26 and December 25 using the exact-time method.

4. Using the exact-time method, calculate the number of days between February 9 and June 9.

Calculating Exact Time Using a Time Table

In Table 8.2 note that the days of the calendar are simply numbered 1 through 365. To calculate the exact number of days between two dates, locate the first date on the table and write down the number it represents. Look up the second date and write down the number it represents. Subtract the two numbers.

Answers to ✔ Check for Understanding
1. 113 days.   **2.** 107 days.   **3.** 243 days.   **4.** 120 days.

TABLE 8.2
Exact Time Table

Day of Month	Jan.	Feb.	Mar.	April	May	June	July	Aug.	Sep.	Oct.	Nov.	Dec.
1	1	32	60	91	121	152	182	213	244	274	305	335
2	2	33	61	92	122	153	183	214	245	275	306	336
3	3	34	62	93	123	154	184	215	246	276	307	337
4	4	35	63	94	124	155	185	216	247	277	308	338
5	5	36	64	95	125	156	186	217	248	278	309	339
6	6	37	65	96	126	157	187	218	249	279	310	340
7	7	38	66	97	127	158	188	219	250	280	311	341
8	8	39	67	98	128	159	189	220	251	281	312	342
9	9	40	68	99	129	160	190	221	252	282	313	343
10	10	41	69	100	130	161	191	222	253	283	314	344
11	11	42	70	101	131	162	192	223	254	284	315	345
12	12	43	71	102	132	163	193	224	255	285	316	346
13	13	44	72	103	133	164	194	225	256	286	317	347
14	14	45	73	104	134	165	195	226	257	287	318	348
15	15	46	74	105	135	166	196	227	258	288	319	349
16	16	47	75	106	136	167	197	228	259	289	320	350
17	17	48	76	107	137	168	198	229	260	290	321	351
18	18	49	77	108	138	169	199	230	261	291	322	352
19	19	50	78	109	139	170	200	231	262	292	323	353
20	20	51	79	110	140	171	201	232	263	293	324	354
21	21	52	80	111	141	172	202	233	264	294	325	355
22	22	53	81	112	142	173	203	234	265	295	326	356
23	23	54	82	113	143	174	204	235	266	296	327	357
24	24	55	83	114	144	175	205	236	267	297	328	358
25	25	56	84	115	145	176	206	237	268	298	329	359
26	26	57	85	116	146	177	207	238	269	299	330	360
27	27	58	86	117	147	178	208	239	270	300	331	361
28	28	59	87	118	148	179	209	240	271	301	332	362
29	29	—	88	119	149	180	210	241	272	302	333	363
30	30	—	89	120	150	181	211	242	273	303	334	364
31	31	—	90	—	151	—	212	243	—	304	—	365

EXAMPLE 5 Calculate the exact number of days between May 26 and September 18.

Solution:

$$261 - 146 = 115$$

- Go down the left-hand column of Table 8.2 to 26, the beginning day of the loan. Move across horizontally to the column headed "May," the beginning month of the loan, and write down 146.
- Do the same for September 18, the ending date of the loan, and write down 261.
- Subtract the two to find the exact number of days.

Section 8.2 The Time Fraction

EXAMPLE 6 Calculate the exact number of days between October 9 and March 19.

Solution: A second calculation is necessary because of changing years:

        282   • Locate the intersection on Table 8.2 of October 9. Write the number down.

  365 − 282 = 83   • Calculate number of days *left* in the year.

Total days + 78   • Locate March 19 on the table and *add* its number of days to the previous step.
            161

CALCULATOR TIP

In figuring exact time, locate the ending date first and enter it into the calculator. Subtract the number representing the beginning date.

In Example 5, enter 261 [−] 146 [=] 115
In Example 6, enter 365 [−] 282 [+] 78 [=] 161

PROBLEM SOLVING STRATEGY

The exact time table does not make adjustments for leap year. If you have a time period involving February 29, add 1 day to your normal calculation. A leap year time table is available if you need it in your business.

✔ CHECK FOR UNDERSTANDING

1. If a loan dated on November 12 was due on February 18, how many exact days were there?

2. If the Harding Company signs loan papers on January 22, 1992, and the loan is due on May 21 of that year, what is the time of the note in exact days?

3. What is the exact number of days between May 2 and October 7?

4. The Picturesque Motel signed a loan on December 5, 1991, for $5,000 that was due on March 9, 1992. How many exact days are in the loan?

SKILL EXERCISES

Using both the 30-day-month and the exact-time methods, compute the number of days for each of the following examples. Watch for leap year problems.

			30-day-month method	Exact-time method
1.	November 16	March 22	_____	_____
2.	January 25	May 4	_____	_____

Answers to ✔ Check for Understanding
1. 98 days.   **2.** 120 days.   **3.** 158 days.   **4.** 95 days.

3. March 31   August 30   _____   _____

4. December 12, 1990   March 20, 1991   _____   _____

5. January 16, 1992   April 4, 1992   _____   _____

6. November 11   February 19   _____   _____

7. June 9   October 14   _____   _____

8. October 7   January 15   _____   _____

9. February 4, 1991   April 26, 1991   _____   _____

10. July 6   November 15   _____   _____

The Denominator of the Time Fraction

The denominator of the time fraction also involves two systems—**ordinary interest** and **exact interest**.

> Ordinary interest is based on 12 months of 30 days each, or a total of 360 days in a year. Exact interest means 365 days, except in leap years when 366 is used.

No calculations are required in getting the denominator. Identify the number of days to use according to problem terminology.

EXAMPLE 7 The Easy-to-Move Transfer and Storage Company needs to borrow $2,000. The loan is dated March 4 and is due May 4, with a stated interest rate of $12\frac{3}{4}\%$. Using 30-day months and ordinary interest, calculate the amount of interest that is due on May 4.

Solution: Unknown is the number of days:

```
      1  +  1
    ┌───┐┌───┐
Mar. 4  Apr. 4  May 4
         2 × 30 = 60 days
```
• Two 30-day months.

Unknown is the interest:

$$P \times R \times T$$
$$2000 \times .1275 \times \frac{60}{360}$$

- Enter variables into formula.
- 2000 is the principal.
- .1275 (12.75%) is the rate.
- $\frac{60}{360}$ is fraction of year.

$$2000 \times .1275 \times \frac{60}{360} = 42.50$$

- Calculate the interest.

ANSWER: $42.50.

Section 8.2   The Time Fraction   **207**

EXAMPLE 8   MacGregor Retail Service applied for a $600 loan on August 8. It will be an ordinary interest loan for four months at an interest rate of $10\frac{1}{2}\%$. What is the interest charge?

Solution: Unknown is four months' interest:

$$P \times R \times T = I$$
$$600 \times .105 \times \frac{4}{12} = 21$$

- Calculate the interest; time in months is ordinary interest. Place 4 months over 12 months or change to 120 days over 360 days.

ANSWER: $21

EXAMPLE 9   Because of its cash-flow requirements, Nutty-Fruity Ice Cream Shoppe had to borrow $500. If the note is dated January 21, 1992, and is due on April 4 at a rate of 9%, what is the amount of interest, based on exact time and exact interest?

Solution: Unknown is the interest involving leap year:

$$P \times R \times T = I$$
$$500 \times .09 \times \frac{74}{366} = 9.10$$

- Calculate interest; the denominator is exact days (365) *plus 1 day* for leap year.

ANSWER: $9.10

Banker's Method

Using exact time to figure the number of days between dates in the loan and using ordinary days (360) as the denominator of the fraction are commonly referred to as the **banker's method.** Using the banker's method results in greater interest than using the exact time over exact days (365 or 366).

EXAMPLE 10   A local bank quoted the following terms to Knee-High Toddler Wear: A loan application dated July 16 for $350 using exact time, ordinary interest at a rate of $12\frac{1}{2}\%$ is due on August 15. What is the total amount due?

Solution: Unknown is total amount due, principal + interest:

$$P \times R \times T = I$$
$$350 \times .125 \times \frac{30}{360} = 3.65$$
$$+350.00$$
$$\overline{\$353.65}$$

- Calculate using 30 exact days and 360 ordinary days.
- Add principal.
- Total due.

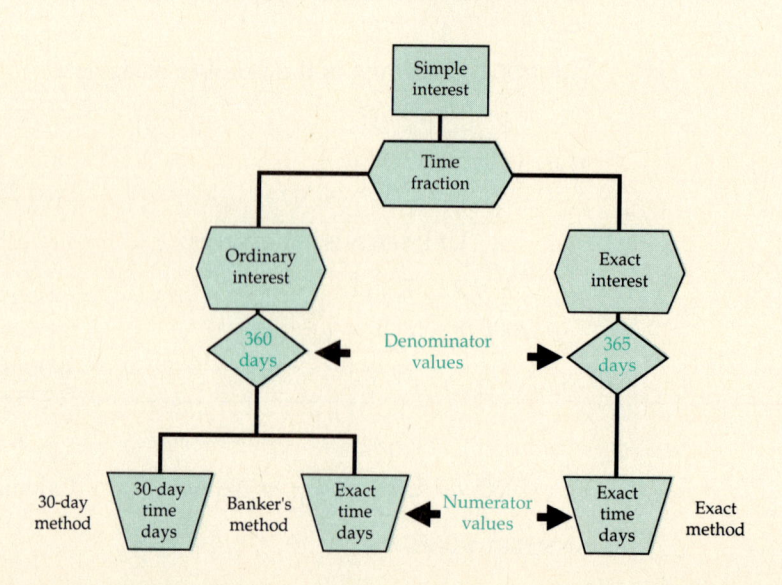

208   Chapter 8   Simple Interest

CHECK FOR UNDERSTANDING

1. Calculate the total amount due on a $1,500, 120-day loan at $11\frac{1}{4}$% using ordinary interest.

2. XYZ Corporation invested $5,000 at $8\frac{3}{4}$%, depositing the money on May 2. Using 30-day months and ordinary interest, calculate the amount of interest due if the money was left on deposit until November 7.

3. If $475 is deposited for 100 days at $13\frac{3}{4}$%, how much interest will be earned, using the exact-interest method?

4. The Eze-Freeze Food Corp. borrowed $6,000 at 10%. If the loan was dated on December 12 and is due on April 11 (not a leap year), what is the total amount due on the loan? Use the banker's method.

5. The Hungry Burger Corporation needs to borrow $10,000 for 75 days. The Ready-to-Loan Finance Company quotes the following terms: $9\frac{3}{4}$%, exact interest. The Third National Bank quotes its terms as $9\frac{3}{4}$% ordinary interest. Which is the better deal for Hungry Burger and by how much?

6. Spread and Soft Margarine Company invested $2,500 on March 26 at $12\frac{3}{8}$%. If the money is left with the financial institution until October 12, and if exact time and exact interest are used, what is the total amount in its account on October 12?

SKILL EXERCISES

Calculate interest using both the ordinary and the exact methods:

	Principal	Rate	Time	Ordinary interest	Exact interest
1.	$13,348	10%	100 days	$ _____	$ _____
2.	$ 7,615	8%	240 days	$ _____	$ _____
3.	$22,930	$9\frac{1}{2}$%	150 days	$ _____	$ _____
4.	$ 850	11%	60 days	$ _____	$ _____
5.	$ 4,235	$7\frac{3}{4}$%	120 days	$ _____	$ _____

Answers to ✔ Check for Understanding
1. $1,556.25.   2. $224.83.   3. $17.89.   4. $6,200.   5. $200.34 vs. $203.13; $2.79 savings with Ready-to-Loan.   6. $2,669.52.

APPLICATIONS

Apply the skills learned in calculating interest to the following problems:

1. The Brandy House signed a loan paper on January 14. If its due date is March 15 and it's not a leap year, how many days are there in a loan term using 30-day months? Using exact time?

2. What is the total repayment on a 60-day note for $325 at 13% if the ordinary method of interest calculation is used?

3. See-Thru Glass has $2,100 to invest. Using exact time and exact interest, calculate how much would be in the account on November 22 if the money is deposited on July 25 at $9\frac{3}{4}$%.

4. Trying to pay the smallest amount of interest possible, U-Drive-It Rental received the following quotes from two banks: Hollywood Bank—$5,000 at $12\frac{1}{4}$% for 90 days using exact interest; Westmoor Bank—$5,000 at $12\frac{1}{2}$% for 90 days using ordinary interest. Which is the better deal for U-Drive-It Rental, and by how much?

Calculate the number of days in both time periods in Problems 5 through 9 using the 30-day-month and the exact-time methods. For calculating exact time, calculate or use the time table.

			30-day month	Exact-time method
5.	February 8	September 19	_____	_____
6.	October 10, 1991	January 10, 1992	_____	_____
7.	January 26, 1992	May 4, 1992	_____	_____
8.	May 9	October 9	_____	_____
9.	December 27, 1989	March 27, 1990	_____	_____

10. U-Pick-Em Tomato Company deposited $800 for six months at $8\frac{3}{8}$%. If interest on the savings account is figured using ordinary interest, how much was in its account at the end of six months?

11. A loan dated February 5 was paid on October 5. If the loan was for $400 with an interest rate of 8% and the institution used the banker's method, how much was paid?

12. Surplus Warehouse Inc. needs to borrow $12,000 to buy a new truck. If it agrees to pay the loan plus interest 120 days later, what is the amount of the check if we use ordinary interest and the bank charges 13%?

Solving for Other Factors in the Simple Interest Formula

8.3

There are times in business when a factor other than interest needs to be calculated. The same formulas used in Chapter 4 will be used here:

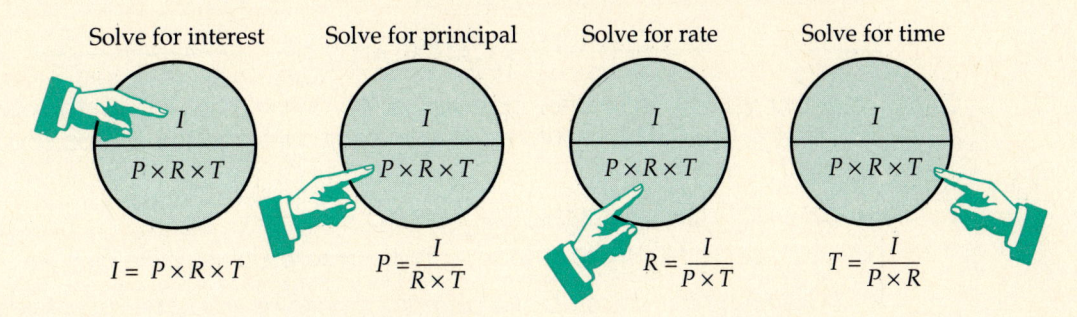

Solve for interest: $I = P \times R \times T$

Solve for principal: $P = \dfrac{I}{R \times T}$

Solve for rate: $R = \dfrac{I}{P \times T}$

Solve for time: $T = \dfrac{I}{P \times R}$

Solving for Principal

When solving for principal, we use the formula: $P = \dfrac{I}{R \times T}$. Divide the amount of interest by the product of the interest rate times the time.

EXAMPLE 11

Suppose you know that at the end of 180 days you will need $500. You also know that the current interest rate is 8%. What you need to calculate is the amount of money (principal) that you need to deposit now to earn $500 in 180 days at 8% if we use ordinary interest.

Solution: Unknown is the principal:

$$P = \dfrac{I}{R \times T}$$ · Identify the proper formula.

$$P = \dfrac{500}{.08 \times \dfrac{180}{360}}$$ · Enter the variables into the formula.
- $500 is the interest.
- .08 (8%) is the rate.
- $\dfrac{180}{360}$ is the time fraction.

$.08 \times \dfrac{180}{360} = .04$ · Calculate the denominator.

$\dfrac{500}{.04} = 12{,}500$ · Calculate the principal.

ANSWER: $12,500 · The principal.

EXAMPLE 12

Front Range Dairy would like to know how much money they would have to invest at $9\frac{1}{2}\%$ for 90 days in order to earn $950 using exact interest.

Solution:

$$P = \dfrac{I}{R \times T}$$ · Identify the proper formula.

$$P = \dfrac{950}{.095 \times \dfrac{90}{365}}$$ · Enter variables into the formula.

$.095 \times \dfrac{90}{365} = .0234246$ · Calculate the divisor.

To preserve the accuracy of your final answer, do not round the divisor—leave as many places as you have calculated!

$$\frac{950}{.0234246} = 40{,}555.66$$ • Calculate the principal.

ANSWER: $40,555.66 • The principal.

CALCULATOR TIP

In Example 11 or 12 after calculating the divisor, place it in memory. After entering the dollars of interest, it can be recalled as the divisor, saving the need to re-enter it:

.095 × 90 ÷ 365 = .0234246 [M+]   Divisor to memory
950 ÷ [MR] = 40,555.66   Divisor recalled to complete problem

Don't round the divisor; leave as many places as you have calculated!

✔ CHECK FOR UNDERSTANDING

1. The Solid Rock Concrete Company needs to earn $600 in interest within 200 days. If the deposit will earn 10% exact interest, how much is the deposit?

2. If simple interest on a deposit left for two months at 14% was $75, how much was the original deposit if the bank uses the ordinary interest method?

3. If ordinary interest on an 11%, 120-day loan was $293.33, what was the principal on the loan?

Solving for Rate

The formula for finding the rate is $R = \dfrac{I}{P \times T}$.

EXAMPLE 13 What rate would be needed to earn $14.06 in interest if we invested $750 for 75 days at ordinary interest?

Solution: Unknown is the rate:

$$R = \frac{I}{P \times T}$$ • Identify the proper formula.

$$\frac{14.06}{750 \times \frac{75}{360}}$$ • Enter variables into formula.

$$750 \times \frac{75}{360} = 156.25$$ • Calculate the divisor.

$$14.06 \div 156.25 = .089984$$ • Calculate the rate.

ANSWER: 9% • The rate.

Answers to ✔ Check for Understanding
1. $10,950.   2. $3,214.29.   3. $7,999.92.

---

212   Chapter 8   Simple Interest

EXAMPLE 14 What interest rate was used if $2,400 invested for 240 days, exact interest, showed total interest of $201.21?

Solution:

$$R = \frac{I}{P \times T}$$ • Identify the proper formula.

$$R = \frac{201.21}{2400 \times \frac{240}{365}}$$ • Enter variables into formula.

$2400 \times \frac{240}{365} = 1578.0821$ • Calculate the divisor.

$201.21 \div 1578.0821 = .1275028$ • Calculate rate.

ANSWER: 12.75% • The rate.

✔ CHECK FOR UNDERSTANDING

1. A construction company needs to earn $400 on money invested during the next year. If it has $25,000 to invest, what is the minimum rate of interest that would be acceptable?

2. If a company needs to borrow $1,200 for the next 60 days and is quoted $17 of ordinary interest as the charge, what rate is it paying?

3. A company paid $369.86 in exact interest on a $15,000 loan for 75 days. What interest rate was the finance company using?

Solving for Time

When solving for time, we use the formula $T = \frac{I}{P \times R}$. Because the formula gives the *time* answer in decimal form, the following examples illustrate two methods of adjusting the formula to show time in days.

EXAMPLE 15 What amount of time would be necessary to earn $106.03 if we invested $2,400 at $7\frac{1}{2}\%$ at exact interest?

Solution 1: Unknown is time in days:

$$T = \frac{I}{P \times R}$$ • Identify the proper formula.

$$T = \frac{106.03}{2400 \times .075}$$ • Enter variables into formula.

$2400 \times .075 = 180$ • Calculate divisor.
$106.03 \div 180 = .5890555$ • Calculate time in decimal form.
$365 \times .5890555 = 215.00572$ • Convert decimal to actual days; multiply number of days in year (365) times .5890555.

ANSWER: 215 days

Note: $2400 × .075 = $180 is the amount of interest earned in one year. When we divide 106.03 by 180 we get .5890555, the fraction of a year in decimal form it takes to earn the interest. Convert this to days by multiplying the decimal times the exact days in the year. (Answer = 215.)

Answers to ✔ Check for Understanding
1. 1.6%. **2.** 8.5%. **3.** 12%.

If we wish to calculate time in the same manner we used to calculate principal and rate, in calculating the divisor we need to incorporate the step of dividing by 365 or 360.

Solution 2:

$$T = \frac{I}{P \times R}$$ · Identify the proper formula.

$$T = \frac{106.03}{2400 \times .075}$$ · Enter variables into formula.

$2400 \times .075 = 180 \div 365 = .4931506$ · Calculate the divisor.
$106.03 \div .4931506 = 215.00531$ · Calculate time.

ANSWER: 215 days

Note: The .4931506 from the first step is the amount of interest earned per day. In order to calculate the number of days it takes to earn the total interest, divide the $106.03 by the interest earned per day—$106.03 \div .4931506 = 215.00531$ days.

EXAMPLE 16 How many days would be needed to earn $90 if we invested $1,800 at 10% ordinary interest?

Solution:

$$T = \frac{I}{P \times R}$$ · Identify the proper formula.

$$T = \frac{90}{1800 \times .10}$$ · Enter variables into formula.

$1800 \times \frac{.10}{360} = .5$ · Calculate the divisor.

$90 \div .5 = 180$ · Calculate time.

ANSWER: 180 days

✔ CHECK FOR UNDERSTANDING

1. For how long will a firm need to leave $4,000 on deposit at 9% if it wishes to earn $500 in ordinary interest?

2. A commercial bank charged interest of $13.81 on a loan of $1,400 at 12%, using exact interest. How many days did the loan run?

3. Two lending institutions quoted the same interest charge of $23.75 on a $2,000 loan at 9.5%. Institution A was using ordinary interest; Institution B, exact interest. What was the length of the loan for each institution?

SKILL EXERCISES

Calculate the principal, the rate, or the time, using ordinary interest for Problems 1–5 and exact interest for Problems 6–10:

	Interest	Principal	Rate	Time
1.	$ 34.50	_____	11.5%	30 days
2.	$ 17.50	$ 600	_____	75 days

Answers to ✔ Check for Understanding
1. 500 days. 2. 30 days. 3. A, 45 days; B, 46 days.

214   Chapter 8   Simple Interest

	Interest	Principal	Rate	Time
3.	$ 57.00	$ 950	12%	_____
4.	$ 29.25	$1,300	9%	_____
5.	$ 20.35	_____	11%	45 days
6.	$912.33	_____	9.25%	45 days
7.	$ 96.16	$ 650	12%	_____
8.	$ 9.12	$ 435	_____	60 days
9.	$ 43.40	$1,100	_____	180 days
10.	$ 16.18	_____	7%	135 days

APPLICATIONS

Apply your new skills to the following set of problems:

1. What is the maximum amount a laundromat can borrow if it can afford to pay only $175 in interest? The lending institution is using ordinary interest, $10\frac{1}{2}$%, and the loan is for 60 days.

2. The Kiddie Land Development Company must borrow $100,000 for 6 months. If it can pay only $6,000 in ordinary interest, what is the maximum rate of interest it can pay?

3. In the previous problem, how much would Kiddie Land save if it could borrow money at 10.25%?

4. In order to pay this year's taxes, AAA Land Company must raise $8,500. If it has $88,000 to invest at 11% exact interest, how many days must it have its money on deposit to raise the necessary tax money?

In Problems 5–7, use exact interest.

	Interest	Principal	Rate	Time
5.	$5,375.34	$ 60,000	_____	300 days
6.	$7,876.71	$125,000	10%	_____
7.	$ 19.57	_____	11.75%	90 days

Section 8.3 Solving for Other Factors in the Simple Interest Formula

8. A firm needs to borrow $4,250 for a period not to exceed 120 days. If a lending institution quotes an interest figure of $155.83, what rate of interest must they be using if they are using ordinary interest?

9. Triple E Concrete will pay $750 in interest on an exact interest loan taken out for 75 days. If the rate is 13.5%, how much did they borrow?

10. The Durable Siding Corp. borrowed $725 at 14% interest. If they must pay $5.64 in interest, what was the length of the loan assuming ordinary interest?

Discounting Negotiable Instruments

8.4

A **negotiable instrument** is a written business paper having value that can be transferred from one person or one business to another. The most common negotiable instrument is a check. A person or business receiving a check may pass that instrument on to another person or business by endorsing it. A **promissory note** may also be negotiable. As Figure 8.1 shows, it is an unconditional promise to pay a certain sum of money within a specified period of time. A promissory note is usually interest bearing.

FIGURE 8.1
Promissory note

(A) $900 Colorado Springs, CO (B) December 12, 19 8X
(C) 90 days AFTER DATE I PROMISE TO PAY TO THE
ORDER OF Chemistry Inc. (D)
AT THE BANK OF COLORADO of Colorado Springs, CO
Nine Hundred and No/100-- Dollars
AND INTEREST OF 9 ½% (E)
NO. 18 DUE March 12, 198X (F)   (G) Fred Peterson

(A) *Principal (face) in figures and words*
(B) *Date*
(C) *Term of note*
(D) *Payee*
(E) *Rate of interest (interest-bearing note)*
(F) *Due date*
(G) *Maker or drawer*

Some negotiable instruments may be noninterest bearing; these include checks, **time and sight drafts,** and **trade acceptances.** In a draft, three parties are involved—the drawer, the drawee, and the payee. Figure 8.2, a sight draft, shows the drawer (Johnnie Horton) is requesting the drawee (Bank of Colorado) to pay the payee (Langley Products Company) $250. Since this is a sight draft, it must be paid or refused on sight (presentation).

FIGURE 8.2
Sight draft

```
_____$250_____  Colorado Springs, CO        January 3  , 19 8X
                At sight                                PAY TO
THE ORDER OF _____Langley Products Company_____
Two Hundred Fifty and No/100------------------------------ Dollars
VALUE RECEIVED AND CHARGE TO ACCOUNT OF
TO  Bank of Colorado                   Johnnie Horton
    1521 South 8th
    Colorado Springs, CO 80906         Langley Products Company
```

In working with time drafts and trade acceptances, the drawee must accept these instruments. If the terms, for example, are 90 days after sight, the term of the draft will not start until the drawee writes his or her acceptance on the note. See Figure 8.3.

FIGURE 8.3
Trade acceptance

```
No.  36      Colorado Springs, CO        August 25 , 19 8X
TO   Best Warehouse         Colorado Springs, CO 80911
ON   September 9   PAY TO THE ORDER OF   Ourselves
ACCEPTED AT   Colorado Springs, CO   ON  August 31 , 19 8X
PAYABLE AT    Bank of Colorado                      BANK
BANK LOCATION  Colorado Springs, CO 80906
BUYER'S SIGNATURE  Best Warehouse
BY AGENT OR OFFICER  Marilyn Wade
                              Rawlings Wholesalers
                              BY  Arlene Beckman
```

The Discounting Process—Interest-Bearing Notes

If negotiable instruments are held to the **maturity date,** the calculation of the amount of any interest due is accomplished by using the simple interest formula. However, many times the instruments are sold to a financial institution before maturity. This process of selling a note is called **discounting,** and the calculation of the proceeds involves several steps:

1. Figure the maturity date.
2. Figure the maturity value.
3. Figure the days in the discount period.
4. Figure the amount of the discount.
5. Figure the amount of the proceeds.

Maturity Date

The **maturity date** is the due date. In calculating the maturity date, time can be quoted in two ways: time in days and time in months or years.

Time in Days. When figuring the maturity date with time quoted in days, use exact time.

EXAMPLE 17 Calculate the maturity date of a note dated August 25 with a time period of 90 days.

Solution:

August 25 = 237	• Determine beginning date from time table.
+ 90	• Add time of note.
Maturity date = 327	• On time table, move down column to 327; match row and column.
ANSWER: 327 = November 23	

Time in Months or Years. When the time is quoted in months or years, the maturity date is that same day of the month, plus the months or years quoted as terms of the note. This is our 30-day-month method.

EXAMPLE 18 What is the maturity date of a note dated February 9 that has a time period of four months?

Solution:

February 9	• Determine beginning date.
+ 4 months	• Add time of note in months.
June 9	• Maturity date is the 9th of the month four months later.

Note: *Do not* change four months to 120 days and use the time table.

Maturity Value

On an interest-bearing note, the **maturity value** is the principal plus the interest for the full term of the note. Interest is calculated using the formula $I = P \times R \times T$.

EXAMPLE 19 The Rapid Tech Engineering Company received a promissory note of $650 at 9% for 60 days. What is the maturity value?

Solution:

$$P \times R \times T = I$$

$$650 \times .09 \times \frac{60}{360} = 9.75$$

• Calculate interest; use interest formula.

$$\begin{array}{r} 9.75 \\ +650.00 \\ \hline 659.75 \end{array}$$

• Add the principal.
• Maturity value.

Note: This text uses ordinary interest throughout the discounting process.

✔ CHECK FOR UNDERSTANDING

1. A local bowling alley signed a promissory note on May 13. If it runs for 6 months, what is the maturity date?

2. Friends Bar and Grill signed a $3,000 promissory note on October 8. If the note runs for 90 days at 10%, what is the maturity date? The maturity value?

3. What is the maturity date and the maturity value of a note dated June 21 running for 180 days, a principal of $9,300, and an interest rate of 8.5%?

Answers to ✔ Check for Understanding
1. November 13.   2. January 6; $3,075.   3. December 18; $9,695.25.

SKILL EXERCISES

Find the maturity date and the maturity value of the following notes:

	Principal	Rate	Time	Note dated	Maturity date	Maturity value
1.	$ 500	11.5%	45 days	Mar. 4	_____	$ _____
2.	$1,200	9.5%	3 months	May 2	_____	$ _____
3.	$ 900	8.0%	6 months	Aug. 18	_____	$ _____
4.	$3,000	14.25%	100 days	Apr. 4	_____	$ _____
5.	$ 350	10.0%	30 days	Nov. 11	_____	$ _____

Discount Period

The **discount period** is the number of days the bank holds the note. Therefore, it is the number of days between the day of discount and the maturity date. There are three important dates in every discounting note situation: the beginning date (day note was dated or accepted); the maturity date, which can be calculated; and the **day of discount** (the day the note is sold to the bank).

EXAMPLE 20 A company received a note dated August 8 with a term of 60 days. It was discounted at the bank on August 30. How many days are there in the discount period?

Solution:

Aug. 8 =	220	• Determine from table the day note is dated.
	+ 60	• Add term of the note.
	280	• Maturity date is October 7.
Aug. 30	− 242	• Subtract day of discount using the number from the time table.
	38	• Days in the discount period. □

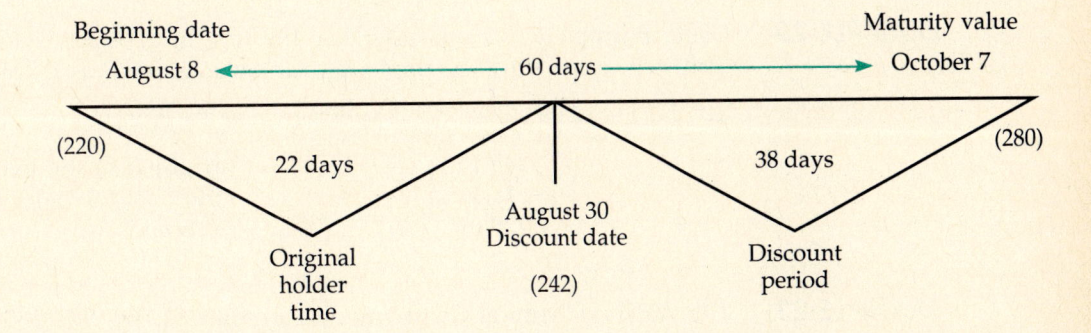

Beginning date — August 8 (220) ←— 60 days —→ Maturity value — October 7 (280)

22 days — Original holder time — August 30 Discount date (242) — 38 days — Discount period

Bank Discount

The **bank discount** is the amount of money the bank charges for discounting. It is calculated by multiplying maturity value times the discount rate times the days in the discount period. Although the names of the components are different, the formula is the same as interest: $I = P \times R \times T$ or Bank discount (I) = Maturity value

Section 8.4 Discounting Negotiable Instruments   **219**

(P) × Discount rate (R) × Discount days (T). The discount rate is the percentage charged by the bank to complete the discounting process. It may or may not be the same as the interest rate on the face of the note.

EXAMPLE 21 A company receives a note for $725 at 10% for 90 days. If it is dated May 21 and is discounted on June 19 at 12%, what is the bank discount?

Solution: Step 1: Calculate the maturity date:

$$\begin{aligned} \text{May 21} &= 141 \\ &+ 90 \\ &\,231 \end{aligned}$$

- Beginning date of note from table.
- Add term of note in days.
- Maturity date, August 19. (Needed in Step 3.)

Step 2: Calculate the maturity value:

$$P \times R \times T = I$$
$$725 \times .10 \times \frac{90}{360} = 18.13$$
$$+725.00$$
$$743.13$$

- Calculate interest.
- Add principal.
- Maturity value. (Needed in Step 4.)

Step 3: Calculate the discount period:

$$\begin{aligned} \text{Maturity date} &= 231 \\ &- 170 \\ \text{Discount days} &\,\,\,\,\,61 \end{aligned}$$

- August 19 from Step 1.
- Subtract *day of discount*; use day from time table for June 19. (Needed in Step 4.)

Step 4: Calculate the bank discount:

Maturity value		Discount rate		Days of discount		Discount
743.13	×	.12	×	$\frac{61}{360}$	=	$15.11

ANSWER: Discount $15.11

Proceeds

The amount of money remaining after the bank discount has been subtracted from the maturity value is called the **proceeds.** The proceeds belong to the person or organization who discounts the note.

EXAMPLE 22 Using Example 21 as our problem, the first four steps have been completed. The fifth step, calculating the proceeds, can be completed as follows:

Solution: Step 5: Calculate the proceeds:

$$\begin{aligned} &743.13 \\ &-\,\,\,15.11 \\ &728.02 \end{aligned}$$

- Begin with the maturity value.
- Subtract the bank discount.
- Proceeds.

EXAMPLE 23 The Watson Chemical Company discounted a $1,700, 9%, 180-day promissory note. If the note was dated on May 20, and was discounted on September 4 at 11%, what were the proceeds?

Solution: Step 1: Calculate maturity date:

$$\begin{aligned} \text{May 20} &= 140 \\ &+180 \\ &\,320 \end{aligned}$$

- Beginning day of note from table.
- Add number of days in the note.
- Maturity date, November 16.

220 Chapter 8 Simple Interest

Step 2: Calculate the maturity value:

$$P \times R \times T = I$$
$$1700 \times .09 \times \frac{180}{360} = 76.50 \quad \text{• Calculate interest.}$$
$$+1700.00 \quad \text{• Add principal. (Use in Step 4.)}$$
$$1776.50$$

Step 3: Calculate the discount days:

$$\begin{array}{r} 320 \\ -247 \\ \hline 73 \text{ days} \end{array}$$

- Maturity date from Step 1.
- Less day of discount from table, September 4.

Step 4: Calculate the discount:

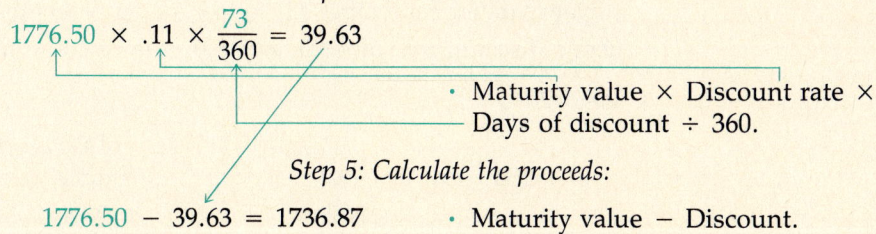

$$1776.50 \times .11 \times \frac{73}{360} = 39.63$$

- Maturity value × Discount rate × Days of discount ÷ 360.

Step 5: Calculate the proceeds:

$$1776.50 - 39.63 = 1736.87 \quad \text{• Maturity value − Discount.}$$

ANSWER: $1736.87

✔ CHECK FOR UNDERSTANDING

1. A $10,000, 8%, 120-day note dated July 12 was discounted on August 26 at 9.5%. What are the proceeds if ordinary interest was used?

2. A bank officer received a $600, $7\frac{3}{4}$%, 30-day note that was dated September 15 for discounting. If the officer uses the same discount rate as the interest rate, what amount of money will the customer receive if it is discounted on September 20?

SKILL EXERCISES

Using the information provided, calculate the discount period in days, the amount of discount, and the amount of proceeds for the following notes:

	Maturity value	Discount rate	Maturity date	Day of discount	Discount period (days)	Discount	Proceeds
1.	$507.19	12%	Apr. 18	Apr. 8	_____	$_____	$_____
2.	$1,279.69	10%	Aug. 2	Jun. 3	_____	$_____	$_____
3.	$936.00	11%	Feb. 18	Jan. 18	_____	$_____	$_____
4.	$3,118.75	15%	Jul. 18	Jun. 1	_____	$_____	$_____
5.	$350.00	10%	Dec. 11	Nov. 29	_____	$_____	$_____

Answers to ✔ Check for Understanding
1. $10,063.48. 2. $600.63.

Discounting Noninterest-Bearing Notes, Drafts, and Trade Acceptances

The discounting of a **noninterest-bearing note,** draft, or trade acceptance is the same as that described in the previous section except there is no maturity value calculation. Since the note contains no interest rate, the principal **(face)** of the note is the maturity value when we calculate the discount.

Noninterest-bearing notes can occur when a bank discounts the promissory note on the same day it is written. The customer receives the face of the note less the discount and repays only the face amount on maturity. Time drafts and trade acceptances are very rarely interest bearing.

EXAMPLE 24 Willow Court Finance Company discounts a 90-day, noninterest-bearing trade acceptance dated September 11, for $4,250 on November 22. If the financial institution uses a discount rate of $9\frac{3}{4}\%$, what are the discount and the proceeds?

Solution:

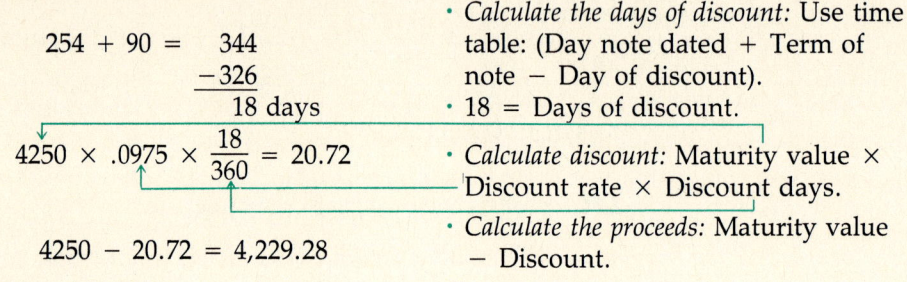

$$254 + 90 = 344$$
$$-326$$
$$18 \text{ days}$$

$$4250 \times .0975 \times \frac{18}{360} = 20.72$$

$$4250 - 20.72 = 4,229.28$$

- *Calculate the days of discount:* Use time table: (Day note dated + Term of note − Day of discount).
- 18 = Days of discount.
- *Calculate discount:* Maturity value × Discount rate × Discount days.
- *Calculate the proceeds:* Maturity value − Discount.

ANSWER: $4,229.28

✔ CHECK FOR UNDERSTANDING

1. The Fetch-It Dog Bone Company received a noninterest-bearing note dated May 27 for $450 with terms of three months. It was discounted at the bank on July 8 at 6%. What will the discount and the proceeds be if ordinary interest is used?

2. A $2,200 noninterest-bearing draft dated April 26 with a time period of 100 days was left for discounting on June 4. If the bank uses a discount rate of 5%, what is the amount of the bank discount?

SKILL EXERCISES

Calculate the amount of the discount and the proceeds on the following notes using exact time and ordinary interest.

Note dated	Principal	Rate	Time	Discount rate	Discount date	Discount	Proceeds
1. Jan. 4	$1,000	13%	1 month	13%	Jan. 9	$ _____	$ _____
2. Nov. 25	$1,750	—	45 days	11%	Dec. 20	$ _____	$ _____
3. Aug. 9	$2,400	9.25%	90 days	12%	Aug. 25	$ _____	$ _____

Answers to ✔ Check for Understanding
1. $3.75, $446.25.   2. $18.64.

4. Oct. 20 $1,375   10%   120 days   13%   Nov. 29 $ _____ $ _____

5. May 11 $5,000   —   6 months   9%   Aug. 11 $ _____ $ _____

APPLICATIONS

1. EZE-Roll Lawn Turf Company accepted a promissory note for 1,000 square yards of sod from the Hercules Greenhouse on September 15. Terms of note were $3,200 at 9.25% for 120 days, ordinary interest. If EZE-Roll discounts the note at 12% on October 31 at Greenbriar State Bank, what will the proceeds be?

2. The Hercules Greenhouse issued a trade acceptance for 500 square yards of sod to We'll-Build-Em Construction Company for $1,600. We'll-Build-Em accepted the instrument on August 2 for a period of 60 days, ordinary interest. If Hercules discounts the noninterest-bearing trade acceptance on August 22 at a rate of $13\frac{1}{2}\%$, how much will Hercules receive from the bank?

3. Washer Manufacturing Inc. issued a time draft to Laundromats Inc. for $6,000, payable in 90 days after sight. Laundromats Inc. accepted the draft on March 13. On May 13, Washer discounted the draft at Century Commercial Bank at 12.75%. What were the proceeds?

4. The Rawlings Appliance Company accepted a 45-day note for $350 from customer A. R. Reynolds. The note was dated June 20, with an interest rate of 10.5%. When Rawlings discounted the note on June 30, the bank charged a discount rate of 11%. How much was added to the Rawlings account at the bank?

5. On July 22, T.V. Wholesalers purchased 15 table model color sets for $7,500, giving the Electronic Manufacturing Company $3,000 in cash and a 30-day non-interest-bearing note for the balance. If the manufacturer discounts the note in 10 days at a rate of 10.5%, what will the proceeds be?

6. Calculate the proceeds on a $1,300 note with interest at 8% and a time of 75 days dated December 2 if it is discounted at 9.5% on February 2.

7. Friendly Supermarkets plans to discount a 60-day, $4,000 note at 10% on April 25. If the maturity date of the note is May 25 and it draws interest at 8.75%, how much will Friendly receive in proceeds?

8. The Hughes Landscape Company agreed to repay a $1,500 loan within 105 days. If the bank discounts the note on the day it was dated at 9.5%, what will the bank discount and the proceeds be?

9. The Luft Sporting Goods Corp. received a promissory note for $3,750 dated January 14. The note was for 90 days and carried an interest rate of 10%. If it will be discounted on March 13 at 12.5%, what will the proceeds be?

10. A promissory note for $12,000 was discounted on May 3 at 13%. If the note was for 10% and a period of 3 months, what were the proceeds if the bank held it for 37 days?

Key Terms

Bank discount (219)
Banker's method (208)
Day of discount (219)
Discount period (219)
Discounting (217)
Exact interest (207)
Exact time (203)
Face (222)
Maturity date (217)
Maturity value (218)
Negotiable instruments (216)

Noninterest-bearing note (222)
Ordinary interest (207)
Principal (200)
Proceeds (220)
Promissory note (216)
Sight draft (216)
Simple interest (200)
30-day months (203)
Time draft (216)
Trade acceptance (216)

Looking Back

Your success in this chapter is keyed to understanding the terms. The terms used direct the procedure to be followed. The numerator of the time fraction can be calculated using either exact time or 30-day months. The denominator is determined by whether you are using ordinary or exact interest. Thirty-day months will always have a denominator of 360 days or 12 months. Exact time can be used as a numerator for either ordinary or exact interest. Using exact time as the numerator and ordinary interest as the denominator is commonly referred to as the banker's method.

Although the discounting of negotiable instruments is presented in one continuous process, there are actually two separate transactions taking place. One is calculating the amount that the bank will receive from the instrument, the second is calculating the amount the individual business will receive from the bank after the discount.

Let's Review

1. The Freightway Express Company accepted a noninterest-bearing promissory note, dated May 12, with a face value of $3,600, and a term of 90 days. If the company discounts the note on June 20 at 8%, what will the proceeds be?

2. What is the ordinary interest due on a loan of $725 running for 3 months if it has a rate of 13%?

3. The Bare Furniture Company needs to borrow $18,000 for 120 days. If it can pay a maximum of $630 in ordinary interest, what is the maximum interest rate the company can pay?

4. Lakefront Furniture Company discounts a noninterest-bearing trade acceptance at $10\frac{3}{8}$% on March 22. If it had a face value of $3,300, a time of 180 days, and was dated on December 12, what will the proceeds be?

5. The Realty Credit Union currently is using 14% exact interest on its consumer loans. The Better Rate Finance Company is using 14% ordinary interest. On a 180-day loan of $850, which financial institution will receive the larger amount of interest and by how much?

6. Riteway Dealers Inc. needs to earn $400 in the next 180 days. If the financial institution is using a 10% interest rate and exact interest, how much must be deposited?

7. The Home Food Freezer Corp. accepted a promissory note for $1,200, dated on August 25 for 120 days at 11%. If the firm discounts the note on October 9 at 12%, what will the discount be?

8. The Better Ride Tire Company plans to deposit $6,000 in an account that earns 8% exact interest. If the company wants to earn $150 in interest, how many days must it leave the money on deposit?

9. A promissory note is dated on May 5 with terms of 3 months and 11% interest. If the note is discounted on July 22, how many days are there in the discount period?

10. If Mike Porter borrows $1,450 on July 22 and pays it back on October 11 at 11.5%, how much interest will he pay if the banker's method is used?

Chapter Test

1. Small Rock Sand and Gravel accepted a promissory note on March 19 from Big Tree Nursery for $1,200 at 9.5% for 60 days. If on April 2 the company discounts the note at Third National at 11%, what will the proceeds be?

2. The Barger Company borrows $2,000 on May 22 at 10.5% and plans to repay it on July 15. What will the total payment to the bank be if the terms are 30-day months at ordinary interest?

3. A company has $50,000 to deposit in an account that pays 9% ordinary interest. How long will it take to earn interest of $4,750?

4. If a local laundry puts $2,500 in an account for 120 days and is promised interest of $67.71, what interest rate will be used?

5. A trade acceptance showing no interest rate, a term of 45 days, and an amount of $25,000 was discounted 20 days after it was received. What were the proceeds if the bank charged a 12.5% discount rate?

6. Straight Line Roofing Company will earn $109.25 in simple interest on money deposited at 14.25% for 240 days. What amount was deposited?

7. Calculate the number of days between the following dates using both the 30-day-month and the exact-time methods.

			30-day	Exact-time
A.	January 5, 1992	March 20, 1992	_____	_____
B.	May 11	August 15	_____	_____
C.	December 21, 1992	February 21, 1993	_____	_____
D.	April 16	June 5	_____	_____
E.	July 17	September 11	_____	_____

8. A three-month certificate of deposit for $10,000 will earn 8% interest. If it carries ordinary interest, what is the value of the certificate on its maturity date?

9. A loan of $1,900 was dated on February 21, 1991. It had an interest rate of 10% and a due date of May 20, 1991. Using exact time and exact interest, calculate the amount of interest due on May 20.

10. A loan dated October 31 for $12,000 and a rate of 9% was paid on January 16. Using the banker's method, calculate the amount of interest.

11. Dave Acre needs to borrow $1,250 for three-fourths of a year. Calculate the amount of interest he would pay if he were able to borrow the money at $9\frac{3}{8}\%$.

12. Using the banker's method, calculate the total amount to be repaid on a loan of $4,250 taken out on July 16 and repaid on November 20. The interest rate is 9%.

13. Speedy Bicycle Shop accepted an $800 promissory note from a customer that was dated on November 28. The note runs for 90 days with an interest rate of 11%. If it is discounted on February 1 at a rate of 12.5%, what are the proceeds?

14. Using 30-day months, calculate the amount of interest that will be paid on a loan dated April 29 for $8,260 with an interest rate of 14% that is repaid on October 5.

15. A loan for $3,380 was dated on December 10. If the lending institution uses exact time and exact interest and charges an interest rate of 11.5%, what amount of interest will be paid if the loan is repaid on March 10?

Personal Finance

9

OBJECTIVES

When you complete this chapter you will be able to:

- *Understand and solve for interest charges as they are applied to credit cards and revolving charge accounts. (9.1)*
- *Calculate installment payment amounts for loans using tables and formula methods. (9.2)*
- *Identify disclosure elements needed to satisfy truth-in-lending legislation. (9.2)*
- *Use different methods to figure loan payoff balances. (9.3)*

COMING UP

Both individuals and businesses need help in making credit decisions. It costs money to borrow. Each of us needs to be able to evaluate the competitive offers of loans and to understand the important elements of lending. True costs of loans may vary simply because they are computed using different interest payback methods. Can you evaluate interest rates being offered and the terms of a loan? This chapter shows how to understand consumer interest. It introduces how interest and payment calculations are made. It also presents how interest is applied to account balances for payment and loan payoff.

Credit Cards and Revolving Charge Accounts

9.1

Credit cards and revolving charge accounts are significant sources of consumer credit. These cards charge interest per month on an account balance. As the balance is reduced, the amount of interest becomes less. A specified minimum monthly payment is required, depending on the account balance and charge card policy.

Monthly interest rates for charge cards vary from as low as 8.0% to as high as 21% on an annual basis. Charge card interest rates are disclosed as **interest rate per month.**

> Interest rate per month = Annual percentage rate (APR) ÷ 12

The amount of monthly interest for an account is found by using the part, base, and rate logic. One of two common procedures—the **unpaid balance method** or the **average daily balance method**—is used.

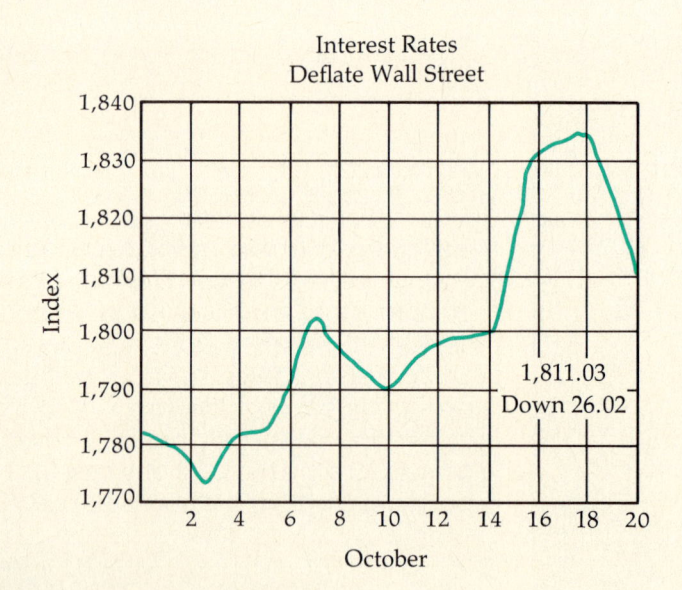

Interest Rates
Deflate Wall Street

[Graph showing index values from 1,770 to 1,840 over October dates 2 through 20, with annotation "1,811.03 Down 26.02"]

Unpaid Balance

The unpaid account balance from the previous month, or **billing period,** is used as the base for interest calculation. With no balance for the previous month, no interest is charged. New purchases made during a month are not assessed interest charges if the purchase is paid in full on the next billing. This provides the customer with the opportunity to use the account interest free as long as it is paid up. To offset the interest-free use for this type of account, many companies bill an annual fee for card use.

PROBLEM SOLVING STRATEGY

Interest on a balance is calculated and added in before new purchases are considered. If the consumer makes a payment less than the balance, the remaining amount becomes eligible for interest the next month. Set up your problem using the $P = B \times R$ strategy. Use a solution sequence of balance $\boxed{+}$ interest $\boxed{+}$ purchase (if any) $\boxed{-}$ payment.

EXAMPLE 1 John made purchases amounting to $500 last month on his credit card. If the interest rate is $1\frac{1}{2}\%$ per month on the unpaid balance, how much will be credited to the reduction of the principal this month when he makes a payment of $50? What will the balance be after the payment is made?

Solution: Find the interest per month, which is a part:

$P = B \times R$	• Formula for the part.
$P = \$500 \times .015$	• Set values into the formula.
	→ $1\frac{1}{2}$ percent or .015 is the rate.
	→ $500 is the base.
$\$500 \times 0.015 = \$7.50$	• Calculate the interest.
$\$500 + \$7.50 = \$507.50$	• Balance including the interest.
$\$50.00$	• Payment by consumer.
$\$507.50 - \$50 = \$457.50$	• Account balance after payment.

The effect of interest on the payment may also be reviewed as:

$\$7.50$	• Monthly interest due.
$\$50 - \$7.50 = \$42.50$	• Amount applied to principal: Payment − Interest = Amount of balance.
$\$500 - \$42.50 = \$457.50$	• New account balance after payment.

CALCULATOR TIP

There is a speedy calculator sequence for problems like that above. The 1 refers to the base. The .015 is the interest per month. The result is 1.015. This shows the interest and the principal in a form that can be used as a multiplier or a divisor. The use of the 1 + interest is the same as using principal plus interest. The principal is the base. Base = 100%, the value 1.

500 $\boxed{\times}$ 1.015 $\boxed{=}$ 507.50	• Find the balance including interest.
507.50 $\boxed{-}$ 50 $\boxed{=}$ 457.50	• Subtract the payment amount.

EXAMPLE 2 A charge account has an unpaid balance of $860, with 1% per month interest on the unpaid balance. If a $50 payment is received, what is the new balance?

Solution: Find the new balance, which is a part:

$P = B \times R$	• Formula for the part.
$\$860 \times .01$	• Set values into the formula.
	→ 1% or .01 is the interest rate.
	→ $860 unpaid balance is the base.
$\$860 \times .01 = \$8.60$	• Calculate interest ($P = B \times R$).
$\$860 + \$8.60 = \$868.60$	• Account balance plus interest.
$\$868.60 - \$50 = \$818.60$	• New balance after payment.

Section 9.1 Credit Cards and Revolving Charge Accounts

Review the interest effect on the payment:

$50.00 − $8.60 = $41.40   • Payment − Interest = Account reduction.

$860 − $41.40 = $818.60   • New account balance.

Incorporate the calculator illustration for solution:

$860 × 1.01 = $868.60   • Balance plus interest.
$868.60 − $50 = $818.60   • Payment reduces total amount owed.

EXAMPLE 3   The $1\frac{1}{2}$% revolving charge account of Juanita Chavez showed a balance of $140 from the previous billing period. If a new purchase was made in the middle of the billing period for $82.40, what would the account balance be if a payment of $60 was made?

Solution: Calculator technique applied to this problem.

Use the sequence: *Balance + Interest + Purchase − Payment:*

$140.00   • Unpaid balance is the base (100%).
100% + 1.5% = 101.5%   • Original balance percent + interest.
101.5% = 1.015   • Decimal form for the base + interest.
$140 × 1.015 = $142.10   • Balance plus interest added ($2.10).
$142.10 + $82.40 = $224.50   • New balance after purchase.
$224.50 − $60 = $164.50   • Payment reduces total account.
$164.50   • New account balance after payment.

✔ CHECK FOR UNDERSTANDING

1. With no new purchases, a customer owes $650 on a revolving credit plan that requires a $1\frac{1}{2}$% rate of interest on the unpaid balance per month. What will the new balance be on September 1 if the following payments are made: June 1, $40.00; July 1, $60.00; and August 1, $75.00?

2. Kathy Herring found that she could borrow either $1,800 from the credit union at a rate of $\frac{3}{4}$% per month on the unpaid balance or could charge her $1,800 purchase on a revolving charge account at $1\frac{1}{2}$% per month. If she were to make payments of $150 per month, how much extra would be repaid on the principal at the credit union in the first month?

3. Susan Savage received the statement below on her retail store charge account. The month-end balance for August was $300.

    September 1   Balance $300
    September 12   Purchase $50
    September 21   Purchase $15

If her retail store charges $1\frac{1}{2}$% on the unpaid balance and she sends in a payment of $65, what is the interest charge, and how much will be credited to her account?

Answers to ✔ Check for Understanding
1. $502.58.   2. $13.50.   3. $4.50; $60.50.

SKILL EXERCISES

Solve the following using the unpaid balance method:

	Unpaid balance	Interest rate per month	Interest	Payment	New balance
1.	$850	$1\frac{1}{2}\%$	$ _____	$55	$ _____
2.	$550	$\frac{3}{4}\%$	$ _____	$50	$ _____
3.	$650	1%	$ _____	$75	$ _____
4.	$425	$1\frac{1}{2}\%$	$ _____	$50	$ _____
5.	$950	$1\frac{1}{4}\%$	$ _____	$120	$ _____

	Unpaid balance	Interest rate per month	Interest	Purchases	Payment	New balance
6.	$850	$1\frac{1}{2}\%$	$ _____	$24.20	$55	$ _____
7.	$582	$1\frac{1}{2}\%$	$ _____	$45.00	$36	$ _____
8.	$712	$1\frac{3}{4}\%$	$ _____	$38.40	$41	$ _____
9.	$244	$1\frac{1}{4}\%$	$ _____	$26.30	$24	$ _____
10.	$175	1%	$ _____	$50.00	$18	$ _____

APPLICATIONS

Calculate the following using the unpaid balance method:

1. What is the APR for the following monthly interest rates?

   a. $\frac{3}{4}\%$ _____   b. 1% _____

   c. $1\frac{1}{2}\%$ _____   d. $1\frac{1}{4}\%$ _____

   e. $1\frac{3}{4}\%$ _____

2. By how much will the account balance be reduced if the unpaid balance on a credit card account is $975 and the interest rate is $1\frac{1}{2}\%$ per month, if a $100 payment is made?

3. Dorla found that the credit card company charged $1\frac{3}{4}\%$ interest per month on the unpaid balance. Her credit union charged $1\frac{1}{4}\%$ interest per month on the unpaid balance. If she borrowed $3,600 and made payments of $127 monthly, by how much would the principal be reduced on the first payment for each of the respective interest rates? **a.** Credit card. **b.** Credit union.

Section 9.1 Credit Cards and Revolving Charge Accounts

4. With no new purchases, apply the following payments to a credit card account that is based upon $1\frac{1}{2}$% interest on the unpaid balance. As of March 1, the account had a balance of $347. What will the new balance be on June 1 if these payments are made?

    April 1 $25
    May 1 $67

5. Fred O'Merrill maintained a revolving credit account with a local florist. The account finance charges were based upon $1\frac{3}{4}$% interest per month on the unpaid balance. If the beginning monthly balance on the account was $26.40 and a $36 purchase was made during the month, what would the balance on the account be after a $27 payment was applied?

6. Carlie Wood's credit card account was based upon $1\frac{1}{2}$% interest on the unpaid balance. Her account was paid in full the previous month. If she made two purchases during the month totaling $127.30, what amount of interest would be due for the current billing month?

7. The balance on a store charge account for the previous month was $640. The account was charged $1\frac{1}{4}$% on the unpaid balance. If an $85 payment was received, what is the remaining balance?

8. Review the following transactions on a credit card account charging $1\frac{1}{2}$% on the unpaid monthly balance:

    Balance   End of June $164.50
    Purchase   July 3 $64.50
    Purchase   July 18 $21.10

   A payment of $120 was made on August 1. What balance would be brought forward?

9. What amount would be due on a $1\frac{1}{4}$% per month credit card account with no previous balance if a purchase of $529.50 was made during the month?

10. A revolving charge account carried an end of month balance of $362. The account interest was calculated on the unpaid balance at $1\frac{1}{8}$% per month. What would the account balance be if an $85 payment were made on this account?

Average Daily Balance

Many companies charge interest using an average daily balance (ADB). With no previous balance, no interest is usually charged on current month purchases, if paid within 25 days of the **account statement.** This benefits the consumer much the same way the unpaid balance method does, by providing a limited ability to use the account without incurring a finance charge. With a balance, interest is calculated using the average of the daily account balances as a base.

$$\text{Average daily balance} = \frac{\text{Total of each daily balance for month (period)}}{\text{Number of days in month (period)}}$$

232 Chapter 9 Personal Finance

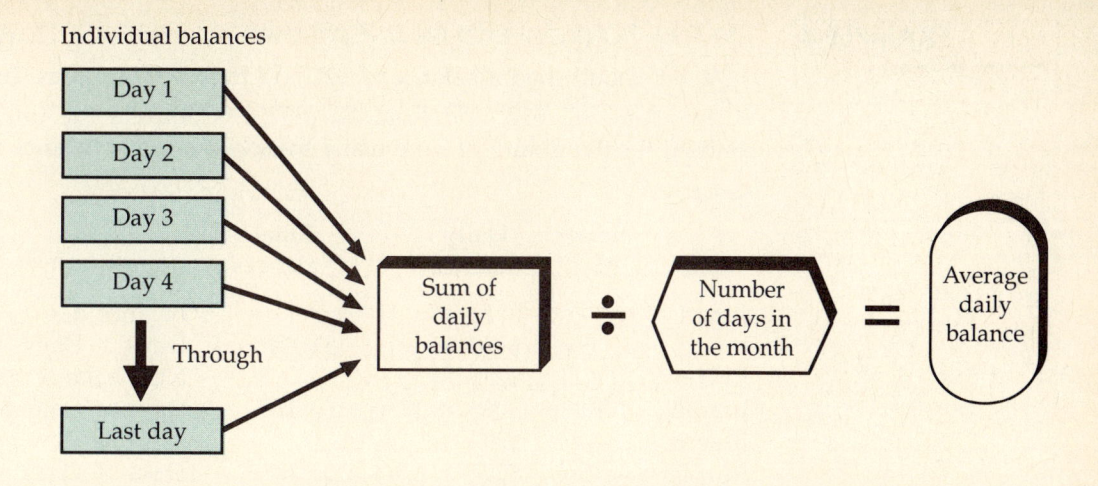

Individual balances

Day 1
Day 2
Day 3
Day 4
↓ Through
Last day

→ Sum of daily balances ÷ Number of days in the month = Average daily balance

PROBLEM SOLVING STRATEGY

The average daily balance procedure uses a balance for each day of the billing month (or billing period). New purchases are added to the balance of the previous day to establish a new balance. This method allows no free days. Purchases count in the balance the same day they are bought. Monthly interest is subtracted from payments. Payment balances are then subtracted from the previous daily balance to find the new daily balance.

7060506053740241100015000004137

YOUR ACCOUNT NUMBER	234-876-123
BILL CLOSING DATE	07/05/90
YOUR NEW BALANCE	$ 104.45
PAYMENT PAST DUE AFTER	08/05/90
MINIMUM DUE THIS MONTH	$ 18.00
PLEASE ENTER THE AMOUNT OF PAYMENT	$

CAR-RT SORT **CR12

CARRIE M. CONSUMER
1234 IRONCLAD DRIVE
ANYWHERE, CO. 89111-0221

MAXIMUM SAVINGS DEPARTMENT STORE

Name Correction _____   Phone Change _____
Address Change _____   City _____ State _____ ZIP _____
Please Send This Portion of Your Statement With Your Check

COME ONE, COME ALL TO OUR FABULOUS MOONLIGHT MADNESS SALE. THE SALE STARTS PROMPTLY AT 10:00 PM ON JULY 9. INCREDIBLE SAVINGS........ DON'T MISS IT !!!!!

Date	Store	Ref.	Dept.	Description	Purchase Debits	Payments-Credits
06/9	702	101	88	PAYMENT, THANK YOU		20.00

| Account Number 234-876-123 | Account Type 4 | No. Days in Billing Cycle 30 | Available Credit 545 | Payment Due Date 08/05/90 |

Bal. Subject to Finance Charge	Portions of Bal. which rates apply	Monthly Rate	Annual Percentage Rate
122.31	Entire Balance	1.75 %	21.0%

Prev. Bal.	Payment & Cr.	+ Purchases & Debits	+ Finance Charge	= New Bal	Amt. Due on New Balance
122.31	20.00	00.00	2.14	104.45	18.00

FIGURE 9.1
Average daily balance statement

EXAMPLE 4 **Previous Balance and New Purchases** A revolving charge account based on $1\frac{1}{2}\%$ per month had a balance of $220 on June 1. Purchases during June were June 6, $65; June 18, $12; and June 24, $87.50. Compute the interest charges on this account for the month of June using the average daily balance method.

Solution:

Date	No. of days	Daily balance	Total balances	
June 1	—	$220		• Balance due.
June 5	5	$220 × 5	$1,100	• Days × Daily balance.
June 6	—	$285		• New balance. ($65 added)
June 17	12	$285 × 12 =	$3,420	• Days × Daily balance.
June 18	—	$297		• Another new balance. ($12 added)
June 23	6	$297 × 6 =	$1,782	• Days × Daily balance.
June 24	—	$384.50		• Another new balance. ($87.50 added)
June 30	7	$384.50 × 7 =	$2,691.50	• Days × Daily balance.
June 30 (30 days)			$8,993.50	• Total daily balance.

$8,993.50 ÷ 30 days = $299.78   • Average daily balance.
ADB $299.78 × 0.015 = $4.50   • Monthly interest ($B \times R$).

The principal component of a payment is subtracted from the previous day's balance to determine a new daily balance. The monthly interest rate is multiplied by the average daily balance to establish the finance charge for that period.

EXAMPLE 5 **Payment Received During the Billing Period** With monthly interest of $1\frac{3}{4}\%$, use the average daily balance method to determine the interest charge for the August billing period. Billing date for the account is the 4th of the month. The balance on the account as of the 4th of August is $344.38. The average daily balance for the previous billing period was $352. An August 5th payment was received in the amount of $45. Account purchases were August 9, $42.14; and August 30, $14.96.

Solution: ADB previous $352.00 × .0715 = $6.16 Interest Charge

Date	No. of days	Daily balance	Total balances	
Aug. 4	1	$344.38	$344.38	• Balance due.
Aug. 5		$45 − 6.16 = $38.84		• Payment − Interest.
Aug. 5		$305.54		• New balance.
Aug. 8	4	$305.54	$1,222.16	• New balance × 4 days.
Aug. 9		$305.45 + $42.14		• Added Aug. 9 new purchase.
Aug. 9		$347.68		• New balance.
Aug. 29	21		$7,301.28	• New balance × 21 days.
Aug. 30		$347.68 + $14.96		• Added Aug. 30 new purchase.
Aug. 30		$362.64		• New balance.
Sep. 3	5		$1,813.20	• New balance × 5 days.
(Aug. 4 to Sep. 3—31 days)				• Days in billing period.
			$10,681.02	• Sum of total balances.

$$\text{ADB} = \frac{\text{Total daily balances}}{\text{Number of days in billing period}}$$

$$= \frac{\$10,681.02}{31}$$

$$= \$344.55 \text{ ADB}$$

ADB $344.55 × Rate .0175 = 6.0296   • August interest = $6.03.

234 Chapter 9 Personal Finance

CHECK FOR UNDERSTANDING

1. Using a monthly interest rate of $1\frac{1}{2}\%$ and the average daily balance method, calculate the account balance for the next month. (Account paid in full as of April 30.)

May 2	Purchase	$85.00
May 12	Purchase	$92.00
May 26	Purchase	$64.00
June 1	Payment	$125.00

2. What is the average daily balance and the interest charges for an account billed monthly at $1\frac{3}{4}\%$? The balance as of March 1 was $641.20 with a purchase of $64.25 made on March 26.

3. On a revolving account, determine the balance after payment is applied. Use the average daily balance method at $1\frac{3}{4}\%$ and a billing date of the 7th of the month.

Balance from previous billing period		$131.60
November 9	Purchase	$42.60
November 21	Purchase	$16.70
December 8	Payment	$75.00

SKILL EXERCISES

Complete the following using the average daily balance method:

	Account balance	Dates of balance	Number of balance days	Total daily balance
1.	$ 142.60	Nov. 3–Nov. 12	_____	$ _____
2.	$ 28.31	Mar. 30–Apr. 2	_____	$ _____
3.	$ 144.52	June 26–July 4	_____	$ _____
4.	$1,021.12	May 3–May 17	_____	$ _____
5.	$ 377.92	Aug. 12–Aug. 29	_____	$ _____

Complete the following average daily balance situations to find the amount of interest due:

	Account balance	Balance days	Account balance	Balance days	Interest rate	ADB	Amount of interest due
6.	$ 64.80	20	$ 96.50	11	$1\frac{1}{2}\%$	$ _____	$ _____
7.	$ 141.40	10	$ 164.80	21	$1\frac{3}{4}\%$	$ _____	$ _____
8.	$ 196.50	4	$ 144.80	26	1%	$ _____	$ _____

Answers to ✔ Check for Understanding
1. $118.31. 2. ADB = $653.64; Interest = $11.44. 3. ADB = $180.27; Interest = $3.15; Balance = $119.05.

9. $1,426.40   12 $1,240.10   19 $1\frac{1}{4}$% $ _____ $ _____

10. $ 341.00   22 $ 711.10   8 $1\frac{1}{2}$% $ _____ $ _____

APPLICATIONS

Solve the following problems for average daily balance credit accounts:

1. J.L. had a balance of $350 on a credit card account on August 1. He made purchases of $25 on August 4; $42 on August 12; and $38 on August 22. Compute the interest due for August using the average daily balance method and a monthly interest rate of $1\frac{1}{2}$%.

2. Heinrick's revolving charge account at the clothiers showed a balance at the beginning of September of $624.80. The account carries a $1\frac{1}{4}$% interest rate per month on the average daily balance. If his payment resulted in a principal reduction of $75 on September 18, and a purchase was made on September 26 for $21.20, what is his average daily balance? What is the interest charge for September?

3. A credit card account carried terms of $1\frac{3}{4}$% interest on the average daily balance. The beginning balance on June 1 was $573.28. If no purchases were made for the month, how much interest would be due on the account for June?

4. The billing date for a revolving charge was the 11th of the month. Interest rate on the account is $1\frac{1}{2}$%. Given the following data, compute the average daily balance and interest due:

    March 11   Balance $146.80
    March 16   Purchase $4.50
    March 18   Purchase $24.60
    March 20   Payment $35.00
          (Principal to be applied)
    March 30   Purchase $6.84

5. Use a monthly finance charge of $1\frac{1}{4}$% and the average daily balance method to determine the interest charge for the November billing. The billing date for Andrea Polski was the 3rd of the month. The balance on the account as of the 3rd of November is $526.40.

    November 6   Purchase $16.80
    November 21   Purchase $24.40
    December 1   Purchase $8.80

Installment Loans and Purchases

9.2

Other **installment period** lengths allow consumers to borrow amounts for larger items such as furniture, automobiles, televisions, and appliances.

Truth-in-lending legislation encompassed by **Regulation Z** directs that lending agencies present loan information to consumers in a manner which ensures clear interpretation. Figure 9.2 illustrates information which must be included in the loan information.

Read the following and sign the promissory note.

FEDERAL DISCLOSURE STATEMENT

Annual Percentage Interest Rate	Finance Charge	Amount Financed	Total of Payments
Cost of My Credit as a Yearly Rate	Dollar Cost to Me	Total of Credit Allowed	Amount I Will Pay in Total
19.00%	$1,600.72	$3,678.32	$5,279.04

My Payment Schedule Will Be:

Number of Payments	Amount of Each Payment	When Due
48	$109.98	5th of Month

Prepayment: If I pay off my loan early, I will not have to pay a penalty.

_____ Date: _____

FIGURE 9.2
Federal disclosure example

Care must be taken in interpreting installment transactions. In an **add-on interest** contract, the payback begins immediately and continues throughout the contract period. This differs from a simple interest contract, in which the total principal and interest are paid back at the end of the loan period. Each time a payment is made, the amount of the principal is reduced. Because the amount of the principal continually reduces and the interest paid each month does not, the true rate of interest goes up. Use Table 9.1 and follow this add-on interest example.

TABLE 9.1
Payment Schedule for $100 Borrowed for One Year at 8%*
(Note the balance due reduces monthly, interest does not.)

Date	Payment	Credit to Principal	Balance Due	Credit to Interest
Feb. 1	$9.00	$8.333	$91.667	$0.667
Mar. 1	$9.00	$8.333	$83.334	$0.667
Apr. 1	$9.00	$8.333	$75.001	$0.667
May 1	$9.00	$8.333	$66.668	$0.667
June 1	$9.00	$8.333	$58.335	$0.667
July 1	$9.00	$8.333	Mid-Yr. (50.002)	$0.667
Aug. 1	$9.00	$8.333	Bal $41.669	$0.667
Sep. 1	$9.00	$8.333	$33.336	$0.667
Oct. 1	$9.00	$8.333	$25.003	$0.667
Nov. 1	$9.00	$8.333	$16.670	$0.667
Dec. 1	$9.00	$8.333	$8.337	$0.667
Jan. 1	$9.00	$8.333	$.004	$0.667

* Interest allocated evenly for each month.

If $100 is borrowed for one year at an interest rate of 8% to be repaid on 12 equal payments, we find:

$100	• Principal to be borrowed.
8% = .08	• Interest in decimal form.
$100 × 0.08 × 1 = $8.00	• Interest found by $I = P \times R \times T$.
$100 + $8 = $108	• Interest added for total owed.
$108 ÷ 12 = $9.00	• Total ÷ 12 is the monthly payment.
$100 ÷ 12 = $8.33	• Principal ÷ 12 is monthly principal.
$8 ÷ 12 = $.67	• Interest ÷ 12 is interest per month.

Review the schedule to determine the effect of early payback.

By mid-year you have repaid nearly one-half of the loan. Effectively, you have use of only one-half of the money borrowed. The **annual percentage rate (APR)** reflects the actual interest rate.

The Federal Reserve Board prepares interest tables to assist lenders by providing annual percentage rate information. These tables reflect an accurate interest annual percentage rate (APR) for the installment period. If **Federal Reserve tables** are not available, an APR formula may be used to approximate the table values. The formula uses interest apportioned equally for each month and will usually overstate the Federal Reserve APR.

Formula Approximation for APR

$$APR = \frac{2 \times \text{Payment periods in one year} \times \text{Amount of interest}}{\text{Amount borrowed (principal)} \times (\text{Total payments} + 1)}$$

Where:
2 is a constant multiplier.
Payment periods are 12 for monthly payments; 52 for weekly payments.
Amount of interest is the cost of installments.
Amount borrowed is actual amount financed.
Total payments is the number of payments to pay off the loan.

Look at the previous example, $100 borrowed for one year at 8%.

$$APR = \frac{2 \times 12 \times \$8.00}{\$100 \times (12 + 1)} = .1477 \text{ or } 14.8\%$$

CALCULATOR TIP

In the type of problem above, the calculation can be done all in one step. Set the information into sequence and complete the calculation using a chain multiplication and division:

2 [×] 12 [×] 8 [÷] 100 [÷] 13 [=] .1477

Add-On Interest

Using add-on interest, the interest is calculated on the amount borrowed for the full length of the loan, then added to the loan principal. Other **loan fee/service charges** may also be added. The total to be repaid is divided by the planned number of payments to establish the payment amount. The total to be repaid is referred to as the **total contract price**. This includes the principal, interest, and other fees or service charges.

$$\text{Pmt} = \frac{P + I + F}{n}$$

Where:
Pmt = Payment amount
P = Principal
I = Total interest
F = Fee or service charge
n = Number of payments

EXAMPLE 6 **Simple Loan** If Mose Inc. borrows $500 at 9% add-on interest to be paid in 12 equal monthly payments, how much will the monthly payment be? What is the APR?

Solution: The first unknown is interest, which is a part:

Part = Base × Rate	· Formula for the part.
$500 × .09	· Set values in formula.
$500 × .09 = $45	· Calculate the interest.
$500 + $45 = $545	· P + I = total contract cost.
$545 ÷ 12 = $45.42	· Monthly payment.

Federal Reserve tables are used to establish an APR for add-on interest loans. Complete tables are found in Appendix D. To find the correct APR,

· Determine the total interest and fee charges per $100 borrowed.
· Enter into the table the interest and fee per $100 amount and the number of payments in the loan to find the APR. The table amount closest to the interest per $100 is used. Since it is illegal to understate the APR to a customer, business people would choose the **closest greater table APR** rather than the **closest numerical table value.**

For the Example 6 problem, the Federal Reserve APR procedure is:

$500	· Amount borrowed.
$45	· Total interest due on the contract.
500 ÷ 100 = 5	· Number of hundreds borrowed.
$45 ÷ 5 = $9.00	· Interest per hundred borrowed.
$9.02 (closest)	· Table value for 12 months (closest).
16.25%	· The column APR = 16.25%.
16.25	· Interest to be disclosed to consumer.

Annual Percentage Rate

Number of Payments	13.50%	13.75%	14.00%	14.25%	14.50%	14.75%	15.00%	15.25%	15.50%	15.75%	16.00%	16.25%	16.50%	16.75%
	Finance Charge per $100 of Amount Financed													
8	5.13	5.22	5.32	5.42	5.51	5.61	5.71	5.80	5.90	6.00	6.09	6.19	6.29	6.38
9	5.71	5.82	5.92	6.03	6.14	6.25	6.35	6.46	6.57	6.68	6.78	6.89	7.00	7.11
10	6.29	6.41	6.53	6.65	6.77	6.88	7.00	7.12	7.24	7.36	7.48	7.60	7.72	7.84
11	6.88	7.01	7.14	7.27	7.40	7.53	7.66	7.79	7.92	8.05	8.18	8.31	8.44	8.57
12	7.46	7.60	7.74	7.89	8.03	8.17	8.31	8.45	8.59	8.74	8.88	9.02	9.16	9.30
13	8.05	8.20	8.36	8.51	8.66	8.81	8.97	9.12	9.27	9.43	9.58	9.73	9.89	10.04
14	8.64	8.81	8.97	9.13	9.30	9.46	9.63	9.79	9.96	10.12	10.29	10.45	10.62	10.78
15	9.23	9.41	9.59	9.76	9.94	10.11	10.29	10.47	10.64	10.82	11.00	11.17	11.35	11.53
16	9.83	10.02	10.20	10.39	10.58	10.77	10.95	11.14	11.33	11.52	11.71	11.90	12.09	12.28
17	10.43	10.63	10.82	11.02	11.22	11.42	11.62	11.82	12.02	12.22	12.42	12.62	12.83	13.03

EXAMPLE 7 Loan and Fee   Snowy River Arabians Inc. borrowed $1,800 for a new feeder. If a $12\frac{1}{2}\%$ add-on interest rate plus a $25 initiation fee was charged for a 24-month loan, what were the payments? What was the APR?

Number of Payments	\multicolumn{13}{c}{Annual Percentage Rate}
	20.50%	20.75%	21.00%	21.25%	21.50%	21.75%	22.00%	22.25%	22.50%	22.75%	23.00%	23.25%	23.50%	23.75%
	\multicolumn{14}{c}{Finance Charge per $100 of Amount Financed}
20	18.90	19.14	19.38	19.63	19.87	20.11	20.36	20.60	20.84	21.09	21.33	21.58	21.82	22.07
21	19.85	20.11	20.36	20.62	20.87	21.13	21.38	21.64	21.90	22.16	22.41	22.67	22.93	23.19
22	20.81	21.08	21.34	21.61	21.88	22.15	22.42	22.69	22.96	23.23	23.50	23.77	24.04	24.32
23	21.77	22.05	22.33	22.61	22.90	23.18	23.46	23.74	24.03	24.31	24.60	24.88	25.17	25.45
24	22.74	23.03	23.33	23.62	23.92	24.21	24.51	24.80	25.10	25.40	25.70	25.99	26.29	26.59
25	23.71	24.02	24.32	24.63	24.94	25.25	25.56	25.87	26.18	26.49	26.80	27.11	27.43	27.74
26	24.68	25.01	25.33	25.65	25.97	26.29	26.62	26.94	27.26	27.59	27.91	28.24	28.56	28.89
27	25.67	26.00	26.34	26.67	27.01	27.34	27.68	28.02	28.35	28.69	29.03	29.37	29.71	30.05
28	26.65	27.00	27.35	27.70	28.05	28.40	28.75	29.10	29.45	29.80	30.15	30.51	30.86	31.22
29	27.64	28.00	28.37	28.73	29.09	29.46	29.82	30.19	30.55	30.92	31.28	31.65	32.02	32.39

Solution: Use $I = P \times R \times T$ and Federal Reserve tables:

$1,800	• Principal of the loan is the base.
$12\frac{1}{2}\%$ = .125	• $12\frac{1}{2}\%$ in decimal form is .125.
$1,800 × .125 × 2 = $450	• Values set into formula.
$25.00	• Added loan fee charge.
$1,800 + 450 + 25 = $2,275	• Total contract price.
$450 + $25 = $475	• Total combined charges (interest plus fee).
1,800 ÷ 100 = 18	• Number of hundreds borrowed.
$475 ÷ 18 = $26.39	• Interest and fee cost per hundred.
23.75% (See Table)	• Table value 24 periods and 24.69.
APR = 23.75%	(Note: Since 23.50% is numerically closest to your calculated value, it would understate the APR.)
$2,275 ÷ 24 = $94.79	• Monthly payment (rounded).

EXAMPLE 8 Purchase—No Down Payment   If a TV set sells for $975 and can be purchased for no down payment and 36 monthly payments of $36.75, what is the annual percentage rate (APR) for the contract?

Number of Payments	\multicolumn{14}{c}{Annual Percentage Rate}
	20.50%	20.75%	21.00%	21.25%	21.50%	21.75%	22.00%	22.25%	22.50%	22.75%	23.00%	23.25%	23.50%	23.75%
	\multicolumn{14}{c}{Finance Charge per $100 of Amount Financed}
32	30.64	31.05	31.45	31.85	32.26	32.67	33.07	33.48	33.89	34.30	34.71	35.12	35.53	35.94
33	31.65	32.07	32.49	32.91	33.33	33.75	34.17	34.59	35.01	35.44	35.86	36.29	36.71	37.14
34	32.67	33.10	33.53	33.96	34.40	34.83	35.27	35.71	36.14	36.58	37.02	37.46	37.90	38.34
35	33.68	34.13	34.58	35.03	35.47	35.92	36.37	36.83	37.28	37.73	38.18	38.64	39.09	39.55
36	34.71	35.17	35.63	36.09	36.56	37.02	37.49	37.95	38.42	38.89	39.35	39.82	40.29	40.77
37	35.74	36.21	36.69	37.16	37.64	38.12	38.60	39.08	39.56	40.05	40.53	41.02	41.50	41.99
38	36.77	37.26	37.75	38.24	38.73	39.23	39.72	40.22	40.72	41.21	41.71	42.21	42.71	43.22
39	37.81	38.31	38.82	39.32	39.83	40.34	40.85	41.36	41.87	42.39	42.90	43.42	43.93	44.45
40	38.85	39.37	39.89	40.41	40.93	41.46	41.98	42.51	43.04	43.56	44.09	44.62	45.16	45.69
41	39.89	40.43	40.96	41.50	42.04	42.58	43.12	43.66	44.20	44.75	45.29	45.84	46.39	46.94

Chapter 9 Personal Finance

Solution:

$975	• Cost of TV set.
$36.75	• Monthly payment.
$36.75 × 36 = $1,323	• Total amount for all payments.
$1,323 − $975 = $348	• Amount − Cost = Installment cost.
975 ÷ 100 = 9.75	• Number of hundreds borrowed.
$348 ÷ $9.75 = $35.69	• Cost per $100 for installments.
36 months and 35.69	• Use for Federal Reserve table.
21.25%	• Table APR. (21% is the closest percent to the calculated value. However, since it would understate the APR, choose 36.09 or 21.25%.)

EXAMPLE 9 **Purchase with Down Payment** A snow blower retails for $1,085.50. With 10% down, it may be financed for 36 months at $36.10 per month. What are the APR and total contract price for this sale?

Number of Payments	Annual Percentage Rate												
	17.00%	17.25%	17.50%	17.75%	18.00%	18.25%	18.50%	18.75%	19.00%	19.25%	19.50%	19.75%	20.00%	20.25%
	Finance Charge per $100 of Amount Financed												
32	25.07	25.46	25.86	26.25	26.65	27.04	27.44	27.84	28.24	28.64	29.04	29.44	29.84	30.24
33	25.88	26.29	26.70	27.11	27.52	27.93	28.34	28.75	29.16	29.57	29.99	30.40	30.82	31.23
34	26.70	27.12	27.54	27.97	28.39	28.81	29.24	29.66	30.09	30.52	30.95	31.37	31.80	32.23
35	27.52	27.96	28.39	28.83	29.27	29.71	30.14	30.58	31.02	31.47	31.91	32.35	32.79	33.24
36	28.35	28.80	29.25	29.70	30.15	30.60	31.05	31.51	31.96	32.42	32.87	33.33	33.79	34.25
37	29.18	29.64	30.10	30.57	31.03	31.50	31.97	32.43	32.90	33.37	33.84	34.32	34.79	35.26
38	30.01	30.49	30.96	31.44	31.92	32.40	32.88	33.37	33.85	34.33	34.82	35.30	35.79	36.28
39	30.85	31.34	31.83	32.32	32.81	33.31	33.80	34.30	34.80	35.30	35.80	36.30	36.80	37.30
40	31.68	32.19	32.69	33.20	33.71	34.22	34.73	35.24	35.75	36.26	36.78	37.29	37.81	38.33
41	32.52	33.04	33.56	34.08	34.61	35.13	35.66	36.18	36.71	37.24	37.77	38.30	38.83	39.36

Solution: Use formulas Part = Base × Rate:

Total contract price = Payment × No. of payments

$1,085.50	• Original retail price.
$1,085.50 × .10 = $108.55	• Down payment $P = B \times R$.
$1,085.50 − $108.55 = $976.95	• Amount to be financed.
$36.10 × 36 = $1,299.60	• Total amount of all payments.
$1,299.60 − $976.95 = $322.65	• Contract − Amount financed = Interest.
976.95 ÷ 100 = 9.7695	• Number of hundreds borrowed.
$322.65 ÷ 9.7695 = $33.02	• Interest per $100.
36 months and 33.02	• Use for Federal Reserve table.
19.75%	• Table APR.
$1,299.60 (payment × no. of payments)	• Total contract price.

EXAMPLE 10 Living room furniture is quoted to Cheryl and Don for their new store at $1,755. The furniture can be financed for 48 months with 15% down, $14\frac{1}{2}$% add-on interest, and a $10 loan initiation fee. What would their payments be? What is the total interest? What is the APR?

Number of Payments	24.00%	24.25%	24.50%	24.75%	25.00%	25.25%	25.50%	25.75%	26.00%	26.25%	26.50%	26.75%	27.00%	27.25%
					Finance Charge per $100 of Amount Financed									
44	51.31	51.91	52.51	53.11	53.71	54.31	54.92	55.52	56.13	56.74	57.35	57.96	58.57	59.19
45	52.59	53.21	53.82	54.44	55.06	55.68	56.30	56.92	57.55	58.17	58.80	59.43	60.06	60.69
46	53.89	54.52	55.15	55.78	56.42	57.05	57.69	58.33	58.97	59.61	60.26	60.90	61.55	62.20
47	55.18	55.83	56.48	57.13	57.78	58.44	59.09	59.75	60.40	61.06	61.72	62.39	63.05	63.71
48	56.49	57.15	57.82	58.49	59.15	59.82	60.50	61.17	61.84	62.52	63.20	63.87	64.56	65.24
49	57.80	58.48	59.16	59.85	60.53	61.22	61.91	62.60	63.29	63.98	64.68	65.37	66.07	66.77
50	59.12	59.81	60.51	61.21	61.92	62.62	63.33	64.03	64.74	65.45	66.16	66.88	67.59	68.31
51	60.44	61.15	61.87	62.59	63.31	64.03	64.75	65.48	66.20	66.93	67.66	68.39	69.12	69.86
52	61.77	62.50	63.23	63.97	64.70	65.44	66.18	66.92	67.67	68.41	69.16	69.91	70.66	71.41
53	63.10	63.85	64.60	65.35	66.11	66.86	67.62	68.38	69.14	69.90	70.67	71.43	72.20	72.97

Annual Percentage Rate

Solution: Use formulas with principal, interest, rate, and time:

$1,755 × .15 = $263.25	• Down payment (15%).
$1,755 − $263.25 = $1,491.75	• Amount financed = Principal.
$1,491.75 × .145 × 4 = $865.22	• Interest = $P \times R \times T$.
$10.00	• Loan fee.
$865.22 + $10.00 = $875.22	• Total interest and fees.
$1,491.75 + $865.72 + $10 = $2,366.97	• Total contract price.
1,491.75 ÷ 100 = 14.9175	• Number of hundreds borrowed.
$875.22 ÷ 14.9175 = $58.67	• Interest per $100 financed.
48 months and 58.76	• Use for Federal Reserve table.
25.0%	• Table APR.
$2,366.97 ÷ 48 = $49.31	• Total contract ÷ Number of payments = Monthly payment.

CALCULATOR TIP

Solve Example 10 with a calculator:

1755 × .15 = 263.25 M+	• Down payment
1755 − MR = 1491.75	• Principal
1491.75 × .145 × 4 = 865.22	• Interest
865.22 + 1491.75 + 10 = 2366.97	• Total contract
2366.97 ÷ 48 = 49.31	• Monthly contract payment

✓ CHECK FOR UNDERSTANDING

1. The cash price of an automobile is $4,250. It could be bought for $650 down and 42 equal monthly payments of $109.60.
   (a) What is the amount of add-on interest?
   (b) What will the total cost of the automobile be if the installment method of payment is used?
   (c) What is the APR?

2. A restaurant owner borrowed $1,850 to pay for a new satellite antenna for his television system. He is quoted $13\frac{1}{4}$% add-on interest to be repaid in 24 months. How much will the monthly payments be? What is the loan APR?

3. Dale was told that his new store cash register will cost $984.60. If he were to pay 15% down and finance the remaining amount at 12% add-on interest for 18 months, with a $15 loan application fee, what would his payments be? What is the loan APR?

Chapter 9 Personal Finance

4. A sprinkler system was quoted to a prospective buyer at $2,600. The terms were 10% down and financing for 36 months. Total interest on the financing would amount to $610. What was the monthly payment? What is the APR?

SKILL EXERCISES

Use add-on interest method and Federal Reserve tables to find APR:

	Cash price	Down payment	Amount financed	No. of payments	Interest/ Rate of interest	Monthly payment	Annual percentage rate (APR)
1.	$1,426	15%	$ _____	30	14%	$ _____	_____ %
2.	$ 826	5%	$ _____	24	$122.00	$ _____	_____ %
3.	$3,220	10%	$ _____	36	15%	$ _____	_____ %
4.	$ 367.50	none	$ _____	18	$ 51.00	$ _____	_____ %
5.	$ 519.80	10%	$ _____	24	11%	$ _____	_____ %

	Total amt. loan interest	Number months	Loan fee/ Svc. charge	Principal borrowed	Finance chg./$100	APR
6.	$1,337	40	none	$5,000	$ _____	_____ %
7.	$ 225	24	$10	$ 674	$ _____	_____ %
8.	$ 549	48	none	$1,348	$ _____	_____ %
9.	$ 142	30	$20	$ 384.50	$ _____	_____ %
10.	$ 799	60	$35	$1,941.60	$ _____	_____ %

APPLICATIONS

Complete the following problems using the add-on interest method:

1. The Hardwood Furniture Store advertised lawn furniture groups for $275 cash or no down payment and 18 equal monthly payments of $19.65. What is the APR for this credit plan?

2. What is the annual percentage rate of interest on a loan of $700 if it is repaid in 20 equal monthly payments of $39.95?

Answers to ✓ Check for Understanding
1. (a) $1,003.20; (b) $5,253.20; (c) 14.5%.   2. $97.51; 23.75%.   3. $55.70; 23.75%.
4. $81.94; 15.75%.

TABLE 9.2
Installment Amortization Table

%	Months 12	24		%	30	36	Months 42	48	60		%	72	Months 84	96
12	1.06617	1.12975		12	1.16244	1.19570	1.22955	1.26398	1.33464		12	1.40760	1.48276	1.56019
12.25	1.06758	1.13256		12.25	1.16598	1.19998	1.23463	1.26988	1.34220		12.25	1.41696	1.49402	1.57344
12.50	1.06898	1.13536		12.50	1.16952	1.20430	1.23975	1.27584	1.34982		12.50	1.42639	1.50536	1.58668
12.75	1.07040	1.13817		12.75	1.17306	1.20862	1.24488	1.28174	1.35750		12.75	1.43582	1.51670	1.60003
13	1.07180	1.14098		13	1.17663	1.21294	1.25000	1.28769	1.36518		13	1.44532	1.52804	1.61347
13.25	1.07320	1.14381		13.25	1.18020	1.21730	1.25512	1.29364	1.37286		13.25	1.45483	1.53955	1.62691
13.50	1.07462	1.14664		13.50	1.18377	1.22166	1.26029	1.29964	1.38054		13.50	1.46433	1.55097	1.64044
13.75	1.07602	1.14945		13.75	1.18734	1.22601	1.26546	1.30564	1.38828		13.75	1.47398	1.56256	1.65398
14	1.07744	1.15228		14	1.19094	1.23037	1.27062	1.31164	1.39608		14	1.48356	1.57416	1.66761
14.25	1.07884	1.15514		14.25	1.19454	1.23476	1.27579	1.31769	1.40388		14.25	1.49320	1.58575	1.68134
14.50	1.08026	1.15797		14.50	1.19814	1.23912	1.28100	1.32369	1.41168		14.50	1.50292	1.59742	1.69507
14.75	1.08168	1.16080		14.75	1.20174	1.24354	1.28620	1.32979	1.41948		14.75	1.51264	1.60910	1.70889
15	1.08309	1.16366		15	1.20534	1.24794	1.29145	1.33584	1.42734		15	1.52244	1.62086	1.72272
15.25	1.08451	1.16652		15.25	1.20897	1.25233	1.29666	1.34193	1.43526		15.25	1.53223	1.63270	1.73664
15.50	1.08592	1.16937		15.50	1.21257	1.25676	1.30191	1.34803	1.44318		15.50	1.54202	1.64455	1.75056
15.75	1.08734	1.17223		15.75	1.21620	1.26118	1.30716	1.35417	1.45110		15.75	1.55188	1.65639	1.76467
16	1.08876	1.17511		16	1.21986	1.26565	1.31245	1.36032	1.45908		16	1.56175	1.66840	1.77868
16.25	1.09018	1.17796		16.25	1.22349	1.27008	1.31775	1.36646	1.46706		16.25	1.57168	1.68033	1.79289
16.50	1.09160	1.18084		16.50	1.22715	1.27454	1.32304	1.37265	1.47504		16.50	1.58169	1.69234	1.80700
16.75	1.09303	1.18372		16.75	1.23078	1.27900	1.32833	1.37880	1.48308		16.75	1.59163	1.70444	1.82131
17	1.09444	1.18660		17	1.23444	1.28347	1.33366	1.38504	1.49112		17	1.60171	1.71654	1.83561
17.25	1.09587	1.18948		17.25	1.23813	1.28797	1.33900	1.39123	1.49922		17.25	1.61172	1.72872	1.85001
17.50	1.09730	1.19236		17.50	1.24179	1.29247	1.34433	1.39747	1.50732		17.50	1.62187	1.74090	1.86441
17.75	1.09873	1.19527		17.75	1.24548	1.29697	1.34971	1.40371	1.51542		17.75	1.63195	1.75316	1.87881
18	1.10016	1.19817		18	1.24917	1.30147	1.35508	1.41000	1.52358		18	1.64210	1.76542	1.89340

18.25	1.10158	1.20108	18.25	1.25286	1.30597	1.36046	1.41624	1.53174
18.50	1.10301	1.20398	18.50	1.25655	1.31050	1.36584	1.42252	1.53996
18.75	1.10444	1.20688	18.75	1.26027	1.31504	1.37125	1.42886	1.54818
19	1.10587	1.20979	19	1.26396	1.31961	1.37667	1.43520	1.55640
19.25	1.10730	1.21272	19.25	1.26768	1.32415	1.38209	1.44153	1.56468
19.50	1.10874	1.21562	19.50	1.27140	1.32872	1.38755	1.44787	1.57296
19.75	1.11016	1.21855	19.75	1.27515	1.33329	1.39301	1.45425	1.58124
20	1.11160	1.22148	20	1.27887	1.33786	1.39847	1.46064	1.58958
20.25	1.11304	1.22443	20.25	1.28262	1.34247	1.40393	1.46702	1.59798
20.50	1.11448	1.22736	20.50	1.28637	1.34704	1.40943	1.47345	1.60632
20.75	1.11591	1.23028	20.75	1.29012	1.35165	1.41493	1.47988	1.61472
21	1.11735	1.23324	21	1.29387	1.35630	1.42044	1.48632	1.62318
21.25	1.11879	1.23619	21.25	1.29765	1.36090	1.42598	1.49280	1.63164
21.50	1.12023	1.23914	21.50	1.30143	1.36555	1.43148	1.49928	1.64010
21.75	1.12168	1.24209	21.75	1.30521	1.37019	1.43707	1.50576	1.64856
22	1.12312	1.24507	22	1.30899	1.37484	1.44261	1.51228	1.65708
22.25	1.12456	1.24802	22.25	1.31277	1.37948	1.44820	1.51876	1.66566
22.50	1.12602	1.25100	22.50	1.31698	1.38416	1.45374	1.52534	1.67418
22.75	1.12746	1.25397	22.75	1.32036	1.38884	1.45937	1.53187	1.68282
23	1.12891	1.25695	23	1.32417	1.39352	1.46496	1.53844	1.69140
23.25	1.13036	1.25992	23.25	1.32801	1.39824	1.47058	1.54502	1.70004
23.50	1.13180	1.26290	23.50	1.33182	1.40292	1.47621	1.55164	1.70868
23.75	1.13325	1.26590	23.75	1.33566	1.40763	1.48184	1.55822	1.71738
24	1.13470	1.26890	24	1.33947	1.41235	1.48751	1.56484	1.72602

18.25	1.65232	1.77777	1.90800	
18.50	1.66255	1.79012	1.92259	
18.75	1.67277	1.80255	1.93728	
19	1.68307	1.81507	1.95196	
19.25	1.69344	1.82750	1.96675	
19.50	1.70373	1.84010	1.98163	
19.75	1.71417	1.85262	1.99651	
20	1.72454	1.86530	2.01148	
20.25	1.73498	1.87790	2.02646	
20.50	1.74549	1.89067	2.04153	
20.75	1.75600	1.90335	2.05660	
21	1.76659	1.91620	2.07177	
21.25	1.77710	1.92897	2.08694	
21.50	1.78776	1.94191	2.10220	
21.75	1.79834	1.95476	2.11747	
22	1.80907	1.96770	2.13283	
22.25	1.81972	1.98072	2.14819	
22.50	1.83045	1.99374	2.16364	
22.75	1.84125	2.00684	2.17910	
23	1.85205	2.01994	2.19465	
23.25	1.86285	2.03305	2.21020	
23.50	1.87372	2.04624	2.22585	
23.75	1.88460	2.05942	2.24150	
24	1.89547	2.07270	2.25724	

Section 9.2 Installment Loans and Purchases

EXAMPLE 13   A Problem That May Be Solved with Table 9.2. Check your understanding of the formula.   Yung-Min wants to start a business venture. He is offered $10,000 by a regional banker to be repaid at 14% APR over 2 years. What would his monthly payment be if no additional loan fees were charged?

Solution:

$10,000	• Principal (amount borrowed).
14% or .14	• Annual percentage rate.
.14 ÷ 12 = .0116667	• Interest rate per month.
2 × 12 = 24	• Number of months for payments.

Step 1

$$\$10{,}000 \times \frac{(.0116667)(1 + .0116667)^{24}}{[(1 + .0116667)^{24} - 1]}$$ • Set values into the formula.

Step 2

$$\$10{,}000 \times \frac{(.0116667) \times (1.3209881)}{(1.3209881) - 1}$$ • Remove the exponents using your calculator.

Step 3

$$\$10{,}000 \times \frac{(.0154116)}{(.3209881)}$$ • Compute within the parentheses.

Step 4 $10,000 × .048013   • Complete the division.

Step 5 $10,000 × .048013 = $480.13   • Complete the multiplication.
            $480.13 = monthly payment

Check: Table solution:
     Factor = 1.15228   • (Table rounding of factors is the penny difference.)
     $10,000 × 1.15228 = $11,522.80 ÷ 24
                            = $480.12

EXAMPLE 14   Amortization with Fee   First Bank offered Vicki a $1,000 loan amortized at 10% for 12 months. The loan carried a $25 prepaid finance charge. What will her payments be? What is her APR?

Solution:

Principal $1,000 + Fee $25 = $1,025	• Amount to be financed.
10% or .10 ÷ 12 = .0083333	• Monthly interest rate.
12 months	• Total loan period.

Step 1

$$\$1{,}025 \times \frac{(.0083333)(1 + .0083333)^{12}}{[(1 + .0083333)^{12} - 1]}$$ • Set values into formula.

Step 2

$$\$1{,}025 \times \frac{(.0083333)(1.1047126)}{(1.1047126 - 1)}$$ • Remove exponents.

Step 3

$$\$1{,}025 \times \frac{(.0092056)}{(.1047126)}$$ • Compute within parentheses.

248   Chapter 9   Personal Finance

Step 4

$1,025 × .0879127 = $90.11	· Monthly payments.
$90.11 × 12 = $1,081.33	· Total payback.
$1,081.33 − $1,000 = $81.33	· Total interest.
1,000 ÷ 100 = 10	· Number of hundreds borrowed.
$81.33 ÷ 10 = $8.13	· Interest per $100.
8.13 and 12 months	· Use for Federal Reserve tables.
14.75%	· Federal Reserve APR.

Note: This differs from the stated problem APR due to the additional loan fee.

✔ CHECK FOR UNDERSTANDING

1. Gilberto was interested in buying a new car. The dealer offered to finance $4,800 for 30 months at $14\frac{1}{2}$%. The loan carried a $64 loan processing charge. **(a)** What would his payments be? **(b)** What is the APR?

2. A loan for $968 was to be financed for 48 months at $19\frac{3}{4}$%. What were the monthly payments?

3. What are **(a)** the payments and **(b)** the APR on a loan for $3,000 if 16 percent APR is charged with a $25 loan fee and it is amortized over 42 months?

4. If a new piano costing $1,748 is financed at 18% interest for $5\frac{1}{2}$ years, what will the monthly payment be? (Use formula.)

SKILL EXERCISES

Use table factor or formula to find the following monthly payments:

	Amount financed	No. of months	Interest APR	Finance fee	Table factor	Monthly payment
1.	$ 3,000	30	$13\frac{3}{4}$	none	_____	$ _____
2.	$ 8,000	84	$16\frac{1}{4}$	$20	_____	$ _____
3.	$ 6,750	36	$15\frac{1}{2}$	none	_____	$ _____
4.	$ 1,280	24	$19\frac{1}{2}$	none	_____	$ _____
5.	$ 2,000	15	18	none	formula	$ _____
6.	$ 750	12	21	$10	_____	$ _____
7.	$18,000	96	17	none	_____	$ _____

Answers to ✔ Check for Understanding
1. (a) $194.26; **(b)** 25.75%. **2.** $29.33. **3. (a)** $94.53; **(b)** 17.00%. **4.** $41.91.

8.	$ 4,150	60	14	$40	_____	$ _____
9.	$ 9,880	72	$15\frac{1}{2}$	$25	_____	$ _____
10.	$ 7,500	18	12	$25	formula	$ _____

APPLICATIONS

1. If $8,700 were amortized on 30 installments at $15\frac{1}{2}\%$, what would the payments be?

2. Lynne's new sport power boat was financed at $14\frac{1}{2}\%$ for 84 months. If the boat costs $13,800, what are the monthly amortization payments?

3. A business loan for $8,000 was amortized for 36 months at 15% interest. If a $50 loan initiation fee was charged, what was the APR for the loan?

4. A $900 consumer loan is amortized for 18 months at 12% interest. What are the monthly payments?

5. An investor borrowed $6,200 for 48 months to buy a new horse trailer. If the interest rate was 17%, what were the monthly payments?

6. Arlie Jean borrowed $14,800 to pay the balance on her new motor home. A loan fee of $100 was charged. If the amortization period was for 60 months at 16%, what was her payment?

7. What would the monthly amortization payment be for a business loan of $5,000 financed for 18 months at 20.5%?

8. How much difference would there be in monthly payments if an $8,000 automobile was amortized for 48 months or for 60 months, if the interest rate was $14\frac{3}{4}\%$?

9. An inventory expansion loan for $7,750 was amortized for 24 months at 21%. What were the payments?

10. A $3,744 hot tub was amortized over 36 months at $18\frac{1}{2}\%$ interest. What were the payments?

Loan Payoff

9.3

A loan payoff is used to complete an installment contract early. Contracts rarely use an even-interest apportionment payment schedule. A contract payoff may be calculated using two methods: interest per payment and the Rule of 78.

Interest-per-Payment Method

The interest-per-payment method calculates the amount of simple interest from the date of last payment received. For consumer loans, the time equation uses the exact number of days and a 365/366-day year. For business or commercial loans, the time equation uses the exact number of days and a 360-day year.

EXAMPLE 15 A business loan with a current principal balance of $14,254 was in effect at $16\frac{1}{2}\%$ interest. The previous payment was made on March 16. What would the payoff be if made on April 8?

Solution: Use formula: Payoff = Balance − Interest due:

$14,254	• Principal balance.
March 16th to April 8th = 23 days	• Days of interest due.
$14,254 × .165 = (23 ÷ 360) = $150.26	• Interest amount due.
$14,254 + 150.26 = $14,404.26	• Total payoff.

✔ CHECK FOR UNDERSTANDING

1. On September 12, a loan payoff was made on a $14\frac{1}{2}\%$ business loan. The balance remaining on the loan was $6,200. If the interest-per-payment method is used, what amount of interest would be due with a previous payment receipt date of August 15?

2. A 16% consumer loan with a balance of $620 was to be paid off on January 28. What is the payoff amount if the previous payment had been made on December 24?

SKILL EXERCISES

Complete the following using the interest-per-payment method for payoff:

	Loan balance	Date of last payment	Date of payoff	Interest rate	Type of loan	No. of interest days	Interest due
1.	$1,784	Mar. 1	Apr. 3	8%	Consumer	_____	$ _____
2.	$341.60	Oct. 12	Nov. 11	12%	Commercial	_____	$ _____
3.	$2,120	June 10	July 10	15%	Commercial	_____	$ _____
4.	$195.50	Apr. 6	May 8	16%	Consumer	_____	$ _____
5.	$847	Nov. 3	Dec. 4	22%	Consumer	_____	$ _____

Answers to ✔ Check for Understanding
1. $69.92.   2. $629.51.

APPLICATIONS

1. Mike Cabot bought a $1,625 wedding ring on 12 installments at 18% simple interest. His payment of April 4 brought the account balance down to $846.20. On May 5, he desired to pay the account in full. What total amount was due if the interest-per-payment method was used?

2. A consumer loan with a principal balance of $865.20 carried an interest rate of 19%. If the last payment had been made on August 16, what would the total payoff be when made on September 1 using the interest-per-payment method?

3. What final amount of interest would be charged for a payoff on June 16 using the interest-per-payment method? The 13% commercial loan carried a balance of $2,140 and had its last payment made on May 20.

4. A $13\frac{3}{4}$% consumer loan was paid off on October 10. If the loan account carried a balance of $344.80 and the previous payment had been made on September 10, using the interest-per-payment method, what was the total payoff?

5. A consumer loan was effective on June 20 for $1,200 at 17%. If the interest-per-payment method is used on the account, how much of the first $65 payment would be applied to reduce the principal if payment was made on July 20?

Rule of 78

A lender using **Rule of 78** maximizes interest earned on a loan. The Rule of 78 derives its name from determining interest per payment using a fraction. The denominator of the fraction is 78 if found for one year. For periods longer than a year use the formula below to find the denominator.

$$\frac{\text{Number of payments} \times (\text{Number of payments} + 1)}{2}$$

For example: one year has months 1, 2, 3, 4, 5, 6, 7, 8, 9, 10, 11, and 12. The summation of these numbers is 78. The formula could also be used:
(12 × 13) ÷ 2 = 78.

The numerator of the fractions is the sum of the month numbers in the loan period used in reverse order. For example: A year has 1, 2, 3, 4, 5, 6, 7, 8, 9, 10, 11, 12 months. If a borrower desired to pay back his loan after 4 months, the numerator would be calculated using 9 + 10 + 11 + 12 = 42. The denominator would be 78. Therefore $\frac{42}{78}$ of the annual interest would be due on the loan. (Notice this differs from the $\frac{1}{3}$ interest expected.)

Table 9.3 shows how interest calculations compare using the Rule of 78 and two other common methods: the even allocation and the interest-per-payment methods. A $1,200 interest amount is assumed.

Rule of 78 Procedure. To use the Rule of 78 to compute the amount of interest due on a loan:

a. Use formula to find the denominator for the fraction.
b. Sum the numerators of the months used in the loan.
c. Set the fraction to represent the interest due. (The sum for either the number of payments remaining or the number already made can be used.)

TABLE 9.3
Interest Due Each Month

Month	Even Allocation	Per Payment*	Rule of 78
1	$100	$1200 \times \frac{31}{365} = \$101.92$	$1200 \times \frac{12}{78} = \$184.61$
2	$100	$1200 \times \frac{28}{365} = \$92.04$	$1200 \times \frac{11}{78} = \$169.25$
3	$100	$1200 \times \frac{31}{365} = \$101.92$	$1200 \times \frac{10}{78} = \$153.84$
4	$100	$1200 \times \frac{30}{365} = \$98.63$	$1200 \times \frac{9}{78} = \$138.46$
5	$100	$1200 \times \frac{31}{365} = \$101.92$	$1200 \times \frac{8}{78} = \$123.08$
6	$100	$1200 \times \frac{30}{365} = \$98.63$	$1200 \times \frac{7}{78} = \$107.69$
7	$100	$1200 \times \frac{31}{365} = \$101.92$	$1200 \times \frac{6}{78} = \$92.31$
8	$100	$1200 \times \frac{31}{365} = \$101.92$	$1200 \times \frac{5}{78} = \$76.92$
9	$100	$1200 \times \frac{30}{365} = \$98.63$	$1200 \times \frac{4}{78} = \$61.54$
10	$100	$1200 \times \frac{31}{365} = \$101.92$	$1200 \times \frac{3}{78} = \$46.15$
11	$100	$1200 \times \frac{30}{365} = \$98.63$	$1200 \times \frac{2}{78} = \$30.77$
12	$100	$1200 \times \frac{31}{365} = \$101.92$	$1200 \times \frac{1}{78} = \$15.38$
Totals	$1,200	$1,200.00	$1,200.00

* Note: Assumes payment on first of each month. Commercial loans using 360-day year will pay more than the $1,200 interest.

Illustrations:

- Sum for 12 payments 12 × 13 ÷ 2 = 78 (from equation).
- Sum for 48 payments 48 × 49 ÷ 2 = 1176.
- For numerators of the fraction use the month numbers for the total payments in reverse order.

12 payments 1st month $\frac{12}{78}$

2nd month $\frac{11}{78}$

3rd month $\frac{10}{78}$

48 payments 1st month $\frac{48}{1176}$

2nd month $\frac{47}{1176}$

3rd month $\frac{46}{1176}$

Section 9.3 Loan Payoff

d. The fractional allocation for each month is multiplied by the total interest due on a loan. That is, $1,650 interest due on a 4-year loan:

$$\text{1st month interest } \$1650 \times \frac{48}{1176} = \$67.35$$

$$\text{2nd month interest } \$1650 \times \frac{47}{1176} = \$65.94$$

EXAMPLE 16 Joanie borrowed $600 for her business to be repaid over a 12-month period. The loan charge was $13\frac{1}{2}\%$ simple interest, Rule of 78 applied. Monthly payments were $56.75. After making four monthly payments Joanie wants to pay off the loan. What amount is due?

Solution:

$56.75 × 12 = $681	· Total amount to be paid.
$681 − 600 = $81.00	· Total amount of interest.
1st month $\frac{12}{78}$	· Fractional amount of interest. (Note the reverse number order of the numerators and $[n \times (n+1)] \div 2 = 78$ as the denominator.)
2nd month $\frac{11}{78}$	
3rd month $\frac{10}{78}$	
4th month $\frac{9}{78}$	
Total $\frac{42}{78}$	· Total interest paid.
$81.00 × $\frac{42}{78}$ = $43.62	· Amount of interest paid.
$56.75 × 4 = $227.00	· Total paid on account to date.
$227.00 − $43.62 = $183.38	· Amount of principal paid.
$600 − $183.38 = $416.62	· Payoff amount.

✔ **CHECK FOR UNDERSTANDING**

1. The Cabot family was charged $842 interest on a recent 3-year loan. The Rule of 78 applied to the loan. How much interest had been paid on this loan for the first 8 months?

2. Harcourt borrowed $1,000 to be paid back over an 18-month period at 15% simple interest at a rate of $68.06 per month. What was the principal balance after the first five payments if the Rule of 78 is used to amortize the interest?

SKILL EXERCISES

Complete the following payoff information using the Rule of 78:

	Total loan interest	Monthly payment period	Rule 78 denominator	1st month interest	Total payoff month	Fraction earned interest
1.	$1300.00	2 years	_____	$ _____	10th	$ _____
2.	$ 872.40	18 months	_____	$ _____	14th	$ _____

Answers to ✔ Check for Understanding
1. $328.71.   2. $764.96.

254   Chapter 9   Personal Finance

3. $ 66.20   1 year   _____ $ _____   8th $ _____

4. $2144.00   3 years   _____ $ _____   20th $ _____

5. $ 95.40   12 months   _____ $ _____   6th $ _____

APPLICATIONS

Apply the Rule of 78 to the following payoff problems:

1. On an installment loan for $1,100 to be repaid in 18 months, the customer has already made 12 payments. The total amount to be repaid was $1,347.50. Using the Rule of 78, determine the remaining amount of interest due on the loan.

2. Commercial office equipment costing $1,848 was purchased at 14% for 6 months' simple interest. When the company made its fourth payment it desired to pay the total outstanding amount. How much interest would be saved if the Rule of 78 were used?

3. Hesser borrowed $750 to be repaid in 14 monthly payments. The total interest charged was $140. Using the Rule of 78, what is the first month's interest charge?

4. If a purchase for $510 were repaid in 36 monthly installments with a total interest charge of $183.60, what amount of interest would be saved if paid in full after 10 months? Use the Rule of 78.

5. Lea Highcliff borrowed $800 for her business for 8 months. The monthly payments were $116.50. At the end of the 5th month, she paid off the loan. Using the Rule of 78, what was the payoff amount?

Key Terms

Account statement (232)
Add-on interest (237)
Amortization (244)
Annual percentage rate (APR) (238)
Average daily balance method (228, 232)
Billing period (228)
Federal Reserve tables (238)
Installment period (236)
Interest-per-payment method (251)

Interest rate per month (228)
Loan fee/service charges (238)
Payoff amount (250)
Regulation Z (236)
Rule of 78 (252)
Total contract price (239)
Truth in lending (236)
Unpaid balance method (228)

Looking Back

Total expenses for a credit card or revolving charge must include the annual fees. Watch for the stated interest rate per month. Multiply the monthly rate by 12 and add the annual fee for the account. This is the total cost to evaluate.

The amortization method shows the same charges as the Federal Reserve tables. The tables are needed for the APR when there is a fee applied on the loan.

The purpose of the truth-in-lending provision is to ensure meaningful disclosure of credit terms to consumers. It imposes specific rules for lenders to follow. As a component of the consumer act, Regulation Z applies only to consumer credit and lease transactions. It does not apply to other business and commercial loans issued on time payback.

The Rule of 78 cannot be used for consumer loans but is appropriate for business and commercial transactions. The method or dollar amount of interest must be disclosed at the time of loan signing.

Let's Review

1. What will the new credit card balance be if a previous balance of $194.20 received a $40 payment on account? The account carries a $1\frac{1}{2}$% interest charge per month on the unpaid balance.

2. Phillip borrowed $950 at $10\frac{1}{2}$% add-on simple interest to be paid in 16 monthly installments. How much will the installment payments be? What is the APR?

3. A 15% APR consumer loan with a balance of $847 received its last payment on April 12. The borrower wished to make a payoff on the loan on May 15. Using the interest-per-payment method, what is the payoff amount?

4. What is the average daily balance and interest charge for an account billed monthly at $1\frac{1}{4}$% if the balance as of September 1 was $128.40 and a purchase of $104.40 was made on September 15?

5. Helen borrows $1,280 to be amortized over 24 months. If the lender quotes $16\frac{1}{2}$% APR, what will her payments be? What is the total interest charge for the loan?

6. New bathroom fixtures costing $4,164 were financed with 20% down and 18 installments of $210.30. What was the total interest on this contract? If this was an add-on interest transaction, what was the APR?

7. Franco Marcotti's revolving charge account showed a last-month balance of $543.20. If the account was charged $1\frac{1}{2}$% interest per month on the unpaid balance, and he purchased $44.80 during the month, what would the new balance be after a $220 payment?

8. Judy Cedain purchased equipment for her new office business. The $3,400 purchase was financed for 20 months with monthly payments of $212.50. For the 6th payment she wanted to pay off the account. Use the Rule of 78 to compute her payoff.

9. A $1,500 consumer loan was to be financed for 30 months at $14\frac{3}{4}$% APR. What were the monthly payments on the amortization schedule?

10. The billing date on a credit card was the 17th of the month. The card carried charges of $1\frac{1}{4}$% monthly on the average daily balance. Given the following data, compute the amount of interest on the account for the current billing period.

June 17 (end of period)	Balance	$208.00
June 20	Purchase	$ 16.80
July 4	Purchase	$ 61.20

11. What final amount would be due for a consumer loan payoff on October 11th using the interest-per-payment method if the 14% loan carried a balance of $547.30 and the most recent payment was made on September 10?

12. Carol was told her new equipment would cost $9,500. She could amortize it for 60 months. If the bank charges $15\frac{1}{2}$% interest APR, what would her total interest cost be?

Chapter Test

1. Sam Polski borrows $1,350 at $9\frac{1}{2}$% add-on interest to be paid in 18 equal monthly installments. How much will the payment be? What is the APR?

2. A new audio-sound amplifier costing $2,377 is amortized at 18% APR for 18 months. What will the monthly payment be?

3. A $1\frac{1}{4}$% revolving charge account showed a balance of $721 from the previous month. If a new purchase was made during the following month for $33.27, what is the new account balance if the unpaid balance method is being used?

4. Wilda wants to borrow $1,640 for landscaping improvements. If a 12% add-on interest loan plus a $15 application fee was charged on an 18-month installment contract, what were her payments? What was the APR?

5. Tayco Screens borrowed $7,200 to be repaid over 9 months. The loan charge was 14% simple interest, Rule of 78 applied. Monthly payments were $884. After making four payments, Tayco desired to pay off the loan on the next payment date. What amount would be due?

6. Tony was told that his new mower would cost $428.70. If he were to pay 15% down and finance the remainder at 14% add-on interest for 24 months, what would his payment be? What is the loan APR?

7. If a new truck costing $8,970 were fully amortized for 36 months at $13\frac{1}{2}$% APR and the loan carried a $75 processing fee, what would the payment be? What is the APR?

8. What final payment would be due for a payoff made on May 23 using the interest-per-payment method? The 15% consumer loan carried a balance of $1,200 and had its last payment made on April 22.

9. If a 2-year loan is issued for $3,290 at 16% add-on interest plus a $25 initiation fee, what is the monthly payment? What is the APR?

10. A credit card account based on $1\frac{1}{2}$% per month had a balance of $86 on April 1. Purchases during April were April 7, $42; and April 23, $16.20. Compute the interest charge for this account using the average daily balance method.

Mortgages, Taxes, and Insurance

10

OBJECTIVES

When you have completed this chapter you will be able to:

- *Calculate home mortgage amortization schedules and understand the major elements of a total principal, interest, taxes, and insurance (PITI) payment. (10.1)*
- *Know how taxes are assessed against real property and be able to calculate the primary elements of a tax system. (10.2)*
- *Become knowledgeable about the four categories of insurance and how rates under each are calculated. Know how to apply co-insurance concepts to loss determination. (10.3)*

COMING UP

A home, a condo, perhaps a townhouse. . . . We all dream of the time when we can say, "It's mine!" But most of us thinking of acquiring property are aware of the reality of ownership: We must usually settle for "it's ours," since the property will probably belong to us *and* the mortgage holder. And with ownership come other responsibilities, such as taxes and insurance.

Three financial issues that involve major expenses for both business and consumers are home mortgages, property taxes, and insurance. You must be able to evaluate the impact of various interest rates and **mortgage periods.** Taxes are applied annually against both personal and **real property.** Whether the property is purchased or leased, the need for insurance and taxes incurs an expense. The potential for loss can seriously affect the ability of a business to grow, as well as the personal life of an individual. The major risk categories including life, auto, property, and liability should be considered to protect your property.

Home Mortgages

10.1

For most of us, the purchase of a home is a major expenditure involving a long-term mortgage. All mortgages are based on simple interest with payments prorated over the life of the mortgage. The interest is calculated on the unpaid balance from month to month. The mainstay of the typical home mortgage is a **fixed-rate mortgage.** This includes a fixed interest rate on the principal and a payment amount which pays back the principal and interest (PI) over the mortgage period. Mortgage periods may be 15, 20, 25, or 30 years. Mortgage interest rates vary considerably during different economic cycles.

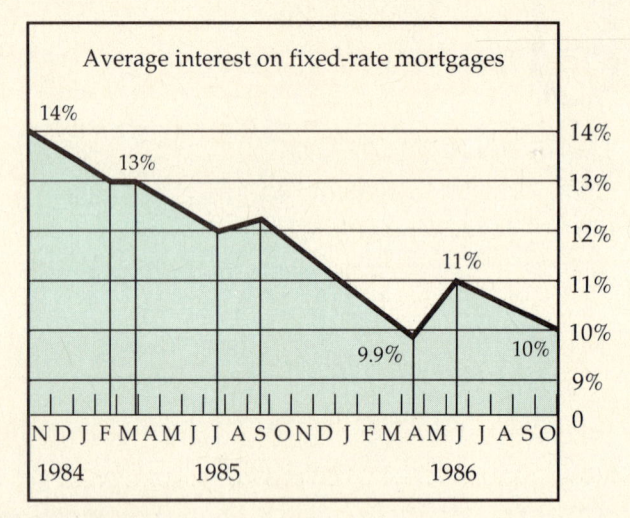

Amortization Schedule

An **amortization schedule** for home mortgages is calculated using the same formula shown in Chapter 9. The schedule is created for owners to give them an instant reference to a payoff amount on the property. The amounts of principal and interest are shown, including the balance established after payment is made each month. The payment amount for a fixed-rate mortgage will not change over the entire term of the mortgage. Mortgage payment tables are frequently provided by mortgage loan departments to calculate payment amounts. Table 10.1 provides a typical example. It shows four standard mortgage periods and a range of common interest rates. To use this table follow these steps:

- Divide the total mortgage amount by 1,000. This gives the principal per $1,000.
- Find the interest rate and length of the mortgage on the computation table.
- Read the multiplier from the table.
- Multiply this amount times the principal per $1,000. This will establish the principal and interest (PI) payment for the mortgage term.

260   Chapter 10   Mortgages, Taxes, and Insurance

TABLE 10.1
PI Payment Computation Table

Interest Rate	30 Years	25 Years	20 Years	15 Years
7 % per $1,000	6.65320	7.06780	7.75300	8.98840
7.5 % per $1,000	6.99220	7.39000	8.05600	9.27020
8 % per $1,000	7.33780	7.71820	8.36460	9.55660
8.5 % per $1,000	7.68920	8.05240	8.67840	9.84740
9 % per $1,000	8.04640	8.39200	8.99740	10.14280
9.5 % per $1,000	8.40860	8.73700	9.32140	10.44240
10 % per $1,000	8.77580	9.08720	9.65040	10.74620
10.5% per $1,000	9.14740	9.44200	9.98380	11.05400
11 % per $1,000	9.52340	9.80120	10.32200	11.36600
11.5% per $1,000	9.90300	10.16480	10.66440	11.68200
12 % per $1,000	10.28620	10.53240	11.01100	12.00180
12.5% per $1,000	10.67260	10.90360	11.36160	12.32540
13 % per $1,000	11.06200	11.27840	11.71580	12.65260
13.5% per $1,000	11.45420	11.65660	12.07380	12.98320
14 % per $1,000	11.84880	12.03780	12.43540	13.31760
14.5% per $1,000	12.24560	12.42180	12.80000	13.65520

EXAMPLE 1 Determine the payment for a 25-year, 10% mortgage taken on a $63,500 property.

Solution: Use Table 10.1:

$63,500 ÷ 1,000 = 63.5 • Find the principal per $1,000.
25 years, 10% rate • Use these factors for the table.
9.0872 • Locate the table payment factor.
63.5 × 9.0872 = 577.0372 • Value/1,000 × Factor = Payment.
$577.04 • Monthly PI payment.

EXAMPLE 2 What would the principal and interest (PI) payment be if a $120,000 home was purchased with a 20% down payment, at an interest rate of $9\frac{1}{2}$% for 30 years?

Solution: Use Table 10.1:

$120,000 × .80 = $96,000 • Mortgage 80% of cost.
96,000 ÷ 1,000 = 96 • Principal per $1,000.
30 years, 9.5% • Factors for the table.
8.40860 • Locate the table factor.
96 × 8.40860 = 807.2256 • Value/1,000 × Factor = Payment.
$807.23 • Monthly PI payment.

PROBLEM SOLVING STRATEGY

Once the amount of monthly principal and interest payment is determined, the amortization schedule can be established. Since the principal and interest payback amounts are included in the PI payment, the procedure becomes one of establishing how much of the payment each month is allocated to principal and how much to interest. The balance owed is reduced with each payment by the amount of principal. The interest for the following month is then calculated using the new balance. (See also Appendix A.)

Section 10.1 Home Mortgages

To determine how to calculate an amortization schedule, follow these steps:

> **Step 1.** Find the total annual interest.
> **Step 2.** Determine the monthly interest due.
> **Step 3.** Establish the amount of PI payment that is principal.
> **Step 4.** Find the new balance.

Follow Table 10.2 to evaluate the procedure. Use the example of a mortgage balance of $29,000 carried at 9% interest and a $265 per month PI payment.

TABLE 10.2
Calculation of Monthly Interest Payment Allocation

Total annual interest	=	Balance	×	Annual interest rate
	=	$29,000	×	.09
	=	$2,610.		
Monthly interest	=	Annual interest	÷	Months in a year
	=	$2,610	÷	12
	=	$217.50.		
Principal payment	=	Monthly payment	−	Monthly interest
	=	$265	−	$217.50
	=	$47.50.		
New balance	=	Previous balance	−	Principal payment
	=	$29,000	−	$47.50
	=	$28,952.50.		

The calculation sequence continues for the total number of months in the mortgage period; 30 years, for example, would be 360 months, 20 years, 240 months, etc. The first year of the amortization schedule for this example problem is illustrated in the following table:

Payment Number	Monthly Payment (PI)	Interest	Principal	Balance
1	$265	$217.50	$47.50	$28,952.50
2	$265	$217.14	$47.86	$28,904.64
3	$265	$217.78	$48.22	$28,856.42
4	$265	$216.42	$48.58	$28,807.84
5	$265	$216.06	$48.94	$28,758.90
6	$265	$215.69	$49.31	$28,709.59
7	$265	$215.32	$49.68	$28,659.91
8	$265	$214.95	$50.05	$28,609.86
9	$265	$214.57	$50.43	$28,559.43
10	$265	$214.20	$50.80	$28,508.63
11	$265	$213.81	$51.19	$28,457.44
12	$265	$213.43	$51.57	$28,405.87

CALCULATOR TIP

A complete payment schedule involves only the continued computation of the simple interest per month and subtraction. The calculator sequence for the Table 10.2 example problem would be:

29000 × .09 ÷ 12 = 217.50   • Interest per month (Mortgage × Rate ÷ Months in year).

217.50 − 265 = −47.50   • Amount principal reduced (Payment − Interest).

−47.50 + 29000 = 28952.50   • New balance for that month (Balance − Principal).

(Can be done in one sequence.)

EXAMPLE 3   Show the 1st month's principal and interest allocation for a $76,500 mortgage that is taken for 25 years at $11\frac{1}{2}$%.

Solution:

10.1648	• Table factor per $1,000.
76,500 ÷ 1,000 = 76.5	• Mortgage per $1,000.
76.5 × 10.1648 = 777.61	• Monthly payment.
76,500 × .115 ÷ 12 = 733.13	• 1st month interest.
777.61 − 733.13 = 44.48	• 1st month principal.
76,500 − 44.48 = 76,455.52	• 1st month balance.

Payment	Interest	Principal	Balance
$777.61	$733.13	$44.48	$76,455.52

EXAMPLE 4   What is the balance on a $48,000, 30-year, 12% mortgage after the first two monthly payments have been applied? Use the calculator sequence and the schedule format.

Solution:

10.2862	• Table factor per $1,000.
48 × 10.2862 = $493.74	• Monthly payment.
12% = .12	• Annual interest.

Payment	Payment	Interest	Principal	Balance
#1	493.74	480.00	13.74	47,986.26
#2	493.74	479.86	13.88	47,972.38

Balance after 2nd payment: $47,972.38.

✓ CHECK FOR UNDERSTANDING

1. The Smyths bought a home for $48,000 at 9% and made a $12,000 down payment. The lender quoted payments of $325 per month (PI). Set up the first two monthly payment allocations of principal and interest.

2. What is the monthly PI payment if an $87,000 house was purchased with 10% down, $8\frac{1}{2}$% interest for 20 years?

3. What amount would be paid per month per $1,000 for a 13% loan taken for 15 years?

4. How much of the first month's payment would be allocated to the principal if the transaction involved an $83,000 mortgage, at 10% for 25 years?

5. What would the balance be on a 9%, 20-year mortgage taken for $63,500 after the first two monthly payments have been applied?

Total Home Payment (PITI)

Amortization schedules with principal and interest (PI) do not reflect the total monthly payment requirements for a property owner. Many home payments also include taxes and insurance (TI). Lending institutions hold money paid for taxes and insurance in an **escrow account.** The taxes and insurance are paid from this account when due. The total home payment would include the amortized principal and interest plus taxes and insurance **(PITI).**

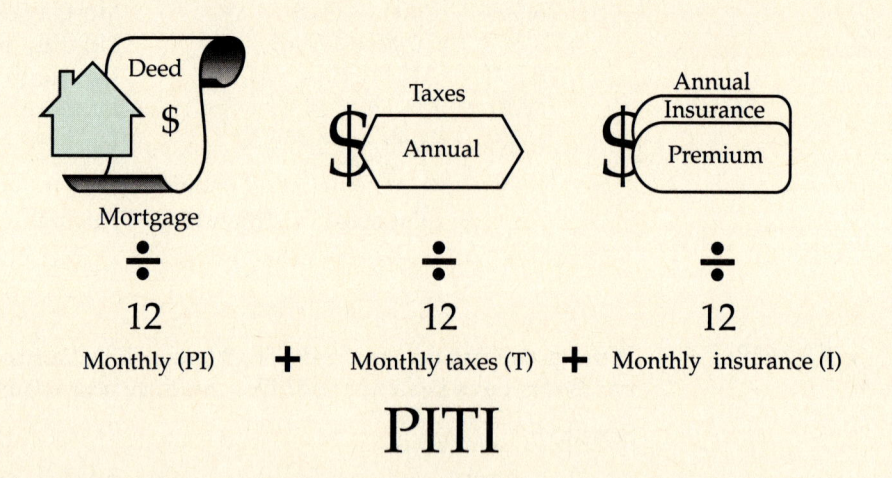

$$\frac{\text{Mortgage}}{12} \text{ Monthly (PI)} + \frac{\text{Annual Taxes}}{12} \text{ Monthly taxes (T)} + \frac{\text{Annual Insurance Premium}}{12} \text{ Monthly insurance (I)}$$

PITI

To find the escrow values, use these formulas:

> Escrow tax = Total annual tax ÷ 12
>
> Escrow insurance = $\frac{\text{Total insurance premium cost}}{\text{Total no. months of policy coverage}}$
>
> PITI payment = (Monthly) (PI payment + Tax + Insurance)

Answers to ✓ Check for Understanding

1.
Payment	Interest	Principal	Balance
$325	$270.00	$55.00	$35,945.00
$325	$269.59	$55.41	$35,889.59

2. $679.52.   3. $12.65.   4. $62.57.   5. $63,309.13.

EXAMPLE 5 The addition of $890 in taxes per year and $210 annual insurance cost to a mortgage payment of $275 would result in what PITI payment?

Solution:

$275	• (PI) Principal and interest.
$890 ÷ 12 = $74.17	• (T) Taxes per month.
$210 ÷ 12 = $17.50	• (I) Insurance per month.
$275 + $74.17 + $17.50 = $366.67	• (PITI) Add total payment.
$366.67	• PITI payment.

EXAMPLE 6 A new mortgage for $52,000 was taken at $11\frac{1}{2}\%$ for 30 years. Estimates of $294 annual insurance and $1,164 in taxes were planned. What would the total PITI payment be?

Solution:

$52,000 ÷ 1,000 = 52	• Loan principal per $1,000.
52 × 9.903 = $514.96	• (PI) Value/1,000 × Factor.
$1,164 ÷ 12 = $97.00	• (T) Monthly tax due.
$294 ÷ 12 = $24.50	• (I) Monthly insurance due.
$514.96 + $97.00 + $24.50 = $636.46	• (PITI) Add total payment.
$636.46	• PITI payment.

✔ CHECK FOR UNDERSTANDING

1. What is the monthly escrow total if taxes on a property were $978 and a two-year insurance policy on the property was quoted at $685.20?

2. A total PITI payment on a property was $744 per month. If annual taxes were $840 and insurance was billed at $372 per year, what was the monthly PI payment?

3. The Ballance family bought a home for $87,500. They paid 20% down and obtained a 12% mortgage on the balance. The monthly PI payments were $720.03. With annual taxes of $749.40 and insurance costs of $328.20, what were the monthly PITI payments?

4. With a monthly deposit of $74 per month for taxes and $22.40 for insurance, what would the total of the escrow be in one year on the purchase of a business property?

5. The Zapnar family purchased a $78,000 home by making an $11,000 down payment and agreeing to a $10\frac{1}{2}\%$, 25-year mortgage. If taxes were estimated at $1,240.20 and insurance for one year was $417, what was the PI payment and the PITI payment?

Answers to ✔ Check for Understanding
1. $110.05.   2. $643.   3. $809.83.   4. $1,156.80.   5. $632.61; $770.71.

SKILL EXERCISES

Calculate the following mortgage payments:

	Cost of property	Down payment	Mortgage amount	Interest rate	Term (years)	Payment (PI)
1.	$135,000	30%	$ _____	$8\frac{1}{2}$%	15	$ _____
2.	$ 89,000	22%	$ _____	11%	30	$ _____
3.	$145,000	$65,000	$ _____	12%	25	$ _____
4.	$ 76,000	$24,000	$ _____	14%	20	$ _____
5.	$ 92,500	42%	$ _____	$11\frac{1}{2}$%	15	$ _____
6.	$ 56,000	$12,000	$ _____	7%	20	$ _____
7.	$ 79,200	$35,000	$ _____	$9\frac{1}{2}$%	25	$ _____
8.	$109,300	45%	$ _____	13%	30	$ _____
9.	$ 98,600	26%	$ _____	10%	25	$ _____
10.	$194,000	$85,000	$ _____	$14\frac{1}{2}$%	30	$ _____

Calculate the following total PITI payments:

	Mortgage	PI Payment	Annual tax	Annual insurance	PITI
11.	$48,500	$412.50	$ 586.20	$440.16	$ _____
12.	$56,200	$701.00	$ 667.68	$368.16	$ _____
13.	$95,400	$912.40	$1,467.00	$412.20	$ _____
14.	$86,570	$795.40	$ 982.20	$ _____	$ 918.18
15.	$74,380	$804.70	$ _____	$441.60	$ 925.20
16.	$92,000	$ _____	$1,740.00	$612.00	$1,204.40
17.	$36,500	$ _____	$ 456.00	$285.00	$ 448.15
18.	$57,900	$ _____	$ 954.00	$398.16	$ 612.80

266   Chapter 10   Mortgages, Taxes, and Insurance

19.	$63,400	$ _____	$ 699.00	$390.00	$ 675.75
20.	$76,600	$800.40	$1,351.20	$540.96	$ _____

APPLICATIONS

Solve the following problems using home mortgage concepts:

1. A home was purchased for $86,000. It carried a $68,000 mortgage. If the mortgage was written at $10\frac{1}{2}\%$ for 25 years, what was the PI payment? What was the mortgage balance after the first two payments had been applied?

2. A property was purchased for $98,000 with 15% down. If it carried a 13%, 20-year mortgage, what would the first month's interest be? What is the monthly PI payment?

3. Allocate the first three months' principal and interest payments for an $86,000 mortgage at $11\frac{1}{2}\%$ for 30 years. Monthly payments are $851.66.

4. What would the total amount of monthly escrow be if the annual taxes were $1,288.32 with a three-year insurance policy costing $945?

5. A PI mortgage payment is $486 monthly and the annual taxes are $1,086, with annual insurance premiums of $172.20. What is the PITI payment?

6. The Backup Plumbing Company bought a building for $75,000. After a down payment of 20%, a 10% mortgage was taken on the balance. The PI payment was $625 a month. What is the mortgage balance after the second month?

7. The PITI payment on a home was $946. The home was purchased with a mortgage of $73,200 and was taken at 11% for 25 years. If the annual insurance policy for the property cost $480, what are the total annual taxes?

Section 10.1   Home Mortgages

8. A house purchaser was presented the following information:

> Home mortgage: $86,000
> Mortgage rate: $8\frac{1}{2}$%, 30 years
> Annual property tax: $1,149.60
> 2-year property insurance: $795.12

What is the PITI for this property?

9. The total PITI payment on a property was $672.40. Annual insurance costs were $364.20 with property taxes listed at $650.16. If the property was mortgaged for $52,500 at 12%, what would the first month's principal payment be on an amortization schedule?

10. A property purchased for $128,000 with 18% down, carried a $12\frac{1}{2}$% mortgage for 30 years. What is the PI payment? What is the first month's principal component on an amortization schedule?

Property Taxes

10.2

Property taxes are a major expense. Any person planning property acquisition should understand the way taxes are determined. The county collects taxes. **Tax rates** are determined by the county and are set by formulas, which may vary by state. An assessor determines the **market value** of each property in the county. Each state prescribes a percent called an **assessed rate,** which is applied against the market value to determine the **assessed value** for taxation. Depending upon how a given state approaches property assessment, different assessed rates would be used for various categories of property, such as homes, business, or industrial. Tax rates are used with assessed values to determine taxes due.

School district mill* levies

School districts	Proposed '90 budget**	'90 mill levy	Mill levy increase over '89
Colorado Springs District 11	$111.6	53.62	0.81
Academy District 20	$39.6	66.13	3.83
Harrison District 2	$37.4	68.3	7.66
Widefield District 3	$26.3	75.7	7.81
Cheyenne Mountain District 12	$10.3	63.12	0.59
Falcon District 49	$8.7	77.51	6.73

*$1 for every $1,000 of assessed property
**In millions of dollars

FIGURE 10.1
Property tax elements

```
                    INDIVIDUAL CALCULATIONS

Assessed Value      =   Market Value        ×   Assessed Rate
     Part           =        Base           ×        Rate

Tax Rate (per dollar) =  Total Budget Needs ÷   Total Assessed Value
     Rate           =        Part           ÷        Base

Property Taxes      =   Total Assessed Value ×  Tax Rate (per dollar)
     Part           =        Base           ×        Rate

                   IN SEQUENCE THE PROCESS IS:

Market Value        ×   Assessed Rate       =   Assessed Value
     B              ×        R              =        P

Assessed Value      ×   Tax Rate            =   Taxes
     B              ×        R              =        P


Tax Rate            =   Annual Budget       ÷   Total Assessed Value of Property
     R              =        P              ÷        B
```

Several agencies or governing bodies within a typical county boundary may tax property. For instance, the city, county, school district, library district, fire district, water district, all tax property. The level of tax for any of these agencies is based upon their individual operating budgets. Their budgets are consolidated by the county to determine total tax levels needed to generate their annual requirements.

A preliminary calculation is needed to establish an assessed rate. The assessed rate becomes the base of computation for both the tax rate and taxes. Figure 10.1 shows the calculations required to generate property taxes. Note that each involves the application of the base, rate, and part concepts.

Follow these steps:

- Determine the assessed value.
- Establish the tax rate per dollar.
- Calculate the property taxes.

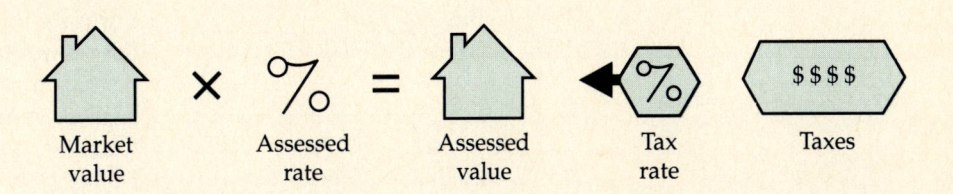

Market value × Assessed rate = Assessed value ← Tax rate — Taxes

The calculated tax rate is a rate "per dollar" of assessed value. Since these rates frequently involve decimal expressions, the use of a **mill levy** is common for expressing tax rates. The mill levy represents the dollar amount of taxes per $1,000 of assessed property value. A mill is an expression used to represent 1,000.

- Mill levy = Taxes per dollar × 1,000 (3 decimals right).
- Taxes per dollar = Mill levy ÷ 1,000 (3 decimals left).

To illustrate, assume:

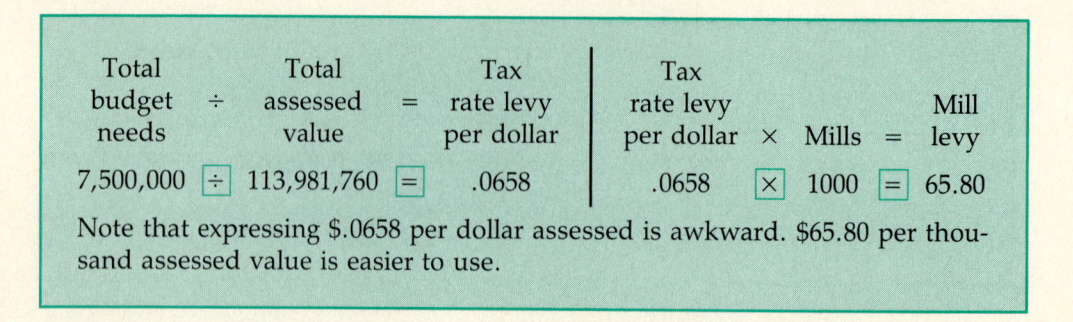

Total budget needs	÷	Total assessed value	=	Tax rate levy per dollar		Tax rate levy per dollar	×	Mills	=	Mill levy
7,500,000	÷	113,981,760	=	.0658		.0658	×	1000	=	65.80

Note that expressing $.0658 per dollar assessed is awkward. $65.80 per thousand assessed value is easier to use.

EXAMPLE 7 If the budget for Mesa county is $24,400,000, the total market value of property in the county is $945,736,430, and the assessed rate is 30 percent for all categories, what is the tax rate? What is the mill levy?

Solution: The unknown is a tax rate, the rate:

945,736,430 × .30 = 283,720,929   • $P = B \times R$, assessed value.
Rate = Part ÷ Base   • Formula for the rate.
Rate = 24,400,000 ÷ 283,720,929   • Set values into formula.
24,400,000 ÷ 283,720,929 = .086   • Find tax rate per dollar.
.086 × 1,000 = 86.00   • Convert tax rate to mills.
$86.00   • Mill levy.

CALCULATOR TIP

Find the mill levy using this calculator sequence:

945,736,430 × .30 = 283,720,929 [M+]   • Assessed value.
24,400,000 ÷ (283,720,929) [MR] = .086   • Tax rate (dollar).
.086 × 1,000 = 86   • Mills.

EXAMPLE 8 A property with a $135,000 market value was assessed at a 42% rate. If the tax rate was 45.72 mills, what were the annual taxes?

Solution: The unknown is annual taxes, a part:

Part = Base × Rate   • Formula for the part.
Part = 135,000 × .42   • Set values into formula.
   • Assessed rate.
   • Market value.
135,000 × .42 = 56,700   • Calculate the assessed value.
45.72 ÷ 1,000 = .04572   • Mill levy to tax per dollar.
56,700 × .04572 = 2,592.32   • $P = B \times R$, calculate taxes.
$2,592.32   • Annual taxes.

EXAMPLE 9 A property was taxed $85.84 by the regional library district. If the library district tax rate was .75 mills, what was the assessed value of the property?

270   Chapter 10   Mortgages, Taxes, and Insurance

Solution: The unknown is assessed value, a base:

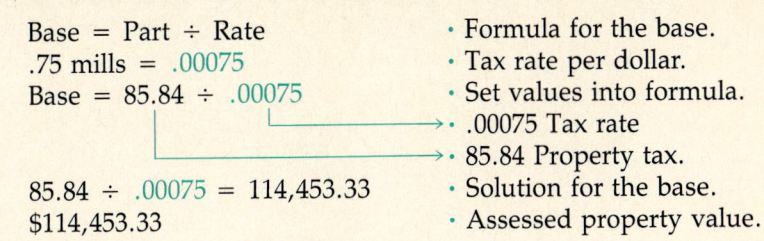

Base = Part ÷ Rate	• Formula for the base.
.75 mills = .00075	• Tax rate per dollar.
Base = 85.84 ÷ .00075	• Set values into formula.
	→ .00075 Tax rate
	→ 85.84 Property tax.
85.84 ÷ .00075 = 114,453.33	• Solution for the base.
$114,453.33	• Assessed property value.

EXAMPLE 10 A business building had an assessed value of $245,900. If the taxes were $8,803.22, what was the mill levy?

Solution: The unknown is the mill levy, a rate.

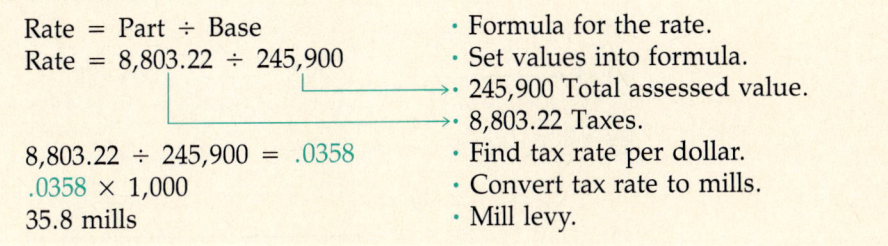

Rate = Part ÷ Base	• Formula for the rate.
Rate = 8,803.22 ÷ 245,900	• Set values into formula.
	→ 245,900 Total assessed value.
	→ 8,803.22 Taxes.
8,803.22 ÷ 245,900 = .0358	• Find tax rate per dollar.
.0358 × 1,000	• Convert tax rate to mills.
35.8 mills	• Mill levy.

✔ CHECK FOR UNDERSTANDING

1. The budget for the county is $15,865,000, and the assessed valuation is $193,925,000. What is the tax rate? What is the mill levy?

2. The market value of a small business is $250,000. If the assessed rate is 25%, what is the assessed value?

3. The tax rate is 15.82 mills. If a property has an assessed value of $36,000, what are the annual taxes?

SKILL EXERCISES

Apply the appropriate base, rate, and part relationships to find the missing values:

	Market value	Assessed rate	Assessed value	Tax rate	Taxes
1.	$ 87,000	30%	$ _____	.0972	$ _____
2.	$ _____	25%	$47,000	_____	$3,525
3.	$ 46,000	_____ %	$16,100	.0875	$ _____
4.	$ 69,500	_____ %	$18,765	92 mills	$ _____
5.	$ _____	40%	$ _____	.0765	$ 975

Answers to ✔ Check for Understanding
1. 0.08181 per $1; 81.81 mills.   2. $62,500.   3. $569.52.

Section 10.2 Property Taxes   271

6.	$168,000	_____%	$84,000	_____	$8,760	
7.	$ _____	32%	$ _____	76.5 mills	$1,566.72	
8.	$ _____	42%	$16,000	.0832	$ _____	
9.	$ 49,600	_____%	$17,360	_____	$1,597	
10.	$135,000	_____%	$78,420	_____ mills	$6,480	
11.	$ _____	60%	$ _____	.0975	$8,287.50	
12.	$ _____	50%	$84,000	.0444	$ _____	
13.	$286,000	40%	$ _____	12.36 mills	$ _____	
14.	$ 48,440	_____% $ _____	.0426	$ 822.00		
15.	$111,363	_____% $ _____	46.4 mills	$1,136.80		

APPLICATIONS

Apply property tax concepts to the following problems:

1. The Out-of-Bounds Golf Manufacturing Company has a warehouse with a market value of $227,000. If the assessed rate is 25% and the tax rate is 67 mills, what is the tax?

2. If the Low-Neck Chicken Ranch has a tax bill of $3,750 and the assessed value of its buildings is $49,020, what is the tax rate per dollar of assessed value?

3. If the Best-Break Cement Company has a group of buildings with a market value of $387,000, the assessed rate is 30%, and the tax rate is 9.31 mills, what is the tax?

4. If the tax rate is 67.3 mills and the taxes are $877.65, what is the assessed value?

5. The market value of property owned by Gretchen's Boutique is $97,500. If the assessed rate is 28% and the taxes are $3,600, what is the tax rate per dollar?

6. Given the following tax information, what would the total taxes be on a property with an assessed value of $48,500?

    City: 11.21 mills
    County: 22.3 mills
    School district: 56.2 mills
    Regional library: 0.15 mills
    Water district: 1.82 mills

7. If the tax rate for a school district was 61.3 mills and the total assessed property value for the district was $87,525,000, what was the school district's budget?

8. The Big-Wave water conservation district taxed a property for $28.40. If the tax rate was .000234 per dollar, what was the budget for the water district?

9. Ruth's Ceramics Factory had a total tax bill of $2,720. If the tax rate was 52.5 mills and the property assessed rate was 28%, what was the market value of the property?

10. The Red-Center Target Company paid $4,250 in property taxes last year. The tax rate was 50 mills. If the tax bill this year increased 12%, what are this year's taxes? How much is the assessed value?

Insurance

10.3

Insurance provides compensation for damage or loss of property, life, acts of another, or various other types of risks that one may experience. The four risk categories that cause loss are property, legal liability, life or earning power, and dishonesty. The loss of property is one of the most common risks. Another major insurance category covers personal injury compensation for employees and customers. Some of this coverage is required by law, such as workmen's compensation, unemployment insurance, and old age and survivor's benefits (social security) as discussed in Chapter 6.

Life Insurance

There are four basic types of payment plans for life insurance: **term, ordinary** (or whole life), variable **pay life,** and **endowment.** Any other plan available is some variation of one of these four. The difference in cost among the various types of policies varies because of the different lengths in payment periods. Insurance tables show rates as an amount per $1,000 of coverage. The rates vary depending on the age of the insured at the time of purchase and the type of insurance needed.

> Policy cost = Table rate per $1,000 × Coverage per $1,000

Table 10.3 illustrates monthly rates for the four basic categories of insurance. The additional column "ADB" means additional death benefits. This feature pays double the policy coverage in the event of death by accident. The rates in Table 10.3 should be considered only as one example.

EXAMPLE 11 Partners Stepp (age 28) and Fetch (age 30) decided to take out $25,000 ordinary life policies in favor of each other. What would the respective annual premiums be? What is the expense of the combined premium for the company?

Solution: Use the ordinary life column of Table 10.3:

Stepp: $1.64 per month per $1,000   · Table value.
Table value × Thousands × Months
           ÷ year   · Premium calculation.
$1.64 × 25 × 12 = $492   · Annual cost.
Fetch: $1.75 per month per $1,000   · Table value.
$1.75 × 25 × 12 = $525   · Annual cost.
$492 + $525 = $1,017   · Combined premium.

TABLE 10.3
Premium Rates per Month per $1,000 for Adults 16–50: Basic Policy Categories

Plan Age	Ordinary Life $10,000 Minimum Premium	ADB	20-Pay Life Premium	ADB	Endowment @ 65 Premium	ADB	15-Year Term 12-Pay Premium	20-Year Term 16-Pay Premium
16	1.19	.11	2.40	.13	1.69	.11		
17	1.22	.11	2.44	.13	1.73	.11		
18	1.25	.11	2.48	.13	1.78	.11		
19	1.28	.11	2.52	.13	1.83	.11		
20	1.32	.11	2.57	.13	1.88	.11	.25	.25
21	1.35	.11	2.61	.13	1.94	.11	.25	.25
22	1.39	.11	2.66	.13	2.00	.11	.25	.26
23	1.43	.11	2.71	.13	2.06	.11	.26	.26
24	1.47	.11	2.75	.13	2.12	.11	.26	.27
25	1.51	.11	2.80	.13	2.19	.11	.26	.27
26	1.55	.11	2.86	.13	2.27	.11	.27	.28
27	1.60	.11	2.91	.13	2.34	.11	.27	.29
28	1.64	.11	2.96	.13	2.43	.11	.28	.30
29	1.69	.11	3.02	.13	2.51	.11	.29	.31
30	1.75	.11	3.08	.13	2.60	.11	.30	.32
31	1.80	.11	3.14	.13	2.70	.11	.31	.33
32	1.86	.11	3.21	.13	2.80	.11	.32	.34
33	1.92	.11	3.27	.13	2.91	.11	.33	.36
34	1.99	.11	3.34	.13	3.02	.11	.34	.38
35	2.05	.11	3.41	.13	3.15	.11	.36	.40
36	2.13	.11	3.49	.13	3.28	.11	.38	.43
37	2.20	.11	3.57	.13	3.42	.11	.40	.46
38	2.28	.11	3.65	.13	3.58	.11	.43	.49
39	2.36	.11	3.74	.13	3.74	.11	.46	.52
40	2.45	.13	3.83	.13	3.91	.13	.49	.56
41	2.54	.13	3.92	.13	4.09	.13	.52	.60
42	2.64	.13	4.02	.13	4.30	.13	.56	.65
43	2.74	.13	4.12	.13	4.52	.13	.60	.70
44	2.85	.13	4.23	.13	4.75	.13	.65	.75
45	2.97	.13	4.34	.13	5.02	.13	.70	.81
46	3.09	.13	4.45	.13	5.31	.13	.75	.87
47	3.22	.13	4.58	.13	5.65	.13	.81	.94
48	3.36	.13	4.71	.13	6.01	.13	.88	1.02
49	3.50	.13	4.85	.13	6.42	.13	.95	1.11
50	3.66	.15	4.99	.15	6.88	.15	1.03	1.21

EXAMPLE 12 What would the annual cost be for a 32-year-old business person to insure himself with a $100,000, 15-year term, 12-pay policy?

Solution: Use the 15-year term, 12-pay column of Table 10.3:

- 32 years old = .32 monthly · Table rate for term.
- $.32 × 12 = $3.84 · Annual rate for $1,000.
- $3.84 × 100 = $384 · Coverage for $100,000.

✔ CHECK FOR UNDERSTANDING

1. From Table 10.3, find the amount the Jacobs Company will have to pay monthly for a $35,000 ordinary life policy on 38-year-old Ted Jacobs.

274 Chapter 10 Mortgages, Taxes, and Insurance

2. The Hope-Rite Computer Company decided to insure the lives of its two top executives—Mr. Agee, 43, and Ms. Botee, 41—for $25,000 each. How much more would the monthly premium be for a whole life policy than for a 15-year term, 12-pay policy on each executive?

Auto Insurance

Auto insurance costs are complex and involve two major issues. The number of various coverage categories is the first issue; the complicated decision making process to determine risk class for **premiums** is the other. In addition, there are different levels of protection to consider. So that we might see the interaction of these issues, we will focus on a single "typical" category.

Table 10.4 shows the basic categories of insurance coverage and the purpose of each coverage. Table 10.5 shows a general six-month rate schedule for rate class A1. Although insurance companies have many rate classes, once determined, the procedures for each are identical.

TABLE 10.4
Auto Insurance Coverages

Type of Insurance Coverage	Extent of Coverage
Liability (Bodily Injury and Property)	Bodily injuries to other people in your car. Damage to property caused by your car.
Uninsured Motorist	Bodily injuries to you caused by either uninsured motorist or hit-and-run driver.
Personal Injury Protection	Pays for medical expenses to you regardless of fault. Pays a predetermined portion of lost income. Pays medical expenses for others in your car.
Comprehensive	Pays for damage to your car caused by circumstances other than collision or upset.
Collision	Pays for damage to your car caused by collision with any object or by upset.

Table 10.5 shows the five categories of coverage. The headings at the top of the table list three of the categories—**BI/PD (Liability), UM (Uninsured Motorist),** and **No Fault (Personal Injury).** The letters and numbers (H, J, K, etc.) in the leftmost column designate the value of the insured vehicle by class. "Ded" is an abbreviation for "deductible," or the portion of damages the insured party is responsible for paying.

Answers to ✔ Check for Understanding
1. $79.80.   **2.** Agee, $53.50; Botee, $50.50.

TABLE 10.5
Typical Rate Classification Table (Semi-Annual Rates—Accident-Free)

BI/PD	1 Car	Multi		UM	1 Car	Multi		No Fault	
10/20/10	53.30	45.30		25/50	6.50	6.50			50 Ded	100 Ded
25/50/15	67.20	57.10		50/100	7.90	7.90		50,000	29.90	23.90
50/100/50	76.20	64.80		100/300	11.10	11.10		100,000	28.90	22.90
100/300/50	82.60	70.20		250/500	13.00	13.00				
250/500/100	90.10	76.60								

Comprehensive—One Car

	1985			1984			1983			1982			1981			1980 and Prior		
	50 Ded	100 Ded	500 Ded	50 Ded	100 Ded	500 Ded	50 Ded	100 Ded	500 Ded	50 Ded	100 Ded	500 Ded	50 Ded	100 Ded	500 Ded	50 Ded	100 Ded	500 Ded
H	29.10	22.10	12.20	27.70	21.00	11.60	24.90	18.90	10.40	23.50	17.90	9.90	20.80	15.80	8.70	19.40	14.70	8.10
J	32.70	24.80	13.80	31.10	23.60	13.10	28.00	21.20	11.80	26.40	20.10	11.10	23.30	17.70	9.80	21.80	16.50	9.20
K	39.90	30.30	16.80	38.00	28.90	16.00	34.20	26.00	14.40	32.30	24.60	13.60	29.50	21.70	12.00	26.60	20.20	11.20
L	58.10	44.10	24.40	55.30	42.00	23.20	49.80	37.80	20.90	47.00	35.70	19.70	41.50	31.50	17.40	36.70	29.40	16.20
M	72.60	55.10	30.60	69.10	52.50	29.10	62.20	47.30	26.20	58.70	44.60	24.70	51.80	39.40	21.80	48.40	36.80	20.40
N	80.50	61.20	35.70	76.70	58.30	34.00	69.00	52.50	30.60	65.20	49.60	28.90	57.50	43.70	25.50	53.70	40.80	23.80
O	87.80	66.80	41.20	83.60	63.60	39.20	75.20	57.20	35.30	71.10	54.10	33.30	62.70	47.70	29.40	58.50	44.50	27.40
P	95.80	72.80	46.40	91.20	69.30	44.20	82.10	62.40	39.80	77.50	58.90	37.60	68.40	52.00	33.20	63.80	48.50	30.90
Q	104.50	79.40	51.60	99.50	75.60	49.10	89.60	68.00	44.20	84.60	64.30	41.70	74.60	56.70	36.80	69.70	52.90	34.40
R	112.50	85.50	56.70	107.10	81.40	54.00	96.40	73.30	48.60	91.00	69.20	45.90	80.30	61.10	40.50	75.00	57.00	37.80
S	121.90	92.70	63.10	116.10	88.30	60.10	104.50	79.50	54.10	96.70	75.10	51.10	87.10	66.20	45.10	81.30	61.80	42.10
T	131.40	99.90	69.20	125.10	95.10	65.90	112.60	85.60	59.30	106.30	80.80	56.00	93.80	71.30	49.40	87.60	66.00	46.10
U	140.80	107.00	75.40	134.10	101.90	71.80	120.70	91.70	64.60	114.00	86.60	61.00	100.60	76.40	53.90	93.90	71.30	50.30
V	151.00	114.80	81.80	143.80	109.30	77.90	129.40	98.40	70.10	122.20	92.90	66.20	107.90	82.00	58.40	100.70	76.50	54.50
W	160.40	121.90	87.90	152.80	116.10	83.70	137.50	104.50	75.30	129.90	96.70	71.10	114.60	87.10	62.80	107.00	81.30	58.60
X	170.50	129.60	94.00	162.40	123.40	89.50	146.30	111.10	80.60	138.00	104.90	76.10	121.80	92.60	67.10	113.70	86.40	62.70
Y	183.60	139.50	102.20	174.90	132.90	97.30	157.40	119.60	87.60	148.70	113.00	82.70	131.20	99.70	73.00	122.40	93.00	68.10
Z	199.60	151.70	112.60	190.10	144.50	107.20	171.10	130.10	96.50	161.60	122.80	91.10	142.60	108.40	80.40	133.10	101.20	75.00
1	215.60	163.80	123.00	205.30	156.00	117.10	184.80	140.40	105.40	174.50	132.60	99.50	154.00	117.00	87.80	143.70	109.20	82.00
2	232.30	176.50	133.00	221.20	168.10	126.70	199.10	151.30	114.00	188.00	142.90	107.70	165.90	126.10	95.00	154.80	117.70	88.70

Comprehensive—Multi-Car

	1985			1984			1983			1982			1981			1980 and Prior		
	50 Ded	100 Ded	500 Ded	50 Ded	100 Ded	500 Ded	50 Ded	100 Ded	500 Ded	50 Ded	100 Ded	500 Ded	50 Ded	100 Ded	500 Ded	50 Ded	100 Ded	500 Ded
H	26.10	19.80	11.00	24.90	18.90	10.50	22.40	17.00	9.50	21.20	16.10	8.90	18.70	14.20	7.90	17.40	13.20	7.40
J	29.40	22.40	12.40	28.00	21.30	11.80	25.20	19.20	10.60	23.80	18.10	10.00	21.00	16.00	8.90	19.60	14.90	8.30
K	35.90	27.30	15.10	34.20	26.00	14.40	30.80	23.40	13.00	29.10	22.10	12.20	25.70	19.50	10.80	23.90	18.20	10.10
L	52.30	39.70	21.90	49.60	37.80	20.90	44.80	34.00	18.80	42.30	32.10	17.80	37.40	28.40	15.70	34.90	26.50	14.00
M	65.30	49.70	27.50	62.20	47.30	26.20	56.00	42.60	23.00	52.90	40.20	22.30	46.70	35.50	19.70	43.50	33.10	18.30
N	72.60	55.10	32.10	69.10	52.50	30.60	62.20	47.30	27.50	58.70	44.60	26.00	51.80	39.40	23.00	48.40	36.80	21.40
O	79.10	60.10	37.10	75.30	57.20	35.30	67.80	51.50	31.80	64.00	48.60	30.00	56.50	42.90	26.50	52.70	40.00	24.70
P	86.20	65.50	41.70	82.10	62.40	39.70	73.90	56.20	35.70	69.80	53.00	33.70	61.60	46.80	29.80	57.50	43.70	27.80
Q	94.10	71.50	46.40	89.60	68.10	44.20	80.60	61.30	39.80	76.20	57.90	37.60	67.20	51.10	33.20	62.70	47.70	30.90
R	101.20	77.00	51.00	96.40	73.30	48.60	86.80	66.00	43.80	81.90	62.30	41.30	72.30	55.00	36.50	67.50	51.30	34.00
S	109.70	83.40	56.80	104.50	79.40	54.10	94.10	71.50	48.70	88.80	67.50	46.00	78.40	59.60	40.60	73.20	55.60	37.90
T	118.20	89.90	62.40	112.60	85.60	59.40	101.30	77.00	53.50	95.70	72.80	50.50	84.50	64.20	44.60	78.80	59.90	41.00
U	126.70	96.30	67.80	120.70	91.70	64.60	108.60	82.50	56.10	102.60	77.90	54.90	90.50	68.80	48.50	84.50	64.20	45.23
V	135.90	103.20	73.60	129.40	98.30	70.10	116.50	88.50	63.10	110.00	83.60	59.60	97.10	73.70	52.60	90.60	68.80	49.10
W	144.40	109.70	79.10	137.50	104.50	75.30	123.80	94.10	67.00	116.90	88.80	64.00	103.10	78.40	56.30	96.30	73.20	52.70
X	153.50	116.70	84.50	146.20	111.10	80.50	131.60	100.00	72.50	124.30	94.40	68.40	109.70	83.30	60.40	102.30	77.80	56.40
Y	165.30	125.60	92.00	157.40	119.60	87.60	141.70	107.60	78.80	133.80	101.70	74.50	118.10	89.70	65.70	110.20	83.70	61.30
Z	179.70	136.50	101.30	171.10	130.00	96.50	154.00	117.00	86.90	145.40	110.50	82.00	128.30	97.50	72.40	119.80	91.00	67.60
1	194.00	147.40	110.70	184.80	140.40	105.40	166.30	126.40	94.90	157.10	119.30	89.60	138.60	105.30	79.10	129.40	98.30	73.80
2	209.10	158.90	119.70	199.10	151.30	114.00	179.20	136.20	102.60	169.20	128.60	96.90	149.30	113.50	85.50	139.40	105.90	79.80

276 Chapter 10 Mortgages, Taxes, and Insurance

Collision—One Car

1982

	100 Ded	200 Ded	500 Ded
H	54.90	42.30	20.20
J	65.70	50.60	26.40
K	76.50	58.90	33.00
L	87.30	67.20	40.00
M	96.10	75.60	47.10
N	105.90	81.60	51.90
O	114.80	88.40	56.50
P	122.60	94.40	61.30
Q	131.40	101.20	66.00
R	139.30	107.30	70.70
S	148.10	114.10	75.40
T	158.00	120.10	80.20
U	164.80	126.90	84.80
V	172.60	132.90	89.50
W	181.50	130.70	94.30
X	191.30	147.30	98.90
Y	207.00	159.40	108.40
Z	222.60	171.40	117.80
1	238.30	183.50	127.20
2	254.10	195.60	136.70

1981

	100 Ded	200 Ded	500 Ded
H	48.50	37.40	17.90
J	58.00	44.60	23.30
K	67.50	52.00	29.10
L	77.00	59.30	35.30
M	86.60	66.70	41.60
N	93.50	72.00	45.80
O	101.30	78.00	49.90
P	108.20	83.30	54.10
Q	116.00	89.30	58.20
R	122.90	94.70	62.40
S	130.70	100.70	66.50
T	137.60	106.00	70.70
U	145.40	112.00	74.90
V	152.30	117.30	79.00
W	160.10	123.30	83.20
X	168.80	130.00	87.30
Y	182.60	140.60	95.60
Z	196.40	151.30	104.00
1	210.30	161.90	112.30
2	224.20	172.60	120.60

1980 and Prior

	100 Ded	200 Ded	500 Ded
H	45.20	34.90	16.70
J	54.10	41.70	21.70
K	63.00	48.50	27.20
L	71.90	55.40	33.00
M	80.80	62.20	38.80
N	87.20	67.20	42.70
O	94.50	72.80	46.60
P	100.90	77.80	50.50
Q	108.20	83.40	54.30
R	114.70	88.30	58.20
S	121.90	93.90	62.10
T	128.50	96.90	68.00
U	135.70	104.50	69.90
V	142.20	109.50	73.70
W	149.50	115.10	77.60
X	157.50	121.30	81.50
Y	170.50	131.30	89.30
Z	183.30	141.20	97.00
1	196.30	151.10	104.80
2	209.20	161.10	112.60

Collision—Multi-Car

1982

	100 Ded	200 Ded	500 Ded
H	49.50	38.10	18.30
J	59.20	45.60	23.70
K	68.90	53.00	29.70
L	78.50	60.50	36.00
M	88.30	68.00	42.40
N	95.40	73.40	46.70
O	103.30	79.60	50.90
P	110.30	85.00	55.20
Q	118.30	91.10	59.40
R	125.40	96.50	63.60
S	133.30	102.00	67.80
T	140.30	108.00	72.10
U	148.30	114.20	76.30
V	155.40	119.60	80.60
W	163.30	125.70	84.80
X	172.10	132.50	89.10
Y	186.20	143.40	97.60
Z	200.30	154.30	106.00
1	214.50	165.20	114.50
2	228.70	176.00	123.00

1981

	100 Ded	200 Ded	500 Ded
H	43.70	33.60	16.10
J	52.20	40.20	20.90
K	60.80	46.80	26.20
L	69.30	53.40	31.80
M	77.90	60.00	37.40
N	84.20	64.80	41.20
O	91.10	70.20	44.90
P	97.40	75.00	48.70
Q	104.40	80.40	52.40
R	110.60	85.10	56.10
S	117.00	90.50	59.90
T	123.80	95.30	63.60
U	130.90	100.70	67.40
V	137.10	105.50	71.10
W	144.10	110.50	74.90
X	151.90	116.90	78.60
Y	164.30	126.50	86.10
Z	176.80	136.10	93.50
1	189.30	145.70	101.00
2	201.80	155.30	108.50

1980 and Prior

	100 Ded	200 Ded	500 Ded
H	40.70	31.40	15.10
J	48.70	37.50	19.50
K	56.70	43.70	24.40
L	64.70	49.80	29.70
M	72.70	56.00	34.90
N	78.50	60.50	38.40
O	85.10	65.50	41.90
P	90.90	70.00	45.40
Q	97.40	75.00	48.90
R	103.30	79.50	52.40
S	109.80	84.50	55.90
T	115.60	89.00	58.40
U	122.20	94.00	62.90
V	128.00	98.50	66.40
W	134.50	103.50	69.90
X	141.80	109.10	73.40
Y	153.40	118.10	80.40
Z	165.00	127.10	87.30
1	176.70	136.00	94.30
2	188.30	145.00	101.30

Collision Plus 3.30
Towing 3.00
Death-Dismemberment

5,000 — 1.90
10,000 — 3.40
15,000 — 4.90
25,000 — 7.90

Disability — 600 Weekly 2.50
Full CCD = 129% of $50 Deductible CCD

Collision—One Car

1985

	100 Ded	200 Ded	500 Ded
H	67.80	52.30	25.00
J	81.20	62.50	32.60
K	94.50	72.60	40.70
L	107.80	83.10	49.50
M	121.20	93.30	58.20
N	130.80	100.80	64.10
O	141.80	109.20	69.80
P	151.40	116.70	75.70
Q	162.30	125.10	81.50
R	172.10	132.50	87.40
S	182.90	140.90	93.10
T	192.70	148.40	99.00
U	203.60	156.80	104.80
V	213.30	164.20	110.60
W	224.20	172.60	116.40
X	236.30	182.00	122.20
Y	255.70	196.90	133.90
Z	275.00	211.80	145.50
1	294.40	226.70	157.20
2	313.80	241.60	168.80

1984

	100 Ded	200 Ded	500 Ded
H	64.60	49.80	23.80
J	77.30	59.50	31.00
K	90.00	69.30	38.80
L	102.70	79.10	47.10
M	115.40	88.90	55.40
N	124.60	96.00	61.00
O	135.00	104.00	66.50
P	144.20	111.10	72.10
Q	154.60	119.10	77.60
R	163.90	126.20	83.20
S	174.20	134.20	88.70
T	183.50	141.30	94.30
U	193.90	149.30	99.80
V	203.10	156.40	105.30
W	213.50	164.40	110.90
X	225.00	173.30	116.40
Y	243.50	187.50	127.50
Z	261.90	201.70	138.60
1	280.40	215.90	149.70
2	298.90	230.10	160.80

1983

	100 Ded	200 Ded	500 Ded
H	58.10	44.80	21.40
J	69.60	53.60	27.90
K	81.00	62.40	34.90
L	92.40	71.20	42.40
M	103.90	80.00	49.90
N	112.10	86.40	54.90
O	121.50	93.60	59.90
P	129.80	100.00	64.90
Q	139.10	107.20	69.80
R	147.50	113.60	74.90
S	156.80	120.00	79.80
T	165.20	127.20	84.90
U	174.50	134.40	89.80
V	182.80	140.80	94.80
W	192.20	148.00	99.80
X	202.50	156.00	104.80
Y	219.20	168.80	114.80
Z	235.70	181.50	124.70
1	252.40	194.30	134.70
2	269.00	207.10	144.70

Collision—Multi-Car

1985

	100 Ded	200 Ded	500 Ded
H	61.10	47.00	22.60
J	73.10	56.30	29.30
K	85.10	65.50	36.60
L	97.00	74.80	44.50
M	100.10	84.00	52.40
N	117.80	90.70	57.60
O	127.60	98.30	62.90
P	136.30	105.00	68.10
Q	146.20	112.60	73.40
R	154.90	119.20	78.50
S	164.60	126.70	83.80
T	173.40	133.50	89.00
U	183.20	141.00	94.30
V	191.90	147.70	99.50
W	201.70	155.30	104.80
X	212.60	163.70	110.00
Y	230.10	177.10	120.50
Z	247.50	190.60	130.90
1	265.00	204.00	141.40
2	282.50	217.50	151.90

1984

	100 Ded	200 Ded	500 Ded
H	58.20	44.80	21.50
J	69.60	56.60	27.90
K	81.00	62.40	34.90
L	92.40	71.20	42.40
M	103.90	80.00	49.90
N	112.20	86.40	54.90
O	121.50	93.60	59.90
P	129.80	100.00	64.90
Q	139.20	107.20	69.90
R	147.50	113.50	74.80
S	156.80	120.70	79.60
T	165.10	127.10	84.80
U	174.50	134.30	89.80
V	182.80	140.70	94.80
W	192.10	147.90	99.80
X	202.50	155.90	104.80
Y	219.10	168.70	114.80
Z	235.70	181.50	124.70
1	252.40	194.30	134.70
2	269.00	207.10	144.70

1983

	100 Ded	200 Ded	500 Ded
H	52.40	40.30	19.40
J	62.60	48.20	25.10
K	72.90	56.20	31.40
L	83.20	64.10	38.20
M	93.50	72.00	44.90
N	101.00	77.80	49.40
O	109.40	84.20	53.90
P	116.80	90.00	58.40
Q	125.30	96.50	62.90
R	132.80	102.20	67.30
S	141.10	108.60	71.90
T	148.60	114.40	76.30
U	157.10	120.90	80.00
V	164.50	126.60	85.30
W	172.90	133.10	89.80
X	182.30	140.30	94.30
Y	197.20	151.80	103.30
Z	212.10	163.40	112.20
1	227.20	174.90	121.20
2	242.10	186.40	130.20

Section 10.3 Insurance

BI/PD. The BI/PD categories represent rates for single vehicles and multiple cars (two or more). Levels of coverage are listed for five categories. To interpret the BI/PD codes, read them as follows:

$10,000 / $20,000 / $10,000

| Personal injury; maximum for one person per accident. | Total personal injury; maximum for all involved per accident. | Property damage; maximum per accident. |

UM. The uninsured motorist categories are interpreted as follows:

$25,000 / $50,000

| Personal injury; maximum for one person per accident. | Total personal injury; maximum for all involved per accident. |

This coverage relates to individuals injured as pedestrians or as bicycle riders injured by hit-and-run or uninsured motorists. This category can also be accessed legally if liability–no fault expenses range beyond the $50,000 per person coverage.

No Fault (Personal Injury). This table shows one-level coverage for $50,000. Another rate is provided if a $100 deductible feature is chosen. This category protects the driver and all passengers of the owner's car from medical and hospital expenses. Work disability rehabilitation expenses are also included in this category.

Figure 10.2 includes the elements of the decision making processes for rate classification. Once a general rate level is established, it is used with a property value symbol to find the proper rate in Table 10.5.

EXAMPLE 13 Karla Krashbinder must insure her automobile. She feels that adequate protection includes liability and property damage, uninsured motorist, and personal injury. What would her six-month premium be if her choices of coverage were

        25/50/15   BI/PD
        50/100   UM
        100 Deductible No fault—PI

Solution: Use the one-car column of Table 10.5:

    $ 67.20   • BI/PD.
    $ 7.90   • Uninsured motorist.
 +$ 28.90   • No fault—PI
    $104.00   • Total premium.

EXAMPLE 14 Joe "Bumper" Fenders is ready to review his business expenses for his company's two vehicles. Vehicle A is a 1983 (value symbol S); vehicle B is a 1985 (value symbol W). His risk management portfolio requires that he carry liability BI/PD; uninsured motorist; no fault medical; $100 deductible comprehensive; and $200 deductible collision. For the following levels of coverage, what should he budget for annual vehicle insurance expenses?

        BI/PD   250/500/100
        UM   250/500
        No Fault—PI No deductible

Use the two-vehicle column.

TABLE 10.6a
Typical Property Insurance Schedule Groups 01–02

Amount of Insurance	Premium Group 01 Basic	Broad	Special	Premium Group 02 Basic	Broad	Special	Amount of Insurance	Premium Group 01 Basic	Broad	Special	Premium Group 02 Basic	Broad	Special
10,000	69	76	77	77	84	85	91,000	135	149	150	150	165	167
15,000	70	77	78	78	86	87	92,000	137	150	152	152	167	169
20,000	72	79	80	80	88	89	93,000	139	152	154	154	169	171
25,000	74	81	82	82	90	91	94,000	140	154	156	156	171	173
30,000	75	83	84	84	92	93	95,000	142	156	158	158	173	175
31,000	76	84	85	85	93	94	96,000	143	157	158	158	174	176
32,000	76	84	85	85	93	94	97,000	144	158	160	160	176	178
33,000	77	85	86	86	94	95	98,000	146	160	162	162	178	180
34,000	78	85	86	86	95	96	99,000	147	162	164	164	180	182
35,000	79	86	87	87	96	97	100,000	149	164	166	166	182	184
36,000	79	86	87	87	96	97	101,000	151	166	167	167	184	186
37,000	79	87	88	88	97	98	102,000	152	167	169	169	186	188
38,000	80	88	89	89	98	99	103,000	153	168	170	170	187	189
39,000	80	88	89	89	98	99	104,000	155	170	172	172	189	191
40,000	81	89	90	90	99	100	105,000	156	172	174	174	191	193
41,000	82	90	91	91	100	101	106,000	158	174	176	176	193	195
42,000	83	91	92	92	101	102	107,000	160	175	177	177	195	197
43,000	83	92	93	93	102	103	108,000	160	176	178	178	196	198
44,000	84	93	94	94	103	104	109,000	162	178	180	180	198	200
45,000	86	94	95	95	105	106	110,000	164	180	182	182	200	202
46,000	87	95	96	96	106	107	111,000	165	182	184	184	202	204
47,000	87	96	97	97	107	108	112,000	167	183	185	185	204	206
48,000	88	97	98	98	108	109	113,000	168	184	186	186	205	207
49,000	89	98	99	99	109	110	114,000	169	186	188	188	207	209
50,000	90	99	100	100	110	111	115,000	171	188	190	190	209	211
51,000	91	100	101	101	111	112	116,000	173	190	192	192	211	213
52,000	91	100	101	101	111	112	117,000	174	191	194	194	213	215
53,000	92	101	102	102	112	113	118,000	175	192	194	194	214	216
54,000	92	101	102	102	112	113	119,000	177	194	196	196	216	218
55,000	92	101	103	103	113	114	120,000	178	196	198	198	218	220
56,000	93	102	104	104	114	115	121,000	180	198	200	200	220	222
57,000	93	102	104	104	114	115	122,000	181	199	202	202	222	224
58,000	94	103	104	104	115	116	123,000	183	201	203	203	224	226
59,000	94	103	104	104	115	116	124,000	185	203	205	205	226	228
60,000	95	104	105	105	116	117	125,000	186	205	207	207	228	230
61,000	96	105	106	106	117	118	130,000	194	213	215	215	237	239
62,000	97	107	108	108	119	120	135,000	201	221	223	223	246	248
63,000	98	108	109	109	120	121	140,000	208	229	231	231	254	257
64,000	99	109	110	110	121	122	145,000	215	237	239	239	263	266
65,000	100	110	112	112	123	124	150,000	223	245	248	248	272	275
66,000	101	111	113	113	124	125	155,000	230	253	256	256	281	284
67,000	102	112	113	113	125	126	160,000	237	261	264	264	290	293
68,000	103	113	114	114	126	127	165,000	245	270	273	273	300	303
69,000	104	115	116	116	128	129	170,000	253	278	281	281	309	312
70,000	105	116	117	117	129	130	175,000	260	286	289	289	318	321
71,000	107	117	119	119	131	132	180,000	267	294	297	297	327	330
72,000	108	118	120	120	132	133	185,000	275	303	306	306	337	340
73,000	109	120	122	122	134	135	190,000	283	311	314	314	346	349
74,000	111	122	123	123	136	137	195,000	290	319	322	322	354	358
75,000	113	124	125	125	138	139	200,000	297	327	330	330	363	367
76,000	113	125	126	126	139	140	210,000	312	343	347	347	381	385
77,000	115	126	128	128	141	142	220,000	327	360	364	364	400	404
78,000	117	128	130	130	143	144	230,000	342	376	380	380	418	422
79,000	117	129	131	131	144	145	240,000	357	392	397	397	437	441
80,000	119	131	132	132	146	147	250,000	372	409	413	413	454	459
81,000	121	133	134	134	148	149	260,000	387	425	430	430	473	478
82,000	122	134	136	136	149	151	270,000	402	441	446	446	491	496
83,000	123	135	137	137	150	152	280,000	417	458	464	464	510	515
84,000	125	137	139	139	152	154	290,000	432	474	480	480	528	533
85,000	126	139	140	140	154	156	300,000	447	491	497	497	546	552
86,000	128	141	142	142	156	158	310,000	462	507	513	513	564	570
87,000	130	142	144	144	158	160	320,000	476	523	529	529	582	588
88,000	130	143	145	145	159	161	330,000	492	540	546	546	601	607
89,000	132	145	147	147	161	163	340,000	506	556	563	563	619	625
90,000	134	147	149	149	163	165	350,000	521	572	579	579	637	643
							Addl 1000s	1.46	1.60	1.62	1.62	1.78	1.80

Section 10.3 Insurance

TABLE 10.6b
Typical Property Insurance Schedule Groups 03–04

Amount of Insurance	Premium Group 03 Basic	Broad	Special	Premium Group 04 Basic	Broad	Special	Amount of Insurance	Premium Group 03 Basic	Broad	Special	Premium Group 04 Basic	Broad	Special
10,000	77	85	86	84	93	94	91,000	152	167	169	165	182	184
15,000	79	87	88	86	95	96	92,000	154	169	171	167	184	186
20,000	81	89	90	88	97	98	93,000	156	171	173	169	186	188
25,000	83	91	92	90	99	100	94,000	157	173	175	171	189	190
30,000	85	93	94	92	101	102	95,000	159	175	177	173	191	193
31,000	86	94	95	93	102	103	96,000	160	176	178	174	192	194
32,000	86	94	95	93	102	103	97,000	162	178	180	176	194	196
33,000	86	95	96	94	104	105	98,000	164	180	182	178	196	198
34,000	87	96	97	95	105	106	99,000	166	182	184	180	198	200
35,000	88	97	98	96	106	107	100,000	167	184	186	182	201	202
36,000	88	97	98	96	106	107	101,000	169	186	188	184	203	205
37,000	89	98	99	97	107	108	102,000	171	188	190	186	205	207
38,000	90	99	100	98	108	109	103,000	172	189	191	187	206	208
39,000	90	99	100	98	108	109	104,000	174	191	193	189	208	210
40,000	91	100	101	99	109	110	105,000	176	193	195	191	210	212
41,000	92	101	102	100	110	111	106,000	177	195	197	193	213	215
42,000	93	102	103	101	111	112	107,000	179	197	199	195	215	217
43,000	94	103	104	102	112	113	108,000	180	198	200	196	216	218
44,000	95	104	105	103	113	114	109,000	182	200	202	198	218	220
45,000	96	106	107	105	116	117	110,000	184	202	204	200	220	222
46,000	97	107	108	106	117	118	111,000	186	204	206	202	222	224
47,000	98	108	109	107	118	119	112,000	187	206	208	204	225	227
48,000	99	109	110	108	119	120	113,000	188	207	209	205	226	228
49,000	100	110	111	109	120	121	114,000	190	209	211	207	228	230
50,000	101	111	112	110	121	122	115,000	192	211	213	209	230	232
51,000	102	112	113	111	122	123	116,000	194	213	215	211	232	234
52,000	102	112	113	111	122	123	117,000	196	215	217	213	234	237
53,000	103	113	114	112	123	124	118,000	197	216	218	214	235	238
54,000	103	113	114	112	123	124	119,000	198	218	220	216	238	240
55,000	104	114	115	113	124	125	120,000	200	220	222	218	240	242
56,000	105	115	116	114	125	127	121,000	202	222	224	220	242	244
57,000	105	115	116	114	125	127	122,000	204	224	226	222	244	246
58,000	106	116	117	115	126	128	123,000	206	226	228	224	246	249
59,000	106	116	117	115	126	128	124,000	207	228	230	226	249	251
60,000	106	117	118	116	128	129	125,000	209	230	232	228	251	253
61,000	107	118	119	117	129	130	130,000	217	239	241	237	261	263
62,000	109	120	121	119	131	132	135,000	226	248	250	246	270	273
63,000	110	121	122	120	132	133	140,000	234	257	260	254	280	283
64,000	111	122	123	121	133	134	145,000	242	266	269	263	290	293
65,000	113	124	125	123	135	136	150,000	250	275	278	272	300	303
66,000	114	125	126	124	136	138	155,000	258	284	287	281	310	312
67,000	115	126	127	125	137	139	160,000	267	293	296	290	319	322
68,000	116	127	128	126	138	140	165,000	276	303	306	300	330	333
69,000	117	129	130	128	141	142	170,000	284	312	315	309	340	343
70,000	118	130	131	129	142	143	175,000	292	321	324	318	350	353
71,000	120	132	133	131	144	145	180,000	300	330	333	327	360	363
72,000	121	133	134	132	145	146	185,000	309	340	343	337	371	374
73,000	123	135	136	134	147	149	190,000	318	349	352	346	380	384
74,000	125	137	138	136	149	151	195,000	326	358	362	354	390	394
75,000	126	139	140	138	152	153	200,000	334	367	371	363	400	404
76,000	127	140	141	139	153	154	210,000	350	385	389	381	420	424
77,000	129	142	143	141	155	156	220,000	368	404	408	400	440	444
78,000	131	144	145	143	157	158	230,000	384	422	426	418	460	464
79,000	132	145	146	144	158	160	240,000	401	441	445	437	481	485
80,000	134	147	148	146	160	162	250,000	418	459	464	454	500	505
81,000	136	149	150	148	162	164	260,000	435	478	483	473	521	526
82,000	137	151	153	149	165	166	270,000	451	496	501	491	541	546
83,000	138	152	154	150	166	167	280,000	469	515	520	510	561	567
84,000	140	154	156	152	168	169	290,000	485	533	538	528	581	586
85,000	142	156	158	154	170	172	300,000	502	552	558	546	602	607
86,000	144	158	160	156	172	174	310,000	519	570	576	564	621	627
87,000	146	160	162	158	174	176	320,000	535	588	594	582	641	647
88,000	147	161	163	159	175	177	330,000	552	607	613	601	662	668
89,000	148	163	165	161	178	179	340,000	569	625	631	619	681	688
90,000	150	165	167	163	180	182	350,000	585	643	649	637	701	707
							Addl 1000s	1.64	1.80	1.82	1.78	1.96	1.98

natural disasters is significant for the risk manager. Annual rates will vary and are determined by using cost of replacement. Property values are used with the type of coverage to find rates of cost from tables.

Many insurance companies require property owners or the lessee of a property to carry insurance on a minimum replacement value of the property. This special type of consideration is called **co-insurance.** If the property owner decides to carry an amount of insurance other than the amount specified by the co-insurance percent, any loss on the property will be prorated using the following formula:

$$\text{Loss} \times \frac{\text{Amount of insurance carried}}{\text{Amount of insurance required}}$$

The required amount of co-insurance usually ranges from 80% to 100% of the property value. Assume, for instance, a building with an 80% co-insurance clause has a replacement value of $100,000. If the building is insured for $40,000 (one-half the required $80,000) the insurance company would pay only one-half of any loss up to the $40,000 face value of the policy. Table 10.7 shows how liability is calculated with and without co-insurance.

EXAMPLE 16 Find the annual broad-form insurance premium for a Premium Group 3 property valued at $145,000.

Solution: Premium Group 03–Broad

$266	• Table value for $145,000.
$266	• Annual premium.

EXAMPLE 17 What would the annual premium be for a Premium Group 4, special coverage policy if the property was valued at $260,000? What would the premium be if a 90% co-insurance clause was included in the policy and it was insured at the co-insurance rate?

Solution: *Part A:* Premium Group 04–Special

$526 • Table value for $260,000.

Part B: 90% Co-insurance required

Co-insurance percent × Value = Co-insurance calculation

.90 × $260,000 = $234,000	• Required coverage.
$464	• Table value for $230,000.
$1.98 × 4 = $7.92 (extra)	• $1.98 each added $1,000.
$464 + $7.92 = $471.92	• Total premium. (See bottom of table for the calculation factors to calculate premiums for additional $1,000s.)

TABLE 10.7
Property Loss

Policy Condition	Reimbursement
Without co-insurance	Full value of category covered by policy
With co-insurance	Liability calculated by: $$\frac{\text{Loss} \times \text{Amount of coverage}}{\text{Amount of coverage required by co-insurance}}$$

Calculated reimbursement will not be paid beyond policy coverage limits.

EXAMPLE 18 A property valued at $135,000 was insured with an 85% co-insurance policy. *Part A:* On what value would the premiums be calculated? *Part B:* Assuming the required coverage was carried, what amount would the insurance company pay on a $12,000 fire loss?

Solution: Use Part = Base × Rate:

Part A:
135,000 (base) · Property value.
85% = .85 (rate) · Co-insurance coverage rate.
$135,000 × .85 = $114,750 · Required coverage amount.

Part B: Loss × Amount of coverage ÷ Amount required:

12,000 × 114,750 ÷ 114,750 = 12,000 · Amount paid.

(Full loss paid because of full coverage.)

EXAMPLE 19 A property was insured with a policy containing a 90% co-insurance clause. The property value was placed at $180,000. The owner insured the property for $137,700 coverage. If a loss of $40,000 occurs, what will the insurance company's liability be?

Solution:

.90 Co-insurance · Amount coverage required.
180,000 × .90 = 162,000 · Required policy value.
Loss × Amount of coverage ÷
   Amount required · Loss coverage.
40,000 × 137,700 ÷ 162,000 = $34,000 · Liability.
$40,000 · Actual loss amount.
$34,000 · Insurance co-liability.

✔ CHECK FOR UNDERSTANDING

1. What are the insurance premiums per $1,000 for a property policy with basic coverage in Premium Group 2 if it is valued at $125,000?

2. A company with buildings valued at $169,000 carries needed insurance from an 80% co-insurance policy. If the company suffers a loss of $56,000:
   (a) How much will the insurance company pay on the loss?
   (b) If the loss was $147,000, how much would the insurance company cover?
   (c) If the insured carried coverage of $108,160 instead of the required 80%, how much would the insurance company cover of the $147,000 loss?

Other Insurance

Many other types of insurance are available to protect business people from financial loss. **Workmen's compensation,** for example, is required by all companies with at least one employee. The rate of premium is based on the accident experience of the business and the type of business. **Unemployment insurance** is determined in the same manner. If there are considerable layoffs in a company, the rate for the company's unemployment insurance increases.

Unemployment insurance is set at a current rate of 5.4% for the state plus 0.8% for federal. These are adjusted according to a company's level of unemployment. If

Answers to ✔ Check for Understanding
1. $1.656 or $1.66.   2. (a) $56,000.   (b) $135,200.   (c) $117,600.

unemployment is high, the rate may be raised; if it is low, it can be reduced. This program is administered through state departments of employment. See Chapter 6 for more information on unemployment.

The costs of unemployment insurance are based upon job risk, number of employees, and level of payroll (dollar value). The original charge is approximately 0.8% for a new business. This percent is applied to the first $14,000 worth of salary per year for each employee. The rates may vary by state.

Personal liability insurance is another coverage business owners must consider. The costs vary considerably, depending on the nature of the business. If a business is hazardous, its premiums will be higher. It would be impractical to attempt to quote rates for the various types of policies available for personal liability insurance, but you should be aware of the necessity of carrying it.

EXAMPLE 20 The Seacor Company has sales of $560,000, buildings and equipment valued at $800,000, and a payroll of $200,000 subject totally to workmen's compensation and unemployment tax. Casualty rates are $1.85 per $1,000 of value. Liability insurance costs are $865 per year per employee. Workmen's compensation is 0.5% of payroll, and unemployment insurance is 5.4% of payroll. What percent of sales would the total insurance costs be for the company?

Solution:

800 (thousands) × 1.85 = $1,480   • Casualty cost.
865   • Liability cost.

Workmen's compensation and unemployment:

200,000 × 0.054 = 10,800   • Unemployment insurance.
200,000 × 0.005 = 1,000   • Workmen's compensation.
1,480 + 865 + 10,800 + 1,000
 = 14,145   • Total cost calculation.
14,145 (total cost) ÷ 560,000 (sales)
 = 0.0252589   • Find rate.
0.0252589 rounds to 2.53%   • Percent of sales.

✔ CHECK FOR UNDERSTANDING

1. The BYD Company had the following operating expenses:

Sales	$185,000
Building and equipment	375,000
Payroll	95,000

Its insurance costs were:

Unemployment insurance	2.3% of payroll
Workmen's compensation	0.6% of payroll
Liability insurance	$436
Casualty insurance	$1.98 per $1,000 with an 80% co-insurance

(a) What is the cost of insurance?
(b) What percent of sales is the insurance cost?

Answers to ✔ Check for Understanding
1. (a) $3,785. (b) 2.05%.

SKILL EXERCISES

Determine the following life insurance annual premiums:

	Age	Amt. of ins.	Type of insurance	Premium
1.	36	$27,000	20-term, 16-pay	$ _____
2.	26	$15,000	Endowment at 65	$ _____
3.	42	$30,000	20-pay, life	$ _____
4.	25	$15,000	20-pay, life + ADB	$ _____
5.	22	$10,000	Ordinary life + ADB	$ _____

Determine the following per-vehicle 6-month premiums:

	Type of coverage	Level/ type	Year of car	No. of cars	Premium
6.	BI/PD	100/300/50	1986	one	$ _____
7.	$500 deductible comprehensive	Symbol L	1984	multi	$ _____
8.	$100 deductible collision	Symbol Z	1982	one	$ _____
9.	BI/PD	25/50/15	1987	multi	$ _____
10.	$50 deductible comprehensive	Symbol R	1985	one	$ _____
11.	$100 deductible comprehensive	Symbol 2	1983	multi	$ _____
12.	No fault	100 Ded.	1987	multi	$ _____
13.	$200 deductible collision	Symbol K	1984	one	$ _____
14.	$500 deductible collision	Symbol P	1983	multi	$ _____
15.	Uninsured motorist	250/500	1986	one	$ _____

Find the following values of the liability that will be assumed by the insurance company:

	Property value	Required co-insurance	Amount carried	Loss	Ins. company liability
16.	$130,000	None	Full	$28,000	$ _____

17.	$ 95,000	None	90%	$12,000	$ _____
18.	$ 62,500	90%	50%	$36,000	$ _____
19.	$ 69,000	90%	$42,000	$18,000	$ _____
20.	$127,000	80%	$67,000	$52,000	$ _____
21.	$ 82,000	70%	40%	$27,000	$ _____
22.	$ 97,000	90%	$87,300	$65,000	$ _____
23.	$ 65,000	80%	$42,000	$29,000	$ _____
24.	$ 87,000	70%	70%	$80,000	$ _____
25.	$ 75,000	80%	60%	$27,000	$ _____

APPLICATIONS

Solve the following insurance problems:

1. The World Wide Benevolence Company wanted to insure its 48-year-old president. They wanted a $30,000 ordinary life policy with ADB. What would the monthly expense be?

2. The Red Flannel Foundation wanted to compare costs of insuring the president of the company, who was 45 years old. The company wanted $50,000 worth of insurance, and had budgeted $2,850 annually as the maximum it could spend. Consider ordinary life and 20-pay life policies. What is the largest policy it could buy for the amount budgeted? (Round to the closest thousand.)

3. What would it cost the Brian Bullseye Company in annual premiums to insure its employees with 15-year term, 12-pay policies for $15,000 each based on the following information:

Stanley	30 years old	$ _____
Roxanne	27 years old	$ _____
Donald	34 years old	$ _____
George	22 years old	$ _____
Maureen	32 years old	$ _____
Total premium		$ _____

4. The Cost-Conscious Clothing Emporium wants to insure the life of the owner of the company, who is now 50 years old, for $40,000. Compare the annual costs of ordinary life, 20-pay life, and endowment at 65, without ADB.

5. Ms. Hasty, 42 years old, needed insurance to cover a loan of $35,000 for her business. How much would a 15-year term, 12-pay policy cost per year? If the company allowed a discount of 9% for paying premiums annually, what would the cost be?

6. Instead of another retirement plan, the Gross Company decided to insure its key personnel. If the executives to be insured were 45 and 49 years old, respectively, how much would it cost per month to write a $65,000 endowment at 65 without ADB policies on them?

7. Heather insured her 1984 automobile (value symbol T) as an only vehicle with the following choice of coverage:

BI/PD	50/100/50
UM	100/300
No fault	Full amount
$200 deductible collision	

What was her total premium for a six-month period?

8. How much will be saved if you choose a $500 deductible level instead of a $100 deductible level for a multi-car comprehensive policy if the vehicles are both 1985 models and both classed with the value symbol X?

9. What insurance class would a male driver fall into if he is unmarried, under 20, and owns a car?

10. Luther wanted to insure a just-purchased 1985 vehicle, value code V, with the following coverage. What was his six-month premium?

    BI/PD   100/300/50
    UM   50/100
    Full no fault personal injury
    $100 deductible collision

11. Find the annual premium cost for a 1983 automobile which has been classified under multi-car rates, with value code M, with coverages of:

    BI/PD   25/50/15
    UM   50/100
    No fault with $100 deductible
    $200 deductible collision

12. Use the following information:

    Payroll $250,000
    Value of building and equipment $1,750,000
    Sales for the period $1,250,000
    Liability insurance $975

    The total payroll is subject to FICA at 7.51%; unemployment insurance at 2.7%; and workmen's compensation at 0.8%. The casualty insurance is at a rate of $1.86 per $1,000 of value, and an 80% co-insurance property policy is carried.
    (a) What is the total insurance cost?
    (b) What percent is insurance cost of sales?

13. The Blind-Bend Corporation had buildings valued at $127,000. Amen Insurance Company carried the coverage and required a 90% co-insurance. If the company had a fire loss of $63,000 and was insured for $92,000, what would the liability of the insurance company be? How much will Blind-Bend Corporation have to pay?

14. At the time a casualty policy was issued, Dale's farm building was valued at $264,000. The policy contained an 85% co-insurance clause. The policy was written for $175,000. The farm suffered a major fire, and the loss was estimated at $250,000. What was the insurance company's liability?

15. What is the annual building insurance premium rate on property listed as Premium Group 1, if broad coverage was desired and the property value was $90,000?

Key Terms

Amortization schedule (260)
Assessed rate (268)
Assessed value (268)
Bodily injury (275)
Co-insurance (283)
Collision (275)
Comprehensive (275)
Endowment (273)
Escrow account (264)
Fixed-rate mortgage (260)
Market value (268)
Mill levy (269)
Mortgage periods (260)

No fault (275, 278)
Ordinary life (273)
Pay life (273)
Personal liability (285)
PI (principal and interest) (260)
PITI (264)
Premium (275)
Real property (259)
Tax rate (268)
Term insurance (273)
Unemployment insurance (284)
Uninsured motorist (UM) (275)
Workmen's compensation (284)

Looking Back

There is a significant dollar difference between a PI mortgage payment and a PITI house payment. On a fixed-rate mortgage, the PI mortgage payment will not change once the amortization schedule is set. On a variable-rate mortgage, a new schedule is established as each interest increment changes.

Property tax is based on assessed value. The assessed rate that is used to convert market price of real property to assessed value varies considerably with different communities. If the assessed base is low, the tax rate (mill levy) is usually higher. If the mill levy is high, the assessed value is usually lower. The net effect of these variables is that the government taxing agency will meet its budget.

Insurance is a significant investment for individuals and businesses. Attempting to hold down expenses on insurance premiums by having a larger co-insurance agreement may result in a significant cash loss when a claim is paid. Decide carefully on the face amount of your insurance policies. Watch for the amount of co-insurance you must be responsible to pay.

Let's Review

1. Set up the payment schedule for the first two payments (PI) on a mortgage of $34,000 with a $9\frac{1}{2}$% rate and monthly payments of $336.

2. A mortgage of $30,000 has an interest rate of $13\frac{1}{2}$% and payments of $397 (PI). The taxes are $865 per year with insurance premiums costing $876 for three years. What are the PITI payments?

290   Chapter 10   Mortgages, Taxes, and Insurance

3. A $126,000 home was purchased with 22% down and a 30-year fixed mortgage at $8\frac{1}{2}$%. What would the monthly principal and interest payment be?

4. The tax rate in Johnson County is 76.3 mills. If the tax on Joan's business is $878.60, what is the assessed value of her property?

5. The Gaddies purchased a condo for $89,500 and paid 15% down. The mortgage was for 25 years at 12%. Find the monthly PI payment and set up the first two months' interest, principal, and loan balance schedule.

6. The county budget is as follows:

    School district $7,865,000
    County $6,525,000
    City $1,325,000

    If the assessed value in the county is $187,500,000, what is the mill levy for each taxing district?

    School district: _____ mills

    County: _____ mills

    City: _____ mills

7. What is the monthly PITI payment on a condo purchased for $62,000 with 10% down? The 20-year mortgage was carried at 9%. Taxes were projected to be $735 and insurance for two years was $684.

8. Assessed value for a property was $36,400. If the taxes were $939.12, what was the mill levy?

9. If the tax rate on a property is 42.6 mills, the assessed rate is 35%, and taxes were $746.20, what is the market value of the property?

10. Visionville Medical Supply Company wanted to take out two 20-pay life key man policies on its two chief corporate officers. Each policy would be for $150,000. If the ages of the officers were 33 and 42, respectively, what would the total premium costs be per month?

11. For the same coverage in Problem 10, how much would the company save per month if it carried two $150,000, 15-year term, 12-pay policies on their officers instead of the 20-pay life policies?

12. One state required a minimum insurance package for all vehicles registered within the state. The minimum package included bodily injury and property damage (BI/PD) and no fault personal injury (No Fault). Marquita wanted to insure her 1984 vehicle (value symbol Q) for 50/100/50 BI/PD and $100 deductible no fault. What would her annual cost be for premiums on this coverage?

Let's Review

13. Jaime Manufacturing was budgeting for insurance coverage for next year. The three company vehicles are:

>1985 (value symbol M)
>1985 (value symbol M)
>1984 (value symbol P)

Company policy required vehicles to be insured for:

>BI/PD   250/500/100
>UM   100/300
>No fault   Full
>$200 deductible collision
>$100 deductible comprehensive

What is the company's annual insurance budget for these vehicles?

14. Helen was reviewing her auto insurance coverage. She owned a 1985 (value symbol S) vehicle. How much would she save on her collision insurance for six months by purchasing $500 deductible instead of $100 deductible?

15. What would the annual premiums be for a special coverage policy on a Premium Group 2 property valued at $124,000?

16. A property valued at $142,000 was insured with a policy containing an 85% co-insurance policy. The owner paid premiums on a $100,000 policy covering property loss. Later in the year a $35,000 loss was experienced due to fire. What was the insurance company's liability on this loss?

17. A property valued at $88,000 was covered with a 90% co-insurance policy for $75,000. If a loss of $12,500 was incurred, what would the owner's liability be on the loss?

18. A small company with qualified employee earnings of $14,000 was charged unemployment insurance at the 5.4% rate. What was the company's unemployment insurance expense?

19. What will the six-month premiums be for a 1983 vehicle (value symbol L) if the selected coverage includes:

>BI/PD   100/300/50
>UM   50/100
>No fault   Full
>Comprehensive $100 Deductible
>Collision $200 Deductible

20. A company carried a $186,500 annual payroll. Workmen's compensation for this company was rated at 0.0625%. What would the company's workmen's compensation expense be?

Chapter Test

1. What is the balance after the first three payments have been made on a $42,800, 13% mortgage if it has a $484 monthly payment?

2. A new $145,000 home was purchased with 40% down. The balance was financed with a 30-year mortgage at $10\frac{1}{2}$%. What will the monthly PI payment be?

3. A property with an assessed value of $48,300 was taxed a total of 63.32 mills. What was the annual tax bill?

4. A property with a 25-year, 14% mortgage of $56,000 carried property tax of $1,485. It also had an annual insurance premium of $420.96. What was the PITI monthly payment?

5. A public library district contained property with a total assessed value of $242,000,000. If the total operating budget for the year was $1,748,600, what is the mill levy for the library district?

6. Wilmot's 1985 vehicle carried both comprehensive and collision insurance. The vehicle qualified for multi-car rates and its value symbol was Z. If $100 deductible coverage is desired in each category, what would the six-month premium be for this coverage?

7. Allocate the first two months' principal and interest payments for a $96,000 property. The property was purchased with 38% down and the remainder financed at 11% for 30 years.

8. Find the annual premium for a 33-year-old female executive. She is insured for $175,000 with a 20-year term 16-pay policy.

9. A $152,000 property was insured with a loss-protection policy which contained a 90% co-insurance clause. The premiums were paid on a $125,000 policy coverage. If a $22,000 loss was experienced, what would the insurance company's liability be?

10. Given an assessed rate of 30% and a tax rate of 51.362 mills, what are the taxes on a property with a market value of $96,400?

PART IV
Financial Applications

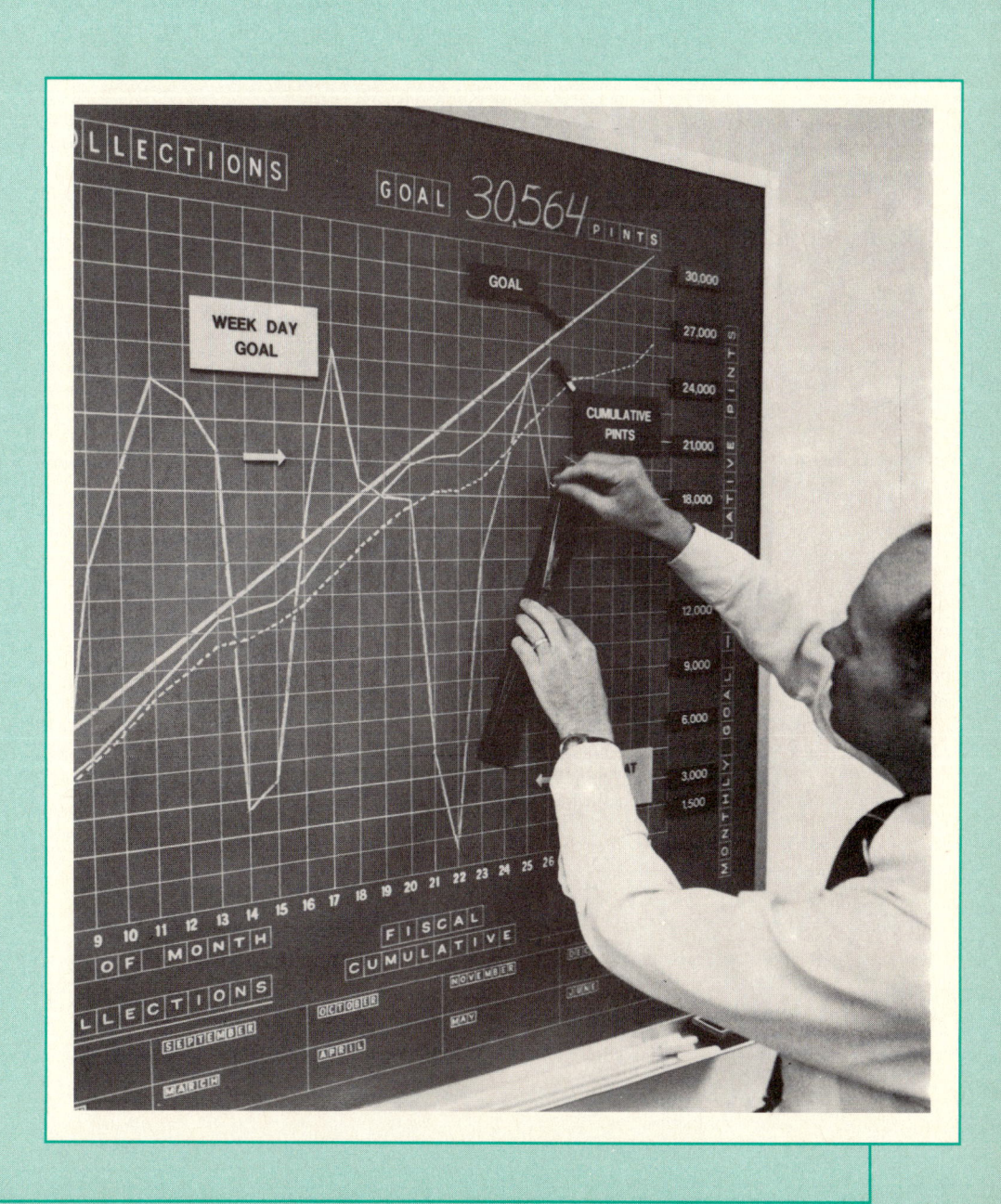

Depreciation and Inventory Valuation

11

OBJECTIVES

When you complete this chapter you will be able to:
- *Calculate the depreciation of various assets using the common methods of straight line, sum of the years' digits, units of production, and declining balance. (11.1)*
- *Calculate the depreciation of various assets for tax purposes using the ACRS method. (11.2)*
- *Calculate the value of the ending inventory using FIFO, LIFO, weighted average, and specific identification methods. (11.3)*

COMING UP

Collection of information that supports financial decision making is one of the principal responsibilities of the accounting department. Although each of us may not be planning a career in accounting, we may be responsible for assisting in making decisions using information provided by our company's financial department. These decisions very frequently affect the amount of the business's profit or loss.

Two of the common accounting procedures that influence profit are depreciation and inventory valuation. This chapter introduces you to several depreciation methods. It also shows some of the alternatives that can be used to determine the value of a company's inventory.

Depreciation

11.1

Depreciation is a portion of the cost of a tangible asset allocated as an expense over its estimated useful life. **Tangible property,** such as buildings or equipment, can be seen or touched. **Intangible property** such as patents, copyrights, goodwill, and franchises can be amortized (a certain percent of their value allocated to an expense), if a **useful life** can be calculated. In this text we will discuss tangible property only. In general, property can be depreciated if it meets the following criteria:

1. It must be used in business or held for the production of income.
2. It must have a useful life of at least one year and we must be able to determine that life.
3. It must be something that wears out, ages, gets used up, becomes obsolete, or loses value from natural causes.

The other factor that has significantly influenced figuring depreciation for tax purposes is the **Economic Recovery Tax Act of 1981.** This act was passed to greatly accelerate the amount of depreciation used for figuring tax liability. Since the act was passed, it has been modified several times. The text reflects the modifications in the Tax Reform Act of 1986.

Even though the accelerated cost recovery system (ACRS) method is required for federal tax purposes, many companies still use other methods of figuring depreciation on their financial statements. Some states also do not permit the use of the ACRS method for figuring state tax liability. The four common depreciation methods other than ACRS are straight line, sum-of-the-years' digits, units of production, and declining balance, each of which is discussed below.

There are four factors involved when working with depreciation: cost, salvage or scrap value, accumulated depreciation, and book value. **Cost** is the total amount paid for the asset, which would include normal transportation charges and cost of installation. **Salvage or scrap value** is the estimated amount the asset will be worth after its useful life with the business has ended.

Accumulated depreciation is the running total of depreciation. **Book value** is the value of an asset as recorded in your books. It is cost minus the accumulated depreciation. The book value during the first year is equal to the cost.

Straight Line Method

The most common method of calculating depreciation is the **straight line method.** Under this method, the amount of depreciation allocated to each year is the same. The formula is:

$$\text{Annual depreciation} = \frac{\text{Cost} - \text{Salvage value}}{\text{Useful life in years}}$$

EXAMPLE 1 A company purchases a $16,000 delivery truck that has a useful life of 5 years and a salvage value of $1,000. Calculate the annual depreciation. Develop a depreciation schedule showing the depreciation and the book value for the 5 years.

Solution:

$$\text{Annual depreciation} = \frac{\text{Cost} - \text{Salvage}}{\text{Years of life}}$$ • Identify the formula.

$$\frac{16,000 - 1000}{5}$$ • Set values into the formula and solve.

$$\frac{15,000}{5} = 3000$$ • Annual depreciation.

$$\text{Book value} = \text{Cost} - \text{Accumulated depreciation}$$ • Calculate book value.

$$16,000 - 3000 = 13,000$$
• Continue in like manner for each additional year.
• Develop the depreciation schedule.

Year	Cost	Annual Depreciation	Accumulated Depreciation	End-of-Year Book Value
				$16,000 = Cost
1	$16,000	$3,000	$ 3,000	$13,000
2	$16,000	$3,000	$ 6,000	$10,000
3	$16,000	$3,000	$ 9,000	$ 7,000
4	$16,000	$3,000	$12,000	$ 4,000
5	$16,000	$3,000	$15,000	$ 1,000*

* Note: $1,000, the final book value, is the amount of the original salvage. Never depreciate a property below its salvage value.

EXAMPLE 2 Gates Fence Company uses straight line depreciation and a life of 8 years on all of its digging equipment. If the equipment costs $10,000 and has a salvage value of $400, prepare the depreciation schedule for the first 3 years.

Solution:

$$\text{Annual depreciation} = \frac{\text{Cost} - \text{Salvage}}{\text{Years of life}}$$ • Identify the formula.

$$\frac{10,000 - 400}{8}$$ • Set values into the formula and solve.

$$\frac{9600}{8} = 1200$$ • Annual depreciation.

$$10,000 - 1200 = 8800$$
• Calculate book value.
• Prepare the depreciation schedule.

Year	Cost	Annual Depreciation	Accumulated Depreciation	End-of-Year Book Value
				$10,000 = Cost
1	$10,000	$1,200	$1,200	$ 8,800
2	$10,000	$1,200	$2,400	$ 7,600
3	$10,000	$1,200	$3,600	$ 6,400

Partial Year Depreciation

Partial year depreciation is calculated by multiplying the annual amount times the fractional part of the year the property was in use. Whether the month of purchase should be counted or ignored is determined by the date of purchase. One rule used is that for property purchased on or before the fifteenth of the month, the entire month is counted. However, for any property purchased on or after the sixteenth, that month is not counted. This system will be used in this text. The formula is:

> Partial year = Annual depreciation × Fractional part of year in use

PARTIAL YEAR

To count a depreciation month:

If purchased between the 1st and 15th of the month, count the month in the depreciation year:

| 1 | 2 | 3 | 4 | 5 | 6 | 7 |
| 8 | 9 | 10 | 11 | 12 | 13 | 14 |
| 15 |

If purchased between the 16th and the end of the month, do not count the month as a depreciation month:

16	17	18	19	20	21
22	23	24	25	26	27	28
29	30	31

For a May 12 purchase, depreciate for:

MAY JUN JUL AUG SEP OCT NOV DEC = 8 Months

First-year depreciation is 8/12 of the total year

EXAMPLE 3 O'Reilly Corporation purchased a typewriter for $1,400 on April 4. It has a useful life of 5 years and a salvage value of $200. Calculate the annual depreciation, the depreciation for the partial year, and develop a depreciation schedule showing the depreciation and the book value for the 5 years.

Solution:

$1400 - 200 = 1200$
$1200 \div 5 = 240$

- Calculate annual depreciation.

$240 \times \frac{9}{12} = 180$

- Calculate partial year depreciation: use April through December, or $\frac{9}{12}$ of a year. April is counted; purchased before April 16.
- Develop depreciation schedule.

Year	Cost	Depreciation	End-of-Year Book Value	
			$1,400 =	Cost
1	$1,400	$180	$1,220	
2	$1,400	$240	$ 980	See
3	$1,400	$240	$ 740	Strategy
4	$1,400	$240	$ 500	on Page 301.
5	$1,400	$240	$ 260	
6*	$1,400	$ 60	$ 200	

* Because only nine months of depreciation were taken during Year 1, there is a carryover of three months' depreciation to Year 6.

PROBLEM SOLVING STRATEGY

Although the definition of book value is cost minus accumulated depreciation, book value can be calculated by subtracting the current year's depreciation from last year's book value. This method lends itself to keeping the running book value in your calculator's memory.

✔ CHECK FOR UNDERSTANDING

1. McGraw Company purchased an office machine with a useful life of 10 years for $4,000. The machine has a salvage value of $200. What is the annual depreciation?

2. Construct a depreciation schedule including the book value for the following piece of property. An air conditioner was purchased for $5,000 on January 10. It has a salvage value of $500 and a useful life of 3 years.

3. The Sell-All Novelty Company purchased a display case for $750 on May 21. It has a salvage value of $50 and a useful life of 20 years. Calculate the first two calendar years' depreciation. The first calendar year will be a partial year calculation.

4. Are-You-There Answering Service purchased a secretarial desk for $1,400 on September 13. The desk has a useful life of 15 years and a salvage value of $50. What is the book value at the end of the second calendar year?

SKILL EXERCISES

Use the straight line method to calculate the first calendar year's depreciation and the book value in the following problems:

	Cost	Salvage	Life in years	Date of purchase	1st year depreciation	End-of-year book value
1.	$1,100	$300	4	6/11	$ _____	$ _____
2.	$2,700	$500	6	5/16	$ _____	$ _____
3.	$1,500	$100	5	1/12	$ _____	$ _____
4.	$8,000	$750	6	8/19	$ _____	$ _____
5.	$625	$75	3	2/15	$ _____	$ _____

Answers to ✔ Check for Understanding
1. $380.

2.
Year	Depreciation	End-of-Year Book Value
		$5,000 = Cost
1	$1,500	$3,500
2	$1,500	$2,000
3	$1,500	$ 500

3. $20.42; $35.   4. $1,280.

Section 11.1 Depreciation   **301**

6. $ 1,200	–0–	10	11/11	$ _____	$ _____
7. $ 6,400	$ 200	7	1/10	$ _____	$ _____
8. $15,000	$1,000	5	7/21	$ _____	$ _____
9. $ 3,600	–0–	4	4/16	$ _____	$ _____
10. $ 2,150	$ 25	8	9/12	$ _____	$ _____

APPLICATIONS

1. The Better Management Group purchased 4 office desks for $375 each. If they use straight line depreciation, a life of 12 years, and no salvage, what is the annual depreciation for all of the 4 desks?

2. Ace Auto Repair purchased a self-contained mechanics work station on March 12 for $4,450. Calculate each of the first two calendar years' depreciation using the straight line method assuming a salvage value of $200 and life of 10 years.

3. A local moving and storage company purchased several hand appliance carts for $145 each. If they use the straight line method, a life of 13 years, and no salvage, what is the book value at the end of the fifth year?

4. A copy machine cost $3,745 when it was purchased on September 9. If the salvage value is estimated to be $650 and the estimated life is 6 years, what is the book value using the straight line method at the end of the third calendar year?

5. Prepare a depreciation schedule showing the depreciation and the book value for the first 4 years for a large freezer unit that costs $11,350 using the straight line method. The unit was purchased on January 14, has a scrap value of $150, and has a life of 8 years.

6. A building that was purchased on October 5 for $62,500 has a life of 20 years and no salvage value. Use the straight line method and calculate the depreciation for each of the first 3 years.

7. The See-Thru-Glass Company purchased a small computer system on May 18 that cost $12,000. The system has an estimated life of 8 years and $1,250 salvage value. If we use straight line depreciation, what would the accumulated depreciation be at the end of the fourth year? The book value?

8. The stadium used by the Mid-Town Raiders cost $22 million. If the scrap value is estimated to be $2 million and the estimated life is 40 years, what is the annual depreciation using the straight line method?

9. Interstate Properties installed a truck washing facility for $190,000 that began operation on November 1. The estimated life of the facility is 30 years. If we use straight line depreciation and no salvage, what is the book value at the end of the tenth year?

10. The Crags Office System purchased 50 posture chairs for their electronic work stations. Each chair cost $375 and has an estimated salvage value of $25 and a life of 7 years. What is the accumulated depreciation and book value on all 50 chairs at the end of Year 4 if we use the straight line method?

Sum-of-the-Years'-Digits Method

Because many pieces of property do not depreciate at the same fixed rate each year, the **sum-of-the-years'-digits** method was developed. It provides the largest amount of depreciation the first year with a gradual decrease each year throughout the life of the property.

The name "sum-of-the-years" comes from the mathematical process performed to calculate the denominator of the fraction used for each year's depreciation. If the life of the property is four years, for example, we sum, or add, the years together. Thus, starting with the life in years, we add $4 + 3 + 2 + 1$ to get 10, the denominator. Depreciation is then calculated by taking $\frac{4}{10}$ for Year 1; $\frac{3}{10}$ for Year 2; $\frac{2}{10}$ for Year 3; and $\frac{1}{10}$ for Year 4. Like straight line, this method also considers *salvage as a reduction in cost* to determine the base. The formula is:

$$\text{Annual depreciation} = (\text{Cost} - \text{Salvage}) \times \text{Fractional part allocated}$$

EXAMPLE 4 The Rent-A-Truck Corporation depreciates its fleet of trucks using the sum-of-the-years'-digits method. On January 8 it purchased a truck for $11,000 having a life of 3 years and a salvage value of $2,000. Calculate the depreciation and book value for each of the 3 years.

Solution:

$3 + 2 + 1 = 6$
- Calculate the denominator: begin with life in years and add all years down to zero.
- Identify the depreciation formula.

$$\frac{\text{Annual}}{\text{depreciation}} = (\text{Cost} - \text{Salvage}) \times \frac{\text{Fractional part}}{\text{allocated}}$$

$11{,}000 - 2000 = 9000$ (base) • Calculate the base: Cost − Salvage.

$9000 \times \frac{3}{6} = 4500$
- Calculate first year; use numerator equal to life in years and denominator calculated above. Multiply the fraction times the base calculated in previous step.

$$\frac{\text{Book}}{\text{value}} = \text{Cost} - \frac{\text{Accumulated}}{\text{depreciation}}$$
- Identify formula to calculate book value.

$11{,}000 - 4500 = 6500$ • Set numbers in formula and solve for Year 1 book value.

Section 11.1 Depreciation

$9000 \times \dfrac{2}{6} = 3000$ • Calculate Year 2 depreciation; reduce numerator by one; base is the same.

$11{,}000 - 7500 = 3500$ • Calculate Year 2 book value.*

$9000 \times \dfrac{1}{6} = 1500$ • Calculate Year 3 depreciation; reduce numerator by one; base is the same.

$11{,}000 - 9000 = 2000$ • Calculate Year 3 book value.*

*Book value can also be calculated by subtracting the current year's depreciation from the previous year's book value. □

PROBLEM SOLVING STRATEGY

When figuring the denominator of the fraction, you may find the following formula helpful:

$$\text{Denominator} = \dfrac{n \times (n+1)}{2}, \text{ where } n = \text{life in years.}$$

Using Example 4 and the truck life of 3 years, calculate the denominator:

$$\dfrac{3 \times (3+1)}{2} = \dfrac{3 \times 4}{2} = \dfrac{12}{2} = 6.$$

CALCULATOR TIP

When calculating the dollar amount of depreciation, you may find it easier to calculate the last year's depreciation first. This dollar value then *becomes a calculator constant.* In Example 4, 9000 $\boxed{\times}$ $\dfrac{1}{6}$ (last year fraction) $\boxed{=}$ 1500, the constant. Every sixth is equal to $1,500. Complete the problem by multiplying 1500 times the numerator in each year. The calculator sequence for Example 4 is:

9000 $\boxed{\times}$ $\dfrac{1}{6}$ $\boxed{=}$ 1500 $\boxed{\times}$ • Constant.

3 $\boxed{=}$ 4500 • First year depreciation.

2 $\boxed{=}$ 3000 • Second year depreciation.

See Example 5.

EXAMPLE 5   A property having a life of 8 years and costing $11,000 is estimated to have a salvage value of $2,000. Calculate the amount of depreciation for each of the 8 years, using the sum-of-the-years'-digits method.

Solution:

$\dfrac{8 \times (8+1)}{2} = \dfrac{72}{2} = 36$ • Calculate the denominator.

$11{,}000 - 2000 = 9000$ • Calculate the dollar base.

$9000 \times \dfrac{1}{36} = 250$ • Calculate the *eighth year*, $\dfrac{1}{36}$ first to get *constant*; see schedule on page 305.

---

304 Chapter 11 Depreciation and Inventory Valuation

- Calculate depreciation for remaining years by entering each numerator and the $=$ key.

Year	$\frac{1}{36}$ Times Each Numerator
1	8 $=$ 2,000
2	7 $=$ 1,750
3	6 $=$ 1,500
4	5 $=$ 1,250
5	4 $=$ 1,000
6	3 $=$ 750
7	2 $=$ 500

First calculate year 8: $11,000 - 2,000 = 9,000$; $9,000 \div 36 \left(\text{or} \times \frac{1}{36}\right) = 250$. □

CALCULATOR TIP

If the problem in Example 5 also asked for the book value, we can use calculator memory to keep a running book value. Begin by entering this sequence:

11000 $\boxed{M+}$ $\boxed{-}$ 2000 $\boxed{=}$ 9000 $\boxed{\div}$ 36 $\boxed{=}$ 250 $\boxed{\times}$

(A) The 11000 $\boxed{M+}$ stores cost in memory for subtraction of each year's depreciation.
(B) The 9000 is the base, which when divided by 36 yields 250, the constant.
(C) The $\boxed{\times}$ key sets up the 250 to be constantly multiplied by the numerator of each yearly fraction.
(D) In the display below, the $\boxed{M-}$ subtracts the yearly depreciation from memory. The $\boxed{MR}$ displays the book value at the end of each current year.

Numerator	Depreciation	End-of-Year Book Value	
		11,000 = Cost	
8 $=$	2000 $\boxed{M-}$ $\boxed{MR}$	9000	Year 1
7 $=$	1750 $\boxed{M-}$ $\boxed{MR}$	7250	Year 2
6 $=$	1500 $\boxed{M-}$ $\boxed{MR}$	5750	Year 3
5 $=$	1250 $\boxed{M-}$ $\boxed{MR}$	4500	Year 4
4 $=$	1000 $\boxed{M-}$ $\boxed{MR}$	3500	Year 5
3 $=$	750 $\boxed{M-}$ $\boxed{MR}$	2750	Year 6
2 $=$	500 $\boxed{M-}$ $\boxed{MR}$	2250	Year 7
1 $=$	250 $\boxed{M-}$ $\boxed{MR}$	2000	Year 8

✓ **CHECK FOR UNDERSTANDING**

1. Using the sum-of-the-years'-digits method and a life of 4 years, compute the depreciation for each of the 4 years on a property purchased on January 2 for $750 with a salvage value of $50.

2. A concrete-mixing company bought a mixer for $150,000 on January 11. It has a life of 15 years and no salvage. Prepare a schedule of depreciation, showing both the amount of yearly depreciation and the book value for the first 5 years. Use the sum-of-the-years'-digits method.

Section 11.1 Depreciation

3. In the previous problem, use a life expectancy of 18 years to compute the first, tenth, and eighteenth years of depreciation. See problem solving strategy (p. 304).

4. A building was purchased for $304,500. If the building has no salvage value and a life of 20 years, calculate the depreciation for Years 3, 12, and 15.

SKILL EXERCISES

Calculate the denominator, record the fraction for the year listed, and calculate the amount of depreciation for each horizontal problem. Problem 0 is given as an example.

	Base	Life in years	Denom-inator	Year	Fraction for year	Depreciation
0.	$ 4,200	6	21	3	$\frac{4}{21}$	$ 800
1.	$ 890	4	_____	2	_____	$ _____
2.	$21,000	9	_____	7	_____	$ _____
3.	$ 1,450	5	_____	5	_____	$ _____
4.	$ 600	3	_____	1	_____	$ _____
5.	$10,000	8	_____	6	_____	$ _____
6.	$ 5,400	12	_____	10	_____	$ _____
7.	$ 4,750	2	_____	2	_____	$ _____
8.	$ 3,175	11	_____	11	_____	$ _____
9.	$ 2,950	7	_____	4	_____	$ _____
10.	$15,250	15	_____	9	_____	$ _____

Answers to ✔ Check for Understanding
1. $280; $210; $140; $70.

2. Depreciation   End-of-Year Book Value
                  $150,000 = Cost
   $18,750 $131,250
   $17,500 $113,750
   $16,250 $ 97,500
   $15,000 $ 82,500
   $13,750 $ 68,750

3. $15,789.47; $7,894.74; $877.19.   4. $26,100; $13,050; $8,700.

APPLICATIONS

1. New Klean Laundry purchased a large commercial dryer for $1,860. If it has no salvage value and a life of 8 years, what is the depreciation for the third year using the sum-of-the-years'-digits method?

2. A large construction crane was purchased for $180,000. It has an estimated life of 12 years and a salvage value of $4,000. Calculate the depreciation for the second year using the sum-of-the-years'-digits method.

3. If we have a building with a life of 30 years, what is the denominator of the fraction used to figure depreciation under the sum-of-the-years'-digits method?

4. Try-Us Life Insurance Company bought 5 cars on January 6 for $8,400 each. The cars have a salvage value of $2,000 and a life of 3 years. Calculate the book value at the end of the second calendar year for all 5 cars using the sum-of-the-years'-digits method.

5. A large generator with a life of 14 years was purchased on January 10. If it cost $230,000 and has a scrap value of $25,000, what is the third calendar year's depreciation using the sum-of-the-years'-digits method?

6. Exercise equipment was purchased for $80,000. The salvage value is $5,000 and the life is 5 years. Prepare a schedule of the first 3 years using the sum-of-the-years'-digits method showing the depreciation and the book value.

7. A log splitter was purchased for $2,300 on January 10. What is the second-year depreciation using the sum-of-the-years'-digits method if it has a 9-year life and a salvage value of $300?

8. Calculate the first-year depreciation on a delivery van purchased for $17,500. Use the sum-of-the-years'-digits method, a life of 4 years, and a salvage value of $4,500.

9. Prepare a depreciation schedule showing the calendar year depreciation and the book value on an electronic typewriter purchased for $1,100. Assume a 4-year life and a salvage value of $300 and use the sum-of-the-years'-digits method.

10. Calculate each of the first 3 years of depreciation on a commercial dishwasher using the sum-of-the-years'-digits method. The dishwasher cost $3,400 with a life of 8 years and no salvage.

Units of Production

The **units-of-production** method calculates depreciation using a life stated in the number of units the machine will produce, the number of hours it will operate, or the number of miles it will travel. Salvage value, which might be called **scrap** value, is subtracted from cost to determine the dollar base. The dollar base is then divided by the life in units to obtain the rate per unit. This rate is multiplied by the number of units used. The formula is:

$$\text{Annual depreciation} = \frac{\text{Cost} - \text{Scrap}}{\text{Life in units}} \times \text{Number of units produced, hours operated, or miles driven}$$

There is no special calculation for a partial year of use. If a production machine is purchased on September 25 and produces 45,000 units during the calendar year, the depreciation is based on the 45,000 units it produced. It is of no consequence that it was in use only three full months.

EXAMPLE 6 A large production-line machine was purchased 4 years ago for $250,000 and was expected to produce 1,000,000 units during its lifetime. It has a scrap value of $10,000. Calculate the depreciation for the first 4 years if the machine produced the following number of units: first year, 75,000; second year, 135,000; third year, 425,000; and fourth year, 60,000 units.

Solution:

$$\frac{\text{Cost} - \text{Scrap}}{\text{Life in units}} = \frac{250{,}000 - 10{,}000}{1{,}000{,}000}$$

- Calculate the depreciation rate per unit.

$$= 24 \text{ cents/unit (rate)}$$

$.24 \times 75{,}000 = 18{,}000$

- Calculate Year 1 depreciation: Calculated rate × Units used.
- Calculate each additional year's depreciation: Rate × Units used. Set the rate up as a constant multiplier.

Year	Depreciation per Unit	Units Produced	Depreciation
1	24 cents	75,000	$ 18,000
2	24 cents	135,000	$ 32,400
3	24 cents	425,000	$102,000
4	24 cents	60,000	$ 14,400

□

PROBLEM SOLVING STRATEGY

With this method, as with any method, do not depreciate below the salvage or scrap value. If the machine is used to produce more units than were originally estimated, you need to adjust the final year to depreciate only the remaining units. Incorporate special steps into your routine to ensure that you don't overdepreciate. See Example 7.

EXAMPLE 7 A refrigeration compressor has a useful life of 5,000 hours. If it was purchased for $7,000 and has a scrap value of $500, what is the amount of depreciation for the first 4 years of use, using the following information: first year, 2,000 hours; second year, 900 hours; third year, 1,500 hours; and fourth year, 2,200 hours? Set up a depreciation schedule showing the depreciation and the book value for each of the 4 years.

Solution:

$$\frac{7000 - 500}{5000} = \$1.30$$

- Calculate the depreciation per unit.

$1.30 \times 2000 = 2600$

- Calculate first-year depreciation: Depreciation per unit × Units used.

$7000 - 2600 = 4400$

- Calculate end of year book value: Cost − Accumulated depreciation.
- Repeat the sequence for the remaining years.

Year	Depreciation per Unit	Hours of Use	Depreciation	End-of-Year Book Value
				$7,000 = Cost
1	$1.30	2,000	$2,600	$4,400
2	$1.30	900	$1,170	$3,230
3	$1.30	1,500	$1,950	$1,280
4	$1.30	2,200	$ 780*	$ 500

*The depreciation for Year 4 is $2,860 (i.e., $1.30 × 2,200 hours), but we can list only $780. The final-year depreciation cannot force the book value below salvage or zero. To calculate the maximum amount of depreciation allowed in Year 4, subtract salvage ($500) from the previous year's book value ($1,280) to arrive at $780. Another system is to keep a running total of the hours used after each year. If the accumulated hours exceed the life of the property, an adjustment must be made during that year.

Year 1   2000 hours used
Year 2 + 900 hours used
            2900 subtotal   • Compared to maximum life of 5,000 hours, it's OK.

Year 3 + 1500
            4400 subtotal   • Compared to maximum of 5,000 hours, it's OK.

Year 4 + 2200
            6600 subtotal   • Compared to maximum of 5,000 hours, it exceeds the total; an adjustment is necessary.

Determine the maximum number of hours permitted in Year 4 by subtracting the previous year's subtotal (4,400) from the total life expectancy (5,000), or 600 hours. Multiply the maximum hours times the rate:

600 hours × 1.30 = 780, the maximum for Year 4.

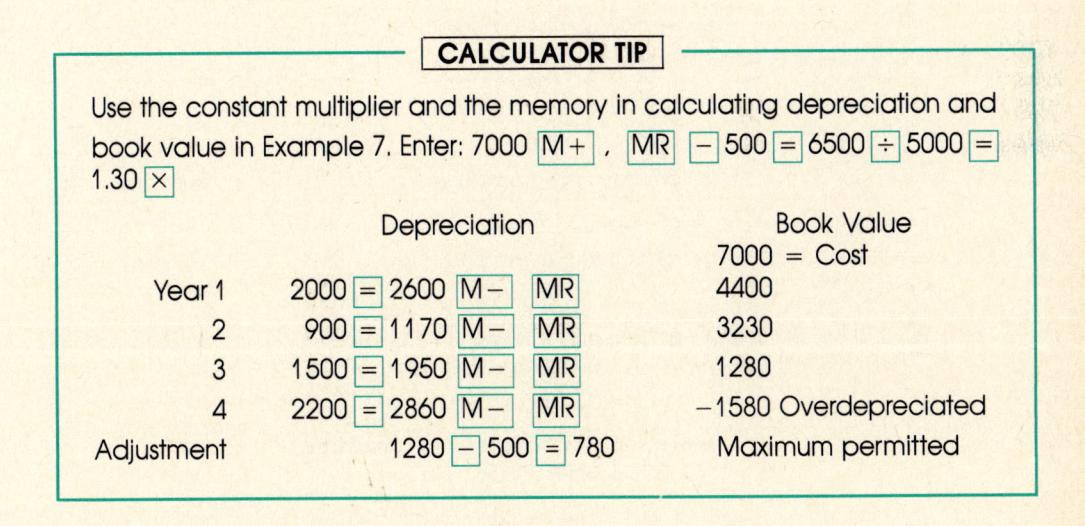

CALCULATOR TIP

Use the constant multiplier and the memory in calculating depreciation and book value in Example 7. Enter: 7000 [M+], [MR] [−] 500 [=] 6500 [÷] 5000 [=] 1.30 [×]

	Depreciation	Book Value
		7000 = Cost
Year 1	2000 [=] 2600 [M−] [MR]	4400
2	900 [=] 1170 [M−] [MR]	3230
3	1500 [=] 1950 [M−] [MR]	1280
4	2200 [=] 2860 [M−] [MR]	−1580 Overdepreciated
Adjustment	1280 [−] 500 [=] 780	Maximum permitted

✓ **CHECK FOR UNDERSTANDING**

1. An airplane engine has a useful life of 3,500 hours. Using the unit of production method, a cost of $13,000, and a scrap value of $750, figure the depreciation for the first 3 years if the engine was used as follows: Year 1, 750 hours; Year 2, 1,500 hours; Year 3, 500 hours.

2. A large dirt-moving machine is used 1,800 hours the first year; 2,200 hours the second year; 1,300 hours the third year; and 2,200 hours the fourth year. If its life is 6,500 hours and it has a cost of $133,125 with a salvage of $8,000, compute the depreciation for the 4 years, showing the book value as well.

3. Calculate the book value at the end of the second year of this production machine that has an estimated life of 6 years and 300,000 units. It cost the company $63,000 and has an estimated scrap value of $6,000. It produced units as follows: Year 1, 33,000; Year 2, 128,000; Year 3, 90,000; Year 4, 60,000; Year 5, 55,000; and Year 6, 28,000.

SKILL EXERCISES

In each of the following problems, calculate the depreciation per unit (rate), the depreciation for Year 1, and book value at the end of Year 1:

	Cost	Life in units	Depreciation per unit	Units used, year 1	Depreciation	End-of-year book value
1.	$60,000	150,000	$ _____	40,000	$ _____	$ _____
2.	$24,000	120,000	$ _____	18,500	$ _____	$ _____
3.	$250,000	1,000,000	$ _____	33,000	$ _____	$ _____
4.	$175,000	70,000	$ _____	5,385	$ _____	$ _____
5.	$8,500	80,000	$ _____	16,300	$ _____	$ _____
6.	$17,850	3,000	$ _____	515	$ _____	$ _____
7.	$32,844	184,000	$ _____	11,680	$ _____	$ _____
8.	$36,225	115,000	$ _____	21,785	$ _____	$ _____
9.	$2,384,550	105,000	$ _____	4,750	$ _____	$ _____
10.	$5,850	90,000	$ _____	16,925	$ _____	$ _____

Answers to ✓ Check for Understanding
1. $2,625; $5,250; $1,750.

2.
	Depreciation	Book Value
		$133,125 = Cost
Year 1	$34,650	$98,475
Year 2	$42,350	$56,125
Year 3	$25,025	$31,100
Year 4	$23,100	$8,000

3. $32,410.

APPLICATIONS

Solve for depreciation in the years indicated:

1. A large utility company uses the hours of operation to determine the depreciation of its large generators. On January 4 it purchased a $60,000 generator having a scrap value of $6,000 and a useful life of 105,000 hours. The generator operated 7,000 hours in Year 1, 7,600 hours in Year 2, and 8,050 hours in Year 3. Calculate the depreciation for the first 3 years.

2. Over-the-Road Trucking uses 125,000 miles as the life of its large diesel motors. The scrap value on a $9,000 motor is estimated to be $300. Compute the depreciation and the book value for the following: Year 1, 28,000 miles; Year 2, 46,000 miles; Year 3, 44,000 miles; and Year 4, 32,000 miles.

3. Substitute the following schedule of miles into Problem 2: Year 1, 48,250; Year 2, 61,000; Year 3, 25,000; and Year 4, 10,000. In what year will the company be unable to take the full amount of depreciation because of dropping below salvage? Also determine the amount of depreciation that will be allowed during that year.

4. An assembly line stamping machine was purchased on September 14 for $33,750. The machine has an estimated life of 750,000 units and a scrap value of $350. If the machine produces 105,000 units in Year 1, 89,000 in Year 2, and 241,000 in Year 3, what is the depreciation for each of those years?

5. Wholesale Inc. trades in its fleet of cars when they reach 65,000 miles at a guaranteed trade-in of $2,750. If the cars cost $9,050 each, what is the depreciation rate per mile? What is the depreciation in a year in which a car travels 22,000 miles?

6. Large dirt-moving machines have an engine life of 8,000 hours before replacement. If one costs $8,000 and has a salvage value of $1,500, figure the depreciation for the following years using the units of production method: Year 1, 1,750 hours; Year 2, 2,850 hours; Year 3, 3,725 hours; Year 4, 2,100 hours; Year 5, 1,680 hours.

7. The following information is available on a production machine: purchase price, $39,000; scrap, $3,500; life of 10 years or 125,000 units. Calculate the depreciation for each of the following years: Year 1, 39,000 units; Year 2, 23,400 units; Year 3, 48,650 units; Year 4, 21,900 units.

8. A large generator costs $145,000 with an estimated life of 200,000 hours. If the generator has scrap value of $7,000 and the following hours of use: Year 1, 8,000 hours; Year 2, 7,990 hours; Year 3, 8,100 hours; Year 4, 7,780 hours, calculate the book value at the end of Year 4.

9. Manufacturers General uses 85,000 miles as the life of their auto sales fleet. If they buy 8 cars at a cost of $8,200 each, which have a trade-in value of $2,800 each, what is the depreciation in Years 1 and 2 when Car A was driven 15,600 miles and 19,250 miles?

10. A machine lathe will handle 315,000 cuts during its life. The lathe cost $16,485 and has a scrap value of $815. Calculate the depreciation and the book value for each of the first 3 years using the following information: Year 1, 21,500; Year 2, 18,260 units; Year 3, 26,115 units.

Declining Balance

The **declining balance** method is an accelerated method of depreciation with more expense the first year and smaller amounts in Years 2, 3, etc. Many types of assets do not depreciate at the same amount each year—a delivery truck is a good example.

The salvage value is *not* subtracted from cost to determine the base. Even so, we *never* depreciate below the salvage value. The declining balance rate is $1\frac{1}{4}$, $1\frac{1}{2}$, or 2 times the straight line rate. These rates are commonly listed as 125%, 150%, or 200% of the straight line rate. The rate is multiplied times the book value at the beginning of each year to calculate the depreciation. The method's name originates from the fact that the book value (base) gets smaller each year (declines) as the rate stays constant. The formula is:

> Annual depreciation = Book value (beginning of year) × Declining balance rate

EXAMPLE 8 A company buys a delivery van for $15,000 on January 10. It has a $1,000 trade-in value and a life of 6 years. Using 150% of the straight line rate, calculate the depreciation for the 6 years.

Solution:

100% ÷ 6 = 16.6667%	· Calculate the straight line rate: 100% ÷ life in years.
16.6667 × 1.5 = 25%	· Calculate declining balance rate.
15000 × .25 = 3750	· Calculate Year 1 depreciation: Cost is book value to begin Year 1.
(15000 − 3750) × .25 = 2812.50	· Calculate new book value and Year 2 depreciation.
(11250 − 2812.50) × .25 = 2109.38	· Calculate new book value and Year 3 depreciation.
(8437.50 − 2109.38) × .25 = 1582.03	· Calculate new book value and Year 4 depreciation.
(6328.12 − 1582.03) × .25 = 1186.52	· Calculate new book value and Year 5 depreciation.
(4746.09 − 1186.52) × .25 = 889.89	· Calculate new book value and Year 6 depreciation.
3559.57 − 889.89 = 2669.68 Book value compared to 1,000 salvage—No!	· Compare final book value to salvage; is it overdepreciated?

312   Chapter 11   Depreciation and Inventory Valuation

> **CALCULATOR TIP**
>
> Use the constant multiplier, the memory for keeping a running book value (base), and proper use of the MR key to reduce the number of steps in Example 8. Enter 15000 [M+], 1 [÷] 6 [=] .166667 [×] 1.5 [=] .25 [×] [MR] [=] 3750 [M−], [MR] 11250
>
> 1.0 [÷] 6 [=] .166667 is the decimal form of 100% [÷] 6 [=] 16.6667%
>
> Constant (.25) [×] base from memory (15000) [=] Depr. (3750) subtracted from memory (M−) and recalled (MR) = new base (11,250)
>
> [=] 2812.50 [M−]   [MR] 8437.50   The cycle continues without re-entering.
> [=] 2109.37 [M−]   [MR] 6328.13
> [=] 1582.03 [M−]   [MR] 4746.10
> [=] 1186.52 [M−]   [MR] 3559.58
> [=] 889.89 [M−]   [MR] 2669.68

EXAMPLE 9 A microcomputer work station costing $4,700 was installed on January 6. If the salvage value is $1,000, it has a life of 5 years, and uses 200% of the straight line rate, prepare a depreciation schedule showing the base for calculating each year's depreciation, the annual depreciation, and the book value at the end of each year.

Solution:

100% ÷ 5 = 20% × 2 = 40%   · Calculate the declining balance rate.
4700 × .40 = 1880   · Calculate Year 1 depreciation.
(4700 − 1880) × .40 = 1128   · Calculate book value and Year 2 depreciation.
· Complete the schedule.

Year	Rate	Depreciation Base	Depreciation	End-of-Year Book Value
				$4,700 = Cost
1	.40	$4,700	$1,880	$2,820
2	.40	$2,820	$1,128	$1,692
3	.40	$1,692	$ 676.80	$1,015.20
4	.40	$1,015.20	$ 15.20*	$1,000.00

* Year 4 normal depreciation is $1,015.20 × .40, or $406.08. Subtracting $406.08 from the previous book value of $1,015.20 leaves $609.12, which is less than the salvage value of $1,000. The maximum depreciation in Year 4 is the difference between the book value at the end of Year 3 ($1,015.20) minus the salvage ($1,000) or $15.80. □

✓ CHECK FOR UNDERSTANDING

1. The Move-a-Long Company purchased a heavy-duty conveyor machine for $20,000 on January 6. It had a salvage value of $2,000 and an estimated life of 10 years. Using the declining balance method at 200% of the straight line rate, calculate the depreciation for the third year.

2. The declining balance method at $1\frac{1}{2}$ times straight line is used by a company for figuring depreciation on its fleet of delivery vans. The company purchased a van

for $12,000 with a salvage value of $1,500 after 6 years of use. Prepare a depreciation schedule for the first 4 years of use, showing the amount of depreciation and the book value for those years.

3. An air cargo company depreciated its airplane engines on the declining balance method over a life of 4 years. If the engines are purchased for $20,000 and have a scrap value of $3,000, what would the fourth year's depreciation be, using 200% of the straight line rate?

4. The Murphy Company purchased a large production machine on January 8 for $135,000. If the machine has a salvage value of $5,000 and a life of 8 years, what would the depreciation be for each of the first 2 years using the declining balance method at twice the straight line rate?

SKILL EXERCISES

Using life in years, calculate the straight line rate. Using the declining balance multiplier in Column C, calculate the declining balance rate as a decimal. Lastly, calculate the first-year depreciation using the declining balance rate and the cost that is given. Problem 0 is given as an example.

	(A) Life in years	(B) Straight line rate in decimal	(C) Percent of straight line rate	(D) Declining balance rate in decimal	(E) Cost	(F) Year 1 depreciation
0.	5	.20	200%	.40	$7,200	$2,880
1.	4	_____	200%	_____	$7,350	$_____
2.	8	_____	200%	_____	$12,000	$_____
3.	6	_____	150%	_____	$8,000	$_____
4.	10	_____	125%	_____	$6,000	$_____
5.	12	_____	200%	_____	$9,600	$_____
6.	5	_____	150%	_____	$21,000	$_____

Answers to ✓ Check for Understanding

1. $2,560

2.
Depreciation	End-of-Year Book Value
	$12,000 = Cost
$3,000	$9,000
$2,250	$6,750
$1,687.50	$5,062.50
$1,265.63	$3,796.87

3. 0.   4. $33,750; $25,312.50.

7.	3	_____	150%	_____	$ 4,000 $ _____
8.	15	_____	150%	_____	$63,500 $ _____
9.	7	_____	200%	_____	$45,500 $ _____
10.	20	_____	125%	_____	$20,000 $ _____

APPLICATIONS

1. Try-Us Rent-a-Car purchased an automobile for $8,600 with a salvage value of $1,000 and a life of 4 years. What is the book value at the end of the third year if they use a rate twice straight line?

2. Atlas Construction purchased a building that cost $120,000 with no salvage and a life of 15 years. If they use a rate of $1\frac{1}{2}$ times straight line, what is the depreciation for the third year?

3. Calculate the depreciation for the fourth year on a delivery van purchased on January 12 for $21,000. The company uses 200% of the straight line rate, a life of 5 years, and a $3,000 salvage value.

4. Sell-All Hardware's cash register cost $3,840. They use no salvage, a life of 8 years, and 200% of the straight line rate. Calculate the second year's depreciation.

5. EZE-Rent's mini-warehouses cost $660,000 with an estimated salvage value of $20,000. If they use a life of 20 years and a rate twice straight line, what is the depreciation for each of the first 3 years?

6. Prepare a five-year depreciation schedule showing the yearly depreciation and the book value on a microcomputer that costs $4,500. The company uses a rate of 200% of the straight line and an estimated salvage of $500.

7. A bank purchased a new sound system with a life of 10 years for $5,600. If it has no salvage, what would the book value be at the end of 5 years if they use a rate that is 200% of straight line?

8. Hay Seed Farm just purchased a used combine for $85,000 on January 13. Calculate the depreciation for each of the first 3 years if it has no salvage value, a life of 10 years, and they use a rate that is 150% of straight line.

9. Ocean World purchased a very large aquarium on January 1 for $6,200. They estimated it would have a life of 15 years and no salvage value. Calculate the first calendar year's depreciation if they use a rate 200% of straight line.

10. Calculate the fourth year's depreciation expense on the following asset: moving van that cost $90,000 with a life of 8 years, a salvage value of $10,000, and a rate that is 200% of straight line.

Method Comparison

Comparing the depreciation of a $6,000 asset under the three different methods is very revealing. If it has a life of 5 years and no salvage value:

Year	Straight Line Depreciation	Book Value	Sum-of-the-Years' Digits Depreciation	Book Value	Declining Balance 200% of Straight Line Depreciation	Book Value
1	$1,200	$4,800	$2,000	$4,000	$2,400	$3,600
2	$1,200	$3,600	$1,600	$2,400	$1,440	$2,160
3	$1,200	$2,400	$1,200	$1,200	$ 864	$1,296
4	$1,200	$1,200	$ 800	$ 400	$ 518*	$ 778
5	$1,200	–0–	$ 400	–0–	$ 311*	$ 467

*Rounded to whole dollars.

This relationship can be seen better in Figure 11.1.

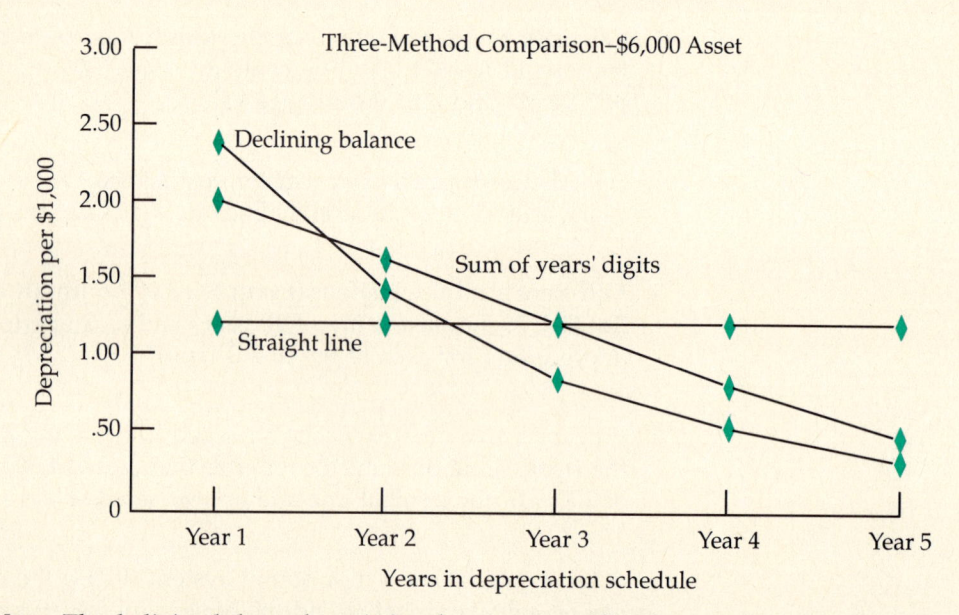

FIGURE 11.1
Depreciation comparison

Note: *The declining balance depreciation drops very rapidly after starting with the most depreciation in Year 1. The decline, however, slows considerably toward the end of the asset life. Because the units-of-production method has no set pattern of depreciation, it is not included in the comparison.*

Partial Year—Sum-of-the-Years'-Digits Method and Declining Balance

As we saw in working with partial year depreciation using the straight line method, an adjustment is necessary when a property is purchased during a month that doesn't match the calendar or fiscal year the company is using. Partial year calculations are required under sum-of-the-years'-digits and declining balance methods also, except they require more than the first-year adjustment. Let's use Example 3 from page 300 to illustrate.

Sum-of-the-Years'-Digits Method

EXAMPLE 10 O'Reilly Corporation purchased a typewriter for $1,400 on April 4. It has a useful life of 5 years and a salvage value of $200. Using sum-of-the-years'-digits method, calculate the *calendar* year depreciation for each of the 5 years.

Sum-of-the-Years'-Digits Partial Depreciation

Calendar Year	Calculation	Depreciation	Book Value
1 Apr.–Dec.	$\frac{5}{15} \times 1200 \times \frac{9}{12}$	$300.00	$1,400 = Cost 1,100.00 (1,400 − 300)
2 Jan.–Mar.	$\frac{5}{15} \times 1200 \times \frac{3}{12}$	$100.00	
2 Apr.–Dec.	$\frac{4}{15} \times 1200 \times \frac{9}{12}$	$240.00	
2	Calendar year total	$340.00	760.00 (1,100 − 340)
3 Jan.–Mar.	$\frac{4}{15} \times 1200 \times \frac{3}{12}$	$ 80.00	
3 Apr.–Dec.	$\frac{3}{15} \times 1200 \times \frac{9}{12}$	$180.00	
3	Calendar year total	$260.00	500.00 (760 − 260)
4 Jan.–Mar.	$\frac{3}{15} \times 1200 \times \frac{3}{12}$	$ 60.00	
4 Apr.–Dec.	$\frac{2}{15} \times 1200 \times \frac{9}{12}$	$120.00	
4	Calendar year total	$180.00	320.00 (500 − 180)
5 Jan.–Mar.	$\frac{2}{15} \times 1200 \times \frac{3}{12}$	$ 40.00	
5 Apr.–Dec.	$\frac{1}{15} \times 1200 \times \frac{9}{12}$	$ 60.00	
5	Calendar year total	$100.00	220.00 (320 − 100)
6 Jan.–Mar.	$\frac{1}{15} \times 1200 \times \frac{3}{12}$	$ 20.00	200.00 (220 − 20)

Solution:

- Visualize the number of months in each part of the calculation:

Calendar Year 1 April through December: $\frac{9}{12}$ of full year

Calendar Year 2 January through March: $\frac{3}{12}$ of old year *plus* April through December: $\frac{9}{12}$ of new total.

Calendar Years 3 to 5   • Same months and fractions as Calendar Year 2.

$$\frac{n \times (n+1)}{2} = \frac{5 \times 6}{2} = 15$$ • Calculate the denominator.

$\frac{5}{15} \times 1200 \times \frac{9}{12} =$ $300   • Year 1 (April–December).

$\frac{5}{15} \times 1200 \times \frac{3}{12} =$ 100   • Year 2 (January–March) plus (April–December).

$\frac{4}{15} \times 1200 \times \frac{9}{12} =$ (+)240

Calendar Year 2 total $340
See schedule on page 317.   • Continue the pattern through Year 5.

Declining Balance Partial Year Depreciation

Partial year depreciation using the declining balance method requires an adjustment for Year 1. Solution A shows the same logic as that used in sum-of-the-years'-digits method. Solution B shows an easier method. Let's use the same problem in Example 10.

EXAMPLE 11   O'Reilly Corporation purchased a typewriter for $1,400 on April 4. It has a useful life of 5 years and a salvage value of $200. Calculate the calendar year depreciation for the 5 years of life using twice the straight line rate.

Solution A:

• Visualize the months in each part of the transaction:

Calendar Year 1   April through December: $\frac{9}{12}$ of full year

Calendar Year 2   January through March: $\frac{3}{12}$ of old year
plus April through December: $\frac{9}{12}$ of new year.

Calendar Years 3 to 5   • The pattern continues as in Year 2:

100% ÷ 5 = 20%   • Calculate the rate at twice straight line.
20% × 2 = 40%

$.40 \times 1400 \times \frac{9}{12} =$ $420   • Year 1 (April–December).

$.40 \times 1400 \times \frac{3}{12} =$ 140   • Year 2 (January–March) *plus* (April–December).

$.40 \times 840^* \times \frac{9}{12} =$ (+)252

Calendar Year 2 total $392
*1400 − 420 − 140 = 840
   • Book value at beginning of Year 2.
   • The pattern continues through Year 5.

* Calendar Year 2 was figured in much the same manner as was the sum-of-the-years'-digits method. However, there is an easier way. Because the rate remains constant, after figuring the partial year on Calendar Year 1, the remaining years can be figured in the regular declining balance fashion.

Solution B:

- Visualize the months in the first year of the transaction:

Calendar Year 1

April through December: $\frac{9}{12}$ of full year

$100\% \div 5 = 20\%$
$20\% \times 2 = 40\%$

Calculate the rate using twice straight line:

$.40 \times 1400 \times \dfrac{9}{12} = \$420$

- Year 1 (April–December).

$.40 \times 980 = 392$
$(1400 - 420)$

- Year 2.

$.40 \times 588 = 235.20$
$(980 - 392)$

- Year 3.

See schedule below.

- The pattern continues. □

Declining Balance Partial Year Depreciation

Calendar Year	Calculation	Depreciation	Book Value
			$1,400.00 = Cost
1 Apr.–Dec.	$1400 \times .40 \times \dfrac{9}{12}$	$420.00	$980.00 (1,400 − 420)
2	$980 \times .40$	$392.00	$588.00 (980 − 392)
3	$588 \times .40$	$235.20	$352.80 (588 − 235.20)
4	$352.80 \times .40$	$141.12	$211.68 (352.80 − 141.12)
5	$211.68 \times .40$	$ 11.68*	$200.00 (211.68 − 11.68)

* The depreciation in Year 5 is $84.67 ($211.68 × .40) but do not depreciate below the salvage of $200.

Because partial year depreciation is covered extensively in most accounting programs, additional practice problems are not provided in this text.

Accelerated Cost Recovery System (ACRS) Method

11.2

For most tangible property placed in service after 1980, the **accelerated cost recovery system (ACRS,** pronounced "acres") must be used for tax purposes. Under this method as modified by the Tax Reform Act of 1986, **personal property** placed in service after December 31, 1986, is assigned a recovery period (estimated life) and a method of calculating depreciation. Personal property may be assigned a life of 3 years, 5 years, 7 years, 10 years, 15 years, or 20 years. **Real property** (real estate) is assigned 27.5 or 31.5 years, depending upon whether it is residential, rental, or other real property.

Under ACRS, both new and used properties are treated the same. The cost is the base for each calculation—salvage is not considered. The double declining balance method (200%) is used for properties in the 3-, 5-, 7-, and 10-year classes. The 15- and 20-year classes use the 150% declining balance method. All classes switch to the straight line method at the appropriate time in order to maximize the allowance. Table 11.1 shows the recovery periods and common types of properties that fall into each category. Since the new system prescribes a depreciation method rather than statutory depreciation percentages, Table 11.2 rates were established to make the depreciation calculation easier. The rates in Table 11.2 also reflect the **mid-year convention** rule. This means that personal property will receive one-half year of depreciation in the first year regardless of the month placed into service. One-half year of depreciation will also be allowed in the year of disposition or sale.

TABLE 11.1
ACRS Recovery Periods and Common Types of Properties in Each Period Placed in Service after December 31, 1986

Recovery Period	Types of Properties
3-year	Useful life 4 years or less; special tools and handling devices in manufacture of food and beverages, rubber products, finished plastic products, fabricated metal products, or motor vehicles; breeding hogs.
5-year	Useful lives of more than 4 and less than 10 years; automobiles, light trucks, computers, typewriters, copiers, duplicating equipment, heavy general purpose trucks, computer-based central office switching equipment, semiconductor manufacturing equipment, research and experimentation property.
7-year	Useful lives of more than 10 and less than 16 years; all properties not falling into other categories; office furniture, fixtures and equipment, single-purpose agriculture, or horticultural structures.
10-year	Useful lives of more than 16 and less than 20 years; petroleum-refining equipment, assets used in manufacture of tobacco products or certain food products.
15-year	Useful lives of more than 20 and less than 25 years; waste-water treatment plants, telephone distribution plants, and comparable equipment used for two-way exchange of voice and data communications.
20-year	Useful lives of 25 years and more; other than real property with an asset depreciation range life of 27.5 or longer; sewer pipes.
27.5-year	Residential rental property, elevators, escalators.
31.5-year	Nonresidential real property.

SOURCE: Much of the information taken from Prentice-Hall's *Explanation of the Tax Reform Act of 1986*, September 27, 1986, Bulletin 51 Extra, Prentice-Hall Information Services, Paramus, NJ 07652.

Once the recovery period is determined from Table 11.1 for each class of property, the effective rates to calculate depreciation are taken from Table 11.2.

TABLE 11.2
ACRS Depreciation Rates for Each Class of *Personal Property*

If the Recovery Year Is:	\multicolumn{6}{c}{The Applicable Percentage for the Class of Property Is:}
	3-Year	5-Year	7-Year	10-Year	15-Year	20-Year
1	33.33%	20.00%	14.29%	10.00%	5.00%	3.750%
2	44.45	32.00	24.49	18.00	9.50	7.219
3	14.81*	19.20	17.49	14.40	8.55	6.677
4	7.41	11.52*	12.49	11.52	7.70	6.177
5		11.52	8.93*	9.22	6.93	5.713
6		5.76	8.92	7.37	6.23	5.285
7			8.93	6.55*	5.90*	4.888
8			4.46	6.55	5.90	4.522
9				6.56	5.91	4.462*
10				6.55	5.90	4.461
11				3.28	5.91	4.462
12					5.90	4.461
13					5.91	4.462
14					5.90	4.461
15					5.91	4.462
16					2.95	4.461
17						4.462
18						4.461
19						4.462
20						4.461
21						2.231

3-, 5-, 7-, and 10-year classes are 200% of declining balance method. 15- and 20-year classes are 150% of declining balance method. All classes switch to the straight line method at a time to maximize the depreciation allowance. The asterisk in each column shows where that point was reached.
SOURCE: IRS Revised Proceedings 87-57, Issued October 1987.

Real Property Depreciation. Residential rental property placed in service after December 31, 1986, has a recovery period of 27.5 years. Nonresidential real property's recovery period is 31.5 years. In addition, both types will use the straight line method rather than double or 150% declining balance methods used for personal property. The **mid-month convention** rather than the mid-year convention applies. Therefore, rather than getting a half-year's depreciation in the first year regardless of when the property was purchased (mid-year), the month of the purchase must be considered in the calculation.

> ACRS depreciation is calculated by multiplying the cost times the rates in Table 11.2.

EXAMPLE 12 Calculate the depreciation for each year in the life of an automobile purchased for $7,500 on November 10 having a salvage value of $2,500.

Solution:

    Autos = 5 years
    20%, 32%, 19.2%, 11.52%,
      11.52%, 5.76%
    Year 1: 7500 × .20   = 1500
    Year 2: 7500 × .32   = 2400
    Year 3: 7500 × .192 = 1440
    Year 4: 7500 × .1152 = 864
    Year 5: 7500 × .1152 = 864
    Year 6: 7500 × .0576 = 432

- Determine years of life from Table 11.1.
- Determine yearly percents from Table 11.2.
- Cost × Annual rate.

PROBLEM SOLVING STRATEGY

Note 1: No salvage is used to calculate the base. *Note 2:* Even though the auto was purchased in November, one-half year of depreciation is allowed in the first year. This is reflected in the rate used for the first year (20%). Remember in the double declining balance method 100% is divided by life in years and then doubled (100% ÷ 5 is 20% × 2 = 40%). To show only a half year, the regular rate (40%) is divided by 2 and 20% is used. *Note 3:* When the auto is disposed of, one-half year of depreciation will be allowed in the year of disposition or sale. See Example 13 for its application.

EXAMPLE 13 Only Us Placement Service purchased an office desk and chair for $1,000. They had a salvage value of $175 and were placed in service on April 10. Prepare a depreciation schedule showing depreciation and book value for the life of the office furniture.

Solution:

    Equipment = 7 years
    (1) 14.29% (2) 24.49% (3) 17.49%
    (4) 12.49% (5) 8.93% (6) 8.92%
    (7) 8.93% (8) 4.46%

- Determine years of life from Table 11.1.
- Determine the percents from Table 11.2.
- Set up a table with given information and then calculate the required:

Year	Cost Base		Rate		Depreciation	End-of-Year Book Value
						$1,000.00 = Cost
1	$1000	×	.1429	=	$142.90	$ 857.10
2	$1000	×	.2449	=	$244.90	$ 612.20
3	$1000	×	.1749	=	$174.90	$ 437.30
4	$1000	×	.1249	=	$124.90	$ 312.40
5	$1000	×	.0893	=	$ 89.30	$ 223.10
6	$1000	×	.0892	=	$ 89.20	$ 133.90
7	$1000	×	.0893	=	$ 89.30	$ 44.60
8	$1000	×	.0446	=	$ 44.60*	–0–

* Notice the schedule shows an eighth year. This is the carryover because only one-half year's depreciation was allowed in Year 1. Remember, salvage is not considered in the ACRS system.

Chapter 11   Depreciation and Inventory Valuation

✓ CHECK FOR UNDERSTANDING

1. The Always Solid Canning Company purchased food processing equipment for $28,000. It has a salvage value of $4,000. What is the depreciation under the ACRS system for the second year?

2. A telephone distribution plant was purchased for $82,000 on August 25. If it has no scrap value, what is the depreciation for the fourth year if we use ACRS?

3. A light duty truck costing $12,500 was purchased by Ever-Faithful Electric Company on February 15. If it has a salvage value of $5,000, what is the depreciation for Year 1?

4. A used microcomputer with monitor, disk drives, and printer were purchased for $2,800. If the salvage value is $700, what is the depreciation for the third year?

5. What is the book value at the end of Year 3 on a copier purchased for $6,560? It was purchased on November 12 and has a salvage value of $500.

SKILL EXERCISES

Use the type of property in Column B to determine the retention period. Use the retention period and Table 11.2 to determine the appropriate rate to be entered in Column D. Multiply the rate in Column D times the cost to calculate the dollars of depreciation. Problem 0 is given as an example.

	(A) Cost	(B) Type of property	(C) Depreciation year	(D) Depreciation rate	(E) Dollars of depreciation
0.	$18,000	Computer	3	19.20 %	$ 3,456
1.	$ 685	Collator	4	_____ %	$ _____
2.	$36,000	Refining equipment	8	_____ %	$ _____
3.	$ 8,000	Auto	2	_____ %	$ _____
4.	$13,600	Light duty truck	3	_____ %	$ _____
5.	$ 6,500	Desks & chair	1	_____ %	$ _____
6.	$21,300	Telecommunications equip.	5	_____ %	$ _____

Answers to ✓ Check for Understanding
1. $12,446. 2. $6,314. 3. $2,500. 4. $537.60. 5. $1,889.28.

Section 11.2 Accelerated Cost Recovery System (ACRS) Method

7.	$18,000	Word processor	4	_____ %	$ _____
8.	$16,000	Heavy duty truck	2	_____ %	$ _____
9.	$40,000	Special tools, rubber products mfg.	3	_____ %	$ _____
10.	$32,000	Office fixtures	5	_____ %	$ _____

Partial Year ACRS

Except for the mid-year convention, there isn't partial year depreciation of tangible personal property. Real property having 27.5 and 31.5 recovery years does use mid-month convention. Depreciation calculations must consider the month of purchase and therefore the beginning and ending year are partial years. This text does not cover real property depreciation.

APPLICATIONS

1. Using the ACRS method, figure the depreciation for the first 3 years on a typewriter purchased for $830.

2. A sewage treatment plant costing $750,000 was put into service on October 5. Using the ACRS depreciation method, calculate the depreciation for Year 7.

3. Lite-Weight Manufacturing purchased special tools for use in their metal fabrication shop. They were purchased for $41,700 on June 16 and have an estimated scrap value of $850. What is the depreciation for Years 1 and 2?

4. Forever Grow Sod Farm uses the ACRS method of depreciation on its 18-inch sod cutters. If they cost $6,350 and have a salvage value of $1,200, what is the depreciation for Year 4?

5. Prepare a depreciation schedule showing the annual depreciation and the book value for a light duty truck that costs $12,850. The company uses the ACRS method for the truck, which has a salvage value of $4,500.

6. A telephone distribution plant costing $450,000 was placed in service on August 1. Calculate depreciation for Years 1, 5, and 10 under the ACRS method.

7. Meadowland Manufacturing Corporation, a semiconductor manufacturing company, purchased new production line equipment for $46,450 on April 1. If the equipment has a scrap value of $850 and the corporation uses the ACRS method, what is the depreciation for Year 4?

8. Determine the book value at the end of Year 4 on a word processor that costs $12,000. The company uses the ACRS method and no salvage.

9. Horton Beverage Packers Inc. purchased special production line handling equipment for $58,000 on May 21. If they use the ACRS method, what is the depreciation for the second year? The book value?

10. Used office furniture was placed in service in September for $18,500. Using the ACRS method, calculate the depreciation for Years 1 and 2.

Inventory Valuation

11.3

Inventory is typically the merchandise a company has on hand for sale. It is also the goods held for consumption in a manufacturing business. Management must place a dollar cost on that inventory in order to calculate a profit or loss. As with depreciation, there are several methods of calculating that dollar value.

The computation must be based on a **physical inventory** (an actual count of the items on hand), or on a **perpetual inventory** (a figure calculated from the company's books). There are four common methods used in valuing inventory: specific identification; first-in, first-out (FIFO); last-in, first-out (LIFO); and weighted average.

Specific Identification Method

The **specific identification** method uses items valued at their specific actual costs. If items are large and easily identified without a large amount of fluctuation in their cost, this method may be appropriate. Types of businesses that might use this method are auto dealers, large appliance stores, furniture stores, computer outlets, and others. Because each item can be easily identified, its cost can be traced through company records. The cost may also be recorded on the back of the sales tag in some type of company code.

> Total inventory value = Cost of items in the same class added together

EXAMPLE 14 The Underwater Waterbed Outlet generates a list of inventory on December 31 of its king-size beds showing the following:

Date of Purchase	Model	Cost
March 20	TR-15	$183.50
June 1	WT-28	$270.00
August 11	WT-42	$335.75
October 5	TR-30	$215.00
December 10	WT-28	$282.00

Using the specific identification method, calculate the value of the ending inventory.
Solution:

183.50 + 270 + 335.75 + 215 + 282 = $1286.25   • Add all costs together.

CHECK FOR UNDERSTANDING

1. Whiz Bang Furniture Outlet is able to identify six living room groups in its physical inventory on December 31. Calculate the value of the inventory using the specific identification method:

Date	Cost	Date	Cost
February 2	$675	Aug. 11	$1,080
April 16	$952	Oct. 12	$1,350
May 6	$595	Nov. 10	$ 875

2. Speedy TV Outlet has four console televisions in stock on March 31. Using the specific identification method, calculate the ending inventory value:

Model	Cost	Model	Cost
BR164	$318	SL256	$296
SL256	$426	SL416	$450

First-In, First-Out (FIFO)

Inventories are normally valued under the **FIFO** system: the first items brought into the inventory are the first items to be used or sold (see Figure 11.2). The ending inventory is then valued by starting with the last purchase in the period and adding on as many purchases as necessary to account for the inventory total. As we add on purchases, we work through the dates from the last purchase in the period back to the first.

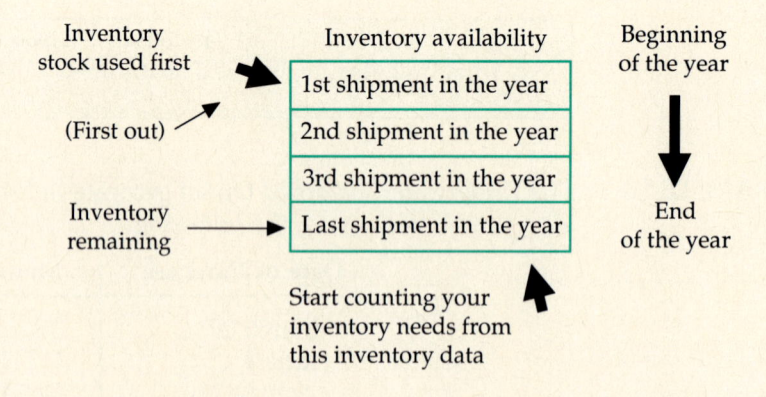

FIGURE 11.2
FIFO—first-in, first-out illustration

Answers to ✓ Check for Understanding
1. $5,527.   2. $1,490.

326 Chapter 11 Depreciation and Inventory Valuation

EXAMPLE 15 During the year, the Lawn Mower Exchange shows the following information on its Model 10 grass catchers:

Purchase Date	Quantity	Cost
		(each)
Beginning inventory	4	$17.00
February 22	10	$18.50
March 19	15	$18.75
June 6	8	$19.25
August 20	4	$19.35

There are 6 catchers in the physical inventory on December 31. Calculate their value, using the FIFO method.

Solution:

```
    4 at 19.35 =  $ 77.40        · Start with the August 20 purchase.
  +2 at 19.25 =     38.50        · We need only 2 more items from
                                   June 6.
    6             $115.90        · Total inventory value.
```

Note: We don't use the other 6 items from the June 6 purchase or any items from March, February, or Beginning Inventory because the total (6) was accounted for using only the August 20 and June 6 purchases.

✔ CHECK FOR UNDERSTANDING

1. A company shows the following information on its Model C hair dryer:

Beginning inventory	26 at $10.50
March 15	50 at $10.65
June 21	75 at $11.00
September 2	100 at $10.25
November 28	50 at $11.10

    The ending inventory shows 92 hair dryers on hand. Calculate their value using the FIFO method.

2. The Park Distributing Corporation shows an ending inventory of 525 units. The yearly summary shows:

1st purchase	1,500 units at $2.50
2nd purchase	2,500 units at $2.75
3rd purchase	250 units at $3.25
4th purchase	150 units at $3.35

    Calculate the value of the inventory under the FIFO method.

3. The Galaxy Company has a total of 1,250 $\frac{3''}{4} \times 3''$ bolts on hand. Calculate the value of these bolts, using the following information and the FIFO method:

Beginning inventory	750 bolts at 12 cents
April 4	500 bolts at 14 cents
August 8	500 bolts at 15 cents

Answers to ✔ Check for Understanding
1. $985.50.   2. $1,658.75.   3. $175.

Last-In, First-Out (LIFO)

The **LIFO** method is the reverse of the FIFO method. We assume the last items brought into the system are the first used or sold (see Figure 11.3). In placing a value on the inventory, we start with the beginning inventory, if there is one, and using date ordered proceed from the first purchase to the last in the period. As was true in the FIFO method, we use as many of the purchases as are necessary to cover the actual count.

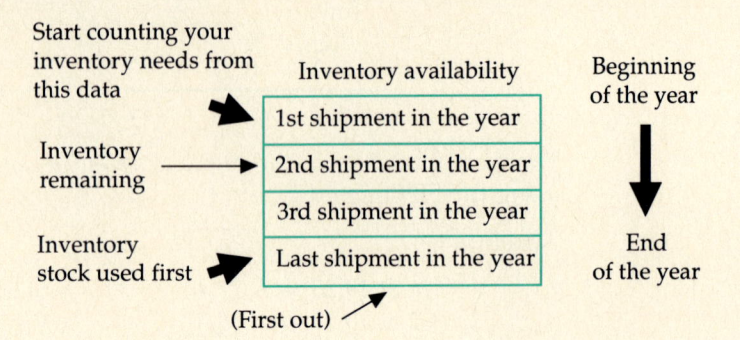

FIGURE 11.3
LIFO—last-in, first-out illustrated

EXAMPLE 16 During the year, the Lawn Mower Exchange shows the following information on its Model 10 grass catchers:

Purchase Date	Quantity	Cost
		(each)
Beginning inventory	4	$17.00
February 22	10	$18.50
March 19	15	$18.75
June 6	8	$19.25
August 20	4	$19.35

There are 6 catchers in the physical inventory on December 31. Calculate their value, using the LIFO method.

Solution:

$$\begin{array}{rl} 4 \text{ at } 17.00 = & \$\ 68.00 \\ +2 \text{ at } 18.50 = & \underline{\ \ 37.00} \\ \overline{6} \quad\quad\quad = & \$105.00 \end{array}$$

- Start with *beginning inventory*.
- We need 2 more items from *February*.
- Total inventory value.

Note: Although a company might not actually use or sell its latest purchased items first, they are permitted to use this method in theory to value their inventory. □

CHECK FOR UNDERSTANDING

1. A company using the LIFO method has 1,134 units on hand on December 31. The following information is available:

Beginning inventory	126 units at $3.36
1st purchase	800 units at $3.40
2nd purchase	650 units at $3.42

   Calculate the value of the ending inventory.

2. The Modern Glass Company's inventory of 6 feet × 8 feet glass pieces on December 31 showed 16. Since this was the first year of operation, there was no beginning inventory but the following purchases were made:

> January 6   8 units at $60.00
> May 11   24 units at $59.50
> October 14 12 units at $60.25

Calculate the inventory value based on the LIFO method.

3. At Sewing Unlimited the purchasing department lists the following information on its model 4G pinking shears:

> January 1, inventory   10 shears at $6.75
> April 26, purchase   12 shears at $6.80
> July 24, purchase   24 shears at $6.60

If the inventory on December 31 is 23, what is the value of the inventory using the LIFO method?

Weighted Average Method

In using the **weighted average** method, we calculate the total amount paid for all like units during the period. That figure is then divided by the total number of units purchased to yield the average cost per unit. The ending inventory is then multiplied times the average cost per unit to calculate the total value.

EXAMPLE 17 During the year, the Lawn Mower Exchange shows the following information on its Model 10 grass catchers:

Purchase Date	Quantity	Cost
		(each)
Beginning inventory	4	$17.00
February 22	10	$18.50
March 19	15	$18.75
June 6	8	$19.25
August 20	4	$19.35

There are 6 catchers in the physical inventory on December 31. Calculate their value, using the weighted average method.

Solution:
- Calculate the total cost of each purchase. Multiply the quantity purchased times the unit cost.
- Add the units and total cost columns.

Units		Unit Cost	Total Cost
4	×	$17.00	$ 68.00
10	×	$18.50	$185.00
15	×	$18.75	$281.25
8	×	$19.25	$154.00
4	×	$19.35	$ 77.40
Totals 41			$765.65

Answers to ✓ Check for Understanding
1. $3,854.72.   2. $956.   3. $155.70.

$$765.65 \div 41 = 18.67439*$$
- Calculate the *average price* per unit; divide the total cost by the total number of units.

$$6 \times 18.67439 = \$112.05$$
- Total inventory value; number of units in inventory times average price per unit.

Because each purchase is "weighted" by the number of items purchased and a varying cost, it is referred to as a weighted average. □

*Do not round to whole cents in using this figure.

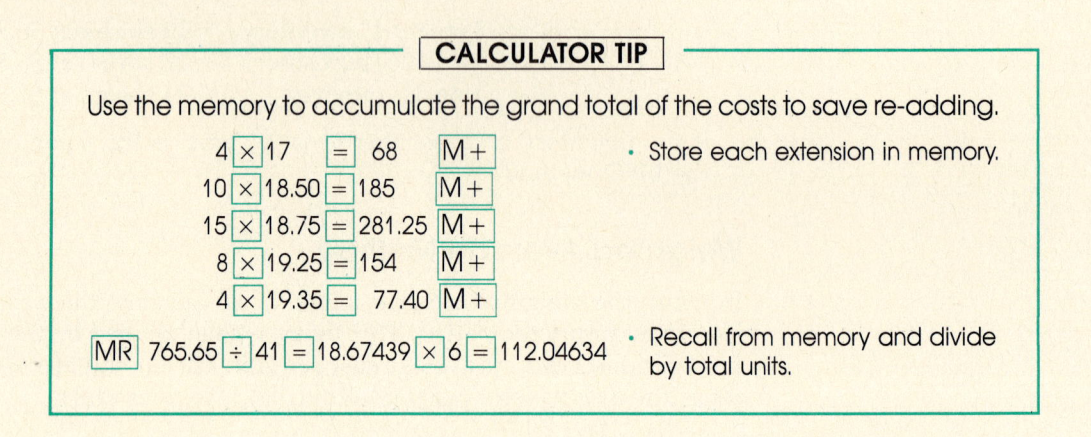

CALCULATOR TIP

Use the memory to accumulate the grand total of the costs to save re-adding.

4 × 17 = 68 M+	• Store each extension in memory.
10 × 18.50 = 185 M+	
15 × 18.75 = 281.25 M+	
8 × 19.25 = 154 M+	
4 × 19.35 = 77.40 M+	
MR 765.65 ÷ 41 = 18.67439 × 6 = 112.04634	• Recall from memory and divide by total units.

The weighted average method normally yields an inventory value that falls between the FIFO and LIFO values. Typically the FIFO is higher because it is based on units purchased later in the year, which under an inflationary economy would have a higher cost. The LIFO value is usually lower because its base is with the earliest purchases (lower cost) in the time period. Since Examples 20, 21, and 22 are the same problem worked under the three systems, their answers show this normal pattern: FIFO, $115.90 is the highest; weighted average, $112.05 falls in the middle; and LIFO, $105 is the lowest (see Figure 11.4).

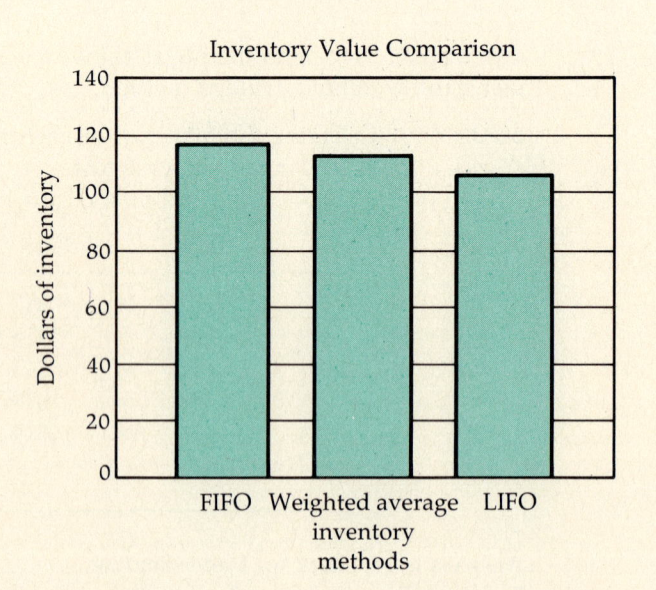

FIGURE 11.4
Inventory value comparison

Inventory Value Comparison — bar chart showing FIFO, Weighted average, and LIFO inventory methods (Dollars of inventory, 0 to 140).

✔ CHECK FOR UNDERSTANDING

1. Ride-to-Health Bicycle Shop shows the following information for the year on its ten-speed Model 20 bicycles:

Beginning inventory	3 at $188.00
April 20	5 at $190.00
July 10	12 at $191.00
Ending inventory	4

   Calculate the cost of the ending inventory using the weighted average method.

2. A hardware store counted 13 Model C power saws in its December 31 inventory. The purchasing history of the saw during the year indicates:

Opening inventory	None
February 15, purchase	8 at $14.75
May 2, purchase	12 at $14.90
August 11, purchase	24 at $14.00

   Calculate the cost of the ending inventory using the weighted average method.

3. The following information is available on a Series D lamp shade:

Beginning inventory	9 at $4.25
1st purchase	12 at $4.25
2nd purchase	6 at $4.35
3rd purchase	12 at $4.37
Ending inventory	11

   Using the weighted average, compute the value of the ending inventory.

APPLICATIONS

1. The following information is available for the standard refrigerator-freezer at All-Nite Appliances:

May 2	Model D	$390
July 16	Model D11	$435
September 12	Model D	$400
December 3	Model EF2	$472

   Find the value of the ending inventory using the specific identification method.

2. Yum Yum Cookie Bakery listed their purchases of sorghum the past year as follows:

April 11	16 barrels at $36.00
June 6	12 barrels at $36.35
August 12	18 barrels at $36.35
November 29	20 barrels at $36.38

   Determine the value of the ending inventory of 26 barrels using FIFO, LIFO, and weighted average methods.

Answers to ✔ Check for Understanding
1. $761.20. 2. $186.96. 3. $47.33.

3. We-Never-Close Hardware uses a fiscal year ending September 30. Their ending inventory of rose trellises shows 36. Using the following history of purchases, calculate the value of the inventory under the FIFO method:

Date	Quantity	Cost
October 6	48	$3.15
March 12	12	$3.65
May 20	72	$3.60
August 8	18	$3.60

4. Sports Wear Outlet shows an inventory of 32 pairs of men's high-top sports shoes. Their purchases during the fiscal year ending March 31 were as follows:

April 21	6 pairs at $32.75
June 1	24 pairs at $33.10
June 25	36 pairs at $33.10
August 19	12 pairs at $32.90
December 5	24 pairs at $32.80

Calculate the inventory value using FIFO, LIFO, and weighted average methods.

5. Sports Wear Outlet uses the specific identification method for its weight bench sets. Their purchases during the year showed:

May 1	$310.75
August 24	$315.00
December 12	$315.00
February 12	$310.00

If they only have the benches purchased on August 24 and February 12 in stock, what is the value of their inventory?

6. The ending inventory of 80-column expansion boards at Micros Unlimited was 15. If they use the LIFO method of inventory valuation and the purchasing history shows the following, calculate the value:

January 12	4 at $72.50
May 18	3 at $73.25
June 1	8 at $68.75
September 2	6 at $68.75
December 12	5 at $67.50

7. Electronics Wholesale lists this purchasing history of computer monitors:

July 3	4 at $182.00
September 9	2 at $180.50
November 21	10 at $175.00
February 28	3 at $175.00
May 3	4 at $172.50

If they use a fiscal year ending on June 30, calculate the value of 8 monitors using the FIFO, LIFO, and weighted average methods.

8. Purchasing records show the following on 50-foot, $\frac{5}{8}$-inch garden hoses:

March 1	18 at $4.10
April 6	24 at $4.25
June 20	72 at $3.00
August 15	12 at $4.25

   Calculate the value of 24 hoses in stock on December 31 using FIFO, LIFO, and weighted average methods.

9. The ending inventory of $5\frac{1}{4}$-inch floppy disks at Electronics-for-You showed 16 boxes, 10 per box. The records indicate their purchases were:

April 19	6 boxes at $8.90
May 30	10 boxes at $8.75
September 20	10 boxes at $8.75
November 12	18 boxes at $8.25
February 5	6 boxes at $8.10

   Calculate the value of ending inventory using weighted average.

10. Ten porch glider swings were in stock on December 31. Calculate their value using the following information and the FIFO, LIFO, and weighted average methods:

May 10	8 at $25.00
June 1	4 at $25.75
July 18	6 at $24.25
August 2	15 at $23.00

Key Terms

Accelerated cost recovery system (ACRS) method (319)
Accumulated depreciation (298)
Book value (298)
Cost (298)
Declining balance method (312)
Depreciation (298)
Economic Recovery Tax Act of 1981 (298)
First-in, first-out (FIFO) (326)
Intangible property (298)
Inventory (325)
Last-in, first-out (FIFO) (328)
Mid-month convention (321, 324)
Mid-year convention (320)

Partial year depreciation (299, 317)
Perpetual inventory (325)
Personal property (319)
Physical inventory (325)
Real property (319, 321)
Salvage value (298, 312)
Scrap value (298, 307)
Specific identification method (325)
Straight line method (298)
Sum-of-the-years'-digits method (303)
Tangible property (298)
Units-of-production method (307)
Useful life (298)
Weighted average method (329)

Looking Back

Many businesses choose to use one set of depreciation methods for financial statement purposes and a different method for taxes. For tax purposes, businesses are required to use the accelerated methods prescribed by the Internal Revenue code. For financial statement purposes, businesses may elect to depreciate property over a longer period of time. Since the ACRS methods are being analyzed and adjusted continuously, you need to stay current by watching for published changes in the allowable life and/or the rates of depreciation.

Because the value of the ending inventory greatly affects the amount of gross profit, choosing the proper method of valuing inventory is very important. Regardless of the method chosen, it must be used for both tax computation and financial statement reporting.

Let's Review

1. A large executive desk that cost $1,200 with $125 salvage was purchased on January 6. If it has a life of 12 years, what is the first year's depreciation using the straight line method?

2. The Colorado Regional Sales Team purchased a fleet of 8 autos for its salespeople. Each car cost $8,750 and had a salvage value of $3,500. If the company uses the ACRS method, what is the depreciation per car for the second year?

3. Seaside Condominiums installed a computer-based central telephone switching device on August 12. The switch cost $56,000 and has a scrap value of $3,200. Calculate the depreciation of each of Years 1 and 2 using the ACRS method.

4. A microcomputer with a life of 7 years was purchased on January 10 for $2,500. If it has a salvage value of $750 and the company uses the sum-of-the-years'-digits method, what is the depreciation for the second year?

5. Furniture Warehouse's fiscal year inventory on June 30 showed 13 plastic stack chairs in stock. Their purchase history reveals the following:

July 7	12 units	$6.75 each
August 13	18 units	$6.75 each
October 1	24 units	$6.80 each
December 20	36 units	$6.50 each
March 1	10 units	$6.80 each

    Use the FIFO, LIFO, and weighted average methods to calculate the value of the ending inventory under each method.

6. All Occasion Trailers uses the specific identification method of valuing their inventory. Their records indicate the following fold-out camping trailers still in stock on December 31:

March 31	Model 6	$1,150
May 31	Model 6D	$1,412
July 31	Model 6	$1,175
September 30	Model 6E	$1,340

    Calculate the ending inventory.

7. A pickup used for delivery cost All Season Tool Rental $7,350. They purchased it on January 1 and estimated salvage to be $1,200. If they use the declining balance method, twice the straight line rate, and a life of 5 years, prepare a depreciation schedule calculating the required information. Use the following format.

Year	Rate	Depreciation	Book Value
1			
2			
3			
4			
5			

8. Large motors used in construction have an estimated life of 8,000 hours. If Model A16-AE costs $14,500 and has a scrap value of $650, calculate the depreciation for each of the following years: Year 1, 1,400 hours; Year 2, 2,100 hours; Year 3, 2,275 hours; Year 4, 2,080 hours; Year 5, 1,850 hours.

9. Research equipment costing $38,750 was purchased on February 22. It has a salvage value of $6,000. Calculate the book value at the end of Year 4 using the ACRS method of depreciation.

10. A large furniture outlet just completed its year-end inventory on June 30: 137 sofa pillows are on hand. Purchases for the year show: July 8, 100 pillows @ $4.37; October 12, 75 pillows @ $4.25; February 2, 150 pillows @ $4.50; May 9, 50 pillows @ $4.10. Using the FIFO, LIFO, and weighted average methods, calculate the value of the ending inventory.

11. A local airline depreciates its jet engines over a 4-year period at twice the straight line rate. One engine costs $12,000 on a March 1 purchase and has a scrap value of $1,500. Prepare a 4-year depreciation schedule, including the book value for this airline.

Year	Rate	Depreciation	Book Value
1			
2			
3			
4			

12. Equipment used in petroleum refining was purchased for $225,000 on September 1. Calculate the depreciation for each of the first 3 years using the ACRS method.

13. Flair Manufacturing purchased 4 microcomputer work stations for $15,000. Using the ACRS method, calculate the depreciation for each of Years 1 and 2.

14. The Box Tool and Die Corporation purchased a machine on January 1 for $22,000. It is estimated to have a life of 7 years and a scrap value of $750. Calculate the depreciation for each of the first 3 calendar years using the sum-of-the-years'-digits method.

15. Over-the-Road Trucking uses 150,000 miles as the life of its large diesel motors. The scrap value on a $9,600 motor is estimated to be $600. Compute the depreciation and the book value for the following year: Year 1, 28,000 miles; Year 2, 46,000 miles; Year 3, 44,000 miles; and Year 4, 32,000 miles.

16. The Offset Press Company depreciates its office desks over a period of 17 years, with no salvage value. An executive desk was purchased on January 9 for $2,150. Using the straight line method, calculate the book value at the end of the third year.

17. A used car dealer had the following inventory of used pickups on June 30:

Description	Cost
1 black short bed, half ton	$3,850
1 red short bed, step side half ton	$3,225
1 burgundy, half ton	$4,895
1 green short bed, half ton	$3,600

Using the specific identification method, calculate the value of the ending inventory.

18. Office typewriters are being depreciated at $1\frac{1}{2}$ times the straight line rate over 6 years. The typewriters were purchased for $4,750 with a guaranteed trade-in of $500 (treat as a salvage value). What is the book value at the end of the third year using the declining balance method?

19. Ace Secretarial Service purchased a dedicated word processing system for $11,000 on July 7. To assist them in their tax planning, calculate the first 3 years of depreciation under the ACRS method.

20. A delivery truck was purchased on March 11 for $9,500. If it has an estimated life of 6 years and a trade-in value of $1,250, what is the depreciation for the first two calendar years using the straight line method?

Chapter Test

1. The Video TV Repair Shop used the straight line method in depreciating all of its testing equipment. One ohm tester was purchased for $300 with a life of 7 years. If the tester has no salvage value, what is the book value at the end of the third year?

2. Which inventory method—FIFO, LIFO, or weighted average—produces the lowest cost on the 12 units remaining in stock at the end of the year?

Beginning inventory	8 units @ $32.15
April 12, purchase	24 units @ $31.65
August 18, purchase	18 units @ $32.40
November 6, purchase	6 units @ $29.95

3. A heavy duty general purpose truck was purchased on October 11 for $25,000. If it has no salvage, what is the depreciation for the first two calendar years using the ACRS method?

4. A microcomputer bought on January 11 for $16,000 has an expected life of 9 years and an estimated trade-in of $2,500. If the company uses 200% of the straight line rate, what is the depreciation for the first two calendar years under the declining balance method?

5. What is the book value at the end of the third year on a forklift purchased for $32,000? Its salvage value is $3,000, it has a life of 6 years, and the company uses the sum-of-the-years'-digits method of depreciation.

6. A chief executive's car that cost $12,000 is depreciated under the ACRS method for tax purposes. What is the first year's depreciation?

7. A large utility company uses the hours of operation to determine the depreciation of its large generators. On January 4 it purchased a $160,000 generator having a scrap value of $6,000 and a useful life of 105,000 hours. The generator operated 700 hours in Year 1, 7,600 hours in Year 2, and 8,050 hours in Year 3. Calculate the depreciation for the first 3 years using the units of production method.

8. The Computer Shop has 5 microcomputers in stock on December 31 that have memory of 128K. Using the specific identification method, calculate the total cost of the ending inventory:

    Model AP5068 $1,200
    Model RS9114 $ 960
    Model AT6445 $1,450
    Model IB7050 $1,975
    Model CA8468 $1,050

9. Calculate the depreciation for the first 3 years on a copying machine under the ACRS method if the cost is $8,275.

10. A large petroleum refinery purchased some new equipment on July 11 for $350,000. If the estimated scrap under the ACRS method is $3,500, what is the depreciation for the first 2 calendar years?

11. The Franklin Company depreciates its display cases over a 20-year period. It purchased 3 cases at a cost of $625 each on May 3. Set up a depreciation schedule that includes all 3 cases and shows depreciation and book value for the first 3 calendar years, assuming a scrap value of $25 each and the straight line method.

12. Use 150% of the straight line rate and the declining balance method to compute the first 2 years of depreciation. The property costs $3,400, has a life of 8 years and no salvage, and was installed on January 1.

Investments

12

OBJECTIVES

When you complete this chapter you will be able to:

- *Calculate compound interest using a table or a calculator. (12.1)*
- *Understand the difference between an ordinary annuity and an annuity due and calculate the annuity value using a table. (12.2)*
- *Calculate the present value of any compound interest investment or annuity using a table. (12.3)*
- *Understand a stock market quotation and be able to calculate the total cost of buying or amount received when selling stock. (12.4)*
- *Understand a bond market quotation and how to calculate the total cost of buying or the amount received from selling bonds. (12.5)*

COMING UP

Companies and individuals borrow money. We saw in previous chapters that for loans, interest charges were typically calculated using simple interest. When individuals and companies invest, however, their investments may earn interest. Investment interest is called compound interest. Compounding means as interest is earned, it may be left in the account so it too can earn additional interest. Earnings on a savings account or earnings on a pension plan are good examples of interest being compounded.

Investing involves setting objectives and considering the risks. Overall risk can be minimized by diversifying investments. The more risk you are willing to accept, generally the better the return. Investments and the degree of risk can range from savings accounts and certificates of deposit to annuities, bonds, stocks, and others. Each one needs to be considered for its return on investment and its growth possibilities.

Although present value is not a type of investment, it is an excellent planning tool. It is used to calculate how much money you will need to put away today to meet your financial objectives sometime in the future.

Compound Interest

12.1

The interest earned in savings accounts, certificates of deposit (CDs), money market accounts, and other, similar accounts is called **compound interest.** With compound interest, the interest earned in a specified period is re-invested or added to the previous balance in the account. This means interest is earned on interest and has a compounding effect.

Although there are easier ways to calculate compound interest, working a problem out the "long way" helps in understanding the theory behind it. (*Note:* In this chapter, rates of interest are quoted as annual rates unless specified otherwise.)

EXAMPLE 1   A company deposits $1,800 at 8% for 3 years, to be compounded annually. How much interest will the company earn?

Solution:

$1800.00	*Original deposit*	• Calculate Year 1 interest.
× .08	*Annual interest rate*	
$ 144.00	*Interest for Year 1*	
$1800.00	*Original deposit*	
+144.00	*First year's interest*	
$1944.00	*Account total at beginning of year is* new base	
× .08	*Annual interest rate*	• Calculate Year 2 interest.
$ 155.52	*Interest for Year 2*	
$1944.00	*Account total at beginning of Year 2*	
+155.52	*Interest for Year 2*	
$2099.52	*Account total at beginning of Year 3 is* new base	
× .08	*Annual interest rate*	• Calculate Year 3 interest.
$ 167.96	*Interest for Year 3*	
$2099.52	*Account total at beginning of Year 3*	
+167.96	*Interest for Year 3*	
$2267.48	*Account total at end of Year 3*	• Calculate total interest earned.
$ 2267.48	*Account total*	
−1800.00	*Original deposit*	
$ 467.48	*Compound interest earned over three years*	

Your first reaction is probably, "There has to be an easier way!" Fortunately, there are easier ways of calculating compound interest: using a compound interest table, a compound interest formula, or a standard calculator. Whether you use the formula, the table, or a calculator, there are two common steps:

1. Determine the number of periods.
2. Determine the rate per period.

Number of compound periods in one year

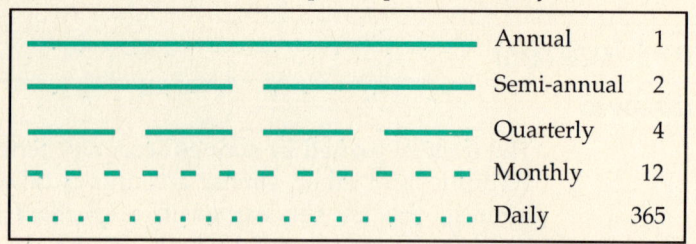

Annual	1
Semi-annual	2
Quarterly	4
Monthly	12
Daily	365

FIGURE 12.1
Compound periods

Compound Interest—Using a Table

To use the table method, we look up a predetermined factor that reflects the relationship between the number of periods and the rate per period. Multiply the factor times the amount invested.

EXAMPLE 2 Granite Rock Quarry deposited $1,400 in an account that paid 7% interest compounded annually. If they leave it on deposit for 5 years, how much is in their account at the end of that time?

Solution:

- *Step 1:* Calculate the number of **compounding periods:**

> Formula: Multiply the number of compounding periods per year times the number of years in the deposit.

Since the deposit was compounded only once per year and left for five years, multiply 1 (period) × 5 (years) = 5.

- *Step 2:* Calculate the **rate per compounding period:**

> Formula: Annual rate of interest divided by the number of compounding periods per year.

Since the deposit was compounded once each year (annually) there is no adjustment, because 7% divided by 1 is 7%.

- *Step 3:* Select the correct factor from the compound interest table in Appendix D at the back of the book. Locate the number of periods from Step 1 in the first or last column of the compound interest table in Appendix D on page A–53. Locate the interest rate from Step 2 across the top of the table. At the point where the column and row intersect, read and enter that factor in your calculator: 1.40255173.

340 Chapter 12 Investments

Step 4: Calculate the total in the account. Multiply the factor on the table times the dollars of investment:

1.40255173 × 1400 = $1963.5723 or $1963.57 total dollars in the account.

Note: The heading on the compound interest table states, "The Compound Interest for $1." The factor we used from the table, 1.40255173, or $1.40 rounded to the nearest cent, is the value of $1 invested at compound interest of 7% for 5 periods. Since we invested $1,400, we multiply the compound value of $1 times our investment of $1,400 to get the total in the account: 1.40255173 × 1400 = 1963.5723 or $1963.57.

EXAMPLE 3

RWT Corp. deposited $2,600 in an account that earned 8% compound interest. If they leave it for 3 years and the interest compounds *quarterly*, how much is in the account at the end of 3 years?

Solution:

4 × 3 = 12 periods	• *Step 1:* Calculate the number of periods. **Quarterly** compounding means 4 times per year; number of periods per year times number of years on deposit.
8% ÷ 4 = 2%	• *Step 2:* Calculate the quarterly interest rate: Annual interest rate ÷ Number of periods *per year.*
1.26824179	• *Step 3:* Determine the *table factor* from the compound interest table in Appendix D on page A–49. Match 23 periods from Step 1 with 2% from Step 2.
1.26824179 × 2600 = $3297.43	• *Step 4:* Calculate the total in the account. Multiply the factor from the table times dollars invested.

EXAMPLE 4

You-Rent-It deposited $850 in an account that compounds interest semi-annually. If the interest rate is 9% and they leave their deposit for 5 years, how much interest will they earn?

Solution:

2 × 5 = 10 periods	• *Step 1:* Calculate the number of compounding periods. **Semi-annual** equals 2 times per year; number of periods per year times the number of years.
9% ÷ 2 = $4\frac{1}{2}$%	• *Step 2:* Calculate the semi-annual interest rate: Annual rate (9%) ÷ 2 periods.
1.55296942	• *Step 3:* Select the factor from the compound interest table in Appendix D on page A–52. Match 10 periods with $4\frac{1}{2}$%.
1.55296942 × 850 = $1320.02	• *Step 4:* Calculate the total in the account. Multiply table factor times dollars invested.
1320.02 − 850 = $470.02	• *Step 5:* Calculate the interest earned. Subtract the original deposit from the account total.

✎ CHECK FOR UNDERSTANDING

1. A $3,200 deposit was made in a savings account that compounds interest semi-annually. If the institution is currently paying 7% interest, what is the amount in the account if it is left for 4 years?

2. North Side Savings compounds quarterly at a rate of 10%. If a $600 deposit is made, what is the balance in the account after 5 years?

3. How much interest is earned on a deposit of $1,100 if it is left for 3 years and the institution pays 8% compounded annually?

4. A savings and loan compounds interest quarterly and is quoting a rate of 6%. How much interest would be earned if a deposit of $1,600 is left for 6 years?

SKILL EXERCISES

Using the compound interest table in Appendix D, compute the following account totals and the compound interest:

	Principal	Rate	Time (years)	Compound period	Account total	Compound interest
1.	$ 4,500	8%	12	Annual	$ _____	$ _____
2.	$20,000	10%	3	Quarterly	$ _____	$ _____
3.	$ 600	14%	9	Semi-annual	$ _____	$ _____
4.	$ 1,400	12%	2	Monthly	$ _____	$ _____
5.	$ 750	8%	10	Semi-annual	$ _____	$ _____
6.	$ 1,100	6%	6	Quarterly	$ _____	$ _____
7.	$ 330	18%	$1\frac{1}{2}$	Monthly	$ _____	$ _____
8.	$ 1,525	9%	$12\frac{1}{2}$	Semi-annual	$ _____	$ _____
9.	$ 735	8%	12	Annual	$ _____	$ _____
10.	$ 1,450	8%	5	Quarterly	$ _____	$ _____

Compound Interest—Using a Calculator

Compound interest can be figured using a calculator by incorporating the constant multiplier, which we have been using throughout the text. It can also be done using the exponent key, which will be discussed later.

Answers to ✎ Check for Understanding
1. $4,213.79.   2. $983.17.   3. $285.68.   4. $687.20.

EXAMPLE 5 A deposit of $1,200 is made in an account that pays 8% interest compounded annually. If the deposit is left for 3 years, what is the balance in the account?

Solution:

Annual = 3 periods	• *Step 1:* Calculate the number of compounding periods.
Annual = 8%	• *Step 2:* Calculate the interest rate.
	• *Step 3:* Calculate the interest.

Let's visualize the process:

1200 × .08 = 96	• Interest for one year
1200 + 96 = 1296	• Beginning deposit plus interest is the year end total in the account.

Remember, the $1,200 is base or 100%, the rate is 8%, which makes the total of $1,296 = 108% of the original deposit. To save the long process we saw in Example 1, use 108% as the rate:

Base	+	Interest	=	Account Total
$1,200	+	$96	=	$1296
100%	+	8%	=	108%

```
1st year =    1200      Base
            × 1.08      (decimal)
              1296      Principal plus interest

2nd year =    1296      New base
            × 1.08
            1399.68     Principal plus interest

3rd year =  1399.68
            ×   1.08
            1511.65     Principal plus interest
```

Note: The number that is common to all three calculations is the rate, 1.08%. If you enter 1.08 in the constant position in your calculator, it won't have to be re-entered each time. *Try it:*

1.08 × 1200 = 1296	• Principal and interest Year 1.
= 1399.68	• Principal and interest end of second year. Although your calculator displayed only the answer, it actually multiplied the 1296 from Step 1 times the constant 1.08.
= 1511.65	• Principal and interest end of third year. Same rationale as Step 2. □

CALCULATOR TIP

If your constant is the second number in the sequence, reverse the order of Step 1 (1200 × 1.08); the remaining steps are the same. If you have a k (constant) key on your calculator, remember to enter 1.08 × k 1200 = and the remaining steps will be the same.

Section 12.1 Compound Interest

EXAMPLE 6 Roadside Swap Shop deposited $450 in an account paying 6% interest compounded quarterly. If they leave the deposit for 4 years, how much interest will it earn?

Solution:

$4 \times 4 = 16$ periods • Calculate the number of periods.

The 16 periods can be used on the table or can be used as the number of times to depress the ⃞= key.

6% ÷ 4 = 1.5% or .015 • Calculate the rate.
1.015 ⃞× 450 ⃞= (16 times) is $571.04 • Calculate the account total. Enter rate from previous step plus 100% in *constant position*; multiply times dollars on deposit; depress ⃞= key 16 times.

571.04 − 450 = 121.04 • Calculate the interest: Account total − Original deposit.

Note: Since the account total from the previous step is still in the calculator and can be used if we press a function key, touch the minus key ⃞−, enter the 450 ⃞= without having to clear the calculator and re-enter.

CALCULATOR TIP

The calculator steps in Example 6 can be chained together to make the process simpler:

.06 ⃞÷ 4 ⃞= .015 ⃞+ 1 ⃞= 1.015 ×   • Enter 6% plus 100% in decimal form.
450 ⃞= key 16 times   • Enter dollars and depress the ⃞= key the number of compounding periods.
571.04 ⃞− 450 ⃞= 121.04   • Calculate the interest.

EXAMPLE 7 A local credit union uses a rate of 6% compounded daily. If a deposit of $500 is made and left 15 days, what amount of interest is earned?

Solution:

15 (given in problem) • Determine number of periods.
.06 ÷ 365 = .0001643 • Calculate the rate: Annual rate in decimal form divided by 365* plus 100% in decimal form.
.0001643 + 1.0 = 1.0001643
1.0001643 ⃞× 500 ⃞= (15 times) 501.23 • Calculate the account total.
501.23 − 500 = 1.23 • Calculate the interest: Account total − Original deposit.

✓ CHECK FOR UNDERSTANDING

1. Calculate the total in an account on a deposit of $675 if it is left for 3 years. The institution is paying 5% interest compounded quarterly.

2. If a credit union pays 5.75% interest compounded daily, how much interest is earned on a $10,000 deposit that is left for 15 days?

* This text will use 365 days for all daily compounding problems.

3. A credit union in your area is paying 9% interest compounded monthly. A savings and loan, however, is paying 9% compounded quarterly. If you were to make a deposit of $5,000 in each of them and leave it for one year, which type of account would earn more interest and by how much?

SKILL EXERCISES

Calculate the following account totals and the compound interest. Use your calculator and chain the steps together.

	Principal	Rate	Time	Period	Account total	Interest
1.	$ 200	$11\frac{1}{2}$	6 years	Annual	$ _____	$ _____
2.	$ 175	12	2 years	Quarterly	$ _____	$ _____
3.	$ 350	$7\frac{3}{4}$	4 years	Semi-annual	$ _____	$ _____
4.	$ 650	10	3 years	Annual	$ _____	$ _____
5.	$1,000	8	2 years	Quarterly	$ _____	$ _____
6.	$9,000	9	2 years	Monthly	$ _____	$ _____
7.	$7,000	$8\frac{1}{4}$	12 days	Daily	$ _____	$ _____
8.	$1,250	7	5 years	Annual	$ _____	$ _____
9.	$1,000	5	20 days	Daily	$ _____	$ _____
10.	$1,300	6	$1\frac{1}{2}$ years	Monthly	$ _____	$ _____

CALCULATOR TIP

If your calculator has an **exponent key** y^x or x^y, the compound interest calculation may be simplified further. Let's use the example we discussed earlier about the company depositing $1,800 at 8% for 3 years to be compounded annually. Enter 1.08 y^x (exponent key), enter 3 equals $=$. At this point your screen may go blank or you will see the rapid multiplication of the rate 1.08 being multiplied times itself 3 times. The answer of this step (1.259712) is the value of $1 invested at 8% for 3 periods. This is the same factor that appears on the compound interest table when we match 3 periods with 8%. This factor (1.259712) is multiplied times the dollars invested ($1,800) to give the account total. It makes more sense if we see the uninterrupted sequence: 1.08 y^x 3 $=$ 1.259712 $\times$ 1800 $=$ 2267.48. Your exponent key sequence may be different. Consult your owner's manual.

Answers to ✔ Check for Understanding
1. $783.51.   2. $23.64.   3. $ 469.03   Credit Union
                              −465.42   S & L
                              $ 3.61   More in the Credit Union

Comparison of Compounding Periods

There are two advantages to investing money in accounts using a shorter compounding period: (1) you will earn more interest on the same dollar deposit with shorter compounding periods and (2) as you invest in shorter compounding periods, you have greater flexibility for early withdrawal.

A comparison of a $1,000 deposit invested at 6% interest using different compounding periods illustrates point number one.

TABLE 12.1
Comparison of Earnings on $1,000 Invested for One Year Using Different Compounding Periods

Amount	Nominal* Rate	Compounding Period	Interest Earned	Effective** Rate
$1,000	6%	Annual	$60.00	6.00%
$1,000	6%	Semi-annual	$60.90	6.09%
$1,000	6%	Quarterly	$61.36	6.14%
$1,000	6%	Monthly	$61.68	6.17%
$1,000	6%	Daily	$61.83	6.18%

* The **nominal rate** is the stated rate.
** The last column shows the true rate or **effective rate.** It is figured by dividing the interest earned by the original deposit.

The second advantage means that if you withdraw your money before the date interest is figured for the current period, you lose the interest for that period. For example, if you make a deposit on January 1 in an account that is compounded quarterly and you withdraw your money on March 15, you lose the interest that would have been added to the account on March 31.

In daily compounding, even though you plan to leave your money for a full quarter but find you must withdraw it after 70 days, you still earn interest for 70 days. It should be noted, however, that in many types of accounts such as certificates of deposit, there is a loss of interest or a penalty or both if you withdraw early.

APPLICATIONS

Use either your calculator or the compound interest table to calculate the following interest:

1. Wind-Safe Awning Company was able to invest $4,350 for 4 years. If their savings and loan pays interest compounded semi-annually at a rate of 8%, how much interest did the company earn?

2. The officers of the Log Cabin Savings and Loan need to make a decision on the compound interest rate to pay its customers during the next year. The institution pays interest quarterly and has an average of $6,500,000 on deposit during the year. If it raises the rate from $5\frac{1}{2}$% to 6%, how much additional interest would it pay?

3. If White Sands National Bank compounds interest monthly at 8%, how much would your company earn in interest on a deposit of $3,000 left for $1\frac{1}{2}$ years?

4. If Garth Auto Parts deposits $1,600 for 3 years in a bank that compounds semi-annually at 8 percent and Freeway Auto Salvage deposits $1,600 for 3 years in a bank that compounds quarterly at 8%, which company earns more and by how much?

5. Hold-Your-Own Safe Company deposits all of its receipts in a savings account and when needed transfers it to a checking account by phone. If they were able to leave $12,000 in the savings account for 18 days at 6% compounded daily before having to transfer it, how much interest did the company earn?

6. What is the account balance after 5 years on a deposit of $10,000 in an account that pays 8% and compounds quarterly?

7. Always-Kool Awnings deposited $825 in an account that earns compound interest at a rate of 6.25%. If the institution compounds monthly and the deposit is left for 17 months, what will the ending balance be?

8. Bloomington Iron Works deposited $5,000 in an account paying 7.5% interest compounded daily. If they transfer the entire balance to their checking account after 20 days, what amount will be transferred?

9. What amount of interest is earned on a $1,350 deposit if the institution pays 9% compounded annually and the money is left for 7 years?

10. The Three Star State Bank pays 7% compounded monthly. The Westside Credit Union pays 7.25% compounded quarterly. On a deposit of $10,000 left for 1 year, which account earns more interest and by how much?

Annuities

12.2

An **annuity** is a series of periodic deposits or payments of a specific amount of money. If you are establishing an annuity account, you would make a series of deposits. If you are benefiting from an annuity, you would be given a series of payments. Common examples of annuities are retirement plans under Social Security or company-sponsored pension plans. Individuals might also establish an annuity fund to have money available for a college education, a vacation, or to supplement their Social Security retirement.

Although an annuity can be established by a lump sum payment, it is more commonly thought of as a series of deposits that are made and will earn compound interest. Annuities can also be described as an ordinary annuity or an annuity due. An **ordinary annuity** is one in which the deposit is made at the end of the period, such as a salary payment or bond interest. An **annuity due,** however, requires the deposit to be made at the beginning of the period, such as in car insurance premiums, rent, or a mortgage payment.

Ordinary Annuity

EXAMPLE 8 How much money will a company have in its account at the end of 3 years if it deposits $500 annually in an ordinary annuity that is compounded at 6%? (Remember that ordinary annuity deposits are made at the end of the period.)

Solution: Although there are better ways of calculating the value of an annuity, let's do it the long way to see how it is actually done. *Remember*—the first deposit is made at the end of Year 1; therefore, no interest is earned during Year 1.

End of Year 1	$500	First Deposit
	+ 30	Interest (500 × 6%) Year 2
	$530	Value at end of Year 2 before second deposit
End of Year 2	+500	Second Deposit
	$1030	Value to begin Year 3
	+61.80	Interest (1030 × 6%) Year 3
	$1091.80	Value at end of Year 3 before third deposit
	+500.00	Third Deposit
	$1591.80	Ending value of a 3-year annuity after final deposit

Calculating the value of an annuity is greatly simplified by using the ordinary annuity table shown in Appendix D on pages A–48 to A–56. Calculating the value of an annuity is similar to calculating the value of a compound interest deposit, except we use a different table. Let's use the same problem illustrated in Example 8.

EXAMPLE 9   How much money will a company have in its account at the end of 3 years if it deposits $500 annually in an ordinary annuity that is compounded at 6%?

Solution:

Annual compounding = 3	• Determine number of periods (also the number of deposits).
Annual rate = 6%	• Determine rate per period.
3.1836	• Determine annuity table factor. Match number of periods from columns on either side with rate stated at the top of the table.
3.1836 × 500 = 1591.80	• Calculate the value of the annuity. Multiply table factor times dollars invested; same amount calculated above.

If the series of annuity deposits is made other than annually, we again use the same solution steps we did in calculating compound interest using the table.

EXAMPLE 10   The Green Manufacturing Company plans to begin an annuity fund to have money available to replace machines that wear out. If they make $300 quarterly payments in an ordinary annuity that pays 8% compound interest, what is the value of the annuity at the end of 6 years?

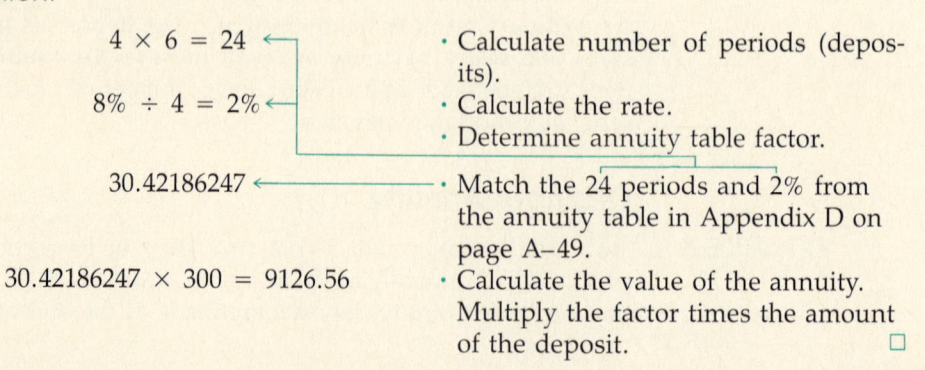

Solution:

4 × 6 = 24	• Calculate number of periods (deposits).
8% ÷ 4 = 2%	• Calculate the rate.
	• Determine annuity table factor.
30.42186247	• Match the 24 periods and 2% from the annuity table in Appendix D on page A–49.
30.42186247 × 300 = 9126.56	• Calculate the value of the annuity. Multiply the factor times the amount of the deposit.

✔ CHECK FOR UNDERSTANDING

1. To provide for future expansion, FTW Manufacturing Company decides to deposit $5,000 semi-annually in an ordinary annuity that pays 9% compound interest. After making these deposits for 10 years, what is the value of the company's annuity?

2. The Smith Construction Company deposits $750 monthly in an ordinary annuity that is compounded at 12%. What is the balance of the account after 2 years?

3. By investing money semi-annually at 10% in an ordinary annuity, the Ever-Watchful Private Detective Agency hopes to have enough money to purchase a three-acre tract of land. If the agency puts away $2,500 semi-annually for 9 years, how much money will accumulate?

4. Peters Herbicide Company is investing in an ordinary annuity that pays 6% interest compounded quarterly. If the company makes a series of deposits of $800 each for $3\frac{1}{2}$ years, what is the value of its annuity?

SKILL EXERCISES

Calculate the value of each of the following ordinary annuities using the ordinary annuity table in Appendix D:

	Deposit	Rate	Time in years	Type of period	Value of annuity
1.	$ 100	12%	$1\frac{1}{2}$	Monthly	$ _____
2.	$ 350	8%	$6\frac{1}{2}$	Semi-annually	$ _____
3.	$ 750	10%	6	Quarterly	$ _____
4.	$1,200	9%	$12\frac{1}{2}$	Semi-annually	$ _____
5.	$ 200	16%	5	Quarterly	$ _____
6.	$ 250	8%	25	Annually	$ _____
7.	$6,000	7%	7	Semi-annually	$ _____
8.	$ 650	$4\frac{1}{2}$%	19	Annually	$ _____
9.	$ 375	3%	5	Semi-annually	$ _____
10.	$1,000	10%	4	Quarterly	$ _____

Answers to ✔ Check for Understanding
1. $156,857.11.   2. $20,230.10.   3. $70,330.96.   4. $12,360.31.

Annuity Due

Annuity due deposits are made at the beginning of each period rather than at the end as is done for ordinary annuities. As a result, an adjustment in our calculations is necessary. There are two common ways to calculate an annuity due: (1) create and use an annuity due table or (2) use the ordinary annuity table with slight modifications.

We will use the ordinary annuity table with two modifications. We need to add one period to our normal period calculation table and subtract one deposit from the ending annuity balance. Example 11 clarifies the process.

EXAMPLE 11 Man-Made Crafts deposited $900 in an annuity due that compounds interest annually. If the interest rate is 7% and deposits are made for 10 years, what is the value of the annuity due?

Solution:

Annual payments = 10 periods · Calculate the number of deposits.
Annual rate = 7% · Calculate the rate.
10 + 1 = 11 · *Adjust* the number of periods. To the number of periods calculated in the first step, add 1 period. Since the annuity due deposits money at the beginning of each period and the ordinary annuity table considers the deposit as being made at the end, we must add 1 period.

15.78359932 · Determine the table factor. Match the periods from columns on either side with the rate stated at the top of the table. Be sure to use 11 periods.

15.78359932 × 900 = $14,205.24 · Calculate the value of the annuity.

14,205.24 − 900 = $13,305.24 · Adjust the ending value. *Subtract one deposit* from the annuity value. Remember, in the ordinary annuity table deposits are made at the end of the period. Because in annuity due the payments are made at the beginning of each period, we must subtract the payment made at the end of the tenth year.

EXAMPLE 12 Flagstone Rock Quarry plans to deposit $400 semi-annually in an annuity due account. If the account pays 7% compounded interest and they leave it for $5\frac{1}{2}$ years, what will be the value of the annuity?

Solution:

$2 \times 5\frac{1}{2} = 11$ periods · Calculate the number of periods.
$7\% \div 2 = 3\frac{1}{2}\%$ · Calculate the rate.
11 + 1 = 12 periods · *Adjust* the periods for annuity due.
14.60196164 · Determine annuity table factor.
14.60196164 × 400 = 5840.78 · Calculate the annuity value.
5840.78 − 400 = 5440.78 · Adjust the annuity value.
Subtract one deposit.

Ordinary Annuity—Calculating the Periodic Payment

The ordinary annuity table can also be used as another type of planning tool for investments. If we know how much money we need and when we need it, we can use the table to help us figure the amount of each periodic payment. For example, if we want $8,000 5 years from now for a down payment on some property, we can calculate the amount of each payment whether it is monthly, quarterly, semi-annually, or annually.

EXAMPLE 13 Tom Gonzales wants $12,000 4 years from now to buy a new car. If he deposits money quarterly in an account paying 8% compound interest, what is the amount of each deposit? Base your calculation on an ordinary annuity.

Solution:

4 × 4 = 16 periods	• Calculate number of deposits.
8% ÷ 4 = 2%	• Calculate quarterly rate.
18.63928525	• Determine table factor.
12,000 ÷ 18.63928525 = 643.80*	• Calculate the quarterly payment. Divide the ending value needed in the annuity by the factor from the previous step.

✔ CHECK FOR UNDERSTANDING

1. An annuity due is set up by the Orange County Safe & Vault Company on an annual basis at 8%. If the company makes a payment of $1,200 for the next 6 years, what is the value of the annuity at the end of that time?

2. An annuity due was established on a quarterly basis at a rate of 8%. If the amount of each deposit is $2,500 for a period of 6 years, what is the ending value of the annuity?

3. A 2-year 12% annuity due was established by Coker Distributing Company. If deposits of $3,600 are made monthly, what is the ending value of the annuity?

4. White Water Rafting Inc. needs $4,800 3 years from now. How much will the firm's quarterly payments be on an ordinary annuity if the current rate is 6%?

5. John and Alice Johnson are planning an around-the-world cruise 5 years from now and want $10,000 available for their vacation. If they make semi-annual payments that are earning 7% interest, how much must each of their payments in an ordinary annuity be in order to have $10,000 in 5 years?

*Note: This payment is also referred to as the **sinking fund payment;** such a fund is established to receive periodic payments. When these payments and the interest they earn are added together, they will equal the amount they are supposed to pay off (sink). Sinking funds are more commonly used in retiring bonds.

Answers to ✔ Check for Understanding
1. $9,507.36.   2. $77,575.75.   3. $98,075.51.   4. $368.06.   5. $852.41.

SKILL EXERCISES

Calculate the number of periods for each problem and then calculate the value of each annuity. Consider each problem as annuity due and use the ordinary annuity table. Problem 0 is completed as an example.

	Payment	Rate	Term	Frequency of deposit	Number of annuity due periods	Value of annuity
0.	$ 500	5%	19 years	Annual	20	$ 16,032.98
1.	$ 600	5%	10 years	Annual	_____	$ _____
2.	$ 250	12%	18 months	Monthly	_____	$ _____
3.	$ 3,000	5%	12 years	Semi-annual	_____	$ _____
4.	$ 1,100	6%	3 years	Quarterly	_____	$ _____
5.	$10,000	8%	5 years	Quarterly	_____	$ _____
6.	$ 5,500	7%	22 years	Annual	_____	$ _____
7.	$ 475	7%	7 years	Semi-annual	_____	$ _____
8.	$ 925	18%	22 months	Monthly	_____	$ _____
9.	$ 1,800	10%	$4\frac{1}{2}$ years	Quarterly	_____	$ _____
10.	$ 300	9%	9 years	Semi-annual	_____	$ _____

APPLICATIONS

1. The Canvas Back Awning Company is investing $2,200 each quarter in an ordinary annuity. If the annuity is paying a rate of 10% and extends for 4 years, what is the value of the annuity at the end of that time?

2. An ordinary annuity paying 9% interest compounded semi-annually has been established for Onyx Tile Company. What is the value of the annuity after 8 years if the company makes $700 deposits on a semi-annual basis?

3. Calculate the value of an annuity due if Metro Used Cars makes annual deposits of $3,000 for 5 years. The annuity is set up using 5% compound interest.

4. Secretarial Services Inc. will need a new dedicated word processing system in 3 years that will cost $12,000. If the current rate is 6%, what will be the amount of the quarterly payments in order to have the funds available?

5. The Brown Chocolate Candy Company invests $350 monthly in a 2-year ordinary annuity. What is the ending value of the annuity if the rate of interest is 12%?

6. Hardwood Floors Inc. is comparing the annuity due with the ordinary annuity plan. If the firm has $400 to deposit quarterly for 4 years, and the rate is 8%, what would the value of the ordinary annuity be? The annuity due?

7. If the current rate on a semi-annual ordinary annuity is 9%, what is the value of a 10-year annuity if semi-annual deposits of $500 are made?

8. Ray Long invests $250 quarterly in an annuity due for 3 years. If Ray gets an interest rate of 6%, what will be the value of the annuity?

9. Tom Mason wants to have $20,000 available in 16 years for his son's education. What will his annual payments into an ordinary annuity have to be if the current rate is 6%?

10. Alice Young is investing $325 semi-annually in an annuity due that is paying 6% interest. What will be the value of the annuity after 11 years?

Present Value

12.3

In working with compound interest and annuities, we calculated the future value of the account and the value of an account on a date in the future, knowing the amount and rate of current investment. In **present value,** we know the needed future value but must calculate the amount of the deposit invested today that will grow to that value.

Present Value—Compound Interest

Although there is a formula for calculating present value, we will use the factors shown in the present value–compound interest table in Appendix D on pages A–48 to A–56 to solve for present value. The steps used are similar to those used for working with compound interest and annuities.

EXAMPLE 14   Taylor Pipe needs $8,000 4 years from now to replace its work van. The best compound interest rate today is 7% annually. How much must it deposit today to realize its goal?

Solution:

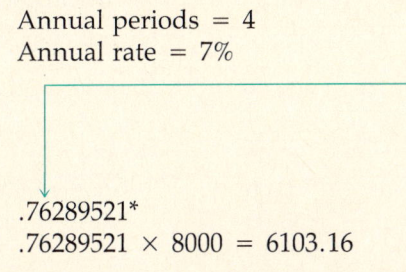

Annual periods = 4   · Calculate number of periods.
Annual rate = 7%   · Determine rate.
                      · Determine *present value table factor* from present value—compound interest table in Appendix D. Match 4 periods with 7%. Be sure to use Column 2, present value.
.76289521*
.76289521 × 8000 = 6103.16   · Calculate the lump sum deposit.

* Note: This factor is the present value of $1. If one dollar is needed 4 years from now and the interest rate is 7%, we need to invest .76289521 or .76 cents today to accomplish this.

EXAMPLE 15 Mary Jensen wants to have $6,000 available to pay for her wedding. The current compound interest rate is 12%. If Mary needs this money in 3 years and the credit union compounds quarterly, how much must her deposit be?

Solution:

4 × 3 = 12 periods	• Calculate number of periods.
12% ÷ 4 = 3%	• Calculate the rate.
.70137988	• Determine present value table factor.
.70137988 × 6000 = 4208.28	• Calculate the lump sum deposit.

✔ CHECK FOR UNDERSTANDING

1. Grant Garcia needs $1,500 in 2 years to buy a dirt bike. What amount must he deposit today to realize his goal if it earns 10% semi-annual interest?

2. Image Corporation needs to replace its $2,400 copy machine in 18 months. What amount must it deposit if the institution is paying 12% compounded monthly?

3. Don and Marilyn Johnson are planning a vacation 8 months from now and believe they need $2,800 for the trip. If their credit union is paying 18% compounded monthly, how much must they deposit today to realize their dream?

Present Value—Annuities

There are two ways to think of the **present value of an annuity:** (1) a lump sum deposit today that will give us the same annuity value we calculated earlier by using a series of payments; or (2) a lump sum deposit today that will give us a series of equal periodic withdrawals. We will use the present value of annuities table in Appendix D on pages A–48 to A–56. We calculate the interest rate and the number of periods the same way we calculated the present value of compound interest. Let's first try an example of the lump sum deposit that will permit a series of periodic withdrawals.

EXAMPLE 16 John Rogers wants to know how much he must invest today to withdraw $4,000 annually for 3 years. The financial institution he is working with uses 8% interest.

Solution:

Annual periods = 3	• Calculate number of periods.
Annual rate = 8%	• Determine rate.
2.57709699	• Determine the present value factor from present value annuity table.
2.57709699 × 4,000 = $10,308.39	• Calculate the lump sum payment: $10,308.39 deposited today at 8% will provide the money needed for 3 annual withdrawals of $4,000 each.

Let's check the calculation just completed:

$10,308.39	*Lump sum deposit*
+ 824.67	*Interest (10,308.39 × 8%) for Year 1*
11,133.06	*Value, end of Year 1 before withdrawal*
−4,000.00	*Withdrawal No. 1*
7,133.06	*Balance at end of Year 1*

Answers to ✔ Check for Understanding
1. $1,234.05.   2. $2,006.44.   3. $2,485.59.

	Year 2	$ 7,133.06	*Balance to begin Year 2*
		+ 570.64	*Interest (7,133.06 × 8%) earned Year 2*
		7,703.70	*Value before Withdrawal No. 2*
		−4,000.00	*Withdrawal No. 2*
		3,703.70	*Balance to end Year 2*
	Year 3	$ 3,703.70	*Balance to begin Year 3*
		+ 296.30	*Interest (3,703.70 × 8%) earned Year 3*
		4,000.00	*Value before Withdrawal No. 3*
		−4,000.00	*Withdrawal No. 3*
		-0-	*Balance at end of Year 3*

PROBLEM SOLVING STRATEGY

This example can also be used to show that the lump sum deposit will have the same value as a series of periodic deposits when both use the same rate and the same periods. If we use the information from Example 16—$4,000 invested at 8% in an ordinary annuity account for three years—the value of that annuity is as follows: Factor from ordinary annuity table for 3 periods at 8% is 3.2464; 3.2464 × 4,000 = $12,985.60. If we use the lump sum payment calculated in Example 16 and invest it at 8% compound interest for 3 years, we discover: Factor from compound interest table for 3 periods at 8% is 1.259712; 1.259712 × 10,308.39 = $12,985.60. They are the same!

EXAMPLE 17 Micrographic Services Inc. would like to have $600 available every 6 months for the next 4 years to upgrade equipment. How much money would have to be invested today at 6% to realize the company's goal?

Solution:

2 × 4 = 8 periods · Calculate the number of periods.
6% ÷ 2 = 3% · Calculate rate.
7.01969219 · Determine present value table factor.
7.01969219 × 600 = 4211.82 · Calculate the lump sum deposit.

✔ CHECK FOR UNDERSTANDING

1. The Peterson Family wants to have $7,000 available for each of the next 4 years to be paid annually to cover college tuition. If the current rate is 5%, what is the lump sum deposit needed to meet this objective?

2. In order to retire several pieces of equipment, Blackhawk Leather Works needs $1,200 each 6 months for 8 years. How large a deposit is necessary if the current rate is 10%?

3. Calculate the lump sum deposit that would be needed today to permit $600 quarterly withdrawals for the next 5 years if the interest rate is 8%?

4. The winner of the $1,000,000 state lottery will receive $50,000 each year for the next 20 years. If the current rate is 8%, what lump sum deposit must the state make today to fund the payoff?

Answers to ✔ Check for Understanding
1. $24,821.65.   2. $13,005.32.   3. $9,810.86.   4. $490,907.37.

SKILL EXERCISES

Using the present value tables, calculate the present value of Problems 1–5 involving compound interest. Then calculate the present value of Problems 6–10 involving annuities.

	Amount needed	Time period	No. of years	Rate	Present value
1.	$9,400	Annual	9	4%	$ _____
2.	$3,200	Quarterly	6	8%	$ _____
3.	$ 800	Monthly	2	12%	$ _____
4.	$2,200	Semi-annual	5	10%	$ _____
5.	$5,000	Quarterly	4	6%	$ _____

	Amount of withdrawal	Frequency of withdrawal	No. of years	Rate	Present value
6.	$8,000	Annual	13	4%	$ _____
7.	$ 750	Semi-annual	11	8%	$ _____
8.	$2,200	Quarterly	4	6%	$ _____
9.	$ 650	Monthly	2	12%	$ _____
10.	$ 600	Semi-annual	$7\frac{1}{2}$	10%	$ _____

APPLICATIONS

1. A professional baseball player wants to receive $15,000 each year for the next 20 years. How much is the lump sum annuity going to be if the current interest rate is 8%?

2. In order to pay off a serial bond issue, Atlantic Railway needs $200,000 each year for 5 years. What amount needs to be deposited in an annuity now at the rate of 7% in order to meet the company's obligations?

3. What is the present value of a $1,600 compound interest account if it is established for 3 years at an annual rate of 11%?

4. The Green County Soccer Club plans to remodel its stadium. The current compound interest rate is 6% compounded quarterly. How much must be deposited today in a compound interest account to provide $300,000 in 4 years?

5. Every 3 months for the next 6 years Susan Wolphiel wants to withdraw $500 to help her through college. Her credit union quoted her an investment rate of 8% and her bank quoted a rate of 6%. Which institution will need the smaller lump sum deposit and by how much?

6. The Minger Family needs a $2,000 vacation fund 2 years from now. If their compound interest account pays 12% compounded monthly, what lump sum deposit needs to be made today to make the vacation possible?

7. The president of Wood Products Inc. is retiring and the company plans to pay him $6,000 every 6 months for the next 10 years. If the best investment rate they could get was 14%, what amount must be deposited today that will permit this repayment schedule?

8. Tony Owen plans to buy a new car 5 years from now and believes it will take $9,000. If the compound interest account uses 12% compounded quarterly, how much must Tony deposit today?

9. The professional athletes' association must plan now for pensions of retiring players for the next 20 years. If they need $750,000 each year and the current rate is 8%, what lump sum annuity deposit must be made?

10. A local church plans to establish a carpet fund to mature in 3 years. The current rate is 8% compounded semi-annually. What amount must they deposit in a compound interest account in order to have $4,500 in their carpet fund?

Stocks

12.4

Another type of investment used by both individuals and businesses is stock. When corporations wish to raise money either when they start the corporation or when they wish to expand, they may sell shares of stock. The most frequently issued stock is **common stock.** Common stock shows ownership in the corporation and is also the voting stock. **Preferred stock,** as the name implies, is preferred or ahead of common stock when dividends are distributed or when claims are made on property if the corporation has to liquidate. Ownership of either type is shown by a stock certificate stating the number of shares owned in the corporation.

Investment in stock has two objectives: (1) to earn a good return on investment by receiving good periodic dividend checks; and (2) to have an investment grow over a period of time if the stock increases in value. It could then be sold at the higher price—realizing a gain, the difference between the purchase price and the selling price. Very rarely can both of these objectives be achieved by investing in one company.

Reading the Stock Market Listing

To understand the buying and selling of stock on one of the exchanges, we need to understand how to read stock transactions printed in the daily paper. The newspaper in your town may or may not have all the columns illustrated in Table 12.2, which is taken from *The Wall Street Journal*.

TABLE 12.2
Stock Market Listing—Eastman Kodak

Net High	Low	Stock	Sym	Div.	52 weeks Yld %	P.E. Ratio	Sales 100's	High	Low	Close	Chg
$70\frac{5}{8}$ $-\frac{1}{4}$	$39\frac{3}{4}$	EKodak	EK	1.80	4.1	12	8925	$44\frac{1}{4}$	$43\frac{1}{2}$	$43\frac{7}{8}$	$-\frac{1}{4}$
(A)	(B)	(C)	(D)	(E)	(F)	(G)	(H)	(I)	(J)	(K)	(L)

(A) **High:** *The highest price ($70.625) the stock traded for in the last 52 weeks. The dollar quotations are made in eighths of a dollar. One-eighth is equal to 12.5 cents.*

(B) **Low:** *The lowest price ($39.75) the stock traded for in the last 52 weeks. The quotation can be read $39\frac{3}{4}$ points. Each point on the stock market is equal to $1.*

(C) **Stock:** *The name of the stock, Eastman Kodak, in abbreviated form.*

(D) **Symbol:** *EK—stock symbol for Eastman Kodak.*

(E) **Dividend:** *Kodak paid an annual dividend of $1.80 per share.*

(F) **Yield %:** *The dividend is divided by the closing price per share to calculate the yield percent. The yield percent will therefore fluctuate almost daily as the closing price changes: 1.80/43.875 = 4.1%.*

(G) **P.E. Ratio:** *The price/earnings ratio: (12) The market price is divided by the earnings per share. The earnings per share is calculated by dividing the earnings by the number of outstanding shares of common stock.*

(H) **Sales in 100's:** *The number of stocks traded this day quoted in blocks of 100 shares each, 8925. To calculate the total number of shares traded, just add 2 zeros to the quoted number of shares: multiply 8925 × 100 = 892,500 shares.*

(I) **High:** *The highest price ($44.25) a share was sold for today.*

(J) **Low:** *The lowest price ($43.50) a share was sold for today.*

(K) **Close:** *The price ($43.875) of the last trade today.*

(L) **Net Change:** *The difference between the closing price today and the closing price on the previous day of trading $\left(-\frac{1}{4}\right)$. The closing price of $43\frac{7}{8}$ is down $\frac{1}{4}$ point from the previous close of $44\frac{1}{8}$ $\left(43\frac{7}{8} + \frac{1}{4} = 44\frac{1}{8}\right).$*

When buying or selling stock, you must work through either a full-fledged or discount broker, who charges a commission stated as a percent of the total stock transaction. Commission rates vary among brokerage firms.

EXAMPLE 18 Marge Keeler decides to buy 200 shares of ANOC listed at $35\frac{3}{4}$. If her broker charges a 2% commission, what is her total cost?

Solution:

$$200 \times \$35.75 = \$7150$$
$$7150 \times .02 = \underline{(+)\ 143}$$
$$\$7293$$

- Calculate the cost of the stock.
- Calculate the commission.
- Add to get total cost.   □

The commission will also vary if the number of shares involved in the transaction is an odd lot. An **odd lot** is any number of shares less than a full 100. One hundred shares is considered to be a **round lot**. The stock quotation in Table 12.2 showed

358 Chapter 12 Investments

sales in 100s or round lots. Typically, another $\frac{1}{8}$ point is added to the commission charge for each share in an odd lot if the share lists for $40 or less. If more than $40, the charge is $\frac{1}{4}$ point.

EXAMPLE 19 Maria Delgado plans to buy 250 shares of MSVR at $16\frac{7}{8}$. If her broker uses a 2% commission and another $\frac{1}{8}$ point for the odd lot shares, what is her total cost?

Solution:

250 × 16.875 = $4218.75	• Calculate the cost of the shares.
4218.75 × .02 = (+) 84.38	• Calculate the basic commission.
50 × .125 = (+) 6.25	• Calculate odd lot commission.
$4309.38	• Add to get total cost.

Selling Stock

When selling stock, there are two other charges that must be considered in addition to the commission rate and the odd lot differential. The Securities and Exchange Commission (SEC), a federal regulatory agency, levies a fee of $.01 per $500 of value or fraction thereof. Some states and local governments also charge a transfer tax paid by the seller.

The amount the seller receives then will be the total sales price minus the broker's commission; odd lot differential if it applies; SEC fee; and any transfer tax that might apply. The brokerage firm subtracts all charges and fees before writing the net amount on the check.

EXAMPLE 20 Barger Equipment Company is selling 500 shares of common stock at $62\frac{1}{8}$ per share. If the commission rate is 2% and the combination SEC fee and transfer tax is $1.53, what amount will they receive from their broker?

Solution:

500 × 62.125 = $31,062.50	• Calculate the selling price.
31,062.50 × .02 = (−) 621.25	• Less commission of 2%.
= (−) 1.53	• Less SEC fee and transfer tax.
$30,439.72	• Subtract for net amount of sale.

EXAMPLE 21 Don Murphy is selling 250 shares of a stock listed at $72\frac{1}{4}$. The commission rate is 2% and the odd lot differential is 25 cents per share. If the transfer taxes and fees were $1.28, how much did Don receive?

Solution:

250 × 72.25 = 18,062.50	• Calculate the selling price.
18,062.50 × .02 = (−) 361.25	• Less commission of 2%.
50 × .25 = (−) 12.50	• Less odd lot differential.
(−) 1.28	• Less SEC fee and transfer tax.
$17,687.47	• Subtract to get net amount.

✓ CHECK FOR UNDERSTANDING

1. Gates Ironworks wants to buy 300 shares of a common stock that lists for $21\frac{5}{8}$. If the commission rate is $1\frac{1}{2}$%, what is the total cost?

2. Tom Nujen purchased 175 shares of common stock at $15\frac{1}{2}$. The commission rate is 2% and the odd lot differential is $12\frac{1}{2}$¢. What is Tom's cost?

Section 12.4 Stocks   359

3. Marilyn Jones wants to know how much money she will have left if she sells 100 shares of stock for $13\frac{3}{8}$. Charges she must consider are broker's commission of $2\frac{1}{2}\%$ and fees and taxes of $.86. What will you tell Marilyn?

4. Determine the net amount left on a sale of 625 shares of stock at $18\frac{1}{4}$. The commission rate is $1\frac{1}{2}\%$ with an odd lot adjustment of 12.5 cents per share. The SEC fee and transfer taxes total $1.73.

SKILL EXERCISES

Using the information given below, calculate the total cost if you are buying or the net amount if you are selling.

	Market price	Shares bought (B) sold (S)	Commission rate	Odd lot difference	Fees and taxes	Total cost or net amount
1.	6	100B	2%	N/A	N/A	$ _____
2.	$8\frac{3}{8}$	325B	2%	$12\frac{1}{2}¢$	N/A	$ _____
3.	$77\frac{1}{4}$	400S	$1\frac{1}{2}\%$	N/A	N/A	$ _____
4.	$32\frac{5}{8}$	260S	$2\frac{1}{2}\%$	$12\frac{1}{2}¢$	9.30	$ _____
5.	$48\frac{1}{8}$	115S	$1\frac{3}{4}\%$	25¢	4.15	$ _____
6.	$115\frac{7}{8}$	100B	2%	N/A	N/A	$ _____
7.	$82\frac{1}{2}$	680S	$1\frac{1}{2}\%$	25¢	2.73	$ _____
8.	$14\frac{3}{4}$	245B	2%	$12\frac{1}{2}¢$	N/A	$ _____
9.	$27\frac{5}{8}$	355S	2%	$12\frac{1}{2}¢$	1.25	$ _____
10.	$10\frac{3}{8}$	700B	$1\frac{1}{4}\%$	N/A	N/A	$ _____

APPLICATIONS

1. Monte Jackson is selling 365 shares of stock at $18\frac{1}{4}$. If there is a 2% commission, a $12\frac{1}{2}¢$ odd lot charge, and fees and taxes of $2.85, what amount does he have left after the sale?

Answers to ✓ Check for Understanding
1. $6,584.81.   2. $2,776.32.   3. $1,303.20.   4. $11,230.30.

2. Front Range Nursery is buying 430 shares of common stock at a cost of $5\frac{7}{8}$. What is the total cost if the rate of commission is 2% and the odd lot differential is 12.5 cents per share?

3. Peg Board Interiors is paying a $1\frac{1}{2}$% broker's commission and SEC fees and transfer taxes of $.94. If they sell 200 shares of stock at $10\frac{3}{4}$, what amount will they have left?

4. Debby Peterson's broker charges $1\frac{1}{4}$% commission and $12\frac{1}{2}$¢ for odd lot shares. What is her total cost on a purchase of 65 shares of stock listed at $5\frac{1}{4}$?

5. The market price for ISTA is $65\frac{3}{8}$. The broker for Brown's Landscaping Services typically charges $1\frac{3}{4}$% commission. What is the total cost on a purchase of 400 shares?

6. Mark Cushman purchased 15 shares of stock at $111\frac{1}{4}$ per share. If the commission rate is $1\frac{1}{2}$% and the odd lot charge is 25¢ per share, what is Mark's total cost?

7. Rite-Way Plumbing sold 270 shares of stock with its broker charging a 2% commission and an odd lot fee of 12.5 cents per share. If SEC fees and transfer taxes totaled $1.21 and the selling price was $31\frac{7}{8}$, what net amount did they realize?

8. Peggy Thompson plans to sell 100 shares of stock to meet an emergency. If the market price is $42\frac{3}{8}$, what amount will she have left if the broker's rate is 2% and there are no fees or taxes?

9. Laundry Machine Service plans to buy 290 shares of a stock listing at $40 per share. The service's broker charges a $1\frac{1}{2}$% commission and an odd lot fee of 12.5 cents per share. What will be the total cost of this purchase?

10. The market price of EMLC is $136\frac{5}{8}$. If the commission rate is 2%, the odd lot charge is 25¢ per share and there are no taxes and fees on the transaction, how much will Raw Furniture realize from a sale of 53 shares?

Calculating Dividends

When a corporation realizes a net income at the end of their quarter, a decision must be made as to how much if any of the net income is to be distributed. The amount distributed to the stockholders (owners) is in the form of a **dividend.** If there are both common and preferred stockholders, preferred stockholders will receive their dividends first. If there is any money left, common stockholders will receive a dividend. Preferred stockholders receive a fixed amount or a fixed percent of the par value of the stock.

EXAMPLE 22 Long Range Movers Inc. has allocated $120,000 to be distributed to stockholders. They have 20,000 shares of preferred stock and 80,000 shares of common stock outstanding. If the board of directors declares an $.80 per share dividend for preferred stockholders, how much will the common stockholders receive per share?

Solution:

$120,000	• Determine earnings allocated for dividends.
20,000 × .80 = (−) 16,000	• Less preferred dividends.
$104,000	• Balance to be distributed to common shares.
104,000 ÷ 80,000 = $1.30	• Calculate dividends per share for common stock (balance of dividends ÷ number of common shares outstanding). □

EXAMPLE 23 Linda Newman has 200 shares of common stock. Her corporation just completed its 2nd quarter and shows the following: declared dividends, $430,000; 50,000 shares of preferred stock outstanding with a dividend of $2.20 per share; and 200,000 shares of common stock outstanding. What is Linda's total dividend for the year?

Solution:

$430,000	• Determine earnings available for common dividends.
50,000 × 2.20 = (−)110,000	• Less preferred dividend.
320,000	• Balance available for common shares.
$320,000 ÷ 200,000 = $1.60	• Calculate dividends per share of common stock.
$1.60 × 200 = $320	• Calculate Linda's total dividend. □

Earnings per Share Calculation

Earnings per share is calculated by dividing the net income by the number of common shares outstanding. It is not the same as dividends per share. The formula is:

$$\text{Earnings per share} = \frac{\text{Net income}}{\text{Number of common shares outstanding}}$$

EXAMPLE 24 Eastside Mobile Park Inc. had net income last year of $857,500 with a preferred stock dividend of $130,000. If there are 175,000 shares of common stock outstanding, what are the earnings per share?

Solution:

$\dfrac{\text{Net income}}{\text{Number of common shares outstanding}}$	• Determine the formula.
$\dfrac{\$857,500}{175,000}$	• Substitute figures and solve.
$\dfrac{\$857,500}{175,000} = \$4.90$ earnings per share	□

Price/Earnings (P/E) Ratio Calculation

The price/earnings ratio, which is shown in the stock listing in Table 12.2, is a frequently used indicator that shows the relationship between the price paid for stock and its earnings. It is calculated by dividing the market price by the earnings per share. The formula is:

$$\text{P/E ratio} = \text{Market price} \div \text{Earnings per share}$$

362 Chapter 12 Investments

EXAMPLE 25 The current market price of common stock at Easler Construction Inc. is $66.75. If earnings per share are $5.25, calculate the P/E ratio.

Solution:

$$\frac{\text{Market value}}{\text{Earnings per share}}$$ • Determine the P/E ratio formula.

$$\frac{66.75}{5.25} = 12.7 \text{ to } 1$$ • Substitute into the formula and solve.

ANSWER: 13 to 1 • Typically rounded to whole number. □

✔ CHECK FOR UNDERSTANDING

1. The total amount allocated from net income for dividends at Burns Manufacturing Inc. last year was $1,250,000. There are 100,000 shares of preferred stock with a declared dividend of $2.50 and 800,000 common shares outstanding. What is the dividend per share on common stock?

2. Andy Worthington has 750 shares of common stock in Trailers Inc. The company's end-of-quarter information indicates 15,000 shares of preferred stock outstanding with a dividend of 20 cents per share; 80,000 common shares outstanding; and amount allocated for dividends of $67,000. Calculate the amount of Andy's dividend check.

3. The total net income at Happy Trails Inc. was $1,750,000 with preferred stockholders receiving $450,000 in dividends. If there are 400,000 common shares outstanding, what are the earnings per share?

4. Using an earnings per share of $3.25 and a market value of $34.50, calculate the price/earnings ratio rounded to the nearest whole number.

SKILL EXERCISES

For Problems 1–5, calculate the total preferred dividends and record your answer in Column D. Calculate the total available for common stockholders and record that amount in Column E. Calculate the common dividend per share and record that in Column G.

	(A) Earnings for dividends	(B) No. of preferred shares	(C) Preferred dividend	(D) Total preferred dividend	(E) Amount for common dividend	(F) No. of common shares	(G) Dividend per share
1.	$375,000	15,000	$2.00	$ _____	$ _____	150,000	$ _____
2.	$1,800,000	80,000	$4.30	$ _____	$ _____	400,000	$ _____
3.	$635,000	60,000	$2.25	$ _____	$ _____	200,000	$ _____
4.	$975,000	120,000	$2.60	$ _____	$ _____	300,000	$ _____
5.	$1,400,000	200,000	$4.50	$ _____	$ _____	1,000,000	$ _____

Answers to ✔ Check for Understanding
1. $1.25.   2. $600.   3. $4.38.   4. 11.

Using earnings available for common stock, calculate the earnings per share and record it in Column C. Then, calculate the P/E ratio and record it in Column E.

	(A) Earnings available common	(B) No. of common shares	(C) Earnings per share	(D) Market value	(E) P/E ratio
6.	$ 400,000	80,000	$ _____	$65.00	_____
7.	$ 120,000	60,000	$ _____	$18.50	_____
8.	$ 620,000	400,000	$ _____	$ 8.75	_____
9.	$1,200,000	600,000	$ _____	$12.00	_____
10.	$ 525,000	100,000	$ _____	$48.25	_____

APPLICATIONS

1. David Brewer owns 340 shares of common stock in a corporation that has this 4th quarter summary: earnings allocated for dividends, $450,000; preferred shares outstanding, 50,000 with a declared dividend of $3; and common shares outstanding, 120,000. How much is available for common stockholders? How much will David receive in dividends?

2. The net income at Market Square Inc. last year was $1,800,000. If there are 70,000 common shares outstanding, what are the earnings per share?

3. Lyle Webb's stock has a market value of $32\frac{3}{8}$. If the earnings per share are $8, what is the current P/E ratio?

4. The 80,000 preferred shares are earning a dividend of $2.75 each. There is a total of $720,000 allocated for dividends. If there are 120,000 common shares outstanding, how much is the dividend per share?

5. Moffets Inc. posted the following partial 3rd quarter summary of activity: net income $2,485,000; preferred dividend of $3.50 with 120,000 shares outstanding; and 350,000 common shares outstanding. Calculate the earnings per share.

6. The market value of common shares at Greenleaf Inc. is $24\frac{7}{8}$. If the earnings per share are $3.15, what is the current P/E ratio?

7. Commonwealth Inc. has $360,000 available for dividends. There are 10,000 preferred shares outstanding that will receive a dividend of 75 cents each. If there are 100,000 common shares outstanding and Kate Morris has 500, how much will she receive?

8. If the following information is available at Tatun Manufacturing, calculate the earnings per share and the P/E ratio:

    Net income $375,000   Preferred dividends $60,000
    Common shares 200,000   Market value common stock $10.25

9. Braxton Inc. has 25,000 preferred shares outstanding that receive $1.75 each. If the amount declared for dividends is $92,000 and they have 60,000 common shares outstanding, what will be the dividend per share for common stock?

10. There are 200,000 common shares of stock outstanding at Munson Products Inc. and Brad Paxton has 28 of them. Preferred stockholders will receive $40,000 out of the $460,000 available for dividends. What amount will Brad receive in dividends?

Bonds

12.5

Issuing bonds is another method that companies can use to raise money. Companies and individuals can also invest in bonds and receive interest as a source of income. Each **bond** is an agreement to repay the principal (face value) on the maturity date and to pay annual interest at a rate stated on the bond. Because the bond is a debt to the company issuing it, the interest must be paid and the face value must be repaid. For the investor, bond interest is a more certain source of income than stock dividends.

Although there are different types of bonds, they are typically issued for $1,000 and interest is normally paid semi-annually. However, once the bonds are on the market, the price is subject to the laws of supply and demand. Therefore, a $1,000 bond can sell for less than the face value (at a **discount**) or at more than face value (at a **premium**).

Reading the Bond Market Listing

TABLE 12.3
Bond Market Listing of Two Bonds

(A) Bonds	(B) Current Yield	(C) Volume	(D) Close*	(E) Net Change
GMA $11\frac{3}{4}$ 00	11.1	7	106	-2
IBM $9\frac{3}{8}$ 04	9.4	386	$99\frac{1}{2}$	$+\frac{1}{4}$

(A) Bonds: *This column includes the name of the company, the annual interest rate, and the year the bond matures. GMA is the name of the company; the annual interest rate is 11.75%; the year of maturity is 2000. If we multiply the $1,000 face value times the rate of interest, 11.75%, the annual interest is $117.50.*

(B) Current Yield: *The current yield is calculated by dividing the annual interest by the closing price: $117.50 ÷ $1,060 = 11.1%. Notice that because the amount invested in the GMA bond is more than $1,000 (premium) the yield is lower than the stated interest rate. The IBM bond shows a closing price of $995, which is lower than the face value of $1,000 (discount); therefore, the yield is higher than the stated interest rate.*

(C) Volume: *The number of bonds sold. We do not multiply the number 7 or the number 386 times 100 as we did in the stock listing. The listing shows the actual number of bonds sold.*

(D) Close: *The price paid on the last sale of the trading day. GMA = $1,060 (106 × $1,000); IBM = $995 ($99\frac{1}{2}$ × $1,000).*

(E) Net Change: *The GMA bond closed down 2 points from the close of the previous trading day or $20 (1000 × .02). The IBM bond closed up $\frac{1}{4}$ point or $2.50 (1000 × .0025).*

* Some bond listings may still list highs and lows for the day as was illustrated for the stocks in Table 12.2.

Bond market listings are very similar to stock listings. The major difference is, the bond point is $10 rather than $1. The close of 106 for the GMA bond seen in Table 12.3 must be multiplied times $10 to arrive at its dollar value, 106 × $10 = $1,060. Another way of calculating the price is to treat the point listing as a percent—106%—and multiply that times the face value of $1,000.

Buying and Selling Bonds

In addition to the purchase price, other costs must be considered when dealing with bonds. Both the buyer and seller must pay a broker's commission, which is stated as a dollar cost per bond. The commission does vary and is frequently based on the number of bonds in the transaction. The interest is paid to the owner of the bond, which means the buyer may have to reimburse the seller for the interest earned from the last interest payment to the date of sale. Finally, the SEC fee of $.01 per $500 or fraction thereof of value must be paid by the seller. In this text only the commission charge will be included.

EXAMPLE 26 Madeline Tilley plans to buy 5 bonds currently listed at $98\frac{5}{8}$. If the commission charge is $5 per bond, what is her total cost? How much semi-annual interest will she receive if the interest rate is 9%?

Solution:

1000 × .98625 = $ 986.25	• Calculate cost of 1 bond.
986.25 × 5 = $4931.25	• Calculate cost of 5 bonds.
5 × $5 = (+)25.00	• Add commission on 5 bonds.
$4956.25	• Add for total cost.
1000 × .09 ÷ 2 = $45	• Calculate semi-annual interest.

EXAMPLE 27 Downtown Auto Salvage wants to sell 12 bonds currently listed at $101\frac{3}{4}$. What net amount will they receive if the commission rate is $5 per bond?

Solution:

1000 × 1.0175 = $ 1017.50	• Calculate selling price of 1 bond.
1017.50 × 12 = $12,210.00	• Calculate selling price of 12 bonds.
$5 × 12 = (−) 60.00	• Calculate commission.
$12,150.00	• Subtract for net amount received.

✓ CHECK FOR UNDERSTANDING

1. The closing price on AZTN bonds was $68\frac{7}{8}$. Murray Auto Supply bought 8 bonds and paid a commission of $7.50 per bond. What was their total cost?

2. Lester Pack bought 3 bonds that were quoted at $105\frac{1}{8}$. If the commission charge was a flat $25, what was Lester's total cost? If the interest rate is 11.25%, what is his semi-annual interest?

3. Children's Wear is selling 15 bonds at $139\frac{1}{4}$ each. How much will they receive if the commission charge is $5 per bond?

4. Downtown Brokers indicated the selling price on NZET bonds would be $75\frac{5}{8}$ and that their commission would be $7 per bond up to a total of 10. If Wayne Tuttle sells 7 bonds, what net amount will he receive?

SKILL EXERCISES

Using the bond listing given, answer the following questions:

Bond	Yield	Vol.	High	Low	Close	Net Chg.
Mattel $11\frac{5}{8}$ 03	12.7	10	$93\frac{5}{8}$	$91\frac{1}{4}$	$91\frac{1}{4}$	$-\frac{5}{8}$

1. What year will the bond mature? _____

2. Is it being sold at a discount or a premium? _____

3. What is the closing price of one bond in dollar and cents? _____

4. What is the annual interest rate in percent? _____

5. How many bonds were sold? _____

6. What was the close on the previous day of trading? _____

7. What would the total cost of 19 bonds be using the closing price as the base? _____

8. How much would you save on a purchase of 10 bonds if you bought at the low price rather than the high? _____

9. How much is the annual interest in dollars? _____

10. What percent greater is the yield rate compared to the interest rate? _____

APPLICATIONS

1. The bond quotation for a large financial business read in part: high of $96\frac{5}{8}$ and low of $94\frac{3}{4}$. Brad Davis bought 6 bonds at the daily high. Had he waited until he could have bought at the daily low, how much would he have saved?

2. Branson Irrigation Systems sold 24 bonds: 18 were quoted at $107\frac{3}{8}$ and 6 were quoted at $93\frac{1}{2}$. If the commission is $75, what net amount did they realize?

Answers to ✔ Check for Understanding
1. $5,570.   2. $3,178.75; $56.25   3. $20,812.50.   4. $5,244.75.

Section 12.5 Bonds

3. What is the total cost of a purchase of 10 bonds listed at $126\frac{7}{8}$ if the commission charge is $5 per bond?

4. A partial listing of bonds shows: NNON $9\frac{3}{8}$ 08. How much do the bondholders receive in semi-annual interest?

5. Eight bonds were sold for $107\frac{1}{4}$. If the seller originally purchased them at face value, how much premium did he receive on the sale?

6. A large corporation purchased a block of 200 bonds for $84\frac{1}{2}$. Assuming the commission charge would be the same in both cases, how much did they save by waiting for the bonds to drop from $85\frac{7}{8}$ to their current level of $84\frac{1}{2}$?

7. The net change figure on a bond quotation for today is $+2\frac{5}{8}$, and you purchase 5 bonds at the closing price of $94\frac{1}{4}$. How much would you have saved had you bought them at the closing price yesterday?

8. Radcliff and Associates sold 12 bonds at $94\frac{3}{4}$. If they purchased the bonds at face value, what was the total amount of discount on the sale?

9. Wyman Brokers purchased 25 bonds at $106\frac{1}{8}$ and paid a commission charge of $5 per bond. What was the total cost? Calculate the semi-annual interest on each bond if the rate is $15\frac{1}{4}\%$.

10. The latest quotation on a bond maturing in 2005 is $99\frac{1}{4}$. If a corporation buys 10 bonds and pays a commission of $6.50 per bond, what is the total cost? If the corporation holds them until maturity, how much will it receive in additional principal over what it paid?

Key Terms

Annuity (347)
Annuity due (347, 350)
Bond (365)
Bond discount (365)
Bond premium (365)
Common stock (357)
Compound interest (339)
Compounding periods (340)
Dividend (361)
Effective rate (346)
Exponent key (345)
Nominal rate (346)

Odd lot (358)
Ordinary annuity (347)
P/E ratio (362)
Preferred stock (357)
Present value (353)
Present value of an annuity (354)
Quarterly (340, 341)
Rate per compounding period (340)
Round lot (358)
Semi-annual (340, 341)
Sinking fund payment (351)
Yield (365)

Looking Back

The calculations in the chapter for compound interest, annuities, and present value are made primarily from tables. Remember, the tables are based on mathematical formulas that can also be used to calculate those values. There are also programmable calculators and computer software packages available to meet those needs.

When working with annuities, remember the payment is made at the end of the period for an ordinary annuity and at the beginning of the period for an annuity due.

The tables for present value of a compound interest account are different from the present value tables for annuities. The compound interest account will be paid out in one lump sum, whereas the annuity will be dispersed in a series of equal periodic payments.

There are many types of stocks and bonds that need to be investigated before any investment is made. They vary in degrees of risk and rate of return. You should choose brokerage firms and/or brokers carefully; their rates and kinds of services vary.

Let's Review

1. Old Sod Farm established a savings account that pays 9% interest compounded monthly. If they deposit $4,500 and leave it for 14 months, how much interest will it earn?

2. Valley Instrumentation wants to establish a pension fund for its employees and to fund it the company has been checking various annuity account setups. What is the present value of an annuity set up to return $15,000 every 6 months for 10 years if the current compound rate is 12%?

3. The Jackson Family wants to buy 10 acres of mountain property. The seller wants to receive 5 annual payments of $4,000 each. If the current annual interest rate is 6%, what amount would have to be deposited now in an annuity account to meet the seller's terms?

4. How much would the Knutson Family have to deposit today in a compound interest account that is paying 9% semi-annual interest, if they want a vacation fund of $3,800 3 years from now?

5. Pete Bridges wants to set up an ordinary annuity that will pay $18,000 twelve years from now. The best annuity rate he can get is 10% semi-annually. Using the annuity table, calculate the amount of each of Jeff's deposits.

6. Quaker Oats common stock closed at $43\frac{7}{8}$ with a net change of $+\frac{3}{8}$. If 125 shares are purchased at the closing price with a 2% rate of commission and an odd lot differential of 25¢, what is the total cost? What was the closing quotation on the previous day's trading?

7. How much would Fran Beatty have in her credit union account that compounds interest quarterly at 6% if she deposits $3,100 and leaves it for 5 years?

8. The Safe-Net Communication Corporation wants to have $8,000 available each year for the next 8 years to upgrade communication systems. The current compound interest rate is 7%. What amount must be deposited today so that the plan will be properly funded?

9. Rite-Way bonds are selling at $102\frac{1}{2}$. What would the net amount received be if they sold 5 bonds that had a commission charge of $7.50 per bond? If the interest rate is $8\frac{3}{8}\%$, what will the buyer's first full semi-annual interest check be?

10. The state lottery's top price is $4.5 million dollars to be paid by 25 annual payments of $180,000. If the state deposits a lump sum amount in an annuity today that earns 10%, how much will the deposit need to be?

11. Solid Rock Concrete Company was able to leave $8,500 on deposit for 13 days in its savings account before transferring the money to checking. If the account pays 6% compounded daily, how much interest did the company earn?

12. Art and Dorla Patterson are supplementing their retirement income by investing in an annuity due account that pays 8% compounded quarterly. If they are able to deposit $750 each quarter for 6 years, how much will be in their annuity at the end of that time?

13. David Martin wants to sell 145 shares of QMAC at the closing price of $13\frac{5}{8}$. What net amount will he receive if the SEC fee and transfer tax totals $1.37 and the odd lot charge is 12.5 cents per share?

14. Margarita Garcia received a quote of $92\frac{7}{8}$ on a purchase of 4 bonds. If the commission charge is $20, what total will she pay for the bonds?

15. Rod Larson is selling 5 bonds for $97\frac{1}{2}$ that he paid $85\frac{1}{4}$ for 3 years ago. How much will Rod make on the sale if the commission charge is $4.50 per bond?

16. Each of the 5,000 preferred shares is earning a dividend of .75 at McKnight Welding Inc. There are 15,000 common shares outstanding and the total amount available for dividends is $12,000. How much will the dividend per share of common stock be?

17. Market Hunters Inc. common stock has current market value of $21\frac{3}{4}$ and has earnings per share of $1.90. What is the price/earnings ratio?

Chapter Test

1. The winner of the $1,000,000 state lottery will receive $50,000 every 6 months for 10 years. Assuming an interest rate of 12%, what lump sum deposit must the state make now in an ordinary annuity to meet its obligation?

2. The East End Football Club needs $250,000 each year for the next 4 years. The current interest rate is 9% on annual payments. What lump sum deposit must be made in an ordinary annuity to provide the necessary money?

3. A savings and loan is paying 12% compounded monthly. If the Black Water Conservation District deposits $8,500 and leaves it for 3 years, how much interest will it earn?

4. Bill Burke is selling 450 shares of Eze-Wheeze at $37\frac{3}{8}$. The brokerage firm charges a commission rate of 2% and the transfer tax and SEC fee are $1.64. If the odd lot charge is $12\frac{1}{2}$ cents per share, what is the net amount of the sale?

5. In order to have $5,000 available in 4 years to make a down payment on some land, Brooke Greenberg opened an ordinary annuity account that is paying 10% compounded quarterly. How much must she deposit quarterly to realize her goal?

6. French, Morrison, and Franks, Attorneys at Law, P.C., deposited $5,000 in a compound interest account paying 10%. If it is compounded quarterly and left for 6 years, how much interest will be earned?

7. Lockyear Inc. deposits $500 monthly in an annuity due account. The account is paying 12% and is left for 18 months. What is the ending value of the annuity?

8. Angela and Rick Jones want $7,500 in 6 years. What amount must be deposited in an account paying 10% compounded semi-annually for them to achieve their goal?

9. At the end of 5 years, David Marsh would like to have $3,500 in his compound interest account. If the account earns 7% interest compounded semi-annually, what lump sum deposit does David need to make today to realize his goals?

10. Custer County Implement Dealers wants to have $6,000 available in 4 years to replace some office equipment. What would the quarterly payments have to be, assuming an ordinary annuity paying 8%, in order for the organization to reach its goal?

11. Harms, Gedding and Associates, P.C., plan to deposit $950 each quarter in an ordinary annuity fund to be used as a pension fund. What is the value of the account after 5 years if it is paying 16% interest?

12. Black Forest Manufacturing has decided to buy 185 bonds using the following quotation: GMA $10\frac{3}{8}$ 95 and a close of $103\frac{7}{8}$. If the total commission is $75, what is the total cost? When the company receives its first full semi-annual interest payment, how much will it be?

PART V
Retail Pricing and Profit

Pricing the Product

13

OBJECTIVES

When you complete this chapter you will be able to:
- *Perform markup functions and establish prices based on cost. (13.1)*
- *Know how margin identifies the manager's component of the price structure and be able to price using the margin system. (13.2)*
- *Understand markdowns from the retail price. (13.3)*
- *Convert markup pricing to margin system for decision making. (13.4)*
- *Convert margin pricing to the markup system. (13.5)*

COMING UP

We all can relate to prices. We respond to them daily as we evaluate our consumer choices. Pricing is the single most important business activity that affects customers and profit levels. Proper pricing requires a thorough understanding of its fundamentals.

Some pricing is done using the cost of merchandise as the base for calculation. Other pricing uses the retail price as its base of determination. The type of business usually dictates which pricing method is appropriate. This chapter explains both systems, illustrates their differences, and shows the conversion from one method to the other.

Markup (Pricing on Cost)

13.1

The cost-based pricing structure uses the base, rate, and part formula for its calculations. Under this system, the base for determining the price is cost. Cost becomes the base for all reference calculations. **Markup** is a dollar amount that is added to the cost to determine a price. Operating expenses and desired profit levels are considered when figuring the amount. Figure 13.1 shows markup pricing and how it refers to cost for the base.

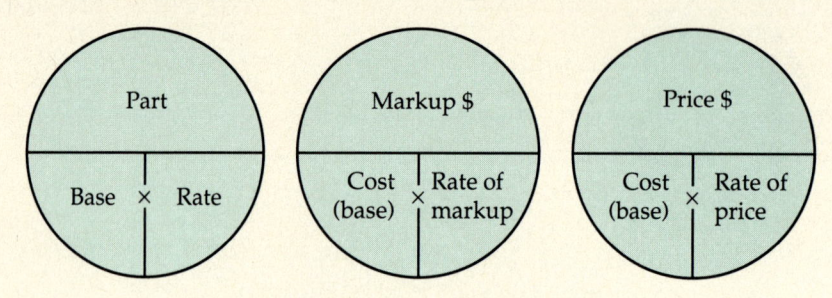

FIGURE 13.1
Pricing with markup

Part	Markup $	Price $
Base × Rate	Cost (base) × Rate of markup	Cost (base) × Rate of price

PROBLEM SOLVING STRATEGY

When using markup, the cost component is always the base or the 100% value. Since Cost + Markup = Price, the rate of price in this method will exceed 100%. The dollar amount of markup is added to the cost to find the price. The amount of markup and price are both parts for calculation purposes. Note these other relationships as well:

$$\text{Markup \$} = \text{Price \$} - \text{Cost \$}$$
$$\text{Markup \%} = \text{Price \%} - \text{Cost \%}$$
$$\text{Cost \$} = \text{Price \$} - \text{Markup \$}$$
$$\text{Markup \%} = \text{Price \%} - \text{Cost (100\%)}$$

Markup for pricing can be summarized as follows:

Step 1. Review the variable relationships:

$$\text{Cost \$} + \text{Markup \$} = \text{Sales price \$}$$

Step 2. Identify the possible problem components:

$$\$ \underline{\quad\text{Base}\quad} + \$ \underline{\quad(P_1)\quad} = \$ \underline{\quad(P_2)\quad}$$
$$\;\;\text{Cost} \qquad\quad + \quad\text{Markup} \quad = \quad\text{Sales price}$$
$$\underline{\quad\text{Base 100}\quad}\% + \underline{\quad(R_1)\quad}\% = \underline{\quad(R_2)\quad}\%$$

376 Chapter 13 Pricing the Product

Step 3. The numbers of (P) and (R) above identify which part goes with which rate to use the base, rate, and part formula. Fill in the blanks with the problem information. Solve for the missing element:

$$\text{Cost} \times \text{Markup rate} = \text{Dollar markup}$$
$$\text{Base} \times \quad (R_1) \quad = \quad (P_1)$$

$$\text{Cost} \times \text{Sales price rate} = \text{Sales price}$$
$$\text{Base} \times \quad (R_2) \quad = \quad (P_2)$$

$$\text{Dollar markup} \div \text{Markup rate} = \text{Cost}$$
$$(P_1) \quad \div \quad (R_1) \quad = \text{Base}$$

$$\text{Sales price} \div \text{Sales price rate} = \text{Cost}$$
$$(P_2) \quad \div \quad (R_2) \quad = \text{Base}$$

EXAMPLE 1 A microwave cost a dealer $234. If a 62% markup rate was used, what would the dealer's sales price be?

Solution: The unknown is the selling price, a part:

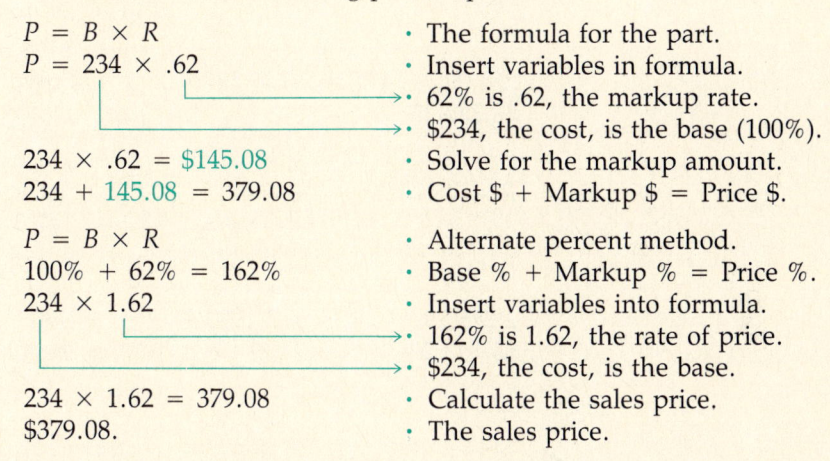

$P = B \times R$ · The formula for the part.
$P = 234 \times .62$ · Insert variables in formula.
 · 62% is .62, the markup rate.
 · $234, the cost, is the base (100%).
$234 \times .62 = \$145.08$ · Solve for the markup amount.
$234 + 145.08 = 379.08$ · Cost $ + Markup $ = Price $.

$P = B \times R$ · Alternate percent method.
$100\% + 62\% = 162\%$ · Base % + Markup % = Price %.
234×1.62 · Insert variables into formula.
 · 162% is 1.62, the rate of price.
 · $234, the cost, is the base.
$234 \times 1.62 = 379.08$ · Calculate the sales price.
$379.08. · The sales price.   □

EXAMPLE 2 A rider lawn mower was priced at $850. If the markup rate was 60%, what was the dealer's cost?

Solution: The unknown is the cost, the base 100%:

Price % = Cost % + Markup %
$100\% + 60\% = 160\%$ · The price percent, or 1.60.
$B = P \div R$ · Formula for the base.
$B = 850 \div 1.60$ · Insert variables into formula.
 · 1.60, the rate of price.
 · $850, the price, is the part.
$850 \div 1.60 = 531.25$ · Solve for the cost.
$531.25 · Dealer's cost for mower.   □

Section 13.1 Markup (Pricing on Cost)

EXAMPLE 3 A glider plane costing $8,345 is priced at $11,432.65. What is the rate of markup?

Solution: The unknown is the rate of markup:

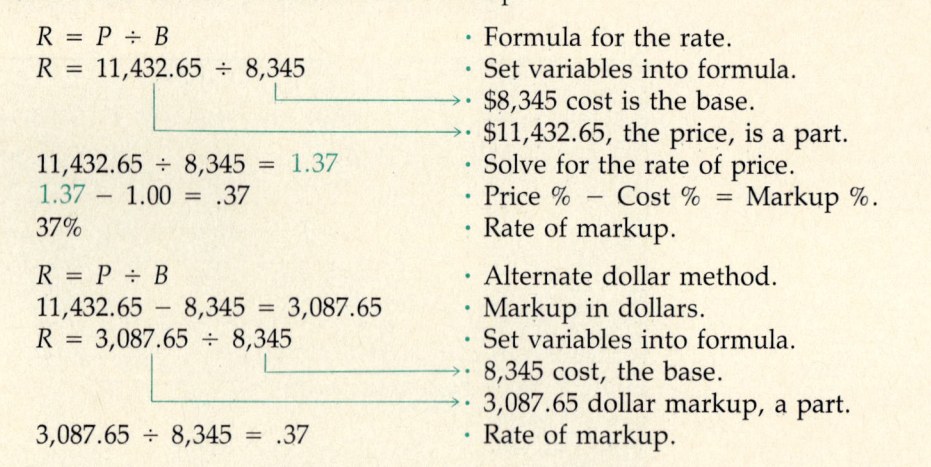

$R = P \div B$ · Formula for the rate.
$R = 11{,}432.65 \div 8{,}345$ · Set variables into formula.
→ · $8,345 cost is the base.
→ · $11,432.65, the price, is a part.
$11{,}432.65 \div 8{,}345 = 1.37$ · Solve for the rate of price.
$1.37 - 1.00 = .37$ · Price % − Cost % = Markup %.
37% · Rate of markup.

$R = P \div B$ · Alternate dollar method.
$11{,}432.65 - 8{,}345 = 3{,}087.65$ · Markup in dollars.
$R = 3{,}087.65 \div 8{,}345$ · Set variables into formula.
→ · 8,345 cost, the base.
→ · 3,087.65 dollar markup, a part.
$3{,}087.65 \div 8{,}345 = .37$ · Rate of markup.

EXAMPLE 4 The markup rate on a new hot tub is 43.5%. If the amount of markup is $968.00, what is the retail price of the hot tub?

Solution: The unknowns are cost and price:
The cost is the base 100%.
The price is a part.

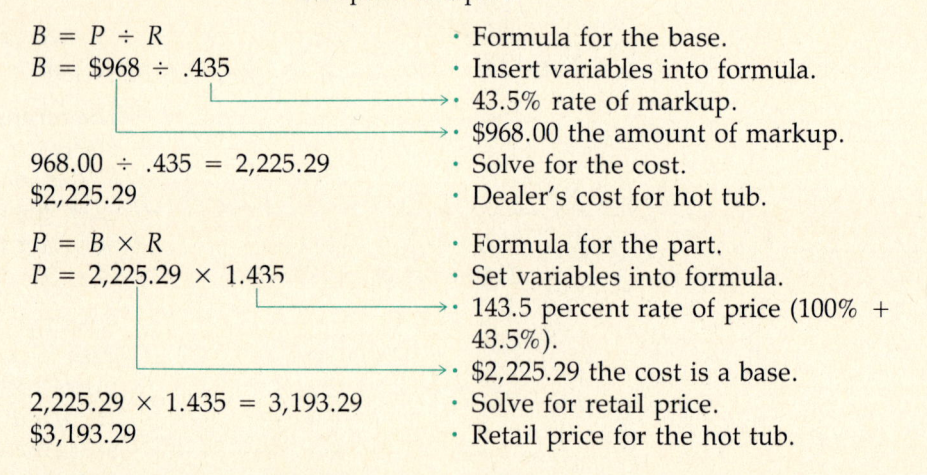

$B = P \div R$ · Formula for the base.
$B = \$968 \div .435$ · Insert variables into formula.
→ · 43.5% rate of markup.
→ · $968.00 the amount of markup.
$968.00 \div .435 = 2{,}225.29$ · Solve for the cost.
$\$2{,}225.29$ · Dealer's cost for hot tub.

$P = B \times R$ · Formula for the part.
$P = 2{,}225.29 \times 1.435$ · Set variables into formula.
→ · 143.5 percent rate of price (100% + 43.5%).
→ · $2,225.29 the cost is a base.
$2{,}225.29 \times 1.435 = 3{,}193.29$ · Solve for retail price.
$\$3{,}193.29$ · Retail price for the hot tub.

✔ CHECK FOR UNDERSTANDING

1. An invoice which lists 4 items shows costs to a retailer of $2,241.82. If the retailer applies a markup of 40% to these items, what is the total price for the combined goods?

2. If Bruce Hardware Store received a rowing machine to sell for $679.38, and its markup was 56%, what was the store's cost?

3. Wholesale Merchants sold a shipment of clothing to a local retailer for $23,690. If its cost was $14,357.58, what was the rate of markup?

Answers to ✔ Check for Understanding
1. $3,138.55. 2. $435.50. 3. 65%.

Chapter 13 Pricing the Product

SKILL EXERCISES

Review the following data and solve for the missing element:

	Cost	Rate of markup	Markup	Price
1.	$ 42.59	_____ %	$ _____	$ 65.00
2.	$ 12.34	_____ %	$ _____	$ 17.45
3.	$ 84.00	_____ %	$ 47.00	$ _____
4.	$ 6.27	_____ %	$ 2.56	$ _____
5.	$ 23.45	_____ %	$ _____	$ 32.95
6.	$ 64.97	54%	$ _____	$ _____
7.	$ 34.67	62%	$ _____	$ _____
8.	$ _____	47%	$ _____	$ 56.97
9.	$ _____	_____ %	$ 12.56	$ 43.24
10.	$ 9.95	_____ %	$ 6.78	$ _____
11.	$ _____	40%	$ 125.00	$ _____
12.	$ _____	32%	$ 32.00	$ _____
13.	$ _____	80%	$ 560.00	$ _____
14.	$ _____	_____ %	$ 125.00	$ 330.00
15.	$1,825.00	61%	$ _____	$ _____

APPLICATIONS

Use the base, rate, and part formula to solve the following problems:

1. If an item cost the retailer $34.50 and was to be marked up 56% on cost, what is the retail price?

2. Ranch Retail Outlet sells a bridle for $67.50 retail. It has a markup of 53%. What is the company's cost?

3. What is the selling price of a micro-cable that costs $34.75 if the wholesaler takes a 62% markup?

4. Plumbing Supplier takes a markup of $75 on its new shower fixtures. If the markup is 53%, what is the company's cost?

5. With a cost of $44.44, what would the retail price be if the markup rate were 47%?

6. What is the markup rate of an item that cost the Merchant Wholesaler $37.50 if it is sold for $52.90?

7. All-Night convenience store buys beer for $10.40 a case of 24. If it uses a 63% markup, what will each bottle sell for?

8. What is the rate of markup on an indirect lighting fixture if it costs the retailer $137.50 and it is priced at $226.88?

9. What is the rate of selling price if a heating element costs $67.80 and is sold for $103.25?

10. A new construction grade hammer cost the Handi Hardware Company $27.80. If it is sold for $38.95, what is the markup rate?

11. Classic Hi-Fi wishes to obtain 48% markup on its new line of stereos. If the company purchases the stereos for $358 each, what will they retail for?

12. Slug-Fest softball bats cost the retailer $12.50. If they retail for $19.50, what is the percent of markup?

13. Melt-in-Your-Mouth ice cream bonbons retail for $2.95 a box. If the markup is $.95, what is the rate of markup?

14. Personal computer disks sell to the retailer for $.80. If the retailer prices them at $1.80, what is the markup?

15. Galixstar telescopes retail for $655. If the markup is $155, what is the rate of markup?

Margin (Pricing on Retail)

13.2

The cash register sales receipt provides an important source of decision making data for managers. Because of its availability, the selling price is used as the base of the pricing system. When the selling price is the pricing base, it is found with a **margin**.

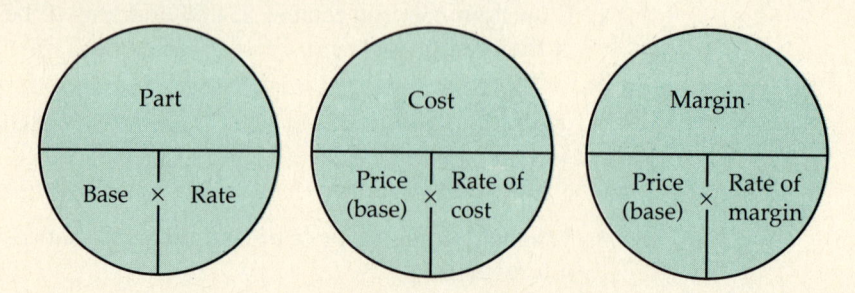

FIGURE 13.2
Pricing with margin

As with markup, margin is the dollar amount difference between cost and the selling price. The pricing elements are similar but the relationships of cost and price are reversed for calculation. The price is the base, margin is a part, and cost also becomes a part for the calculation sequences. Figure 13.2 shows the relationships for margin.

PROBLEM SOLVING STRATEGY

Since the base is the selling price, it is now going to be the largest dollar amount of the three elements in the pricing component. The sum of the cost and margin elements will equal the price in dollars. The sum of the percent figures for cost and margin always equals 100%. Notice these additional relationships:

$$\text{Price } \$ - \text{Margin } \$ = \text{Cost } \$$$
$$\text{Price \%} - \text{Margin \%} = \text{Cost \%}$$

The relationships appropriate for margin pricing can also be summarized.

Step 1. Review the variable relationships:

$$\text{Cost } \$ + \text{Margin } \$ = \text{Sales price } \$$$

Step 2. Identify the possible problem components:

$$\$ \underline{\quad (P_2) \quad} + \$ \underline{\quad (P_1) \quad} = \$ \underline{\quad \text{Base} \quad}$$
$$\text{Cost} \quad + \quad \text{Margin} \quad = \quad \text{Sales price}$$
$$\underline{\quad (R_2) \quad} \% + \underline{\quad (R_1) \quad} \% = \underline{\quad \text{Base (100\%)} \quad}$$

Step 3. The numbers of (P) and (R) above identify the respective parts and rates used to solve with the base, rate, and part formula relationship. Notice that the price is now a base. Review the procedures to solve for these missing elements:

$$\text{Price} \times \text{Margin rate} = \text{Dollar margin}$$
$$\text{Base} \times \quad (R_1) \quad = \quad (P_1)$$

$$\text{Price} \times \text{Cost rate} = \text{Dollar cost}$$
$$\text{Base} \times \quad (R_2) \quad = \quad (P_2)$$

$$\text{Dollar margin} \div \text{Margin rate} = \text{Price}$$
$$(P_1) \quad \div \quad (R_1) \quad = \text{Base}$$

$$\text{Dollar cost} \div \text{Cost rate} = \text{Price}$$
$$(P_2) \quad \div \quad (R_2) \quad = \text{Base}$$

EXAMPLE 5   If an item has a retail price of $38.50 with a margin rate of 42%, what is the cost?

Solution: The unknown is the cost, a part:

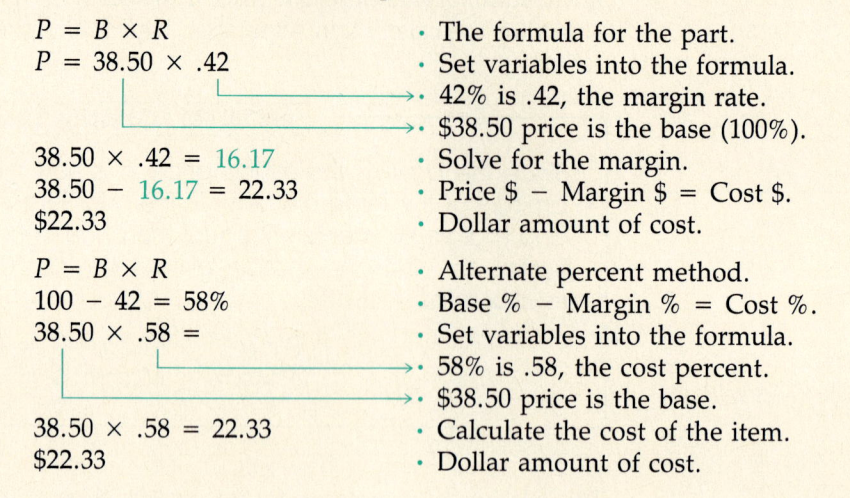

$P = B \times R$ • The formula for the part.
$P = 38.50 \times .42$ • Set variables into the formula.
    → 42% is .42, the margin rate.
    → $38.50 price is the base (100%).
$38.50 \times .42 = 16.17$ • Solve for the margin.
$38.50 - 16.17 = 22.33$ • Price $ − Margin $ = Cost $.
$22.33   • Dollar amount of cost.

$P = B \times R$ • Alternate percent method.
$100 - 42 = 58\%$ • Base % − Margin % = Cost %.
$38.50 \times .58 =$ • Set variables into the formula.
    → 58% is .58, the cost percent.
    → $38.50 price is the base.
$38.50 \times .58 = 22.33$ • Calculate the cost of the item.
$22.33   • Dollar amount of cost.

EXAMPLE 6   If an item costs $57.50 and has a margin of 38%, what will the retail selling price be?

Solution: The unknown is the price, the base:

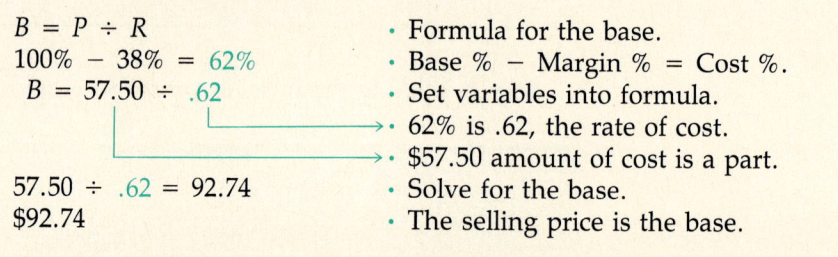

$B = P \div R$ • Formula for the base.
$100\% - 38\% = 62\%$ • Base % − Margin % = Cost %.
$B = 57.50 \div .62$ • Set variables into formula.
    → 62% is .62, the rate of cost.
    → $57.50 amount of cost is a part.
$57.50 \div .62 = 92.74$ • Solve for the base.
$92.74   • The selling price is the base.

EXAMPLE 7   A Whizzer camping generator costs the retailer $256. If it is sold at retail for $640 what is the amount of margin? What is the rate of margin?

Solution: The margin amount and margin rate are unknowns:

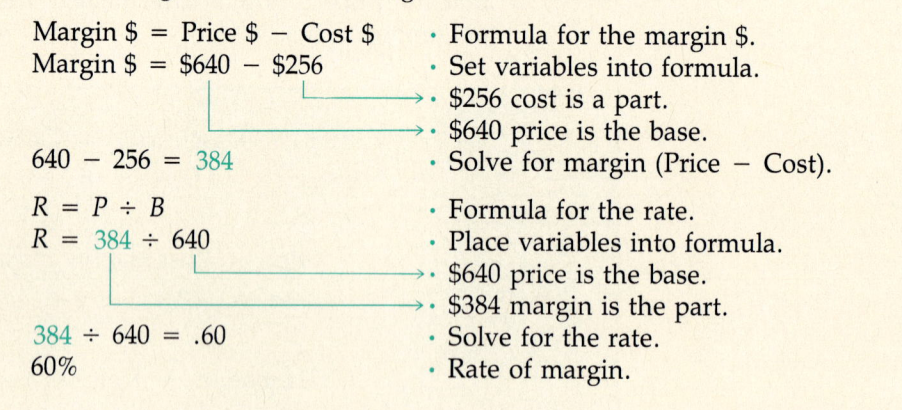

Margin $ = Price $ − Cost $ • Formula for the margin $.
Margin $ = $640 − $256   • Set variables into formula.
    → $256 cost is a part.
    → $640 price is the base.
$640 - 256 = 384$ • Solve for margin (Price − Cost).

$R = P \div B$ • Formula for the rate.
$R = 384 \div 640$ • Place variables into formula.
    → $640 price is the base.
    → $384 margin is the part.
$384 \div 640 = .60$ • Solve for the rate.
60%   • Rate of margin.

EXAMPLE 8   The Clarity Glassware retailer displayed a set of crystal stemware for sale. The stemware was assigned a margin rate of 86%. If the planned amount of margin is $125.00 per set, what is the retail price of the stemware?

Solution: The unknown is the retail price, a base:

$B = P \div R$ · Formula for the base.
$125 \div .86$ · Set variables into formula.
→ 86% is rate of margin.
→ $125 margin amount is a part.
$125 \div .86 = 145.348$ · Solve for the retail price.
$145.35 · The retail price.

✔ CHECK FOR UNDERSTANDING

1. An appliance retailer offers a new side-by-side refrigerator for $960. If it cost him $528, what is the margin rate?

2. Model-Line Blazers offers the new spring model for $128. The margin is 52%. What is the cost?

3. Breakpole, a ski wholesaler, sells its new race ski to the retailer for $236. If the retailer plans a 52% margin, what will the retail price be for the ski?

SKILL EXERCISES

Analyze the following data and calculate the missing component:

	Retail price	Rate of margin	Margin	Cost
1.	$ _____	_____ %	$ 16.50	$ 32.50
2.	$ _____	_____ %	$ 7.90	$ 12.50
3.	$ _____	38%	$ _____	$ 16.26
4.	$ 87.25	_____ %	$ 48.50	$ _____
5.	$ 23.50	_____ %	$ 15.95	$ _____
6.	$ _____	_____ %	$ 31.23	$ 42.80
7.	$ _____	42%	$ _____	$ 56.34
8.	$ 10.25	_____ %	$ _____	$ 6.74
9.	$ 53.87	_____ %	$ _____	$ 34.98
10.	$ 17.98	_____ %	$ _____	$ 12.35

Answers to ✔ Check for Understanding
1. 45%. **2.** $61.44. **3.** $491.67.

Section 13.2 Margin (Pricing on Retail)

11.	$125.00	_____ %	$ 55.00	$ _____
12.	$ _____	31%	$ 62.00	$ _____
13.	$ _____	25%	$ 45.50	$ _____
14.	$325.00	_____ %	$ _____	$123.70
15.	$ _____	_____ %	$ 55.00	$ 76.00

APPLICATIONS

Use part, base, and rate to solve the following problems:

1. A wholesale distributor of food sells breakfast food for $8.80 per 12-package case. Using this as his cost, the retail grocer must add a margin of 27%. What will the grocer's retail price be per package?

2. Strauss Company bought slacks for $22.86 each. At what price must they be sold for the store to realize a 42% margin?

3. The Globe Paper Company sells its paper for $3.85 a ream. If the cost is $2.45, what is the margin rate?

4. Makke Products Company buys goods for $87,000. If the company is to maintain a 35% margin, what sales must it generate?

5. If the gross margin to run a business is 38%, and if the anticipated sales for the year are $685,000, what is the maximum the owner can pay for the merchandise?

6. Bendite Company needed a margin of 43% to operate its store. If this percentage is the standard margin, what was the cost of a coffee pot that was selling for $17.50?

7. If an item cost a retailer $54.65 and was to be sold with a margin of 38%, what is the retail price?

8. A computer was listed by the Digitgrab Corporation for $1,800 and carried a margin of 27%. What did it cost the retailer?

9. The net cost to a retailer for a sectional davenport is $456.78. The margin rate is 44%. What is the retail price for the sectional unit?

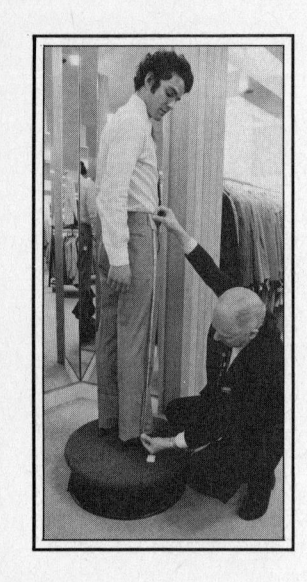

10. If a retail price is $47.60 and the margin rate is 39%, what is the cost?

11. Maxcorp Supply sold hardware with a 38% margin. The amount of margin for a pipe shipment totaled $780. What was the cost of the pipe?

12. Static Electronics retailed its most impressive television for $2,800. The margin was $1,050. What percent of retail did the television cost?

13. Harbor Boat Line offered new fishing skiffs at $275. If the margin on the sale was 35%, what did the skiff cost the company?

14. A video disk unit cost a distributor $485. If the usual margin is 42%, what will the price of the unit be?

15. The cost of a new vacuum is listed at $67.50. If this cost is 42% of the retail price, what is the amount of margin?

Markdown

13.3

There are various retail periods during a business year when reductions in the retail price are appropriate. Such events include product changeover, new incoming fashions, seasonal product clearance, and excess inventory. These events usually result in a **markdown** on the retail price, which results in a **sale price**.

Retail price	= Sale price ÷ Rate of sale price
Markdown	= Retail price − Sale price
Markdown	= Retail price × Rate of markdown
Sale price	= Retail price − Markdown
Rate of markdown	= Markdown ÷ Retail price
Rate of sale price	= Sale price ÷ Retail price

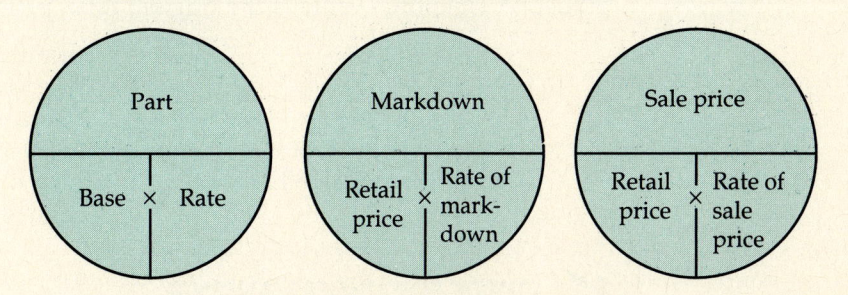

The base, rate, and part formula is used to establish the sale price. The original **retail price** is the base for the markdown calculation.

EXAMPLE 9   A new power hand saw retailing for $63.75 was sale priced at $52.00. What was the amount of markdown? What was the rate of markdown?

Solution: The unknowns are markdown amount, a part, and rate of markdown, a percent:

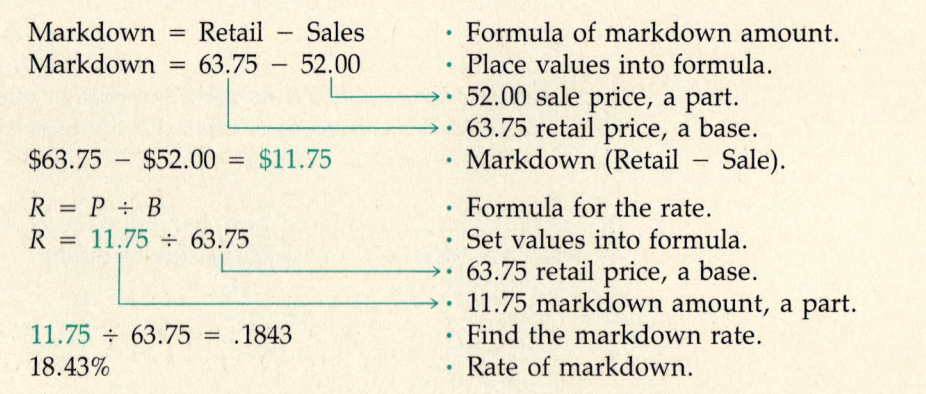

Markdown = Retail − Sales	• Formula of markdown amount.
Markdown = 63.75 − 52.00	• Place values into formula.
	• 52.00 sale price, a part.
	• 63.75 retail price, a base.
$63.75 − $52.00 = $11.75	• Markdown (Retail − Sale).
R = P ÷ B	• Formula for the rate.
R = 11.75 ÷ 63.75	• Set values into formula.
	• 63.75 retail price, a base.
	• 11.75 markdown amount, a part.
11.75 ÷ 63.75 = .1843	• Find the markdown rate.
18.43%	• Rate of markdown.

EXAMPLE 10   A floor lamp was sale priced at $76.85. The sale tag indicated that the lamp had a markdown of 30%. What was the original retail price? What was the amount of markdown?

Solution: Unknown values are retail price, a base, and markdown amount, a part:

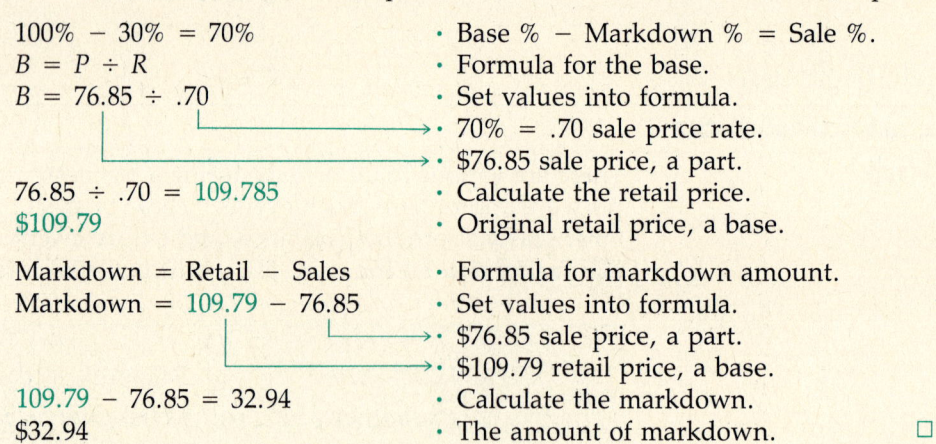

100% − 30% = 70%	• Base % − Markdown % = Sale %.
B = P ÷ R	• Formula for the base.
B = 76.85 ÷ .70	• Set values into formula.
	• 70% = .70 sale price rate.
	• $76.85 sale price, a part.
76.85 ÷ .70 = 109.785	• Calculate the retail price.
$109.79	• Original retail price, a base.
Markdown = Retail − Sales	• Formula for markdown amount.
Markdown = 109.79 − 76.85	• Set values into formula.
	• $76.85 sale price, a part.
	• $109.79 retail price, a base.
109.79 − 76.85 = 32.94	• Calculate the markdown.
$32.94	• The amount of markdown.

EXAMPLE 11   A proud new car owner boasted that he saved $1,200 on a dealer promotion markdown. If the dealer used a 15% markdown rate, what was the original price of the car.

Solution: Unknown value is the original retail price, a base:

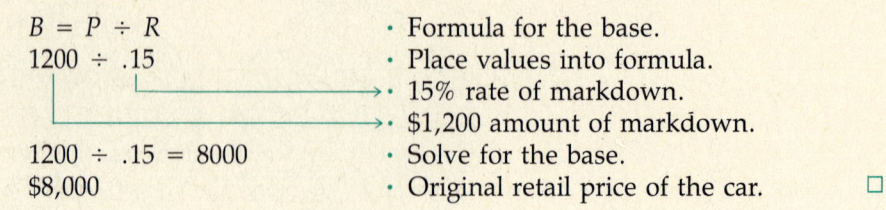

B = P ÷ R	• Formula for the base.
1200 ÷ .15	• Place values into formula.
	• 15% rate of markdown.
	• $1,200 amount of markdown.
1200 ÷ .15 = 8000	• Solve for the base.
$8,000	• Original retail price of the car.

✓ **CHECK FOR UNDERSTANDING**

1. Merchants' Mall sale priced an IBM-compatible software package for $51.25 after an 18% markdown had been applied. What was the original selling price?

386   Chapter 13   Pricing the Product

2. A new line of under-the-counter microwaves was retail priced at $225. If a 26% holiday season markdown was offered, what would the sale price be?

SKILL EXERCISES

Analyze the following data and calculate the missing component:

	Retail price base 100%	Amount markdown	Percent markdown	Sales price	Percent sales price
1.	$488.50	$ _____	_____ %	$ _____	20%
2.	$ _____	$ 5.25	15%	$ _____	_____ %
3.	$ _____	$ _____	_____ %	$69.80	50%
4.	$144.20	$ _____	_____ %	$93.73	_____ %
5.	$ 76.40	$ _____	25%	$ _____	_____ %

APPLICATIONS

1. A power rake normally retailing for $345.75 was being listed at the sale price of $297.35. What rate of markdown was being offered?

2. A consumer boasted that she paid only $56.00 for tableware. She claimed that it was being sold at 60% off the retail price. What was the original retail price?

3. A small retail shop owner was being forced to clear out some excess inventory. If an item originally priced at $1,280 was being offered for $998.40, what markdown rate was he using?

4. Clearance! Clearance! 45% off! What would it cost you for a new jacket originally priced at $149.99?

5. Save $125.00, accept our offer of 20% off! What sale price would you pay for this item?

Answers to ✓ Check for Understanding
1. $62.50.   **2.** $166.50.

Section 13.3 Markdown

Converting Markup to Margin

13.4 Many small businesses fail because they lack understanding of the difference between margin and markup. Although the margin dollars and the markup dollars may look identical, they represent entirely different things. The rate of markup and the rate of margin are different simply because they refer to different decision bases, one cost and the other retail price. This difference is extremely important in planning to meet operational expenses. If a certain percent of margin is needed on sales and that percent is used against a cost figure (markup) by mistake, a retailer will underprice his goods. Review the illustrations of the difference below.

a. To show the difference between markup and margin, assume the same percent for each and watch the different effect in the prices. The percents will be applied against a common cost figure.

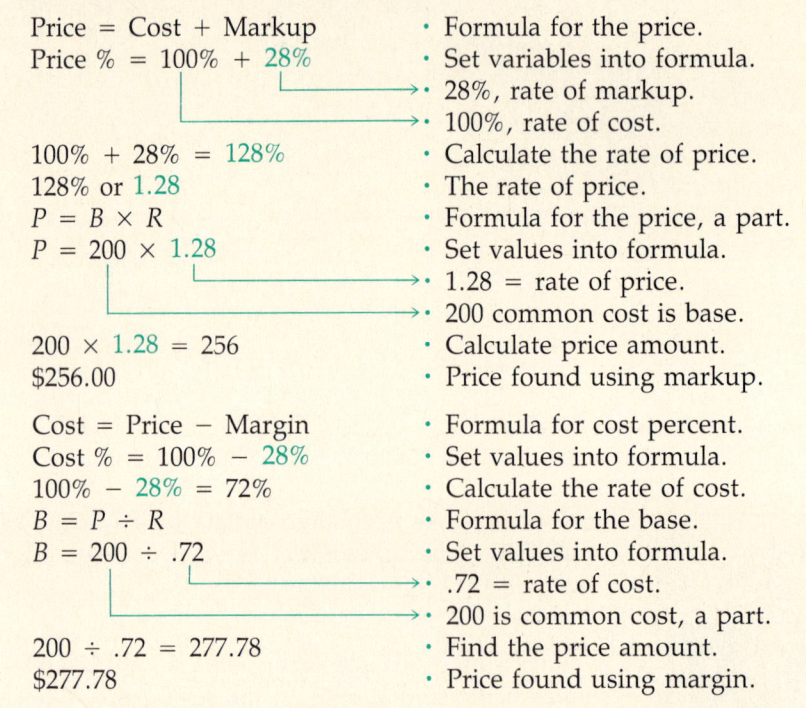

Price = Cost + Markup	• Formula for the price.
Price % = 100% + 28%	• Set variables into formula.
	→ 28%, rate of markup.
	→ 100%, rate of cost.
100% + 28% = 128%	• Calculate the rate of price.
128% or 1.28	• The rate of price.
P = B × R	• Formula for the price, a part.
P = 200 × 1.28	• Set values into formula.
	→ 1.28 = rate of price.
	→ 200 common cost is base.
200 × 1.28 = 256	• Calculate price amount.
$256.00	• Price found using markup.
Cost = Price − Margin	• Formula for cost percent.
Cost % = 100% − 28%	• Set values into formula.
100% − 28% = 72%	• Calculate the rate of cost.
B = P ÷ R	• Formula for the base.
B = 200 ÷ .72	• Set values into formula.
	→ .72 = rate of cost.
	→ 200 is common cost, a part.
200 ÷ .72 = 277.78	• Find the price amount.
$277.78	• Price found using margin.

A cost of $200 with a markup of 28% gives a selling price of $256, while a cost of $200 with a margin of 28% gives a selling price of $277.78.

b. Markup versus margin. Use the retail price of $260 and a cost of $200 to find the markup and margin percents.

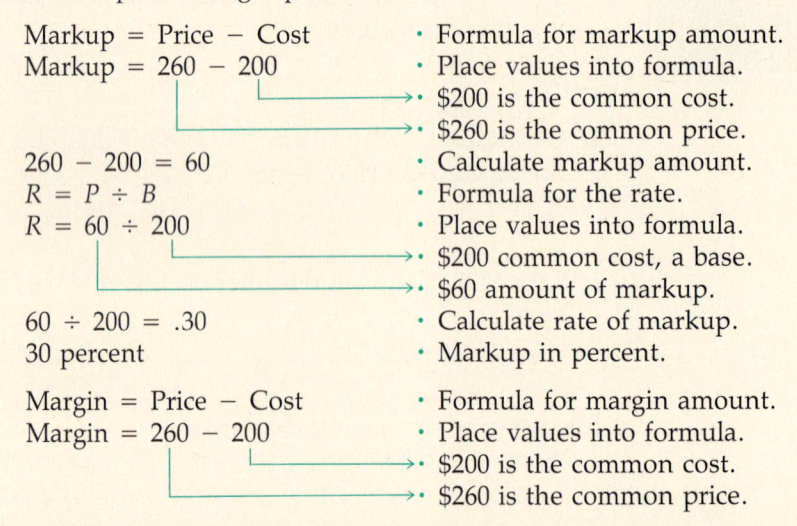

Markup = Price − Cost	• Formula for markup amount.
Markup = 260 − 200	• Place values into formula.
	→ $200 is the common cost.
	→ $260 is the common price.
260 − 200 = 60	• Calculate markup amount.
R = P ÷ B	• Formula for the rate.
R = 60 ÷ 200	• Place values into formula.
	→ $200 common cost, a base.
	→ $60 amount of markup.
60 ÷ 200 = .30	• Calculate rate of markup.
30 percent	• Markup in percent.
Margin = Price − Cost	• Formula for margin amount.
Margin = 260 − 200	• Place values into formula.
	→ $200 is the common cost.
	→ $260 is the common price.

260 − 200 = 60	• Calculate margin amount.
R = P ÷ B	• Formula for the rate.
R = 60 ÷ 260	• Set values into formula.
	• $260 common price, a base.
	• $60 margin amount.
60 ÷ 260 = .2308	• Calculate the margin.
.2308	• Rate of margin or 23.08%.
23.08%	• Margin in percent.

A cost of $200 and a selling price of $260 represents a 30% markup but only a 23.08% margin.

The dollar cost amount is smaller than the retail price. To calculate an equal price amount, the percent used for markup (on cost) must be larger than the margin percent, which uses the retail price as a base. To use margin and markup effectively in retail operations, you must be able to convert margin and markup to equivalent values. This prevents misunderstanding by retail employees of how products should be priced and allows for flexibility in planning usable revenues with cost data. Table 13.1 provides some of the common margin to markup conversions for quick reference. More importantly, however, you should be able to perform the conversions yourself. Most tables do not include all possible conversion needs.

To convert markup rate to margin rate use the formula:

$$\text{Rate of Margin} = \frac{\text{Rate of markup}}{\text{Rate of price}}$$

Note: Rate of price = 1.00 + rate of markup.

EXAMPLE 12 An item that costs $34 has a markup rate of 40%. What is the margin rate for this item?

Solution:

1.00 + .40 = 1.40	• Rate of price (see note).
Rate of margin = Rate of markup ÷ Rate of price	
Rate of margin = .40 ÷ 1.40	• Set values into formula.
	• 1.40 rate of price.
	• .40 rate of markup.
.40 ÷ 1.40 = .2857	• Calculate the margin rate.
28.57%	• Rate of margin.

EXAMPLE 13 Convert a 60% markup to margin.

Solution:

1.00 + .60 = 1.60	• Rate of price (see note).
Rate of margin = Rate of markup ÷ Rate of price	
Rate of margin = .60 ÷ 1.60	• Set values into formula.
	• 1.60 rate of price.
	• .60 rate of markup.
.60 ÷ 1.60 = .375	• Calculate the margin rate.
37.5%	• Rate of margin.

TABLE 13.1
Conversion from Margin Rate to Markup Rate

Margin %	Markup %	Margin %	Markup %	Margin %	Markup %
16.67	20	31.97	47	42.53	74
17.01	20.5	32.20	47.5	42.69	74.5
17.36	21	32.43	48	42.86	75
17.7	21.5	32.66	48.5	43.02	75.5
18.03	22	32.89	49	43.18	76
18.37	22.5	33.11	49.5	43.34	76.5
18.7	23	33.33	50	43.5	77
19.03	23.5	33.55	50.5	43.66	77.5
19.35	24	33.77	51	43.82	78
19.68	24.5	33.99	51.5	43.98	78.5
20	25	34.12	52	44.13	79
20.32	25.5	34.43	52.5	44.29	79.5
20.63	26	34.64	53	44.44	80
20.95	26.5	34.85	53.5	44.6	80.5
21.26	27	35.06	54	44.75	81
21.57	27.5	35.28	54.5	44.9	81.5
21.88	28	35.48	55	45.05	82
22.18	28.5	35.69	55.5	45.21	82.5
22.48	29	35.9	56	45.36	83
22.78	29.5	36.1	56.5	45.5	83.5
23.08	30	36.31	57	45.65	84
23.37	30.5	36.51	57.5	45.8	84.5
23.67	31	36.71	58	45.95	85
23.95	31.5	36.91	58.5	46.09	85.5
24.24	32	37.11	59	46.24	86
24.53	32.5	37.3	59.5	46.38	86.5
24.81	33	37.5	60	46.52	87
25.09	33.5	37.69	60.5	46.67	87.5
25.37	34	37.89	61	46.81	88
25.65	34.5	38.08	61.5	46.95	88.5
25.93	35	38.27	62	47.09	89
26.2	35.5	38.46	62.5	47.23	89.5
26.47	36	38.65	63	47.37	90
26.74	36.5	38.84	63.5	47.51	90.5
27.01	37	39.02	64	47.64	91
27.27	37.5	39.21	64.5	47.78	91.5
27.54	38	39.39	65	47.92	92
27.8	38.5	39.58	65.5	48.05	92.5
28.06	39	39.76	66	48.19	93
28.32	39.5	39.94	66.5	48.32	93.5
28.57	40	40.12	67	48.45	94
28.82	40.5	40.3	67.5	48.59	94.5
29.08	41	40.48	68	48.72	95
29.33	41.5	40.65	68.5	48.85	95.5
29.57	42	40.83	69	48.98	96
29.82	42.5	41	69.5	49.11	96.5
30.07	43	41.18	70	49.24	97
30.31	43.5	41.35	70.5	49.37	97.5
30.56	44	41.52	71	49.49	98
30.8	44.5	41.69	71.5	49.62	98.5
31.03	45	41.86	72	49.75	99
31.27	45.5	42.03	72.5	49.87	99.5
31.51	46	42.20	73	50.00	100
31.74	46.5	42.36	73.5		

EXAMPLE 14 What margin rate is expected if a markup of 81.5% is used?

Solution:

$1.00 + .815 = 1.815$ • Rate of price (see note).

Rate of margin = Rate of markup ÷ Rate of price

Rate of margin = .815 ÷ 1.815 • Set values into formula.
- 181.5% rate of price.
- 81.5% rate of markup.

.815 ÷ 1.815 = .4490358 • Calculate the margin rate.
44.9% • Rate of margin.

✔ CHECK FOR UNDERSTANDING

1. If the markup rate on a lawn mower is 63%, what is the margin rate?

2. The markup on an item that costs $64 is $43. What is the rate of margin?

3. A retail manager needs to convert markup to margin for pricing. If he is using a 77% markup, what will the percent of margin be?

SKILL EXERCISES

For the following data, compute the missing component:

	Cost	Markup	Markup %	Margin %
1.	$35.98	$22.18	_____ %	_____ %
2.	$90.00	$ _____	56%	_____ %
3.	$27.50	$ _____	48%	_____ %
4.	$ 3.56	$ 2.67	_____ %	_____ %
5.	$48.90	$ _____	54%	_____ %
6.	$78.65	$ _____	66%	_____ %
7.	$65.98	$ _____	63%	_____ %
8.	$ 7.50	$ 5.96	_____ %	_____ %
9.	$42.50	$36.67	_____ %	_____ %
10.	$88.88	$ _____	100%	_____ %

Answers to ✔ Check for Understanding
1. 38.65%.   2. 40.19%.   3. 43.5%.

Section 13.4 Converting Markup to Margin

APPLICATIONS

Solve for the matching margin rates:

1. Convert a 140% markup rate to a margin rate.

2. Convert a 96% markup rate to a margin rate.

3. If the cost is $24.60 and the markup rate is 76%, what is the margin rate?

4. Is cost or price the base when markup is used?

5. Convert 80% markup to a margin rate.

6. What is the equivalent margin rate for a 123% markup?

7. What margin rate is the same as an 87% markup rate?

8. Is cost or price the base when margin is used?

9. Convert 95% markup rate to a margin rate.

10. What is the margin rate that would equate to a 78% markup rate?

Converting Margin to Markup

13.5

Converting margin to markup is often used in assisting the retail work force to price a product. Most retail managers use retail figures in their planning. It is necessary to be able to convert margin rates to markup rates fairly quickly for use with cost pricing methods.

The formula for converting a margin rate to a markup rate is:

$$\text{Rate of markup} = \frac{\text{Rate of margin}}{\text{Rate of cost}}$$

Note: Rate of cost = 1.00 − Margin rate.

EXAMPLE 15 Convert a margin rate of 40% to a markup rate.

Solution:

    1.00 − .40 = .60   • Rate of cost (see note).

    Markup rate = Rate of margin ÷ Rate of cost

    Markup rate = .40 ÷ .60   • Set values into formula.
                                • .60 rate of cost.
                                • .40 rate of margin.

    .40 ÷ .60 = .666667   • Calculate the markup rate.
    66.7%   • Rate of markup.

EXAMPLE 16 A retail manager must convert a needed 37% margin rate to a markup rate for pricing. What is the markup rate equivalent?

Solution:

    1.00 − .37 = .63   • Rate of cost (see note).

    Markup rate = Rate of margin ÷ Rate of cost

    Markup rate = .37 ÷ .63   • Set values into formula.
                                    • .63 rate of cost.
                                • .37 rate of margin.

    .37 ÷ .63 = .5873   • Calculate the markup rate.
    58.73%   • Rate of markup.

(Note: The equivalent markup rate will always be higher than the margin rate due to the cost base being a smaller number than price.)

EXAMPLE 17 If a 44.75% margin is needed for income planning, what markup should be used to price the item?

Solution:

    1.00 − .4475 = .5525   • Rate of cost (see note).

    Markup rate = Rate of margin ÷ Rate of cost

    Markup rate = .4475 ÷ .5525   • Set variables into formula.
                                      • 55.25% rate of cost.
                                    • 44.75% margin rate.

    .4475 ÷ .5525 = .8099547   • Calculate the markup rate.
    81%   • Rate of markup.

✔ CHECK FOR UNDERSTANDING

1. If the margin rate is 43%, what is the markup rate?

2. Convert a margin rate of 56% to a markup rate.

3. What is the equivalent markup rate for a 52% margin?

Answers to ✔ Check for Understanding
1. 75.44%.   **2.** 127.27%.   **3.** 108.3%.

SKILL EXERCISES

Use the following data to find the missing component:

	Cost	Retail	Markup rate	Margin rate
1.	$38.50	$ _____	_____ %	42%
2.	$12.34	$ 17.50	_____ %	_____ %
3.	$ 3.56	$ 6.25	_____ %	_____ %
4.	$ _____	$ 87.90	_____ %	38%
5.	$44.56	$ _____	_____ %	27%
6.	$ 6.78	$ 9.95	_____ %	_____ %
7.	$50.75	$ _____	_____ %	44%
8.	$ 4.30	$ 7.26	_____ %	_____ %
9.	$78.24	$117.56	_____ %	_____ %
10.	$ 7.90	$ _____	_____ %	38%

APPLICATIONS

Complete the following margin conversions:

1. Convert a margin rate of 36% to a markup rate.

2. If an item sells for $54.87 and has a margin rate of 43%, what is its markup rate?

3. Convert a margin rate of 47.96% to its equivalent markup rate.

4. If the difference between cost and retail is the same, which will be the larger—markup rate or margin rate?

5. Convert a margin rate of 87% to a markup rate.

6. The housewares department manager wishes to maintain a 57.8% margin. Because of the need to price an extensive quantity of goods, the manager must convert margin to a markup. What would the equivalent markup rate be?

7. What would the equivalent markup rate be for a margin rate of 21%?

8. The electronics department carries a 61% margin. What would that be if markup were used?

394   Chapter 13   Pricing the Product

9. Convert a 67% margin rate to its markup rate.

10. If the margin rate is 33%, what is the equivalent markup rate?

Key Terms

Cost (376)
Margin (380)
Markdown (385)
Markup (376)

Price (376)
Retail price (385)
Sale price (385)
Selling price (380)

Looking Back

There are two ways that goods can be priced. In the business community, price is calculated using either cost or selling price as the base. If the same rate of markup is used for the margin, you will not arrive at the same price.

The basis for the markup system is cost. All references to its calculation or the percents involved use the amount of cost as the base or 100% figure.

Margin is used most often by retail management for pricing. It is more compatible with planning sales quotas and calculating gross profit percentages.

Some retail systems calculate the markdown and show the percent of markdown by shifting the base to the sale price. Whether or not it has been determined by using markup or margin, markdown is based on the established retail price.

Margin and markup can be easily converted from one to the other. The denominator for the fraction describing the new value is either the rate of cost or the rate of price.

Let's Review

1. The amount of markup for a uni-gym is $286. If this markup is 45%, what is the retail price for the uni-gym?

2. If an item costs $345 and has a markup of 89%, what is the retail price?

3. The Boxem Shoppe bought cartons for $234.90 a gross. If the shop needs a margin rate of 43%, what should it charge per box?

4. Sheila, the department manager for home decorations, was responsible for maintaining a 38% margin. What would the equivalent markup rate be?

5. The Linda Looma Lap Cover Co. bought car blankets for $45 each. If the required margin is 42%, what does the store sell them for?

6. The Cut-Em-Up Company received an invoice that listed the price of a lawn mower at $346. If the company carried a margin of 44%, what was its cost?

7. What would an equivalent margin rate be for a 225% markup?

8. Refrigerators cost a dealer $465 each. If the margin is 33%, what is the retail price on these units? What would the sale price be if the dealer offered the units with a 15% markdown?

9. Jim's Service Station installed a new transmission in Dr. Grapple's car. The station's cost for the transmission is $475. A 36% margin is required. The labor costs are $125. What is the total bill to Dr. Grapple? (Note: there is no margin on labor cost.)

10. What would the margin rate be for a 54.5% markup rate?

11. A discount store wants to sell a popular brand of refrigerator for $20 less than its competitor. If the competitor sells the refrigerator for $695, what is the maximum amount the discount store can pay for the refrigerator and still have a 23% margin rate?

12. A videotape recorder was priced at $450. The store maintained a 45% gross margin. What was the cost of the recorder? If the recorder was sale priced at $360, what was the percent markdown?

13. The LaVerne Nursery sold large palm trees for $235. They maintained a markup rate of 63%. What was the cost of the tree to the nursery?

14. Forty-five dollars was the markup for car seat cushions. If this amount was 76% of cost, what was the price of a cushion?

15. When a markup rate is 124%, what is the equivalent margin rate?

Chapter Test

1. Convert the following markup rates to margin rates:
   (a) 76% (b) 89% (c) 123% (d) 88% (e) 234% (f) 23%

2. Convert the following margin rates to markup rates:
   (a) 43% (b) 53% (c) 65% (d) 34% (e) 58% (f) 41%

3. What amount of sales is needed for merchandise that costs $57,000 if we expect to maintain a 35% margin rate?

4. If the cost of goods sold is $45,000 and the markup rate is 76%, what is the retail value of the goods?

5. The Lick-Em-Over Animal Supply Co. sold pet grooming kits for $5.65. If the markup rate was 123%, what did the kits cost the company?

6. When the cost of goods is $43.56, what is the retail price if the margin rate is 43%?

7. Convert a margin rate of 54% to its equivalent markup rate.

8. If the retail price of a car is $9,765 and the markup rate is 54%, what is the cost of the car? What is the sale price if the dealer offers a 12% markdown from retail?

9. A set of metric wrenches lists for $54.89 retail. If the margin rate is 43%, what is its cost?

10. Convert a 234% markup rate to a margin rate.

Retail Operations

14

OBJECTIVES

When you complete this chapter you will be able to:

- *Understand how to calculate inventory turnover from business information and its effect on retail decision making. (14.1)*
- *Use given planning information to establish an open to buy budget. (14.2)*
- *Know the importance of maintaining a retail average margin. Perform the calculations for determining an average margin during buying activities. (14.3)*

COMING UP

From the large department stores, such as Macy's and Sears, to the small Mom and Pop shops, all retail stores have one thing in common—they buy goods and resell them to consumers for a profit. The work of retailing involves certain basic processes, which are the same whether a store is large or small. Common tasks that are performed include buying merchandise, maintaining profit margin, controlling inventory turnover, and staying within budget.

A retailer must consider maintaining a higher margin on some items to offset a lower margin on others. Planning ahead is really necessary to maintain an overall average margin. The retail manager must also determine what goods are selling and in what volume in order to gauge inventory replacement orders.

The buyer usually establishes the quantity and value of goods to be purchased. The money needed to acquire these goods is identified as the buyer's budget. The budget information is used with the average margin for purchase and profitability planning.

Inventory Turnover

14.1

Goods purchased for resale are known as **inventory.** The more often goods can be bought and resold, the more money can be earned. If inventory is kept too low, sales may be lost. Retailers seek a balance of enough inventory for sales but not too much to tie up excess dollars.

Inventory turnover is the number of times a typical stock level has been purchased and resold. It is a measure of the volume of business. If $100,000 worth of merchandise is resold often enough to buy $400,000 in replacement goods in a given period, a retailer has four stock turnovers. Inventory turnover is calculated by using either the cost of the product or its retail price. It is found by either

a. Dividing total sales by the **average inventory** at retail; or
b. Dividing **cost of goods sold** by average inventory at cost.

Average inventory is found by adding either the retail value of the inventories taken or the cost of the inventories taken and dividing by the number of inventories taken. The formula is:

$$\text{Turnover} = \frac{\text{Total sales}}{\text{Average inventory (retail)}}$$

or

$$\frac{\text{Cost of goods}}{\text{Average inventory (cost)}}$$

EXAMPLE 1 Clockheimers' store has recorded retail inventories of $12,000, $14,000, $12,000, $16,000, $14,000, and $16,000 during the past six months. During this period, total sales were $60,000. What was the inventory turnover?

Solution: 12 + 14 + 12 + 16 + 14 + 16 = 84 inventory sum.

| 84,000 | · Total of 6 inventories. |
| 84,000 ÷ 6 = 14,000 | · Average inventory (retail). |

$$\text{Turnover} = \frac{\text{Total sales}}{\text{Average inventory (retail)}}$$

T = 60,000 ÷ 14,000 · Set variables into formula.
· 14,000 average inventory.
· 60,000 total sales.

60,000 ÷ 14,000 = 4.2857 · Turnover calculation.
4.29 · Inventory turnover, retail.

EXAMPLE 6 Cost of goods sold for the first quarter sales period totaled $68,700. Inventories taken for this period were taken at retail. Beginning inventory was $18,200 and ending inventory totaled $16,400. If the average margin is 46%, what was the turnover for the period?

Solution:

$18,200 + 16,400 = 34,600$ · Sum of the two inventories.
$34,600 \div 2 = 17,300$ · Average inventory, retail.
$100\% - 46\% = 54\%$ · Cost percent (Retail − Margin).

Average inventory (retail) × Rate of cost = Average inventory (cost)

$17,300 \times .54$
- Set variables into conversion formula.
- .54 cost percent.
- 17,300 average inventory, retail.

$17,300 \times .54 = \$9,342$ · Convert retail inventory to cost.

Turnover = Cost of goods ÷ Average inventory (cost)

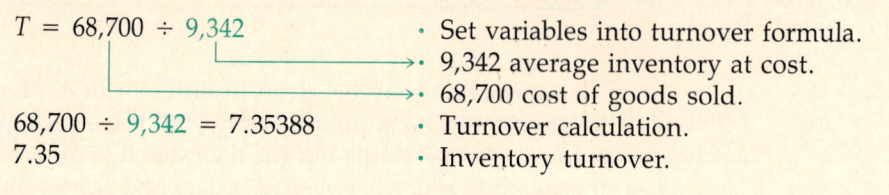

$T = 68,700 \div 9,342$
- Set variables into turnover formula.
- 9,342 average inventory at cost.
- 68,700 cost of goods sold.

$68,700 \div 9,342 = 7.35388$ · Turnover calculation.
7.35 · Inventory turnover.

CHECK FOR UNDERSTANDING

1. The Go-Fast Bicycle Shop had the following retail information:

	Inventories	Sales
January 1	$15,000	$19,000
February 1	$12,000	$17,500
March 1	$14,500	$18,500
April 1	$17,250	$12,500
May 1	$16,200	$26,600
June 1	$12,800	$22,000
June 30	$14,000	

What is the inventory turnover?

2. The average inventory at cost is $26,000. If sales for the period are $146,000, and the average margin is 37%, what is the stock turnover?

3. Inventories taken at cost for the accounting period were beginning inventory, $43,500; ending inventory, $54,100. Cost of goods sold for the period totaled $314,000. What was the inventory turnover?

Answers to ✓ Check for Understanding
1. 7.99.   2. 3.54.   3. 6.43.

EXAMPLE 6 Cost of goods sold for the first quarter sales period totaled $68,700. Inventories taken for this period were taken at retail. Beginning inventory was $18,200 and ending inventory totaled $16,400. If the average margin is 46%, what was the turnover for the period?

Solution:

18,200 + 16,400 = 34,600	• Sum of the two inventories.
34,600 ÷ 2 = 17,300	• Average inventory, retail.
100% − 46% = 54%	• Cost percent (Retail − Margin).

Average inventory (retail) × Rate of cost = Average inventory (cost)

17,300 × .54
 • Set variables into conversion formula.
 • .54 cost percent.
 • 17,300 average inventory, retail.

17,300 × .54 = $9,342 • Convert retail inventory to cost.

Turnover = Cost of goods ÷ Average inventory (cost)

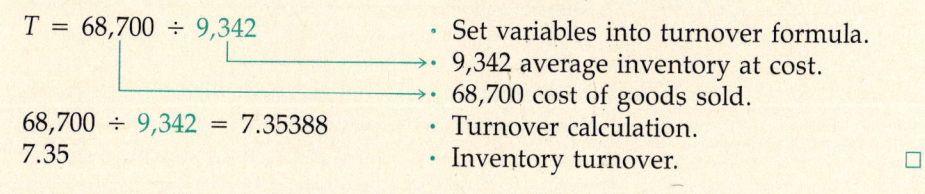

T = 68,700 ÷ 9,342
 • Set variables into turnover formula.
 • 9,342 average inventory at cost.
 • 68,700 cost of goods sold.

68,700 ÷ 9,342 = 7.35388
7.35
 • Turnover calculation.
 • Inventory turnover.

✔ CHECK FOR UNDERSTANDING

1. The Go-Fast Bicycle Shop had the following retail information:

	Inventories	Sales
January 1	$15,000	$19,000
February 1	$12,000	$17,500
March 1	$14,500	$18,500
April 1	$17,250	$12,500
May 1	$16,200	$26,600
June 1	$12,800	$22,000
June 30	$14,000	

What is the inventory turnover?

2. The average inventory at cost is $26,000. If sales for the period are $146,000, and the average margin is 37%, what is the stock turnover?

3. Inventories taken at cost for the accounting period were beginning inventory, $43,500; ending inventory, $54,100. Cost of goods sold for the period totaled $314,000. What was the inventory turnover?

Answers to ✔ Check for Understanding
1. 7.99. 2. 3.54. 3. 6.43.

$$\text{Turnover} = \frac{\text{Cost of goods sold}}{\text{Average inventory (cost)}}$$

    $T = 364{,}098 \div 92{,}940.50$ • Set variables into formula.
                                      • 92,940.50 average inventory, cost.
                                      • 364,098 cost of goods sold.

    $364{,}098 \div 92{,}940.50 = 3.9175$ • Calculate the turnover.
    3.92   • Inventory turnover.

PROBLEM SOLVING STRATEGY

The key procedure for solving turnover problems with these formulas is to have both elements of the formula in the same type of unit. Both should be either at cost or at retail. Check the problem to see how the values are stated. If one of the formula elements needs to be changed use the $P = B \times R$ analysis to convert one of the values given. Review the procedures described below.

Information may be given in different units. For instance, inventory data could be at cost and be supported only with total sales information. You would have two elements for a formula but the data stated in different type units. Chapter 13 showed that the difference between cost data and sales data is the margin. If average margin is provided, it can be used to change either the cost information to retail or sales data to cost. This conversion places the data in the same units. Then it is possible to proceed with the formula calculation.

> Sales × Rate of cost = Cost of goods
> Average inventory (retail) × Rate of cost = Average inventory (cost)

EXAMPLE 5   Average inventory at cost for a period totals $52,570. Sales for the same period were $412,200. If average margin for the store is 39.6%, what is the turnover for the period?

Solution:

    39.6   • Average margin in percent.
    $100 - 39.6 = 60.4$ • Price % − Margin % = Cost %.

    Sales × Rate of cost = Cost of goods

    $412{,}200 \times .604$ • Set variables into formula.
                                 • .604 is 60.4%, cost percent.
                                 • 412,200 retail sales in period.

    $\$412{,}200 \times .604 = \$248{,}968.80$ • Calculate the cost of goods.

    Turnover = Cost of goods ÷ Average inventory (cost)

    $T = 248{,}968.80 \div 52{,}570$ • Set values into formula.
                                 • 52,570 average inventory, cost.
                                 • 248,968.80 cost of goods.

    $248{,}968.80 \div 52{,}570 = 4.7359$ • Calculate the turnover.
    4.74   • Inventory turnover.

> **CALCULATOR TIP**
>
> The previous problem can be done in one calculator sequence. Add the inventories, find the average, and divide average inventory into total sales (all thousands):
>
> 12 [+] 14 [+] 12 [+] 16 [+] 14 [+] 16 [=] 84
> 84 [÷] 6 [=] 14 [M+]
> 60 [÷] [MR] [=] 4.2857 (turnover)
>
> Before you can divide, both values must be the same type of units, either both retail or both cost.
> Note: For the calculation, the zeros can be dropped and the results will be the same.

EXAMPLE 2   A retail beginning inventory for the period was $234,000 and the ending inventory totaled $183,870. Sales for the same period showed a total of $2,345,857. What was the turnover for the period?

Solution:

234,000 + 183,870 = 417,870	• Two inventory totals (retail).
417,870 ÷ 2 = 208,935	• Average inventory (retail).

$$\text{Turnover} = \frac{\text{Total sales}}{\text{Average inventory (retail)}}$$

T = 2,345,857 ÷ 208,935	• Set variables into formula.
	→ • 208,935 average inventory (retail).
	→ • 2,345,857 sales (retail).
2,345,857 ÷ 208,935 = 11.228	• Turnover calculation.
11.23	• Inventory turnover. ☐

EXAMPLE 3   With inventories at cost of $12,000, $15,000, $13,000, $17,000, and $14,000, and cost of goods sold at $86,000, what is the inventory turnover?

Solution:

12 + 15 + 13 + 17 + 14 = 71	• Total inventory (thousands).
71,000 ÷ 5 = $14,200	• Average inventory at cost.

$$\text{Turnover} = \frac{\text{Cost of goods sold}}{\text{Average inventory (cost)}}$$

T = 86,000 ÷ 14,200	• Set variables into formula.
	→ • 14,200 average inventory, cost
	→ • 86,000 cost of goods sold.
$86,000 ÷ $14,200 = 6.06	• Turnover calculation.
6.06	• Inventory turnover. ☐

EXAMPLE 4   What would the inventory turnover be if beginning inventory at cost was $87,125 and ending inventory at cost totaled $98,756? Cost of goods for the same period was $364,098.

Solution:

87,125 + 98,756 = 185,881	• Total inventory at cost.
185,881 ÷ 2 = 92,940.50	• Average inventory.

Inventory Turnover

14.1

Goods purchased for resale are known as **inventory**. The more often goods can be bought and resold, the more money can be earned. If inventory is kept too low, sales may be lost. Retailers seek a balance of enough inventory for sales but not too much to tie up excess dollars.

Inventory turnover is the number of times a typical stock level has been purchased and resold. It is a measure of the volume of business. If $100,000 worth of merchandise is resold often enough to buy $400,000 in replacement goods in a given period, a retailer has four stock turnovers. Inventory turnover is calculated by using either the cost of the product or its retail price. It is found by either

a. Dividing total sales by the **average inventory** at retail; or
b. Dividing **cost of goods sold** by average inventory at cost.

Average inventory is found by adding either the retail value of the inventories taken or the cost of the inventories taken and dividing by the number of inventories taken. The formula is:

$$\text{Turnover} = \frac{\text{Total sales}}{\text{Average inventory (retail)}}$$

or

$$\frac{\text{Cost of goods}}{\text{Average inventory (cost)}}$$

EXAMPLE 1   Clockheimers' store has recorded retail inventories of $12,000, $14,000, $12,000, $16,000, $14,000, and $16,000 during the past six months. During this period, total sales were $60,000. What was the inventory turnover?

Solution: 12 + 14 + 12 + 16 + 14 + 16 = 84 inventory sum.

| 84,000 | • Total of 6 inventories. |
| 84,000 ÷ 6 = 14,000 | • Average inventory (retail). |

$$\text{Turnover} = \frac{\text{Total sales}}{\text{Average inventory (retail)}}$$

T = 60,000 ÷ 14,000
• Set variables into formula.
• 14,000 average inventory.
• 60,000 total sales.

60,000 ÷ 14,000 = 4.2857   • Turnover calculation.
4.29   • Inventory turnover, retail.

SKILL EXERCISES

Find the average inventory at cost in the following problems:

	Jan.	Feb.	Mar.	Apr.	May	Average
1.	$28,000	$22,000	$18,500	$23,500	$27,000	$ _____
2.	$12,225	$13,750	$10,200	$18,725	$14,500	$ _____
3.	$18,000	$16,000	$13,750	$15,500	$ 8,500	$ _____
4.	$67,500	$52,800	$48,250	$69,000	$65,000	$ _____

If the average margin rate is 38%, and the following inventories are at cost, find the average of these inventories at retail:

	Jan.	Feb.	Mar.	Apr.	May	Average
5.	$15,000	$12,250	$14,780	$13,870	$15,690	$ _____
6.	$ 6,850	$ 5,790	$ 9,800	$ 7,650	$ 5,600	$ _____
7.	$27,650	$36,420	$28,970	$29,860	$32,450	$ _____
8.	$72,800	$86,700	$67,800	$75,900	$86,700	$ _____
9.	$97,600	$57,800	$45,000	$34,500	$46,450	$ _____

Given the following data, find the inventory stock turnover:

	Average inventory (cost)	Cost of goods	Turnover
10.	$ 46,000	$136,590	_____
11.	$ 37,500	$148,650	_____
12.	$ 12,600	$ 68,900	_____
13.	$ 48,500	$215,800	_____

What is the stock turnover if the average margin rate is 38%?

	Average inventory (cost)	Sales	Turnover
14.	$ 24,500	$126,000	_____
15.	$ 16,700	$ 86,000	_____
16.	$138,000	$765,000	_____
17.	$ 36,500	$267,000	_____

Section 14.1 Inventory Turnover

APPLICATIONS

1. If the average inventory at retail is $34,500, and the sales for a period are $117,565, what is the inventory turnover?

2. If cost of goods sold is $457,890, and the average inventory at cost for the period is $87,975, what is the inventory turnover?

3. The following inventories were taken at retail: $34,000, $23,000, $27,000, $36,000, $29,000, and $24,000. If sales for the period were $116,000, what was the turnover?

4. If the cost of goods sold is $34,000, and the average inventory at retail is $11,000 with an average margin rate of 39%, what is the inventory turnover?

5. If the stock turnover in the Amanda Trivia Shop is 5.4, and the average inventory at cost is $7,890, what is the cost of goods sold for the period?

6. Ruth's Excel Shop had sales of $34,000 during the period and a stock turnover of 5.6. What was the average inventory at retail?

7. With inventories at retail of $3,000, $5,000, $4,000, $6,000, and $7,000, and cost of goods sold of $23,500, what will the turnover be if the average margin rate is 42%?

8. If the average inventory at cost is $136,890, and the cost of goods sold is $765,000, what is the stock turnover?

9. If the cost of goods sold is $457,000, and the inventory turnover is 4.56, what is the average inventory at cost?

10. The average margin rate for Irene's Grandmother Craft Shop is 42%. The average inventory at retail is $3,985 with the cost of goods sold for the period $11,560. What is the inventory stock turnover?

Open to Buy

14.2

Each person responsible for buying merchandise works within limits on how much resale stock can be maintained at any given time. These limits are similar to the limits that govern our personal budgets. The **open to buy (OTB)** calculation establishes the amount needed to replace the goods sold. Open to buy is the difference between the amount of merchandise needed and the merchandise already available.

Generally the total amount of goods needed includes the end-of-month inventory plus merchandise planned for sales and markdowns. Sales and markdown items are considered separately since they reduce the total dollars of sales due to their reduced margin. Merchandise available typically includes beginning inventory, actual sales, and actual markdowns plus any merchandise in the ordering stage (pending or received). The formula to compute open to buy is shown below. Since retail planning is conducted using sales forecasts, all data in the formula is *listed at retail*. The final OTB solution is attained when OTB retail is converted to cost using the average margin procedure.

> $$\text{OTB retail} = \text{Merchandise needed} - \text{Merchandise available}$$
>
> (Note: Convert OTB retail to OTB cost.)

PROBLEM SOLVING STRATEGY

The OTB conversion of retail to cost uses the average margin. The final expense must be stated as a cost. Since the original problem data is given at retail, the average margin is used to convert the difference to cost. Subtract average margin from 100% (price) to find the cost percent. Multiply the retail OTB by the cost percent to find OTB at cost.

EXAMPLE 7 The buyer for the notions department of the Upper-Class Department Store gathered the following information: Inventory on hand at retail is $17,000, planned sales for the period are $16,000, and planned ending inventory is $14,000. She already has had $3,000 in sales and has placed $4,000 on order at retail. Average margin for the department is 39%. What is the OTB at cost?

Solution:

Available	Needed
$17,000 Opening inventory	$14,000 Ending inventory
3,000 Sales	16,000 Planned sales
4,000 Items on order	
$24,000 available	$30,000 needed.

OTB = Needed − Available • OTB formula.
OTB = 30,000 − 24,000 • Set into formula, retail.
30,000 − 24,000 = $6,000 • Calculate OTB at retail.
100% − 39% = 61% • Cost percent (Retail − Margin).
Retail × Cost percent = Cost • Conversion formula.
6,000 × .61 • Set variables into formula.
• 61% or .61, cost percent.
• 6,000 open to buy at retail.
6,000 × .61 = 3,660 • Calculate OTB at cost.
$3,660 • Open to buy at cost.

EXAMPLE 8 The retail inventory on January 1 for the sporting goods department of the U-Buy Department Store was $16,000, and the planned inventory for February 1 was $22,000. Planned sales for the month were $19,000, and planned markdowns were $3,000. On January 16, actual sales for month to date were $6,000, and actual markdowns were $1,500. Purchases were $4,000 at retail, and orders for $8,000 at retail had been placed but not received. What is the January 16 OTB at cost if the average margin rate is 38%?

Solution:

Available	Needed
$16,000 Opening inventory	$22,000 Ending inventory
6,000 Actual sales	19,000 Planned sales
1,500 Actual markdown	3,000 Planned markdowns
4,000 Goods received	
8,000 Goods ordered	

· $35,500 available · $44,000 needed.

OTB = Needed − Available · OTB formula.
OTB = 44,000 − 35,500 · Set into formula, retail.
44,000 − 35,500 = 8,500 · Calculate OTB at retail.
100% − 38% = 62% · Cost percent (Retail − Margin).
Retail × Cost percent = Cost · Cost conversion formula.
8,500 × .62 · Set variables into formula.
→ · 62% or .62, cost percent.
→ · 8,500 OTB at retail.
8,500 × .62 = 5,270 · Calculate OTB at cost.
$5,270 · Open to buy at cost.

✓ CHECK FOR UNDERSTANDING

1. The blouse department has a beginning inventory of $23,800. The manager plans sales of $19,500 for the month. Planned markdowns are $2,500, and the ending inventory is planned for $19,200. If the average margin rate is 36%, what is the (a) OTB retail; (b) OTB cost?

2. The sporting goods department of the Tri-Level Department Store had a beginning inventory at retail of $65,000, planned sales of $21,400, and planned ending inventory at retail of $63,500. When the buyer analyzed his position in the middle of the period, he found that the actual sales to that point were $22,000, actual markdowns $2,200, and merchandise on order was $8,000. If average margin is 35%, what was (a) OTB at retail; (b) OTB at cost?

SKILL EXERCISES

Place a check mark in the column that properly identifies the item as available or needed.

Identity	Available	Needed
1. Planned sales	_____	_____
2. Beginning inventory	_____	_____
3. Sales	_____	_____
4. Planned markdowns	_____	_____

Answers to ✓ Check for Understanding
1. (a) $17,400. (b) $11,136.   2. (a) $12,300. (b) $7,995.

5. Markdowns   _____ _____

6. Ending inventory   _____ _____

7. Goods on order   _____ _____

8. Goods received   _____ _____

9. Returns   _____ _____

Review the following information and calculate the missing value:

	Available	Needed	Rate of margin	OTB (cost)
10.	$ 27,000	$ 46,000	42%	$ _____
11.	$ 18,000	$ 52,000	35%	$ _____
12.	$135,000	$215,000	38%	$ _____
13.	$ 56,000	$ 87,000	40%	$ _____
14.	$ 6,000	$ 11,500	39%	$ _____
15.	$ 67,000	$ 85,400	_____ %	$12,890
16.	$ 23,600	$ _____	42%	$17,700
17.	$ 47,900	$ _____	38%	$24,675
18.	$122,000	$285,000	_____ %	$96,170
19.	$ _____	$167,975	62%	$38,000
20.	$ 43,900	$ 74,120	44%	$ _____

APPLICATIONS

1. The total goods available for sale are $45,000 at retail, and the total goods needed for the period are $57,800 at retail. What is the OTB at cost if the average margin is 42%?

2. Find the OTB at cost from the following information: sales $12,000; planned sales, $37,000; planned markdowns, $2,000; beginning inventory, $16,000; goods on order, $4,500; ending inventory, $27,000; actual markdowns, $1,200; and an average margin rate of 37%.

3. Planned ending inventory of $53,400 and planned sales of $142,000 are matched with total goods available of $68,750. If the average margin is 40%, what is the open to buy at cost?

4. Given the following retail planning information for Quick Buy Discount Store, what is your open to buy decision at retail? In-stock inventory, $23,000; orders pending, $19,300; planned ending inventory, $35,000; and planned sales, $42,000?

5. Calculate the OTB at cost for the Hybred Bird Store: beginning inventory, $12,400; orders pending, $4,300; actual sales, $1,240; actual markdowns, $4,700; ending inventory, $14,600; planned sales, $26,700; and planned markdowns, $8,200. Average margin is 44%.

Average Margin and Maintained Margin

14.3

Management establishes the total margin rate that a retail operation must receive on its sales. They consider sales volume, cost of goods, overhead, and profit objectives. Retail buyers use their knowledge of the margin as they make their purchase decisions.

Average Margin

An **average margin** is a composite figure. Stores combine the margins on various categories of goods into one percent. For instance, a typical department store sells housewares, clothing, notions, gifts, jewelry, etc. Each merchandise category maintains its own margin rate. All departments combined contribute to the average margin of the store.

> **PROBLEM SOLVING STRATEGY**
>
> The calculation for average margin involves grouping the individual category margins into one combined number. The calculation can be used for a single retail department or an entire store. Simply stated, the average margin is found by multiplying each individual margin on sales by its respective percent of sales for the retail operation. The computation sequence is shown below.

Average Margin Calculation

I. Margin percent × Total percent sales = Percent average margin

II. Margin percent × Total percent sales = Percent average margin

III. Margin percent × Total percent sales = Percent average margin

Sum of percent average margin

Sum of percent average margin = Average margin

408 Chapter 14 Retail Operations

EXAMPLE 9 B-Made Retail Outlet has 5 principal categories of sale items. Each category has its individual margin. For the percent of sale indicated, calculate the average margin for the outlet store.

I.	Shoes	43% margin	23% of sales
II.	Outerwear	39% margin	12% of sales
III.	Accessories	68% margin	14% of sales
IV.	Sporting Goods	42% margin	35% of sales
V.	Electronics	55% margin	16% of sales
			100% of sales

Solution: Category margin × Percent sales = Category %

Category I	.43	×	.23	=	.0989
Category II	.39	×	.12	=	.0468
Category III	.68	×	.14	=	.0952
Category IV	.42	×	.35	=	.147
Category V	.55	×	.16	=	.088
		Average margin		=	.4759
		Average margin		=	47.59%

EXAMPLE 10 Harrison Dry Goods carried 4 categories of retail goods. Each category has a separate margin. The first category was the company's primary line, contributing 53% of sales. Each of the other categories contributed the following to sales: Category II, 17%; Category III, 12%; and Category IV, 18%. If the margins were 32%, 45%, 67%, and 38%, respectively, what was the company's average margin?

Solution: Margin × Percent sale = Contribution

Category I	.32	×	.53	=	.1696
Category II	.45	×	.17	=	.0765
Category III	.67	×	.12	=	.0804
Category IV	.38	×	.18	=	.0684
	Harrison Dry average margin			=	.3949
	Average margin			=	39.49%

Maintained Margin

Average margin reflects a target for profitability. Buyers use the average margin as they make their purchases. Certain goods are planned for sale at a very low margin; others are planned for a high margin sale. The planned total margin earned on the sale of the goods being bought must be equal to the average margin rate. This is referred to as the **maintained margin** since it represents the minimum needed margin rate on all goods bought for resale.

PROBLEM SOLVING STRATEGY

The key procedure for the maintained margin calculation is to begin with a pair of open to buy figures. You need open to buy at cost and at retail. Calculate the OTB not provided using average margin.

EXAMPLE 11 The average margin that must be maintained for company profitability is 40%. A buyer is working with $30,000 open to buy at cost. On January 1, purchases of $5,000 were made with a planned sales price of $8,500. On January 7, purchases of $4,000 were made to sell for $6,200. On January 12, a fast-sale item is bought for $8,000 and marked to sell for $13,000. What margin must be obtained on the remaining purchases in order to maintain the average margin?

Solution: Total budget $30,000 (cost)

  Retail % − Average margin % = Cost %

  100% − 40%
          · Set variables into formula.
          · 40% rate of average margin.
          · 100% rate of retail (base).
  100% − 40% = 60% · Calculate the rate of cost.

  Cost ÷ Rate of cost = Amount of budget at retail

  $30,000 ÷ .60
          · Set variables into formula.
          · .60 rate of cost.
          · $30,000 total budget (cost).
  30,000 ÷ .60 = 50,000 · Calculate OTB retail.
          · OTB cost 30,000; OTB retail 50,000.

Purchases to date:	1/1,	$5,000		Retail	$ 8,500
	1/7,	$4,000		Retail	$ 6,200
	1/12,	$8,000		Retail	$13,000
Total purchases:		$17,000		Total retail:	$27,700
OTB cost:		$30,000		OTB retail:	$50,000
Less purchases:		(−17,000)		Less total retail:	(−27,700)

Remaining purchases: $13,000   Remaining retail: $22,300

Remaining purchases of $13,000 must get $22,300 at retail in order to maintain the average margin of 40%. The base of the calculation is retail price.

  22,300 − 13,000 = 9,300 · Price − Cost = Margin.
  R = P ÷ B   · Formula for the rate.
  9,300 ÷ 22,300 = .417   · Margin ÷ Price = Rate of margin.

Remaining purchases need a margin of 41.7%. □

EXAMPLE 12 The problems can also be shown with each purchase margin being calculated as you acquire purchases. HIDECK Lumber had $25,000 open to buy at cost. It must maintain an average margin of 39% on all purchases. On June 4, the buyer purchased $7,500 worth of materials to sell for $11,750. On June 7, he purchased $12,400 more of materials that he planned to retail for $21,300. What margin must he achieve on remaining purchases to maintain the average margin?

Solution: OTB $25,000 (cost)

  Retail % − Average margin % = Cost %

  100% − 39%
          · Set variables into formula.
          · 39% rate of average margin.
          · 100% rate of retail, base.
  100% − 39% = 61% · Calculate the rate of cost.

  Cost ÷ Rate of cost = Amount of budget at retail

  $25,000 ÷ .61
          · Set variables into formula.
          · .61 rate of cost.
          · $25,000 OTB (budget at cost).
  25,000 ÷ .61 = 40,983.61 · Calculate OTB (budget at retail).
  OTB cost: $25,000   · OTB retail: $40,983.61.

Purchases to date: 6/4, $ 7,500 Retail $11,750 Margin: 36.2%
       6/7, $12,400 Retail $21,300

Total purchases:	$19,900	Total retail: $33,050	Margin: 39.8%
Total OTB cost:	$25,000	OTB retail: $40,983.61	
Less purchases:	(−19,900)	Less total retail: (−33,050.00)	

Remaining purchases: $5,100   Retail: $7,933.61

Retail − Cost = Amount of margin

 7,933.61 − 5,100 = 2,833.61 • Calculate needed margin.
 R = P ÷ B   • Formula for the rate.
 2,833.61 ÷ 7,933.61 = .357   • Rate of margin.

The buyer will maintain a 39% average margin with purchased goods planned for a minimum 35.7% margin. ☐

✔ CHECK FOR UNDERSTANDING

1. The Bi-Model Department Store's women's fashion department had $25,000 to invest for the month of February and needed to maintain a 37% margin. On February 7, the department bought $4,500 to be sold at $6,800; on February 12, $7,200 to be sold at $13,800. What is the maintained margin after each purchase? At what margin rate must the balance of merchandise needed be bought to maintain the average margin?

2. On July 1, the buyer for the budget infant wear department of the Hi-Line Department Store received her budget for the month. It showed that she had $18,000 for purchases. She needed to maintain an average margin rate of 42.5%. On July 3, she bought $4,000 to sell for $6,250; on July 12, she bought $7,000 to sell for $12,850. What was the maintained margin after each purchase? What margin rate must be maintained on the balance of purchases?

SKILL EXERCISES

Review the following data and solve for the missing factor:

	OTB cost	OTB retail	($) Margin	Needed margin
1.	$ 4,000	$ 7,230	$ _____	_____ %
2.	$17,450	$ _____	$13,567	_____ %
3.	$ 1,234	$ 2,087	$ _____	_____ %
4.	$17,890	$24,760	$ _____	_____ %
5.	$ 7,875	$ _____	$ 4,675	_____ %

Answers to ✔ Check for Understanding
1. 33.82%; 43.20%; 30.30%. 2. 36%; 42.41%; 42.64%.

6.	$54,785	$ _____	$ _____	42%
7.	$ _____	$32,675	$ _____	36%
8.	$ _____	$ _____	$ 7,864	39%
9.	$ _____	$87,980	$54,870	_____ %
10.	$ _____	$ 4,450	$ _____	40%

APPLICATIONS

1. Given the following margin categories and percents of sales, calculate the average margin:

Category I	48% margin	24% sales
Category II	24% margin	34% sales
Category III	31% margin	42% sales

2. If the open to buy for the Chelsea House is $46,897, and the average margin needed is 42%, what amount of sales is needed to meet the budget?

With anticipated sales of $74,000 and an average margin rate of 42%, calculate the maintained margin rates from the information provided in Problems 3–6.

3. $14,000 to sell at $23,500.

4. An additional $22,000 to sell at $40,785.

5. An additional $3,000 to sell at $5,175.

6. What margin must be attained on the remaining purchases to maintain a 42% average margin?

7. As the buyer for the LeakProof Pool Co., you have the following information: investment capital, $44,000; planned return, $95,960. Your purchases have been as listed, with anticipated sales on each major purchase figured. Calculate the maintained margin rate after each major purchase and the margin rate needed on the balance of purchases.

Purchases	Anticipated return
Jan. 12 $12,000	$33,350
Feb. 3 $17,000	$44,350

412 Chapter 14 Retail Operations

8. Use the information provided by GOODM's Candy Co. to calculate its needed average margin.

Hard candy	48% margin	22% sales
Chocolates	67% margin	44% sales
Vendor grade	33% margin	15% sales
Soft jell	48% margin	19% sales

9. What is the average margin rate if purchases are to be $67,000, and the sales are planned to be $114,000?

10. If anticipated sales are $45,985 and the average margin rate is 41%, what is the greatest amount that can be invested in the cost of goods?

11. If cost of goods for the period is $325,000 and the average margin rate is 37%, what will the needed retail sales be?

12. Find the margin rate needed on the balance of purchases given the following information:

OTB cost: $56,000	OTB retail: $90,300
Purchases:	Anticipated revenue:
$17,675	$29,600
$14,860	$23,000

Key Terms

Average inventory (399)
Average margin (408)
Cost of goods sold (399)
Inventory (399)
Inventory turnover (399)

Maintained margin (409)
Margin rate (401)
Open to buy (404)
Planned markdowns (404)

Looking Back

All retail merchandise sold is not priced using the same margin. The average margin is a planning margin. It includes the combined effect for all margins used.

The method used on financial statements to calculate cost of goods sold adds purchases to the beginning inventory and then subtracts the ending inventory. You may also use the average margin to convert sales to cost of goods sold.

Turnover is not a percent, units, or dollars. It is the volume of sales for a type of inventory. In a year, for a turnover of 12, it would mean that the typical inventory carried for that category was sold once per month. When turnover can be compared to other years or to industry standards, it takes on managerial importance.

Open to buy is calculated using the retail or selling price figures. It is then converted to cost. Cost is needed to plan the expense of purchasing additional merchandise. The retail figures are used to relate to sales and revenue planning.

Let's Review

1. If the cost of goods sold is $345,678.90 and the average inventory at cost is $72,345.56, what is the turnover?

2. Given the following information, find the open to buy at cost. Planned ending inventory, $65,000; planned sales, $430,000; actual markdowns, $1,200; actual sales, $16,000; opening inventory, $63,780; planned markdowns, $2,300; actual purchases in period, $12,345. All factors are at retail and the average margin rate is 38%.

3. Bon Retail Store carried three major categories of goods, each with a different margin. Analyze the data and calculate the average margin.

Category A	23% margin	28% sales
Category B	64% margin	32% sales
Category C	39% margin	40% sales

4. Sales for the period were $246,800 and the average inventory at retail for the period was $31,864. What was the stock turnover?

5. If the average inventory at cost is $23,890 and the sales for the period are $85,765 with an average margin rate of 39%, what is the inventory stock turnover?

6. The garden supply department of the Gopher Farm Store had the following inventories, each given at cost: $24,875, $32,865, $22,345, $32,864, $36,984. During the period the cost of goods sold was $106,374. What was the stock turnover?

7. The budget for the men's department of the Tall Shoppe was $76,800 at cost. They worked on an average margin rate of 44%. Find the maintained margin rate after each purchase and the margin rate needed to maintain the average margin for the total purchase.

Purchases	Anticipated return
$18,980	$35,675
$34,000	$58,900
$11,670	$25,358

8. Calculate the average margin from these analyses:

Category 1	34% margin	23% sales
Category 2	45% margin	23% sales
Category 3	39% margin	33% sales
Category 4	58% margin	21% sales

9. Jeanette had projected sales for the period of $27,674. The average margin rate for her shop is 39%. Use the following data to determine her open to buy at cost: planned markdowns, $800; beginning inventory at retail, $6,000; purchases not yet delivered, $4,780 at retail; ending inventory, $16,000 at retail; actual sales, $2,000; and actual markdowns, $300.

10. If the average inventory at retail is $87,980 and the cost of goods sold is $235,000 with an average margin rate of 36%, what is the stock turnover?

11. Maida went to the furniture mart to purchase inventory for the Settle Furniture Store. She had an allowance of $346,000. She was required to maintain an average margin of 37%. What was her anticipated return at retail?

When Maida reviewed her purchases she found the following data. What is the cumulative margin for each purchase?

	Purchase	Anticipated return	Cumulative margin
12.	$ 76,000	$120,000	_____
13.	$ 84,700	$116,900	_____
14.	$112,800	$164,500	_____

15. Find the margin rate Maida needs on the balance of the purchases to maintain the average margin.

Chapter Test

1. From the following information, find the stock turnover: average inventory at cost, $378,980; cost of goods sold, $1,365,870.

2. What is the average margin for the Wholesale Merchants Inc.?

    Category 1   43% margin   35% sales
    Category 2   39% margin   49% sales
    Category 3   27% margin   16% sales

3. Carl's Farm Store developed an open to buy at cost. When checking the information for the period, Carl found the following: planned sales, $45,000; planned markdowns, $2,000; beginning inventory at retail, $72,000; planned ending inventory, $90,000; actual sales, $12,000; and actual markdowns, $1,300. If the average margin rate is 42%, what is the open to buy?

4. In Donna's Scandinavian Painting and Creating Place the cost of goods sold for the period is $24,000. The average margin rate is 38%. What is the inventory stock turnover if the average inventory at retail is $8,980?

5. If average inventory at retail for the period is $43,765 and sales for the same period are $156,875, what is the inventory stock turnover?

6. Beginning inventory is $38,700. Orders pending receipt total $23,489. Planned ending inventory is $47,200 with expected sales for the period being $55,000. What is the open to buy at cost if the average margin is 42%?

Use the following for Problems 7–10.

When planning purchases for his company Leo found the following information: planned purchases for the period were $486,900. The average margin rate needed was 41%. Purchases to date and the anticipated revenue for each are listed below. Calculate the maintained margin after each purchase and the margin rate needed for the balance of the purchases to maintain the average margin.

	Purchases	Anticipated revenue	Margin rate
7. May 1	$96,800	$154,000	_____
8. May 16	$87,000	$152,000	_____
9. May 22	$168,000	$293,000	_____

10. Find the margin rate needed on the balance of the purchases.

Determining Profit

15

OBJECTIVES

When you finish this chapter you will be able to:

- Identify general categories of fixed and variable costs and calculate the various components of cost using base, rate, and part formulas. (15.1)
- Understand the components of markup by applying fixed and variable costs to profit elements for the pricing of a product. (15.2)
- Apply the concepts of cost and pricing to establish the difference between gross and net profit. (15.3)

COMING UP

Profit is an imposing word. It is the force behind the motivation of many people, a measure of effort, the result of a little luck, and the drive behind fundamentally sound business systems. It doesn't happen without involving the element of cost.

In this chapter we study cost as it refers to services, commodities, time, raw materials, or other elements useful in making a product. By identifying cost components, we are able to see how markup is established and used to price a product. With price we can determine how profit comes about. In our economy there are several different forces that affect price. In simplest terms, the manufacturer establishes price based on costs and anticipated profit. The consumer then sets the quantity demand for the product at that price.

Profit comes from the pricing structure . . . of that there is no doubt. This chapter shows the relationship between cost, markup, and price and how profit is determined.

Types of Cost

15.1

Cost is an expense of business. The first step in creating managerial information is to determine costs for a product and properly categorize them as fixed or variable.

Fixed Costs

Fixed cost is the foundation of the total cost base. In other words, fixed costs exist even when the production plant creates no products. Although this list is not complete, the following types of fixed costs will be used in the examples and problems in this book:

Type	Examples
Building	Rent or mortgage
Utilities	Heat, light, air conditioning
Licenses	Operating and revenue tax licenses
Security	Guards, physical restraint systems
Communications	Telephone, video data systems
Land	Cost of land used for buildings
Administrative salaries	Salaries for managerial people in the company

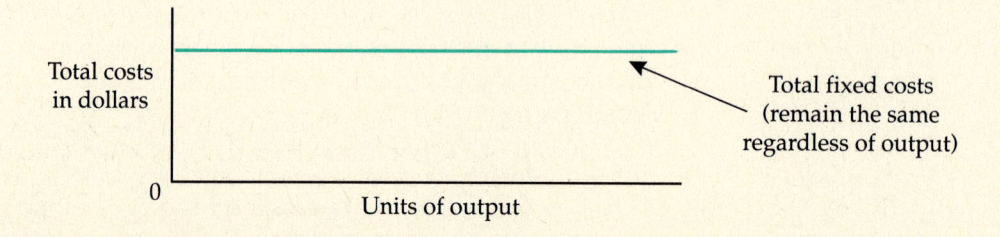

FIGURE 15.1
Completely fixed costs

[Graph: Total costs in dollars vs. Units of output, showing a horizontal line labeled "Total fixed costs (remain the same regardless of output)"]

EXAMPLE 1

Mainline Manufacturing Inc. has determined that 40% of its costs are fixed costs. If the fixed costs of operation are $260,000, what are its total costs?

Solution: Unknown is total cost, a base:

Base = Part ÷ Rate   • Formula for the base.
Base = 260,000 ÷ .40   • Set values into formula.
                          • 40% or .40, the rate of fixed cost.
                          • 260,000 fixed cost is a part.
260,000 ÷ .40 = 650,000   • Calculate total costs, the base.
$650,000   • Total operation costs.

418   Chapter 15   Determining Profit

EXAMPLE 2 The sum of fixed costs for the Hi-Way Company, not including administrative salaries, amounted to $245,680. If the administrative salaries for the company were $16,583.40, what percent of total fixed costs did they amount to?

Solution: Unknown is administrative salaries percent, a rate:

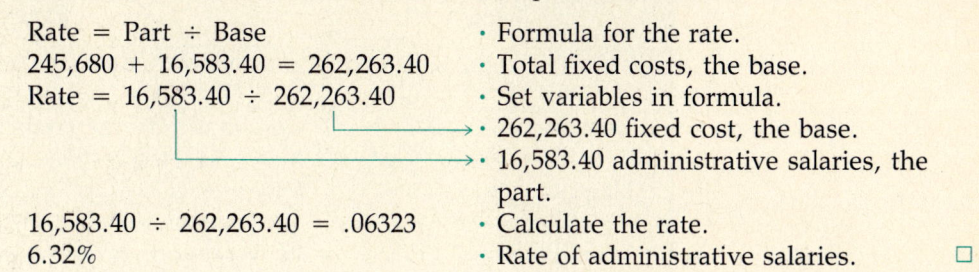

Rate = Part ÷ Base	• Formula for the rate.
245,680 + 16,583.40 = 262,263.40	• Total fixed costs, the base.
Rate = 16,583.40 ÷ 262,263.40	• Set variables in formula.
	• 262,263.40 fixed cost, the base.
	• 16,583.40 administrative salaries, the part.
16,583.40 ÷ 262,263.40 = .06323	• Calculate the rate.
6.32%	• Rate of administrative salaries.

✔ CHECK FOR UNDERSTANDING

1. Trekke Truck Leasing Company computes its annual total fixed costs output to be buildings, $128,000; utilities, $18,500; licenses, $1,600; security, $8,000; communications, $7,600; and administrative salaries, $188,000. If the total of all costs for the company is $975,000, what percent of the total costs is fixed cost?

2. Getlot Manufacturing Company is worried that its fixed costs are increasing because of administrative salaries. Last year's salaries were 18% of the company's total costs. This year's budget reflects administrative salaries of $220,000, with other expenses being $150,000 for buildings, $245,000 for utilities, and the total of all other fixed costs amounting to $365,500. What is this year's percent of administrative salary? How much change in percent is there?

Variable Costs

Variable costs include the costs of manufacturing a component. When the materials, labor, and other necessary elements for making an item are established, these are the costs that will vary based upon how many items are made. Figure 15.2 illustrates how the costs vary with output.

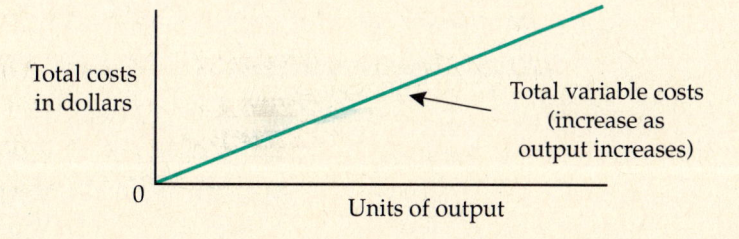

FIGURE 15.2
Completely variable costs

Total variable costs refer to costs for the level of output at a given period of time. This is not to be confused with a cost that varies over a period of time. As more products are made, more material, machine, and labor expenses are usually incurred.

Answers to ✔ Check for Understanding
1. 36.1%.   2. 22.4%; 4.4%.

Section 15.1 Types of Cost

Typically then, variable costs increase with an increased output of units. Some of the costs that qualify as variable costs for our examples in this book are as follows:

Type	Examples
Labor	That which is directly involved in the production of goods or services
Shipping-in	Cost to receive materials
Raw materials	Materials used to make a product
Maintenance	Expenses necessary to keep equipment in operating condition
Supplies	Items other than raw materials used in production
Pre-manufactured parts	Pre-assembled items provided in a manufactured form from other sources

Having reviewed both fixed cost and variable cost components, we can establish their relationship to total costs:

$$\text{Total costs (Sum of all costs)} = \text{Fixed cost} + \text{Variable cost}$$

EXAMPLE 3 In a general budget review, HIHUMP Manufacturing Co. analyzed its costs. The following data was presented:

Building $92,000
Communications $4,260
Administrative salaries $190,000
Maintenance $8,000
Shipping $15,000

Utilities $6,590
Security $1,274
Materials $62,000
Labor $220,000
Supplies $6,000

a. What percent of total costs is variable costs?
b. What percent of total variable costs is materials?
c. If last year's material cost of $75,000 was 21% of total variable costs, what were the variable costs?

Solution: Use the formulas: Part = Base × Rate

$$\text{Total costs} = \text{Fixed cost} + \text{Variable cost}$$

$605,124		· Total costs are the sum of all costs.
62,000	*Materials*	· Variable cost element.
8,000	*Maintenance*	· Variable cost element.
220,000	*Labor*	· Variable cost element.
15,000	*Shipping*	· Variable cost element.
6,000	*Supplies*	· Variable cost element.
311,000	*Total*	· Total variable costs.

a. Rate = 311,000 ÷ 605,124 · Set variables into formula.
· 605,124 total costs, the base.
· 311,000 variable cost, the part.

311,000 ÷ 605,124 = .5139 · Calculate the rate.
51.39% · Rate of variable cost.

420 Chapter 15 Determining Profit

b. Rate = 62,000 ÷ 311,000
- Set variables into formula.
- 311,000 variable cost, the base.
- 62,000 materials, the part.

62,000 ÷ 311,000 = .1994
19.94%
- Calculate the rate.
- Percent materials.

c. Base = 75,000 ÷ .21
- Set variables into formula.
- .21 rate of materials.
- 75,000 materials, the part.

75,000 ÷ .21 = 375,142.86
$375,142.86
- Calculate the base.
- Variable costs last year.

PROBLEM SOLVING STRATEGY

Total cost means the sum of all variable and fixed costs. The total cost is always the base. The total fixed and total variable costs are respective parts of the base. The elements comprising either fixed or variable costs are parts and the total fixed and total variable costs are used as a base.

✔ CHECK FOR UNDERSTANDING

1. A review of material costs for units of output showed that

    100 units cost $2,000
    150 units cost $3,000
    200 units cost $4,750

    (a) What percent increase in cost is incurred when production moves from 100 units to 150 units?
    (b) What percent increase in cost is incurred when production moves from 150 units to 200 units?
    (c) What logical reason is there for the difference in percent between the answers for (a) and (b) above?

2. Total costs incurred for manufacturing bicycles included $482,000 variable cost and $362,000 fixed cost. What percent of the total costs was variable?

3. Variable costs for materials were $10,500, which constituted 28.25% of the total variable costs. What were the total variable costs?

4. Total variable costs of product manufacture were $862,000. Of this total, labor costs were $246,000 and materials were $187,000. What percent greater were the costs of labor over those of materials?

Answers to ✔ Check for Understanding
1. (a) 50%. (b) 58.33%. (c) Not all costs stay constant. Additional production could incur overtime and therefore the cost of labor would increase as more units are produced.
2. 57.11%.   3. $37,168.14.   4. Labor, 28.54%; materials, 21.69%. Labor is 6.85% higher than materials.

SKILL EXERCISES

Use the base, rate, and part formulas to solve for the missing components.

	Base		Part	Rate (nearest tenth of percent)
1. Total costs	$ 84,500	Fixed cost	$ 26,000	_____ %
2. Total costs	$ 12,750	Fixed cost	$ 6,000	_____ %
3. Total costs	$ 9,480	Fixed cost	$ 4,400	_____ %
4. Total costs	$161,000	Fixed cost	$ _____	61%
5. Total costs	$ 57,750	Fixed cost	$ _____	49%
6. Total costs	$104,205	Fixed cost	$ _____	52%
7. Total costs $ _____		Fixed cost	$ 65,184	60%
8. Total costs $ _____		Fixed cost	$ 10,240	42%
9. Total costs $ _____		Fixed cost	$ 3,800	25%
10. Total costs $ _____		Fixed cost	$ 72,000	72%
11. Total costs	$ 93,250	Variable cost	$ 43,000	_____ %
12. Total costs	$104,643	Variable cost	$ 63,000	_____ %
13. Total costs	$ 6,597	Variable cost	$ 1,242	_____ %
14. Total costs	$ 15,942	Variable cost $ _____		85%
15. Total costs	$ 18,464	Variable cost $ _____		72%
16. Total costs	$143,920	Variable cost $ _____		58%
17. Total costs $ _____		Variable cost	$ 62,000	20%
18. Total costs $ _____		Variable cost	$ 24,000	44%
19. Total costs $ _____		Variable cost	$ 19,500	64%
20. Total costs $ _____		Variable cost	$164,000	76%

Chapter 15 Determining Profit

APPLICATIONS

Solve the following using fixed and variable cost logic:

1. Last year's fixed costs for building were $85,500. This year's building expense is $93,400. What percent change was experienced?

2. Fixed costs for Dingbow Manufacturing Inc. for the last fiscal year were $635,000. This was 65% of total costs. What were total costs?

3. Total budgeted costs for X-RITE Corp. are $674,259, of which 42% are fixed costs. What are the budgeted fixed costs?

4. The fixed costs in next year's budget are buildings, $84,000; utilities, $12,500; communications, $6,200; security, $4,570; and licenses, $1,230. What percent of fixed costs does each category represent?

5. Typical estimation of a production run has determined that labor is 52% of variable cost; materials, 30%; shipping, 3%; supplies, 10%; and maintenance, 5%. The total costs of production are calculated at $975,000. Fixed cost is 43% of the total. What are the variable costs by category?

6. The following problem relates to the cost data listed below:

Buildings	$ 62,500
Utilities	$ 8,750
Communications	$ 4,200
Security	$ 18,000
Labor	$100,000
Materials	$126,000
Administrative salaries	$ 79,000
Maintenance	$ 9,500
Supplies	$ 19,000
Shipping-in	$ 15,250
	$442,200 Total cost

    (a) What percent of total cost are total labor and administrative salaries?
    (b) What percent of total cost are materials, labor, and shipping?
    (c) What percent of total costs is the variable cost?

7. If variable costs were $82,575 and represented 60.5% of the total costs, what were the total costs?

8. Yum-Yum Oriental Food Producers determined that the cost of food before preparation was $287,000. The cost of preparing the food adds another 18%. If the total cost of the food plus preparation equals 44% of the total costs of operation, what are the total production operating costs?

9. Total costs of production were $86,588. Total fixed costs were 34%. Labor was 41% of the total variable costs. How much was labor?

10. Total variable costs were 78.5% of the total costs of manufacture. If the total fixed costs amounted to $214,670, what were the total manufacturing costs?

Production Price and Markup

15.2

Up to this point, we have been using "part is equal to the base times the rate" for solving problems. We have already studied the other basic relationship that is important to establish a product price:

$$\text{Cost} + \text{Markup} = \text{Price}$$

Recall from Chapter 13, this relationship uses the pricing method that refers to the total manufacturing cost as the base for pricing.

The cost of the production process can be measured and therefore becomes a basis for pricing. Once production costs are determined, a markup is added on to the cost. This creates the price, which the customer must pay for the product. In order to identify the different categories of profit, this chapter looks at markup in more detail than Chapter 13.

Markup has two components. One part of markup is **profit.** The second part of markup is that which allows the manufacturer to recover the *costs of selling* the product. (See Figure 15.3.) These include the costs of maintaining a sales force, advertising, shipping, and other expenses involved in housing the sales activity of the company. The **total markup,** then, *is established by combining, either in percent or dollars, the profit desired and the cost of selling the product.*

Fixed Costs	Cost of Selling
Land	Sales force
Buildings	Advertising
Utilities	Shipping out
Licenses	Sales overhead
Security	Damaged goods
Communications	
Administrative salaries	
and	and
Variable Costs	**Net Profit (derived from)**
Raw materials	Competition profit or
Pre-manufactured parts	Demand profit or
Labor	Maintenance profit or
Shipping in	Management-determined combination of above
Maintenance	
Supplies	

Total production costs + Markup = Price

FIGURE 15.3
Determinants of pricing

PROBLEM SOLVING STRATEGY

The values of markup and price may be expressed either as a dollar amount or as a percent of cost. As we saw in Chapter 13, using the base, rate, and part, these relationships evolve:

- The total production cost is always the base (B).
- The amount of markup is a part (P).
- The rate of markup (R) refers to cost as the base (B).
- The dollar price is always a part (P).
- The rate of price (R) refers to cost as the base (B).
- Total costs + Markup = Price.

Let's illustrate how the price is determined under this concept:

$3,000 *Raw material or pre-manufactured component*
$4,000 *Variable cost of production*
$2,000 *Fixed cost of production overhead*
$9,000 *Total costs of production*

Using a 75% markup, establish the price:

Total costs	+ Markup	= Price	• The pricing formula.
$9,000	+ 75%	= Price	• Set the variables.
9,000 × .75	= 6,750		• Calculate the markup.
			→ • .75, rate of markup.
			→ • 9,000 total cost, the base.
$9,000	+ $6,750	= $15,750	• Markup added to cost.
$15,750			• The calculated price.

If the total production price of $15,750 results in the creation of 100 units of production, the **unit price** would be calculated as (15,750 ÷ 100) or $157.50 per unit.

To calculate a production price, use the following sequence:

- Calculate the total costs of production (fixed and variable).
- Establish the desired markup (cost of selling and desired profit).
- If markup is expressed as a percent, multiply the percent (R) by the base (total production costs) to obtain the amount of markup.
- Once the amount of markup is determined (can be provided in dollar amount), add the markup amount to the total production costs.
- The sum of these two values is the total production price.
- The total production price divided by the amount of units provided in the production run will provide the unit price.

EXAMPLE 4   The Shoot-Em-Up Gun Company is planning a production of 1,000 small bore rifles. The basic raw materials of wood, steel, and pre-manufactured components are $18,000. Other costs of manufacture are shipping in, $250; supplies, $3,000; and labor, $8,000. Combined fixed costs of overhead are $15,000. Management had determined that its markup for a competitive profit would be 50%.
   a. What is the total price for the rifles?
   b. What is the unit price for each rifle?
   c. What percent of the total costs is the price?
(Note: markup in this problem is a combined amount.)

Solution: Use formulas: Cost + Markup = Price; Part = Base × Rate

a.
$18,000	*Raw materials*	
250	*Shipping in*	
3,000	*Supplies*	
8,000	*Labor*	
$29,250	*Total variable costs*	• Sum of variable costs.
$15,000	*Fixed costs*	• Total of fixed costs.
$44,250	*Total production costs*	• Find the total costs.

The unknown markup is a part, use Part = Base × Rate:

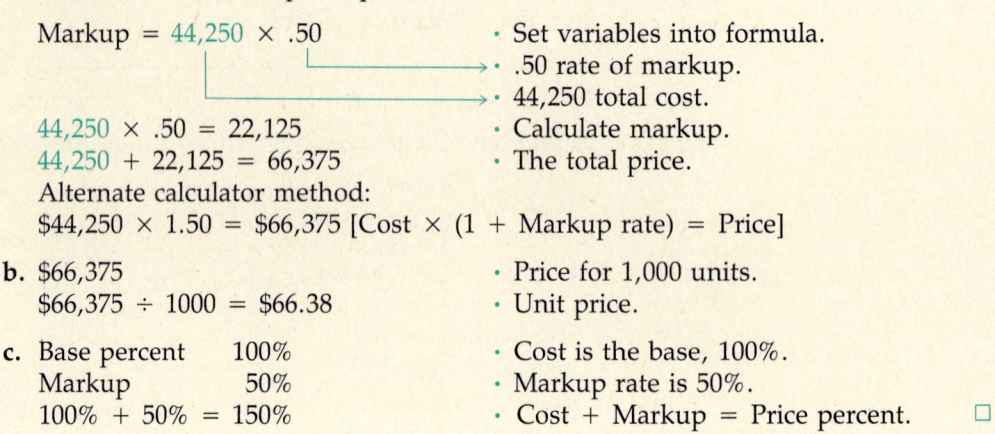

Markup = 44,250 × .50   • Set variables into formula.
                          → • .50 rate of markup.
                          → • 44,250 total cost.

44,250 × .50 = 22,125   • Calculate markup.
44,250 + 22,125 = 66,375   • The total price.

Alternate calculator method:
$44,250 × 1.50 = $66,375 [Cost × (1 + Markup rate) = Price]

b. $66,375   • Price for 1,000 units.
    $66,375 ÷ 1000 = $66.38   • Unit price.

c. Base percent   100%   • Cost is the base, 100%.
    Markup   50%   • Markup rate is 50%.
    100% + 50% = 150%   • Cost + Markup = Price percent.

EXAMPLE 5

The total variable costs for a manufacturing production run of 85 mini-coolers are $1,088. Fixed costs for the production batch are 39% of the total variable costs. If the profit amount is expected to be $850 and the cost of selling is 26% of the total production costs,

     a. What is the manufactured price per unit for the cooler?
     b. What is the rate of markup?

(Note: In this problem, markup is given in its components.)

Solution:

a. 1,088.00   • Total variable costs.
    1,088 × .39 = 424.32   • Fixed costs, 39% of variable costs.
    1,088 + 424.32 = 1,512.32   • Total production costs, the base.

Markup components:
$850   • Profit.
26%   • Selling cost rate.
1,512.32 × .26 = $393.20   • Selling cost, 26% of base.
$850 + $393.20 = $1,243.20   • Total markup.
Price = Cost + Markup   • Formula for total price.
1,512.32 + 1,243.20   → • 1,243.20 total markup.
                        → • 1,512.32 total cost.
1,512.32 + 1,243.20 = $2,755.52   • Total manufactured price.
85   • Coolers manufactured.
$2,755.52 ÷ 85 = 32.4179 or $32.42.   • Price per cooler.

b. Use Rate = Part ÷ Base for the unknown rate of markup:
    Rate = 1,243.20 ÷ 1,512.32   • Set variables into formula.
                               → • 1,512.32 cost is the base.
                               → • 1,243.20 Markup $ is the part.

    1,243.20 ÷ 1,512.32 = .822   • Calculate the markup rate.
    82.2%   • Rate of markup.

✔ CHECK FOR UNDERSTANDING

1. JOBBO Workbench Manufacturers have just received an order for a production run of 1,500 home workbenches. The materials estimate is $45,000; other variable production costs are $14,000; fixed production costs are 62% of total variable costs. The total markup is 80%. What is the unit price? What percent of the total production costs is variable cost?

2. Ringo Tire Company manufactures a steel-belted snow tire. The price per unit of a production batch of 5,000 tires is $21. If the total selling costs are 32% and the profit component is 40%, what are the total production costs?

3. An electric saw with a unit cost of $19.60 is marked up 90%. What is the unit price?

4. Basic materials and all other variable costs for a job lot of 100 men's overcoats is $5,000. The fixed cost of production is 33.2% of variable costs. If the unit price of a coat is $94.60, what is the percent of markup?

SKILL EXERCISES

Solve the following using the base, rate, and part formulas:

	Base		Part		Rate

Calculate the rate:

1. Cost	$62,930	Markup	$ 29,000	Percent	_____ %
2. Cost	$41,000	Markup	$ 15,800	Percent	_____ %
3. Cost	$86,000	Markup	$ 21,000	Percent	_____ %
4. Cost	$51,750	Markup	$ 21,000	Percent	_____ %
5. Cost	$36,400	Markup	$ 16,000	Percent	_____ %

Calculate the part:

6. Cost	$92,500	Markup $ _____	Percent	61%
7. Cost	$ 8,418	Markup $ _____	Percent	85%
8. Cost	$12,132	Markup $ _____	Percent	44%
9. Cost	$25,500	Markup $ _____	Percent	72%
10. Cost	$43,680	Markup $ _____	Percent	42%

Answers to ✔ Check for Understanding
1. $114.70; 61.73%. 2. $61,046.51. 3. $37.24. 4. 42.04%.

Calculate the base:

11. Cost $ _____ Markup $ 61,000 Percent 50%

12. Cost $ _____ Markup $ 38,900 Percent 62%

13. Cost $ _____ Markup $ 58,400 Percent 26%

14. Cost $ _____ Markup $ 98,475 Percent 37%

15. Cost $ _____ Markup $127,300 Percent 42%

Find the missing component:

	Cost	Markup	Price
16.	$132,560	46.8%	$ _____
17.	$ 45,700	38.5%	$ _____
18.	$ 23,120	62.8%	$ _____
19.	$ 65,400	51.5%	$ _____
20.	$ 48,400	_____ %	$ 83,200
21.	$ 65,000	_____ %	$ 95,500
22.	$ 51,370	_____ %	$ 64,726
23.	$ _____	40%	$ 28,000
24.	$ _____	68%	$ 45,230
25.	$ _____	112%	$228,400

APPLICATIONS

Use the base, rate, and part formulas and cost plus markup to find the following values:

1. A specialty item producer priced products at $2.80 each. If the total costs of production per unit are $1.70, what is the percent of markup?

2. Total costs of radio component materials are $6,000; costs of shipping in are $320; other variable production costs are $14,000; and fixed costs are $6,800.
   (a) What are the total costs of production?
   (b) If the production run is 1,800 units, what is the cost per unit?
   (c) If the price per unit is $19, what is the markup percent?
   (d) If the profit component is $2.10, what is the percent of profit?

3. Total costs of production per unit are $157. If the profit markup is 84% and the cost of sales is $14, what is the unit price?

4. A dress manufacturer desires to obtain a $4.50 markup per dress. If the markup is 80% of cost, what is the price?

5. Stark's Unpainted Furniture Factory produces a desk for a unit cost of $36.50. If all variable costs of production except materials are 32% of the unit cost, and the fixed costs of production are 20% of the unit cost, how much is the dollar expenditure for materials per unit?

6. The manufactured cost of a table television is $56.70. If the selling costs of markup are $10 and profit is 40%, what is the price of the product?

7. The total costs of a manufacturing run are $14,200. The profit component of markup is 30% and the cost of selling was $2,800. If there were 1,200 units manufactured, what was the price per unit?

8. The total costs of manufacturing a product are $26,400. If the price for the product is established at $35,376, what is the percent of markup?

9. Variable and fixed costs of manufacturing a product are $149. If the price is $250 and the profit is $50, what is the selling cost percent of markup?

10. If the markup of a product is $82.50, or 40% of the cost, what is the selling price?

Gross and Net Profit

15.3

Total revenue (or income) is the amount of dollars the company receives from the sale of a product. From it, the company deducts the costs of producing and selling to determine the amount of profit. Terms describing profit evolve from the procedure.

By subtracting the fixed and variable costs of producing the product from the revenue, we arrive at a value called **gross profit.**

> Gross profit = Total revenue − Fixed and variable production costs

Gross profit is the total amount of dollars generated from the sale of a product that is in excess of the cost of manufacturing the product.

PROBLEM SOLVING STRATEGY

Recall that the price of a product is a calculation of cost plus markup. Since revenue is what is received from the sale of a product (price), total revenue can be determined by multiplying the unit price by the number of units sold. Another important element shows that since the gross profit equals total revenue minus the cost of production, *total markup and gross profit are identical.* Gross profit may also be identified as the total of the markup per unit multiplied by the total number of units sold.

The procedure for expressing gross profit is illustrated using these formulas:

> Price = Cost + Markup
> Total revenue = Unit price × Units sold
> Gross profit = Total revenue − Total production cost
> Gross profit = Unit markup × Number of units sold
> Gross profit = Total markup

We also look for another type of profit called **net profit**. Net profit is a value derived by subtracting all incurred costs from the revenue—not just the cost of manufacturing. As shown in Figure 15.3, markup includes both the profit and selling costs of a product. If we begin with a price and remove the cost from markup as well as the manufacturing cost, what remains is *net profit—the same as the profit component of markup.* Net profit can be found using any of these methods:

> Net profit = Total markup − Selling costs
> Net profit = Total revenue − Production and selling costs
> Net profit = Profit per unit × Number of units sold
> Net profit = Profit component of markup

EXAMPLE 6 The XYZ Manufacturing Company has provided the following information about the production of its Burn-Up Toaster. Production costs for 1,000 toasters are:

Raw materials and pre-manufactured parts	$4,000
Labor	$2,500
Fixed costs of production	$1,500
Sales cost	$1,000
Profit return	50%

a. Determine total production costs per unit.

Solution:

Materials + Labor + Fixed costs = Total costs
$4,000 + $2,500 + $1,500 = $8,000   • Compute total cost.
Total costs ÷ Number of units = Cost per unit
$8,000 ÷ 1,000 = $8.00   • Find cost per unit.

b. Determine the sales–cost portion of markup in percent.

Solution:

Cost of sales ÷ Total costs = Percent cost of sales
$1,000 ÷ $8,000 = 0.125   • Calculate the percent.
12.5%   • Percent cost of sales.

c. What is the total markup in percent?

Solution:

Percent sales cost + Percent profit = Markup percent
12.5% + 50% = 62.5%   • Markup percent.

d. What is the markup per unit?

Solution:

Profit markup + Cost of sales = Total markup
$4,000 + $1,000 = $5,000   • Find total markup.
Total markup ÷ Number of units = Unit markup
$5,000 ÷ 1,000 = $5.00   • Determine unit markup.

e. What is the price per unit?

Solution:

Total costs + Markup = Total price
8,000 + 5,000 = 13,000   • Calculate total price.
Price ÷ Units = Unit price
13,000 ÷ 1,000 = 13.00   • Compute unit price.

f. What is the total revenue (income) on this product?

Solution:

Price per unit × No. units sold = Total revenue
$13.00 × 1,000 = $13,000   • Find total revenue.

g. What is the gross profit on the sale?

Solution:

Total revenue − Production costs = Gross profit
$13,000 − $8,000 = $5,000   • Calculate gross profit.
(Note: Gross profit = Total markup)

h. What is net profit?

Solution:

Gross profit − Cost of sales = Net profit
$5,000 − $1,000 = $4,000   • Calculate net profit.
(Note: Net profit = Profit component of markup)

✓ CHECK FOR UNDERSTANDING

1. A garden hose manufacturer is planning a production of 30,000 hoses. The estimation of costs and markup is as follows:

    Production costs
       Raw materials and pre-manufactured parts $75,000
       Labor $12,000
       Fixed costs $28,000
    Markup
       Cost of sales   20%
       Profit return   180%

    (a) What is the expected revenue from the total production?
    (b) What is the gross profit?
    (c) What is the net profit per hose?

2. The cost data for the production of 5,000 microwave ovens revealed the following:
   Materials and parts $350,000
   Labor $100,000
   Fixed costs of overhead $ 25,000

   If the cost of sales was $120,000 and the company desired a 70% profit return, what would the unit price to a distributor be for the oven? What is the net profit per unit?

SKILL EXERCISES

Use the base, rate, and part formulas to find the missing component:

	Production cost	Sales cost	Percent profit	Total price
1.	$ 64,000	$28,000	_____ %	$134,000
2.	$ 28,000	$36,000	_____ %	$ 95,000
3.	$126,000	$14,000	68%	$ _____
4.	$ 62,000	$28,000	91%	$ _____
5.	$ 18,000	$31,000	45.2%	$ _____

Solve for the missing component:

	Production cost	Percent cost of sales	Profit	Total price
6.	$56,000	26%	$12,000	$ _____
7.	$14,500	42%	$13,950	$ _____
8.	$26,280	_____ %	$46,000	$ 96,000
9.	$93,720	_____ %	$50,000	$182,000
10.	$74,000	_____ %	$26,500	$134,000

Solve for the missing component:

	Production cost	Percent cost of sales	Percent profit	Total price
11.	$82,400	36%	49%	$ _____
12.	$96,752	18%	62%	$ _____

Answers to ✓ Check for Understanding
1. (a) $345,000. (b) $230,000. (c) $6.90.   2. $185.50; $66.50.

13. $ _____	26%	84%	$127,000
14. $ _____	57%	73%	$185,000
15. $ _____	13%	97%	$226,000

APPLICATIONS

Use the base, rate, and part formulas with cost and profit formulas to find the needed solution:

1. A dress manufacturer is planning to make 1,500 dresses.

   Production costs
   - Material $ 7,500
   - Labor $10,500
   - Fixed costs $12,000

   Markup
   - Cost of sales   6,000
   - Profit return   90%

   (a) What is the total revenue from the dresses?
   (b) What is the gross profit?
   (c) What is the net profit per dress?

2. A macrame potholder manufacturer estimates that costs and markup for 3,000 deluxe units are as follows:

   - Materials $ 3,300
   - Labor $ 7,000
   - Fixed costs $ 1,000
   - Profit return $15,700
   - Cost of sales $ 1,000

   (a) What percent of revenue is the gross profit?
   (b) What percent of cost is the net profit?
   (c) What is the total markup percent?

3. A sporting goods company produces 2,000 units of tennis equipment:

   Production
   - Variable costs $ 68,000
   - Fixed costs $ 30,000

   Markup
   - Cost of sales $ 62,800
   - Profit return $140,000

   (a) What is the unit price?
   (b) What is the gross profit per unit?

4. The total price of a 2,200-unit production run is $426,000. If profit is 63% and cost of sales is 48%, what are the production costs per unit?

5. Production costs to produce a binary code decoder unit is $16,200 and the percent of sales cost is 14%. If the product profit is $22,000, what is the total price?

Section 15.3 Gross and Net Profit

6. For the following production data of 500 units, determine the unit price and the net profit per unit sold:

Production	
Variable costs	$26,000
Fixed costs	$ 6,000
Markup	
Cost of sales	$19,200
Profit return	$38,000

7. If total revenue from the sale of a product is $114,000 and the gross profit is $64,000, what percent of the revenue is the total production cost?

8. Jigkowski Irish Linen Company projects income from a manufacturing product at $450,000. Total production costs are $250,000. If the cost of sales is 20% of the total production costs, what is the markup percent of profit?

9. Production costs for 2,000 products are $115,000 and profit markup is 61%. With a total selling price of $207,000, what is the cost of sales per unit?

10. The total price for a 6,500-unit production batch is $144,000. If cost of sales is 32% and profit markup is 38%, what are the production costs per unit?

Key Terms

Competition profit (424)
Cost (418)
Demand profit (424)
Fixed cost (418)
Gross profit (429)
Markup (424)
Net profit (430)

Profit (424)
Shipping-in (420)
Total markup (424)
Total revenue (429)
Unit cost (430)
Variable cost (419)

Looking Back

Although total costs may be the same for two different manufacturers, the mix of fixed costs and variable costs can provide a distinctly different profit structure. (See Appendix B.)

Total markup is generally referred to as gross profit. However, markup is not all net profit; it also contains selling costs. Net income is used on financial statements rather than net profit.

The concepts of profit discussed in this chapter use cost as a reference. Profit can be expressed with margin as well. There are no manufacturing costs incurred in the wholesale and retail levels, so the cost of the goods is used in place of total manufacturing cost. Operating costs are included in selling costs; therefore, all of the formula expressions for profit (gross and net) would be the same.

Let's Review

1. Dimore Company has just received its annual cost structure:

Buildings	$120,000
Utilities	$ 8,500
Labor	$240,000
Raw materials	$ 88,000
Production supplies	$ 78,000
Security	$ 3,900
Pre-manufactured parts	$143,000
Administrative salaries	$116,000
Telephone	$ 5,200
Licenses	$ 2,700

   (a) What are the total fixed costs?
   (b) What are the total variable costs?
   (c) What percent of variable costs is labor?
   (d) What percent of total costs are administrative salaries?

2. Variable costs were 48% of total costs. If variable costs were $150,000, what were the total costs?

3. Fixed costs this year were reduced 16.5% from last year. This year's total costs are $675,000 and variable costs are $375,000. What were last year's fixed costs?

4. Total costs of a company ran $127,000 for the year. If its total fixed costs were $27,559, what percent of total costs were variable?

5. Total costs for a company ran $748,000 for the year. If the variable costs were 54%, what was the amount of fixed costs?

6. A coffee table costs $88 to produce. If the total markup is $66, what is the percent of markup? What is the price?

7. HOTO Electrical, a component maker, prices its component Number A-68-7 at $12.42. If the markup is 45%, what does the component cost to manufacture?

8. A shoe manufacturer desires to obtain a markup of $3.60 per pair of shoes. If the markup is 72%, what is the cost of the shoe to the manufacturer?

9. Raw materials and other variable costs of a product total $65,000. If the price of the product is $142,000 and total markup is 50%, what are the fixed costs?

10. Hangfire Casket Company received an order for 100 new units. The materials and other production costs total $125,600. If the markup is 83.7%, what is the unit price per casket?

11. Gogone Scooter Works has provided the following information on the production of its new Bustum Scooter. For production of 2,500 scooters, costs are

Raw materials and pre-manufactured parts	$105,000
Labor	$ 60,000
Fixed costs	$ 35,000
Sales costs	$ 8,000
Profit return	40%

    (a) What is the production cost per unit?
    (b) What is the selling price per unit?
    (c) What is the markup percent?
    (d) What is total revenue?
    (e) What is total net profit?

12. If production costs are $65,000, cost of sales is 80%, and desired profit is $15,000, what is the total price?

13. Production costs for a product batch are $62,000. If sales costs are $17,000 and the total price is $105,000, what is the profit percent of markup?

14. The total price for a 6,500-unit production batch is $144,000. If the cost of sales is 32% and profit markup is 38%, what are the production costs per unit?

15. The gross profit for a production run is $86,000. The total price for all of the units is $231,000. If the selling cost is 12%, what is the total net profit?

16. A production run of 1,000 units had a total markup of $12,600. The profit component of markup was $7,500. If the percent of markup profit was 35%, what was the unit price for the product? What was the total selling cost?

17. Total variable costs for a production run were $67,300. If the fixed costs were 28% of total costs, what were the fixed costs?

18. The unit price of a product was $106.40. The total markup was 74%. If the variable cost percent for production was 42%, what was the amount of fixed cost for production?

19. The total markup of a product amounted to $486.20. The rate of markup was 55%. What was the product price?

20. The total manufactured price for 800 units amounted to $226,000. If the profit percent of markup was 32% and the selling cost percent was 28%, what was the production cost per unit?

Chapter Test

1. Analyze the following production cost data:

Buildings	$ 26,000
Licenses	$ 1,200
Communications	$ 3,650
Administrative salaries	$ 29,200
Labor	$ 36,400
Materials and supplies	$128,500
Shipping-in	$ 6,350

   (a) What percent of total costs is fixed?
   (b) What percent of variable cost is labor?

2. If variable costs of production total $46,200 and they are 54% of total costs, what is the amount of total fixed costs?

3. The total price of a production run is $240,000. The total markup is 41% and the fixed costs of production are 26%. What are the variable costs of production?

4. Total costs of production for a manufacturing component are $36.80. If the component sells for $74, what is the rate of markup?

5. A manufacturer priced a product at $2,460. The total costs of production were $896 and the selling cost amounted to 48%. What was the amount of net profit for the product?

6. A production run of 500 units carried a total production cost of $36,300. If the markup was 62%, what was the price per unit? What was the total gross profit?

7. Total costs for a production run of 2,000 units were $142,000. The total markup was 78%. If the cost of selling was $28,224.72, what was the net profit per unit?

8. Variable costs of production for 600 units were $36,742. Fixed costs totaled $28,218. If the total markup was 84%, what was the unit price?

9. Fixed costs of production totaled $74,000. This was 24% of total costs. If the total price for the product was $560,000, what was the amount of gross profit?

10. Total production costs for a production run of 5,000 units were listed at $72,500. The total markup was 66%. The percent of markup needed to cover selling cost was 18%.
    (a) What was the unit price?
    (b) What was the amount of net profit per unit?
    (c) What was the amount of gross profit?

PART VI
Mathematics for Business Decisions

Financial Statements and Ratios

16

OBJECTIVES

When you complete this chapter you will be able to:

- *Conduct vertical analyses of various categories on the balance sheet and income statement. (16.1)*
- *Perform horizontal analyses of each category from different years on the balance sheet and income statement. (16.2)*
- *Calculate performance ratios such as the current ratio, acid-test ratio, debt-to-equity ratio, and income-to-equity ratio from financial statements. (16.3)*

COMING UP

Owners, managers, investors, union officials, bankers, employees, and government agencies all want the same type of information—information contained in financial statements. These statements show how a business is doing. Do you know how to evaluate the information you have in order to tell them?

The two most common statements created by businesses are the balance sheet and the income statement. Your ability to analyze these documents can be greatly enhanced if you understand how to show comparisons and ratios. This chapter tells you what the important analysis elements are and shows you how to calculate these relationships.

Vertical Analysis

16.1

A **financial statement** is a periodic report showing some phase of the financial condition of an organization. **Vertical analysis** is the comparison of two numbers on the same financial statement. The relationship between the two numbers (that is, the relationship of a part to a base), expressed as a percentage, is a rate. In itself, such a rate is not meaningful; it yields meaningful information only when compared with rates in previous financial statements or when compared with an industry standard.

For example, let's say that a comparison of advertising expenses (the part) to net sales (the base) on a given financial statement yields a rate of 4%. This doesn't mean much without some standard of comparison. Is this higher (or lower) than it should be? Compared with the industry standard for advertising, which nationwide shows a rate of 5.5% for this year, 4% is low. Management can use this comparison alone, or several comparisons that show a trend, to decide the appropriate course of action to take.

Vertical Analysis—Balance Sheet

The **balance sheet** is a financial statement showing the **assets** (what is owned), the **liabilities** (what is owed), and the **owner's equity** (what he/she is worth) on a specific date. Figure 16.1 shows the balance sheet for The Banner Company for December

THE BANNER COMPANY
Balance Sheet
December 31, 198X

Assets (owned)

Cash	$ 7,250	
Accounts receivable	$13,000	
Merchandise inventory	$ 3,075	
Equipment	$ 6,150	
Total assets		$29,475

Liabilities (owed)

Accounts payable	$ 3,150	
Notes payable	$ 4,750	
Total liabilities		$ 7,900

Owner's Equity (worth)

James Banner, capital		$21,575
Total liabilities and owner's equity		$29,475

Balance sheet

31, 198X. It shows several asset and liability accounts and one equity account. In addition, it shows the total assets of $29,475 are the same as the total liabilities plus total equity, $29,475. This is the **fundamental accounting equation** [Assets (A) = Liabilities (L) + Owner's Equity (OE)]. It also shows that there are two groups with claims on the assets of The Banner Company, the owners and the **creditors,** those that are owed money. The percent each group has of the total assets is important and is discussed in the section on ratios.

The formula for vertical analysis is one we have used before. To solve for rate, we use $R = P \div B$. The vertical analysis of the asset section uses total assets as its base. Therefore, when the analysis is completed, all of the rates of the items in the asset section added together will equal 100%. The analysis of the liability and owner's equity section uses the total liabilities and owner's equity as the base. Therefore, when all of those rates are added together, they should also equal 100%. Occasionally isolated percents in some problems are rounded up in order to equal 100%.

EXAMPLE 1 Using The Banner Company balance sheet that follows, calculate the rate of each asset, liability, and owner equity account. Use *total assets* as the base for the assets and *total liabilities* and *owner's equity* as the base for liability and equity accounts.

THE BANNER COMPANY
Balance Sheet
December 31, 198X

Assets (owned)

	Dollars	Rate
Cash	$ 5,250	23.73%
Merchandise inventory	11,000	49.72%
Accounts receivable	1,025	4.63%
Equipment	4,850	21.92%
Total assets	$22,125	100.00%

Liabilities (owed)

	Dollars	Rate
Accounts payable	$ 2,375	10.73%
Notes payable	4,000	18.08%
Total liabilities	$ 6,375	28.81%

Owner's Equity (worth)

	Dollars	Rate
James Banner, capital	$15,750	71.19%
Total liabilities and owner's equity	$22,125	100.00%

Solution:

- Compare each asset account to total assets using the formula $R = P \div B$. Percents must add to 100 for each section.

$5250 \div $22,125 = .2373
or 23.73%*

- Calculate the rate of cash to total assets.
- Calculate the rates of merchandise inventory, accounts receivable, and equipment in the same manner.

* Note: All rates in this chapter are rounded to hundredths place.

23.73% + 49.72% + 4.63%
  + 21.92% = 100.0%

$2375 ÷ $22,125 = .1073 = 10.73%

- Total the four percents = 100%.
- Calculate the rate of accounts payable; use liabilities and owner's equity as base.
- Calculate notes payable and James Banner, capital, in the same manner.

10.73% + 18.08% + 71.19% = 100.0%
$6375 ÷ $22,125 = 28.81%

- Total the three percents.
- Calculate the total liabilities. This figure is also the total of accounts payable (10.73%) plus notes payable (18.08%).

CALCULATOR TIP

Use your constant divisor throughout this chapter to improve accuracy and save time of re-entry. Use Example 1 as an illustration:

Cash	5250 ÷ 22125 = .237288	• Total asset base (22125) is now in constant divisor position.
Mdse. inventory	11000 = .497175	
Accts. receivable	1025 = .046328	
Equipment	4850 = .219209	
Accts. payable	2375 = .107345	• New base, but the number is actually the same, so don't re-enter.
Notes payable	4000 = .180791	
Capital	15750 = .711864	
Total liabilities	6375 = .288146	• Proving total of liabilities.

✓ CHECK FOR UNDERSTANDING

1. Make a vertical analysis of the balance sheet for The Computer Store. Use total assets as the base for the asset section and use the total of the liabilities and owner's equity sections as the base for those two.

THE COMPUTER STORE
Balance Sheet
December 31, 198X

Assets (owned)

Cash	$ 20,000	_____ %
Securities	40,000	_____ %
Accounts receivable	14,000	_____ %
Merchandise inventory	68,000	_____ %
Building	135,000	_____ %
Equipment	21,000	_____ %
Total assets	$298,000	100.00%

Answers to ✓ Check for Understanding
1. Cash = 6.71%; securities = 13.42%; accounts receivable = 4.70%; merchandise inventory = 22.82%; building = 45.30%; equipment = 7.05%; accounts payable = 1.34%; notes payable = 6.04%; payroll taxes payable = .67%; mortgage payable = 17.45%; Fred Barnes, capital = 49.66%; Betty Barnes, capital = 24.83%.

Liabilities (owed)

Accounts payable	$ 4,000	_____%
Notes payable	18,000	_____%
Payroll taxes payable	2,000	_____%
Mortgage payable	52,000	_____%
Total liabilities	$ 76,000	25.50%

Owner's Equity (worth)

Fred Barnes, capital	148,000	_____%
Betty Barnes, capital	74,000	_____%
Total owner's equity	$222,000	74.50%
Total liabilities and owner's equity	$298,000	100.00%

SKILL EXERCISES

In Problems 1–5, calculate the rate of each asset account using the total assets as the base. In Problems 6–10, calculate the rate of each liability and owner equity account using total liabilities and owner's equity as the base. Problems 1–5 are not related to Problems 6–10.

1. Cash	$ 8,570	_____%
2. Accounts receivable	12,340	_____%
3. Merchandise inventory	21,772	_____%
4. Building	80,000	_____%
5. Land	27,000	_____%
Total assets	$149,682	100.00%
6. Accounts payable	$ 11,115	_____%
7. Notes payable	5,830	_____%
8. Mortgage payable	41,175	_____%
9. James Ashton, capital	89,644	_____%
10. Bill Lofton, capital	33,416	_____%
Total liabilities and owner's equity	$181,180	100.00%

Vertical Analysis—Income Statement

The **income statement** shows the amount of revenue, the cost of goods sold if the business sells merchandise, the expenses, and the net income or net loss for a period of time. See Figure 16.2.

THE WOODWARD COMPANY
Income Statement
For the Year Ended December 31, 198X

Revenue:		
Consultant fees		$62,000
Operating expenses:		
Salaries	$32,000	
Advertising	$ 4,100	
Rent	$ 5,100	
Vehicle maintenance	$ 200	
Utilities	$ 2,600	
Miscellaneous	$ 375	
Total operating expenses		$44,375
Net income		$17,625

FIGURE 16.2
Income statement

The analysis is performed in the same manner as the balance sheet except there is only one base, the net sales (net revenue) figure. As a result, every category is compared to net sales (100%).

EXAMPLE 2   Calculate the rate of each income statement entry using net sales as the base.

THE MMM CHEESE CORPORATION
Income Statement
For the Year Ended June 30, 198X

	Dollars	Rate
Revenue:		
Sales	$ 375,750	102.04%
Sales returns and allowances	− 7,515	− 2.04%
Net sales	368,235	100.00%
Cost of goods sold	−220,941	− 60.00%
Gross profit	$ 147,294	40.00%
Expenses:		
Advertising	$ 22,094	6.00%
Delivery	29,459	8.00%
Salaries and wages	36,824	10.00%
Utilities	4,840	1.32%
Maintenance	3,200	.87%
Miscellaneous	1,150	.31%
Total expenses	− 97,567	− 26.50%
Net income	$ 49,727	13.50%

Solution:

$375,750 \div $368,235 = 1.0204$
or 102.04%

- Compare each item to net sales; use the formula $R = P \div B$.
- Calculate the rate of sales to net sales; rate is over 100%.
- Calculate the rate of sales returns and allowances, cost of goods sold, and gross profit in the same manner.
- Calculate the rate of each expense; divide each dollar figure by $368,235.

$97,567 \div $368,235 = 26.50%$

- Calculate the rate of total expense. Should agree with the *total* of four expense rates.

$26.50\% + 13.50\% = 40\%$

- Verify the rates of total expense and net income; must equal rate of gross profit.
- Verify the rates of gross profit and cost of goods sold; add them together.

$40\% + 60\% = 100\%$

EXAMPLE 3   Calculate the rate of each entry in the Woodward Company income statement using the consultant fees as the base.

THE WOODWARD COMPANY
Income Statement
For the Year Ended March 31, 198X

	Dollars	Rate
Revenue:		
Consultant fees	$56,000	100.00%
Operating expenses:		
Salaries	24,000	42.86%
Advertising	4,000	7.14%
Rent	4,800	8.57%
Vehicle maintenance	250	.45%
Utilities	2,400	4.29%
Miscellaneous	500	.89%
Total expenses	$35,950	64.20%
Net income	$20,050	35.80%

Solution:

$24,000 \div $56,000 = 42.86\%$

$20,050 \div $56,000 = 35.80\%$
$35,950 \div $56,000 = 64.20\%$

$35.80\% + 64.20\% = 100\%$

- Compare each item to the consultant fees using the formula $R = P \div B$.
- Calculate the rate of salaries.
- Calculate the rate of each expense in the same manner.
- Calculate the rate of net income.
- Calculate the rate of total expenses; verify by adding all expense rates together.
- Verify the correctness; add the net income rate and the total expenses rate to arrive at 100%.

CHECK FOR UNDERSTANDING

1. Do a vertical analysis on the following income statement using net sales as the base:

MERCHANDISE WAREHOUSE
Income Statement
For the Quarter Ended December 31, 198X

	Dollars	Rate
Revenue:		
Sales	$ 28,685.00	_____ %
Sales returns and allowances	− 430.00	_____ %
Net sales	28,255.00	100.00%
Cost of goods sold	−18,358.40	_____ %
Gross margin	$ 9,896.60	_____ %
Expenses:		
Salaries	$ 3,285.00	_____ %
Delivery	480.00	_____ %
Utilities	382.00	_____ %
Advertising	970.00	_____ %
Payroll tax	230.00	_____ %
Total expenses	$ 5,347.00	18.92%
Net income	$ 4,549.60	_____ %

SKILL EXERCISES

Using professional fees as the base on the following partial income statement, calculate the rate that each expense represents.

Professional fees	$107,500	100.00%
1. Salary expense	$ 27,786	_____ %
2. Delivery expense	$ 8,348	_____ %
3. Advertising expense	$ 7,000	_____ %
4. Utilities expense	$ 1,386	_____ %
5. Depreciation expense	$ 6,935	_____ %

Answers to ✔ Check for Understanding
1. Sales 101.52%; sales returns and allowances −1.52%; cost of goods sold 64.97%; gross margin 35.03%; salaries 11.62%; delivery 1.70%; utilities 1.35%; advertising 3.43%; payroll tax .81%; net income 16.10%.

APPLICATIONS

1. Perform a vertical analysis on the balance sheet for the Long's Peak Pharmaceutical Company.

LONG'S PEAK PHARMACEUTICAL COMPANY
Balance Sheet
June 30, 198X

Assets

	Dollars	Rate
Cash	$ 4,550	_____%
Securities	7,150	_____%
Accounts receivable	1,440	_____%
Merchandise inventory	62,125	_____%
Building	92,335	_____%
Equipment	1,160	_____%
Total assets	$168,760	100%

Liabilities

	Dollars	Rate
Accounts payable	$ 545	_____%
Notes payable	715	_____%
Taxes payable	250	_____%
Mortgage payable	61,950	_____%
Total liabilities	$ 63,460	_____%

Owner's Equity

	Dollars	Rate
Mary C. Blake, capital	$105,300	_____%
Total liabilities and owner's equity	$168,760	100%

2. Perform a vertical analysis on the following income statement for the years 198X and 198Y using net sales as the base.

FURNITURE SALES
Income Statement
For the Years Ended March 31, 198X and 198Y

	198X Dollars	198X Rate	198Y Dollars	198Y Rate
Revenue:				
Sales	$132,425.00	____%	$139,920.00	____%
Less sales returned	−11,850.00	____%	−11,235.00	____%
Net sales	120,575.00	100%	128,685.00	100%
Cost of goods sold	66,316.25	____%	71,742.00	____%
Gross margin	$ 54,258.75	____%	$ 56,943.00	____%

(continued)

	198X Dollars	198X Rate	198Y Dollars	198Y Rate
Expenses:				
Salary	$ 11,936.25	____%	$ 12,105.00	____%
Delivery	3,370.00	____%	3,000.00	____%
Advertising	16,800.00	____%	14,450.00	____%
Insurance	1,500.00	____%	1,620.00	____%
Depreciation	8,000.00	____%	6,000.00	____%
Total expenses	$ 41,606.25	____%	$ 37,175.00	____%
Net income	$ 12,652.50	____%	$ 19,768.00	____%

3. Complete the vertical analysis of the following balance sheet for both 198X and 198Y.

Assets

	198X Dollars	198X Rate	198Y Dollars	198Y Rate
Cash	$ 4,850	____%	$ 4,150	____%
Accounts receivable	1,750	____%	2,835	____%
Merchandise inventory	15,250	____%	16,975	____%
Equipment	3,150	____%	3,715	____%
Total assets	$25,000	100%	$27,675	100%

Liabilities

Accounts payable	480	____%	950	____%
Notes payable	1,220	____%	600	____%
Total liabilities	$ 1,700	____%	$ 1,550	____%

Stockholder's Equity

Capital	20,000	____%	20,000	____%
Retained earnings	3,300	____%	6,125	____%
Total stockholder's equity	23,300	____%	26,125	____%
Total liabilities and stockholder's equity	$25,000	100%	$27,675	100%

4. Perform a vertical analysis on the income statement for the Coto Real Estate Corp. for the quarter ended March 31, 198X.

Revenue:		
Fees	$18,335	100.00 %
Expenses:		
Advertising	1,968	____%
Depreciation	3,175	____%

Expenses (continued):

Utilities	435	_____%
Insurance	157	_____%
Wages	3,400	_____%
Total expenses	$ 9,135	_____%
Net income	$ 9,200	_____%

Horizontal Analysis

16.2

Horizontal analysis is a comparison of like figures on a balance sheet or income statement from different years, the same quarter from different years, or the same month from different years. When we analyze, we compare like items and calculate the increase or decrease and the rate of increase or decrease.

As in vertical analysis, we use the formula $R = P \div B$ to calculate the rate of increase or decrease. Use the oldest time information as the base.

Horizontal Analysis—Balance Sheet

EXAMPLE 4 Analyze the balance sheet for The Banner Company showing both the dollars and rates of increase or decrease. Place all negative amounts in parentheses.

THE BANNER COMPANY
Balance Sheet
December 31, 198X and 198Y

Assets

	198X	198Y	Dollars Increase/(Decrease)	Rate Increase/(Decrease)
Cash	$ 5,250	$ 5,750	$ 500	9.52%
Merchandise inventory	11,000	8,000	$(3,000)	(27.27%)
Accounts receivable	1,025	1,500	$ 475	46.34%
Equipment	4,850	5,050	$ 200	4.12%
Total assets	$22,125	$20,300	$(1,825)	(8.25%)

Liabilities

Accounts payable	$ 2,375	$ 1,565	$ (810)	(34.11%)
Notes payable	4,000	2,750	$(1,250)	(31.25%)
Total liabilities	$ 6,375	$ 4,315	$(2,060)	(32.31%)

Owner's Equity

James Banner, capital	15,750	15,985	$ 235	1.49%
Total liabilities and owner's equity	$22,125	$20,300	$(1,825)	(8.25%)

Solution:

- Calculate the dollars of increase or decrease; compare each item in 198X with the same item in 198Y and find the difference. If 198Y is larger, there is an increase; if smaller, a decrease.

$5750 - $5250 = $500
- Calculate the cash increase or decrease: since 198Y is larger, there is an increase.

$500 ÷ $5250 = 9.52%
- Calculate the rate of cash increase or decrease; use $R = P \div B$. Base is the oldest date; that is the number that changed (198X).
- Proceed in the same manner through the remaining items, calculating dollars of increase or decrease and then the rate of increase or decrease. Place all negative amounts or rates in parentheses. □

CALCULATOR TIP

If you always enter the figure for the most recent year in the calculator first (198Y in Example 4), the calculator will correctly display whether it is a positive change (increase) or a negative change (decrease). For example on merchandise inventory:

Enter 8000 [−]
11000 [=] −3000
[÷] 11000 [=] −27.27%

- 198Y data entered first.
- Decrease between years.
- Percent of decrease as negative.

Your calculator will divide a negative number by a positive number and display the correct rate change. Only the first two items on the balance sheet will be completed to give you the pattern: 5750 − 5250 = 500 ÷ 5250 = .0952 (positive); 8000 − 11000 = −3000 ÷ 11000 = −.2727 (negative); etc.

✓ **CHECK FOR UNDERSTANDING**

1. Make a horizontal analysis of the 198X and 198Y years on the balance sheet for Artful Crafts Inc. Place all negative figures in parentheses.

ARTFUL CRAFTS INC.
Balance Sheet
December 31, 198X and 198Y

Assets

	198X	198Y	Dollars Increase/(Decrease)	Rate Increase/(Decrease)
Cash	$ 8,085.50	$ 9,555.00	$ _____	_____%
Accounts receivable	1,175.00	975.00	$ _____	_____%
Merchandise inventory	13,235.00	15,200.00	$ _____	_____%
Equipment	6,800.00	7,000.00	$ _____	_____%
Total assets	$29,295.50	$32,730.00	$3,434.50	11.72%

Liabilities

Accounts payable	$ 2,025.00	$ 3,425.00	$ _____	_____ %
Taxes payable	175.00	190.00	$ _____	_____ %
Long-term liabilities	4,875.00	3,600.00	$ _____	_____ %
Total liabilities	$ 7,075.00	$ 7,215.00	$140	1.98%

Stockholder's Equity

Capital	$15,000.00	$15,000.00	$ -0-	-0-%
Retained earnings	7,220.50	10,515.00	$ _____	_____ %
Total stockholder's equity	$22,220.50	$25,515.00	$3,294.50	14.83%
Total liabilities and stockholder's equity	$29,295.50	$32,730.00	$3,434.50	11.72%

Horizontal Analysis—Income Statement

EXAMPLE 5 Using the 198X and 198Y data on the Woodward Company income statement, make a horizontal analysis. Calculate both the dollars and rate of increase or decrease. Place any negative figures in parentheses.

THE WOODWARD COMPANY
Income Statement
For the Years Ended December 31, 198X and 198Y

	198X	198Y	Dollars Increase/ (Decrease)	Rate Increase/ (Decrease)
Revenue:				
Consultant fees	$56,000	$62,000	$6,000	10.71%
Operating expenses:				
Salaries	$24,000	$32,000	$8,000	33.33%
Advertising	4,000	4,100	100	2.50%
Rent	4,800	5,100	300	6.25%
Vehicle maintenance	250	200	(50)	20.00%
Utilities	2,400	2,600	200	8.33%
Miscellaneous	500	375	(125)	(25.00)%
Total operating expenses	$35,950	$44,375	$8,425	23.44%
Net income	$20,050	$17,625	$(2,425)	(12.09)%

Solution:

Consultant fees
$62,000 − $56,000 = $6000

- Calculate the amount of increase or decrease; compare 198X data to 198Y data and find the difference. If 198Y is larger, there is an increase; if smaller, a decrease.

Answers to ✓ Check for Understanding
1. Cash $1469.50 and 18.17%; accounts receivable ($200) and (17.02%); merchandise inventory $1,965 and 14.85%; equipment $200 and 2.94%; accounts payable $1,400 and 69.14%; taxes payable $15 and 8.57%; long-term liabilities ($1,275) and (26.15%); retained earnings $3,294.50 and 45.63%.

$6000 \div \$56,000 = 10.71\%$

- Calculate the rate of increase or decrease; use the formula $R = P \div B$. Oldest date is base.
- Proceed in the same manner for each item; place all negatives in parentheses.

✔ CHECK FOR UNDERSTANDING

1. Compare the 198X and 198Y income statement figures for Unique Antique Shops Inc. Calculate the amount and rate of increase or decrease for each item on the statement. Place all negative figures in parentheses. Verify the totals where possible.

UNIQUE ANTIQUE SHOPS INC.
Income Statement
For the Years Ended December 31, 198X and 198Y

	198X	198Y	Dollars Increase/ (Decrease)	Rate Increase/ (Decrease)
Revenue:				
Sales	$ 80,000	$ 97,500	$ _____	_____%
Less sales returned	− 2,275	− 2,775	$ _____	_____%
Net sales	$ 77,725	$ 94,725	$ _____	_____%
Cost of goods sold	−48,000	−57,780	$ _____	_____%
Gross margin	$ 29,725	$ 36,945	$ _____	_____%
Operating expenses:				
Salary	$ 13,000	$ 13,800	$ _____	_____%
Supplies	575	595	$ _____	_____%
Rent	2,200	2,375	$ _____	_____%
Utilities	900	1,050	$ _____	_____%
Total operating expenses	$ 16,675	$ 17,820	$ _____	_____%
Profit before taxes	$ 13,050	$ 19,125	$6,075	46.55%
Less federal taxes	1,957.50	3,346.90	$1,389.40	70.98%
Net income	$ 11,092.50	$ 15,778.10	$ _____	_____%

SKILL EXERCISES

Use the balance sheet figures from 198X and 198Y to compute the increase or decrease and the rate of increase or decrease for Problems 1–5. Enclose all negative figures in parentheses. Complete income statement Problems 6–10 in the same manner.

Answers to ✔ Check for Understanding
1. Sales $17,500 and 21.875%; sales returned $500 and 21.98%; net sales $17,000 and 21.87%; cost of goods sold $9,780 and 20.375%; gross margin $7,220 and 24.29%; salary $800 and 6.15%; supplies $20 and 3.48%; rent $175 and 7.95%; utilities $150 and 16.67%; total operating expenses $1,145 and 6.87%; net income $4,685.60 and 42.24%.

	198X	198Y	Dollars Increase/ (Decrease)	Rate Increase/ (Decrease)
1. Cash	$ 6,745	$ 7,125	$ _____	_____%
2. Equipment	$15,450	$ 12,770	$ _____	_____%
3. Notes payable	$ 3,984	$ 8,258	$ _____	_____%
4. Mortgage payable	$24,752	$ 21,990	$ _____	_____%
5. J. Mark, capital	$47,585	$ 51,885	$ _____	_____%
6. Sales	$89,228	$110,576	$ _____	_____%
7. Depreciation expense	$ 7,776	$ 5,998	$ _____	_____%
8. Delivery expense	$ 1,143	$ 1,538	$ _____	_____%
9. Supplies expense	$ 660	$ 414	$ _____	_____%
10. Utilities	$ 968	$ 1,040	$ _____	_____%

APPLICATIONS

1. Using the balance sheet figures for 198X and 198Y, compute the amount of increase or decrease and the rate of increase or decrease for each item on the ABC Auto Parts statement. Place all negative figures in parentheses. Verify totals.

ABC AUTO PARTS
Balance Sheet
March 31, 198X and 198Y

Assets

	198X	198Y	Dollars Increase/ (Decrease)	Rate Increase/ (Decrease)
Current assets				
Cash	$ 5,500	$ 7,050	$ _____	_____%
Accounts receivable	3,750	3,975	$ _____	_____%
Notes receivable	1,850	500	$ _____	_____%
Merchandise inventory	25,375	28,650	$ _____	_____%
Prepaid insurance	1,000	650	$ _____	_____%
Total current assets	$ 37,475	$ 40,825	$ _____	_____%

(continued)

Assets (continued)

	198X	198Y	Dollars Increase/ (Decrease)	Rate Increase/ (Decrease)
Long-term assets				
Land	$ 13,450	$ 13,450	$ _____	_____%
Buildings	62,695	59,250	$ _____	_____%
Equipment	6,000	9,000	$ _____	_____%
Total long-term assets	$ 82,145	$ 81,700	$ _____	_____%
Total assets	$119,620	$122,525	$ _____	_____%

Liabilities

	198X	198Y		
Current liabilities				
Accounts payable	$ 13,000	$ 14,870	$ _____	_____%
Notes payable	62,695	59,250	$ _____	_____%
Taxes payable	1,015	1,305	$ _____	_____%
Total current liabilities	$ 16,790	$ 18,605	$ _____	_____%
Long-term liabilities				
Mortgage payable	$ 28,525	$ 28,225	$ _____	_____%
Total liabilities	$ 45,315	$ 46,830	$ _____	_____%

Owner's Equity

Harvey Martin, capital	73,305	75,695	$ _____	_____%
Total liabilities and owner's equity	$119,620	$122,525	$ _____	_____%

2. Make a horizontal comparative analysis of the income statement for the Security Supply Company, showing both the amount and rate of increase or decrease between 198X and 198Y. Place all negative figures in parentheses.

SECURITY SUPPLY COMPANY
Income Statement
For the Years Ended June 30, 198X and 198Y

	198X	198Y	Amount	Rate
Revenue:				
Sales	$200,365	$217,880	$ _____	_____%
Less sales returns	− 8,365	− 8,925	$ _____	_____%
Net sales	$192,000	$208,955	$ _____	_____%
Cost of goods sold				
Merchandise inventory, January 1	$ 62,385	$ 86,000	$ _____	_____%
Purchases	152,255	141,500	$ _____	_____%
Goods available for sale	$214,640	$227,500	$ _____	_____%
Less merchandise inventory, Dec. 31	−86,000	−87,500	$ _____	_____%
Cost of goods sold	$128,640	$140,000	$ _____	_____%

Gross margin	$ 63,360	$ 68,955	$ _____	_____ %
Operating expenses:				
Salaries	$ 19,750	$ 20,935	$ _____	_____ %
Warehouse rental	9,000	10,200	$ _____	_____ %
Depreciation—equipment	800	800	$ _____	_____ %
Depreciation—building	5,415	5,415	$ _____	_____ %
Payroll tax expense	1,185	1,275	$ _____	_____ %
Total operating expenses	$ 36,150	$ 38,625	$ _____	_____ %
Net operating income	$ 27,210	$ 30,330	$ _____	_____ %
Other income and expense				
Interest expense	575	0	$ _____	_____ %
Net income	$ 26,635	$ 30,330	$ _____	_____ %

3. Calculate the amount and rate of increase or decrease on a horizontal comparison of 198X and 198Y items on the following balance sheet. Verify your totals.

SECURITY SUPPLY COMPANY
Balance Sheet
June 30, 198X and 198Y

Assets

	198X	198Y	Amount	Rate
Current assets				
Cash	$ 11,500	$ 11,950	$ _____	_____ %
Accounts receivable	28,750	29,175	$ _____	_____ %
Notes receivable	8,250	7,980	$ _____	_____ %
Merchandise inventory	86,000	87,000	$ _____	_____ %
Total current assets	$134,500	$136,605	$ _____	_____ %
Long-term assets				
Equipment	8,000	7,200	$ _____	_____ %
Building	65,000	59,585	$ _____	_____ %
Land	225,000	225,000	$ _____	_____ %
Total long-term assets	298,000	291,785	$ _____	_____ %
Total assets	$432,500	$428,390	$ _____	_____ %

Liabilities

Current liabilities				
Accounts payable	$ 35,000	$ 33,900	$ _____	_____ %
Wages payable	1,645	1,875	$ _____	_____ %
Taxes payable	295	305	$ _____	_____ %
Notes payable	0	3,500	$ _____	_____ %
Real estate taxes payable	4,555	0	$ _____	_____ %

(continued)

Liabilities (continued)

Long-term liabilities
 Mortgage payable   63,380 60,210 $ _____ _____ %

 Total liabilities $104,875 $ 99,790 $ _____ _____ %

Owner's Equity

Russel Thompson, capital 218,415 219,070 $ _____ _____ %

Maxine Thompson, capital 109,210 109,530 $ _____ _____ %

 Total owner's equity $327,625 $328,600 $ _____ _____ %

 Total liabilities and
  owner's equity $432,500 $428,390 $ _____ _____ %

4. Using the comparative income statements for 198X and 198Y, complete a horizontal analysis showing both amounts and rates of increase or decrease. Put any negative figures in parentheses. Verify your totals.

	198X	198Y	Dollars Increase/ (Decrease)	Rate Increase/ (Decrease)
Revenue:				
Sales	$140,025	$152,618	$ _____	_____ %
Less sales returns	− 2,520	− 3,110	$ _____	_____ %
Net sales	137,505	149,508	$ _____	_____ %
Cost of goods sold	85,940	88,205	$ _____	_____ %
Gross margin	$ 51,565	$ 61,303	$ _____	_____ %
Expenses:				
Salary	$ 32,118	$ 37,742	$ _____	_____ %
Delivery	3,850	3,975	$ _____	_____
Payroll tax	2,052	2,205	$ _____	_____ %
Utilities	1,308	1,478	$ _____	_____ %
Depreciation—equip.	275	50	$ _____	_____ %
Depreciation—bldg.	1,350	350	$ _____	_____ %
Miscellaneous	119	75	$ _____	_____ %
Total expenses	$ 41,072	$ 45,875	$ _____	_____ %
Net income	$ 10,493	$ 15,428	$ _____	_____ %

Ratios

16.3

A **ratio** is a comparison of two numbers found by dividing the first number by the second. For example, the relationship of 4 to 2 is calculated by dividing 4 by 2. This relationship can be stated as 200%, 2 to 1, or 2:1.

Although many ratios are used, we will calculate only a few of the more common ones: current ratio, acid-test ratio, debt-to-equity ratio, and net-income-to-owner's-equity ratio.

Balance Sheet Ratios

Current Ratio. The most common ratio used in business is the relation of **current assets** to **current liabilities.** "Current" means having a life of one year or less.

Although the ratio can vary depending on the type of business, a ratio of 2 to 1 (2:1) indicates a good financial position. This means that for every $1 of current liabilities, a company has $2 of current assets to repay it. When a company has adequate current assets, it doesn't need to use **long-term assets** (equipment, building, land, etc.) to pay current debts. The formula is:

$$\text{Current ratio} = \frac{\text{Current assets}}{\text{Current liabilities}}$$

EXAMPLE 6 Calculate the current ratio for Friendly Plumbing Supplies using the balance sheet illustrated:

Solution:

$\dfrac{\text{Current assets}}{\text{Current liabilities}}$ • Identify current ratio formula.

$\dfrac{\$36,600}{\$13,875} = 2.64$ • Set numbers into the formula and solve: Current ratio is 2.64 to 1 or 2.64:1. Friendly Plumbing has $2.64 of current assets to each $1 of current debts. It is in a good position to be able to pay off current debts with current dollars. □

FRIENDLY PLUMBING SUPPLIES
Balance Sheet
December 31, 198X

Assets

Current assets		
Cash	$12,000	
Accounts receivable	2,750	
Notes receivable	635	
Merchandise inventory	21,275	
Total current assets		$36,660
Long-term assets		
Equipment	$ 4,250	
Less accumulated depreciation	− 575	$ 3,675
Building	$28,000	
Less accumulated depreciation	−9,500	$18,500
Total long-term assets		$22,175
Total assets		$58,835

Liabilities

Current liabilities	
Accounts payable	$ 7,000
Notes payable	6,500
Interest payable	150
Taxes payable	225
Total current liabilities	$13,875

(continued)

Liabilities (continued)

Long-term liabilities		
Mortgage payable	$11,265	
Total liabilities		$25,140

Owner's Equity

John Friendly, capital		$33,695
Total liabilities and owner's equity		$58,835

Acid-Test Ratio. The acid-test ratio uses only the current assets of cash, accounts receivable, notes receivable, and marketable securities and relates them to current liabilities. This ratio takes into consideration that the merchandise inventory and any prepaid assets may not be as **liquid** (easy to convert into cash). They are, therefore, eliminated when calculating the total current assets for this test. The current liabilities are not adjusted. Many accountants believe that this is a much better test of current company financial health.

Although this ratio also varies depending on the type of business, a minimum standard of 1 to 1 is normally acceptable. The formula is:

$$\text{Acid-test ratio} = \frac{\text{Current assets} - \text{Merchandise inventory} - \text{Prepaid expenses}}{\text{Current liabilities}}$$

EXAMPLE 7 Calculate the acid-test ratio for Friendly Plumbing Supplies using the balance sheet illustrated in Example 6.

Solution:

- Identify the formula.

$$\frac{\text{Current assets} - \text{Merchandise inventory} - \text{Prepaid expenses}}{\text{Current liabilities}}$$

$\dfrac{\$36,660 - \$21,275}{\$13,875}$ • Set values into the formula and solve.

$\$36,660 - \$21,275 = \$15,385$ • Calculate the top value.

$\dfrac{\$15,385}{\$13,875} = 1.11$ • Calculate the ratio.

Acid-test ratio = 1.11 to 1 • $1.11 currently available to pay off every $1 of current debt.

Debt-to-Equity Ratio. One of the important relationships in any business is how much of the business the owners own and how much the creditors own. The financial community and suppliers use this ratio when they are asked to lend a business more money or to charge more merchandise or supplies. This ratio is commonly stated as a percent. The formula is:

$$\text{Debt-to-equity ratio} = \frac{\text{Total liabilities}}{\text{Owner's equity}}$$

EXAMPLE 8 Calculate the debt-to-equity ratio for Friendly Plumbing Supplies. Use the information in the balance sheet in Example 6.

Solution:

$$\frac{\text{Total liabilities}}{\text{Owner's equity}}$$ • Identify the formula.

$$\frac{\$25,140}{\$33,695} = 74.61\%$$ • Set values into the formula and solve. □

This ratio means that the creditors have 74.61% as much at risk as does the owner. The standard varies widely with different industries. In many, there would be concern if the rate were in the 20 to 30% range; in others it may still be acceptable in the 90 to 100% range. Past experience or an industry goal would be the standard.

Net-Income-to-Owner's-Equity Ratio. The relationship of net income to owner's equity is normally stated as a percent and shows management and investors the rate of return on the money invested. It involves the use of both financial statements: the owner's equity from the balance sheet and the net income from the income statement. To give a truer picture, especially if there has been considerable fluctuation in the owner's equity account, the equity can be averaged before setting it into the formula. Thus, if the ratio is being figured for a one-year period, an average of the equity values at the end of each quarter might be a more accurate figure than only the one at the end of the year. The formula is:

$$\text{Net-income-to-owner's-equity ratio} = \frac{\text{Net income}}{\text{Owner's equity}}$$

EXAMPLE 9 Calculate the net-income-to-owner's-equity ratio using the balance sheet of Friendly Plumbing Supplies illustrated earlier and a net income of $13,956.65. Because only one figure is used from the income statement, it is not illustrated.

Solution:

$$\frac{\text{Net income}}{\text{Owner's equity}}$$ • Identify the formula.

$$\frac{\$13,956.65}{\$33,695} = 41.42\%$$ • Set values into the formula and solve.

This is an excellent rate of return and may indicate that an average equity might be more appropriate in the calculation. □

✔ CHECK FOR UNDERSTANDING

1. Using the balance sheet of Ceramic Wholesale Distributors shown on page 462 and a net income of $23,847, calculate the following ratios:
   (a) Current ratio
   (b) Acid-test ratio
   (c) Debt-to-equity ratio
   (d) Net-income-to-owner's-equity ratio

CERAMIC WHOLESALE DISTRIBUTORS
Balance Sheet
September 30, 198X

Assets

Current assets		
Cash	$16,050	
Accounts receivable	28,890	
Notes receivable	3,210	
Merchandise inventory	29,560	
Total current assets		$ 77,710
Long-term assets		
Equipment	$58,422	
Less accumulated depreciation	−7,062	
Total long-term assets		51,360
Total assets		$129,070

Liabilities

Current liabilities		
Accounts payable	$11,556	
Notes payable	7,496	
Taxes payable	209	
Total current liabilities		$ 19,261
Long-term liabilities		32,100
Total liabilities		$ 51,361

Owner's Equity

George Jameson, capital	$ 77,709
Total liabilities and owner's equity	$129,070

2. The following information is available for a local manufacturer:

   Current assets: cash, $10,550; accounts receivable, $4,715; merchandise inventory, $24,860; prepaid expenses, $550. Current liabilities: $3,174. Long-term liabilities: $11,770. Owner's equity averaged: $45,731. Net income: $13,350.

   What is the
   (a) Debt-to-equity ratio? (c) Current ratio?
   (b) Acid-test ratio? (d) Net-income-to-owner's-equity ratio?

SKILL EXERCISES

Use the following information to calculate the ratios in Problems 1–4:

Current assets	$16,875
Merchandise inventory	$ 2,248
Prepaid expenses	$ 750
Current liabilities	$ 7,112
Long-term liabilities	$13,889
Owner's equity	$60,300
Net income	$11,700

Answers to ✓ Check for Understanding
1. (a) 4.03 to 1. (b) 2.5 to 1. (c) 66.09%. (d) 30.69%. 2. (a) 32.68%. (b) 4.81 to 1. (c) 12.82 to 1. (d) 29.19%.

1. Current ratio _____

2. Net-income-to-owner's-equity ratio _____

3. Debt-to-equity ratio _____

4. Acid-test ratio _____

APPLICATIONS

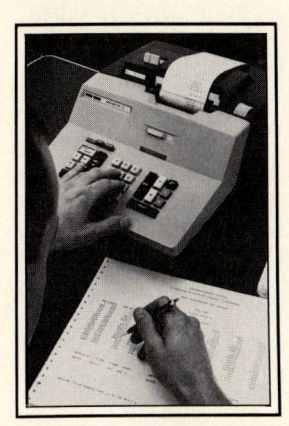

Problems 1–4 use the following balance sheet as the source of information:

NINE TO NINE VARIETY STORE
Balance Sheet
December 31, 198X

Assets

Current assets		
Cash	$ 7,725	
Securities	2,800	
Merchandise inventory	19,884	
Prepaid insurance	664	
Total current assets		$31,073
Plant and equipment		
Equipment	3,850	
Building	62,750	
Total plant and equipment		$66,600
Total assets		$97,673

Liabilities

Current liabilities		
Accounts payable	4,562	
Short-term notes payable	1,200	
Interest payable	179	
Total current liabilities		$ 5,941
Long-term liabilities		
Long-term notes payable	6,000	
Mortgage payable	22,955	
Total long-term liabilities		$28,955
Total liabilities		$34,896

Owner's Equity

Owner's equity		62,777
Total liabilities and owner's equity		$97,673

1. Calculate the debt-to-equity ratio in percent for the Nine to Nine Variety Store.

2. Calculate the acid-test ratio, making it correct to the hundredths position.

3. Using a net income of $12,230 and information from the balance sheet, calculate the net-income-to-equity-ratio in percent.

4. Calculate the current ratio correct to the hundredths place.

Problems 5–8 are based on the following information:

Merchandise inventory	$ 34,850
Total long-term assets	32,875
Total assets	14,560
Total current liabilities	262,519
Total long-term liabilities	344,804
Total liabilities	61,442
Total owner's equity	87,704
Accounts receivable	149,146
Net income	195,658
Cash	47,971

5. What is the ratio of net income to owner's equity?

6. What is the current ratio correct to the hundredths place?

7. What is the debt-to-equity ratio correct to the hundredths place?

8. What is the acid-test ratio correct to the hundredths place?

Key Terms

Acid-test ratio (460)
Assets (442)
Balance sheet (442, 451)
Cost of goods sold (446, 454)
Creditors (443)
Current assets (459)
Current liabilities (459)
Current ratio (459)
Debt-to-equity ratio (460)
Financial statement (442)
Fundamental accounting equation (443)
Gross margin (449, 454)
Horizontal analysis (451–453)
Income statement (446, 453)

Liabilities (442)
Liquid (460)
Long-term assets (459)
Long-term liabilities (459)
Net income (446, 453)
Net-income-to-owner's-equity ratio (461)
Operating expenses (446, 453)
Owner's equity (442)
Plant and equipment (459)
Ratio (458)
Revenue (446, 453)
Vertical analysis (442, 446)

Looking Back

Financial statements are used to inform interested parties of financial happenings and the conditions of a company's business. Vertical and horizontal analyses plus ratio analysis take the financial statement figures one more step in determining whether the company is healthy or needs some adjustment in its financial planning.

Financial comparisons are relatively meaningless unless there is a base with which to compare. That base can be past financial comparisons in a company or industrial data that has been summarized over a period of time.

Many ratios other than the ones in this text are available for use in checking various financial elements of a business. Ratios are only an indication of current conditions and do not in themselves tell a company how to proceed to change or make adjustments.

Let's Review

1. The following information is available on Ford's Computer Outlet: Current assets: cash, $1,563; accounts receivable, $850; merchandise inventory, $12,519; current liabilities, $1,235. Calculate the current ratio and the acid-test ratio for the store.

2. The owner's equity for Ford's Computer Outlet averaged $46,160 for the year. If the net income for the year was $10,569, what is the net-income-to-equity ratio to the nearest hundredth percent?

For Problems 3–8 use the balance sheet for Security Supply Company.

SECURITY SUPPLY COMPANY
Balance Sheet
March 31, 198X and 198Y

Assets

	198X	198Y	Vertical 198X	Vertical 198Y	Dollars Increase/ (Decrease)	Rate Increase/ (Decrease)
Current assets						
Cash	$ 5,475	$ 4,795	____%	____%	$ ____	____%
Marketable securities	11,190	16,540	____%	____%	$ ____	____%
Accounts receivable	14,337	15,870	____%	____%	$ ____	____%
Merchandise inventory	83,553	88,784	____%	____%	$ ____	____%
Total current assets	$114,555	$125,989	____%	____%	$ ____	____%
Long-term assets						
Truck	$ 11,190	$ 8,427	____%	____%	$ ____	____%
Equipment	4,453	5,987	____%	____%	$ ____	____%
Building	126,224	121,175	____%	____%	$ ____	____%
Land	92,000	92,000	____%	____%	$ ____	____%
Total long-term assets	$233,867	$227,589	____%	____%	$ ____	____%
Total assets	$348,422	$353,578	____%	____%	$ ____	____%

(continued)

Liabilities

Current liabilities							
Accounts payable	$ 18,719	$ 19,068	____%	____%	$ _____	____%	
Wages payable	1,352	1,655	____%	____%	$ _____	____%	
Notes payable	0	925	____%	____%	$ _____	____%	
Taxes payable	203	248	____%	____%	$ _____	____%	
Total current liabilities	$ 20,274	$ 21,896	____%	____%	$ _____	____%	
Long-term liabilities							
Notes payable	4,200	1,200	____%	____%	$ _____	____%	
Mortgage payable	85,000	81,750	____%	____%	$ _____	____%	
Total long-term liabilities	$ 89,200	$ 82,950	____%	____%	$ _____	____%	
Total liabilities	$109,474	$104,846	____%	____%	$ _____	____%	

Owner's Equity

Fred Taylor, capital	$159,299	$165,821	____%	____%	$ _____	____%	
Maxine Taylor, capital	79,649	82,911	____%	____%	$ _____	____%	
Total owner's equity	$238,948	$248,732	____%	____%	$ _____	____%	
Total liabilities and owner's equity	$348,422	$353,578	____%	____%	$ _____	____%	

3. Using the two columns titled vertical, make a vertical analysis for each separate year using the total assets as the base for the asset section and total liabilities and owner's equity as the base for the liabilities and owner's equity sections.

4. Make a horizontal analysis of the balance sheet in calculating both the amount and rate of increase or decrease. Use the oldest date as the base of all rate calculations and place your answers in the last two columns. Place all negative figures in parentheses and verify totals where possible.

5. Using the balance sheet, calculate the acid-test ratio for both 198X and 198Y.

6. Calculate the debt-to-equity ratio for 198X and 198Y using the information on the Security Supply Company balance sheet.

7. Security Supply had net income of $30,292 in 198X and $33,669 in 198Y. Use additional information from the balance sheet and calculate the net-income-to-owner's-equity ratio for both years.

8. Calculate the current ratio for 198X and 198Y using the Security Supply Company balance sheet.

For Problems 9 and 10 use the income statement for Security Supply Company illustrated on page 467.

9. Do a vertical analysis for 198X and 198Y. Put the 198X figures in the first blank column and the 198Y figures in the second blank column. Use the net sales figures as your base.

10. Make a horizontal analysis of the income statement. Calculate both the amount and rate of increase or decrease. Place all negative figures in parentheses and use 198X as your base. Verify totals wherever possible.

SECURITY SUPPLY COMPANY
Income Statement
For the Years Ended March 31, 198X and 198Y

	198X	198Y	Vertical 198X	Vertical 198Y	Dollars Increase/ (Decrease)	Rate Increase/ (Decrease)
Revenue:						
Sales	$198,884	$204,539	____%	____%	$ ____	____%
Less sales returns	3,580	3,273	____%	____%	$ ____	____%
Net sales	$195,304	$201,266	____%	____%	$ ____	____%
Cost of goods						
Merchandise inventory, January 1	58,484	78,770	____%		$ ____	____%
Purchases	147,950	133,200	____%	____%	$ ____	____%
Goods available for sale	206,434	211,970	____%	____%	$ ____	____%
Less merchandise inventory, December 31	78,770	83,554	____%	____%	$ ____	____%
Cost of goods sold	$127,664	$128,416	____%	____%	$ ____	____%
Gross margin	$ 67,640	$ 72,850	____%	____%	$ ____	____%
Operating expenses:						
Salaries	24,215	25,095	____%	____%	$ ____	____%
Warehouse rental	9,000	9,500	____%	____%	$ ____	____%
Depreciation—truck	1,275	1,275	____%	____%	$ ____	____%
Depreciation—equipment	800	800	____%	____%	$ ____	____%
Depreciation—building	4,335	4,162	____%	____%	$ ____	____%
Payroll tax expense	3,100	3,156	____%	____%	$ ____	____%
Total operating expenses	42,725	43,988	____%	____%	$ ____	____%
Net operating income	24,915	28,862	____%	____%	$ ____	____%
Income expense	436	231	____%	____%	$ ____	____%
Net income	$ 24,479	$ 28,631	____%	____%	$ ____	____%

Chapter Test

1. Make a vertical analysis of the Electronic Parts Inc. income statement shown on page 468 for each of the years 198X and 198Y. Use net sales as your base.

ELECTRONIC PARTS INC.
Income Statement
For the Years Ended June 30, 198X and 198Y

	198X	198Y				
Revenue:						
Sales	$91,305	$98,201	____%	____%	$_____	____%
Sales returns	692	727	____%	____%	$_____	____%
Net sales	$90,613	$97,474	____%	____%	$_____	____%
Cost of goods						
Merchandise inventory, July 1	22,650	18,992	____%	____%	$_____	____%
Purchases	28,815	36,662	____%	____%	$_____	____%
Goods available for sale	$51,465	$55,654	____%	____%	$_____	____%
Less merchandise inventory, June 30	18,992	22,592	____%	____%	$_____	____%
Cost of goods sold	32,473	33,062	____%	____%	$_____	____%
Gross margin	$58,140	$64,412	____%	____%	$_____	____%
Operating expenses:						
Advertising	$ 1,629	$ 1,427	____%	____%	$_____	____%
Salaries and wages	21,950	23,048	____%	____%	$_____	____%
Utilities	816	778	____%	____%	$_____	____%
Depreciation	1,100	1,100	____%	____%	$_____	____%
Delivery	3,626	3,866	____%	____%	$_____	____%
Total operating expenses	29,121	30,219	____%	____%	$_____	____%
Net income	$29,019	$34,193	____%	____%	$_____	____%

2. Make a horizontal analysis of the Electronics Parts Inc. income statement calculating both the amount and the rate of increase or decrease. Place all negative figures in parentheses.

3. The following information is available from the financial statements of Pre-Cast Molding Corporation for the year ended December 31:

Current Assets			
Cash	$ 5,600	Current liabilities	$ 8,584
Accounts receivable	$ 1,824		
Merchandise inventory	$ 4,654	Total liabilities	$32,616
Prepaids	$ 1,210	Owner's equity	$92,196
Total assets	$124,812	Net income	$17,818

(a) Calculate the ratio of net income to owner's equity.
(b) Calculate the current ratio.
(c) Calculate the debt-to-equity ratio.
(d) Calculate the acid-test ratio.

Use the Electronics Parts Inc. balance sheet for Problems 4–8.

4. Make a vertical analysis of the Electronic Parts Inc. balance sheet. Use the first blank column for your 198X analysis and the second blank column for 198Y.

ELECTRONIC PARTS INC.
Balance Sheet
June 30, 198X and 198Y

Assets

	198X	198Y				
Current assets						
Cash	$ 3,142	$ 3,487	____%	____%	$ _____	____%
Marketable securities	6,500	7,800	____%	____%	$ _____	____%
Accounts receivable	2,398	2,141	____%	____%	$ _____	____%
Merchandise inventory	18,992	22,592	____%	____%	$ _____	____%
Prepaid insurance	1,193	216	____%	____%	$ _____	____%
Total current assets	$ 32,225	$ 36,236	____%	____%	$ _____	____%
Long-term assets						
Equipment	$ 8,540	$ 8,724	____%	____%	$ _____	____%
Building	84,996	79,896	____%	____%	$ _____	____%
Land	40,000	40,000	____%	____%	$ _____	____%
Total long-term assets	$133,536	$128,620	____%	____%	$ _____	____%
Total assets	$165,761	$164,856	____%	____%	$ _____	____%

Liabilities

Current liabilities						
Accounts payable	$ 3,197	$ 3,020	____%	____%	$ _____	____%
Notes payable	4,655	4,775	____%	____%	$ _____	____%
Wages payable	634	684	____%	____%	$ _____	____%
Total current liabilities	$ 8,486	$ 8,479	____%	____%	$ _____	____%
Long-term liabilities						
Mortgage payable	41,950	39,852	____%	____%	$ _____	____%
Total liabilities	$ 50,436	$ 48,331	____%	____%	$ _____	____%

Owner's Equity

Owner's equity	$115,325	$116,525	____%	____%	$ _____	____%
Total liabilities and owner's equity	$165,761	$164,856	____%	____%	$ _____	____%

5. Make a horizontal analysis of the Electronics Parts Inc. balance sheet calculating both the dollars and rates of increase or decrease for each item. Place all negative figures in parentheses.

6. Calculate the current ratio and the acid-test ratio of Electronic Parts Inc. for 198X and 198Y.

	198X	198Y
Current ratio	_____	_____
Acid-test ratio	_____	_____

7. Using the balance sheet of Electronic Parts Inc., calculate the debt-to-equity ratio for each of the two years.

8. Using the information in both of the financial statements of Electronics Parts Inc., calculate the net-income-to-equity ratio for both 198X and 198Y.

Business Statistics and Graphs

17

OBJECTIVES

When you complete this chapter you will be able to:

- *Understand the major differences between and uses of the mean, the median, and the mode and calculate them from ungrouped data. (17.1)*
- *Understand the basic techniques for presenting statistical information with tables and charts. (17.2)*
- *Know which type of presentation to use for the type of decision being made. (17.3)*
- *Understand the use of dispersion measurements in statistics and compute a standard deviation. (17.4)*

COMING UP

People in business need to analyze information. They often use statistical methods to describe what is occurring and make summary statements about different levels of production and retail operations. Relationships of fixed and variable costs are evaluated to determine profit levels. The statistical results are then placed into presentation format for decision making. These tasks require understanding of the fundamentals of making charts and graphs. It all leads to this: decision making requires the use of good calculation techniques and concise presentation formats. To misinform is to mislead.

Statistical Measures

17.1   Three of the more common measures used in business are the **mean**, the **median**, and the **mode**. In **statistics**, they are referred to as **averages**. Each of the terms represents a separate characteristic of data. The characteristic is intended to be "typical" of all values in the data. We will show you how to calculate these values using methods for **ungrouped data**. Ungrouped data uses the actual numbers rather than summarized numbers. Other calculation methods using information in summary form are presented in a statistics course and are not considered relevant for business mathematics.

The proper use of these averages depends on a solid understanding of their meanings. Because each illustrates a specific characteristic of the data, using the wrong average for a particular application leads to improper conclusions. Let's look at the differences.

> Mean: used to show numerical likeness.

The mean is affected by extremely low or high numbers. It is proper to use the mean as a representative value when the numbers being evaluated have few extreme values within a set. The mean should "say" to the user that this number is typical of all the values being summarized. For example, if we state that the mean salary for our department is $18,000, it implies that the typical individual who works in the department makes approximately $18,000. If the actual data shows that most make $12,000 and several make $38,000, the mean would not describe typical department salaries and would therefore be misleading.

> Median: focuses upon the middle value of data.

The median represents a number that holds the center position in the data. It is the "middle" number and therefore one-half of the numbers are larger than the median and one-half of the numbers are smaller. In our above example, if $18,000 was said to be the median, it would indicate that one-half earn above $18,000 and one-half below.

> Mode: the number that occurs most often.

In our above example for the mean, if most of the department personnel earned $18,000, the mode would be used because it is a better interpretation of the data. If,

Chapter 17   Business Statistics and Graphs

however, most of the employees earn $12,000, this number should be presented as the most descriptive average.

Finding the Mean

The **mean** is the value commonly referred to as **"the average."** In general math, we are shown the average as the sum of a series of numbers divided by the number of numbers used in the summation. Since statistics uses more than one average to describe data, we use the more precise term, *mean*.

$$\text{Mean} = \frac{\text{Sum of a series of numbers}}{\text{Number of numbers in the series}}$$

EXAMPLE 1 Compute the mean sales from the monthly report of salespersons:

$5,976	$12,584	$15,848	$ 5,143
$3,271	$ 6,231	$ 9,682	$ 6,898
$4,961	$ 1,144	$ 7,130	$10,040

Solution:

$88,908   • Sum of the numbers.
12   • Number of numbers used.
$\frac{88,908}{12}$ • Set variables into formula.
88,908 ÷ 12 = 7,409   • Calculate the mean.
$7,409   • Mean sales.

By calculating the mean we have determined that $7,409 in sales is the **arithmetic center** of the sales data. □

✔ CHECK FOR UNDERSTANDING

1. In 15 jobs, the costs for producing a component were:

$3.95	$4.05	$4.01	$4.60	$4.44
$4.32	$4.16	$4.08	$4.32	$4.61
$5.01	$3.98	$4.56	$4.12	$4.10

What is the mean production cost (rounded to the nearest cent)?

2. Analyze the cost of labor for the given 15-month period. Determine the mean.

$12,430	$11,960	$36,293	$12,462	$13,260
$15,060	$12,420	$10,587	$14,490	$15,175
$ 8,980	$18,444	$ 6,424	$17,840	$14,240

Finding the Median

Whereas the mean is the arithmetic center for a series of data, the **median** is the number that is located in the middle of the number group. We say it holds the center position. Using ungrouped data, there are two separate procedures for calculating the median. The procedure to be used depends on *the number of numbers* being considered. The number of numbers could be odd or even.

Answers to ✔ Check for Understanding
1. $4.29. 2. $14,671.

The first step in computing the median from a number series is to place the numbers in numerical order. The statistical term for this is an **array**.

EXAMPLE 2 Set ungrouped data into an array:

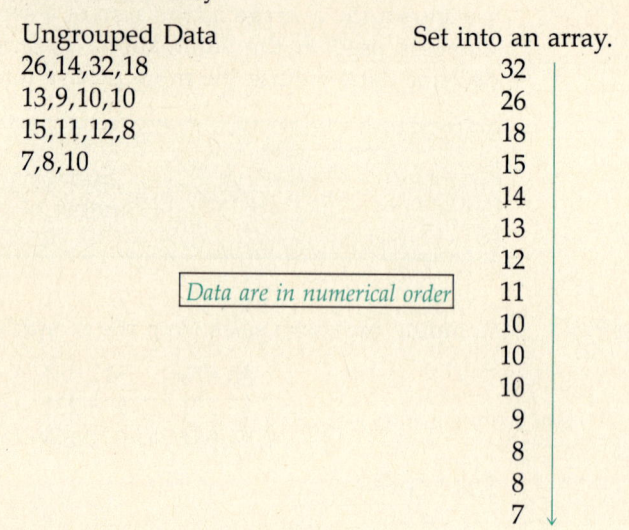

Ungrouped Data	Set into an array.
26,14,32,18	32
13,9,10,10	26
15,11,12,8	18
7,8,10	15
	14
	13
	12
Data are in numerical order	11
	10
	10
	10
	9
	8
	8
	7

Solution: To determine the median once the array is established, follow these two steps.

- *Step 1.* If the number of numbers you are analyzing is *odd*, find the number that is in the middle of the array. That number is the median because it holds the center position.
- *Step 2.* If the number of numbers in the array is *even*, find the two middle numbers. Calculate the mean of those numbers (add them and divide by two). This will give you the arithmetic center of the position between the two middle array values. The arithmetic center becomes the median. ☐

EXAMPLE 3 The following array of salaries has an odd number of data. Find the median:

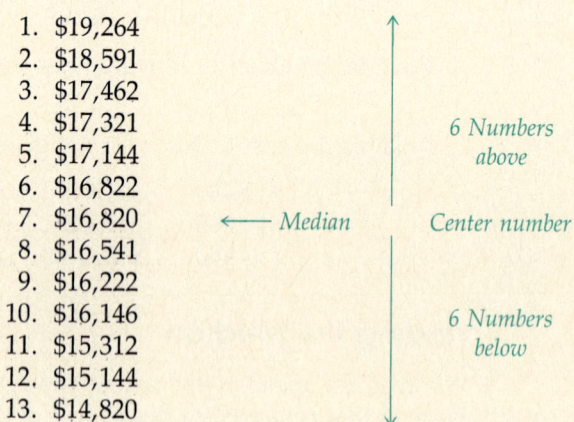

1. $19,264
2. $18,591
3. $17,462
4. $17,321   6 Numbers
5. $17,144   above
6. $16,822
7. $16,820 ← Median   Center number
8. $16,541
9. $16,222
10. $16,146   6 Numbers
11. $15,312   below
12. $15,144
13. $14,820

Solution:

- There are 13 salaries: 13 ÷ 2 = 6.5.
- Count in 6 whole numbers from either end of the array. The next number is $16,820—the median. ☐

474 Chapter 17 Business Statistics and Graphs

EXAMPLE 4 The following is an array of utilities costs for the year. What was the median cost?

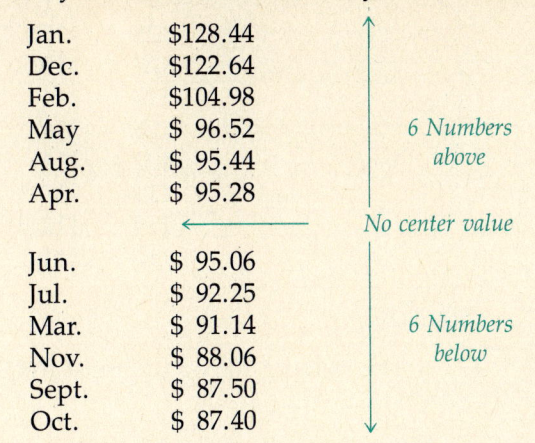

Jan.	$128.44	
Dec.	$122.64	
Feb.	$104.98	
May	$ 96.52	6 Numbers above
Aug.	$ 95.44	
Apr.	$ 95.28	
		← No center value
Jun.	$ 95.06	
Jul.	$ 92.25	
Mar.	$ 91.14	6 Numbers below
Nov.	$ 88.06	
Sept.	$ 87.50	
Oct.	$ 87.40	

Solution: Proceed using the even number step:

- 1. Twelve monthly costs ÷ 2 = 6.
- 2. Count in six from either end.
- 3. Find the mean of the two middle values (the sixth and seventh numbers).

$95.28
+ 95.06
$190.34 ÷ 2 = $95.17 median.

✔ CHECK FOR UNDERSTANDING

1. Set the following data into an array and determine the median:

42	36	15	18	24	22	26	41
16	17	17	19	21	21	23	25
32	19	27	27	25	26	27	16

2. From the list of different prices for an automobile engine part, determine the median price.

$3.20	$3.17	$3.24	$3.18	$3.36
$3.15	$3.16	$3.18	$3.22	$3.20
$3.19				

Finding the Mode

The **mode** describes the number in a set of numbers that appears most frequently. Its intent is to show that a number is typical of all of the data because it occurs most often. By setting the numbers into an array, one can examine and determine which number occurs most frequently. (Note: the array is not needed for the mode; however, it can be very useful to establish how many numbers have a like value. The array is not necessary for the computation of the mean, since we are only concerned with the values of the numbers, not their positions.)

Answers to ✔ Check for Understanding
1. 23.5. 2. $3.19.

EXAMPLE 5   Establish the mode from the following array:

128	117	110	105	95
128	115	110	104	95
127	114	109	104	94
126	114	106	101	92
122	114	106	101	91
119	113	106	100	88
118	112	106	100	88
117	111	105	96	85

Solution:

- The number 106 occurs most frequently; therefore, the mode = 106.

Note: If two numbers occur the same number of times, it is called a *bi-modal distribution*. Two density points are being reflected in the same distribution. It is also possible that no mode can be found in a distribution of ungrouped data because numbers are not repeated. Too many numbers repeated the same number of times also invalidates the mode.

✔ CHECK FOR UNDERSTANDING

1. Determine the mode from the following series of data:

745	740	739	620
620	619	738	598
1195	621	697	582
250	621	821	570
1825	1146	840	619
564	1050	620	980
462	571	974	1006
373	482	808	986

2. What is the mode height, in inches, for the people of Mons Township?

58	57	59	68	62	71
62	57	62	78	65	75
62	59	61	74	70	70
60	62	61	75	71	56
61	61	51	69	70	66
60	60	68	67	75	67
59	68	62	66	71	68
70	68	75	50	70	68

3. Given the following ungrouped test measurement data, establish the mode:

123.7	131.4	233.8	412.4
144.9	287.9	169.7	333.7
187.6	591.6	374.3	201.5

Answers to ✔ Check for Understanding
1. 620.   2. 62, 68 (bi-modal).   3. No mode evident.

> **PROBLEM SOLVING STRATEGY**
> The quickest and most reliable way to solve for the mean, median, and mode is to use the array. Once the numbers are arranged numerically, addition and division can be performed for the mean, the array can be counted for the median, and a quick scan of the array can support the determination of the mode. An array is not needed to solve for the mean; however, if more than one average is required, it does expedite the solution.

SKILL EXERCISES

Compute the mean of the following to the nearest hundredth:

1. 22, 28, 26, 20, 27   mean = _____

2. 528, 864, 193, 121, 365   mean = _____

3. 16.3, 49.7, 86.4, 91.2, 107.9   mean = _____

4. 0.236, 0.714, 0.808, 0.523, 0.667   mean = _____

5. 68.92, 27.41, 15.99, 47.66, 51.98   mean = _____

Set the following data into an array and determine the median:

6. 27, 16, 28, 29, 32, 37, 21   median = _____

7. 27.2, 28.6, 27.9, 29.4, 28.4, 29.1, 27.8, 28.0   median = _____

8. 586, 854, 972, 827   median = _____

9. 9, 2, 2, 7, 5, 6, 3, 1, 8, 8, 4   median = _____

10. 0.231, 0.664, 0.754, 0.669   median = _____

Analyze the following problem data and determine the mode:

11. 2, 7, 5, 4, 2, 2, 5, 4, 6, 8, 6, 7   mode = _____

12. 26, 24, 23, 21, 26, 25, 25, 21, 26, 28, 23   mode = _____

13. 581, 580, 583, 580, 582, 581, 583, 584, 581   mode = _____

14. 165, 167, 168, 165, 168, 162, 163, 161, 161, 163, 165   mode = _____

15. 13, 17, 14, 19, 17, 13, 17, 19   mode = _____

Section 17.1 Statistical Measures

APPLICATIONS

Evaluate and calculate the appropriate statistical measures.

1. Analyze the tabulated sales information. Compute the mean, median, and mode. Which measure do you think is most representative of the data set? Why?

$356	$365	$222	$522
$358	$370	$414	$580
$362	$380	$816	$464
$391	$382	$354	$350
$407	$395	$621	$640
$398	$586	$355	$712
$360	$127	$474	$703

2. Analyze the tabulated cost information. Compute the mean, median, and mode. Select the average you believe is most representative of the data. Explain your reason.

$86	$91	$86
$85	$85	$86
$84	$86	$92
$84	$87	$98
$86	$87	$91
$87	$84	$91
$92	$83	$85
$90	$92	$83
$91	$90	$83
$84	$90	$80
$85	$61	$82
$90	$74	$81

3. Analyze the tabulated price information. Compute the mean, median, and mode. Select the average you feel is most representative of the data. Explain your reason.

$126	$ 81	$ 83	$ 81	$ 81
$143	$125	$112	$ 80	$ 81
$ 82	$ 82	$ 84	$ 81	$ 80
$ 81	$110	$ 86	$106	$ 92
$ 91	$ 84	$ 80	$112	$108
$101	$ 81	$ 81	$144	$ 94
$ 80	$ 82	$ 80	$ 81	$ 84

4. Product ZEBO has increased sales this year. Review the previous sales data. How much difference is there between this year's mean sales and last year's? (Round to the nearest cent.) What percent difference is there between the means? (Use base, rate, and part formulas.)

	Last Year	This Year		Last Year	This Year
Jan.	$ 8,964	$ 9,754	Jul.	$10,600	$ 9,224
Feb.	$ 8,882	$ 9,980	Aug.	$11,400	$12,846
Mar.	$ 6,214	$10,125	Sept.	$ 9,720	$12,931
Apr.	$ 5,100	$ 7,312	Oct.	$ 8,140	$11,410
May	$ 7,880	$ 6,924	Nov.	$ 4,220	$ 7,156
Jun.	$ 9,400	$ 8,141	Dec.	$ 6,810	$ 7,040

Chapter 17 Business Statistics and Graphs

5. An analysis of customers showed that they had been in business for various numbers of years. From the business data provided below, determine the mean, median, and mode of the typical age of the customer's companies. What would you conclude about the most typical number of years after reviewing the averages?

3.2	4.6	5.0	7.8	12.0	9.0
3.4	3.0	3.6	2.4	6.0	5.6
2.4	3.2	4.6	4.8	3.9	5.3
6.2	4.7	4.6	3.7	2.8	1.4
5.4	4.6	3.2	3.8	6.4	7.3

Statistical Tables and Charts

17.2

The next step in developing skills for working with statistical information involves **tables** and **charts**. Eventually every person in business will be required to develop, organize, prepare, or present some type of business information. The task isn't difficult, but some fundamental procedures should be considered. The chart or table format chosen must provide clear communication of the information to the decision maker.

The four major categories of information for presentation include

- Trend or activity information over time
- Effort or results comparison
- Allocation of a quantity into its parts
- Numbers with narrative explanation

Four of the major formats that can be used to show information are

- Bar charts
- Line charts
- Pie charts
- Tables

Deciding which type of chart or table to use depends on the objective. To prepare information properly for a chart or table, select the form of presentation that best matches one of the four categories above. To do this, identify the type of decision to be made. Then match it to the type of chart or table that best illustrates the type of decision pattern. Consider these recommended matching patterns:

Bar chart	Use for data comparison
Line chart	Use for trend or change
Pie chart	Use for allocation of quantities
Table	Use when actual data values and category breakdown must be clear

Chart and Table Format

Bar Charts. When the information objective is to compare results for a business effort, a **bar chart** is preferred. A bar chart uses linear bars—either horizontal or vertical—and a quantitative scale to show the information measure. Such measures could include things such as statistical averages, inventory levels for various commodities, or output levels by category. The bar chart concept can also be used to show multiple results by showing component parts of the various bars. The single data bar shown in Figure 17.1 illustrates the ability to compare results.

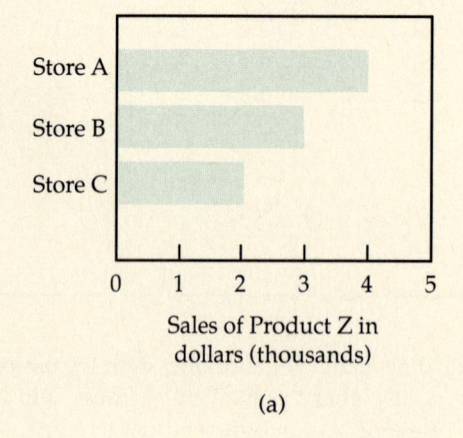

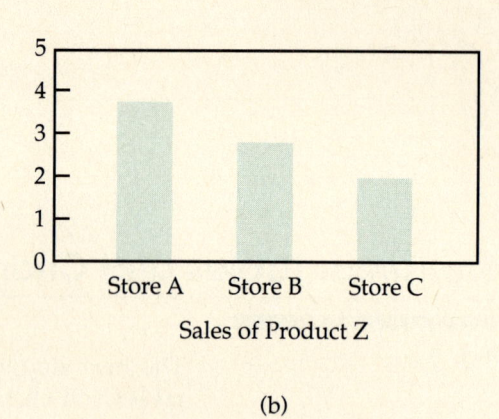

FIGURE 17.1
Illustration of a horizontal (a) and vertical (b) bar chart

Line Charts. The type of chart used to show trend or change is a **line chart**. It is fundamentally a two-axis chart. The left, or vertical, axis breaks the data being shown into various number scales, depending on the type of information. The horizontal axis typically displays the information over some time period, usually months or years. Each line plotted represents the results of one information component. As the line progresses from left to right over time, the plotted results depict the trend or change that has taken place. Multiple comparisons can also be shown by plotting more than one information category. For example, exports can be shown as a solid line, imports as a dotted line, and balance of trade as solid bars (see Figure 17.2).

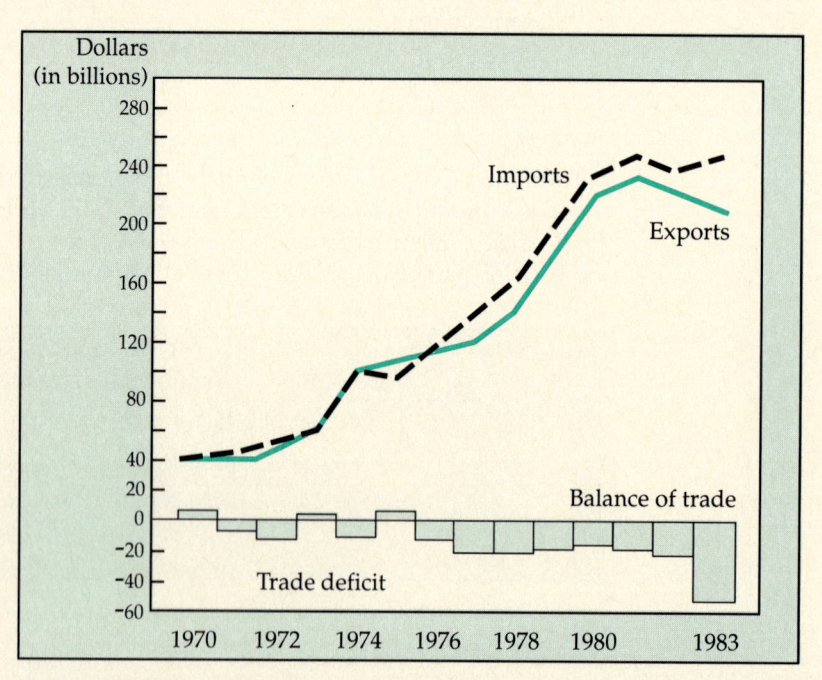

FIGURE 17.2
Illustration of a line chart

Balance of Trade. A nation's balance of trade is the value of its exports minus the value of its imports, during a given time. When a country exports more than it imports, it has a favorable balance of trade.
SOURCE: Federal Reserve Bank of Chicago, International Letter No. 521, March 9, 1984.

480   Chapter 17   Business Statistics and Graphs

Pie Charts. The **pie chart** is circular in form and is used to show the allocation of a particular resource or effort. This type of presentation is used to show such things as sources of tax revenue, categories of a total business budget, or the allocation of time spent on certain jobs. The circle represents 100% of the resource. The 360-degree circle is divided into sections proportional to data categories. Lines are drawn from the center which divide the circle into categories (see Figure 17.3).

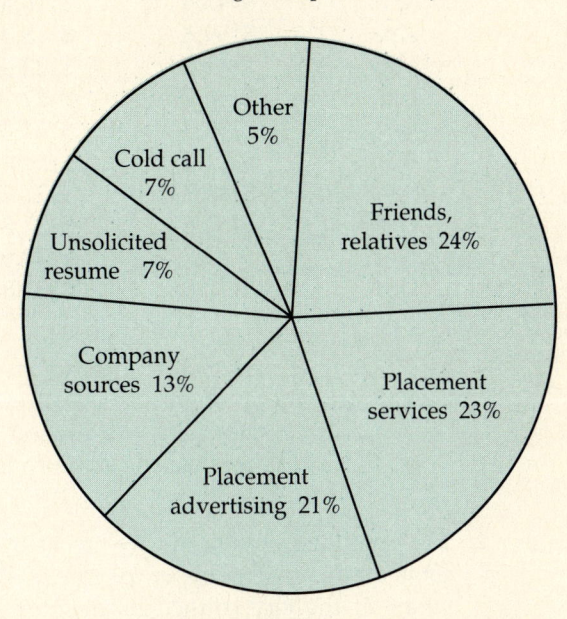

How managers acquired their jobs

- Other 5%
- Cold call 7%
- Unsolicited resume 7%
- Company sources 13%
- Placement advertising 21%
- Placement services 23%
- Friends, relatives 24%

FIGURE 17.3
Illustration of a pie chart

SOURCE: Administrative Management Society.

Table Information. The objective of a graphic presentation is to provide a visual effect rather than an exact interpretation of the data being used. The disadvantage is that the values represented by the bars, lines, or pie segments are only approximations. If exact numbers with identified information categories are needed, the *table* format should be used.

The structure of a table is similar to a line chart. It is usually designed around a two-axis presentation. The vertical axis identifies the general categories of information being reported. The horizontal axis identifies the information components being presented. (Table 17.1 gives an example.)

TABLE 17.1
Company Operating Expenses by Category (Dollars)

	Annual Expenses		
Category	1987	1988	1989
Labor	$126,000	$127,582	$129,641
Utilities	18,541	18,967	19,828
Insurance	1,751	1,882	1,906
Security	2,500	2,644	2,741
Support	62,144	63,226	62,876
Miscellaneous	28,151	16,332	24,562
Total	$239,078	$230,633	$241,554

✔ CHECK FOR UNDERSTANDING

1. Select the appropriate type of chart or table presentation needed for the following sales data for the given objective.

   a. Data: Sales (thousands of dollars)

Month	Location A	Location B
Jan.	$164.3	$117.2
Feb.	$158.3	$121.6
Mar.	$145.4	$116.4
Apr.	$159.8	$118.8
May	$161.2	$122.4
Jun.	$140.7	$122.7
Jul.	$138.3	$124.8
Aug.	$121.2	$120.4
Sept.	$141.7	$121.2
Oct.	$161.6	$123.8
Nov.	$165.7	$130.6
Dec.	$172.8	$131.8

   b. Objectives
   1. Comparison of total sales for two locations.
   2. Comparison of annual sales trends for two locations.
   3. Monthly sales total information by location.
   4. Percent of total sales each location provides.

2. The population of Boom City has been expanding rapidly. Along with growth has come an increase in the crime rate in all categories. Your boss is making a presentation to the city council in an attempt to obtain more funds for an expanded police force. You have been given the crime statistics and asked to prepare two charts to support your boss's arguments. Which two would you choose to meet the objectives? How would each be organized?

SKILL EXERCISES

Place the letter of the type of chart next to the information to be displayed. You may use each letter more than once.

Type to use

A. Bar chart
B. Line chart
C. Pie chart
D. Table

Situation

1. _____ Store location with the greatest sales volume (six locations).

2. _____ Ethnic segments of population makeup in a school system.

3. _____ Changes in labor costs expended over the last four years.

Answers to ✔ Check for Understanding
1. Bar chart, line chart, table, and pie chart. 2. Bar chart—Comparison of crime growth by category; line chart—different lines for categories plotting trend over time.

Type to use		Situation
A. Bar chart	4. _____	Plot of manufacturing error tolerance.
B. Line chart		
C. Pie chart	5. _____	Allocation of total budget by category.
D. Table		
	6. _____	Types and dollar values of construction contracts.
	7. _____	Cost factors for computer components by year.
	8. _____	Growth in customer complaints for the last four years (by month).
	9. _____	Comparison of returns on investment for equipment components.
	10. _____	Allocation of school district cost components in an annual budget.

APPLICATIONS

1. You need to show the amount of change in new energy location attempts for 6 western states over a 3-year period.

Test Drillings (hundreds)

State	1983	1986
California	60	75
Colorado	30	43
Arizona	24	28
Texas	18	26
Wyoming	47	54
Nevada	16	34

What type of chart is most appropriate for the information objective? What type of chart is best if the amount of total activity by state is desired?

Presentation of Tables and Charts

17.3

The objective of the information presentation can usually be addressed by choosing the proper chart or table format. In order to complete the design, certain construction policies should be followed. In addition to the data, there are additional items needed to create a good presentation. These include titles, scales, column headings, category breakdowns, footnotes, and source notes. Figure 17.4 shows the components for a chart. Figure 17.5 identifies the organization needs of a table.

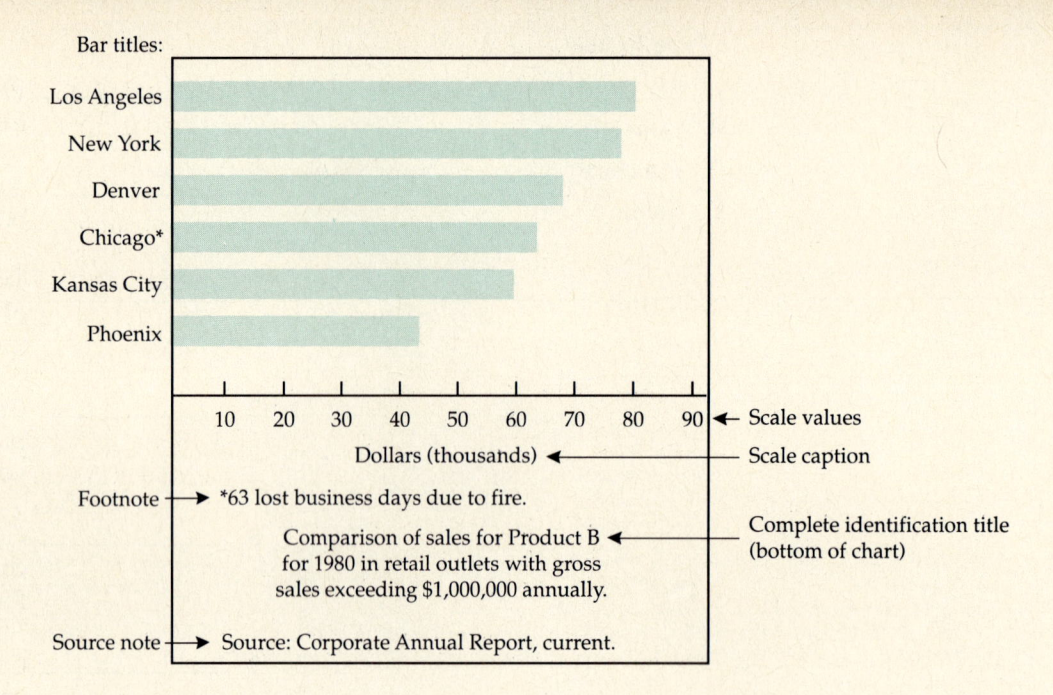

FIGURE 17.4
Chart components

Bar titles: Los Angeles, New York, Denver, Chicago*, Kansas City, Phoenix

Scale values: 10 20 30 40 50 60 70 80 90
Scale caption: Dollars (thousands)

Footnote → *63 lost business days due to fire.

Complete identification title (bottom of chart): Comparison of sales for Product B for 1980 in retail outlets with gross sales exceeding $1,000,000 annually.

Source note → Source: Corporate Annual Report, current.

FIGURE 17.5
Table components

Complete identification title (top of table):
Figure 17.5 Comparison of Product B and Product Z in 1990 in retail outlets grossing $1 million in sales annually

| | Total sales | |
City	Product B	Product Z
Los Angeles	$78,526	$124,593
New York	76,652	127,622
Denver	68,789	89,664
Chicago*	55,462	73,849
Kansas City	50,176	61,331
Phoenix	41,628	52,582
Total	$371,233	$529,641

Column heading → Total sales
Column subheadings → Product B, Product Z
Category breakdown → (city list)

Footnote → *63 lost business days due to fire.
Source note → *Source*: Corporate Annual Report, 1990.

Identification Title
The title introduces the data to the reader; therefore, it must be complete and informative. It usually includes **what** is in the table, **where** the information originated, **when** it was collected, and **how** the information is categorized.

Scale Caption
The axis scales must be clearly marked and labeled. The units represented by the scale should be clearly identified so the reader will know what they mean; e.g., hundreds, thousands, millions, per day, per month, dollars, percents.

Column Headings
Column headings identify the breakdown of the information displayed on the horizontal axis. They identify the basic components to be compared.

Category Breakdowns
These show the breakdown categorization of information organized vertically. They formulate the pattern in which the information being presented will be reviewed.

Footnotes
Footnotes refer to a specific part of the table or chart and are used to explain omissions or to give additional information not found in the data arrangement. They can be used to define terms, explain limitations, show differences, etc.

Source Notes
A source note identifies the origin of the data. Statistics may be from the World Almanac, Statistical Abstract of the United States, *internal company reports, industry surveys*, etc. The sources should be presented in proper business bibliographical reference form.

✓ CHECK FOR UNDERSTANDING

Select the correct description for each chart component. Place the letter of the chart component next to the number of the descriptor which identifies it best.

Chart component descriptors

A. Title
B. Column heading
C. Category breakdown
D. Scale caption
E. Footnote
F. Source note

1. _____ Gives complete reference for the origin of the data.

2. _____ Identifies the quantity being expressed by line marks.

3. _____ Sets the information into groups to be compared.

4. _____ Provides complete information on what is being presented.

5. _____ Gives additional information not expressed by the chart or table.

6. _____ Organizes information into a pattern for review.

SKILL EXERCISES

Match the completion component with the type of data. Place the component letter next to the number which identifies the data type for a chart (or table).

Completion component

A. Title
B. Scale caption
C. Column heading
D. Category breakdown
E. Footnote

Type of data

1. _____ Company A, Company B, Company C.

2. _____ Special Report 1986, Blue Ribbon Panel on Crop Analysis; U.S. Farm Bureau, Washington, D.C.

3. _____ Total production in tons.

4. _____ Does not include trainees with less than six months' service.

5. _____ Sales, cost of goods, operating expenses, net profit (or loss).

Answers to ✓ Check for Understanding
1. F.   2. D.   3. B.   4. A.   5. E.   6. C.

APPLICATIONS

1. Complete the definitions of the identified terms used in the construction of charts, graphs, and tables.

Term	Description and purpose
1. Bar chart	
2. Graph	
3. Line chart	
4. Footnote	
5. Scale caption	
6. Pie chart	
7. Source note	
8. Table	
9. Category	
10. Title	

2. Given the following data, select the proper format for presentation and prepare a chart or table using all of the components for a proper business presentation to aid the decision being made:

Student ages	Number in 1985	Number in 1986	Number in 1987	Number in 1988
6–8	114	126	132	125
9–11	67	88	75	78
12–14	44	24	28	33
15–18	109	131	120	110

   SOURCE: School District 89, Annual Report, Spring 1987
   Decision to be made: What change is taking place—e.g., growth or decline—and what is the change impact by group?

3. The Com-Pare Shoe Corporation projected its total expense budget for the next operating year. An evaluation of the representative categories is to be made. Select and prepare the chart or table you feel is most appropriate for this format.

Cost of manufactured goods	$1,200,000
Administrative salaries	$ 280,500
Labor	$ 840,000
All utilities	$ 68,000
Operating expenses	$ 164,000
Miscellaneous expenses	$ 85,000

The Standard Deviation— Statistical Dispersion

17.4

The mean, median, and mode presented earlier in this chapter represent measures of **central tendency.** Their principal use was to describe a typical middle value for a set of numbers. Business also needs to be able to describe how much variation, or spread, exists in a set of numbers; it indicates how close the numbers are in value. For example, the number of sales for a product in North Carolina ranges from 1,000 to 1,150 for a company's sales force. This might indicate consistency in their sales effort. Another set of data for New England might reflect sales varying from 825 to 1,400 for the sales force. Although other elements could influence the variation, it represents a performance difference between the two areas, which might be significant.

A measurement of **dispersion** used to describe the numerical spread of numbers is a widely used value called the **standard deviation**. The standard deviation measures *the average amount of numerical difference* by which values in a set differ from their mean; the mean represents the mathematical center of the data. The standard deviation shows how close the individual numbers of the set are to their mean. *The smaller the value of the standard deviation, the more closely the mean represents the individual numbers in the data set.*

The symbol used to identify the standard deviation of *population* data is σ. (Note: A **population** is a set of variables for the entire group of data being studied. It is the most complete data set used for management decision making.) A **sample** differs from a population in that it is only a representative part of the population under study, not the whole population. If a standard deviation of a sample is needed, the formula changes slightly. The symbol for the mean changes from μ to $\bar{x}$ although the calculation procedures remain identical. The symbol for the standard deviation changes from σ to s. The formula value of "N" becomes "$n-1$" (sample size minus one). This difference affects the answer slightly. It is used because the variability of sample means is measured around their own mean rather than the population mean. *The standard deviation problems in this chapter use the population standard deviation formula below.*

Standard Deviation

$$\sigma = \sqrt{\frac{\Sigma(x - \mu)^2}{N}}$$

Alternate Formula

$$s = \sqrt{\frac{\Sigma(x - \bar{x})^2}{n - 1}}$$

Where:

- σ = Standard deviation of a population.
- $\sqrt{}$ = The square root of the value.
- Σ = The sum of the calculations (add them up).
- x = The individual variable numerical values.
- $\bar{x}$ = The symbol to represent the mean of the values for a sample (called "x-bar").
- μ = The symbol to represent the population mean.
- N = The number of numbers in the population.
- n = The number of numbers in the sample.

CALCULATOR TIP

Follow these calculator steps to solve for the standard deviation using the preceding formula:

- Step 1. Calculate the mean of the individual numbers.
- Step 2. Subtract the mean from each individual number and square the difference.
- Step 3. Sum the squared differences. Divide by the number of numbers in the population.
- Step 4. Use the square root key on your calculator.

EXAMPLE 6 Find the standard deviation of the following population data. The values represent time (in minutes).

26 32 58 46 31 29 46 43 49

Solution: The mean for this data is 360 ÷ 9 = 40.

The calculation for the standard deviation is supported by setting the data needed into a table for calculation.

x	μ	$(x - \mu)$	$(x - \mu)^2$
26	40	−14	196
32	40	− 8	64
58	40	+18	324
46	40	+ 6	36
31	40	− 9	81
29	40	−11	121
46	40	+ 6	36
43	40	+ 3	9
49	40	+ 9	81
			948

The sum of differences squared: 948. $N = 9$ identifies the numbers in the population. All the calculated values needed for the standard deviation are now available.

$s = \sqrt{948 \div (9)}$ • Step 1. Calculate 948 ÷ 9.
$s = \sqrt{105.33\overline{3}}$ • Step 2. Calculate the square root (use calculator key for square root).
• Step 3. 10.263202 or 10.26.

The average numerical distance of each variable in the population data from its mean of 40 is 10.3 minutes. □

EXAMPLE 7 What is the standard deviation for this dollar sample data?

64 48 54 62 65 58 56 53

Solution: The mean for this data is 460 ÷ 8 or 57.5. Set the data into a table for calculation.

x	μ	$(x - \mu)$	$(x - \mu)^2$
64	57.5	+6.5	42.25
48	57.5	−9.5	90.25
54	57.5	−3.5	12.25
62	57.5	+4.5	20.25
65	57.5	+7.5	56.25
58	57.5	+0.5	.25
56	57.5	−1.5	2.25
53	57.5	−4.5	20.25
			244.00

The sum of differences squared: 244. $N = 8$ identifies the numbers in the population.

- Step 1. Complete the division 244 ÷ 8.
- Step 2. Take the square root of 30.5.
- Step 3. Standard deviation (σ) is 5.5226805 or 5.52.

The average numerical distance of each of the sample numbers from its mean is $5.52.

✔ CHECK FOR UNDERSTANDING

1. Find the mean and the standard deviation for this sample data. (Measurements are in ounces.)

    9.1   8.8   9.2   10.0   8.9   9.5   9.7   8.8

2. What are the sample mean and standard deviation for these sales transactions?

    23   35   21   39   38   29

3. Twelve compact cars were tested for in-town miles-per-gallon performance. What are the mean and standard deviation of the results?

    30   28   26   23   28   24   25   25   27   23   32   34

SKILL EXERCISES

Calculate the individual variation around the following means:

	Variable	Population mean	$(x - \mu)$	$(x - \mu)^2$
1.	28	12	_____	_____
2.	142.6	84	_____	_____

Answers to ✔ Check for Understanding
1. Mean = 9.25; std. dev. = .415.   2. Mean = 30.8; std. dev. = 7.03.   3. Mean = 27.08; std. dev. = 3.35.

Section 17.4   The Standard Deviation—Statistical Dispersion

3.	59	62.8
4.	32.8	44
5.	84.6	83
6.	12	6
7.	24.1	18.4
8.	74.8	56.2
9.	80	74.1
10.	180.2	177
11.	47	39
12.	76	95
13.	27	34
14.	12.4	9.4
15.	8.2	7.1

Use the following data to compute a population standard deviation:

	Summation $\Sigma(x - \mu)^2$	Population size (N)	Standard deviation (4-place accuracy)
16.	334.6	30	
17.	1285.82	14	
18.	144	18	
19.	2120.92	26	
20.	664.73	17	

APPLICATIONS

1. Calculate the mean and standard deviation for personnel ages in an office complex:

   26   26   28   30   38   42   27   30   18   21

2. A study group received the following grades on a study lab exercise. What were the group mean and standard deviation?

   94   86   54   65   78   80   85

3. Eight brands of beer were tested for alcohol content. Compute the mean and standard deviation of the data.

   4.7   4.6   5.2   3.9   4.4   4.8   5.1   5.8

4. The following reactions to emergency braking tests were recorded for women. What were their mean and standard deviation reaction times? (Data recorded in seconds.)

   1.8   0.9   1.2   1.35   1.4   .96   1.0

5. A study recording the number of peak-period phone calls per minute was conducted. What are the mean and standard deviation of the results below?

   26   14   23   20   18   16   21   20   19   18

6. Part-time hours worked per week by college business students were measured. What are the mean and standard deviation for the following data?

   10   16   20   20   16   12   14   14
   12   12   8   16   20   12   16

7. Test scores for a business math exam reflected the following results. What were the group mean and standard deviation?

   94   82   80   76   72   71   58   64   79   84   86   88

8. College entrance exams were reviewed for a group of applicants. What were the mean and standard deviation of their data?

   440   428   324   496   500   620   580   460   502

9. Weekly amounts of soft drinks consumed were evaluated for 12 local households. The results were recorded as numbers of cans. What were the mean and standard deviation of the data?

   24   18   12   6   14   6   8   24   32   6   12   18

10. A new art form was evaluated by 15 students. The ratings from 1 to 10 were recorded over a 3-day period. What are the mean and standard deviation for their ratings?

    1   8   4   4   3   2   1   9   1   4   5   5   6   2   2

Section 17.4   The Standard Deviation—Statistical Dispersion

Key Terms

Arithmetic center (473)
Array (474)
Average (472, 473)
Bar chart (479)
Central tendency (486)
Dispersion (487)
Line chart (479, 480)
Mean (472, 473)
Median (472, 473)

Mode (472, 475)
Pie chart (479, 481)
Population (487)
Sample (487)
Standard deviation (487)
Statistics (472)
Table (479, 481)
Ungrouped data (472)

Looking Back

The important element regarding the use of statistical averages is the understanding that each average has special characteristics. Each can be used to best meet a particular need to explain data. As the data shows more numerical spread, the mean becomes less desirable to use as the typical value.

The median and the mode can be used instead of the mean when there are extreme values in a data set. They can also be used as a supplement to the mean for making the number dynamics clearer for the decision maker.

Concentrate on the specific purpose for each of the table and chart formats. Do not try to show data to managers without using the format that best represents the data presentation objective. Consider the objectives of the four methods: change, allocation, comparison, and numbers to avoid misleading the decision maker.

Let's Review

1. Calculate the mean and standard deviation for the following results of a speed test:

   100.2   101.4   100.6   102.8   96.3   95.4   99.2   100.3

2. Set the following data into an array. Compute the median.

   26   32   59   84   91   72
   48   51   34   46   47   51

3. Find the mode for the listed data set:

   128   162   171   134   134   128
   134   128   114   118   151   164
   321   151   127   128   143   164

4. That part of a table or chart used to explain omissions or to give additional information not found in the data arrangement is called a _____.

492   Chapter 17   Business Statistics and Graphs

5. The following data represents production reject quantities per 1,000 units produced. What are the mean and the standard deviation of the data?

9.2	10.8	15	12	12.9	9	8.5
12.6	11.4	14	13	10	8	13.2

6. Evaluate the following price information. Determine which typical measure of central tendency (mean, median, or mode) should be used to illustrate the data characteristics. Compute the value of the median.

10.92	24.86	8.41	5.36	29.62
3.24	35.82	12.00	19.80	46.50

7. Evaluate the following dress size data and determine the mode:

10	12	8	8	10	8	6
8	12	10	10	12	10	12
10	6	12	8	6	10	6

8. Compute the mean number of voters for given voting district sizes.

863	924	836	521	634	741
852	1008	532	744	918	823

9. Compute the mean and the standard deviation for the following data set:

126	134	129	144	190
182	163	140	126	138

10. The origin of the data in a statistical chart is found by using the information provided by the _____.

11. Find the median for the following data:

36	41	59	87	93
49	52	71	64	92
32	42	56	75	81

Chapter Test

1. Calculate the mean and standard deviation for the given evaluation ratings:

8.4	9.6	8.4	7.8	9.2	8.8	8.7	9.1	7.4

2. Find the mode in the following set of data:

144	134	126	123	123	144
126	138	114	144	162	126
134	144	123	114	138	162

3. If you wanted to compare major expense categories for a manufacturing company, which type chart would give you the best comparison?

4. Find the median for the following data measurements:

126	132	584	326	189	375
251	199	266	431	340	481
261	332	500	509	312	526

5. A representative segment of a statistical population is called a _____.

6. What type of presentation should be used to illustrate the income areas of a company?

7. What is the mean of the following data? Is it a good representative of the typical variable value?

136.2	890.4	331.2	426.4	380.4
261.3	340.6	450.9	780.6	312.0

8. Using respective data groups, calculate standard deviations for each. Determine which of the two data groups has the greatest amount of dispersion around its respective mean.

Group A			Group B		
15.1	28.2	13.6	15.6	26.4	12.8
19.7	21.4	18.6	19.9	18.6	18.4
19.2	14.3	16.4	13.5	14.2	17.2

9. What is the median of this group of data? Is there a mode?

26	35	15	84	76	29	41	62
52	30	41	47	44	29	86	

10. The following accident information has been gathered by the company quality control/safety department. Review the information and prepare an appropriate chart or table that will support the review of the information regarding how the data is changing.

Source: Accident Study, 1987, Safecat Corp.

Struck by falling object: 1984, 213
         1985, 205
         1986, 225
         1987, 190

Caught accidentally between objects: 1984, 24
              1985, 15
              1986, 31
              1987, 26

Cutting or piercing instruments: 1984, 88
             1985, 90
             1986, 102
             1987, 76

Machinery accident: 1984, 126
         1985, 135
         1986, 133
         1987, 152

Appendix A
An Introduction to MICROPAK Software for Business Mathematics

The MICROPAK disk contains ten IBM-compatible microcomputer programs, and a set of instructions to load and initiate the MICROPAK programs.

Useful Terms

Menu	A list of alternative procedure options offered to the user. The user selects from the alternatives in choosing a program option to run.
Key	A pre-set keyboard key that performs special computer functions such as printing instructions or changing data.
Return key	The keyboard key shown as a right-turn arrow (or RETURN key) that is used to enter instructions into the computer.
Prompt	A screen question that is expected to be answered by the user. The flashing space indicator located at the prompt position indicates where the response should be typed.

MICROPAK Software Selection Menu

Program Name	Menu Number
Loan Payment Schedule	1
Descriptive Statistics	2
Open to Buy	3
Average Margin	4
Breakeven Analysis	5
Annuity Value	6
Inventory Turnover	7
Depreciation Schedule	8
Determine Interest Rate	9
Financial Ratios	10

Computer System Readiness Instructions

MICROPAK software may be used with any IBM-compatible computer using an MS-DOS system. The instructions that follow pertain to a dual floppy disk drive system. For single disk drive or hard disk systems, refer to your systems manuals.

Action Step	Instruction
Turn on computer	• Insert system disk in Drive A.
	• Insert MICROPAK disk in Drive B.
	• Turn on computer.
Load programs	• These programs require an IBM-compatible computer using MS-DOS 2.0 or higher disk operating system.
Screen shows A>	• **Type in** BASIC, BASICA, or GWBASIC, the BASIC language your system uses.

Note: By typing DIR and pressing RETURN, the screen will display a directory of the A disk drive. Look for the type of BASIC language available to your system (BASIC, BASICA, or GWBASIC).

Screen shows "OK"	**Type in** LOAD"B:MP"	RETURN key
Screen shows "OK"	**Type in** RUN	RETURN key

Loan Payment Schedule

> **REFERENCE SECTION:** Chapter 9 Personal Finance
> **PROGRAM NAME:** Loan Payment Schedule Menu #1
> **REQUIRED INPUT:** Annual Interest Rate
> **DATA:** Amount Borrowed
> Loan Time Period in Years

INPUT PROBLEMS

1. What would be the monthly payment and the amount of total interest paid on a loan of $18,300 if it were taken at 10.5% for 6 years?

2. Aspen Glow Lighting borrowed $18,500 for 8 years at 12.5%. What amount of total interest would it have paid the first year?

3. Show a first-year amortization schedule for a $96,000, 30-year, 9% mortgage. What are the monthly payments?

4. Bendo Tubing & Pipe Company wanted to borrow $8,000 for an industry expansion project. If the company paid 11.5% interest for 4 years, would the payments be less than $250 per month? What total interest would they be paying on this loan?

5. What amount of a monthly payment would be applied to the principal on the 36th payment of a 60-payment loan? The interest rate is 9.75% and the amount borrowed was $13,400.

Descriptive Statistics

REFERENCE SECTION: Chapter 17   Business Statistics and Graphs
PROGRAM NAME: Descriptive Statistics   Menu #2
REQUIRED INPUT: Individual Data Variable Values
DATA: Various Business-related Data Items

INPUT PROBLEMS

1. Compute the mean, median, and mode for the following data:

71	83	94	108	91	63	71
56	107	46	48	96	84	77
85	65	73	74	62	88	84
94	94	77	91	82	81	65
81	52	58	65	71	64	63

2. What are the mean and standard deviation for the following cost data?

$ 8.42	$ 9.65	$21.83	$14.80	$14.26
$17.44	$14.65	$12.00	$13.50	$12.82
$19.40	$18.20	$ 9.80	$11.75	$21.42
$16.50	$18.75	$12.60	$15.21	$16.24

3. Enter the following data into your computer and evaluate the mean, median, and mode. Which do you feel represents the data the best?

68	85	101	139	177
124	140	96	130	141
197	164	179	89	126
144	168	148	164	184
156	92	153	176	152
170	152	168	181	95
128	136	144	164	176
135	121	87	174	139

4. What is the standard deviation for the following quality control data?

21.6	36.5	63.9	59.8	60.1
32.5	44.5	52.1	53.6	49.7
48.7	40.4	30.0	28.3	50.1
31.4	32.4	37.6	41.1	52.7
51.4	39.8	42.4	53.9	61.8
47.7	49.7	59.7	60.4	52.6
37.6	57.6	36.5	29.4	26.6

5. Given the following data, calculate the mean, median, and standard deviation:

641.8	806.4	741.2	624.3	701.3
762.1	628.4	862.6	658.4	890.1
693.8	744.5	633.4	671.5	841.5
774.5	636.7	650.6	601.4	706.5
721.3	786.5	701.6	813.7	724.7
821.7	878.6	716.5	836.5	615.4
796.2	642.4	670.1	809.1	834.1
694.5	620.1	711.9	640.3	662.7
809.8	670.9	818.6	712.8	844.3
821.5	690.8	808.4	665.3	751.3
811.6	721.4	635.4	770.9	808.6
834.6	801.6	774.6	821.4	621.4

Open to Buy

> **REFERENCE SECTION:** Chapter 14 Retail Operations
> **PROGRAM NAME:** Open to Buy   Menu #3
> **REQUIRED INPUT:** All Data at Retail
> **DATA:** Average Margin at Retail
> Beginning Inventory
> Actual Sales
> Actual Markdown Sales
> Orders Received
> Planned Ending Inventory
> Orders Pending
> Planned Sales
> Planned Markdown Sales

INPUT PROBLEMS

1. Compute the open to buy at cost for the following retail data. All data at retail.

Orders pending	$42,000
Actual sales	$23,000
Actual markdown sales	$12,400
Beginning inventory	$82,000
Orders received	$66,000
Planned ending inventory	$73,000
Planned sales	$365,000
Planned markdown sales	$42,000

   Average margin is 43.5%.

2. For the following retail situation, calculate the open to buy at cost. All data at retail.

Beginning inventory	$36,000
Planned ending inventory	$52,500
Planned sales	$102,600
Orders received	$21,000
Orders pending	$8,550
Actual sales	$18,400

   Average margin is 46%.

3. Christine Designs required an open to buy decision. What amount should be budgeted to support the open to buy cost with these planning data:

Planned sales	$240,300
Planned markdowns	$68,000
Beginning inventory	$74,800
Planned ending inventory	$85,500
Actual markdowns	$7,400
Actual sales	$47,000
Orders pending	$84,300

   Average margin is 42.8%.

4. Custom Line Foods determined that its sales projections for the next period included the following. All data at retail.

Beginning inventories	$138,000
Planned ending inventories	$225,000
Planned sales	$1,475,300
Orders received	$68,000
Orders pending	$416,800

   If Custom Line's average margin was 26.5%, what would the open to buy at cost be?

5. Find the open to buy at cost for PROLIFE Lawn Food. All data at retail.

Beginning inventories	$63,000
Planned sales	$128,700
Planned ending inventories	$47,200
On order	$12,000
Actual sales	$64,100

   PROLIFE's average margin is 31.4%.

Average Margin

> **REFERENCE SECTION:** Chapter 14 Retail Operations
> **PROGRAM NAME:** Average Margin Menu #4
> **REQUIRED INPUT:** Margin per Category of Sales in Percent
> **DATA:** Sales Volume in Percent of Each Category

INPUT PROBLEMS

1. Hawken Retail carried 6 major categories of items for sale. Each category carried a separate margin. For the data given, determine the average margin:

Category	Margin	Percent of sales
a. Sporting	82%	12%
b. Hardware	47%	18%
c. Housewares	74%	13%
d. Tires	35%	28%
e. Automotive	58%	22%
f. Fixtures	60%	7%

2. What is the average margin for this wholesaler?

Category margin	Percent of sales
42%	30%
38%	23%
18%	32%
22%	15%

3. A department store showed the following category of products schedule. How much would the average margin change if the margin in Category D were doubled?

Category	Margin	Percent of sales
A	84%	12%
B	63%	16%
C	41%	23%
D	12%	21%
E	36%	28%

4. Determine the average margin for the following retail categories:

Department	Margin	Percent of sales
FN	46%	18%
AL	32%	24%
ZY	21%	15%
PB	28%	30%
EF	39%	13%

5. MERKIR Tool & Die Inc. priced its products in three general classifications. For the data provided, determine the average margin on sales.

Category	Margin	Percent of sales
Machined	63%	32%
Fabrication	41%	46%
Assembly	52%	22%

Breakeven Analysis

> **REFERENCE SECTION:** Appendix B   Breakeven Analysis
> **PROGRAM NAME:** Breakeven Analysis   Menu #5
> **REQUIRED INPUT:** Fixed Costs
> Variable Costs
> Total Revenue or Sales Forecast
> Number Units Produced

INPUT PROBLEMS

1. A production run was planned for 18,000 units. Total revenues from sale of this run were projected to be $645,120. With the cost data shown below, what is the breakeven point in units?

	Production		Sales
Variable	$82,000	Variable	$212,000
Fixed	$12,000	Fixed	$6,400

2. Given the following production data, determine the breakeven point in units:

Total units produced	$26,000
Production	
Variable costs	$3,240
Fixed costs	$4,000
Sales	
Variable costs	$5,120
Fixed costs	$1,280
Price per unit	$7.25

3. Analyze the following breakeven information:

Total units produced   3,800
Total revenue from production sales $706,800

Production	
Variable costs	$87,400
Fixed costs	$15,200
Selling	
Variable costs	$15,400
Fixed costs	$8,300

(a) What is the breakeven point in units?
(b) If the total fixed costs could be reduced by 8%, what would happen to the breakeven point?

4. Projected sales for the annual promotion period were forecasted to be $685,000. If fixed costs totaled $122,000 and variable costs came to $260,000, what is the breakeven point as a percent of sales? What dollar amount of sales is breakeven?

5. Find the percent of sales breakeven point for a $1,400,000 sales budget. Total fixed costs are forecasted to be $240,000 and variable costs $650,000.

Annuity Value

> REFERENCE SECTION: Chapter 12 Investments
> PROGRAM NAME: Annuity Value Menu #6
> REQUIRED INPUT: Annual, Monthly, Quarterly Payments
> DATA: Amount of Annuity Payment
> Number of Years of Annuity
> Annual Interest Rate

INPUT PROBLEMS

1. By investing $2,000 annually at 8% compound interest, what amount would be accumulated after 10 years?

2. Tayscreen Company deposits $600 monthly in an annuity compounded at 12.75%. What would the account balance be after 5 years?

3. Future expansion planning required the Harbor Marine Company to deposit $1,500 in a quarterly annuity for 6 years. If the interest rate was 10.5%, how much would Harbor Marine have accumulated after the first 3 years?

4. Bengar Manufacturing is planning to meet its needs for $40,000 three years from now. They have decided to use a monthly annuity savings account to meet their need. If they could get a guaranteed 8%, would a deposit of $1,000 meet their goals?

5. Five years from now a "balloon payment" on a property will become due. The amount owed is $36,000. If an interest rate of 9.5% could be guaranteed, would a quarterly annuity deposit of $1,400 meet the payment?

Inventory Turnover

> **REFERENCE SECTION:** Chapter 14 Retail Operations
> **PROGRAM NAME:** Inventory Turnover Menu #7
> **REQUIRED INPUT:** Inventory Valuations (Cost/Retail)
> **DATA:** Cost of Goods Sold
> Average Inventory (Cost/Retail)
> Total Sales
> Average Margin

INPUT PROBLEMS

1. Average inventory at cost is $32,600. What will the inventory turnover be if the cost of goods sold for the period is $264,000?

2. Tall Tree Nursery showed a beginning inventory at cost of $36,500. Ending inventory at cost was $24,300. If the average margin was 46% and sales for the period totaled $163,200, what was the inventory turnover?

3. Ye Cuppe Corner Gift Shop had inventories for the year at cost of $12,000, $18,600, $24,000, and $18,200. If the average margin was 43.5% and if total sales for the period were $187,400, what was the stock turnover?

4. Elima Wholesale carried an average merchandise level at retail of $284,600. The costs of the goods totaled $102,000. With an average margin of 36%, what was the inventory turnover?

5. Given total sales for the accounting period of $285,000 with a 48.5% average margin, what would the inventory turnover be if beginning and ending inventories at cost were $36,400 and $28,700, respectively?

Depreciation Schedule

> **REFERENCE SECTION:** Chapter 11 Depreciation & Inventory Valuation
> **PROGRAM NAME:** Depreciation Schedule Menu #8
> **REQUIRED INPUT:** Asset Purchase Price
> **DATA:** Added Installed Cost
> Number of Years to Be Depreciated
> Estimated Salvage Value
> Acceleration Factor—Declining Balance
>
> *Special Note:* Type in 0.0 whenever there is no data for input.

INPUT PROBLEMS

1. The cost of a depreciable asset is $9,740. Additional installed costs for placing the equipment into operation total $1,260. Salvage value is estimated at $1,500 with a 7-year useful life. Run a straight line and a sum of the years' digits depreciation schedule. How much difference in depreciation would there be in the second year?

2. The Hacklite Communications Center acquired a new piece of equipment. The asset purchase price was $18,200. There was a $200 salvage value on the equipment. Its useful life was estimated at 6 years. Using a declining balance method and twice the straight line rate, what was the third-year depreciation?

3. The Makemor Bakery bought new ovens at an installed cost of $13,400. The life of the equipment is 5 years, with an estimated salvage value of $4,200. Prepare a depreciation comparison using the straight line, double declining balance, sum of the years' digits, and ACRS methods. Which method has the greatest third-year depreciation?

4. Compare the ACRS and the sum of the years' digits depreciation schedules for a personal computer. Use a 5-year depreciation schedule. The equipment has an installed cost of $6,820 with a $1,500 salvage value. Which method provides the greatest total depreciation for three years?

5. Evaluate the depreciation for an engine analyzer using the straight line, sum of the years' digits, double declining balance, and ACRS methods. The equipment depreciation period is 10 years. Initial costs are $126,000 with a $25,000 salvage value. Which method provides the greatest depreciation in the fifth year?

Determine Interest Rate

> **REFERENCE SECTION:** Chapter 9 Personal Finance
> **PROGRAM NAME:** Determine Interest Rate Menu #9
> **REQUIRED INPUT:** Total Amount Borrowed
> **DATA:** Amount of Monthly Payment
> Length of Loan in Years

INPUT PROBLEMS

1. $70,000 was borrowed to be repaid over 30 years. The monthly payments were $740.60. What interest rate was being used?

2. A new vehicle was purchased with a consumer loan. The amount to be financed was $11,000 over 60 months. If the payments were $253.11 per month, what was the interest rate?

3. Business equipment offered for purchase at $26,000 could be carried with monthly payments for 10 years at $402.62. What would the interest rate be for this offer?

4. A builder has offered you an opportunity to finance your new $105,000 business location. Payments could be made monthly. Two financial alternatives have been presented.
   (a) Fifteen years at $1,305 per month.
   (b) Twelve years at $1,400 per month.
   Which offer carries the best interest rate?

5. You have been offered money to expand your business. Repayment could be done monthly. The offer on the $50,000 loan included 10-year terms of $920 per month. Was this amount greater or less than your 15% desired maximum?

Financial Ratios

REFERENCE SECTION: Chapter 16 Financial Statements and Ratios
PROGRAM NAME: Financial Ratios Menu #10
REQUIRED INPUT: Balance Sheet Information
DATA: Asset and Liability Categories

INPUT PROBLEMS

Compute the debt-to-equity ratio, the current ratio, and the acid-test ratio for the following illustrated balance sheets:

1.
Riteon Screen Company

Current assets		
Cash	$18,400	
Accounts receivable	31,400	
Inventory	16,400	
Notes receivable	8,000	
Total current assets		$ 74,200
Other assets		
Land	20,000	
Buildings	40,000	
Furniture and equipment	28,000	
Total other assets		$ 88,000
Total assets		$162,200
Current liabilities		
Accounts payable	19,200	
Notes payable	45,000	
Total current liabilities		$ 64,200
Other liabilities		
Loans payable	25,600	
Total liabilities		$ 89,200
Owner's equity		$ 73,000
Total liabilities and owner's equity		$162,200

2.

Mountain Glow Rocke

Assets

Current assets
  Cash $8,100
  Accounts receivable 9,900
  Notes receivable 500
  Inventory 26,300
    Total current assets $44,800
Fixed assets
  Land 3,500
  Buildings 69,000
  Equipment and machinery 4,000
    Total fixed assets $76,500

Liabilities

Current liabilities
  Accounts payable 1,950
  Notes payable 24,000
    Total current liabilities $25,950
Fixed liabilities
  Mortgages payable 9,900
  Loans payable 36,200
    Total fixed liabilities $46,100

Stockholders' Equity

Capital stock 10,000
Retained earnings 39,250
  Total $49,250

3.

Happiness Oyster Bar

Assets

Current assets
  Cash $2,700
  Accounts receivable 8,000
  Notes receivable 300
  Inventory 1,000
    Total current assets $12,000
Fixed assets
  Furniture and equipment 13,000
  Long-term notes 2,000
    Total fixed assets $15,000

Liabilities

Current liabilities
  Accounts payable 1,300
  Notes payable 2,500
    Total current liabilities $3,800
Fixed liabilities
  Mortgage payable 8,000
    Total fixed liabilities $8,000

Stockholders' Equity

Capital stock	10,000	
Retained earnings	5,200	
Total		$ 15,200

4. ### Coastline Supply Inc.

Assets

Current assets	
Cash	$ 3,600
Accounts receivable	15,000
Notes receivable	5,400
Inventory	42,000
Fixed assets	
Buildings	50,000
Furnishings	14,000
Long-term note	10,500
Land	10,200

Liabilities

Current liabilities	
Accounts payable	14,400
Taxes payable	2,000
Notes payable	1,600
Long-term liabilities	
Mortgage	30,000

Owner's Equity

Owner, capital	52,500
Retained earnings	50,200

5. ### Southern Stage Decorations

Assets

Current assets	
Cash	$ 60,000
Accounts receivable	160,000
Inventory	200,000
Fixed assets	
Plant facilities	285,000
Equipment	115,000

Liabilities

Current liabilities	
Accounts payable	80,000
Notes payable	104,000
Interest payable	16,000
Long-term liabilities	
Mortgages payable	100,000

Owner's Equity

Owner's equity	520,000

Financial Ratios

Appendix B
Breakeven Analysis

Breakeven Graphical Method

Breakeven analysis is a mathematical approach to determining at what point net profit begins. In constructing a simplified breakeven chart, one uses the components of cost and revenue. The chart can be used to determine where in a production or sales activity fixed costs and variable costs have been recovered.

The simplified chart that follows shows that the vertical axis of the chart reflects a total dollar component for both cost and revenue. The horizontal axis shows a scale of the number of units of the product being produced and sold.

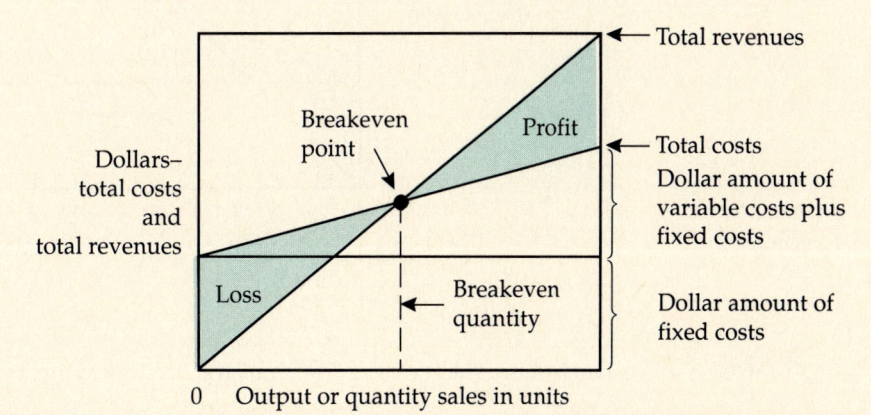

A simplified breakeven chart

Fixed and variable costs are plotted graphically to find the breakeven point. Fixed costs are constant. We draw the line horizontally at its level on the vertical dollar scale.

Variable costs increase each time a new unit is produced. The plot of variable costs starts at the left of the fixed costs line and slants up and to the right, because variable costs are an addition to fixed costs. For this same reason, the line also represents total costs.

Total revenue is a straight line as well. Revenue is incurred from the sale of a unit at its price. Prices do not change within the analysis of any one problem.

Breakeven Graphical Method—Units

The breakeven point for a chart is where the *total revenue* line crosses the *total cost* line. From this point, extend a line down vertically until it intersects the quantity axis. The value on the scale represents the breakeven quantity, which is the number of units that must be sold before any net profit can be accumulated.

EXAMPLE 1 Draw a breakeven analysis chart and determine the breakeven quantity for the Myrad Corporation. The company will be producing a new game for teenagers. Base your chart on 1,000 units of production and the following statistical information:

Fixed costs of production	$1,500
Variable costs of production	$3,000
Fixed costs of sales	$1,000
Variable costs of sales	$1,000
Total profit desired	$\frac{2}{3}$ of the total production costs

Solution:

$4,500 · Total production costs.
$2,000 · Total selling costs.

$4,500 × $\frac{2}{3}$ = $3,000   · Calculated profit.

Production costs + Selling costs + Profit = Total revenue
$4,500 + $2,000 + $3,000 = $9,500   · Total revenue.
Draw your breakeven chart.

ANSWER: Breakeven point approximates 455 units.

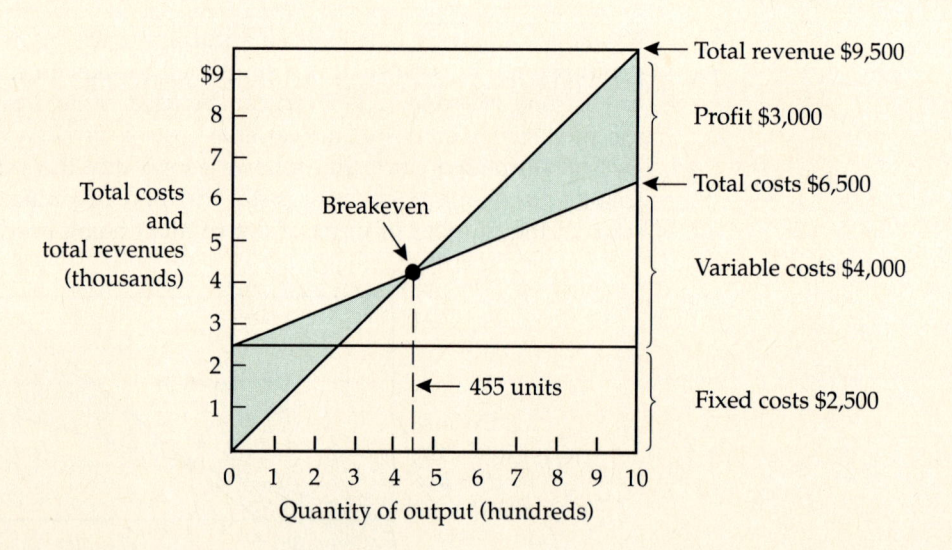

Breakeven chart for Myrad Corporation

EXAMPLE 2 Draw a breakeven analysis chart for the following production problem of 3,000 units:

Production		
	Variable costs	$68,000
	Fixed costs	$30,000
Markup		
	Fixed costs of sales	$12,800
	Variable costs of sales	$50,000
	Profit return	$140,000

Solution: Plot these values:

$42,800	• Total fixed costs.
$118,000	• Total variable costs.
($160,800)	• Total costs.
$300,800	• Total revenue.

ANSWER: Breakeven point approximates 702 units.

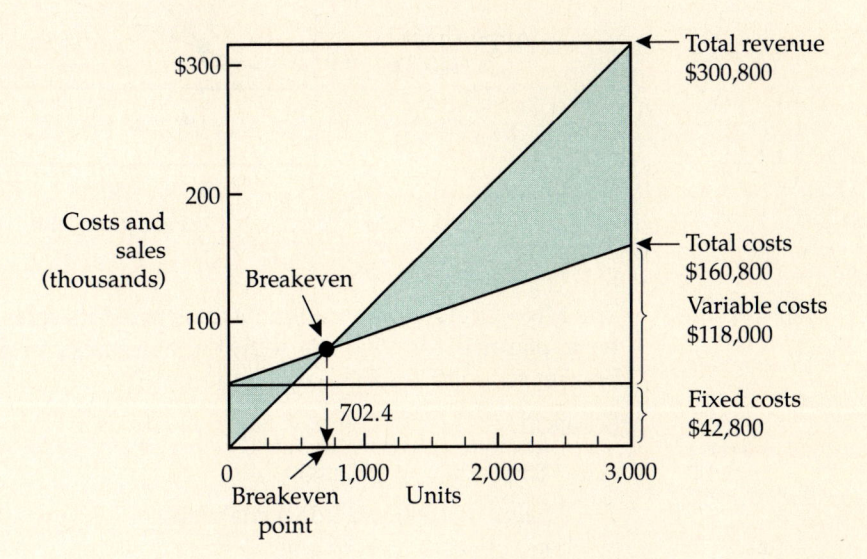

Production breakeven

Breakeven Graphical Method—Sales Percent

The breakeven chart is also commonly used with an amount of expected sales. Fixed and variable costs are plotted in relation to an expected dollar amount of sales. The anticipated level of sales is usually referred to as a percent of sales capacity. If, for instance, the expected level of sales is projected to be $75,000, you can use this figure as a 100% projection of sales to evaluate your expenses and calculate the breakeven point.

EXAMPLE 3   JAZZMO Record Corporation expects a $1.5 million sales year. The total fixed costs for this sales level are $265,000. The total variable costs are calculated to be 36% of sales. Draw a breakeven chart for this sales volume and determine the breakeven point as a percent of sales and as a dollar volume of sales.

Solution:

- Total sales = $1,500,000.
- Sales = 100% on horizontal axis.
- Fixed costs = $265,000.
- Variable costs = .36 × 1,500,000 = $540,000.

ANSWER: Breakeven point approximates 27.6%; $414,062.50.

See chart at top of page A–18

Breakeven Graphical Method   A–17

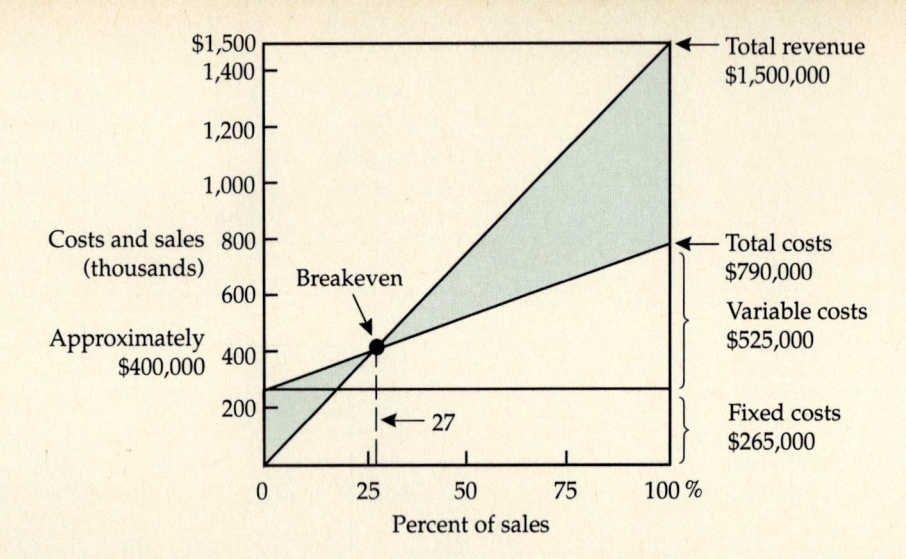

Breakeven chart for JAZZMO Record Corporation

EXAMPLE 4 The Mixo-Grindo Corporation has budgeted its sales volume at $950,000. Fixed costs were planned for $150,000 with variable costs projected at $350,000. What is the breakeven point for this sales projection?

Solution:

- Total sales = $950,000.
- Sales = 100% on horizontal axis.
- Fixed costs = $150,000.
- Variable costs = $350,000.

ANSWER: Breakeven point approximates 25%; $237,500.

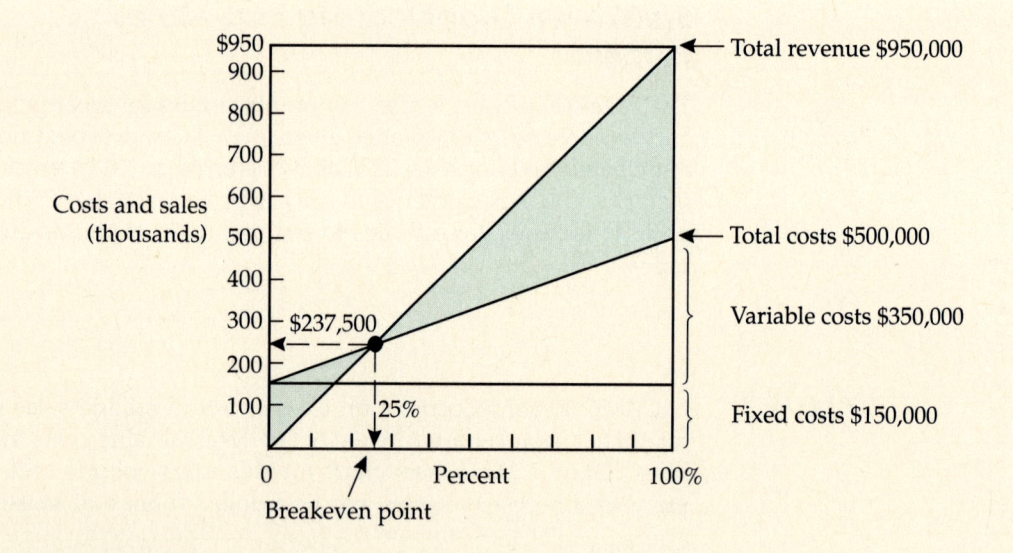

Breakeven chart for Mixo-Grindo Corporation

Breakeven Formula Method

Breakeven positions may also be derived with the use of standard math formulas. The formula method would be used if a statistical chart was not required. The formula method will produce the same breakeven position as the chart presentation.

Breakeven Formula Method—Units

Finding the unit breakeven point with its formula requires that you identify values similar to those previously presented. The values needed to compute the breakeven point include

- **Total fixed costs** for the production run. (Combine the fixed cost of sales and fixed cost of production.)
- **Revenue per unit.** (Divide total revenues from sales by the number of units sold.)
- **Variable costs per unit.** (Divide the total variable costs from production and sales by the total number of units being produced.)

$$\text{Breakeven (in units)} = \frac{\text{Total fixed costs}}{\text{Revenue per unit} - \text{Variable costs per unit}}$$

EXAMPLE 5 Calculate the breakeven point for the BALUP Corporation. The total expected sales for the production run of 25,000 units was $85,642.50. Production costs were summarized as:

Production:	
Fixed costs	$11,300
Variable costs	$18,750
Markup:	
Variable costs of sales	18%
Fixed costs of sales	22%
Profit element of markup	145%

Solution:

11,300	• Fixed costs of production.
18,750	• Variable costs of production.
11,300 + 18,750 = $30,050	• Total production costs.
30,050 × .18 = $5,409	• Variable costs of sales.
30,050 × .22 = $6,611	• Fixed costs of sales.
11,300 + 6,611 = $17,911	• Total fixed costs.
18,750 + 5,409 = 24,159	• Total variable costs.
$\frac{\$85{,}642.50}{25{,}000} = \$3.4257$	• Revenue per unit.
$\frac{24{,}159}{25{,}000} = \$0.96636$	• Variable costs per unit.

$$\text{Breakeven} = \frac{\text{Total fixed costs}}{\text{Revenue per unit} - \text{Variable costs per unit}}$$

$\frac{17{,}911}{(3.4257 - 0.96636)}$	• Breakeven.
7282.85 units or 7283 units	• Breakeven in units.

EXAMPLE 6 What is the unit breakeven point for a production run of 11,000 units of BETHLO masking tape? The following is the planned production cost data:

Fixed costs of production	$8,320
Variable costs of production	$4,262
Variable costs of sales	$9,360
Fixed costs of sales	14% of total production costs
Profit = 42% of production costs	

Solution:

8,320 + 4,262 = 12,582	• Total production costs.
12,582 × .14 = 1,761.48	• Fixed cost of sales.
12,582 × .42 = 5,284.44	• Profit calculation.
9,360 + 1,761.48 = 11,121.48	• Total cost of sales.
11,121.48 + 5,284.44 = 16,405.92	• Total markup.
12,582 + 16,405.92 = 28,987.92	• Revenue.
$\frac{28,987.92}{11,000} = \$2.635$	• Revenue per unit.
13,622	• Total variable cost.
$\frac{13,622}{11,000} = \$1.238$	• Variable cost per unit.

$$\text{Breakeven} = \frac{\text{Total fixed costs}}{\text{Revenue per unit} - \text{Variable costs per unit}}$$

$$\text{Breakeven} = \frac{10,081.48}{2.635 - 1.238}$$

$$\text{Breakeven} \frac{10,081.48}{1.397} = 7,216.5 \text{ units.}$$

Breakeven rounded to whole units = 7,217 units. □

Breakeven Formula Method—Sales Percent

The breakeven point calculation for percent of sales requires that you identify three principal elements:

- **Total fixed costs**—for the sales projection
- **Total variable costs**—for the sales projection
- **Total revenues**—generated on the sales projection.

(Note: If the sales projection is met it then becomes revenue. Therefore, total sales projection is used as the revenue figure.)

Breakeven (percent of sales) Formula

$$\frac{\text{Total fixed costs}}{\text{Total revenues} - \text{Total variable costs}}$$

EXAMPLE 7 Bigthink Software Company projects sales for its new spreadsheet package at $750,000 for the first year. If the cost structure for these sales showed fixed costs to be $120,000 and variable costs to be $185,000, at what percent of sales would the breakeven point fall?

Solution:

$750,000	• Total revenue.
120,000	• Total fixed costs.
185,000	• Total variable costs.

$$\text{Breakeven} = \frac{120,000}{750,000 - 185,000}$$

Breakeven point = .2124 or 21.24% of sales.

EXAMPLE 8 An annual sales budget showed $365,000 fixed costs projection and $212,000 variable costs estimate. With total sales estimated to be $1.25 million, what is the sales level breakeven point? What percent of sales is breakeven?

Solution:

$1,250,000	• Total revenue.
365,000	• Total fixed costs.
212,000	• Total variable costs.

$$\text{Breakeven} = \frac{365,000}{1,250,000 - 212,000}$$

.35164 • Breakeven calculation.
35.16% • Breakeven in percent.
.35164 × 1,250,000 = 439,547.20 • Breakeven amount.

Let's Review

(Also check your chart and formula answers with MICROPAK.)

1. Compute the breakeven in units (closest whole unit) for the following production data on 8,500 units:

   Production:
       Variable costs $21,000
       Fixed costs $ 8,200
   Markup:
       Sales fixed costs $12,000
       Sales variable costs $ 9,400
       Profit component $38,000

2. What is the breakeven point in the closest whole unit for a production run of 12,500 electronic recorders with the following data:

   Production:
       Variable costs $126,000
       Fixed costs $ 28,000
   Markup:
       Sales costs (all variable) $ 38,000
       Profit component $300,000

3. Find the sales breakeven in percent for Klingplant Wholesale. A $2,506,000 sales budget is forecast. Total fixed costs are projected to be $864,000 with total variable costs planned for $962,000.

4. What is the projected sales breakeven level and breakeven sales percentage for the Sleezco Department Store?

> Sales projections $1,244,500
> Total variable costs of sales $ 382,000
> Total fixed costs of sales $ 483,000

5. How many units must be sold before Wanmen Manufacturing can break even on a production run of 26,000 NEWK condensors?

> Production:
>   Variable costs $18,020
>   Fixed costs $9,100
> Markup:
>   Selling costs variable $12,000
>   Selling costs fixed   32% of total production costs
>   Profit   58% of total production costs

6. What is the percent of sales breakeven point for the following sales projections?

> Total sales projected $347,600
> Total variable costs $ 94,000
> Total fixed costs $ 21,200

7. Can Globread Inc. break even at less than 50% of sales if costs and sales projections are:

> Total variable costs $ 464,000
> Total fixed costs $ 872,500
> Total sales projected $2,000,600

8. At what number of units would the breakeven point be for this production sequence?

> Total units produced   10,750
> Total fixed costs of manufacturing $ 28,000
> Total variable costs of manufacturing $126,000
> Profit projection $180,000
> Selling costs (all fixed) $ 32,500

9. Calculate the breakeven in the closest whole unit for Kodeek Cutlery. They are planning production of 125,000 new kitchen slicers. Production data reflects:

> Production:
>   Variable costs $182,400
>   Fixed costs $ 84,600
> Markup:
>   Variable costs of sales $ 12,400
>   Fixed costs of sales $ 8,000
>   Profit return $437,500

10. Define the breakeven dollar level of sales for a projected sales volume of $300,000 with a total fixed costs level of $126,000 and a total variable costs projection of $98,500.

Appendix C
Symbols, Weights, and Measures

The business world is repeatedly being exposed to various systems for expressing weights and measures. In addition to weights and measures, there are business symbols commonly used as a shorthand to communicate information. This appendix provides a brief review of the concepts for your reference.

U.S. Symbols

The more common business symbols have been provided in the table. Other symbols are introduced with weights and measures.

Business Symbols

Symbol	Meaning	Explanation
ea.	Each	Used to refer to the cost of an individual item (watermelons $2 ea.).
@	At	Used to refer to the cost of an individual item, usually when more than one item of the same kind is involved (12 oranges @ .30 = $3.60).
*	Asterisk	Refers a reader to additional information given elsewhere. Usually used when units are larger than usual.
#	Number; Pounds	When preceding a numeral, means "number"; when following, means "pounds" (#94 = number 94; 94# = 94 pounds).
%	Percent	Follows numbers that express ratios of 1 to 100.

(continued)

Business Symbols (continued)

Symbol	Meaning	Explanation
bbl.	Barrel	Unit of liquid or dry measure (barrel of oil; barrel of pork).
rm.	Ream	Approximately 500 sheets of paper.
bx.	Box	Standard-size container.
ctn.	Carton	Container usually holding more than one of the same item.
gr.	Gross	12 dozen, or 144.
rl.	Roll	Cylindrical or spool-like container or package (such as a roll of solder).
$	Dollars	Standard monetary unit.
¢	Cents	$\frac{1}{100}$ of one dollar.
lb.	Pound	16 ounces.
wt.	Weight	Specific gravity of an item.
hdwt.	Hundredweight	Unit comprising 100 pounds.
pkg.	Package	Container in which an item is sold.
"	Double quote	Used to express inches (linear measure) (50.8 mm = 2').
'	Single quote	Used to express feet (linear measure) (24 inches = 2').

SKILL EXERCISES

Identify the following symbols:

1. bbl. _____

2. pkg. _____

3. ctn. _____

4. # _____

5. gr. _____

6. bx. _____

7. hdwt. _____

8. rm. _____

9. rl. _____

10. ea. _____

APPLICATIONS

1. 34 horses @ $575 ea.   = $ _____

2. 375 rm. @ $3.65 ea.   = $ _____

3. 27 pkg. @ $127 ea.   = $ _____

4. 975 lb. @ $27 per hdwt.   = $ _____

5. 72" at $37.50 per 2'   = $ _____

6. 3 pkg., 6 ctn. per pkg., @ $5 per ctn.   = $ _____

7. 1 bx., 10 rm. per bx., @ $3.90 per rm.   = $ _____

8. 12 ctn., 48 rl. per ctn., @ $.80 per rl.   = $ _____

9. 287 bbl. @ $123.56 per bbl.   = $ _____

10. 40 ctn., 30# ea., @ $.15 per #   = $ _____

U.S. Weights and Measures

Typically, weights and measures used in business in the United States are linear measure, square measure, liquid measure, cubic measure, and avoirdupois weight. The following table provides some commonly used conversions for these weights and measures.

U.S. Weights and Measures
Linear Measure

Relationship	Multiply	By	To Obtain
ft. = 12 in.	inches (in.)	0.083333	feet
yd. = 36 in.	inches (in.)	0.027778	yards
	feet (ft.)	12.0	inches
yd. = 3 ft.	feet (ft.)	0.333333	yards
	yards (yd.)	3.0	feet
mi. = 5280 ft.	feet (ft.)	0.0001894	miles
	miles (mi.)	5280.0	feet
mi. = 1760 yd.	yards (yd.)	0.0005682	miles
	miles (mi.)	1760.0	yards

Liquid Measure

Relationship	Multiply	By	To Obtain
4 gl. = 1 pt.	pints (pt.)	4.0	gills
2 pt = 1 qt.	gallons (gal.)	8.0	pints
8 gl. = 1 qt.	gills (gl.)	0.25	pints
	quarts (qt.)	2.0	pints
	pints (pt.)	0.5	quarts
8 pt. = 1 gal.	pints (pt.)	0.125	gallons
4 qt. = 1 gal.	gallons (gal.)	4.0	quarts
	quarts (qt.)	0.25	gallons
31.5 gal. = 1 bbl.	barrels (bbl.)	31.5	gallons
	gallons (gal.)	0.03175	barrels

Avoirdupois Weight

Relationship	Multiply	By	To Obtain
16 dr. = 1 oz.	ounces (oz.)	16.0	dram
	drams (dr.)	0.0625	ounces
16 oz. = 1 lb.	pounds (lb.)	16.0	ounces
	ounces (oz.)	0.0625	pounds
1 hdwt. = 100 lb.	hundredweight (hdwt.)	100.0	pounds
	pounds (lb.)	0.01	hundredweight
2000 lb. = 1 t.	tons (short)	2000.0	pounds
	pounds (lb.)	0.0005	tons

Square Measure

Relationship	Multiply	By	To Obtain
1 sq. ft. = 144 sq. in.	square inches (sq. in.)	0.006945	square feet
	square feet (sq. ft.)	144.0	square inches
1 sq. yd. = 9 sq. ft.	square feet (sq. ft.)	0.11111	square yards
	square yards (sq. yd.)	9.0	square feet

Cubic Measure

Relationship	Multiply	By	To Obtain
1 cu. ft. = 1728 cu. in.	cubic feet (cu. ft.)	1728.0	cubic inches
	cubic inches (cu. in.)	0.000579	cubic feet
1 cu. yd. = 27 cu. ft.	cubic yards (cu. yd.)	27.0	cubic feet
	cubic feet (cu. ft.)	0.037037	cubic yards

SKILL EXERCISES

Enter the conversion number and compute the converted weight or measure.

	Unit	Multiply by	Converted unit
1.	6 mi.	_____	_____ ft.
2.	270 sq. ft.	_____	_____ sq. yd.
3.	48 pt.	_____	_____ gal.
4.	8000 oz.	_____	_____ hundredweight
5.	20 cu. yd.	_____	_____ cu. ft.

Determine the conversion used and compute the original weight or measure.

6.	_____ qt.	_____	40 gal.
7.	_____ sq. yd.	_____	1800 sq. ft.
8.	_____ yd.	_____	612 in.
9.	_____ cu. ft.	_____	112,320 cu. in.
10.	_____ oz.	_____	432 dr.

Enter the conversion number and compute the converted weight or measure.

11.	127 yd.	_____	_____ ft.
12.	344 tons (short)	_____	_____ lb.
13.	1284 pt.	_____	_____ qt.
14.	810 cu. ft.	_____	_____ cu. yd.
15.	792 sq. ft.	_____	_____ sq. yd.
16.	21,520.0 pt.	_____	_____ gal.
17.	601,920 ft.	_____	_____ mi.
18.	300,800 pounds	_____	_____ tons (short)
19.	99 cu. yd.	_____	_____ cu. ft.

U.S. Weights and Measures

20. 2772 in. _____ _____ yd.

21. 1404 sq. ft. _____ _____ sq. yd.

22. 786 qt. _____ _____ gal.

23. 52 bbl. _____ _____ gal.

24. 176 oz. _____ _____ lb.

25. 76 cu. yd. _____ _____ cu. ft.

APPLICATIONS

1. Jim poured a patio 22 feet long and 18 feet wide. If it was 4 inches thick, how many cubic yards of concrete were needed?

2. Kelley Jean needed to air-condition her boutique and measured the building to find that it was 64 feet long, 47 feet wide, and averaged 23 feet high. How many cubic feet were in the building?

3. Jeremy had to excavate the back yard for landscaping. If the yard was 86 feet wide and 92 feet long and an average depth of 5 feet was necessary, how many cubic yards needed to be moved?

4. The cows on Rita's farm produced 864 gallons of milk daily. If milk sold for $.68 cents a quart, how much did she receive daily?

5. Don's yard was 235 feet deep and 87 feet wide. If it cost $3.25 a square foot to put a fence around the yard, what was the cost of fencing?

6. At a speed of 45 miles per hour, how many yards will be traveled in 15 minutes?

7. If the floor in the recreation room is 27 feet long and 15 feet wide how many square yards of carpet will be needed to cover it?

8. If the construction company needs to excavate an area 130 feet long, 45 feet wide, and 7 feet deep, how many loads will it take if the front loader moves 4.25 cubic yards per load?

9. If plate glass costs $27.50 a square foot, how much will a window cost for a frame that is 36 inches high and 48 inches wide?

10. If the store needed 1,764 gallons of vinegar, how many barrels would that be?

Metric Conversions

Sometimes it will be necessary to convert to the metric measurement system from the U.S. measurement system. Usually this is required to complete the necessary calculations for a business transaction. Some of the more common conversions are provided below.

Metric	Prefix	Identifiers
kilo	k	(1,000 basic units)
hecto	h	(100 basic units)
deka	dk	(10 basic units)

Basic unit: meter (m.), liter (l.), gram (g.)

deci	d	(.1 basic units)
centi	c	(.01 basic units)
milli	m	(.001 basic units)

Conversion of U.S. to Metric Measures

Relationship	Multiply	By	To Obtain
cm. = 0.3937 in.	inches	2.54	centimeters
m. = 3.281 ft.	feet	0.3048	meters
m. = 1.0936 yd.	yards	0.9144	meters
km. = 0.62143 mi.	miles	1.6092	kilometers
cu. cm. = 0.061013 cu. in.	cu. inches	16.39	cu. centimeters
cu. m. = 35.3357 cu. ft.	cu. feet	0.0283	cu. meters
cu. m. = 13.0804 cu. yd.	cu. yards	0.07645	cu. meters
sq. cm. = 0.15499 sq. in.	sq. inches	6.452	sq. centimeters
sq. m. = 10.7643 sq. ft.	sq. feet	0.0929	sq. meters
sq. m. = 1.19603 sq. yd.	sq. yards	0.8361	sq. meters
sq. km. = 0.387597 sq. mi.	sq. miles	2.580	sq. kilometers
gr. = 0.564398 dr.	drams	1.7718	grams
gr. = 0.035273 oz.	ounces	28.35	grams
kg. = 2.20264 lb.	pounds	0.454	kilograms
m. ton = 0.90703 ton	tons (short)	1.1025	metric tons (short)
l. = 0.26420 gal.	gallons	3.785	liters
l. = 33.7838 oz.	ounces (fluid)	0.0296	liters
l. = 1.05697 qt.	quarts	0.9461	liters
C. = 32 + (1.8) F.	Fahrenheit	(F−32) × 0.5556	Celsius

Conversion of Metric to U.S. Measures

Relationship	Multiply	By	To Obtain
in. = 2.54 cm.	centimeters	0.3937	inches
ft. = 0.3048 m.	meters	3.281	feet
yd. = 0.9114 m.	meters	1.094	yards
mi. = 1.6092 km.	kilometers	0.6214	miles
cu. in. = 16.39 cu. cm.	cu. centimeters	0.0610	cu. inches
cu. ft. = 0.0283 cu. m.	cu. meters	35.31	cu. feet
cu. yd. = 0.07645 cu. m.	cu. meters	1.308	cu. yards
sq. in. = 6.452 sq. cm.	sq. centimeters	0.155	sq. inches
sq. ft. = 0.0929 sq. m.	sq. meters	10.76	sq. feet
sq. yd. = 0.8361 sq. m.	sq. meters	1.1960	sq. yards
sq. mi. = 2.580 sq. km.	sq. kilometers	0.3861	sq. miles
dr. = 1.7718 g.	grams	0.5644	drams
oz. = 28.35 g.	grams	0.0353	ounces
lb. = 0.454 kg.	kilograms	2.205	pounds
t (s) = 1.1025 t (m)	tons metric (s)	0.90703	tons (short)
gal. = 3.785 l.	liters	0.2642	gallons
qt. = 0.9461 l.	liters	1.057	quarts
oz. = 0.0296 l.	liters	33.78	ounces
F. = (F−32) × 0.55556	Celsius	(C×1.8) + 32	Fahrenheit

SKILL EXERCISES

Convert the following metric measures and weights to U.S. equivalents:

	Unit	Multiply by	Converted to
1.	10 meters	_____	_____ yards
2.	264 kilometers	_____	_____ miles
3.	3 meters	_____	_____ inches
4.	7500 grams	_____	_____ ounces
5.	125 kiloliters	_____	_____ gallons
6.	30 degrees C	_____	_____ Fahrenheit
7.	24 kilograms	_____	_____ pounds
8.	50 liters	_____	_____ quarts
9.	1400 kilometers	_____	_____ miles
10.	7800 meters	_____	_____ yards

Appendix C Symbols, Weights, and Measures

11. 6 kilometers _____ _____ feet

12. 48 liters _____ _____ gallons

Convert the following U.S. weights and measures to metric equivalents:

Unit	Multiply by	Converted to

13. 72 inches _____ _____ centimeters

14. 12 pounds _____ _____ kilograms

15. 125 miles _____ _____ kilometers

16. 150 gallons _____ _____ kiloliters

17. 12 ounces _____ _____ grams

18. 3580 sq. feet _____ _____ sq. meters

19. 61 cu. inches _____ _____ cu. centimeters

20. 490 tons (short) _____ _____ metric tons

21. 150 ounces _____ _____ liters

22. 984 feet _____ _____ meters

23. 140 drams _____ _____ grams

24. 3472 cu. yards _____ _____ cu. meters

25. 97 degrees F _____ _____ degrees C

APPLICATIONS

1. If the temperature at the airport is 86 degrees Fahrenheit, what is the Celsius reading?

2. If J. L. drives 54 miles per hour, how many kilometers will he drive in two and a half hours?

3. If a building measured 68 yards long, how many meters long is it?

4. Linda filled her car with gasoline at a station that indicated the measurement in liters. If she put 48 liters in the tank, how many gallons did she buy?

Metric Conversions

5. Douglas ordered 10,000 kilograms of steel from a plant in Great Britain. How many pounds did he get?

6. If a truck carries $17\frac{1}{2}$ tons of sand, how many kilograms does it carry?

7. An American athlete trains to run the 100 yard dash and must now run the 100 meter dash. How many extra feet must he go?

8. The state police stopped a person for traveling 120 kilometers per hour. How many miles per hour was the person traveling?

9. The temperature in Lake Havasu City was 117 degrees F. What would that convert to in degrees Celsius?

10. When Charles drove in Canada, he filled his tank and it took 38 liters of fuel. If he was measuring his mileage by the gallon, how many gallons did he buy?

Appendix D
Reference Tables

Social Security Employee Tax Table for 1988

Federal Withholding Table for Married Persons—Weekly Payroll Period

Federal Withholding Table for Single Persons—Weekly Payroll Period

Federal Reserve Table for Computing Annual Percentage Rates for Monthly Payment Plans

Compound Interest, Present Value, and Annuity Table

Social Security Employee Tax Table for 1988
7.51% employee tax deductions

Wages at least	But less than	Tax to be withheld	Wages at least	But less than	Tax to be withheld	Wages at least	But less than	Tax to be withheld	Wages at least	But less than	Tax to be withheld
$0.00	$0.07	$0.00	12.72	12.85	.96	25.50	25.64	1.92	38.29	38.42	2.88
.07	.20	.01	12.85	12.99	.97	25.64	25.77	1.93	38.42	38.55	2.89
.20	.34	.02	12.99	13.12	.98	25.77	25.90	1.94	38.55	38.69	2.90
.34	.47	.03	13.12	13.25	.99	25.90	26.04	1.95	38.69	38.82	2.91
.47	.60	.04	13.25	13.39	1.00	26.04	26.17	1.96	38.82	38.95	2.92
.60	.74	.05	13.39	13.52	1.01	26.17	26.30	1.97	38.95	39.09	2.93
.74	.87	.06	13.52	13.65	1.02	26.30	26.44	1.98	39.09	39.22	2.94
.87	1.00	.07	13.65	13.79	1.03	26.44	26.57	1.99	39.22	39.35	2.95
1.00	1.14	.08	13.79	13.92	1.04	26.57	26.70	2.00	39.35	39.49	2.96
1.14	1.27	.09	13.92	14.05	1.05	26.70	26.84	2.01	39.49	39.62	2.97
1.27	1.40	.10	14.05	14.19	1.06	26.84	26.97	2.02	39.62	39.75	2.98
1.40	1.54	.11	14.19	14.32	1.07	26.97	27.10	2.03	39.75	39.89	2.99
1.54	1.67	.12	14.32	14.45	1.08	27.10	27.24	2.04	39.89	40.02	3.00
1.67	1.80	.13	14.45	14.59	1.09	27.24	27.37	2.05	40.02	40.15	3.01
1.80	1.94	.14	14.59	14.72	1.10	27.37	27.50	2.06	40.15	40.28	3.02
1.94	2.07	.15	14.72	14.85	1.11	27.50	27.63	2.07	40.28	40.42	3.03
2.07	2.20	.16	14.85	14.99	1.12	27.63	27.77	2.08	40.42	40.55	3.04
2.20	2.34	.17	14.99	15.12	1.13	27.77	27.90	2.09	40.55	40.68	3.05
2.34	2.47	.18	15.12	15.25	1.14	27.90	28.03	2.10	40.68	40.82	3.06
2.47	2.60	.19	15.25	15.38	1.15	28.03	28.17	2.11	40.82	40.95	3.07
2.60	2.73	.20	15.38	15.52	1.16	28.17	28.30	2.12	40.95	41.08	3.08
2.73	2.87	.21	15.52	15.65	1.17	28.30	28.43	2.13	41.08	41.22	3.09
2.87	3.00	.22	15.65	15.78	1.18	28.43	28.57	2.14	41.22	41.35	3.10
3.00	3.13	.23	15.78	15.92	1.19	28.57	28.70	2.15	41.35	41.48	3.11
3.13	3.27	.24	15.92	16.05	1.20	28.70	28.83	2.16	41.48	41.62	3.12
3.27	3.40	.25	16.05	16.18	1.21	28.83	28.97	2.17	41.62	41.75	3.13
3.40	3.53	.26	16.18	16.32	1.22	28.97	29.10	2.18	41.75	41.88	3.14
3.53	3.67	.27	16.32	16.45	1.23	29.10	29.23	2.19	41.88	42.02	3.15
3.67	3.80	.28	16.45	16.58	1.24	29.23	29.37	2.20	42.02	42.15	3.16
3.80	3.93	.29	16.58	16.72	1.25	29.37	29.50	2.21	42.15	42.28	3.17
3.93	4.07	.30	16.72	16.85	1.26	29.50	29.63	2.22	42.28	42.42	3.18
4.07	4.20	.31	16.85	16.98	1.27	29.63	29.77	2.23	42.42	42.55	3.19
4.20	4.33	.32	16.98	17.12	1.28	29.77	29.90	2.24	42.55	42.68	3.20
4.33	4.47	.33	17.12	17.25	1.29	29.90	30.03	2.25	42.68	42.81	3.21
4.47	4.60	.34	17.25	17.38	1.30	30.03	30.16	2.26	42.81	42.95	3.22
4.60	4.73	.35	17.38	17.51	1.31	30.16	30.30	2.27	42.95	43.08	3.23
4.73	4.87	.36	17.51	17.65	1.32	30.30	30.43	2.28	43.08	43.21	3.24
4.87	5.00	.37	17.65	17.78	1.33	30.43	30.56	2.29	43.21	43.35	3.25
5.00	5.13	.38	17.78	17.91	1.34	30.56	30.70	2.30	43.35	43.48	3.26
5.13	5.26	.39	17.91	18.05	1.35	30.70	30.83	2.31	43.48	43.61	3.27
5.26	5.40	.40	18.05	18.18	1.36	30.83	30.96	2.32	43.61	43.75	3.28
5.40	5.53	.41	18.18	18.31	1.37	30.96	31.10	2.33	43.75	43.88	3.29
5.53	5.66	.42	18.31	18.45	1.38	31.10	31.23	2.34	43.88	44.01	3.30
5.66	5.80	.43	18.45	18.58	1.39	31.23	31.36	2.35	44.01	44.15	3.31
5.80	5.93	.44	18.58	18.71	1.40	31.36	31.50	2.36	44.15	44.28	3.32
5.93	6.06	.45	18.71	18.85	1.41	31.50	31.63	2.37	44.28	44.41	3.33
6.06	6.20	.46	18.85	18.98	1.42	31.63	31.76	2.38	44.41	44.55	3.34
6.20	6.33	.47	18.98	19.11	1.43	31.76	31.90	2.39	44.55	44.68	3.35
6.33	6.46	.48	19.11	19.25	1.44	31.90	32.03	2.40	44.68	44.81	3.36
6.46	6.60	.49	19.25	19.38	1.45	32.03	32.16	2.41	44.81	44.95	3.37
6.60	6.73	.50	19.38	19.51	1.46	32.16	32.30	2.42	44.95	45.08	3.38
6.73	6.86	.51	19.51	19.65	1.47	32.30	32.43	2.43	45.08	45.21	3.39
6.86	7.00	.52	19.65	19.78	1.48	32.43	32.56	2.44	45.21	45.34	3.40
7.00	7.13	.53	19.78	19.91	1.49	32.56	32.69	2.45	45.34	45.48	3.41
7.13	7.26	.54	19.91	20.04	1.50	32.69	32.83	2.46	45.48	45.61	3.42
7.26	7.40	.55	20.04	20.18	1.51	32.83	32.96	2.47	45.61	45.74	3.43
7.40	7.53	.56	20.18	20.31	1.52	32.96	33.09	2.48	45.74	45.88	3.44
7.53	7.66	.57	20.31	20.44	1.53	33.09	33.23	2.49	45.88	46.01	3.45
7.66	7.79	.58	20.44	20.58	1.54	33.23	33.36	2.50	46.01	46.14	3.46
7.79	7.93	.59	20.58	20.71	1.55	33.36	33.49	2.51	46.14	46.28	3.47
7.93	8.06	.60	20.71	20.84	1.56	33.49	33.63	2.52	46.28	46.41	3.48
8.06	8.19	.61	20.84	20.98	1.57	33.63	33.76	2.53	46.41	46.54	3.49
8.19	8.33	.62	20.98	21.11	1.58	33.76	33.89	2.54	46.54	46.68	3.50
8.33	8.46	.63	21.11	21.24	1.59	33.89	34.03	2.55	46.68	46.81	3.51
8.46	8.59	.64	21.24	21.38	1.60	34.03	34.16	2.56	46.81	46.94	3.52
8.59	8.73	.65	21.38	21.51	1.61	34.16	34.29	2.57	46.94	47.08	3.53
8.73	8.86	.66	21.51	21.64	1.62	34.29	34.43	2.58	47.08	47.21	3.54
8.86	8.99	.67	21.64	21.78	1.63	34.43	34.56	2.59	47.21	47.34	3.55
8.99	9.13	.68	21.78	21.91	1.64	34.56	34.69	2.60	47.34	47.48	3.56
9.13	9.26	.69	21.91	22.04	1.65	34.69	34.83	2.61	47.48	47.61	3.57
9.26	9.39	.70	22.04	22.18	1.66	34.83	34.96	2.62	47.61	47.74	3.58
9.39	9.53	.71	22.18	22.31	1.67	34.96	35.09	2.63	47.74	47.87	3.59
9.53	9.66	.72	22.31	22.44	1.68	35.09	35.22	2.64	47.87	48.01	3.60
9.66	9.79	.73	22.44	22.57	1.69	35.22	35.36	2.65	48.01	48.14	3.61
9.79	9.93	.74	22.57	22.71	1.70	35.36	35.49	2.66	48.14	48.27	3.62
9.93	10.06	.75	22.71	22.84	1.71	35.49	35.62	2.67	48.27	48.41	3.63
10.06	10.19	.76	22.84	22.97	1.72	35.62	35.76	2.68	48.41	48.54	3.64
10.19	10.32	.77	22.97	23.11	1.73	35.76	35.89	2.69	48.54	48.67	3.65
10.32	10.46	.78	23.11	23.24	1.74	35.89	36.02	2.70	48.67	48.81	3.66
10.46	10.59	.79	23.24	23.37	1.75	36.02	36.16	2.71	48.81	48.94	3.67
10.59	10.72	.80	23.37	23.51	1.76	36.16	36.29	2.72	48.94	49.07	3.68
10.72	10.86	.81	23.51	23.64	1.77	36.29	36.42	2.73	49.07	49.21	3.69
10.86	10.99	.82	23.64	23.77	1.78	36.42	36.56	2.74	49.21	49.34	3.70
10.99	11.12	.83	23.77	23.91	1.79	36.56	36.69	2.75	49.34	49.47	3.71
11.12	11.26	.84	23.91	24.04	1.80	36.69	36.82	2.76	49.47	49.61	3.72
11.26	11.39	.85	24.04	24.17	1.81	36.82	36.96	2.77	49.61	49.74	3.73
11.39	11.52	.86	24.17	24.31	1.82	36.96	37.09	2.78	49.74	49.87	3.74
11.52	11.66	.87	24.31	24.44	1.83	37.09	37.22	2.79	49.87	50.00	3.75
11.66	11.79	.88	24.44	24.57	1.84	37.22	37.36	2.80	50.00	50.14	3.76
11.79	11.92	.89	24.57	24.71	1.85	37.36	37.49	2.81	50.14	50.27	3.77
11.92	12.06	.90	24.71	24.84	1.86	37.49	37.62	2.82	50.27	50.40	3.78
12.06	12.19	.91	24.84	24.97	1.87	37.62	37.75	2.83	50.40	50.54	3.79
12.19	12.32	.92	24.97	25.10	1.88	37.75	37.89	2.84	50.54	50.67	3.80
12.32	12.46	.93	25.10	25.24	1.89	37.89	38.02	2.85	50.67	50.80	3.81
12.46	12.59	.94	25.24	25.37	1.90	38.02	38.15	2.86	50.80	50.94	3.82
12.59	12.72	.95	25.37	25.50	1.91	38.15	38.29	2.87	50.94	51.07	3.83

Appendix D   Reference Tables

Social Security Employee Tax Table for 1988
7.51% employee tax deductions

Wages at least	But less than	Tax to be withheld	Wages at least	But less than	Tax to be withheld	Wages at least	But less than	Tax to be withheld	Wages at least	But less than	Tax to be withheld
51.07	51.20	3.84	63.72	63.85	4.79	76.37	76.50	5.74	89.02	89.15	6.69
51.20	51.34	3.85	63.85	63.99	4.80	76.50	76.64	5.75	89.15	89.29	6.70
51.34	51.47	3.86	63.99	64.12	4.81	76.64	76.77	5.76	89.29	89.42	6.71
51.47	51.60	3.87	64.12	64.25	4.82	76.77	76.90	5.77	89.42	89.55	6.72
51.60	51.74	3.88	64.25	64.39	4.83	76.90	77.04	5.78	89.55	89.69	6.73
51.74	51.87	3.89	64.39	64.52	4.84	77.04	77.17	5.79	89.69	89.82	6.74
51.87	52.00	3.90	64.52	64.65	4.85	77.17	77.30	5.80	89.82	89.95	6.75
52.00	52.14	3.91	64.65	64.79	4.86	77.30	77.44	5.81	89.95	90.08	6.76
52.14	52.27	3.92	64.79	64.92	4.87	77.44	77.57	5.82	90.08	90.22	6.77
52.27	52.40	3.93	64.92	65.05	4.88	77.57	77.70	5.83	90.22	90.35	6.78
52.40	52.53	3.94	65.05	65.18	4.89	77.70	77.83	5.84	90.35	90.48	6.79
52.53	52.67	3.95	65.18	65.32	4.90	77.83	77.97	5.85	90.48	90.62	6.80
52.67	52.80	3.96	65.32	65.45	4.91	77.97	78.10	5.86	90.62	90.75	6.81
52.80	52.93	3.97	65.45	65.58	4.92	78.10	78.23	5.87	90.75	90.88	6.82
52.93	53.07	3.98	65.58	65.72	4.93	78.23	78.37	5.88	90.88	91.02	6.83
53.07	53.20	3.99	65.72	65.85	4.94	78.37	78.50	5.89	91.02	91.15	6.84
53.20	53.33	4.00	65.85	65.98	4.95	78.50	78.63	5.90	91.15	91.28	6.85
53.33	53.47	4.01	65.98	66.12	4.96	78.63	78.77	5.91	91.28	91.42	6.86
53.47	53.60	4.02	66.12	66.25	4.97	78.77	78.90	5.92	91.42	91.55	6.87
53.60	53.73	4.03	66.25	66.38	4.98	78.90	79.03	5.93	91.55	91.68	6.88
53.73	53.87	4.04	66.38	66.52	4.99	79.03	79.17	5.94	91.68	91.82	6.89
53.87	54.00	4.05	66.52	66.65	5.00	79.17	79.30	5.95	91.82	91.95	6.90
54.00	54.13	4.06	66.65	66.78	5.01	79.30	79.43	5.96	91.95	92.08	6.91
54.13	54.27	4.07	66.78	66.92	5.02	79.43	79.57	5.97	92.08	92.22	6.92
54.27	54.40	4.08	66.92	67.05	5.03	79.57	79.70	5.98	92.22	92.35	6.93
54.40	54.53	4.09	67.05	67.18	5.04	79.70	79.83	5.99	92.35	92.48	6.94
54.53	54.67	4.10	67.18	67.32	5.05	79.83	79.97	6.00	92.48	92.61	6.95
54.67	54.80	4.11	67.32	67.45	5.06	79.97	80.10	6.01	92.61	92.75	6.96
54.80	54.93	4.12	67.45	67.58	5.07	80.10	80.23	6.02	92.75	92.88	6.97
54.93	55.06	4.13	67.58	67.71	5.08	80.23	80.36	6.03	92.88	93.01	6.98
55.06	55.20	4.14	67.71	67.85	5.09	80.36	80.50	6.04	93.01	93.15	6.99
55.20	55.33	4.15	67.85	67.98	5.10	80.50	80.63	6.05	93.15	93.28	7.00
55.33	55.46	4.16	67.98	68.11	5.11	80.63	80.76	6.06	93.28	93.41	7.01
55.46	55.60	4.17	68.11	68.25	5.12	80.76	80.90	6.07	93.41	93.55	7.02
55.60	55.73	4.18	68.25	68.38	5.13	80.90	81.03	6.08	93.55	93.68	7.03
55.73	55.86	4.19	68.38	68.51	5.14	81.03	81.16	6.09	93.68	93.81	7.04
55.86	56.00	4.20	68.51	68.65	5.15	81.16	81.30	6.10	93.81	93.95	7.05
56.00	56.13	4.21	68.65	68.78	5.16	81.30	81.43	6.11	93.95	94.08	7.06
56.13	56.26	4.22	68.78	68.91	5.17	81.43	81.56	6.12	94.08	94.21	7.07
56.26	56.40	4.23	68.91	69.05	5.18	81.56	81.70	6.13	94.21	94.35	7.08
56.40	56.53	4.24	69.05	69.18	5.19	81.70	81.83	6.14	94.35	94.48	7.09
56.53	56.66	4.25	69.18	69.31	5.20	81.83	81.96	6.15	94.48	94.61	7.10
56.66	56.80	4.26	69.31	69.45	5.21	81.96	82.10	6.16	94.61	94.75	7.11
56.80	56.93	4.27	69.45	69.58	5.22	82.10	82.23	6.17	94.75	94.88	7.12
56.93	57.06	4.28	69.58	69.71	5.23	82.23	82.36	6.18	94.88	95.01	7.13
57.06	57.20	4.29	69.71	69.85	5.24	82.36	82.50	6.19	95.01	95.14	7.14
57.20	57.33	4.30	69.85	69.98	5.25	82.50	82.63	6.20	95.14	95.28	7.15
57.33	57.46	4.31	69.98	70.11	5.26	82.63	82.76	6.21	95.28	95.41	7.16
57.46	57.59	4.32	70.11	70.24	5.27	82.76	82.89	6.22	95.41	95.54	7.17
57.59	57.73	4.33	70.24	70.38	5.28	82.89	83.03	6.23	95.54	95.68	7.18
57.73	57.86	4.34	70.38	70.51	5.29	83.03	83.16	6.24	95.68	95.81	7.19
57.86	57.99	4.35	70.51	70.64	5.30	83.16	83.29	6.25	95.81	95.94	7.20
57.99	58.13	4.36	70.64	70.78	5.31	83.29	83.43	6.26	95.94	96.08	7.21
58.13	58.26	4.37	70.78	70.91	5.32	83.43	83.56	6.27	96.08	96.21	7.22
58.26	58.39	4.38	70.91	71.04	5.33	83.56	83.69	6.28	96.21	96.34	7.23
58.39	58.53	4.39	71.04	71.18	5.34	83.69	83.83	6.29	96.34	96.48	7.24
58.53	58.66	4.40	71.18	71.31	5.35	83.83	83.96	6.30	96.48	96.61	7.25
58.66	58.79	4.41	71.31	71.44	5.36	83.96	84.09	6.31	96.61	96.74	7.26
58.79	58.93	4.42	71.44	71.58	5.37	84.09	84.23	6.32	96.74	96.88	7.27
58.93	59.06	4.43	71.58	71.71	5.38	84.23	84.36	6.33	96.88	97.01	7.28
59.06	59.19	4.44	71.71	71.84	5.39	84.36	84.49	6.34	97.01	97.14	7.29
59.19	59.33	4.45	71.84	71.98	5.40	84.49	84.63	6.35	97.14	97.28	7.30
59.33	59.46	4.46	71.98	72.11	5.41	84.63	84.76	6.36	97.28	97.41	7.31
59.46	59.59	4.47	72.11	72.24	5.42	84.76	84.89	6.37	97.41	97.54	7.32
59.59	59.73	4.48	72.24	72.38	5.43	84.89	85.02	6.38	97.54	97.67	7.33
59.73	59.86	4.49	72.38	72.51	5.44	85.02	85.16	6.39	97.67	97.81	7.34
59.86	59.99	4.50	72.51	72.64	5.45	85.16	85.29	6.40	97.81	97.94	7.35
59.99	60.12	4.51	72.64	72.77	5.46	85.29	85.42	6.41	97.94	98.07	7.36
60.12	60.26	4.52	72.77	72.91	5.47	85.42	85.56	6.42	98.07	98.21	7.37
60.26	60.39	4.53	72.91	73.04	5.48	85.56	85.69	6.43	98.21	98.34	7.38
60.39	60.52	4.54	73.04	73.17	5.49	85.69	85.82	6.44	98.34	98.47	7.39
60.52	60.66	4.55	73.17	73.31	5.50	85.82	85.96	6.45	98.47	98.61	7.40
60.66	60.79	4.56	73.31	73.44	5.51	85.96	86.09	6.46	98.61	98.74	7.41
60.79	60.92	4.57	73.44	73.57	5.52	86.09	86.22	6.47	98.74	98.87	7.42
60.92	61.06	4.58	73.57	73.71	5.53	86.22	86.36	6.48	98.87	99.01	7.43
61.06	61.19	4.59	73.71	73.84	5.54	86.36	86.49	6.49	99.01	99.14	7.44
61.19	61.32	4.60	73.84	73.97	5.55	86.49	86.62	6.50	99.14	99.27	7.45
61.32	61.46	4.61	73.97	74.11	5.56	86.62	86.76	6.51	99.27	99.41	7.46
61.46	61.59	4.62	74.11	74.24	5.57	86.76	86.89	6.52	99.41	99.54	7.47
61.59	61.72	4.63	74.24	74.37	5.58	86.89	87.02	6.53	99.54	99.67	7.48
61.72	61.86	4.64	74.37	74.51	5.59	87.02	87.16	6.54	99.67	99.81	7.49
61.86	61.99	4.65	74.51	74.64	5.60	87.16	87.29	6.55	99.81	99.94	7.50
61.99	62.12	4.66	74.64	74.77	5.61	87.29	87.42	6.56	99.94	100.00	7.51
62.12	62.26	4.67	74.77	74.91	5.62	87.42	87.55	6.57			
62.26	62.39	4.68	74.91	75.04	5.63	87.55	87.69	6.58			
62.39	62.52	4.69	75.04	75.17	5.64	87.69	87.82	6.59			
62.52	62.65	4.70	75.17	75.30	5.65	87.82	87.95	6.60			
62.65	62.79	4.71	75.30	75.44	5.66	87.95	88.09	6.61			
62.79	62.92	4.72	75.44	75.57	5.67	88.09	88.22	6.62			
62.92	63.05	4.73	75.57	75.70	5.68	88.22	88.35	6.63			
63.05	63.19	4.74	75.70	75.84	5.69	88.35	88.49	6.64			
63.19	63.32	4.75	75.84	75.97	5.70	88.49	88.62	6.65			
63.32	63.45	4.76	75.97	76.10	5.71	88.62	88.75	6.66			
63.45	63.59	4.77	76.10	76.24	5.72	88.75	88.89	6.67			
63.59	63.72	4.78	76.24	76.37	5.73	88.89	89.02	6.68			

Wages	Taxes
100	$7.51
200	15.02
300	22.53
400	30.04
500	37.55
600	45.06
700	52.57
800	60.08
900	67.59
1,000	75.10

Reference Tables   A–35

MARRIED Persons—WEEKLY Payroll Period
(For Wages Paid After December 1987)

And the wages are—		And the number of withholding allowances claimed is—										
At least	But less than	0	1	2	3	4	5	6	7	8	9	10
			The amount of income tax to be withheld shall be—									
$0	$60	$0	$0	$0	$0	$0	$0	$0	$0	$0	$0	$0
60	65	1	0	0	0	0	0	0	0	0	0	0
65	70	1	0	0	0	0	0	0	0	0	0	0
70	75	2	0	0	0	0	0	0	0	0	0	0
75	80	3	0	0	0	0	0	0	0	0	0	0
80	85	4	0	0	0	0	0	0	0	0	0	0
85	90	4	0	0	0	0	0	0	0	0	0	0
90	95	5	0	0	0	0	0	0	0	0	0	0
95	100	6	0	0	0	0	0	0	0	0	0	0
100	105	7	1	0	0	0	0	0	0	0	0	0
105	110	7	2	0	0	0	0	0	0	0	0	0
110	115	8	2	0	0	0	0	0	0	0	0	0
115	120	9	3	0	0	0	0	0	0	0	0	0
120	125	10	4	0	0	0	0	0	0	0	0	0
125	130	10	5	0	0	0	0	0	0	0	0	0
130	135	11	5	0	0	0	0	0	0	0	0	0
135	140	12	6	1	0	0	0	0	0	0	0	0
140	145	13	7	1	0	0	0	0	0	0	0	0
145	150	13	8	2	0	0	0	0	0	0	0	0
150	155	14	8	3	0	0	0	0	0	0	0	0
155	160	15	9	4	0	0	0	0	0	0	0	0
160	165	16	10	4	0	0	0	0	0	0	0	0
165	170	16	11	5	0	0	0	0	0	0	0	0
170	175	17	11	6	0	0	0	0	0	0	0	0
175	180	18	12	7	1	0	0	0	0	0	0	0
180	185	19	13	7	2	0	0	0	0	0	0	0
185	190	19	14	8	2	0	0	0	0	0	0	0
190	195	20	14	9	3	0	0	0	0	0	0	0
195	200	21	15	10	4	0	0	0	0	0	0	0
200	210	22	16	11	5	0	0	0	0	0	0	0
210	220	23	18	12	7	1	0	0	0	0	0	0
220	230	25	19	14	8	2	0	0	0	0	0	0
230	240	26	21	15	10	4	0	0	0	0	0	0
240	250	28	22	17	11	5	0	0	0	0	0	0
250	260	29	24	18	13	7	1	0	0	0	0	0
260	270	31	25	20	14	8	3	0	0	0	0	0
270	280	32	27	21	16	10	4	0	0	0	0	0
280	290	34	28	23	17	11	6	0	0	0	0	0
290	300	35	30	24	19	13	7	2	0	0	0	0
300	310	37	31	26	20	14	9	3	0	0	0	0
310	320	38	33	27	22	16	10	5	0	0	0	0
320	330	40	34	29	23	17	12	6	1	0	0	0
330	340	41	36	30	25	19	13	8	2	0	0	0
340	350	43	37	32	26	20	15	9	4	0	0	0
350	360	44	39	33	28	22	16	11	5	0	0	0
360	370	46	40	35	29	23	18	12	7	1	0	0
370	380	47	42	36	31	25	19	14	8	2	0	0
380	390	49	43	38	32	26	21	15	10	4	0	0
390	400	50	45	39	34	28	22	17	11	5	0	0
400	410	52	46	41	35	29	24	18	13	7	1	0
410	420	53	48	42	37	31	25	20	14	8	3	0
420	430	55	49	44	38	32	27	21	16	10	4	0
430	440	56	51	45	40	34	28	23	17	11	6	0
440	450	58	52	47	41	35	30	24	19	13	7	2
450	460	59	54	48	43	37	31	26	20	14	9	3
460	470	61	55	50	44	38	33	27	22	16	10	5
470	480	62	57	51	46	40	34	29	23	17	12	6
480	490	64	58	53	47	41	36	30	25	19	13	8
490	500	65	60	54	49	43	37	32	26	20	15	9
500	510	67	61	56	50	44	39	33	28	22	16	11
510	520	68	63	57	52	46	40	35	29	23	18	12
520	530	70	64	59	53	47	42	36	31	25	19	14
530	540	71	66	60	55	49	43	38	32	26	21	15
540	550	73	67	62	56	50	45	39	34	28	22	17
550	560	74	69	63	58	52	46	41	35	29	24	18
560	570	76	70	65	59	53	48	42	37	31	25	20
570	580	77	72	66	61	55	49	44	38	32	27	21
580	590	79	73	68	62	56	51	45	40	34	28	23
590	600	80	75	69	64	58	52	47	41	35	30	24
600	610	82	76	71	65	59	54	48	43	37	31	26

(Continued on next page)

MARRIED Persons—WEEKLY Payroll Period
(For Wages Paid After December 1987)

And the wages are—		And the number of withholding allowances claimed is—										
At least	But less than	0	1	2	3	4	5	6	7	8	9	10
^ ^ ^ ^ ^ ^ ^ ^ ^ ^ ^ ^ ^												
		The amount of income tax to be withheld shall be—										
$610	$620	$83	$78	$72	$67	$61	$55	$50	$44	$38	$33	$27
620	630	85	79	74	68	62	57	51	46	40	34	29
630	640	87	81	75	70	64	58	53	47	41	36	30
640	650	90	82	77	71	65	60	54	49	43	37	32
650	660	93	84	78	73	67	61	56	50	44	39	33
660	670	95	85	80	74	68	63	57	52	46	40	35
670	680	98	88	81	76	70	64	59	53	47	42	36
680	690	101	91	83	77	71	66	60	55	49	43	38
690	700	104	93	84	79	73	67	62	56	50	45	39
700	710	107	96	86	80	74	69	63	58	52	46	41
710	720	109	99	88	82	76	70	65	59	53	48	42
720	730	112	102	91	83	77	72	66	61	55	49	44
730	740	115	105	94	85	79	73	68	62	56	51	45
740	750	118	107	97	86	80	75	69	64	58	52	47
750	760	121	110	100	89	82	76	71	65	59	54	48
760	770	123	113	102	92	83	78	72	67	61	55	50
770	780	126	116	105	95	85	79	74	68	62	57	51
780	790	129	119	108	98	87	81	75	70	64	58	53
790	800	132	121	111	100	90	82	77	71	65	60	54
800	810	135	124	114	103	93	84	78	73	67	61	56
810	820	137	127	116	106	95	85	80	74	68	63	57
820	830	140	130	119	109	98	88	81	76	70	64	59
830	840	143	133	122	112	101	91	83	77	71	66	60
840	850	146	135	125	114	104	93	84	79	73	67	62
850	860	149	138	128	117	107	96	86	80	74	69	63
860	870	151	141	130	120	109	99	88	82	76	70	65
870	880	154	144	133	123	112	102	91	83	77	72	66
880	890	157	147	136	126	115	105	94	85	79	73	68
890	900	160	149	139	128	118	107	97	86	80	75	69
900	910	163	152	142	131	121	110	100	89	82	76	71
910	920	165	155	144	134	123	113	102	92	83	78	72
920	930	168	158	147	137	126	116	105	95	85	79	74
930	940	171	161	150	140	129	119	108	98	87	81	75
940	950	174	163	153	142	132	121	111	100	90	82	77
950	960	177	166	156	145	135	124	114	103	93	84	78
960	970	179	169	158	148	137	127	116	106	95	85	80
970	980	182	172	161	151	140	130	119	109	98	88	81
980	990	185	175	164	154	143	133	122	112	101	91	83
990	1,000	188	177	167	156	146	135	125	114	104	93	84
1,000	1,010	191	180	170	159	149	138	128	117	107	96	86
1,010	1,020	193	183	172	162	151	141	130	120	109	99	88
1,020	1,030	196	186	175	165	154	144	133	123	112	102	91
1,030	1,040	199	189	178	168	157	147	136	126	115	105	94
1,040	1,050	202	191	181	170	160	149	139	128	118	107	97
1,050	1,060	205	194	184	173	163	152	142	131	121	110	100
1,060	1,070	207	197	186	176	165	155	144	134	123	113	102
1,070	1,080	210	200	189	179	168	158	147	137	126	116	105
1,080	1,090	213	203	192	182	171	161	150	140	129	119	108
1,090	1,100	216	205	195	184	174	163	153	142	132	121	111
1,100	1,110	219	208	198	187	177	166	156	145	135	124	114
1,110	1,120	221	211	200	190	179	169	158	148	137	127	116
1,120	1,130	224	214	203	193	182	172	161	151	140	130	119
1,130	1,140	227	217	206	196	185	175	164	154	143	133	122
1,140	1,150	230	219	209	198	188	177	167	156	146	135	125
1,150	1,160	233	222	212	201	191	180	170	159	149	138	128
1,160	1,170	235	225	214	204	193	183	172	162	151	141	130
1,170	1,180	238	228	217	207	196	186	175	165	154	144	133
1,180	1,190	241	231	220	210	199	189	178	168	157	147	136
1,190	1,200	244	233	223	212	202	191	181	170	160	149	139
1,200	1,210	247	236	226	215	205	194	184	173	163	152	142
1,210	1,220	249	239	228	218	207	197	186	176	165	155	144
1,220	1,230	252	242	231	221	210	200	189	179	168	158	147
1,230	1,240	255	245	234	224	213	203	192	182	171	161	150
1,240	1,250	258	247	237	226	216	205	195	184	174	163	153
1,250	1,260	261	250	240	229	219	208	198	187	177	166	156
1,260	1,270	263	253	242	232	221	211	200	190	179	169	158

$1,270 and over — Use Table 1(b) for a **MARRIED** person on page 22. Also see the instructions on page 20.

Reference Tables   A—37

SINGLE Persons—WEEKLY Payroll Period
(For Wages Paid After December 1987)

And the wages are—		And the number of withholding allowances claimed is—										
At least	But less than	0	1	2	3	4	5	6	7	8	9	10
			The amount of income tax to be withheld shall be—										
$0	$25	$0	$0	$0	$0	$0	$0	$0	$0	$0	$0	$0
25	30	1	0	0	0	0	0	0	0	0	0	0
30	35	2	0	0	0	0	0	0	0	0	0	0
35	40	3	0	0	0	0	0	0	0	0	0	0
40	45	3	0	0	0	0	0	0	0	0	0	0
45	50	4	0	0	0	0	0	0	0	0	0	0
50	55	5	0	0	0	0	0	0	0	0	0	0
55	60	6	0	0	0	0	0	0	0	0	0	0
60	65	6	1	0	0	0	0	0	0	0	0	0
65	70	7	1	0	0	0	0	0	0	0	0	0
70	75	8	2	0	0	0	0	0	0	0	0	0
75	80	9	3	0	0	0	0	0	0	0	0	0
80	85	9	4	0	0	0	0	0	0	0	0	0
85	90	10	4	0	0	0	0	0	0	0	0	0
90	95	11	5	0	0	0	0	0	0	0	0	0
95	100	12	6	0	0	0	0	0	0	0	0	0
100	105	12	7	1	0	0	0	0	0	0	0	0
105	110	13	7	2	0	0	0	0	0	0	0	0
110	115	14	8	3	0	0	0	0	0	0	0	0
115	120	15	9	3	0	0	0	0	0	0	0	0
120	125	15	10	4	0	0	0	0	0	0	0	0
125	130	16	10	5	0	0	0	0	0	0	0	0
130	135	17	11	6	0	0	0	0	0	0	0	0
135	140	18	12	6	1	0	0	0	0	0	0	0
140	145	18	13	7	1	0	0	0	0	0	0	0
145	150	19	13	8	2	0	0	0	0	0	0	0
150	155	20	14	9	3	0	0	0	0	0	0	0
155	160	21	15	9	4	0	0	0	0	0	0	0
160	165	21	16	10	4	0	0	0	0	0	0	0
165	170	22	16	11	5	0	0	0	0	0	0	0
170	175	23	17	12	6	0	0	0	0	0	0	0
175	180	24	18	12	7	1	0	0	0	0	0	0
180	185	24	19	13	7	2	0	0	0	0	0	0
185	190	25	19	14	8	3	0	0	0	0	0	0
190	195	26	20	15	9	3	0	0	0	0	0	0
195	200	27	21	15	10	4	0	0	0	0	0	0
200	210	28	22	16	11	5	0	0	0	0	0	0
210	220	29	24	18	12	7	1	0	0	0	0	0
220	230	31	25	19	14	8	3	0	0	0	0	0
230	240	32	27	21	15	10	4	0	0	0	0	0
240	250	34	28	22	17	11	6	0	0	0	0	0
250	260	35	30	24	18	13	7	1	0	0	0	0
260	270	37	31	25	20	14	9	3	0	0	0	0
270	280	38	33	27	21	16	10	4	0	0	0	0
280	290	40	34	28	23	17	12	6	0	0	0	0
290	300	41	36	30	24	19	13	7	2	0	0	0
300	310	43	37	31	26	20	15	9	3	0	0	0
310	320	44	39	33	27	22	16	10	5	0	0	0
320	330	46	40	34	29	23	18	12	6	1	0	0
330	340	47	42	36	30	25	19	13	8	2	0	0
340	350	49	43	37	32	26	21	15	9	4	0	0
350	360	50	45	39	33	28	22	16	11	5	0	0
360	370	52	46	40	35	29	24	18	12	7	1	0
370	380	55	48	42	36	31	25	19	14	8	3	0
380	390	58	49	43	38	32	27	21	15	10	4	0
390	400	60	51	45	39	34	28	22	17	11	6	0
400	410	63	53	46	41	35	30	24	18	13	7	1
410	420	66	55	48	42	37	31	25	20	14	9	3
420	430	69	58	49	44	38	33	27	21	16	10	4
430	440	72	61	51	45	40	34	28	23	17	12	6
440	450	74	64	53	47	41	36	30	24	19	13	7
450	460	77	67	56	48	43	37	31	26	20	15	9
460	470	80	69	59	50	44	39	33	27	22	16	10
470	480	83	72	62	51	46	40	34	29	23	18	12
480	490	86	75	65	54	47	42	36	30	25	19	13
490	500	88	78	67	57	49	43	37	32	26	21	15
500	510	91	81	70	60	50	45	39	33	28	22	16
510	520	94	83	73	62	52	46	40	35	29	24	18
520	530	97	86	76	65	55	48	42	36	31	25	19
530	540	100	89	79	68	58	49	43	38	32	27	21

(Continued on next page)

SINGLE Persons—WEEKLY Payroll Period
(For Wages Paid After December 1987)

And the wages are—		And the number of withholding allowances claimed is—										
At least	But less than	0	1	2	3	4	5	6	7	8	9	10
		The amount of income tax to be withheld shall be—										
$540	$550	$102	$92	$81	$71	$60	$51	$45	$39	$34	$28	$22
550	560	105	95	84	74	63	53	46	41	35	30	24
560	570	108	97	87	76	66	55	48	42	37	31	25
570	580	111	100	90	79	69	58	49	44	38	33	27
580	590	114	103	93	82	72	61	51	45	40	34	28
590	600	116	106	95	85	74	64	53	47	41	36	30
600	610	119	109	98	88	77	67	56	48	43	37	31
610	620	122	111	101	90	80	69	59	50	44	39	33
620	630	125	114	104	93	83	72	62	51	46	40	34
630	640	128	117	107	96	86	75	65	54	47	42	36
640	650	130	120	109	99	88	78	67	57	49	43	37
650	660	133	123	112	102	91	81	70	60	50	45	39
660	670	136	125	115	104	94	83	73	62	52	46	40
670	680	139	128	118	107	97	86	76	65	55	48	42
680	690	142	131	121	110	100	89	79	68	58	49	43
690	700	144	134	123	113	102	92	81	71	60	51	45
700	710	147	137	126	116	105	95	84	74	63	53	46
710	720	150	139	129	118	108	97	87	76	66	55	48
720	730	153	142	132	121	111	100	90	79	69	58	49
730	740	156	145	135	124	114	103	93	82	72	61	51
740	750	158	148	137	127	116	106	95	85	74	64	53
750	760	161	151	140	130	119	109	98	88	77	67	56
760	770	164	153	143	132	122	111	101	90	80	69	59
770	780	167	156	146	135	125	114	104	93	83	72	62
780	790	170	159	149	138	128	117	107	96	86	75	65
790	800	172	162	151	141	130	120	109	99	88	78	67
800	810	175	165	154	144	133	123	112	102	91	81	70
810	820	178	167	157	146	136	125	115	104	94	83	73
820	830	181	170	160	149	139	128	118	107	97	86	76
830	840	184	173	163	152	142	131	121	110	100	89	79
840	850	186	176	165	155	144	134	123	113	102	92	81
850	860	189	179	168	158	147	137	126	116	105	95	84
860	870	193	181	171	160	150	139	129	118	108	97	87
870	880	196	184	174	163	153	142	132	121	111	100	90
880	890	199	187	177	166	156	145	135	124	114	103	93
890	900	203	190	179	169	158	148	137	127	116	106	95
900	910	206	193	182	172	161	151	140	130	119	109	98
910	920	209	197	185	174	164	153	143	132	122	111	101
920	930	212	200	188	177	167	156	146	135	125	114	104
930	940	216	203	191	180	170	159	149	138	128	117	107
940	950	219	207	194	183	172	162	151	141	130	120	109
950	960	222	210	198	186	175	165	154	144	133	123	112
960	970	226	213	201	189	178	167	157	146	136	125	115
970	980	229	217	204	192	181	170	160	149	139	128	118
980	990	232	220	208	195	184	173	163	152	142	131	121
990	1,000	236	223	211	198	186	176	165	155	144	134	123
1,000	1,010	239	226	214	202	189	179	168	158	147	137	126
1,010	1,020	242	230	217	205	193	181	171	160	150	139	129
1,020	1,030	245	233	221	208	196	184	174	163	153	142	132
1,030	1,040	249	236	224	212	199	187	177	166	156	145	135
1,040	1,050	252	240	227	215	203	190	179	169	158	148	137
1,050	1,060	255	243	231	218	206	193	182	172	161	151	140
1,060	1,070	259	246	234	222	209	197	185	174	164	153	143
1,070	1,080	262	250	237	225	212	200	188	177	167	156	146
1,080	1,090	265	253	241	228	216	203	191	180	170	159	149
1,090	1,100	269	256	244	231	219	207	194	183	172	162	151
1,100	1,110	272	259	247	235	222	210	198	186	175	165	154
1,110	1,120	275	263	250	238	226	213	201	189	178	167	157
1,120	1,130	278	266	254	241	229	217	204	192	181	170	160
1,130	1,140	282	269	257	245	232	220	208	195	184	173	163
1,140	1,150	285	273	260	248	236	223	211	198	186	176	165
1,150	1,160	288	276	264	251	239	226	214	202	189	179	168
1,160	1,170	292	279	267	255	242	230	217	205	193	181	171
1,170	1,180	295	283	270	258	245	233	221	208	196	184	174
1,180	1,190	298	286	274	261	249	236	224	212	199	187	177
1,190	1,200	302	289	277	264	252	240	227	215	203	190	179

$1,200 and over   Use Table 1(a) for a **SINGLE person** on page 22. Also see the instructions on page 20.

Reference Tables   A—39

Federal Reserve Table for Computing Annual Percentage Rates for Monthly Payment Plans

Number of Payments	10.00%	10.25%	10.50%	10.75%	11.00%	11.25%	11.50%	11.75%	12.00%	12.25%	12.50%	12.75%	13.00%	13.25%
\multicolumn{15}{c}{Finance Charge per $100 of Amount Financed}
1	0.83	0.85	0.88	0.90	0.92	0.94	0.96	0.98	1.00	1.02	1.04	1.06	1.08	1.10
2	1.25	1.28	1.31	1.35	1.38	1.41	1.44	1.47	1.50	1.53	1.57	1.60	1.63	1.66
3	1.67	1.71	1.76	1.80	1.84	1.88	1.92	1.96	2.01	2.05	2.09	2.13	2.17	2.22
4	2.09	2.14	2.20	2.25	2.30	2.35	2.41	2.46	2.51	2.57	2.62	2.67	2.72	2.78
5	2.51	2.58	2.64	2.70	2.77	2.83	2.89	2.96	3.02	3.08	3.15	3.21	3.27	3.34
6	2.94	3.01	3.08	3.16	3.23	3.31	3.38	3.45	3.53	3.60	3.68	3.75	3.83	3.90
7	3.36	3.45	3.53	3.62	3.70	3.78	3.87	3.95	4.04	4.12	4.21	4.29	4.38	4.47
8	3.79	3.88	3.98	4.07	4.17	4.26	4.36	4.46	4.55	4.65	4.74	4.84	4.94	5.03
9	4.21	4.32	4.43	4.53	4.64	4.75	4.85	4.96	5.07	5.17	5.28	5.39	5.49	5.60
10	4.64	4.76	4.88	4.99	5.11	5.23	5.35	5.46	5.58	5.70	5.82	5.94	6.05	6.17
11	5.07	5.20	5.33	5.45	5.58	5.71	5.84	5.97	6.10	6.23	6.36	6.49	6.62	6.75
12	5.50	5.64	5.78	5.92	6.06	6.20	6.34	6.48	6.62	6.76	6.90	7.04	7.18	7.32
13	5.93	6.08	6.23	6.38	6.53	6.68	6.84	6.99	7.14	7.29	7.44	7.59	7.75	7.90
14	6.36	6.52	6.69	6.85	7.01	7.17	7.34	7.50	7.66	7.82	7.99	8.15	8.31	8.48
15	6.80	6.97	7.14	7.32	7.49	7.66	7.84	8.01	8.19	8.36	8.53	8.71	8.88	9.06
16	7.23	7.41	7.60	7.78	7.97	8.15	8.34	8.53	8.71	8.90	9.08	9.27	9.46	9.64
17	7.67	7.86	8.06	8.25	8.45	8.65	8.84	9.04	9.24	9.44	9.63	9.83	10.03	10.23
18	8.10	8.31	8.52	8.73	8.93	9.14	9.35	9.56	9.77	9.98	10.19	10.40	10.61	10.82
19	8.54	8.76	8.98	9.20	9.42	9.64	9.86	10.08	10.30	10.52	10.74	10.96	11.18	11.41
20	8.98	9.21	9.44	9.67	9.90	10.13	10.37	10.60	10.83	11.06	11.30	11.53	11.76	12.00
21	9.42	9.66	9.90	10.15	10.39	10.63	10.88	11.12	11.36	11.61	11.85	12.10	12.34	12.59
22	9.86	10.12	10.37	10.62	10.88	11.13	11.39	11.64	11.90	12.16	12.41	12.67	12.93	13.19
23	10.30	10.57	10.84	11.10	11.37	11.63	11.90	12.17	12.44	12.71	12.97	13.24	13.51	13.78
24	10.75	11.02	11.30	11.58	11.86	12.14	12.42	12.70	12.98	13.26	13.54	13.82	14.10	14.38
25	11.19	11.48	11.77	12.06	12.35	12.64	12.93	13.22	13.52	13.81	14.10	14.40	14.69	14.98
26	11.64	11.94	12.24	12.54	12.85	13.15	13.45	13.75	14.06	14.36	14.67	14.97	15.28	15.59
27	12.09	12.40	12.71	13.03	13.34	13.66	13.97	14.29	14.60	14.92	15.24	15.56	15.87	16.19
28	12.53	12.86	13.18	13.51	13.84	14.16	14.49	14.82	15.15	15.48	15.81	16.14	16.47	16.80
29	12.98	13.32	13.66	14.00	14.33	14.67	15.01	15.35	15.70	16.04	16.38	16.72	17.07	17.41
30	13.43	13.78	14.13	14.48	14.83	15.19	15.54	15.89	16.24	16.60	16.95	17.31	17.66	18.02
31	13.89	14.25	14.61	14.97	15.33	15.70	16.06	16.43	16.79	17.16	17.53	17.90	18.27	18.63
32	14.34	14.71	15.09	15.46	15.84	16.21	16.59	16.97	17.35	17.73	18.11	18.49	18.87	19.25
33	14.79	15.18	15.57	15.95	16.34	16.73	17.12	17.51	17.90	18.29	18.69	19.08	19.47	19.87
34	15.25	15.65	16.05	16.44	16.85	17.25	17.65	18.05	18.46	18.86	19.27	19.67	20.08	20.49
35	15.70	16.11	16.53	16.94	17.35	17.77	18.18	18.60	19.01	19.43	19.85	20.27	20.69	21.11
36	16.16	16.58	17.01	17.43	17.86	18.29	18.71	19.14	19.57	20.00	20.43	20.87	21.30	21.73
37	16.62	17.06	17.49	17.93	18.37	18.81	19.25	19.69	20.13	20.58	21.02	21.46	21.91	22.36
38	17.08	17.53	17.98	18.43	18.88	19.33	19.78	20.24	20.69	21.15	21.61	22.07	22.52	22.99
39	17.54	18.00	18.46	18.93	19.39	19.86	20.32	20.79	21.26	21.73	22.20	22.67	23.14	23.61
40	18.00	18.48	18.95	19.43	19.90	20.38	20.86	21.34	21.82	22.30	22.79	23.27	23.76	24.25
41	18.47	18.95	19.44	19.93	20.42	20.91	21.40	21.89	22.39	22.88	23.38	23.88	24.38	24.88
42	18.93	19.43	19.93	20.43	20.93	21.44	21.94	22.45	22.96	23.47	23.98	24.49	25.00	25.51
43	19.40	19.91	20.42	20.94	21.45	21.97	22.49	23.01	23.53	24.05	24.57	25.10	25.62	26.15
44	19.86	20.39	20.91	21.44	21.97	22.50	23.03	23.57	24.10	24.64	25.17	25.71	26.25	26.79
45	20.33	20.87	21.41	21.95	22.49	23.03	23.58	24.12	24.67	25.22	25.77	26.32	26.88	27.43
46	20.80	21.35	21.90	22.46	23.01	23.57	24.13	24.69	25.25	25.81	26.37	26.94	27.51	28.08
47	21.27	21.83	22.40	22.97	23.53	24.10	24.68	25.25	25.82	26.40	26.98	27.56	28.14	28.72
48	21.74	22.32	22.90	23.48	24.06	24.64	25.23	25.81	26.40	26.99	27.58	28.18	28.77	29.37
49	22.21	22.80	23.39	23.99	24.58	25.18	25.78	26.38	26.98	27.59	28.19	28.80	29.41	30.02
50	22.69	23.29	23.89	24.50	25.11	25.72	26.33	26.95	27.56	28.18	28.80	29.42	30.04	30.67
51	23.16	23.78	24.40	25.02	25.64	26.26	26.89	27.52	28.15	28.78	29.41	30.05	30.68	31.32
52	23.64	24.27	24.90	25.53	26.17	26.81	27.45	28.09	28.73	29.38	30.02	30.67	31.32	31.98
53	24.11	24.76	25.40	26.05	26.70	27.35	28.00	28.66	29.32	29.98	30.64	31.30	31.97	32.63
54	24.59	25.25	25.91	26.57	27.23	27.90	28.56	29.23	29.91	30.58	31.25	31.93	32.61	33.29
55	25.07	25.74	26.41	27.09	27.77	28.44	29.13	29.81	30.50	31.18	31.87	32.56	33.26	33.95
56	25.55	26.23	26.92	27.61	28.30	28.99	29.69	30.39	31.09	31.79	32.49	33.20	33.91	34.62
57	26.03	26.73	27.43	28.13	28.84	29.54	30.25	30.97	31.68	32.39	33.11	33.83	34.56	35.28
58	26.51	27.23	27.94	28.66	29.37	30.10	30.82	31.55	32.27	33.00	33.74	34.47	35.21	35.95
59	27.00	27.72	28.45	29.18	29.91	30.65	31.39	32.13	32.87	33.61	34.36	35.11	35.86	36.62
60	27.48	28.22	28.96	29.71	30.45	31.20	31.96	32.71	33.47	34.23	34.99	35.75	36.52	37.29

Federal Reserve Table for Computing Annual Percentage Rates for Monthly Payment Plans

Annual Percentage Rate

Number of Payments	13.50%	13.75%	14.00%	14.25%	14.50%	14.75%	15.00%	15.25%	15.50%	15.75%	16.00%	16.25%	16.50%	16.75%
					Finance Charge per $100 of Amount Financed									
1	1.13	1.15	1.17	1.19	1.21	1.23	1.25	1.27	1.29	1.31	1.33	1.35	1.38	1.40
2	1.69	1.72	1.75	1.78	1.82	1.85	1.88	1.91	1.94	1.97	2.00	2.04	2.07	2.10
3	2.26	2.30	2.34	2.38	2.43	2.47	2.51	2.55	2.59	2.64	2.68	2.72	2.76	2.80
4	2.83	2.88	2.93	2.99	3.04	3.09	3.14	3.20	3.25	3.30	3.36	3.41	3.46	3.51
5	3.40	3.46	3.53	3.59	3.65	3.72	3.78	3.84	3.91	3.97	4.04	4.10	4.16	4.23
6	3.97	4.05	4.12	4.20	4.27	4.35	4.42	4.49	4.57	4.64	4.72	4.79	4.87	4.94
7	4.55	4.64	4.72	4.81	4.89	4.98	5.06	5.15	5.23	5.32	5.40	5.49	5.58	5.66
8	5.13	5.22	5.32	5.42	5.51	5.61	5.71	5.80	5.90	6.00	6.09	6.19	6.29	6.38
9	5.71	5.82	5.92	6.03	6.14	6.25	6.35	6.46	6.57	6.68	6.78	6.89	7.00	7.11
10	6.29	6.41	6.53	6.65	6.77	6.88	7.00	7.12	7.24	7.36	7.48	7.60	7.72	7.84
11	6.88	7.01	7.14	7.27	7.40	7.53	7.66	7.79	7.92	8.05	8.18	8.31	8.44	8.57
12	7.46	7.60	7.74	7.89	8.03	8.17	8.31	8.45	8.59	8.74	8.88	9.02	9.16	9.30
13	8.05	8.20	8.36	8.51	8.66	8.81	8.97	9.12	9.27	9.43	9.58	9.73	9.89	10.04
14	8.64	8.81	8.97	9.13	9.30	9.46	9.63	9.79	9.96	10.12	10.29	10.45	10.62	10.78
15	9.23	9.41	9.59	9.76	9.94	10.11	10.29	10.47	10.64	10.82	11.00	11.17	11.35	11.53
16	9.83	10.02	10.20	10.39	10.58	10.77	10.95	11.14	11.33	11.52	11.71	11.90	12.09	12.28
17	10.43	10.63	10.82	11.02	11.22	11.42	11.62	11.82	12.02	12.22	12.42	12.62	12.83	13.03
18	11.03	11.24	11.45	11.66	11.87	12.08	12.29	12.50	12.72	12.93	13.14	13.35	13.57	13.78
19	11.63	11.85	12.07	12.30	12.52	12.74	12.97	13.19	13.41	13.64	13.86	14.09	14.31	14.54
20	12.23	12.46	12.70	12.93	13.17	13.41	13.64	13.88	14.11	14.35	14.59	14.82	15.06	15.30
21	12.84	13.08	13.33	13.58	13.82	14.07	14.32	14.57	14.82	15.06	15.31	15.56	15.81	16.06
22	13.44	13.70	13.96	14.22	14.48	14.74	15.00	15.26	15.52	15.78	16.04	16.30	16.57	16.83
23	14.05	14.32	14.59	14.87	15.14	15.41	15.68	15.96	16.23	16.50	16.78	17.05	17.32	17.60
24	14.66	14.95	15.23	15.51	15.80	16.08	16.37	16.65	16.94	17.22	17.51	17.80	18.09	18.37
25	15.28	15.57	15.87	16.17	16.46	16.76	17.06	17.35	17.65	17.95	18.25	18.55	18.85	19.15
26	15.89	16.20	16.51	16.82	17.13	17.44	17.75	18.06	18.37	18.68	18.99	19.30	19.62	19.93
27	16.51	16.83	17.15	17.47	17.80	18.12	18.44	18.76	19.09	19.41	19.74	20.06	20.39	20.71
28	17.13	17.46	17.80	18.13	18.47	18.80	19.14	19.47	19.81	20.15	20.48	20.82	21.16	21.50
29	17.75	18.10	18.45	18.79	19.14	19.49	19.83	20.18	20.53	20.88	21.23	21.58	21.94	22.29
30	18.38	18.74	19.10	19.45	19.81	20.17	20.54	20.90	21.26	21.62	21.99	22.35	22.72	23.08
31	19.00	19.38	19.75	20.12	20.49	20.87	21.24	21.61	21.99	22.37	22.74	23.12	23.50	23.88
32	19.63	20.02	20.40	20.79	21.17	21.56	21.95	22.33	22.72	23.11	23.50	23.89	24.28	24.68
33	20.26	20.66	21.06	21.46	21.85	22.25	22.65	23.06	23.46	23.86	24.26	24.67	25.07	25.48
34	20.90	21.31	21.72	22.13	22.54	22.95	23.37	23.78	24.19	24.61	25.03	25.44	25.86	26.28
35	21.53	21.95	22.38	22.80	23.23	23.65	24.08	24.51	24.94	25.36	25.79	26.23	26.66	27.09
36	22.17	22.60	23.04	23.48	23.92	24.35	24.80	25.24	25.68	26.12	26.57	27.01	27.46	27.90
37	22.81	23.25	23.70	24.16	24.61	25.06	25.51	25.97	26.42	26.88	27.34	27.80	28.26	28.72
38	23.45	23.91	24.37	24.84	25.30	25.77	26.24	26.70	27.17	27.64	28.11	28.59	29.06	29.53
39	24.09	24.56	25.04	25.52	26.00	26.48	26.96	27.44	27.92	28.41	28.89	29.38	29.87	30.36
40	24.73	25.22	25.71	26.20	26.70	27.19	27.69	28.18	28.68	29.18	29.68	30.18	30.68	31.18
41	25.38	25.88	26.39	26.89	27.40	27.91	28.41	28.92	29.44	29.95	30.46	30.97	31.49	32.01
42	26.03	26.55	27.06	27.58	28.10	28.62	29.15	29.67	30.19	30.72	31.25	31.78	32.31	32.84
43	26.68	27.21	27.74	28.27	28.81	29.34	29.88	30.42	30.96	31.50	32.04	32.58	33.13	33.67
44	27.33	27.88	28.42	28.97	29.52	30.07	30.62	31.17	31.72	32.28	32.83	33.39	33.95	34.51
45	27.99	28.55	29.11	29.67	30.23	30.79	31.36	31.92	32.49	33.06	33.63	34.20	34.77	35.35
46	28.65	29.22	29.79	30.36	30.94	31.52	32.10	32.68	33.26	33.84	34.43	35.01	35.60	36.19
47	29.31	29.89	30.48	31.07	31.66	32.25	32.84	33.44	34.03	34.63	35.23	35.83	36.43	37.04
48	29.97	30.57	31.17	31.77	32.37	32.98	33.59	34.20	34.81	35.42	36.03	36.65	37.27	37.88
49	30.63	31.24	31.86	32.48	33.09	33.71	34.34	34.96	35.59	36.21	36.84	37.47	38.10	38.74
50	31.29	31.92	32.55	33.18	33.82	34.45	35.09	35.73	36.37	37.01	37.65	38.30	38.94	39.59
51	31.96	32.60	33.25	33.89	34.54	35.19	35.84	36.50	37.15	37.81	38.46	39.12	39.79	40.45
52	32.63	33.29	33.95	34.61	35.27	35.93	36.60	37.27	37.94	38.61	39.28	39.96	40.63	41.31
53	33.30	33.97	34.65	35.32	36.00	36.68	37.36	38.04	38.72	39.41	40.10	40.79	41.48	42.17
54	33.98	34.66	35.35	36.04	36.73	37.42	38.12	38.82	39.52	40.22	40.92	41.63	42.33	43.04
55	34.65	35.35	36.05	36.76	37.46	38.17	38.88	39.60	40.31	41.03	41.74	42.47	43.19	43.91
56	35.33	36.04	36.76	37.48	38.20	38.92	39.65	40.38	41.11	41.84	42.57	43.31	44.05	44.79
57	36.01	36.74	37.47	38.20	38.94	39.68	40.42	41.16	41.91	42.65	43.40	44.15	44.91	45.66
58	36.69	37.43	38.18	38.93	39.68	40.43	41.19	41.95	42.71	43.47	44.23	45.00	45.77	46.54
59	37.37	38.13	38.89	39.66	40.42	41.19	41.96	42.74	43.51	44.29	45.07	45.85	46.64	47.42
60	38.06	38.83	39.61	40.39	41.17	41.95	42.74	43.53	44.32	45.11	45.91	46.71	47.51	48.31

Reference Tables   A–41

Federal Reserve Table for Computing Annual Percentage Rates for Monthly Payment Plans

Annual Percentage Rate

Number of Payments	17.00%	17.25%	17.50%	17.75%	18.00%	18.25%	18.50%	18.75%	19.00%	19.25%	19.50%	19.75%	20.00%	20.25%
	Finance Charge per $100 of Amount Financed													
1	1.42	1.44	1.46	1.48	1.50	1.52	1.54	1.56	1.58	1.60	1.63	1.65	1.67	1.69
2	2.13	2.16	2.19	2.22	2.26	2.29	2.32	2.35	2.38	2.41	2.44	2.48	2.51	2.54
3	2.85	2.89	2.93	2.97	3.01	3.06	3.10	3.14	3.18	3.23	3.27	3.31	3.35	3.39
4	3.57	3.62	3.67	3.73	3.78	3.83	3.88	3.94	3.99	4.04	4.10	4.15	4.20	4.25
5	4.29	4.35	4.42	4.48	4.54	4.61	4.67	4.74	4.80	4.86	4.93	4.99	5.06	5.12
6	5.02	5.09	5.17	5.24	5.32	5.39	5.46	5.54	5.61	5.69	5.76	5.84	5.91	5.99
7	5.75	5.83	5.92	6.00	6.09	6.18	6.26	6.35	6.43	6.52	6.60	6.69	6.78	6.86
8	6.48	6.58	6.67	6.77	6.87	6.96	7.06	7.16	7.26	7.35	7.45	7.55	7.64	7.74
9	7.22	7.32	7.43	7.54	7.65	7.76	7.87	7.97	8.08	8.19	8.30	8.41	8.52	8.63
10	7.96	8.08	8.19	8.31	8.43	8.55	8.67	8.79	8.91	9.03	9.15	9.27	9.39	9.51
11	8.70	8.83	8.96	9.09	9.22	9.35	9.49	9.62	9.75	9.88	10.01	10.14	10.28	10.41
12	9.45	9.59	9.73	9.87	10.02	10.16	10.30	10.44	10.59	10.73	10.87	11.02	11.16	11.31
13	10.20	10.35	10.50	10.66	10.81	10.97	11.12	11.28	11.43	11.59	11.74	11.90	12.05	12.21
14	10.95	11.11	11.28	11.45	11.61	11.78	11.95	12.11	12.28	12.45	12.61	12.78	12.95	13.11
15	11.71	11.88	12.06	12.24	12.42	12.59	12.77	12.95	13.13	13.31	13.49	13.67	13.85	14.03
16	12.46	12.65	12.84	13.03	13.22	13.41	13.60	13.80	13.99	14.18	14.37	14.56	14.75	14.94
17	13.23	13.43	13.63	13.83	14.04	14.24	14.44	14.64	14.85	15.05	15.25	15.46	15.66	15.86
18	13.99	14.21	14.42	14.64	14.85	15.07	15.28	15.49	15.71	15.93	16.14	16.36	16.57	16.79
19	14.76	14.99	15.22	15.44	15.67	15.90	16.12	16.35	16.58	16.81	17.03	17.26	17.49	17.72
20	15.54	15.78	16.01	16.25	16.49	16.73	16.97	17.21	17.45	17.69	17.93	18.17	18.41	18.66
21	16.31	16.56	16.81	17.07	17.32	17.57	17.82	18.07	18.33	18.58	18.83	19.09	19.34	19.60
22	17.09	17.36	17.62	17.88	18.15	18.41	18.68	18.94	19.21	19.47	19.74	20.01	20.27	20.54
23	17.88	18.15	18.43	18.70	18.98	19.26	19.54	19.81	20.09	20.37	20.65	20.93	21.21	21.49
24	18.66	18.95	19.24	19.53	19.82	20.11	20.40	20.69	20.98	21.27	21.56	21.86	22.15	22.44
25	19.45	19.75	20.05	20.36	20.66	20.96	21.27	21.57	21.87	22.18	22.48	22.79	23.10	23.40
26	20.24	20.56	20.87	21.19	21.50	21.82	22.14	22.45	22.77	23.09	23.41	23.73	24.04	24.36
27	21.04	21.37	21.69	22.02	22.35	22.68	23.01	23.34	23.67	24.00	24.33	24.67	25.00	25.33
28	21.84	22.18	22.52	22.86	23.20	23.55	23.89	24.23	24.58	24.92	25.27	25.61	25.96	26.30
29	22.64	22.99	23.35	23.70	24.06	24.41	24.77	25.13	25.49	25.84	26.20	26.56	26.92	27.28
30	23.45	23.81	24.18	24.55	24.92	25.29	25.66	26.03	26.40	26.77	27.14	27.52	27.89	28.26
31	24.26	24.64	25.02	25.40	25.78	26.16	26.55	26.93	27.32	27.70	28.09	28.47	28.86	29.25
32	25.07	25.46	25.86	26.25	26.65	27.04	27.44	27.84	28.24	28.64	29.04	29.44	29.84	30.24
33	25.88	26.29	26.70	27.11	27.52	27.93	28.34	28.75	29.16	29.57	29.99	30.40	30.82	31.23
34	26.70	27.12	27.54	27.97	28.39	28.81	29.24	29.66	30.09	30.52	30.95	31.37	31.80	32.23
35	27.52	27.96	28.39	28.83	29.27	29.71	30.14	30.58	31.02	31.47	31.91	32.35	32.79	33.24
36	28.35	28.80	29.25	29.70	30.15	30.60	31.05	31.51	31.96	32.42	32.87	33.33	33.79	34.25
37	29.18	29.64	30.10	30.57	31.03	31.50	31.97	32.43	32.90	33.37	33.84	34.32	34.79	35.26
38	30.01	30.49	30.96	31.44	31.92	32.40	32.88	33.37	33.85	34.33	34.82	35.30	35.79	36.28
39	30.85	31.34	31.83	32.32	32.81	33.31	33.80	34.30	34.80	35.30	35.80	36.30	36.80	37.30
40	31.68	32.19	32.69	33.20	33.71	34.22	34.73	35.24	35.75	36.26	36.78	37.29	37.81	38.33
41	32.52	33.04	33.56	34.08	34.61	35.13	35.66	36.18	36.71	37.24	37.77	38.30	38.83	39.36
42	33.37	33.90	34.44	34.97	35.51	36.05	36.59	37.13	37.67	38.21	38.76	39.30	39.85	40.40
43	34.22	34.76	35.31	35.86	36.42	36.97	37.52	38.08	38.63	39.19	39.75	40.31	40.87	41.44
44	35.07	35.63	36.19	36.76	37.33	37.89	38.46	39.03	39.60	40.18	40.75	41.33	41.90	42.48
45	35.92	36.50	37.08	37.66	38.24	38.82	39.41	39.99	40.58	41.17	41.75	42.35	42.94	43.53
46	36.78	37.37	37.96	38.56	39.16	39.75	40.35	40.95	41.55	42.16	42.76	43.37	43.98	44.58
47	37.64	38.25	38.86	39.46	40.08	40.69	41.30	41.92	42.54	43.15	43.77	44.40	45.02	45.64
48	38.50	39.13	39.75	40.37	41.00	41.63	42.26	42.89	43.52	44.15	44.79	45.43	46.07	46.71
49	39.37	40.01	40.65	41.29	41.93	42.57	43.22	43.86	44.51	45.16	45.81	46.46	47.12	47.77
50	40.24	40.89	41.55	42.20	42.86	43.52	44.18	44.84	45.50	46.17	46.83	47.50	48.17	48.84
51	41.11	41.78	42.45	43.12	43.79	44.47	45.14	45.82	46.50	47.18	47.86	48.55	49.23	49.92
52	41.99	42.67	43.36	44.04	44.73	45.42	46.11	46.80	47.50	48.20	48.89	49.59	50.30	51.00
53	42.87	43.57	44.27	44.97	45.67	46.38	47.08	47.79	48.50	49.22	49.93	50.65	51.37	52.09
54	43.75	44.47	45.18	45.90	46.62	47.34	48.06	48.79	49.51	50.24	50.97	51.70	52.44	53.17
55	44.64	45.37	46.10	46.83	47.57	48.30	49.04	49.78	50.52	51.27	52.02	52.76	53.52	54.27
56	45.53	46.27	47.02	47.77	48.52	49.27	50.03	50.78	51.54	52.30	53.06	53.83	54.60	55.37
57	46.42	47.18	47.94	48.71	49.47	50.24	51.01	51.79	52.56	53.34	54.12	54.90	55.68	56.47
58	47.32	48.09	48.87	49.65	50.43	51.22	52.00	52.79	53.58	54.38	55.17	55.97	56.77	57.57
59	48.21	49.01	49.80	50.60	51.39	52.20	53.00	53.80	54.61	55.42	56.23	57.05	57.87	58.68
60	49.12	49.92	50.73	51.55	52.36	53.18	54.00	54.82	55.64	56.47	57.30	58.13	58.96	59.80

Federal Reserve Table for Computing Annual Percentage Rates for Monthly Payment Plans

Annual Percentage Rate

Number of Payments	20.50%	20.75%	21.00%	21.25%	21.50%	21.75%	22.00%	22.25%	22.50%	22.75%	23.00%	23.25%	23.50%	23.75%
\multicolumn{15}{c}{Finance Charge per $100 of Amount Financed}
1	1.71	1.73	1.75	1.77	1.79	1.81	1.83	1.85	1.88	1.90	1.92	1.94	1.96	1.98
2	2.57	2.60	2.63	2.66	2.70	2.73	2.76	2.79	2.82	2.85	2.88	2.92	2.95	2.98
3	3.44	3.48	3.52	3.56	3.60	3.65	3.69	3.73	3.77	3.82	3.86	3.90	3.94	3.98
4	4.31	4.36	4.41	4.47	4.52	4.57	4.62	4.68	4.73	4.78	4.84	4.89	4.94	5.00
5	5.18	5.25	5.31	5.37	5.44	5.50	5.57	5.63	5.69	5.76	5.82	5.89	5.95	6.02
6	6.06	6.14	6.21	6.29	6.36	6.44	6.51	6.59	6.66	6.74	6.81	6.89	6.96	7.04
7	6.95	7.04	7.12	7.21	7.29	7.38	7.47	7.55	7.64	7.73	7.81	7.90	7.99	8.07
8	7.84	7.94	8.03	8.13	8.23	8.33	8.42	8.52	8.62	8.72	8.82	8.91	9.01	9.11
9	8.73	8.84	8.95	9.06	9.17	9.28	9.39	9.50	9.61	9.72	9.83	9.94	10.04	10.15
10	9.63	9.75	9.88	10.00	10.12	10.24	10.36	10.48	10.60	10.72	10.84	10.96	11.08	11.21
11	10.54	10.67	10.80	10.94	11.07	11.20	11.33	11.47	11.60	11.73	11.86	12.00	12.13	12.26
12	11.45	11.59	11.74	11.88	12.02	12.17	12.31	12.46	12.60	12.75	12.89	13.04	13.18	13.33
13	12.36	12.52	12.67	12.83	12.99	13.14	13.30	13.46	13.61	13.77	13.93	14.08	14.24	14.40
14	13.28	13.45	13.62	13.79	13.95	14.12	14.29	14.46	14.63	14.80	14.97	15.13	15.30	15.47
15	14.21	14.39	14.57	14.75	14.93	15.11	15.29	15.47	15.65	15.83	16.01	16.19	16.37	16.56
16	15.14	15.33	15.52	15.71	15.90	16.10	16.29	16.48	16.68	16.87	17.06	17.26	17.45	17.65
17	16.07	16.27	16.48	16.68	16.89	17.09	17.30	17.50	17.71	17.92	18.12	18.33	18.53	18.74
18	17.01	17.22	17.44	17.66	17.88	18.09	18.31	18.53	18.75	18.97	19.19	19.41	19.62	19.84
19	17.95	18.18	18.41	18.64	18.87	19.10	19.33	19.56	19.79	20.02	20.26	20.49	20.72	20.95
20	18.90	19.14	19.38	19.63	19.87	20.11	20.36	20.60	20.84	21.09	21.33	21.58	21.82	22.07
21	19.85	20.11	20.36	20.62	20.87	21.13	21.38	21.64	21.90	22.16	22.41	22.67	22.93	23.19
22	20.81	21.08	21.34	21.61	21.88	22.15	22.42	22.69	22.96	23.23	23.50	23.77	24.04	24.32
23	21.77	22.05	22.33	22.61	22.90	23.18	23.46	23.74	24.03	24.31	24.60	24.88	25.17	25.45
24	22.74	23.03	23.33	23.62	23.92	24.21	24.51	24.80	25.10	25.40	25.70	25.99	26.29	26.59
25	23.71	24.02	24.32	24.63	24.94	25.25	25.56	25.87	26.18	26.49	26.80	27.11	27.43	27.74
26	24.68	25.01	25.33	25.65	25.97	26.29	26.62	26.94	27.26	27.59	27.91	28.24	28.56	28.89
27	25.67	26.00	26.34	26.67	27.01	27.34	27.68	28.02	28.35	28.69	29.03	29.37	29.71	30.05
28	26.65	27.00	27.35	27.70	28.05	28.40	28.75	29.10	29.45	29.80	30.15	30.51	30.86	31.22
29	27.64	28.00	28.37	28.73	29.09	29.46	29.82	30.19	30.55	30.92	31.28	31.65	32.02	32.39
30	28.64	29.01	29.39	29.77	30.14	30.52	30.90	31.28	31.66	32.04	32.42	32.80	33.18	33.57
31	29.64	30.03	30.42	30.81	31.20	31.59	31.98	32.38	32.77	33.17	33.56	33.96	34.35	34.75
32	30.64	31.05	31.45	31.85	32.26	32.67	33.07	33.48	33.89	34.30	34.71	35.12	35.53	35.94
33	31.65	32.07	32.49	32.91	33.33	33.75	34.17	34.59	35.01	35.44	35.86	36.29	36.71	37.14
34	32.67	33.10	33.53	33.96	34.40	34.83	35.27	35.71	36.14	36.58	37.02	37.46	37.90	38.34
35	33.68	34.13	34.58	35.03	35.47	35.92	36.37	36.83	37.28	37.73	38.18	38.64	39.09	39.55
36	34.71	35.17	35.63	36.09	36.56	37.02	37.49	37.95	38.42	38.89	39.35	39.82	40.29	40.77
37	35.74	36.21	36.69	37.16	37.64	38.12	38.60	39.08	39.56	40.05	40.53	41.02	41.50	41.99
38	36.77	37.26	37.75	38.24	38.73	39.23	39.72	40.22	40.72	41.21	41.71	42.21	42.71	43.22
39	37.81	38.31	38.82	39.32	39.83	40.34	40.85	41.36	41.87	42.39	42.90	43.42	43.93	44.45
40	38.85	39.37	39.89	40.41	40.93	41.46	41.98	42.51	43.04	43.56	44.09	44.62	45.16	45.69
41	39.89	40.43	40.96	41.50	42.04	42.58	43.12	43.66	44.20	44.75	45.29	45.84	46.39	46.94
42	40.95	41.50	42.05	42.60	43.15	43.71	44.26	44.82	45.38	45.94	46.50	47.06	47.62	48.19
43	42.00	42.57	43.13	43.70	44.27	44.84	45.41	45.98	46.56	47.13	47.71	48.29	48.87	49.45
44	43.06	43.64	44.22	44.81	45.39	45.98	46.56	47.15	47.74	48.33	48.93	49.52	50.11	50.71
45	44.13	44.72	45.32	45.92	46.52	47.12	47.72	48.33	48.93	49.54	50.15	50.76	51.37	51.98
46	45.20	45.81	46.42	47.03	47.65	48.27	48.89	49.51	50.13	50.75	51.38	52.00	52.63	53.26
47	46.27	46.90	47.53	48.16	48.79	49.42	50.06	50.69	51.33	51.97	52.61	53.25	53.89	54.54
48	47.35	47.99	48.64	49.28	49.93	50.58	51.23	51.88	52.54	53.19	53.85	54.51	55.16	55.83
49	48.43	49.09	49.75	50.41	51.08	51.74	52.41	53.08	53.75	54.42	55.09	55.77	56.44	57.12
50	49.52	50.19	50.87	51.55	52.23	52.91	53.59	54.28	54.96	55.65	56.34	57.03	57.73	58.42
51	50.61	51.30	51.99	52.69	53.38	54.08	54.78	55.48	56.19	56.89	57.60	58.30	59.01	59.73
52	51.71	52.41	53.12	53.83	54.55	55.26	55.98	56.69	57.41	58.13	58.86	59.58	60.31	61.04
53	52.81	53.53	54.26	54.98	55.71	56.44	57.18	57.91	58.65	59.38	60.12	60.87	61.61	62.35
54	53.91	54.65	55.39	56.14	56.88	57.63	58.38	59.13	59.88	60.64	61.40	62.16	62.92	63.68
55	55.02	55.78	56.54	57.30	58.06	58.82	59.59	60.36	61.13	61.90	62.67	63.45	64.23	65.01
56	56.14	56.91	57.68	58.46	59.24	60.02	60.80	61.59	62.38	63.17	63.96	64.75	65.54	66.34
57	57.26	58.04	58.84	59.63	60.43	61.22	62.02	62.83	63.63	64.44	65.25	66.06	66.87	67.68
58	58.38	59.18	59.99	60.80	61.62	62.43	63.25	64.07	64.89	65.71	66.54	67.37	68.20	69.03
59	59.51	60.33	61.15	61.98	62.81	63.64	64.48	65.32	66.15	67.00	67.84	68.68	69.53	70.38
60	60.64	61.48	62.32	63.17	64.01	64.86	65.71	66.57	67.42	68.28	69.14	70.01	70.87	71.74

Reference Tables   A–43

Federal Reserve Table for Computing Annual Percentage Rates for Monthly Payment Plans

Number of Payments	24.00%	24.25%	24.50%	24.75%	25.00%	25.25%	25.50%	25.75%	26.00%	26.25%	26.50%	26.75%	27.00%	27.25%
	\multicolumn{14}{c}{Finance Charge per $100 of Amount Financed}
1	2.00	2.02	2.04	2.06	2.08	2.10	2.12	2.15	2.17	2.19	2.21	2.23	2.25	2.27
2	3.01	3.04	3.07	3.10	3.14	3.17	3.20	3.23	3.26	3.29	3.32	3.36	3.39	3.42
3	4.03	4.07	4.11	4.15	4.20	4.24	4.28	4.32	4.36	4.41	4.45	4.49	4.53	4.58
4	5.05	5.10	5.16	5.21	5.26	5.32	5.37	5.42	5.47	5.53	5.58	5.63	5.69	5.74
5	6.08	6.14	6.21	6.27	6.34	6.40	6.46	6.53	6.59	6.66	6.72	6.79	6.85	6.91
6	7.12	7.19	7.27	7.34	7.42	7.49	7.57	7.64	7.72	7.79	7.87	7.95	8.02	8.10
7	8.16	8.25	8.33	8.42	8.51	8.59	8.68	8.77	8.85	8.94	9.03	9.11	9.20	9.29
8	9.21	9.31	9.40	9.50	9.60	9.70	9.80	9.90	9.99	10.09	10.19	10.29	10.39	10.49
9	10.26	10.37	10.48	10.59	10.70	10.81	10.92	11.03	11.14	11.25	11.36	11.47	11.58	11.69
10	11.33	11.45	11.57	11.69	11.81	11.93	12.06	12.18	12.30	12.42	12.54	12.67	12.79	12.91
11	12.40	12.53	12.66	12.80	12.93	13.06	13.20	13.33	13.46	13.60	13.73	13.87	14.00	14.13
12	13.47	13.62	13.76	13.91	14.05	14.20	14.34	14.49	14.64	14.78	14.93	15.07	15.22	15.37
13	14.55	14.71	14.87	15.03	15.18	15.34	15.50	15.66	15.82	15.97	16.13	16.29	16.45	16.61
14	15.64	15.81	15.98	16.15	16.32	16.49	16.66	16.83	17.00	17.17	17.35	17.52	17.69	17.86
15	16.74	16.92	17.10	17.28	17.47	17.65	17.83	18.02	18.20	18.38	18.57	18.75	18.93	19.12
16	17.84	18.03	18.23	18.42	18.62	18.81	19.01	19.21	19.40	19.60	19.79	19.99	20.19	20.38
17	18.95	19.16	19.36	19.57	19.78	19.99	20.20	20.40	20.61	20.82	21.03	21.24	21.45	21.66
18	20.06	20.28	20.50	20.72	20.95	21.17	21.39	21.61	21.83	22.05	22.27	22.50	22.72	22.94
19	21.19	21.42	21.65	21.89	22.12	22.35	22.59	22.82	23.06	23.29	23.53	23.76	24.00	24.23
20	22.31	22.56	22.81	23.05	23.30	23.55	23.79	24.04	24.29	24.54	24.79	25.04	25.28	25.53
21	23.45	23.71	23.97	24.23	24.49	24.75	25.01	25.27	25.53	25.79	26.05	26.32	26.58	26.84
22	24.59	24.86	25.13	25.41	25.68	25.96	26.23	26.50	26.78	27.05	27.33	27.61	27.88	28.16
23	25.74	26.02	26.31	26.60	26.88	27.17	27.46	27.75	28.04	28.32	28.61	28.90	29.19	29.48
24	26.89	27.19	27.49	27.79	28.09	28.39	28.69	29.00	29.30	29.60	29.90	30.21	30.51	30.82
25	28.05	28.36	28.68	28.99	29.31	29.62	29.94	30.25	30.57	30.89	31.20	31.52	31.84	32.16
26	29.22	29.55	29.87	30.20	30.53	30.86	31.19	31.52	31.85	32.18	32.51	32.84	33.18	33.51
27	30.39	30.73	31.07	31.42	31.76	32.10	32.45	32.79	33.14	33.48	33.83	34.17	34.52	34.87
28	31.57	31.93	32.28	32.64	33.00	33.35	33.71	34.07	34.43	34.79	35.15	35.51	35.87	36.23
29	32.76	33.13	33.50	33.87	34.24	34.61	34.98	35.36	35.73	36.10	36.48	36.85	37.23	37.61
30	33.95	34.33	34.72	35.10	35.49	35.88	36.26	36.65	37.04	37.43	37.82	38.21	38.60	38.99
31	35.15	35.55	35.95	36.35	36.75	37.15	37.55	37.95	38.36	38.76	39.16	39.57	39.97	40.38
32	36.35	36.77	37.18	37.60	38.01	38.43	38.84	39.26	39.68	40.10	40.52	40.94	41.36	41.78
33	37.57	37.99	38.42	38.85	39.28	39.71	40.14	40.58	41.01	41.44	41.88	42.31	42.75	43.19
34	38.78	39.23	39.67	40.11	40.56	41.01	41.45	41.90	42.35	42.80	43.25	43.70	44.15	44.60
35	40.01	40.47	40.92	41.38	41.84	42.31	42.77	43.23	43.69	44.16	44.62	45.09	45.56	46.02
36	41.24	41.71	42.19	42.66	43.14	43.61	44.09	44.57	45.05	45.53	46.01	46.49	46.97	47.45
37	42.48	42.96	43.45	43.94	44.43	44.93	45.42	45.91	46.41	46.90	47.40	47.90	48.39	48.89
38	43.72	44.22	44.73	45.23	45.74	46.25	46.75	47.26	47.77	48.29	48.80	49.31	49.82	50.34
39	44.97	45.49	46.01	46.53	47.05	47.57	48.10	48.62	49.15	49.68	50.20	50.73	51.26	51.79
40	46.22	46.76	47.29	47.83	48.37	48.91	49.45	49.99	50.53	51.07	51.62	52.16	52.71	53.26
41	47.48	48.04	48.59	49.14	49.69	50.25	50.80	51.36	51.92	52.48	53.04	53.60	54.16	54.73
42	48.75	49.32	49.89	50.46	51.03	51.60	52.17	52.74	53.32	53.89	54.47	55.05	55.63	56.21
43	50.03	50.61	51.19	51.78	52.36	52.95	53.54	54.13	54.72	55.31	55.90	56.50	57.09	57.69
44	51.31	51.91	52.51	53.11	53.71	54.31	54.92	55.52	56.13	56.74	57.35	57.96	58.57	59.19
45	52.59	53.21	53.82	54.44	55.06	55.68	56.30	56.92	57.55	58.17	58.80	59.43	60.06	60.69
46	53.89	54.52	55.15	55.78	56.42	57.05	57.69	58.33	58.97	59.61	60.26	60.90	61.55	62.20
47	55.18	55.83	56.48	57.13	57.78	58.44	59.09	59.75	60.40	61.06	61.72	62.39	63.05	63.71
48	56.49	57.15	57.82	58.49	59.15	59.82	60.50	61.17	61.84	62.52	63.20	63.87	64.56	65.24
49	57.80	58.48	59.16	59.85	60.53	61.22	61.91	62.60	63.29	63.98	64.68	65.37	66.07	66.77
50	59.12	59.81	60.51	61.21	61.92	62.62	63.33	64.03	64.74	65.45	66.16	66.88	67.59	68.31
51	60.44	61.15	61.87	62.59	63.31	64.03	64.75	65.48	66.20	66.93	67.66	68.39	69.12	69.86
52	61.77	62.50	63.23	63.97	64.70	65.44	66.18	66.92	67.67	68.41	69.16	69.91	70.66	71.41
53	63.10	63.85	64.60	65.35	66.11	66.86	67.62	68.38	69.14	69.90	70.67	71.43	72.20	72.97
54	64.44	65.21	65.98	66.75	67.52	68.29	69.07	69.84	70.62	71.40	72.18	72.97	73.75	74.54
55	65.79	66.57	67.36	68.14	68.93	69.72	70.52	71.31	72.11	72.91	73.71	74.51	75.31	76.12
56	67.14	67.94	68.74	69.55	70.36	71.16	71.97	72.79	73.60	74.42	75.24	76.06	76.88	77.70
57	68.50	69.32	70.14	70.96	71.78	72.61	73.44	74.27	75.10	75.94	76.77	77.61	78.45	79.29
58	69.86	70.70	71.54	72.38	73.22	74.06	74.91	75.76	76.61	77.46	78.32	79.17	80.03	80.89
59	71.23	72.09	72.94	73.80	74.66	75.52	76.39	77.25	78.12	78.99	79.87	80.74	81.62	82.50
60	72.61	73.48	74.35	75.23	76.11	76.99	77.87	78.76	79.64	80.53	81.42	82.32	83.21	84.11

A–44 Appendix D Reference Tables

Federal Reserve Table for Computing Annual Percentage Rates for Monthly Payment Plans

Annual Percentage Rate

Number of Payments	27.50%	27.75%	28.00%	28.25%	28.50%	28.75%	29.00%	29.25%	29.50%	29.75%	30.00%	30.25%	30.50%	30.75%
\multicolumn{15}{c}{Finance Charge per $100 of Amount Financed}
1	2.29	2.31	2.33	2.35	2.37	2.40	2.42	2.44	2.46	2.48	2.50	2.52	2.54	2.56
2	3.45	3.48	3.51	3.54	3.58	3.61	3.64	3.67	3.70	3.73	3.77	3.80	3.83	3.86
3	4.62	4.66	4.70	4.74	4.79	4.83	4.87	4.91	4.96	5.00	5.04	5.08	5.13	5.17
4	5.79	5.85	5.90	5.95	6.01	6.06	6.11	6.17	6.22	6.27	6.33	6.38	6.43	6.49
5	6.98	7.04	7.11	7.17	7.24	7.30	7.37	7.43	7.49	7.56	7.62	7.69	7.75	7.82
6	8.17	8.25	8.32	8.40	8.48	8.55	8.63	8.70	8.78	8.85	8.93	9.01	9.08	9.16
7	9.37	9.46	9.55	9.64	9.72	9.81	9.90	9.98	10.07	10.16	10.25	10.33	10.42	10.51
8	10.58	10.68	10.78	10.88	10.98	11.08	11.18	11.28	11.38	11.47	11.57	11.67	11.77	11.87
9	11.80	11.91	12.03	12.14	12.25	12.36	12.47	12.58	12.69	12.80	12.91	13.02	13.13	13.24
10	13.03	13.15	13.28	13.40	13.52	13.64	13.77	13.89	14.01	14.14	14.26	14.38	14.50	14.63
11	14.27	14.40	14.54	14.67	14.81	14.94	15.08	15.21	15.35	15.48	15.62	15.75	15.89	16.02
12	15.51	15.66	15.81	15.95	16.10	16.25	16.40	16.54	16.69	16.84	16.98	17.13	17.28	17.43
13	16.77	16.93	17.09	17.24	17.40	17.56	17.72	17.88	18.04	18.20	18.36	18.52	18.68	18.84
14	18.03	18.20	18.37	18.54	18.72	18.89	19.06	19.23	19.41	19.58	19.75	19.92	20.10	20.27
15	19.30	19.48	19.67	19.85	20.04	20.22	20.41	20.59	20.78	20.96	21.15	21.34	21.52	21.71
16	20.58	20.78	20.97	21.17	21.37	21.57	21.76	21.96	22.16	22.36	22.56	22.76	22.96	23.16
17	21.87	22.08	22.29	22.50	22.71	22.92	23.13	23.34	23.55	23.77	23.98	24.19	24.40	24.61
18	23.16	23.39	23.61	23.83	24.06	24.28	24.51	24.73	24.96	25.18	25.41	25.63	25.86	26.08
19	24.47	24.71	24.94	25.18	25.42	25.65	25.89	26.13	26.37	26.61	26.85	27.08	27.32	27.56
20	25.78	26.03	26.28	26.53	26.78	27.04	27.29	27.54	27.79	28.04	28.29	28.55	28.80	29.05
21	27.11	27.37	27.63	27.90	28.16	28.43	28.69	28.96	29.22	29.49	29.75	30.02	30.29	30.55
22	28.44	28.71	28.99	29.27	29.55	29.82	30.10	30.38	30.66	30.94	31.22	31.50	31.78	32.07
23	29.77	30.07	30.36	30.65	30.94	31.23	31.53	31.82	32.11	32.41	32.70	33.00	33.29	33.59
24	31.12	31.43	31.73	32.04	32.34	32.65	32.96	33.27	33.57	33.88	34.19	34.50	34.81	35.12
25	32.48	32.80	33.12	33.44	33.76	34.08	34.40	34.72	35.04	35.37	35.69	36.01	36.34	36.66
26	33.84	34.18	34.51	34.84	35.18	35.51	35.85	36.19	36.52	36.86	37.20	37.54	37.88	38.21
27	35.21	35.56	35.91	36.26	36.61	36.96	37.31	37.66	38.01	38.36	38.72	39.07	39.42	39.78
28	36.59	36.96	37.32	37.68	38.05	38.41	38.78	39.15	39.51	39.88	40.25	40.61	40.98	41.35
29	37.98	38.36	38.74	39.12	39.50	39.88	40.26	40.64	41.02	41.40	41.78	42.17	42.55	42.94
30	39.38	39.77	40.17	40.56	40.95	41.35	41.75	42.14	42.54	42.94	43.33	43.73	44.13	44.53
31	40.79	41.19	41.60	42.01	42.42	42.83	43.24	43.65	44.07	44.48	44.89	45.30	45.72	46.13
32	42.20	42.62	43.05	43.47	43.90	44.32	44.75	45.17	45.60	46.03	46.46	46.89	47.32	47.75
33	43.62	44.06	44.50	44.94	45.38	45.82	46.26	46.70	47.15	47.59	48.04	48.48	48.93	49.37
34	45.05	45.51	45.96	46.42	46.87	47.33	47.79	48.24	48.70	49.16	49.62	50.08	50.55	51.01
35	46.49	46.96	47.43	47.90	48.37	48.85	49.32	49.79	50.27	50.74	51.22	51.70	52.17	52.65
36	47.94	48.42	48.91	49.40	49.88	50.37	50.86	51.35	51.84	52.33	52.83	53.32	53.81	54.31
37	49.39	49.89	50.40	50.90	51.40	51.91	52.41	52.92	53.42	53.93	54.44	54.95	55.46	55.97
38	50.86	51.37	51.89	52.41	52.93	53.45	53.97	54.49	55.02	55.54	56.07	56.59	57.12	57.65
39	52.33	52.86	53.39	53.93	54.46	55.00	55.54	56.08	56.62	57.16	57.70	58.24	58.79	59.33
40	53.81	54.35	54.90	55.46	56.01	56.56	57.12	57.67	58.23	58.79	59.34	59.90	60.47	61.03
41	55.29	55.86	56.42	56.99	57.56	58.13	58.70	59.28	59.85	60.42	61.00	61.57	62.15	62.73
42	56.79	57.37	57.95	58.54	59.12	59.71	60.30	60.89	61.48	62.07	62.66	63.25	63.85	64.44
43	58.29	58.89	59.49	60.09	60.69	61.30	61.90	62.51	63.11	63.72	64.33	64.94	65.56	66.17
44	59.80	60.42	61.03	61.65	62.27	62.89	63.51	64.14	64.76	65.39	66.01	66.64	67.27	67.90
45	61.32	61.95	62.59	63.22	63.86	64.50	65.13	65.77	66.42	67.06	67.70	68.35	69.00	69.64
46	62.84	63.49	64.15	64.80	65.45	66.11	66.76	67.42	68.08	68.74	69.40	70.07	70.73	71.40
47	64.38	65.05	65.71	66.38	67.06	67.73	68.40	69.08	69.75	70.43	71.11	71.79	72.47	73.16
48	65.92	66.60	67.29	67.98	68.67	69.36	70.05	70.74	71.44	72.13	72.83	73.53	74.23	74.93
49	67.47	68.17	68.87	69.58	70.29	70.99	71.70	72.41	73.13	73.84	74.56	75.27	75.99	76.71
50	69.03	69.75	70.47	71.19	71.91	72.64	73.37	74.10	74.83	75.56	76.29	77.02	77.76	78.50
51	70.59	71.33	72.07	72.81	73.55	74.29	75.04	75.78	76.53	77.28	78.03	78.79	79.54	80.30
52	72.16	72.92	73.67	74.43	75.19	75.95	76.72	77.48	78.25	79.02	79.79	80.56	81.33	82.11
53	73.74	74.52	75.29	76.07	76.85	77.62	78.41	79.19	79.97	80.76	81.55	82.34	83.13	83.92
54	75.33	76.12	76.91	77.71	78.50	79.30	80.10	80.90	81.71	82.51	83.32	84.13	84.94	85.75
55	76.92	77.73	78.55	79.36	80.17	80.99	81.81	82.63	83.45	84.27	85.10	85.93	86.75	87.58
56	78.53	79.35	80.18	81.02	81.85	82.68	83.52	84.36	85.20	86.04	86.89	87.73	88.58	89.43
57	80.14	80.98	81.83	82.68	83.53	84.39	85.24	86.10	86.96	87.82	88.68	89.55	90.41	91.28
58	81.75	82.62	83.48	84.35	85.22	86.10	86.97	87.85	88.72	89.60	90.49	91.37	92.26	93.14
59	83.38	84.26	85.15	86.03	86.92	87.81	88.71	89.60	90.50	91.40	92.30	93.20	94.11	95.01
60	85.01	85.91	86.81	87.72	88.63	89.54	90.45	91.37	92.28	93.20	94.12	95.04	95.97	96.89

Reference Tables

Federal Reserve Table for Computing Annual Percentage Rates for Monthly Payment Plans

Number of Payments	31.00%	31.25%	31.50%	31.75%	32.00%	32.25%	32.50%	32.75%	33.00%	33.25%	33.50%	33.75%	34.00%	34.25%
	\multicolumn{14}{c}{Finance Charge per $100 of Amount Financed}
1	2.58	2.60	2.63	2.65	2.67	2.69	2.71	2.73	2.75	2.77	2.79	2.81	2.83	2.85
2	3.89	3.92	3.95	3.99	4.02	4.05	4.08	4.11	4.14	4.18	4.21	4.24	4.27	4.30
3	5.21	5.25	5.30	5.34	5.38	5.42	5.46	5.51	5.55	5.59	5.63	5.68	5.72	5.76
4	6.54	6.59	6.65	6.70	6.75	6.81	6.86	6.91	6.97	7.02	7.08	7.13	7.18	7.24
5	7.88	7.95	8.01	8.08	8.14	8.21	8.27	8.33	8.40	8.46	8.53	8.59	8.66	8.72
6	9.23	9.31	9.39	9.46	9.54	9.61	9.69	9.77	9.84	9.92	9.99	10.07	10.15	10.22
7	10.60	10.68	10.77	10.86	10.95	11.03	11.12	11.21	11.30	11.39	11.47	11.56	11.65	11.74
8	11.97	12.07	12.17	12.27	12.37	12.47	12.57	12.67	12.77	12.87	12.97	13.07	13.17	13.27
9	13.36	13.47	13.58	13.69	13.80	13.91	14.02	14.14	14.25	14.36	14.47	14.58	14.69	14.81
10	14.75	14.87	15.00	15.12	15.24	15.37	15.49	15.62	15.74	15.86	15.99	16.11	16.24	16.36
11	16.16	16.29	16.43	16.56	16.70	16.84	16.97	17.11	17.24	17.38	17.52	17.65	17.79	17.93
12	17.58	17.72	17.87	18.02	18.17	18.32	18.47	18.61	18.76	18.91	19.06	19.21	19.36	19.51
13	19.00	19.16	19.33	19.49	19.65	19.81	19.97	20.13	20.29	20.45	20.62	20.78	20.94	21.10
14	20.44	20.62	20.79	20.96	21.14	21.31	21.49	21.66	21.83	22.01	22.18	22.36	22.53	22.71
15	21.89	22.08	22.27	22.45	22.64	22.83	23.01	23.20	23.39	23.58	23.76	23.95	24.14	24.33
16	23.35	23.55	23.75	23.95	24.15	24.35	24.55	24.75	24.96	25.16	25.36	25.56	25.76	25.96
17	24.83	25.04	25.25	25.47	25.68	25.89	26.11	26.32	26.53	26.75	26.96	27.18	27.39	27.61
18	26.31	26.54	26.76	26.99	27.22	27.44	27.67	27.90	28.13	28.35	28.58	28.81	29.04	29.27
19	27.80	28.04	28.28	28.52	28.76	29.00	29.25	29.49	29.73	29.97	30.21	30.45	30.70	30.94
20	29.31	29.56	29.81	30.07	30.32	30.58	30.83	31.09	31.34	31.60	31.86	32.11	32.37	32.63
21	30.82	31.09	31.36	31.62	31.89	32.16	32.43	32.70	32.97	33.24	33.51	33.78	34.05	34.32
22	32.35	32.63	32.91	33.19	33.48	33.76	34.04	34.33	34.61	34.89	35.18	35.46	35.75	36.04
23	33.88	34.18	34.48	34.77	35.07	35.37	35.66	35.96	36.26	36.56	36.86	37.16	37.46	37.76
24	35.43	35.74	36.05	36.36	36.67	36.99	37.30	37.61	37.92	38.24	38.55	38.87	39.18	39.50
25	36.99	37.31	37.64	37.96	38.29	38.62	38.94	39.27	39.60	39.93	40.26	40.59	40.92	41.25
26	38.55	38.89	39.23	39.58	39.92	40.26	40.60	40.94	41.29	41.63	41.97	42.32	42.66	43.01
27	40.13	40.49	40.84	41.20	41.56	41.91	42.27	42.63	42.99	43.34	43.70	44.06	44.42	44.78
28	41.72	42.09	42.46	42.83	43.20	43.58	43.95	44.32	44.70	45.07	45.45	45.82	46.20	46.57
29	43.32	43.71	44.09	44.48	44.87	45.25	45.64	46.03	46.42	46.81	47.20	47.59	47.98	48.37
30	44.93	45.33	45.73	46.13	46.54	46.94	47.34	47.75	48.15	48.56	48.96	49.37	49.78	50.19
31	46.55	46.97	47.38	47.80	48.22	48.64	49.06	49.48	49.90	50.32	50.74	51.17	51.59	52.01
32	48.18	48.61	49.05	49.48	49.91	50.35	50.78	51.22	51.66	52.09	52.53	52.97	53.41	53.85
33	49.82	50.27	50.72	51.17	51.62	52.07	52.52	52.97	53.43	53.88	54.33	54.79	55.24	55.70
34	51.47	51.94	52.40	52.87	53.33	53.80	54.27	54.74	55.21	55.68	56.15	56.62	57.09	57.56
35	53.13	53.61	54.09	54.58	55.06	55.54	56.03	56.51	57.00	57.48	57.97	58.46	58.95	59.44
36	54.80	55.30	55.80	56.30	56.80	57.30	57.80	58.30	58.80	59.30	59.81	60.31	60.82	61.33
37	56.49	57.00	57.51	58.03	58.54	59.06	59.58	60.10	60.62	61.14	61.66	62.18	62.70	63.22
38	58.18	58.71	59.24	59.77	60.30	60.84	61.37	61.90	62.44	62.98	63.52	64.06	64.59	65.14
39	59.88	60.42	60.97	61.52	62.07	62.62	63.17	63.72	64.28	64.83	65.39	65.94	66.50	67.06
40	61.59	62.15	62.72	63.28	63.85	64.42	64.99	65.56	66.13	66.70	67.27	67.84	68.42	68.99
41	63.31	63.89	64.47	65.06	65.64	66.22	66.81	67.40	67.99	68.57	69.16	69.76	70.35	70.94
42	65.04	65.64	66.24	66.84	67.44	68.04	68.65	69.25	69.86	70.46	71.07	71.68	72.29	72.90
43	66.78	67.40	68.01	68.63	69.25	69.87	70.49	71.11	71.74	72.36	72.99	73.61	74.24	74.87
44	68.53	69.17	69.80	70.43	71.07	71.71	72.35	72.99	73.63	74.27	74.91	75.56	76.20	76.85
45	70.29	70.94	71.60	72.25	72.90	73.56	74.21	74.87	75.53	76.19	76.85	77.52	78.18	78.84
46	72.06	72.73	73.40	74.07	74.74	75.42	76.09	76.77	77.44	78.12	78.80	79.48	80.17	80.85
47	73.84	74.53	75.22	75.91	76.60	77.29	77.98	78.67	79.37	80.07	80.76	81.46	82.16	82.87
48	75.63	76.34	77.04	77.75	78.46	79.17	79.88	80.59	81.30	82.02	82.74	83.45	84.17	84.89
49	77.43	78.15	78.88	79.60	80.33	81.06	81.79	82.52	83.25	83.98	84.72	85.45	86.19	86.93
50	79.24	79.98	80.72	81.46	82.21	82.96	83.70	84.45	85.20	85.96	86.71	87.47	88.22	88.98
51	81.06	81.81	82.58	83.34	84.10	84.87	85.63	86.40	87.17	87.94	88.71	89.49	90.26	91.04
52	82.88	83.66	84.44	85.22	86.00	86.79	87.57	88.36	89.15	89.94	90.73	91.52	92.32	93.11
53	84.72	85.51	86.31	87.11	87.91	88.72	89.52	90.33	91.13	91.94	92.75	93.57	94.38	95.20
54	86.56	87.38	88.19	89.01	89.83	90.66	91.48	92.30	93.13	93.96	94.79	95.62	96.45	97.29
55	88.42	89.25	90.09	90.92	91.76	92.60	93.45	94.29	95.14	95.99	96.83	97.69	98.54	99.39
56	90.28	91.13	91.99	92.84	93.70	94.56	95.43	96.29	97.15	98.02	98.89	99.76	100.63	101.51
57	92.15	93.02	93.90	94.77	95.65	96.53	97.41	98.30	99.18	100.07	100.96	101.85	102.74	103.63
58	94.03	94.92	95.82	96.71	97.61	98.51	99.41	100.31	101.22	102.12	103.03	103.94	104.85	105.77
59	95.92	96.83	97.75	98.66	99.58	100.50	101.42	102.34	103.26	104.19	105.12	106.05	106.98	107.91
60	97.82	98.75	99.68	100.62	101.56	102.49	103.43	104.38	105.32	106.27	107.21	108.16	109.12	110.07

A–46   Appendix D   Reference Tables

Federal Reserve Table for Computing Annual Percentage Rates for Monthly Payment Plans

Annual Percentage Rate

Number of Payments	34.50%	34.75%	35.00%	35.25%	35.50%	35.75%	36.00%	36.25%	36.50%	36.75%	37.00%	37.25%	37.50%	37.75%
	\multicolumn{14}{c}{Finance Charge per $100 of Amount Financed}
1	2.87	2.90	2.92	2.94	2.96	2.98	3.00	3.02	3.04	3.06	3.08	3.10	3.12	3.15
2	4.33	4.36	4.40	4.43	4.46	4.49	4.52	4.55	4.59	4.62	4.65	4.68	4.71	4.74
3	5.80	5.85	5.89	5.93	5.97	6.02	6.06	6.10	6.14	6.19	6.23	6.27	6.31	6.36
4	7.29	7.34	7.40	7.45	7.50	7.56	7.61	7.66	7.72	7.77	7.83	7.88	7.93	7.99
5	8.79	8.85	8.92	8.98	9.05	9.11	9.18	9.24	9.31	9.37	9.44	9.50	9.57	9.63
6	10.30	10.38	10.45	10.53	10.61	10.68	10.76	10.83	10.91	10.99	11.06	11.14	11.22	11.29
7	11.83	11.91	12.00	12.09	12.18	12.27	12.35	12.44	12.53	12.62	12.71	12.80	12.88	12.97
8	13.36	13.46	13.56	13.66	13.76	13.86	13.97	14.07	14.17	14.27	14.37	14.47	14.57	14.67
9	14.92	15.03	15.14	15.25	15.37	15.48	15.59	15.70	15.82	15.93	16.04	16.15	16.27	16.38
10	16.48	16.61	16.73	16.86	16.98	17.11	17.23	17.36	17.48	17.60	17.73	17.85	17.98	18.10
11	18.06	18.20	18.34	18.47	18.61	18.75	18.89	19.02	19.16	19.30	19.43	19.57	19.71	19.85
12	19.66	19.81	19.96	20.11	20.25	20.40	20.55	20.70	20.85	21.00	21.15	21.31	21.46	21.61
13	21.26	21.43	21.59	21.75	21.91	22.08	22.24	22.40	22.56	22.73	22.89	23.05	23.22	23.38
14	22.88	23.06	23.23	23.41	23.59	23.76	23.94	24.11	24.29	24.47	24.64	24.82	25.00	25.17
15	24.52	24.71	24.89	25.08	25.27	25.46	25.65	25.84	26.03	26.22	26.41	26.60	26.79	26.98
16	26.16	26.37	26.57	26.77	26.97	27.17	27.38	27.58	27.78	27.99	28.19	28.39	28.60	28.80
17	27.82	28.04	28.25	28.47	28.69	28.90	29.12	29.34	29.55	29.77	29.99	30.20	30.42	30.64
18	29.50	29.73	29.96	30.19	30.42	30.65	30.88	31.11	31.34	31.57	31.80	32.03	32.26	32.49
19	31.18	31.43	31.67	31.91	32.16	32.40	32.65	32.89	33.14	33.38	33.63	33.87	34.12	34.36
20	32.88	33.14	33.40	33.66	33.91	34.17	34.43	34.69	34.95	35.21	35.47	35.73	35.99	36.25
21	34.60	34.87	35.14	35.41	35.68	35.96	36.23	36.50	36.78	37.05	37.33	37.60	37.88	38.15
22	36.32	36.61	36.89	37.18	37.47	37.76	38.04	38.33	38.62	38.91	39.20	39.49	39.78	40.07
23	38.06	38.36	38.66	38.96	39.27	39.57	39.87	40.18	40.48	40.78	41.09	41.39	41.70	42.00
24	39.81	40.13	40.44	40.76	41.08	41.40	41.71	42.03	42.35	42.67	42.99	43.31	43.63	43.95
25	41.58	41.91	42.24	42.57	42.90	43.24	43.57	43.90	44.24	44.57	44.91	45.24	45.58	45.91
26	43.36	43.70	44.05	44.40	44.74	45.09	45.44	45.79	46.14	46.49	46.84	47.19	47.54	47.89
27	45.15	45.51	45.87	46.23	46.60	46.96	47.32	47.69	48.05	48.42	48.78	49.15	49.52	49.89
28	46.95	47.33	47.70	48.08	48.46	48.84	49.22	49.60	49.98	50.36	50.75	51.13	51.51	51.89
29	48.77	49.16	49.55	49.95	50.34	50.74	51.13	51.53	51.93	52.32	52.72	53.12	53.52	53.92
30	50.60	51.00	51.41	51.82	52.23	52.65	53.06	53.47	53.88	54.30	54.71	55.12	55.54	55.96
31	52.44	52.86	53.29	53.71	54.14	54.57	55.00	55.43	55.85	56.28	56.72	57.15	57.58	58.01
32	54.29	54.73	55.17	55.62	56.06	56.50	56.95	57.39	57.84	58.29	58.73	59.18	59.63	60.08
33	56.16	56.62	57.07	57.53	57.99	58.45	58.92	59.38	59.84	60.30	60.77	61.23	61.70	62.16
34	58.04	58.51	58.99	59.46	59.94	60.42	60.89	61.37	61.85	62.33	62.81	63.30	63.78	64.26
35	59.93	60.42	60.91	61.40	61.90	62.39	62.89	63.38	63.88	64.38	64.88	65.37	65.87	66.37
36	61.83	62.34	62.85	63.36	63.87	64.38	64.89	65.41	65.92	66.44	66.95	67.47	67.98	68.50
37	63.75	64.27	64.80	65.33	65.85	66.38	66.91	67.44	67.97	68.51	69.04	69.57	70.11	70.64
38	65.68	66.22	66.76	67.31	67.85	68.40	68.95	69.49	70.04	70.59	71.14	71.69	72.25	72.80
39	67.62	68.18	68.74	69.30	69.86	70.43	70.99	71.56	72.12	72.69	73.26	73.83	74.40	74.97
40	69.57	70.15	70.73	71.31	71.89	72.47	73.05	73.63	74.22	74.80	75.39	75.98	76.56	77.15
41	71.53	72.13	72.73	73.32	73.92	74.52	75.12	75.72	76.32	76.93	77.53	78.14	78.74	79.35
42	73.51	74.12	74.74	75.35	75.97	76.59	77.21	77.82	78.44	79.07	79.69	80.31	80.94	81.56
43	75.50	76.13	76.76	77.40	78.03	78.67	79.30	79.94	80.58	81.22	81.86	82.50	83.14	83.79
44	77.50	78.15	78.80	79.45	80.10	80.76	81.41	82.07	82.72	83.38	84.04	84.70	85.36	86.03
45	79.51	80.18	80.85	81.52	82.19	82.86	83.53	84.21	84.88	85.56	86.24	86.92	87.60	88.28
46	81.53	82.22	82.91	83.60	84.28	84.98	85.67	86.36	87.06	87.75	88.45	89.15	89.85	90.55
47	83.57	84.27	84.98	85.69	86.39	87.10	87.81	88.53	89.24	89.95	90.67	91.39	92.11	92.83
48	85.61	86.34	87.06	87.79	88.52	89.24	89.97	90.70	91.44	92.17	92.91	93.64	94.38	95.12
49	87.67	88.41	89.16	89.90	90.65	91.40	92.14	92.89	93.65	94.40	95.15	95.91	96.67	97.42
50	89.74	90.50	91.26	92.03	92.79	93.56	94.33	95.10	95.87	96.64	97.41	98.19	98.96	99.74
51	91.82	92.60	93.38	94.16	94.95	95.74	96.52	97.31	98.10	98.89	99.69	100.48	101.28	102.07
52	93.91	94.71	95.51	96.31	97.12	97.92	98.73	99.54	100.35	101.16	101.97	102.79	103.60	104.42
53	96.01	96.83	97.65	98.47	99.30	100.12	100.95	101.78	102.61	103.44	104.27	105.10	105.94	106.78
54	98.13	98.96	99.80	100.64	101.49	102.33	103.18	104.03	104.88	105.73	106.58	107.43	108.29	109.14
55	100.25	101.11	101.97	102.83	103.69	104.55	105.42	106.29	107.16	108.03	108.90	109.77	110.65	111.53
56	102.38	103.26	104.14	105.02	105.90	106.79	107.67	108.56	109.45	110.34	111.23	112.13	113.02	113.92
57	104.53	105.43	106.32	107.22	108.13	109.03	109.94	110.85	111.75	112.67	113.58	114.49	115.41	116.33
58	106.68	107.60	108.52	109.44	110.36	111.29	112.21	113.14	114.07	115.00	115.93	116.87	117.81	118.74
59	108.85	109.79	110.73	111.67	112.61	113.55	114.50	115.45	116.40	117.35	118.30	119.26	120.22	121.17
60	111.03	111.98	112.94	113.90	114.87	115.83	116.80	117.77	118.74	119.71	120.68	121.66	122.64	123.62

Compound Interest, Present Value, and Annuity Table

RATE 0.5%

PERIODS	COMPOUND INTEREST	PRESENT VALUE	AMOUNT OF ORDINARY ANNUITY	PRESENT VALUE OF ANNUITY
1	1.00500000	0.99502488	1.00000000	0.99502488
2	1.01002500	0.99007450	2.00500000	1.98509938
3	1.01507513	0.98514876	3.01502500	2.97024814
4	1.02015050	0.98024752	4.03010013	3.95049566
5	1.02525125	0.97537067	5.05025063	4.92586633
6	1.03037751	0.97051808	6.07550188	5.89638441
7	1.03552940	0.96568963	7.10587939	6.86207404
8	1.04070704	0.96088520	8.14140879	7.82295924
9	1.04591058	0.95610468	9.18211583	8.77906392
10	1.05114013	0.95134794	10.22802641	9.73041186
11	1.05639583	0.94661487	11.27916654	10.67702673
12	1.06167781	0.94190534	12.33556237	11.61893207
13	1.06698620	0.93721924	13.39724018	12.55615131
14	1.07232113	0.93255646	14.46422639	13.48870777
15	1.07768274	0.92791688	15.53654752	14.41662465
16	1.08307115	0.92330037	16.61423026	15.33992502
17	1.08848651	0.91870684	17.69730141	16.25863186
18	1.09392894	0.91413616	18.78578791	17.17276802
19	1.09939858	0.90958822	19.87971685	18.08235624
20	1.10489558	0.90506290	20.97911544	18.98741915
21	1.11042006	0.90056010	22.08401101	19.88797925
22	1.11597216	0.89607971	23.19443107	20.78405896
23	1.12155202	0.89162160	24.31040322	21.67568055
24	1.12715978	0.88718567	25.43195524	22.56286622
25	1.13279558	0.88277181	26.55911501	23.44563803
26	1.13845955	0.87837991	27.69191059	24.32401794
27	1.14415185	0.87400986	28.83037015	25.19802780
28	1.14987261	0.86966155	29.97452020	26.06768936
29	1.15562197	0.86533488	31.12439461	26.93302423
30	1.16140008	0.86102973	32.28001658	27.79405397
31	1.16720708	0.85674600	33.44141666	28.65079997
32	1.17304312	0.85248358	34.60862375	29.50328355
33	1.17890833	0.84824237	35.78166686	30.35152592
34	1.18480288	0.84402226	36.96057520	31.19554818
35	1.19072689	0.83982314	38.14537807	32.03537132
36	1.19668052	0.83564492	39.33610496	32.87101624
37	1.20266393	0.83148748	40.53278549	33.70250372
38	1.20867725	0.82735073	41.73544942	34.52985445
39	1.21472063	0.82323455	42.94412666	35.35308900
40	1.22079424	0.81913886	44.15884730	36.17222786
41	1.22689821	0.81506354	45.37964153	36.98729141
42	1.23303270	0.81100850	46.60653977	37.79829991
43	1.23919786	0.80697363	47.83957244	38.60527354
44	1.24539385	0.80295884	49.07877030	39.40823238
45	1.25162082	0.79896402	50.32416415	40.20719640
46	1.25787892	0.79498907	51.57578497	41.00218547
47	1.26416832	0.79103390	52.83366390	41.79321937
48	1.27048916	0.78709841	54.09783222	42.58031778
49	1.27684161	0.78318250	55.36832138	43.36350028
50	1.28322581	0.77928607	56.64516299	44.14277635
60	1.34885015	0.74137220	69.77003051	51.72556075
80	1.49033857	0.67098847	98.06771357	65.80230538
100	1.64666849	0.60728678	129.33359842	78.54264477
120	1.81939673	0.54963273	163.87934681	90.07345333
240	3.31020048	0.30209614	462.04089516	139.58077168
360	6.02257521	0.16604193	1004.51504245	166.79161439

RATE 1.0%

PERIODS	COMPOUND INTEREST	PRESENT VALUE	AMOUNT OF ORDINARY ANNUITY	PRESENT VALUE OF ANNUITY
1	1.01000000	0.99009901	1.00000000	0.99009901
2	1.02010000	0.98029605	2.01000000	1.97039506
3	1.03030100	0.97059110	3.03010000	2.94098521
4	1.04060401	0.96098034	4.06040100	3.90196555
5	1.05101005	0.95146569	5.10100501	4.85343124
6	1.06152015	0.94204524	6.15201506	5.79547647
7	1.07213535	0.93271805	7.21353521	6.72819453
8	1.08285671	0.92348322	8.28567056	7.65167775
9	1.09368527	0.91433982	9.36852727	8.56601758
10	1.10462213	0.90528695	10.46221254	9.47130453
11	1.11566835	0.89632372	11.56683467	10.36762825
12	1.12682503	0.88744923	12.68250301	11.25507747
13	1.13809328	0.87866260	13.80932804	12.13374007
14	1.14947421	0.86996297	14.94742132	13.00370304
15	1.16096896	0.86134947	16.09689554	13.86505252
16	1.17257864	0.85282126	17.25786449	14.71787378
17	1.18430443	0.84437749	18.43044314	15.56225127
18	1.19614748	0.83601131	19.61474757	16.39826858
19	1.20810895	0.82773992	20.81089504	17.22600850
20	1.22019004	0.81954447	22.01900399	18.04555297
21	1.23239194	0.81143017	23.23919403	18.85698313
22	1.24471586	0.80339621	24.47158598	19.66037934
23	1.25716302	0.79544179	25.71630183	20.45582113
24	1.26973465	0.78756613	26.97346485	21.24338726
25	1.28243200	0.77976844	28.24319950	22.02315570
26	1.29525631	0.77204796	29.52563150	22.79520366
27	1.30820888	0.76440392	30.82088781	23.55960759
28	1.32129097	0.75683557	32.12909669	24.31644316
29	1.33450388	0.74934215	33.45038766	25.06578530
30	1.34784892	0.74192292	34.78489153	25.80770822
31	1.36132740	0.73457715	36.13274045	26.54228537
32	1.37494068	0.72730411	37.49406785	27.26958947
33	1.38869009	0.72010307	38.86900853	27.98969255
34	1.40257699	0.71297334	40.25769862	28.70266589
35	1.41660276	0.70591420	41.66027560	29.40858009
36	1.43076878	0.69892495	43.07687836	30.10750504
37	1.44507647	0.69200490	44.50764714	30.79950994
38	1.45952724	0.68515337	45.95272361	31.48466330
39	1.47412251	0.67836967	47.41225085	32.16303298
40	1.48886373	0.67165314	48.88637336	32.83468611
41	1.50375237	0.66500311	50.37523709	33.49968922
42	1.51878989	0.65841892	51.87898946	34.15810814
43	1.53397779	0.65189992	53.39777936	34.81000806
44	1.54931757	0.64544546	54.93175715	35.45545352
45	1.56481075	0.63905492	56.48107472	36.09450844
46	1.58045885	0.63272764	58.04588547	36.72723608
47	1.59626344	0.62646301	59.62634432	37.35369909
48	1.61222608	0.62026041	61.22260777	37.97395949
49	1.62834834	0.61411921	62.83483385	38.58807871
50	1.64463182	0.60803882	64.46318218	39.19611753
60	1.81669670	0.55044962	81.66966986	44.95503841
80	2.21871522	0.45111794	121.67152172	54.88820611
100	2.70481383	0.36971121	170.48138294	63.02887877
120	3.30038689	0.30299478	230.03868946	69.70052203
240	10.89255365	0.09180584	989.25536539	90.81941635
360	35.94964133	0.02781669	3494.96413277	97.21833108

Appendix D Reference Tables

Compound Interest, Present Value, and Annuity Table

RATE 1.5%	COMPOUND INTEREST	PRESENT VALUE	AMOUNT OF ORDINARY ANNUITY	PRESENT VALUE OF ANNUITY
1	1.01500000	0.98522167	1.00000000	0.98522167
2	1.03022500	0.97066175	2.01500000	1.95588342
3	1.04567837	0.95631699	3.04522500	2.91220042
4	1.06136355	0.94218423	4.09090338	3.85438485
5	1.07728400	0.92826033	5.15226693	4.78264497
6	1.09344326	0.91454219	6.22955093	5.69718717
7	1.10984491	0.90102679	7.32299419	6.59821396
8	1.12649259	0.88771112	8.43283911	7.48592508
9	1.14338998	0.87459224	9.55933169	8.36051732
10	1.16054083	0.86166723	10.70272167	9.22218455
11	1.17794894	0.84893323	11.86326249	10.07111779
12	1.19561817	0.83638742	13.04121143	10.90750521
13	1.21355244	0.82402702	14.23682960	11.73153222
14	1.23175573	0.81184928	15.45038205	12.54338150
15	1.25023207	0.79985150	16.68213778	13.34323301
16	1.26898555	0.78803104	17.93236984	14.13126405
17	1.28802033	0.77638526	19.20135539	14.90764931
18	1.30734064	0.76491159	20.48937572	15.67256089
19	1.32695075	0.75360747	21.79671636	16.42616837
20	1.34685501	0.74247042	23.12366710	17.16863879
21	1.36705783	0.73149795	24.47052211	17.90013673
22	1.38756370	0.72068763	25.83757994	18.62082437
23	1.40837715	0.71003708	27.22514364	19.33086145
24	1.42950281	0.69954392	28.63352080	20.03040537
25	1.45094535	0.68920583	30.06302361	20.71961120
26	1.47270953	0.67902052	31.51396896	21.39863172
27	1.49480018	0.66898574	32.98667850	22.06761746
28	1.51722218	0.65909925	34.48147867	22.72671671
29	1.53998051	0.64935887	35.99870085	23.37607558
30	1.56308022	0.63976243	37.53868137	24.01583801
31	1.58652642	0.63030781	39.10176159	24.64614582
32	1.61032432	0.62099292	40.68828801	25.26713874
33	1.63447918	0.61181568	42.29861233	25.87895442
34	1.65899637	0.60277407	43.93309152	26.48172849
35	1.68388132	0.59386608	45.59208789	27.07559458
36	1.70913954	0.58508974	47.27596921	27.66068431
37	1.73477663	0.57644309	48.98510874	28.23712740
38	1.76079828	0.56792423	50.71988538	28.80505163
39	1.78721025	0.55953126	52.48068366	29.36458288
40	1.81401841	0.55126232	54.26789391	29.91584520
41	1.84122888	0.54311559	56.08191232	30.45896079
42	1.86884712	0.53508925	57.92314100	30.99405004
43	1.89687982	0.52718153	59.79198812	31.52123157
44	1.92533302	0.51939067	61.68886794	32.04062223
45	1.95421301	0.51171494	63.61420096	32.55233718
46	1.98352621	0.50415265	65.56841398	33.05648983
47	2.01327910	0.49670212	67.55194018	33.55319195
48	2.04347829	0.48936170	69.56521929	34.04255365
49	2.07413046	0.48212975	71.60869758	34.52468339
50	2.10524242	0.47500468	73.68282804	34.99968807
60	2.44321978	0.40929597	96.21465171	39.38026888
80	3.29066279	0.30389015	152.71085247	46.40732349
100	4.43204565	0.22562944	228.80304330	51.62470367
120	5.96932287	0.16752319	331.28819149	55.49845411
240	35.63281555	0.02806402	2308.85437027	64.79573209
360	212.70378089	0.00470137	14113.58539279	66.35324174

RATE 2.0%	COMPOUND INTEREST	PRESENT VALUE	AMOUNT OF ORDINARY ANNUITY	PRESENT VALUE OF ANNUITY
1	1.02000000	0.98039216	1.00000000	0.98039216
2	1.04040000	0.96116878	2.02000000	1.94156094
3	1.06120800	0.94232233	3.06040000	2.88388327
4	1.08243216	0.92384543	4.12160800	3.80772870
5	1.10408080	0.90573081	5.20404016	4.71345951
6	1.12616242	0.88797138	6.30812096	5.60143089
7	1.14868567	0.87056018	7.43428338	6.47199107
8	1.17165938	0.85349037	8.58296905	7.32548144
9	1.19509257	0.83675527	9.75462843	8.16223671
10	1.21899442	0.82034830	10.94972100	8.98258501
11	1.24337431	0.80426304	12.16871542	9.78684805
12	1.26824179	0.78849318	13.41208973	10.57534122
13	1.29360663	0.77303253	14.68033152	11.34837375
14	1.31947876	0.75787502	15.97393815	12.10624877
15	1.34586834	0.74301473	17.29341692	12.84926350
16	1.37278571	0.72844581	18.63928525	13.57770931
17	1.40024142	0.71416256	20.01207096	14.29187188
18	1.42824625	0.70015937	21.41231238	14.99203125
19	1.45681117	0.68643076	22.84055863	15.67846201
20	1.48594740	0.67297133	24.29736980	16.35143334
21	1.51566634	0.65977582	25.78331719	17.01120916
22	1.54597967	0.64683904	27.29898354	17.65804820
23	1.57689926	0.63415592	28.84496321	18.29220412
24	1.60843725	0.62172149	30.42186247	18.91392560
25	1.64060599	0.60953087	32.03029972	19.52345647
26	1.67341811	0.59757928	33.67090572	20.12103576
27	1.70688648	0.58586204	35.34432383	20.70689780
28	1.74102421	0.57437455	37.05121031	21.28127236
29	1.77584469	0.56311231	38.79223451	21.84438466
30	1.81136158	0.55207089	40.56807921	22.39645555
31	1.84758882	0.54124597	42.37944079	22.93770152
32	1.88454059	0.53063330	44.22702961	23.46833482
33	1.92223140	0.52022873	46.11157020	23.98856355
34	1.96067603	0.51002817	48.03380160	24.49859172
35	1.99988955	0.50002761	49.99447763	24.99861933
36	2.03988734	0.49022315	51.99436719	25.48884248
37	2.08068509	0.48061093	54.03425453	25.96945341
38	2.12229879	0.47118719	56.11493962	26.44064060
39	2.16474477	0.46194822	58.23723841	26.90258883
40	2.20803966	0.45289042	60.40198318	27.35547924
41	2.25220046	0.44401021	62.61002284	27.79948945
42	2.29724447	0.43530413	64.86222330	28.23479358
43	2.34318936	0.42676875	67.15946777	28.66156233
44	2.39005314	0.41840074	69.50265712	29.07996307
45	2.43785421	0.41019680	71.89271027	29.49015987
46	2.48661129	0.40215373	74.33056447	29.89231360
47	2.53634352	0.39426836	76.81717576	30.28658196
48	2.58707039	0.38653761	79.35351927	30.67311957
49	2.63881179	0.37895844	81.94058966	31.05207801
50	2.69158803	0.37152788	84.57940145	31.42360589
60	3.28103079	0.30478227	114.05153942	34.76088668
80	4.87543916	0.20510973	193.77195780	39.74451939
100	7.24464612	0.13803297	312.23230591	43.09835164
120	10.76516303	0.09289223	488.25815171	45.35538850
240	115.88873515	0.00862897	5744.43675765	49.56855168
360	1247.56112775	0.00080156	62328.05638744	49.95992180

PERIODS

Reference Tables   A-49

Compound Interest, Present Value, and Annuity Table

RATE 2.5%

PERIODS	COMPOUND INTEREST	PRESENT VALUE	AMOUNT OF ORDINARY ANNUITY	PRESENT VALUE OF ANNUITY
1	1.02500000	0.97560976	1.00000000	0.97560976
2	1.05062500	0.95181440	2.02500000	1.92742415
3	1.07689062	0.92859941	3.07562500	2.85602356
4	1.10381289	0.90595064	4.15251563	3.76197421
5	1.13140821	0.88385429	5.25632852	4.64582850
6	1.15969342	0.86229687	6.38773673	5.50812536
7	1.18868575	0.84126524	7.54743015	6.34939060
8	1.21840290	0.82074657	8.73611590	7.17013717
9	1.24886297	0.80072836	9.95451880	7.97086553
10	1.28008454	0.78119840	11.20338177	8.75206393
11	1.31208666	0.76214478	12.48346631	9.51420871
12	1.34488882	0.74355589	13.79555297	10.25776460
13	1.37851104	0.72542038	15.14044179	10.98318497
14	1.41297382	0.70772720	16.51895284	11.69091217
15	1.44829817	0.69046556	17.93192666	12.38137773
16	1.48450562	0.67362493	19.38022483	13.05500266
17	1.52161826	0.65719506	20.86473045	13.71219772
18	1.55965872	0.64116591	22.38634871	14.35336363
19	1.59865019	0.62552772	23.94600743	14.97889134
20	1.63861644	0.61027094	25.54465761	15.58916229
21	1.67958185	0.59536629	27.18327405	16.18454857
22	1.72157140	0.58086467	28.86285590	16.76541324
23	1.76461068	0.56669724	30.58442730	17.33211048
24	1.80872595	0.55287535	32.34903798	17.88498583
25	1.85394410	0.53939059	34.15776393	18.42437642
26	1.90029270	0.52623472	36.01170803	18.95061114
27	1.94780002	0.51339973	37.91200073	19.46401087
28	1.99649502	0.50087778	39.85980075	19.96488866
29	2.04640739	0.48866125	41.85629577	20.45354991
30	2.09756758	0.47674269	43.90270316	20.93029259
31	2.15000677	0.46511481	46.00027074	21.39540741
32	2.20375694	0.45377055	48.15027751	21.84917796
33	2.25885086	0.44270298	50.35404445	22.29188094
34	2.31532213	0.43190534	52.61288531	22.72378628
35	2.37320519	0.42137107	54.92820744	23.14515734
36	2.43253532	0.41109372	57.30141263	23.55625107
37	2.49334870	0.40106705	59.73394794	23.95731812
38	2.55568242	0.39128492	62.22729664	24.34860304
39	2.61957448	0.38174139	64.78297906	24.73034443
40	2.68506384	0.37243062	67.40255354	25.10277505
41	2.75219043	0.36334695	70.08761737	25.46612200
42	2.82099520	0.35448483	72.83980781	25.82060683
43	2.89152008	0.34583886	75.66080300	26.16644569
44	2.96380808	0.33740376	78.55232308	26.50384945
45	3.03790328	0.32917440	81.51613116	26.83302386
46	3.11385086	0.32114576	84.55403443	27.15416962
47	3.19169713	0.31331294	87.66788530	27.46748255
48	3.27148956	0.30567116	90.85958242	27.77315371
49	3.35327680	0.29821576	94.13107199	28.07136947
50	3.43710872	0.29094221	97.48434879	28.36231168
60	4.39978975	0.22728359	135.99158995	30.90865649
80	7.20956782	0.13870457	248.38271265	34.45181722
100	11.81371635	0.08464737	432.54865404	36.61410526
120	19.35814983	0.05165783	734.32599335	37.93368683
240	374.73796499	0.00266853	14949.51859948	39.89325875

RATE 3.0%

PERIODS	COMPOUND INTEREST	PRESENT VALUE	AMOUNT OF ORDINARY ANNUITY	PRESENT VALUE OF ANNUITY
1	1.03000000	0.97087379	1.00000000	0.97087379
2	1.06090000	0.94259591	2.03000000	1.91346970
3	1.09272700	0.91514166	3.09090000	2.82861135
4	1.12550881	0.88848705	4.18362700	3.71709840
5	1.15927407	0.86260878	5.30913581	4.57970719
6	1.19405230	0.83748426	6.46840988	5.41719144
7	1.22987387	0.81309151	7.66246218	6.23028296
8	1.26677008	0.78940923	8.89233605	7.01969219
9	1.30477318	0.76641673	10.15910613	7.78610892
10	1.34391638	0.74409391	11.46387931	8.53020284
11	1.38423387	0.72242128	12.80779569	9.25262411
12	1.42576089	0.70137988	14.19202956	9.95400399
13	1.46853371	0.68095134	15.61779045	10.63495533
14	1.51258972	0.66111781	17.08632416	11.29607314
15	1.55796742	0.64186195	18.59891389	11.93793509
16	1.60470644	0.62316694	20.15688130	12.56110203
17	1.65284763	0.60501645	21.76158774	13.16611847
18	1.70243306	0.58739461	23.41443537	13.75351308
19	1.75350605	0.57028603	25.11686844	14.32379911
20	1.80611123	0.55367575	26.87037449	14.87747486
21	1.86029457	0.53754928	28.67648572	15.41502414
22	1.91610341	0.52189250	30.53678030	15.93691664
23	1.97358651	0.50669175	32.45288370	16.44360839
24	2.03279411	0.49193374	34.42647022	16.93554212
25	2.09377793	0.47760557	36.45926432	17.41314769
26	2.15659127	0.46369473	38.55304225	17.87684242
27	2.22128901	0.45018906	40.70963352	18.32703147
28	2.28792768	0.43707675	42.93092252	18.76410823
29	2.35656551	0.42434636	45.21885020	19.18845459
30	2.42726247	0.41198676	47.57541571	19.60044135
31	2.50008035	0.39998715	50.00267818	20.00042849
32	2.57508276	0.38833703	52.50275852	20.38876553
33	2.65233524	0.37702625	55.07784128	20.76579178
34	2.73190530	0.36604490	57.73017652	21.13183668
35	2.81386245	0.35538340	60.46208181	21.48722007
36	2.89827833	0.34503243	63.27594427	21.83225250
37	2.98522668	0.33498294	66.17422259	22.16723544
38	3.07478348	0.32522615	69.15944927	22.49246159
39	3.16702698	0.31575355	72.23423275	22.80821513
40	3.26203779	0.30655684	75.40125973	23.11477197
41	3.35989893	0.29762800	78.66329753	23.41239997
42	3.46069589	0.28895922	82.02319645	23.70135920
43	3.56451677	0.28054294	85.48389234	23.98190213
44	3.67145227	0.27237178	89.04840911	24.25427392
45	3.78159584	0.26443862	92.71986139	24.51871254
46	3.89504372	0.25673653	96.50145723	24.77544907
47	4.01189503	0.24925876	100.39650095	25.02470783
48	4.13225188	0.24199880	104.40839598	25.26670664
49	4.25621944	0.23495029	108.54064785	25.50165693
50	4.38390602	0.22810708	112.79686729	25.72976401
60	5.89166310	0.16973309	163.05343680	27.67556367
80	10.64089056	0.09397710	321.36301855	30.20076345
100	19.21863198	0.05203284	607.28773270	31.59890534
120	34.71098714	0.02880932	1123.69957119	32.37302261
240	1204.85262793	0.00082998	40128.42093093	33.30566743

A–50   Appendix D   Reference Tables

Compound Interest, Present Value, and Annuity Table

RATE 3.5%	COMPOUND INTEREST	PRESENT VALUE	AMOUNT OF ORDINARY ANNUITY	PRESENT VALUE OF ANNUITY
1	1.03500000	0.96618357	1.00000000	0.96618357
2	1.07122500	0.93351070	2.03500000	1.89969428
3	1.10871788	0.90194271	3.10622500	2.80163698
4	1.14752300	0.87144223	4.21494287	3.67307921
5	1.18768631	0.84197317	5.36246588	4.51505238
6	1.22925533	0.81350064	6.55015218	5.32855302
7	1.27227926	0.78599096	7.77940751	6.11454398
8	1.31680904	0.75941156	9.05168677	6.87395554
9	1.36289735	0.73373097	10.36849581	7.60768651
10	1.41059876	0.70891881	11.73139316	8.31660532
11	1.45996972	0.68494571	13.14199192	9.00155104
12	1.51106866	0.66178330	14.60196164	9.66333433
13	1.56395606	0.63940415	16.11303030	10.30273849
14	1.61869452	0.61778179	17.67698636	10.92052028
15	1.67534883	0.59689062	19.29568088	11.51741090
16	1.73398604	0.57670591	20.97102971	12.09411681
17	1.79487555	0.55720378	22.70501575	12.65132059
18	1.85748920	0.53836114	24.49969130	13.18968173
19	1.92250132	0.52015569	26.35718050	13.70983742
20	1.98978886	0.50256588	28.27968181	14.21240330
21	2.05943147	0.48557090	30.26947068	14.69797420
22	2.13151158	0.46915063	32.32890215	15.16712484
23	2.20611448	0.45328563	34.46041373	15.62041047
24	2.28332498	0.43795713	36.66652821	16.05836760
25	2.36324498	0.42314699	38.94985669	16.48151459
26	2.44595856	0.40883767	41.31310168	16.89035226
27	2.53156711	0.39501224	43.75906024	17.28536451
28	2.62017196	0.38165434	46.29062734	17.66701885
29	2.71187798	0.36874815	48.91079930	18.03576700
30	2.80679370	0.35627841	51.62267728	18.39204541
31	2.90503148	0.34423035	54.42947098	18.73627576
32	3.00670759	0.33258971	57.33450247	19.06886547
33	3.11194235	0.32134271	60.34121005	19.39020818
34	3.22086033	0.31047605	63.45315240	19.70068423
35	3.33359045	0.29997686	66.67401274	20.00066110
36	3.45026611	0.28983272	70.00760318	20.29049381
37	3.57102543	0.28003161	73.45786930	20.57052542
38	3.69601132	0.27056194	77.02889472	20.84108736
39	3.82537171	0.26141250	80.72490604	21.10249987
40	3.95925972	0.25257247	84.55027775	21.35507234
41	4.09783381	0.24403137	88.50953747	21.59910371
42	4.24125799	0.23577910	92.60737128	21.83488281
43	4.38970202	0.22780590	96.84862928	22.06268870
44	4.54334160	0.22010231	101.23833130	22.28279102
45	4.70235855	0.21265924	105.78167290	22.49545026
46	4.86694110	0.20546787	110.48403145	22.70091813
47	5.03728404	0.19851968	115.35097255	22.89943780
48	5.21358898	0.19180645	120.38825659	23.09124425
49	5.39606459	0.18532024	125.60184557	23.27656450
50	5.58492686	0.17905337	130.99791016	23.45561787
60	7.87809090	0.12693431	196.51688288	24.94473412
80	15.67573754	0.06379285	419.30678685	26.74877567
100	31.19140798	0.03206011	862.61165666	27.65542540
120	62.06431624	0.01611232	1744.69474973	28.11107663
240	3851.9793504	0.00025961	110027.981440	28.56401123

RATE 4.0%	COMPOUND INTEREST	PRESENT VALUE	AMOUNT OF ORDINARY ANNUITY	PRESENT VALUE OF ANNUITY
1	1.04000000	0.96153846	1.00000000	0.96153846
2	1.08160000	0.92455621	2.04000000	1.88609467
3	1.12486400	0.88899636	3.12160000	2.77509103
4	1.16985856	0.85480419	4.24646400	3.62989522
5	1.21665290	0.82192711	5.41632256	4.45182233
6	1.26531902	0.79031453	6.63297546	5.24213686
7	1.31593178	0.75991781	7.89829448	6.00205467
8	1.36856905	0.73069021	9.21422626	6.73274487
9	1.42331181	0.70258674	10.58279531	7.43533161
10	1.48024428	0.67556417	12.00610712	8.11089578
11	1.53945406	0.64958093	13.48635141	8.76047671
12	1.60103222	0.62459705	15.02580546	9.38507376
13	1.66507351	0.60057409	16.62683768	9.98564785
14	1.73167645	0.57747508	18.29191119	10.56312293
15	1.80094351	0.55526450	20.02358764	11.11838743
16	1.87298125	0.53390818	21.82453114	11.65229561
17	1.94790050	0.51337325	23.69751239	12.16566885
18	2.02581652	0.49362812	25.64541288	12.65929697
19	2.10684918	0.47464242	27.67122940	13.13393940
20	2.19112314	0.45638695	29.77807858	13.59032634
21	2.27876807	0.43883360	31.96920172	14.02915995
22	2.36991879	0.42195539	34.24796979	14.45111533
23	2.46471554	0.40572633	36.61788858	14.85684167
24	2.56330416	0.39012147	39.08260412	15.24696314
25	2.66583633	0.37511680	41.64590829	15.62207994
26	2.77246978	0.36068923	44.31174462	15.98276918
27	2.88336858	0.34681657	47.08421440	16.32958575
28	2.99870332	0.33347747	49.96758298	16.66306322
29	3.11865145	0.32065101	52.96628630	16.98371463
30	3.24339751	0.30831867	56.08493775	17.29203330
31	3.37313341	0.29646026	59.32833526	17.58849356
32	3.50805875	0.28505794	62.70146867	17.87355150
33	3.64838110	0.27409417	66.20952742	18.14764567
34	3.79431634	0.26355209	69.85790851	18.41119776
35	3.94608899	0.25341547	73.65222486	18.66461323
36	4.10393255	0.24366872	77.59831385	18.90828195
37	4.26808986	0.23429685	81.70224640	19.14257880
38	4.43881345	0.22528543	85.97033626	19.36786423
39	4.61636599	0.21662061	90.40914971	19.58448484
40	4.80102063	0.20828904	95.02551570	19.79277388
41	4.99306145	0.20027793	99.82653633	19.99305181
42	5.19278391	0.19257493	104.81959778	20.18562674
43	5.40049527	0.18516820	110.01238169	20.37079494
44	5.61651508	0.17804635	115.41287696	20.54884129
45	5.84117568	0.17119841	121.02939204	20.72003970
46	6.07482271	0.16461386	126.87056772	20.88465356
47	6.31781562	0.15828256	132.94539043	21.04293612
48	6.57052824	0.15219476	139.26320604	21.19513088
49	6.83334937	0.14634112	145.83373429	21.34147200
50	7.10668335	0.14071262	152.66708366	21.48218462
60	10.51962741	0.09506040	237.99068520	22.62348997
80	23.04997907	0.04338433	551.24497675	23.91539185
100	50.50494818	0.01980004	1237.62370461	24.50499900
120	110.66256080	0.00903648	2741.56402011	24.77408800
240	12246.2023638	0.00008166	306130.059093	24.99795855

Compound Interest, Present Value, and Annuity Table

RATE 4.5 %	COMPOUND INTEREST	PRESENT VALUE	AMOUNT OF ORDINARY ANNUITY	PRESENT VALUE OF ANNUITY
1	1.04500000	0.95693780	1.00000000	0.95693780
2	1.09202500	0.91572995	2.04500000	1.87266775
3	1.14116612	0.87629660	3.13702500	2.74896435
4	1.19251860	0.83856134	4.27819112	3.58752570
5	1.24618194	0.80245105	5.47070973	4.38997674
6	1.30226012	0.76789574	6.71689166	5.15787248
7	1.36086183	0.73482846	8.01915179	5.89270094
8	1.42210061	0.70318513	9.38001362	6.59588607
9	1.48609514	0.67290443	10.80211423	7.26879050
10	1.55296942	0.64392768	12.28820837	7.91271818
11	1.62285305	0.61619874	13.84117879	8.52891692
12	1.69588143	0.58966386	15.46403184	9.11858078
13	1.77219610	0.56427164	17.15991327	9.68285242
14	1.85194902	0.53997286	18.93210937	10.22282528
15	1.93528244	0.51672044	20.78405429	10.73954573
16	2.02237015	0.49446932	22.71933673	11.23401505
17	2.11337681	0.47317639	24.74170689	11.70719143
18	2.20847877	0.45280037	26.85508370	12.15999180
19	2.30786031	0.43330179	29.06356246	12.59329359
20	2.41171402	0.41464286	31.37142277	13.00793645
21	2.52024116	0.39678743	33.78313680	13.40472388
22	2.63365201	0.37970089	36.30337795	13.78442476
23	2.75216635	0.36335013	38.93702996	14.14777489
24	2.87601383	0.34770347	41.69619631	14.49547837
25	3.00543446	0.33273060	44.56521015	14.82820896
26	3.14067901	0.31840248	47.57064460	15.14661145
27	3.28200956	0.30469137	50.71132361	15.45130282
28	3.42969999	0.29157069	53.99333317	15.74287351
29	3.58403649	0.27901502	57.42303316	16.02188853
30	3.74531813	0.26700002	61.00706966	16.28888854
31	3.91385745	0.25550241	64.75238779	16.54439095
32	4.08998104	0.24449991	68.66624524	16.78889086
33	4.27403018	0.23397121	72.75622628	17.02286207
34	4.46633154	0.22389589	77.03025646	17.24675796
35	4.66734781	0.21425444	81.49661800	17.46101240
36	4.87737846	0.20502817	86.16396581	17.66604058
37	5.09686049	0.19619921	91.04134427	17.86223979
38	5.32621921	0.18775904	96.13820476	18.04999023
39	5.56589908	0.17966549	101.46442398	18.22965572
40	5.81636454	0.17192870	107.03032306	18.40158442
41	6.07810094	0.16452507	112.84668760	18.56610949
42	6.35161548	0.15744026	118.92478854	18.72354975
43	6.63748818	0.15066054	125.27640402	18.87421029
44	6.93612290	0.14417276	131.91384220	19.01838305
45	7.24824843	0.13796437	138.84996510	19.15634742
46	7.57441961	0.13202332	146.09621353	19.28837074
47	7.91526849	0.12633810	153.67263314	19.41470884
48	8.27145557	0.12089771	161.58790163	19.53660654
49	8.64367107	0.11569158	169.85935720	19.65129813
50	9.03263627	0.11070965	178.50302828	19.76200778
60	14.02740793	0.07128901	289.49795398	20.63802204
80	33.83009643	0.02955948	729.55769854	21.56534493
100	81.58851803	0.01225663	1790.85595627	21.94985274
120	196.76817320	0.00508212	4350.40384897	22.10928616
240	38717.713986	0.00002583	860371.4219077	22.22164827

RATE 5.0 %	COMPOUND INTEREST	PRESENT VALUE	AMOUNT OF ORDINARY ANNUITY	PRESENT VALUE OF ANNUITY
1	1.05000000	0.95238095	1.00000000	0.95238095
2	1.10250000	0.90702948	2.05000000	1.85941043
3	1.15762500	0.86383760	3.15250000	2.72324803
4	1.21550625	0.82270247	4.31012500	3.54595050
5	1.27628156	0.78352617	5.52563125	4.32947667
6	1.34009564	0.74621540	6.80191281	5.07569207
7	1.40710042	0.71068133	8.14200845	5.78637340
8	1.47745544	0.67683936	9.54910888	6.46321276
9	1.55132822	0.64460892	11.02656432	7.10782168
10	1.62889463	0.61391325	12.57789254	7.72173493
11	1.71033936	0.58467929	14.20678716	8.30641422
12	1.79585633	0.55683742	15.91712652	8.86325164
13	1.88564914	0.53032135	17.71298285	9.39357299
14	1.97993160	0.50506795	19.59863199	9.89864094
15	2.07892818	0.48101710	21.57856359	10.37965804
16	2.18287459	0.45811152	23.65749177	10.83776956
17	2.29201832	0.43629669	25.84036636	11.27406625
18	2.40661923	0.41552065	28.13238467	11.68958690
19	2.52695020	0.39573396	30.53900391	12.08532086
20	2.65329771	0.37688948	33.06595410	12.46221034
21	2.78596259	0.35894236	35.71925181	12.82115271
22	2.92526072	0.34184987	38.50521440	13.16300258
23	3.07152376	0.32557131	41.43047512	13.48857388
24	3.22509994	0.31006791	44.50199887	13.79864179
25	3.38635494	0.29530277	47.72709882	14.09394457
26	3.55567269	0.28124073	51.11345376	14.37518530
27	3.73345632	0.26784832	54.66912645	14.64303362
28	3.92012914	0.25509364	58.40258277	14.89812726
29	4.11613560	0.24294632	62.32271191	15.14107358
30	4.32194238	0.23137745	66.43884750	15.37245103
31	4.53803949	0.22035947	70.76078988	15.59281050
32	4.76494147	0.20986617	75.29882937	15.80267667
33	5.00318854	0.19987254	80.06377084	16.00254921
34	5.25334797	0.19035480	85.06695938	16.19290401
35	5.51601537	0.18129029	90.32030735	16.37419429
36	5.79181614	0.17265741	95.83632272	16.54685171
37	6.08140694	0.16443563	101.62813886	16.71128734
38	6.38547729	0.15660536	107.70954580	16.86789271
39	6.70475115	0.14914797	114.09502309	17.01704067
40	7.03998871	0.14204568	120.79977424	17.15908635
41	7.39198815	0.13528160	127.83976295	17.29436796
42	7.76158756	0.12883962	135.23175110	17.42320758
43	8.14966693	0.12270440	142.99333866	17.54591198
44	8.55715028	0.11686133	151.14300559	17.66277331
45	8.98500779	0.11129651	159.70015587	17.77406982
46	9.43425818	0.10599668	168.68516366	17.88006650
47	9.90597109	0.10094921	178.11942185	17.98101571
48	10.40126965	0.09614211	188.02539294	18.07715782
49	10.92133313	0.09156391	198.42666259	18.16872173
50	11.46739979	0.08720373	209.34799572	18.25592546
60	18.67918589	0.05353552	353.58371788	18.92928953
80	49.56144107	0.02017698	971.22882134	19.59646048
100	131.50125785	0.00760449	2610.02515693	19.84791020
120	348.91198567	0.00286605	6958.23971334	19.94267895
240	121739.573742	0.00000821	2434771.47490	19.99983571

Appendix D Reference Tables

Compound Interest, Present Value, and Annuity Table

RATE 6.0%

PERIODS	COMPOUND INTEREST	PRESENT VALUE	AMOUNT OF ORDINARY ANNUITY	PRESENT VALUE OF ANNUITY
1	1.06000000	0.94339623	1.00000000	0.94339623
2	1.12360000	0.88999644	2.06000000	1.83339267
3	1.19101600	0.83961928	3.18360000	2.67301195
4	1.26247696	0.79209366	4.37461600	3.46510561
5	1.33822558	0.74725817	5.63709296	4.21236379
6	1.41851911	0.70496054	6.97531854	4.91732433
7	1.50363026	0.66505711	8.39383766	5.58238144
8	1.59384807	0.62741237	9.89746791	6.20979381
9	1.68947896	0.59189846	11.49131598	6.80169227
10	1.79084770	0.55839478	13.18079494	7.36008705
11	1.89829856	0.52678753	14.97164264	7.88687458
12	2.01219647	0.49696936	16.86994120	8.38384394
13	2.13292826	0.46883902	18.88213767	8.85268296
14	2.26090396	0.44230096	21.01506593	9.29498393
15	2.39655819	0.41726506	23.27596988	9.71224899
16	2.54035168	0.39364628	25.67252808	10.10589527
17	2.69277279	0.37136442	28.21287976	10.47725969
18	2.85433915	0.35034379	30.90565255	10.82760348
19	3.02559950	0.33051301	33.75999170	11.15811649
20	3.20713547	0.31180473	36.78559120	11.46992122
21	3.39956360	0.29415540	39.99272668	11.76407662
22	3.60353742	0.27750510	43.39229028	12.04158172
23	3.81974966	0.26179726	46.99582769	12.30337898
24	4.04893464	0.24697855	50.81557735	12.55035753
25	4.29187072	0.23299863	54.86451200	12.78335616
26	4.54938296	0.21981003	59.15638272	13.00316619
27	4.82234594	0.20736795	63.70576568	13.21053414
28	5.11168670	0.19563014	68.52811162	13.40616428
29	5.41838790	0.18455674	73.63979832	13.59072102
30	5.74349117	0.17411013	79.05818622	13.76483115
31	6.08810064	0.16425484	84.80167739	13.92908599
32	6.45338668	0.15495740	90.88977803	14.08404339
33	6.84058988	0.14618622	97.34316471	14.23022961
34	7.25102528	0.13791153	104.18375460	14.36814114
35	7.68608679	0.13010522	111.43477987	14.49824636
36	8.14725200	0.12274077	119.12086666	14.62098713
37	8.63608712	0.11579318	127.26811866	14.73678031
38	9.15425235	0.10923885	135.90420578	14.84601916
39	9.70350749	0.10305552	145.05845813	14.94907468
40	10.28571794	0.09722219	154.76196562	15.04629687
41	10.90286101	0.09171905	165.04768356	15.13801592
42	11.55703267	0.08652740	175.95054457	15.22454332
43	12.25045463	0.08162962	187.50757724	15.30617294
44	12.98548191	0.07700908	199.75803188	15.38318202
45	13.76081083	0.07265007	212.74351379	15.45583209
46	14.59048748	0.06853781	226.50812462	15.52436990
47	15.46591673	0.06465831	241.09861210	15.58902821
48	16.39387173	0.06099840	256.56452882	15.65002661
49	17.37750403	0.05754566	272.95840055	15.70757227
50	18.42015427	0.05428836	290.33590458	15.76186064
60	32.98769085	0.03031434	533.12818089	16.16142771
80	105.79599348	0.00945215	1746.59989137	16.50913077
100	339.30208351	0.00294723	5638.36805857	16.61754623
120	1088.18774784	0.00091896	18119.79579725	16.65135068

RATE 7.0%

PERIODS	COMPOUND INTEREST	PRESENT VALUE	AMOUNT OF ORDINARY ANNUITY	PRESENT VALUE OF ANNUITY
1	1.07000000	0.93457944	1.00000000	0.93457944
2	1.14490000	0.87343873	2.07000000	1.80801817
3	1.22504300	0.81629788	3.21490000	2.62431604
4	1.31079601	0.76289521	4.43994300	3.38721126
5	1.40255173	0.71298618	5.75073901	4.10019744
6	1.50073035	0.66634222	7.15329074	4.76653966
7	1.60578148	0.62274974	8.65402109	5.38928940
8	1.71818618	0.58200910	10.25980257	5.97129851
9	1.83845921	0.54393374	11.97798875	6.51523225
10	1.96715136	0.50834929	13.81644796	7.02358154
11	2.10485195	0.47509280	15.78359932	7.49867434
12	2.25219159	0.44401196	17.88845127	7.94268630
13	2.40984500	0.41496445	20.14064286	8.35765074
14	2.57853415	0.38781724	22.55048786	8.74546799
15	2.75903154	0.36244602	25.12902201	9.10791401
16	2.95216375	0.33873460	27.88805355	9.44664860
17	3.15881521	0.31657439	30.84021730	9.76322299
18	3.37993228	0.29586392	33.99903251	10.05908691
19	3.61652754	0.27650833	37.37896479	10.33559524
20	3.86968446	0.25841900	40.99549232	10.59401425
21	4.14056237	0.24151309	44.86517678	10.83552733
22	4.43040174	0.22671317	49.00573916	11.06124050
23	4.74052986	0.21094688	53.43614090	11.27218738
24	5.07236695	0.19714662	58.17667076	11.46933400
25	5.42743264	0.18424918	63.24903772	11.65358318
26	5.80735292	0.17219549	68.67647036	11.82577867
27	6.21386763	0.16093037	74.48382328	11.98670904
28	6.64883836	0.15040221	80.69769091	12.13711125
29	7.11425705	0.14056282	87.34652927	12.27767407
30	7.61225504	0.13136712	94.46078632	12.40904118
31	8.14511290	0.12277301	102.07304137	12.53181419
32	8.71527080	0.11474113	110.21815426	12.64655532
33	9.32533975	0.10723470	118.93342506	12.75379002
34	9.97811354	0.10021934	128.25876481	12.85400936
35	10.67658148	0.09366294	138.23687835	12.94767230
36	11.42394219	0.08753546	148.91345984	13.03520776
37	12.22361814	0.08180884	160.33740202	13.11701660
38	13.07927141	0.07645686	172.56102017	13.19347345
39	13.99482041	0.07145501	185.64029158	13.26492846
40	14.97445784	0.06678038	199.63511199	13.33170884
41	16.02266989	0.06241157	214.60956983	13.39412041
42	17.14425678	0.05832857	230.63223972	13.45244898
43	18.34435475	0.05451268	247.77649650	13.50696167
44	19.62845959	0.05094643	266.12085125	13.55790810
45	21.00245176	0.04761349	285.74931084	13.60552159
46	22.47262338	0.04449859	306.75176260	13.65002018
47	24.04570702	0.04158747	329.22438598	13.69180764
48	25.72890651	0.03886679	353.27008300	13.73047443
49	27.52992997	0.03832410	378.99899951	13.76679853
50	29.45702506	0.03394776	406.52892947	13.80074629
60	57.94642683	0.01725732	813.52038335	14.03918115
80	224.23438758	0.00445962	3189.06267969	14.22200544
100	867.71632557	0.00115245	12381.66179381	14.26925071
120	3357.78838289	0.00029782	47954.11975557	14.28145978

Reference Tables A—53

Compound Interest, Present Value, and Annuity Table

RATE 8.0 %	COMPOUND INTEREST	PRESENT VALUE	AMOUNT OF ORDINARY ANNUITY	PRESENT VALUE OF ANNUITY
1	1.08000000	0.92592593	1.00000000	0.92592593
2	1.16640000	0.85733882	2.08000000	1.78326475
3	1.25971200	0.79383224	3.24640000	2.57709699
4	1.36048896	0.73502985	4.50611200	3.31212684
5	1.46932808	0.68058320	5.86660096	3.99271004
6	1.58687432	0.63016963	7.33592904	4.62287966
7	1.71382427	0.58349040	8.92280336	6.20637006
8	1.85093021	0.54026888	10.63662763	5.74663894
9	1.99900463	0.50024897	12.48755784	6.24688791
10	2.15892500	0.46319349	14.48656247	6.71008140
11	2.33163900	0.42888286	16.64548746	7.13896426
12	2.51817012	0.39711376	18.97712646	7.53807802
13	2.71962373	0.36769792	21.49529658	7.90377594
14	2.93719362	0.34046104	24.21492030	8.24423698
15	3.17216911	0.31524170	27.15211393	8.55947869
16	3.42594264	0.29189047	30.32428304	8.85136916
17	3.70001805	0.27026895	33.75022569	9.12163811
18	3.99601950	0.25024903	37.45024374	9.37188714
19	4.31570106	0.23171206	41.44626324	9.60359920
20	4.66095714	0.21454821	45.76196430	9.81814741
21	5.03383372	0.19865575	50.42292144	10.01680316
22	5.43654041	0.18394051	55.45675516	10.20074366
23	5.87146365	0.17031528	60.89329557	10.37105895
24	6.34118074	0.15769934	66.76475922	10.52875828
25	6.84847520	0.14601790	73.10593995	10.67477619
26	7.39635321	0.13520176	79.95441515	10.80997795
27	7.98806147	0.12518682	87.35076836	10.93516477
28	8.62710639	0.11591372	95.33882983	11.05107849
29	9.31727490	0.10732752	103.96593622	11.15840601
30	10.06265689	0.09937733	113.28321111	11.25778334
31	10.86766944	0.09201605	123.34586800	11.34979939
32	11.73708300	0.08520005	134.21353744	11.43499944
33	12.67604964	0.07888893	145.95062044	11.51388837
34	13.69013361	0.07304531	158.62667007	11.58693367
35	14.78534429	0.06763454	172.31680368	11.65456822
36	15.96817184	0.06262458	187.10214797	11.71719279
37	17.24562558	0.05798572	203.07031981	11.77517851
38	18.62527563	0.05369048	220.31594540	11.82886899
39	20.11529768	0.04971341	238.94122103	11.87858240
40	21.72452150	0.04603093	259.05651871	11.92461333
41	23.46248322	0.04262123	280.78104021	11.96723457
42	25.33948187	0.03946411	304.24352342	12.00669867
43	27.36664042	0.03654084	329.58300530	12.04323951
44	29.55597166	0.03383411	356.94964572	12.07707362
45	31.92044939	0.03132788	386.50561738	12.10840150
46	34.47408534	0.02907730	418.42606677	12.13747880
47	37.23201217	0.02685861	452.90015211	12.16426741
48	40.21057314	0.02486908	490.13216428	12.18913649
49	43.42741899	0.02302693	530.34273742	12.21216341
50	46.90161251	0.02132123	573.77015642	12.23348464
60	101.25706367	0.00987585	1253.21329584	12.37655782
80	471.95483426	0.00211885	5886.93542831	12.47351441
100	2199.76125634	0.00045459	27484.5157042	12.49431757
120	10252.9929425	0.00009753	128149.9117813	12.49878084

RATE 9.0 %	COMPOUND INTEREST	PRESENT VALUE	AMOUNT OF ORDINARY ANNUITY	PRESENT VALUE OF ANNUITY
1	1.09000000	0.91743119	1.00000000	0.91743119
2	1.18810000	0.84167999	2.09000000	1.75911119
3	1.29502900	0.77218348	3.27810000	2.53129467
4	1.41158161	0.70842521	4.57312900	3.23971988
5	1.53862395	0.64993139	5.98471061	3.88965126
6	1.67710011	0.59626733	7.52333456	4.48591859
7	1.82803912	0.54703424	9.20043468	5.03295284
8	1.99256264	0.50186628	11.02847380	5.53481911
9	2.17189328	0.46042778	13.02103644	5.99524689
10	2.36736367	0.42241081	15.19292972	6.41765770
11	2.58042641	0.38753285	17.56029339	6.80519055
12	2.81266478	0.35553473	20.14071980	7.16072528
13	3.06580461	0.32617865	22.95338458	7.48690392
14	3.34172703	0.29924647	26.01918919	7.78615039
15	3.64248246	0.27453804	29.36091622	8.06068843
16	3.97030588	0.25186976	33.00339868	8.31255819
17	4.32763341	0.23107318	36.97370456	8.54363137
18	4.71712042	0.21199374	41.30133797	8.75562511
19	5.14166125	0.19448967	46.01845839	8.95011478
20	5.60441077	0.17843089	51.16011964	9.12854567
21	6.10880774	0.16369806	56.76453041	9.29224373
22	6.65860043	0.15018171	62.87333815	9.44242544
23	7.25787447	0.13778139	69.53193858	9.58020683
24	7.91108317	0.12640494	76.78981305	9.70661177
25	8.62308066	0.11596784	84.70089623	9.82257960
26	9.39915792	0.10639251	93.32397689	9.92897211
27	10.24508213	0.09760781	102.72313481	10.02657992
28	11.16713952	0.08954845	112.96821694	10.11612837
29	12.17218208	0.08215454	124.13535646	10.19828291
30	13.26767847	0.07537114	136.30753855	10.27365404
31	14.46176953	0.06914783	149.57521702	10.34280187
32	15.76332879	0.06343838	164.03698655	10.40624025
33	17.18202838	0.05820035	179.80031534	10.46444060
34	18.72841093	0.05339481	196.98234372	10.51783541
35	20.41396792	0.04898607	215.71075465	10.56682148
36	22.25122503	0.04494135	236.12472257	10.61176282
37	24.25383528	0.04123059	258.37594760	10.65299342
38	26.43668046	0.03782623	282.62978288	10.69081965
39	28.81598170	0.03470296	309.06646334	10.72552281
40	31.40942005	0.03183758	337.88244504	10.75736020
41	34.23626786	0.02920379	369.29186510	10.78656899
42	37.31753197	0.02679706	403.52813296	10.81336604
43	40.67610984	0.02458446	440.84566492	10.83795050
44	44.33695973	0.02255455	481.52177477	10.86050504
45	48.32728610	0.02069224	525.85873450	10.88119729
46	52.67674185	0.01898371	574.18602060	10.90018100
47	57.41764862	0.01741625	626.86276245	10.91759725
48	62.58523700	0.01597821	684.28041107	10.93357546
49	68.21790833	0.01465891	746.86564807	10.94823436
50	74.35752008	0.01344854	815.08355640	10.96168290
60	176.03129196	0.00568081	1944.79213289	11.04799102
80	986.55166813	0.00101363	10950.5740900	11.09984854
100	5529.04079183	0.00018086	61422.6754630	11.10910152
120	30987.0157492	0.00003227	344289.0638799	11.11075254

A–54 Appendix D Reference Tables

Compound Interest, Present Value, and Annuity Table

RATE 10.%

PERIODS	COMPOUND INTEREST	PRESENT VALUE	AMOUNT OF ORDINARY ANNUITY	PRESENT VALUE OF ANNUITY
1	1.10000000	0.90909091	1.00000000	0.90909091
2	1.21000000	0.82644628	2.10000000	1.73553719
3	1.33100000	0.75131346	3.31000000	2.48685199
4	1.46410000	0.68301346	4.64100000	3.16986545
5	1.61051000	0.62092132	6.10510000	3.79078677
6	1.77156100	0.56447393	7.71561000	4.35526070
7	1.94871710	0.51315812	9.48717100	4.86841882
8	2.14358881	0.46650738	11.43588810	5.33492620
9	2.35794691	0.42409762	13.57947691	5.75902382
10	2.59374246	0.38554329	15.93742460	6.14456711
11	2.85311671	0.35049390	18.53116706	6.49506101
12	3.13842838	0.31863082	21.38428377	6.81369182
13	3.45227121	0.28966438	24.52271214	7.10335620
14	3.79749834	0.26333155	27.97498336	7.36668746
15	4.17724817	0.23939205	31.77248169	7.60607951
16	4.59497299	0.21762914	35.94972986	7.82370864
17	5.05447028	0.19784467	40.54470285	8.02155331
18	5.55991731	0.17985879	45.59917313	8.20141210
19	6.11590904	0.16350799	51.15909045	8.36492009
20	6.72749995	0.14864363	57.27499949	8.51356372
21	7.40024994	0.13513057	64.00249944	8.64869429
22	8.14027494	0.12284597	71.40274939	8.77154026
23	8.95430243	0.11167816	79.54302433	8.88321842
24	9.84973268	0.10152560	88.49732676	8.98474402
25	10.83470594	0.09229600	98.34705943	9.07704002
26	11.91817654	0.08390545	109.18176538	9.16094547
27	13.10999419	0.07627768	121.09994191	9.23722316
28	14.42099361	0.06934335	134.20993611	9.30656651
29	15.86309297	0.06303941	148.63092972	9.36960591
30	17.44940227	0.05730855	164.49402269	9.42691447
31	19.19434250	0.05209868	181.94342496	9.47901315
32	21.11377675	0.04736244	201.13776745	9.52637559
33	23.22515442	0.04305676	222.25154420	9.56943236
34	25.54766986	0.03914251	245.47669862	9.60857487
35	28.10243685	0.03558410	271.02436848	9.64415897
36	30.91268053	0.03234918	299.12680533	9.67650816
37	34.00394859	0.02940835	330.03948586	9.70591651
38	37.40434344	0.02673486	364.04343445	9.73265137
39	41.14477779	0.02430442	401.44777789	9.75695579
40	45.25925557	0.02209493	442.59255568	9.77905072
41	49.78518112	0.02008630	487.85181125	9.79913702
42	54.76369924	0.01826027	537.63699237	9.81739729
43	60.24006916	0.01660025	592.40069161	9.83399753
44	66.26407608	0.01509113	652.64076077	9.84908867
45	72.89048369	0.01371921	718.90483685	9.86280788
46	80.17953205	0.01247201	791.79532054	9.87527989
47	88.19748526	0.01133819	871.97485259	9.88661808
48	97.01723378	0.01030745	960.17233785	9.89692553
49	106.71895716	0.00937041	1057.18957163	9.90629594
50	117.39085288	0.00851855	1163.90852880	9.91481449
60	304.48163954	0.00328427	3034.81639541	9.96715730
80	2048.40021459	0.00048819	20474.00214585	9.99511814
100	13780.61233398	0.00007257	137796.1233982	9.99927434
120	92709.0688178	0.00001079	927080.6881783	9.99989214

RATE 12.%

PERIODS	COMPOUND INTEREST	PRESENT VALUE	AMOUNT OF ORDINARY ANNUITY	PRESENT VALUE OF ANNUITY
1	1.12000000	0.89285714	1.00000000	0.89285714
2	1.25440000	0.79719388	2.12000000	1.69005102
3	1.40492800	0.71178025	3.37440000	2.40183127
4	1.57351936	0.63551808	4.77932800	3.03734935
5	1.76234168	0.56742686	6.35284736	3.60477620
6	1.97382269	0.50663112	8.11518904	4.11140732
7	2.21068141	0.45234922	10.08901173	4.56375654
8	2.47596318	0.40388323	12.29969314	4.96763977
9	2.77307876	0.36061002	14.77565631	5.32824979
10	3.10584821	0.32197324	17.54873507	5.65022303
11	3.47854999	0.28747610	20.65458328	5.93769913
12	3.89597599	0.25667509	24.13313327	6.19437423
13	4.36349311	0.22917419	28.02910926	6.42354842
14	4.87511229	0.20461981	32.39260238	6.62816823
15	5.47356576	0.18269626	37.27971466	6.81086449
16	6.13039365	0.16312166	42.75328042	6.97398615
17	6.86604089	0.14564434	48.88367407	7.11963049
18	7.68996580	0.13003959	55.74971496	7.24967008
19	8.61276169	0.11610678	63.43968075	7.36577686
20	9.64629309	0.10366677	72.05244244	7.46944362
21	10.80384826	0.09255961	81.69873554	7.56200324
22	12.10031006	0.08264251	92.50258380	7.64464575
23	13.55234726	0.07378796	104.60289386	7.71843370
24	15.17862893	0.06588210	118.15524112	7.78431581
25	17.00006441	0.05882331	133.33387006	7.84313911
26	19.04007214	0.05252081	150.33393446	7.89565992
27	21.32488079	0.04693358	169.37400660	7.94255350
28	23.88386649	0.04186927	190.69888739	7.98442277
29	26.74993047	0.03738327	214.58275388	8.02180604
30	29.95992212	0.03337792	241.33268434	8.05518397
31	33.55511278	0.02980172	271.29260646	8.08498569
32	37.58172631	0.02660868	304.84771924	8.11159436
33	42.09153347	0.02375775	342.42944555	8.13535211
34	47.14251748	0.02121227	384.52097901	8.15656438
35	52.79961958	0.01893953	431.66349649	8.17550091
36	59.13557393	0.01691029	484.46311607	8.19241421
37	66.23184280	0.01509848	543.59869000	8.20751269
38	74.17966394	0.01348078	609.83053280	8.22099347
39	83.08122361	0.01203641	684.01019674	8.23302988
40	93.05097044	0.01074680	767.09142034	8.24377668
41	104.21708689	0.00959536	860.14239079	8.25337204
42	116.72313732	0.00856728	964.35947768	8.26193932
43	130.72991380	0.00764936	1081.08261500	8.26958868
44	146.41750346	0.00682978	1211.81252880	8.27641846
45	163.98760387	0.00609802	1358.23003226	8.28251648
46	183.66611634	0.00544466	1522.21763613	8.28796115
47	205.70605030	0.00486131	1705.88375247	8.29282245
48	230.39077633	0.00434045	1911.58980276	8.29716290
49	258.03776949	0.00387540	2141.98057909	8.30103831
50	289.00218983	0.00346018	2400.01824858	8.30449849
60	897.59693349	0.00111409	7471.64111243	8.32404929
80	8658.4830008	0.00011549	72145.69250066	8.33237089

Reference Tables A-55

Compound Interest, Present Value, and Annuity Table

RATE 14.%

PERIODS	COMPOUND INTEREST	PRESENT VALUE	AMOUNT OF ORDINARY ANNUITY	PRESENT VALUE OF ANNUITY
1	1.14000000	0.87719298	1.00000000	0.87719298
2	1.29960000	0.76946753	2.14000000	1.64666051
3	1.48154400	0.67497152	3.43960000	2.32163203
4	1.68896016	0.59208028	4.92114400	2.91371230
5	1.92541458	0.51936866	6.61010416	3.43308097
6	2.19497262	0.45558655	8.53551874	3.88866752
7	2.50226879	0.39963732	10.73049137	4.28830484
8	2.85258642	0.35055905	13.23276016	4.63886389
9	3.25194852	0.30750794	16.08534658	4.94637184
10	3.70722131	0.26974381	19.33729510	5.21611565
11	4.22823230	0.23661738	23.04451641	5.45273302
12	4.81790482	0.20755910	27.27074871	5.66029213
13	5.49241149	0.18206939	32.08865353	5.84236151
14	6.26134910	0.15970999	37.58106503	6.00207150
15	7.13793798	0.14009648	43.84241413	6.14216799
16	8.13724930	0.12289165	50.98035211	6.26505964
17	9.27646420	0.10779969	59.11760141	6.37285933
18	10.57516918	0.09456113	68.39406560	6.46742046
19	12.05569287	0.08294836	78.96923479	6.55036883
20	13.74348987	0.07276172	91.02492766	6.62313055
21	15.66757845	0.06382607	104.76841753	6.68695662
22	17.86103944	0.05598778	120.43599598	6.74294441
23	20.36158496	0.04911209	138.29703542	6.79205650
24	23.21220685	0.04308078	158.65862038	6.83513728
25	26.46191581	0.03779016	181.87082723	6.87292744
26	30.16658403	0.03314926	208.33274304	6.90607670
27	34.38990579	0.02907830	238.49932707	6.93515500
28	39.20449260	0.02550728	272.88923286	6.96066228
29	44.69312158	0.02237481	312.09372546	6.98303709
30	50.95015858	0.01962702	356.78684702	7.00266411
31	58.08318078	0.01721669	407.73700561	7.01988080
32	66.21482609	0.01510236	465.82018639	7.03498316
33	75.48490175	0.01324768	532.03501249	7.04823084
34	86.05278799	0.01162077	607.51991423	7.05985161
35	98.10017831	0.01019366	693.57270223	7.07004528
36	111.83420328	0.00894181	791.67288054	7.07898708
37	127.49099173	0.00784369	903.50708382	7.08683078
38	145.33973058	0.00688043	1030.99807555	7.09371121
39	165.68729286	0.00603547	1176.33780613	7.09974667
40	188.88351386	0.00529427	1342.02509898	7.10504094
41	215.32720580	0.00464410	1530.90861284	7.10968504
42	245.47301461	0.00407377	1746.23581864	7.11375880
43	279.83923665	0.00357348	1991.70883325	7.11733228
44	319.01672979	0.00313463	2271.54806990	7.12046692
45	363.67907196	0.00274968	2590.56479969	7.12321655
46	414.59414203	0.00241200	2954.24387165	7.12562859
47	472.63732191	0.00211579	3368.83801368	7.12774438
48	538.80654698	0.00185595	3841.47533559	7.12960033
49	614.23946656	0.00162803	4380.28188258	7.13122836
50	700.23298846	0.00142810	4994.52134614	7.13265646
60	2595.91865960	0.00038572	18535.13328332	7.14010557

RATE 16.%

PERIODS	COMPOUND INTEREST	PRESENT VALUE	AMOUNT OF ORDINARY ANNUITY	PRESENT VALUE OF ANNUITY
1	1.16000000	0.86206897	1.00000000	0.86206897
2	1.34560000	0.74316290	2.16000000	1.60523187
3	1.56089600	0.64065767	3.50560000	2.24588954
4	1.81063936	0.55229110	5.06649600	2.79818064
5	2.10034166	0.47611302	6.87713536	3.27429365
6	2.43639632	0.41044225	8.97747702	3.68473591
7	2.82621973	0.35382953	11.41387334	4.03856544
8	3.27841489	0.30502546	14.24009307	4.34369090
9	3.80296127	0.26295298	17.51850797	4.60654388
10	4.41143508	0.22668360	21.32146924	4.83322748
11	5.11726469	0.19541690	25.73290432	5.02864438
12	5.93602704	0.16846284	30.85016901	5.19710722
13	6.88579137	0.14522659	36.78619605	5.34233381
14	7.98751799	0.12519534	43.67198742	5.46752915
15	9.26552087	0.10792701	51.65950541	5.57545616
16	10.74800420	0.09304053	60.92502627	5.66849669
17	12.46768488	0.08020735	71.67303048	5.74870404
18	14.46251446	0.06914427	84.14071536	5.81784831
19	16.77651677	0.05960713	98.60322981	5.87745544
20	19.46075945	0.05138546	115.37974658	5.92884090
21	22.57448097	0.04429781	134.84050604	5.97313871
22	26.18639792	0.03818776	157.41498700	6.01132647
23	30.37622159	0.03292049	183.60188492	6.04424696
24	35.23641704	0.02837973	213.97760651	6.07262669
25	40.87424377	0.02446528	249.21402355	6.09709197
26	47.41412277	0.02109076	290.08826732	6.11818273
27	55.00038241	0.01818169	337.50239009	6.13636443
28	63.80044360	0.01567387	392.50277250	6.15203830
29	74.00851458	0.01351196	456.30321610	6.16555026
30	85.84987691	0.01164824	530.31173068	6.17719850
31	99.58585721	0.01004159	616.16160759	6.18724008
32	115.51959437	0.00865654	715.74746480	6.19589662
33	134.00272947	0.00746253	831.26705917	6.20335916
34	155.44316618	0.00643322	965.26978864	6.20979238
35	180.31407277	0.00554488	1120.71295482	6.21533826
36	209.16432441	0.00478093	1301.02702759	6.22011919
37	242.63061632	0.00412149	1510.19135201	6.22424068
38	281.45151493	0.00355301	1752.82196833	6.22779369
39	326.48375732	0.00306294	2034.27348326	6.23085663
40	378.72115849	0.00264047	2360.75724058	6.23349709
41	439.31664385	0.00227626	2739.47839907	6.23577336
42	509.60719087	0.00196230	3178.79494293	6.23773565
43	591.14434141	0.00169163	3688.40213380	6.23942729
44	685.72743603	0.00145831	4279.54647520	6.24088558
45	795.44382580	0.00125716	4965.27391123	6.24214275
46	922.71483793	0.00108376	5760.71773703	6.24322651
47	1070.34921199	0.00093427	6683.43257496	6.24416078
48	1241.60508591	0.00080541	7753.78178695	6.24496619
49	1440.26189966	0.00069432	8995.38687286	6.24566051
50	1670.70380360	0.00059855	10435.64877252	6.24625906
60	7370.20136525	0.00013568	46057.50853281	6.24915199

Appendix D Reference Tables A–56

Glossary

ABA numbers Numbers assigned to each bank by the American Banking Association, which include the city or area in which the bank is located and the number of the bank.
Accelerated cost recovery system (ACRS) method A consistent method of calculating depreciation for tax purposes. Both the recovery period in years and the method of depreciation are specified.
Account statement Document showing the status of a charge account including the balance, finance charges, and payment amount due.
Accumulated depreciation Running total of depreciation.
Acid-test ratio Relationship comparing current assets less merchandise inventory and prepaid expenses to current liabilities.
Add-on interest Loan repayment concept in which the total simple interest due is added to the principal of a loan to establish the installment payment amount.
Addend A number to be added.
Amortization Calculation of a monthly installment payment schedule using a given annual percentage rate for interest, a specified time, and interest calculated on the unpaid balance for each payment period.
Annual percentage rate (APR) Interest rate or equivalent interest rate stated as an annual cost for borrowing money.
Annuity Periodic deposits or payments of a fixed amount of money.
Annuity due Type of annuity in which deposits are made at the beginning of each period as in insurance payments, rent, or mortgage payments.
Approximation Close representation of a solution for a mathematical operation; used to evaluate the result for a business decision.
Arithmetic center A numeric value representing the mathematical center of a set of numbers. When this value is subtracted from each number in the set, the sum of the differences will always be zero.
Array Listing of a set of numbers that have been placed in numerical order.
Assessed rate Percent used on the market value of property to determine the assessed valuation for a tax base.
Assessed value Property value used as the base for computing property tax.
Assets Items of value owned by a company.
Average A typical value. Statistics presents three typical averages for the interpretation of data: the mean, median, and mode.
Average daily balance Method of determining charge account finance charges when the balance for each day of the accounting period is averaged as the base for calculation.
Average inventory Sum of the values of all merchandise counted during all inventories taken divided by the total number of inventories taken.
Average margin Composite figure that reflects the combined margins of the various categories of goods for sale.

Balance sheet Statement that shows the financial condition of a company on a specific date. It shows the assets, liabilities, and the owner's equity.
Bank discount Charge made by a bank for discounting a

note or draft. It is an interest charge collected at the beginning of the time period rather than at the end.
Bank reconciliation Process of adjustment that results in a checkbook balance agreeing with the bank statement balance.
Bank statement Monthly form sent to each checking account holder giving the opening balance, the additions and subtractions to the account, and the closing balance.
Banker's method Interest calculation method that uses exact time in the numerator and 360 days in the denominator.
Bar chart Information summation in which horizontal or vertical bars with value length have been used to facilitate data comparison.
Base Value that represents the whole or total; the point of reference for a change. Represented by 100 percent.
Bill of lading Shipping document listing the number of packages being shipped, their description, and their weights.
Billing period Charge account time period used to bill customers. Typically monthly or a monthly period starting within the month and running for the number of days in that month.
Blank endorsement Type of endorsement that includes only the name of the payee.
Bodily liability Insurance that provides coverage for personal injury to a third party.
Bond Certificate showing indebtedness that is issued to raise money.
Bond discount Amount by which the current market value of a bond is less than the face value of the bond.
Bond premium Amount by which the current market value of a bond is greater than the face value of the bond.
Book value Value of the property in the organization's records. It is the cost minus the accumulated depreciation.
Borrowing Shifting of a digit from a column representing a power of ten to another column of a power of ten. Used frequently in subtraction.
Breakeven point Point in a business operation at which full fixed costs and variable costs of the units sold have been recovered from sales. At this point net profit will be earned on the sale of additional goods.

Cancelled checks Checks that have been processed by a bank's accounting department and returned with the bank statement to the account holder.
Cash discount Discount given on the amount of the goods purchased because of prompt payment of the bill.
Central tendency Natural clustering of variable values around the center values of a number distribution.
Co-insurance Insurance that requires the insured to maintain coverage on property up to a certain amount or percent of the property's value.
Collision Type of automobile insurance that covers an unintended striking of another object with a vehicle.
Commission earnings Amount of money earned by salespersons for selling services or products. The amount is calculated as a percentage of sales dollar value.
Common stock Shares in a corporation whose holders have the last claim to dividends and assets in case of liquidation.
Competition profit Amount of profit derived from the sale of a good that is encountering extreme competition in the marketplace. Typically, a lower level of profit is earned as competition increases.
Complement Either of two parts constituting a whole. Using a base of ten, the complement of 6 would be 4. The complement of 55% would be 45% because percent is based in 100%.
Compound interest Interest calculated on an ever-increasing base. Interest is added to the principal each period, which is described by many as earning interest on interest.
Compounding periods Number of times a financial institution calculates interest over the life of an investment. Calculated by multiplying the number of compounding periods per year times the number of years of investment.
Comprehensive Insurance that protects the policyholder against virtually all automobile risks, except collision or upset, fire, or theft.
Conversion Changing the number form from one type to another: decimal to fraction, fraction to percent, decimal to percent, etc.
Cost The total amount paid for a property, including transportation and any installation costs; the dollar amount needed to create or obtain a product for resale.
Cost of goods sold Cost of goods purchased for resale plus any charges to get them ready for sale. The value of inventory items sold in an accounting period taken at cost.
Creditors Companies or individuals to whom money is owed.
Current assets Items owned that can be turned into cash in less than one year.
Current liabilities Amounts owed that can be paid off in one year or less.
Current ratio Relationship comparing current assets to current liabilities.

Date of invoice Terms of a cash discount in which the beginning date is the date of the invoice.
Day of discount The day the holder of a note sells it to a bank.
Debt-to-equity ratio Comparison of the total amount owed to the total amount owned.
Decimal system A number system for computation based on the number ten.
Declining balance method Accelerated method of depreciation that uses a rate typically 200% of the straight line rate. The base is the book value.
Demand profit Dollar amount of profit obtained from the sale of goods when the effect of competition on the pricing is at a minimum.
Denominator Number in a fraction that appears below the line and gives the number of parts the whole unit is divided into.
Depreciation Portion of the cost of a property that is allocated as an expense during a certain period of time.
Difference Result of a subtraction.
Discount period Number of days between the day of discount and the maturity date.
Discounting Selling a promissory note to a bank. It may also refer to the process that a bank goes through to figure the discount and the proceeds.
Dispersion Numerical spread of number values around a measure of central tendency for the same variable.

Dividend Payment to stockholders from a company's earnings; a number to be divided.
Divisor Number used to divide by.
Double time A pay rate two times the regular rate.

Earnings Total or gross amount earned when working for an employer—before taxes.
Economic Recovery Tax Act of 1981 Act creating the original accelerated cost recovery system (ACRS) of calculating depreciation for tax purposes. It specified that all properties placed in service after 1980 must use the ACRS method. Properties placed in service before 1981 must continue to use the depreciation method at the time of purchase.
Effective rate True rate of interest calculated by dividing the amount of interest by the original deposit. In a compound interest account earning 7% interest compounded monthly, the 7% is the nominal rate but the effective rate would be higher because of the interest that is being added each period.
Employee Earning Record A summary report of payroll information for each employee.
Employer's Quarterly Federal Tax Return (Form 941) Quarterly form filed with the federal government showing the amounts withheld from employees' wages for federal income tax and social security. It also reports the matching amount of employer FICA tax and the amount already deposited during the quarter.
Endowment Type of insurance under which the insurer pays a certain sum to the insured when reaching a specified age or death (if that occurs sooner than the agreed-upon date).
EOM Abbreviation for "end of month." Indicates the beginning date of the terms will be the last day of month in which the invoice is dated.
Equation Two mathematical expressions set equal to each other.
Escrow Money put into the care of a third party, usually a bank, until certain conditions are met. In the case of home buying, the conditions are the receipt of the annual statements for taxes and insurance.
Estimation Non-exact calculation method used to approximate answers to mathematical problems.
Exact interest Method of calculating interest that uses 365 days as the denominator of the time fraction. Leap years use 366 days.
Exact time Method of calculating the exact number of days between two dates using a specified year as the base. This method includes leap year calculations.
Expedite delivery charge Extra charge added to an invoice to pay for an other than regularly scheduled delivery or one needed immediately.
Exponent key Calculator key that raises any positive number to any power.

Face Another name for the principal of a note or draft.
Factor One of the numbers to be multiplied in a multiplication problem.
Federal Reserve tables Interest rate tables provided by the Federal Reserve to assist in the calculation of the annual percentage rates for consumer loans.
FICA tax Official name used for the Social Security Tax created by the Federal Insurance Contributions Act.

Financial statements Reports prepared periodically by businesses that show the financial condition of a company.
First-in, first-out (FIFO) method Method of valuing inventory that uses the first items available in the time period to be the first items used or sold. Thus, the value is obtained by starting with the last items available in the time period.
Fixed cost Cost that exists even when the production plant creates no products to sell; sometimes referred to as "overhead."
Fixed-rate mortgage Mortgage taken on property in which the rate of interest charged is not changed over the time period of the loan.
FOB Abbreviation for "free on board." Shipping is normally done FOB point of origin but can be shipped point of destination.
Fraction Any quantity expressed in terms of a numerator or a denominator.
Fundamental accounting equation Relationship of the balance sheet accounts that shows total assets equal the total of the liabilities added to owner's equity.
FUTA tax Official name for the unemployment tax paid by each employer to the federal government.

Graduated commission system Commission earnings system that uses a gradually increasing rate of commission as sales increase. A beginning rate is applied to a basic dollar range of sales. Only when that dollar value is sold and commissions figured is the new increased rate applied to a second range of dollar sales—and it continues.
Gross earnings Total amount earned by an employee before anything is deducted.
Gross margin Difference between the net sales and the cost of goods sold.
Gross profit Total amount of markup or margin. The amount of total dollar difference between the price of an item and its cost.

Horizontal analysis Comparison of like terms showing both the amount and the rate of increase or decrease between two periods of time using the oldest date as the base.

Improper fraction Fraction whose value is one or greater than one. The numerator is the same size or larger than the denominator.
Income statement Financial statement that shows the net income or net loss for a period of time.
Installment period Total length of time allowed to consumers to pay back borrowed money on a monthly or weekly basis.
Insured Person whose life or property is insured against loss or damage.
Insurer Person or company that insures others against loss or damage.
Intangible property Property not having an easy calculable life in years such as patents, copyrights, goodwill, or franchises.
Integer A whole number.
Interest Cost of borrowing money or the reward for investing it. May be calculated by taking the amount to be borrowed (deposited), the principal, times the rate of in-

terest being charged, times the length of time of the loan (Principal × Rate × Time).
Interest per month Interest calculation method that uses simple interest from the date of last payment.
Interest-per-payment payoff Loan payoff method that calculates the last amount of interest due based upon simple interest and the date of last payment receipt.
Inventory Merchandise or goods being held for resale or goods held for consumption in a manufacturing process.
Inventory turnover Number of times a typical stock level of goods has been purchased and sold during a fiscal period.
Invoice Bill prepared by the seller showing the items purchased and all related costs, normally in response to a purchase order. It includes terms of payment, shipping terms, and all costs.

Last-in, first-out (LIFO) method Method of valuing the ending inventory that considers the last items available in the time period to be the first items used or sold. The value is therefore obtained by starting with the first items available in the time period.
Liability Amount owed by a company.
Line chart Chart used to show trend or change. Fundamentally a two-axis chart; the data is plotted using the scales and a connecting line.
Liquid Degree to which an item that is owned is cash or can be quickly converted to cash.
List price Price in a catalog or published list issued by a manufacturer or wholesaler. It may also be known as the suggested retail price. Used with trade discounts.
Loan fee/service charge Charge other than interest to establish and repay a loan.
Long-term liabilities Amounts owed that will take longer than one year to pay off.
Lowest common denominator Smallest number that all denominators will divide into exactly.

Maintained margin Minimum margin rate needed on all goods bought for resale.
Mandatory deductions Money withheld from each employee's paycheck to be deposited in reserve as required by state and federal laws.
Margin Dollar amount added to the cost to determine the retail price. The base is the retail price; it is used with the rate of margin.
Margin rate Percent used to establish the dollar amount that will be added to cost to determine the retail price.
Markdown Reduction of a retail price; calculated using the retail price as the base and the rate of markdown.
Market value Value of real property in the real estate market; usually established by the amount consumers are willing to pay for comparable property.
Markup Dollar amount added to a base cost to establish a price. The base is the cost.
Maturity date Date a financial obligation is due.
Maturity value Dollar value of a financial obligation on the date of maturity. Normally it is defined as the face value plus interest.
Mean Arithmetic center for a set of data.
Median Number located in the middle of a series of numbers.

Metric system Decimal system of weights and measures in which the gram, liter, and meter are the basic units of measure.
Mid-month convention Accounting practice that places a property in service at the middle of the month purchased.
Mid-year convention Accounting practice that allocates one half year of depreciation to the first year. Property is placed in service at mid-year regardless of the date of purchase.
Mill levy A mill is one-tenth of a cent or a thousandth of a dollar. Used in taxing property, the mill levy expresses the tax cost per thousand dollars of assessed value of a property.
Minuend Number being reduced in a subtraction problem.
Mixed number Number containing a whole number and a fraction.
Mode Most commonly occurring value in a set of numbers.
Monthly period Twelve times a year.
Monthly statement Business form mailed to any customer having an outstanding balance at the end of the month.
Mortgage periods Length of time designated to repay a property mortgage.
Multiplicand Number being multiplied.
Multiplier Number used in multiplication that identifies the number of times a number must be added to determine a product.

Negotiable instruments Business papers, checks, promissory notes, and trade acceptances that can be legally transferred from person to person, person to business, or business to business by endorsing them.
Net income Amount remaining after expenses are subtracted from gross margin.
Net-income-to-owner's-equity ratio Relationship of net income to owner's equity; shows the return on investment.
Net pay "Take-home pay." Amount an employee receives after all deductions have been subtracted from gross earnings.
Net profit Profit component of markup. The amount of dollars remaining after all manufacturing, selling, and administrative costs are subtracted from sales.
No fault Insurance providing coverage for injury while using an automobile without regard to who is at fault.
Nominal rate The stated rate.
Noninterest-bearing note Promissory note or draft that contains no interest rate as part of its terms.
Nonsufficient funds (NSF) check Check that is returned to a depositor. The person or company that wrote the check originally does not have enough money in the account to cover the check.
Numerator Number appearing above the line in a fraction. It represents the number of units available in the base unit described by the denominator.

Odd lot Quantity of stock less than 100 shares.
Open to buy Calculation used to establish the amount of goods needed to replace the goods sold from inventory. The difference between the goods available for retail and the goods needed in a planned sale period.

Operating expenses Expenses resulting from direct operation of a business as opposed to administrative expenses.

Order of operations Sequence in which mathematical operations are performed for a mathematics problem.

Ordinary annuity Type of annuity in which deposits are made at the end of the period such as in bond interest or savings account interest.

Ordinary interest Method of figuring interest that uses 360 days as the denominator of the time fraction.

Ordinary life Type of life insurance in which payment is made for the premiums of the policy for the term of life of the insured.

Outstanding checks Checks that have been written by a depositor but have not been processed by the bank's accounting department before the bank statement is mailed to the account holder.

Outstanding deposit Deposit that has not been processed by the bank's accounting department prior to the bank statement being mailed to the account holder.

Overdraft Result of a depositor's not having enough money in a checking account to cover a check that was written.

Overtime pay Amount earned beyond the normal day, week, or month.

Owner's equity Amount the owners of a company are worth, which is found by subtracting liabilities from assets.

Part Any amount (larger or smaller) that is not a base.

Partial payment Payment received during a cash discount period that is less than the invoice minus the full cash discount.

Partial year depreciation Depreciation calculated for a period less than 12 months.

Pay life Insurance policy on the life of an individual which includes a specific date on which the premiums of the policy are paid up.

Payoff amount Amount of money needed to pay off a loan, which includes the principal and all interest due as of the payoff date.

Payroll register Form that documents all earnings and deductions for each employee in a given payroll period.

Percent A number as a part of 100, usually expressed with the % sign.

Periods Number of times interest is calculated per year. On a long-term investment, the total number of times interest is calculated.

Personal liability Type of insurance that provides protection from claims made by a third party for damage to their person.

Perpetual inventory Inventory that is continually calculated by adding items received and subtracting items sold, lost, stolen, etc., from a beginning base unit.

Personal property Property used in a business that is movable such as automobiles, furniture, equipment, and tools.

P/E ratio Price/earnings ratio, comparing a share's current market value with its earnings per share.

Physical inventory Actual count of items on hand.

PI (principal and interest) Portion of a total house payment that will repay the original amount borrowed and the accrued interest for the mortgage period.

Pie chart Chart drawn in circular form that is used to show the allocation of a resource.

Piece-rate pay Amount of money paid to employees for each unit produced.

PITI A full house payment that includes the principal, interest, taxes, and insurance on a property. The taxes and insurance amounts are usually held by the lending agency in an escrow account.

Place value Position of an integer, as in a decimal number.

Planned markdown Category of goods for sale in which special markdown rates have been applied.

Plant and equipment Items owned by a company that have a life longer than one year.

Population Term used in statistics to refer to all of the group or items being studied.

Preferred stock Shares in a corporation whose holders have the first claim to dividends.

Premium Amount of payment made on an insurance policy to cover its terms.

Prepaid shipping Amount added to an invoice by the seller because he or she is prepaying the shipping costs.

Present value Amount invested today that will produce a given future amount.

Prime number A number that cannot be divided exactly by any number except itself and 1.

Principal Amount borrowed or amount deposited as an investment.

Proceeds Amount of money that remains after subtracting the bank discount from the maturity value.

Product Answer to a multiplication operation.

Production cost Total amount of fixed and variable costs used to manufacture a product. Used as a base for the markup pricing system.

Promissory note Legal promise in writing to pay a certain sum of money at a future date. Generally this promise also includes paying interest at a stated rate.

Proper fraction Fraction whose numerator is smaller than the denominator; a fraction whose value is less than 1.

Purchase order Business form prepared by the buyer and sent to the supplier (vendor) ordering supplies or merchandise.

Purchase requisition In-house business form prepared to indicate the need for supplies or merchandise.

Qualified endorsement Type of endorsement using "without recourse" followed by a signature. It relieves the payee from all responsibility if the check is not honored when presented for payment.

Quantity discount Discount issued because the number of items or the total amount of an invoice exceeds a certain minimum value.

Quarterly Four times a year.

Quotient Answer to a division problem.

Rate An expression in percent, reflecting the ratio of the part value compared to the value of the base.

Rate per compounding period Annual rate divided by the number of times an institution compounds interest each year.

Ratio Relationship of two numbers found by dividing the first by the second.

Real property Property including land and improvements permanently attached to it, such as buildings or trees.

Regulation Z Regulation within truth-in-lending legislation that directs full disclosure of total interest and total contract charges.

Remainder Amount left over when a division problem does not result in an answer of a whole number.

Restrictive endorsement Type of endorsement that restricts the use of the check, such as "for deposit only."

Retail price Dollar amount established in the margin system that customers will pay for a product; the base of the margin pricing system.

Revenue Total income from all sources.

ROG Abbreviation for "receipt of goods." It identifies the beginning date of the terms to be the day the goods are received by the buyer.

Round lot Quantity of stock equal to a 100-share group.

Rounding Arbitrary placement of an end digit when more digits appear in a number than are needed.

Rule of 78 payoff Method of determining interest due on a loan by using a fraction denominator of 78 within a single year.

Rules of rounding Standard procedure for raising the decision digit. When the following digit is 5 or greater, the decision digit is raised by one; if 4 or less, the decision digit remains the same.

Sale price Net price determined by using a markdown on a selling price. Sometimes known as the net price.

Salvage value Estimated amount an asset (property) would be worth after it is fully depreciated.

Sample Term used in statistics to refer to a portion of the group or items being studied.

Scrap value Similar to salvage value but used to describe an asset's value if it has no usefulness to trade in or sell but could be sold for scrap.

Selling price Dollar amount at which an item is offered to its customers. May be established using the markup, margin, or trade discount systems.

Semi-annual Twice a year.

Series trade discount Sequential listing of two or more trade discounts with each having a different base.

Service charge Typically the amount charged by a bank for handling a checking account; frequently includes any charge for bank service.

Shipping-in Cost incurred for sending raw materials and pre-manufactured parts to the manufacturing location.

Sight draft Bill of exchange that is payable on sight or on presentation.

Simple interest Charge for the use of money, calculated on a principle that a borrower has the full use of the principal amount for the entire time period of the loan.

Single equivalent discount rate One number stated in percent that represents a series of two or more trade discounts.

Single equivalent net rate One number stated in percent that is equal to two or more net trade discounts. It represents the net amount to be paid in percent.

Sinking fund Fund established to receive periodic payments that are invested. When payments plus investment interest equals the amount needed, the fund is used to pay off or "sink" the debt.

Special endorsement Type of endorsement that limits who may process the check.

Specific identification method Method of calculating the ending inventory value when items are valued at their actual cost. This method is used when items are identified and their cost is readily available.

Standard deviation Measure of the average amount of numerical difference that values in a set have around the mean of the set.

State unemployment contributions Amount paid by an employer to the state providing a fund from which to pay unemployed workers.

Statistics Numerical data assembled, classified, or tabulated to present information for decision making.

Straight line method Method of calculating depreciation in which the same amount is used for each full year.

Subtrahend Number being subtracted from another number.

Suggested retail price A wholesaler's catalog or list price to retailers.

Sum Result of an addition problem; the total of the addends.

Sum-of-the-years'-digits method Accelerated depreciation method that allocates more depreciation to the first year than to succeeding years. The name derives from the technique of adding the years of life together (sum) to get the denominator of the fraction used for calculating depreciation.

Supplier Common name given to a seller of merchandise or supplies.

Table Information summary shown as a two-axis presentation that expresses and emphasizes units of data.

Table factor Number on a compound interest, annuity, or present value table that is found by matching the number of periods with the interest rate per period.

Tangible property Property that can be seen or touched and that has a life that can be calculated.

Tax rate Percent used to calculate the amount of taxes due on a property.

Term insurance Insurance protection established for a limited time, usually five-year periods.

Thirty-day (30-day) months Method of calculating time that uses 30 days in each month.

Time and a half A pay rate one and a half times the regular rate.

Time draft Bill of exchange payable at future time, either within a certain number of days after sight (presentation), after date written, or on a specified date.

Total contract price Total charges in an installment lending contract, which include costs for the merchandise and all interest charges for the installment period.

Total revenue Income derived from the sale of goods at their selling price.

Trade acceptance Sight or time draft that has been accepted by the drawee for a stated purpose.

Trade discount Discount taken from a list price, either singly or in a series, taken one at a time.

Truth in lending Federal legislation focused on providing clear and accurate information to consumers on all charges relating to a loan.

Unemployment insurance Insurance benefits provided by an employer covering employees who are without work through no fault of their own.

Ungrouped data Data evaluation method that uses the actual numbers in a set rather than summarized numbers.

Uninsured motorist Type of automobile liability insurance which protects the owner from loss suffered from a motorist who is uninsured.

Unit price The manufacturer's price for one unit of a production batch.

Units-of-production method Method of depreciation that uses the number of units produced, the number of hours of use, or the number of miles driven as the life of the assets (property) rather than a life stated in years.

Units position Integer in a decimal number shown directly to the left of the decimal point.

Unpaid balance method Procedure for calculating finance charges on an account where the unpaid balance from the previous month is used as the base for calculation.

Useful life Estimated number of years an asset (property) will be used.

Variable Problem quantity or function of any given value or symbol.

Variable costs Costs incurred in the manufacture of a product. Variable costs increase with the increase in unit output.

Vertical analysis Comparison of items on a financial statement using an established base.

Voluntary deductions Amount of money employees choose to have withheld from their gross earnings.

W-2 (Wage and Tax Statement) Form showing each employee the amount of wages, amounts withheld for federal, state, social security taxes, and in some cases, city taxes.

W-4 (Employee's Witholding Allowance Certificate) Form filled out by each employee showing social security number, number of allowances claimed, and marital status.

Weighted average method Method of calculating the value of the ending inventory by using all of the purchases during the period plus any beginning inventory to calculate the weighted average of one unit. This weighted average is then multiplied by the actual number in stock.

Word problem Mathematics problem with its elements and relationships expressed narratively.

Workmen's compensation Compensation covered by insurance for injuries arising within the course of an employee's work caused by a risk involved in that work.

Yield Rate calculated by dividing the current return on a bond by its market value.

Answers to Even-Numbered Problems

CHAPTER 1

1.1 The Decimal Number System

SKILL EXERCISES, page 7
2. 50, 600, 5,000 **4.** 20, 900, 8,000 **6.** 27,112
8. 958 **10.** 26,409 **12.** 86,410 **14.** 812 **16.** tens
18. thousand **20.** hundred thousands

1.2 Addition

SKILL EXERCISES, page 9
2. 1,564 **4.** 1,331 **6.** 89,874 **8.** 11,944
10. 63,688 **12.** 121,777 **14.** 181,268

APPLICATIONS, page 10
2. $747 **4.** $13,721 **6.** $213 **8.** $9,555
10. 14,150 miles

1.3 Subtraction

SKILL EXERCISES, page 13
2. 112 **4.** 111,827 **6.** 311 **8.** 11 **10.** 23
12. 1,797 **14.** −19,608 **16.** −423 **18.** 2,322
20. 8,867

APPLICATIONS, page 14
2. 397 **4.** 89,246 **6.** 168 **8.** 12,200 **10.** $5,432

1.4 Multiplication

SKILL EXERCISES, page 16
2. 16,992 **4.** 7,140,000 **6.** 39,366 **8.** 1,221
10. 4,410 **12.** 10,070 **14.** 2,744 **16.** 566,918
18. 35 **20.** 17,766

APPLICATIONS, page 17
2. $139,305 **4.** 58,650 **6.** 11,745 **8.** 69,300
10. 10,108

1.5 Division

SKILL EXERCISES, page 19
2. 19 **4.** 1,321 **6.** 22 + 16 remainder **8.** 103
10. 2,427 **12.** 5,126 **14.** 47 **16.** 188 **18.** 24
20. 125 + 27 remainder

APPLICATIONS, page 20
2. 35,968 **4.** 1,250,000 **6.** $71 **8.** 77 **10.** 3 + 9 remaining or 3.5

1.6 Approximating and Estimating

SKILL EXERCISES, page 23
2. E 140,000   A 136,128
4. E 9,000,000   A 7,569,330
6. E 150   A 152 + 49 remainder
8. E 1,400   A 1,384 + 531 remainder
10. E 16   A 14   + 33 remainder

APPLICATIONS, page 23
2. 400,000 **4.** $500,000

1.7 The Calculator

SKILL EXERCISES, page 28
2. 88 **4.** 86 **6.** 1,432.4211 **8.** 43,199 **10.** 5,654
12. 38,874 **14.** 17,112 **16.** .0800361 **18.** .2960692
20. .116956 **22.** 4.7647059 **24.** 950.25
26. 1.2132353 **28.** 238, 216, 1.25, T455.25 **30.** 38

APPLICATIONS, page 29
2. 2,025 miles **4.** $1,914 **6.** 630 saved, 15,330
8. 35,300 people **10.** $245

Let's Review

ADDITION
2. 119 **4.** 85 **6.** 930,474 **8.** 15,167 **10.** 4,063

SUBTRACTION
12. 6 **14.** 43 **16.** 245 **18.** 442 **20.** 354

MULTIPLICATION
22. 46,242 **24.** 1,768

DIVISION
26. 38 **28.** 816 **30.** 40

CHAPTER 2

2.1 Fractions in Use

SKILL EXERCISES, page 36
2. $\frac{30}{34}$ $\frac{81}{85}$ **4.** $\frac{1}{2}$ $\frac{15}{16}$ **6.** $\frac{4}{3}$ $\frac{5}{2}$ **8.** $\frac{8}{7}$ $\frac{17}{16}$
10. $\frac{13}{12}$ $\frac{15}{9}$ **12.** Improper **14.** Mixed **16.** Proper
18. Mixed **20.** Proper

SKILL EXERCISES, page 38
2. $\frac{15}{18}$ **4.** $\frac{14}{16}$ **6.** $\frac{16}{36}$ **8.** $\frac{14}{32}$ **10.** $\frac{16}{28}$ **12.** $\frac{4}{5}$
14. $\frac{3}{4}$ **16.** $\frac{1}{3}$

APPLICATIONS, page 38
2. $\frac{5}{2}$ **4.** $\frac{7}{8}$ **6.** $\frac{10}{15}$ **8.** $\frac{21}{24}$ **10.** $\frac{5}{20}$ **12.** $\frac{12}{32}$
14. $\frac{1}{4}$

2.2 Improper Fractions and Mixed Numbers

SKILL EXERCISES, page 41
2. 62 **4.** $14\frac{1}{9}$ **6.** $19\frac{7}{16}$ **8.** $19\frac{4}{19}$ **10.** $10\frac{3}{7}$

12. $\frac{41}{7}$ **14.** $\frac{53}{3}$ **16.** $\frac{177}{8}$ **18.** $\frac{39}{5}$ **20.** $\frac{100}{3}$

2.3 The Common Denominator

SKILL EXERCISES, page 45
2. 36 $2\frac{13}{36}$ **4.** 60 $14\frac{23}{30}$ **6.** 8 $1\frac{7}{8}$ **8.** 72 $49\frac{61}{72}$
10. 32 $1\frac{13}{32}$ **12.** 8 $\frac{3}{8}$ **14.** 40 $3\frac{11}{40}$ **16.** 8 $\frac{3}{8}$
18. 15 $\frac{4}{15}$ **20.** 20 $45\frac{11}{20}$

APPLICATIONS, page 46
2. $4\frac{3}{4}$ **4.** $442\frac{5}{7}$ **6.** $274\frac{1}{2}$ **8.** $5\frac{15}{16}$ **10.** $244\frac{9}{20}$
12. $5\frac{3}{8}$ **14.** $\frac{37}{60}$

2.4 Multiplication and Division of Fractions and Mixed Numbers

SKILL EXERCISES, page 51
2. $\frac{21}{40}$ **4.** $\frac{20}{27}$ **6.** $1\frac{2}{3}$ **8.** $4\frac{1}{36}$ **10.** $\frac{63}{256}$ **12.** $\frac{4}{5}$
14. $1\frac{11}{24}$ **16.** $4\frac{7}{8}$ **18.** $5\frac{1}{3}$ **20.** $\frac{9}{10}$

APPLICATIONS, page 51
2. $7\frac{7}{10}$ **4.** $31\frac{1}{2}$ **6.** 3 **8.** 9 **10.** $22\frac{2}{7}$
12. $16\frac{4}{5}$ **14.** $528\frac{3}{4}$

Let's Review

2. Improper **4.** Improper **6.** Mixed **8.** $1\frac{11}{24}$
10. $2\frac{25}{48}$ **12.** $\frac{35}{56}$ **14.** $\frac{1}{2}$ **16.** $\frac{7}{10}$ **18.** $4\frac{1}{2}$
20. $1\frac{5}{16}$ **22.** 56 **24.** 18

CHAPTER 3

3.1 The Decimal Point

SKILL EXERCISES, page 59
2. .48 **4.** .03 **6.** .45 **8.** .22 **10.** .89 **12.** .139
14. .915 **16.** .114 **18.** .398 **20.** .5

APPLICATIONS, page 59
2. .87 **4.** .27990 **6.** .7877 **8.** .27962 **10.** .3965

3.2 Converting Fractions to Decimals

SKILL EXERCISES, page 61
2. .125 **4.** .4375 **6.** .111 **8.** 2.2 **10.** 2.6
12. .6 **14.** 4.667 **16.** 5.13 **18.** .778 **20.** 4.5

APPLICATIONS, page 61
2. 6.858 yards   4. $93.75   6. 12.708 loads   8. 210 quarts   10. 3.708   12. 3.269

SKILL EXERCISES, page 63
2. $\frac{948}{1,000}$ 4. $\frac{1}{10,000}$ 6. $\frac{48}{100}$ 8. $\frac{161}{1,000}$ 10. $\frac{625}{1,000}$

APPLICATIONS, page 64
2. 3,675   4. 1022.8667   6. 56   8. 12.5833
10. 82.3   12. 49.8333   14. 123.1

3.3 Changing Fractions and Decimals to Percents

SKILL EXERCISES, page 65
2. 132.4%   4. 19%   6. 75%   8. 166.67%
10. 31.25%   12. 49%   14. 316%   16. 40%
18. 9000%   20. 8%

APPLICATIONS, page 66
2. 34.75%   4. 255%   6. 10.55%   8. 16.6667%
10. 286.3%

SKILL EXERCISES, page 68
2. .006   4. .96   6. .055   8. .001429   10. .299
12. .03   14. 1.22   16. 2.35   18. .000003
20. .00625

APPLICATIONS, page 69
2. .5487   4. .12   6. 3.46   8. .002   10. 8.75

Let's Review

2. .329   4. .765   6. .554   8. .83   10. .44
12. .44   14. $\frac{19}{25}$ 16. $\frac{2431}{2500}$ 18. $\frac{1501}{2000}$ 20. 712.5%
22. 375%   24. .75%   26. .0025   28. .875
30. .022

CHAPTER 4

4.2 Number Progressions

SKILL EXERCISES, page 76
2. minus 21, divide 4
4. plus 12, none
6. minus 7, none plus 8, multiply 2
8. minus 20, none plus 60, multiply 6
10. minus 10, none minus 10, none

4.3 Stating Problem Variables

SKILL EXERCISES, page 78
2. $3x + 5$ 4. $6x - 12$ 6. $x - .12x$ 8. $10 - x$
10. $2x - 3 = 30$

APPLICATIONS, page 79
2. $n = 15$ 4. $6y - 3 = 3y + 18$ 6. $2\frac{1}{2}y = 101$
8. $5y = \$8.00 + \$3.20$ 10. Profit $= 2y - \$15,000$

4.4 Identifying Problem Variables

SKILL EXERCISES, page 82
2. 15,000   4. 85 mph   6. 9.5 hours   8. 855 miles
10. $40,000

APPLICATIONS, page 83
2. Amount of loan, base   4. Travel time, time

4.6 Solving Problems with Formulas

SKILL EXERCISES, page 90
2. $P = B \times R$ 4. $I = P \times R \times T$ 6. $B = P$ divided by R

APPLICATIONS, page 91
2. 42.5%   4. 7.5%   6. $10.95   8. .5%
10. $8,000   12. $33,138   14. $10,238.10

4.7 Solving Problems for Changing Values

SKILL EXERCISES, page 95
2. 80%   4. 129%   6. 113%   8. 92%   10. 54%
12. 118%   14. $2,790   16. 75%   18. $974.40
20. $124.26

APPLICATIONS, page 96
2. 19.4%   4. $40,000   6. 16%   8. $88.35
10. $100,000   12. $142.35   14. $331.25   16. $7.69
18. 68.29%   20. $91.52

Let's Review

2. $2,800   4. $37,500   6. $250,000   8. $120
10. $165.79   12. $216.39   14. $2,660

CHAPTER 5

5.1 Checking Accounts

SKILL EXERCISES, page 106

Currency	$138.00	$241.00	$145.00	$242.00	$294.00
Coin	$3.90	$10.50	$7.90	$10.65	$11.53
Checks	$152.00	$187.00	$215.00	$118.00	$315.00
Total	$293.90	$438.50	$367.90	$370.65	$620.53

APPLICATIONS, page 106
2. $844.57   4. Currency, $67; Coin, $4.67; Checks, $597.95; Total, $669.62.

5.2 Checks

APPLICATIONS, page 110
2. See written form

5.3 The Check Register

APPLICATIONS, page 113
2. $1,326.36 4. $702.90

5.4 Bank Statement Reconciliation

SKILL EXERCISES, page 121
2. Subtract bank statement 4. Subtract check register
6. Subtract check register 8. Subtract check register
10. $350 12. $123 14. $3,497 16. $3,821
18. $1,084

APPLICATIONS, page 122
2. (a) $88.12 (b) no (c) Check for 88.12 not listed in register (d) Check register 4. $735.01 6. $1,398.71

Let's Review

2. $342.53
4. Currency $181.00
   Coin $ 15.00
   Checks $336.82
   Total $532.82
6. Checks $319.20
8. (a) $3,125.52
   (b) $3,089.52
   (c) transposition
   (d) check register

CHAPTER 6

6.1 Computing Gross Earnings

SKILL EXERCISES, page 131
2. $381.73 4. $555.77

SKILL EXERCISES, page 132
2. Carlson 40 hours $186.00
4. Stewart 39 hours $154.05

SKILL EXERCISES, page 134
2. Carlson $ 6.975 $186.00 $62.78 $248.78
4. Romero $10.70 $214.00 $42.80 $256.80
6. Hoyle $ 9.60 $192.00 $96.00 $288.00

APPLICATIONS, page 134
2. $248.60
4. Total $997.43
6. 1. $1,093.75
   2.   789.58
   3.   570.38
   4.   565.50
   5.   743.75
   Total $3,762.96
8. Mannerly $184.00
   Nelson $266.80
   Valdez $282.90
   Reynolds $174.80
10. $359.10

SKILL EXERCISES, page 136
2. $206.25 4. $179.03

SKILL EXERCISES, page 138
2. $1,395.63 4. $1,136.25 6. $281.70 8. $333.50
10. $159.20

APPLICATIONS, page 139
2. $3,950 4. $7,217.19 6. $96.00 8. $510,000
10. $16,250

6.2 Deductions

SKILL EXERCISES, page 142
2. $12.20 4. $107.84 6. $51.60 8. $33.80
10. $28.56

SKILL EXERCISES, page 143
2. $164.09 4. $21.10 6. $22.91 8. $97.63
10. $111.60

SKILL EXERCISES, page 145
2. $58 4. $61 6. $17

APPLICATIONS, page 145
2. Fed. $149
   SS $63.84
   Deductions $212.84
   Total $637.16
4. Ramon: fed. $33 SS $23.28
   Jessie: fed. $34 SS $21.03
6. Total $716.06
   SS $53.78
8. gross $693.25
   SS $52.06

SKILL EXERCISES, page 151
2. $325.00 $325.00
4. $ −0− $320.00
6. $542.00 $542.00

Let's Review

2. Check stub bal. $565.80
4. Employee 2, $386.62
   Employee 3, $207.85
   Employee 4, $524.18
   Employee 5, $292.71
   Employee 6, $1,626.23
6. Unemployment $40.61
   SS $63.84
8. Earnings $345.65
   SS   25.96
   Fed. tax   26.00
   Net pay $293.69
10. Earnings $664.00
    SS $37.17

CHAPTER 7

7.1 Purchasing Supplies and Merchandise

SKILL EXERCISES, page 161
2. 3-inch garden tool $ 67.20
   $1\frac{1}{2}$-inch garden tool $ 46.50
   Long-handled spade $ 27.60
   Kentucky blue grass $255.00
          Total $396.30

SKILL EXERCISES, page 165

2. Dup. paper $ 85.20
   Micro print paper $ 86.50
   Bond letterhead $ 40.75
   Index cards $ 29.50
   Envelopes $138.00
   Total $379.95
   Grand total $408.65
4. $319.40

7.2 Calculating and Preparing the Monthly Statement

SKILL EXERCISES, page 169

2. 12/1 $1,586.50   10. $726.54 Merchandise
   12/6 $1,056.25 $ 21.80 Carton
   12/9 $1,764.61 $ 52.90 Shipping
   12/10 $ 708.36 $801.24 Grand total
   12/17 $1,026.68
   12/19 $ 318.32
   12/26 $1,849.27
   12/27 $1,530.95

APPLICATIONS, page 169

2. Total $948.80
4. Grand total $1,826.44
6. 11/11 $ 512.40
   11/20 $1,017.55
   11/24 $ 505.15
   11/29 $ 835.95
8. Total $238.50
10. Total $801.24

7.3 Quantity Discounts

SKILL EXERCISES, page 174

2. QD $ 4.59   Net amt. $ 224.91
4. QD $17.40   Net amt. $1,142.28

APPLICATIONS, page 174

2. Plugs $ 35.55   4. 87 cases
   Filters $ 203.54
   Points $ 866.25
   Valves $ 902.88
   Total $2,008.22

7.4 Trade Discounts

SKILL EXERCISES, page 177

2. $331.04 60% $496.56   4. 20% 80% $30.40
6. 32.98% $4.93 67.02%   8. 19% $24.20 $103.15
10. $6.75 $1.69 75%

APPLICATIONS, page 177

2. $108.83   4. $141.75, 27%   6. 44.8%   8. $319, 58%   10. $1,590.32

SKILL EXERCISES, page 179

2. $117.75 $182.25   4. $13.87 $23.63
6. $74.59 $100.41   8. $30.19 $74.81
10. $60.93 $119.07

APPLICATIONS, page 180

2. $547.54   4. $91.93

SKILL EXERCISES, page 181

2. 67.68% 32.32%   4. 47.04% 52.96%   6. 45% 55%
8. 66.24% 33.76%   10. 59.85% 40.15%

APPLICATIONS, page 182

2. 57.375%   4. $719.29, 57.73%

7.5 Cash Discounts

SKILL EXERCISES, page 184

2. $28.58 $924.22   4. $381.07 $11.43   6. Nov. 20

APPLICATIONS, page 184

2. $818.97   4. $34.68

SKILL EXERCISES, page 185

2. $29.28 $1,434.72   4. $625.00 $612.50   6. Oct. 15
8. Jul. 15   10. Apr. 10

APPLICATIONS, page 186

2. $1,037.50 Jul. 10   4. Dec. 10 $1,196.98   6. $2,150

SKILL EXERCISES, page 188

2. $9.64 $472.36   4. $1,619.80 $32.40   6. Dec. 18
8. Jun. 21   10. May 16

APPLICATIONS, page 188

2. Total paid $6,465   4. $758.59

SKILL EXERCISES, page 190

2. $382.86   4. $1,416.64   6. $1,984.20   8. $1,054.83

APPLICATIONS, page 191

2. $846.80

Let's Review

2. $428.40   4. $4,636.60   6. $4,423.20   8. 60%
10. $506.63   12. $773.20   14. 50.4%

CHAPTER 8

8.1 Simple Interest

SKILL EXERCISES, page 201

2. $55.00   4. $828.00   6. $238   8. $21.88
10. $97.13

APPLICATIONS, page 202

2. $231.25   4. $507.81   6. $6,200   8. No, $30 more
10. $2,437.50

Answers to Even-Numbered Problems A–69

8.2 The Time Fraction

SKILL EXERCISES, page 206
2. 99 99   **4.** 98 98   **6.** 98 100   **8.** 98 100
10. 129 132

SKILL EXERCISES, page 209
2. $406.13 $400.57   **4.** $15.58 $15.37

APPLICATIONS, page 210
2. $332.04   **4.** Hollywood $5.22   **6.** 90 92
8. 150 153   **10.** $833.50   **12.** $12,520

8.3 Solving for Other Factors in the Simple Interest Formula

SKILL EXERCISES, page 214
2. 14%   **4.** 90 days   **6.** $80,000   **8.** 12.75%
10. $624.94

APPLICATIONS, page 215
2. 12%   **4.** 321 days   **6.** 230 days   **8.** 11%
10. 20 days

8.4 Discounting Negotiable Instruments

SKILL EXERCISES, page 219
2. Aug. 2 $1,228.50   **4.** Jul. 13 $3,118.75

SKILL EXERCISES, page 221
2. 60 days $21.33 $1,258.36
4. 47 days $61.08 $3,057.67

SKILL EXERCISES, page 222
2. $10.69 $1,739.31   **4.** $41.05 $1,379.79

APPLICATIONS, page 223
2. $1,576   **4.** $350.80   **6.** $1,317.14
8. Discount $41.56 Proceeds $1,458.44
10. $12,135.66

Let's Review

2. $23.56   **4.** $3,223.92   **6.** $8,111.11   **8.** 114 days
10. $37.52

CHAPTER 9

9.1 Credit Cards and Revolving Charge Accounts

SKILL EXERCISES, page 231
2. $4.13, $504.13   **4.** $6.38, $381.38   **6.** $12.75, $831.95   **8.** $12.46, $721.86   **10.** $1.75, $208.75

APPLICATIONS, page 231
2. $85.37   **4.** $269.10   **6.** No balance due; none
8. $132.57   **10.** $281.07

SKILL EXERCISES, page 235
2. 4 days $113.24   **4.** 15 days $15,316.80
6. $76.05 $1.14   **8.** $151.69 $1.52
10. $439.69 $6.60

APPLICATIONS, page 236
2. ADB $595.83 Int. $7.45   **4.** ADB $147.43 Int. $2.21

9.2 Installment Loans and Purchases

SKILL EXERCISES, page 243
2. $783.75 $37.74 14.50%
4. $367.50 $23.25 17.00%
6. $26.74 14.75%   **8.** $40.73 18.00%
10. $42.95 15.25%

APPLICATIONS, page 243
2. 15.75%   **4.** 27.25%, $33.68   **6.** $25.73, 28.50%
8. 35.25%, $393.50   **10.** 24.00%

SKILL EXERCISES, page 249
2. 1.68033 $160.43   **4.** 1.21562 $64.83
6. 1.11735 $70.77   **8.** 1.39608 $97.49
10. Formula $458.89

APPLICATIONS, page 250
2. $262.44   **4.** $54.88   **6.** $362.34
8. $32.36 difference   **10.** $136.30

9.3 Loan Payoff

SKILL EXERCISES, page 251
2. $\frac{30}{360}$ $3.42   **4.** $\frac{32}{365}$ $2.74

APPLICATIONS, page 252
2. $872.41   **4.** $348.70

SKILL EXERCISES, page 254
2. 171 $91.83 $821.38   **4.** 666 $115.89 $1,706.19

APPLICATIONS, page 255
2. $18.48   **4.** $96.76

Let's Review

2. 19.25% $67.90   **4.** ADB $184.08 Int. $2.30
6. Int. $454.20 APR 16.75%   **8.** $2,762.50   **10.** $3.12
12. $4,210.21

CHAPTER 10

10.1 Home Mortgages

SKILL EXERCISES, page 266
2. $69,420 $661.11   **4.** $52,000 $646.64

A–70   Answers to Even-Numbered Problems

6. $44,000 $341.13 **8.** $60,115 $664.99
10. $109,000 $1,334.77 **12.** $787.32 **14.** $491.16
16. $1,008.40 **18.** $500.12 **20.** $958.08

APPLICATIONS, page 267
2. $902.42 int. $975.93 pmt. **4.** $133.61
6. $59,748.96 **8.** $790.20 **10.** $1,120.20 PI $26.87

10.2 Property Taxes

SKILL EXERCISES, page 271
2. $188,000 .075 **4.** 27% $1,726.38
6. 50.00% .1042857 **8.** $38,095.24 $1,331.20
10. 58.09% 82.632 **12.** $168,000 $3,729.60
14. 39.83% $19,295.78

APPLICATIONS, page 272
2. .0765 **4.** $13,040.86 **6.** $4,446.48
8. $121,367.52 **10.** $4,760 $85,000

10.3 Insurance

SKILL EXERCISES, page 286
2. $408.60 **4.** $527.40 **6.** $82.60 **8.** $222.60
10. $112.50 **12.** $22.90 **14.** $58.40 **16.** $28,000
18. $20,000 **20.** $34,291.34 **22.** $65,000
24. $60,900

APPLICATIONS, page 287
2. 20 pay/life w/ADB $53,000, ord life w/ADB $76,000
4. ord $1,756.80, 20 pay/life $2,395.20, end/65 $3,302.40
6. @45 $3,915.60, @49 $5,007.60 **8.** Save $32.20
10. $333.70 **12.** $31,104, 2.49% **14.** $175,000 max. coverage

Let's Review

2. $493.41 **4.** $11,515.07 **6.** 41.94667, 34.8, 7.06667
8. 25.8 mills **10.** 33–$490.50, 42–$603.00 T–$1,093.50
12. $210.20 **14.** $89.80 **16.** $28,997.51 **18.** $756
20. $116.56

CHAPTER 11

11.1 Depreciation

SKILL EXERCISES, page 301
2. $213.89 $2,486.11 **4.** $402.78 $7,597.22
6. $20.00 $1,180.00 **8.** $1,166.67 $13,833.33
10. $88.54 $2,061.46

APPLICATIONS, page 302
2. Yr. 1 $354.17
   Yr. 2 $425.00
4. B.V. $2,541.40
6. Yr. 1 $781.25
   Yr. 2 $3,125.00
   Yr. 3 $3,125.00
8. $500,000
10. $10,000, $8,750

SKILL EXERCISES, page 306
2. 45 $\frac{3}{45}$ $1,400 **4.** 6 $\frac{3}{6}$ $300
6. 78 $\frac{3}{78}$ $207.69 **8.** 66 $\frac{1}{66}$ $48.11
10. 120 $\frac{7}{120}$ $889.58

APPLICATIONS, page 307
2. $24,820.51 **8.** $5,200
4. $15,333.33 **10.** $755.56 $661.11 $566.67
6. Yr. 1 $25,000 $55,000
   Yr. 2 $20,000 $35,000
   Yr. 3 $15,000 $20,000

SKILL EXERCISES, page 310
2. .20 $3,700 $20,300 **4.** 2.50 $13,462.50 $161,537.50
6. 5.95 $3,064.25 $14,785.75 **8.** .315 $6,862.28 $29,362.72 **10.** .065 $1,100.13 $4,749.87

APPLICATIONS, page 311
2. Yr. 1 1,948.80 7,051.20
   Yr. 2 3,201.60 3,849.60
   Yr. 3 3,062.40 787.20
   Yr. 4 487.20 300.00
6. $1,421.87
   $2,315.63
   $2,762.50
   –0–
   –0–
4. Yr. 1 $ 4,676
   Yr. 2 $ 3,963.46
   Yr. 3 $10,732.53
8. $123,009.70
10. $1,069.54 $15,415.46
   $ 908.36 $14,507.10
   $1,299.12 $13,207.98

SKILL EXERCISES, page 314
2. .125 .25 $3,000 **4.** .10 .125 $750
6. .20 .30 $6,300 **8.** .066666 .10 $6,350
10. .05 .0625 $1,250

APPLICATIONS, page 315
2. $9,720 **4.** $720
6. Yr. 1 1,800 2,700
   Yr. 2 1,080 1,620
   Yr. 3 648   972
   Yr. 4 388.80 583.20
   Yr. 5 83.20 500.00
8. 1) $12,750
   2) $10,837.50
   3) $9,211.88
10. $9,492.19

11.2 Accelerated Cost Recovery System (ACRS) Method

SKILL EXERCISES, page 323
2. 6.55% $2,358 **4.** 19.2% $2,611.20
6. 6.93% $1,476.09 **8.** 32.0% $5,120
10. 8.93% $2,857.60

APPLICATIONS, page 324
2. $44,250 **8.** $2,073.60
4. $793.12 **10.** Yr. 1 $2,643.65
6. Yr. 1 $22,500   Yr. 2 $4,530.65
   Yr. 5 $31,185
   Yr. 10 $26,550

11.3 Inventory Valuation

APPLICATIONS, page 331
2. FIFO $ 945.70   LIFO $ 939.50   Wt. Avg. $ 943.13
4. FIFO $1,050.40   LIFO $1,057.10   Wt. Avg. $1,055.53
6. $1,059.75
8. FIFO $ 87.00   LIFO $ 99.30   Wt. Avg. $ 83.34
10. FIFO $ 230.00   LIFO $251.50   Wt. Avg. $ 240.45

Let's Review

2. $2,800
4. $375
6. $5,077
8. Yr. 1 $2,423.75
   Yr. 2 $3,635.63
   Yr. 3 $3,938.59
   Yr. 4 $3,601.00
   Yr. 5 $ 251.03
10. FIFO $596.50
    LIFO $594.25
    Wt. Avg. $597.59
12. 1) $22,500   2) $40,500
    3) $32,400
14. 1) $5,312.50
    2) $4,553.57
    3) $3,794.64
16. $1,770.59 book value
18. $2,003.91
20. 1) $1,145.88
    2) $1,375.00

CHAPTER 12

12.1 Compound Interest

SKILL EXERCISES, page 342
2. $26,897.78 $6,897.78   4. $1,777.63 $377.63
6. $1,572.45 $472.45   8. $4,583.29 $3,058.29
10. $2,154.62 $704.62

SKILL EXERCISES, page 345
2. $221.68 $46.68   4. $865.15 $215.15
6. $10,767.71 $1,767.71   8. $1,753.19 $503.19
10. $1,422.11 $122.11

APPLICATIONS, page 346
2. $33,921.80   4. $4.68 Freeway Auto   6. $14,859.47
8. $5,020.58   10. $22.06 Westside Credit Union

12.2 Annuities

SKILL EXERCISES, page 349
2. $5,819.39   4. $53,478.25   6. $18,276.48
8. $18,891.32   10. $19,380.22

SKILL EXERCISES, page 352
2. 19 $4,952.72   4. 13 $15,554.49   6. 23 $288,398.77
8. 23 $24,258.26   10. 19 $8,419.07

APPLICATIONS, page 352
2. $15,903.54   4. $894.71   6. $7,455.71 $7,604.83
8. $3,559.21   10. $10,547.19

12.3 Present Value

SKILL EXERCISES, page 356
2. $1,989.51   4. $1,350.61   6. $79,885.18
8. $31,088.78   10. $6,227.79

APPLICATIONS, page 356
2. $820,039.48   4. $236,409.30   6. $1,575.13
8. $4,983.08   10. $3,556.42

12.4 Stocks

SKILL EXERCISES, page 360
2. $2,779.50   4. $8,253.64   6. $11,819.25
8. $3,691.76   10. $7,353.28

APPLICATIONS, page 360
2. $2,580.53   4. $353.64   6. $1,697.53   8. $4,152.75
10. $7,083.05

SKILL EXERCISES, page 363
2. $344,000; $1,456,000; $3.64   4. $312,000; $663,000;
$2.21   6. $5.00; 13   8. $1.55; 6   10. $525,000;
$5.25; 9

APPLICATIONS, page 364
2. $25.71   4. $4.17   6. 8   8. $1.88; 5   10. $58.80

12.5 Bonds

SKILL EXERCISES, page 367
2. Discount   4. 11.625%   6. $91\frac{7}{8}$ 8. $237.50
10. 1.075%

APPLICATIONS, page 367
2. $24,862.50   4. $93.75   6. $2,750   8. $630
10. $9,990; $75

Let's Review

2. $206,472.46   4. $2,918.00   6. $5,600.31; $43\frac{1}{2}$%
8. $47,770.39   10. $1,633,867.20   12. $22,816.40
14. $3,735   16. $.55

CHAPTER 13

13.1 Markup (Pricing on Cost)

SKILL EXERCISES, page 379
2. 41.41% $5.11   4. 40.83% $8.83   6. $35.08 $100.05
8. $38.76 $18.21   10. 68.14% $16.73
12. $100.00 $132.00   14. $205.00 60.98%

APPLICATIONS, page 379
2. $44.12   4. $141.51   6. 41.07%   8. 65%
10. 40.11%   12. 56%   14. $1.00

A—72   Answers to Even-Numbered Problems

13.2 Margin (Pricing on Retail)

SKILL EXERCISES, page 383
2. $20.40 38.73%   4. 55.59% $38.75
6. $74.03 42.19%   8. 34.24% $3.51
10. 31.31% $5.63   12. $200.00 $138.00
14. 61.94% $201.30

APPLICATIONS, page 384
2. $39.41   4. $133,846.15   6. $9.98   8. $1,314
10. $29.04   12. 62.5%   14. $836.21

13.3 Markdown

SKILL EXERCISES, page 387
2. $35.00 $29.75 85%   4. $50.47 35% 65%

APPLICATIONS, page 387
2. $140.00   4. $82.49

13.4 Converting Markup to Margin

SKILL EXERCISES, page 391
2. $50.40 35.90%   4. 75% 42.86%   6. $51.91 39.76%
8. 79.47% 44.28%   10. $88.88 50.00%

APPLICATIONS, page 392
2. 48.98%   4. Cost   6. 55.16%   8. Price
10. 43.82%

13.5 Converting Margin to Markup

SKILL EXERCISES, page 394
2. 41.82% 29.49%   4. $54.50 61.29%
6. 46.76% 31.86%   8. 68.84% 40.77%
10. $12.74 61.29%

APPLICATIONS, page 394
2. 75.44%   4. Markup rate   6. 136.97%
8. 156.41%   10. 49.25%

Let's Review

2. $652.05   4. 61.29%   6. $193.76   8. $694.03, $589.93   10. 35.28%   12. $247.50 cost, 20.0%
14. $104.21

CHAPTER 14

14.1 Inventory Turnover

SKILL EXERCISES, page 403
2. $13,880   4. $60,510   6. $11,512.90
8. $125,774.19   10. 2.97   12. 5.47   14. 3.19
16. 3.44

APPLICATIONS, page 404
2. 5.20   4. 5.07   6. $6,071.43   8. 5.59   10. 5.00

14.2 Open to Buy

SKILL EXERCISES, page 406
2. Available   4. Needed   6. Needed   8. Available
10. $11,020   12. $49,600   14. $3,355
16. $54,117.24   18. 41%   20. $16,923.20

APPLICATIONS, page 407
2. $20,349   4. OTB retail $34,700

14.3 Average Margin and Maintained Margin

SKILL EXERCISES, page 411
2. $31,017 43.74%   4. $6,870 27.75%
6. $94,456.90 $39,671.90   8. $12,300.10 $20,164.10
10. $2,670 $1,780

APPLICATIONS, page 412
2. $80,856.90   4. 44.00% cumulative   6. 13.66%
8. 54.11%   10. $27,131.15   12. 37.76%

Let's Review

2. $250,464.50   4. 7.75   6. 3.55   8. 43.22%
10. 4.17   12. 36.67%   14. 31.86%

CHAPTER 15

15.1 Types of Costs

SKILL EXERCISES, page 422
2. 47.1%   4. $98,210   6. $54,186.60   8. $24,380.95
10. $100,000   12. 60.2%   14. $13,550.70
16. $83,473,60   18. $54,545.46   20. $215,789.47

APPLICATIONS, page 423
2. $976,923.08   6. (a) 40.48%
4. (a) 77.42%   (b) 54.56%
   (b) 11.52%   (c) 61.00%
   (c) 5.71%   8. $769,681.81
   (d) 4.21%   10. $998,465.12
   (e) 1.13%

15.2 Production Price and Markup

SKILL EXERCISES, page 427
2. 38.54%   4. 40.58%   6. $56,425   8. $5,338.08
10. $18,345.60   12. $62,741.94   14. $266,148.65
16. $194,598.08   18. $37,639.36   20. 71.9%
22. 26.00%   24. $26,922.62

APPLICATIONS, page 428

2. (a) $27,120
   (b) $15.07
   (c) 26.08%
   (d) 13.93%
4. $10.13
6. $89.38
8. 34%
10. $288.75

15.3 Gross and Net Profit

SKILL EXERCISES, page 432

2. 110.71% 4. $146,420 6. $82,560 8. 90.26%
10. 45.27% 12. $174,153.60 14. $80,434.78

APPLICATIONS, page 433

2. (a) 59.64%
   (b) 138.94%
   (c) 147.79%
4. $91.77
6. (a) $178.40
   (b) $76.00
8. 60.00%
10. $13.03

Let's Review

2. $312,500 4. 78.3% 6. 75%; $154 8. $5.00
10. $2,307.27 12. $132,000 14. $13.03
16. $34.03, $5,100 18. $35.47 20. $176.56

CHAPTER 16

16.1 Vertical Analysis

SKILL EXERCISES, page 445

2. 8.24% 4. 53.45% 6. 6.13% 8. 22.73%
10. 18.44%

SKILL EXERCISES, page 448

2. 7.77% 4. 1.29%

APPLICATIONS, page 449

2. 109.83%   108.73%   4. 100.00%
   (9.83)%   (8.73)%   10.73%
   55%   55.75%   17.32%
   45%   44.25%   2.37%
   9.90%   9.41%   .86%
   2.80%   2.33%   18.54%
   13.93%   11.23%   49.82%
   1.24%   1.26%   50.18%
   6.64%   4.66%
   34.51%   28.89%
   10.49%   15.36%

16.2 Horizontal Analysis

SKILL EXERCISES, page 454

2. $(2,680), (17,35)% 4. $(2,762), (11.16)%
6. $21,348, 23.93% 8. $395, 34.56% 10. $72, 7.44%

APPLICATIONS, page 455

2. $17,515   8.74%
   $ 560   6.69%
   $16,955   8.83%
   $23,615   37.85%
   $(10,755) (7.06)%
   $12,860   5.99%
   $ 1,500   1.74%
   $11,360   8.83%
   $ 5,595   8.83%
   $ 1,185   6.00%
   $ 1,200   13.3%
      –0–   –0–
      –0–   –0–
        90   7.59%
   $ 2,475   6.85%
   $ 3,120   11.47%
   $ (575) (100)%
   $ 3,695   13.87%

4. $12,593   8.99%
   $ 590   23.41%
   $12,003   8.73%
   $ 2,265   2.64%
   $ 9,738   18.88%
   $ 5,624   17.51%
   $ 125   3.25%
   $ 153   7.46%
   $ 170   13.00%
   $ (225) (81.82)%
   $(1,000) (74.07)%
   $ (44) (36.97)%
   $ 4,803   11.69%
   $ 4,935   47.03%

16.3 Ratios

SKILL EXERCISES, page 462

2. 19.40% 4. 1.95:1

APPLICATIONS, page 463

2. 1.77:1 4. 5.23:1 6. 1.34:1 8. 1.10:1

Let's Review

2. 22.90%
4.   Assets
   $ (680) (12.42)%
   $ 5,350   47.81%
   $ 1,533   10.69%
   $ 5,231   6.26%
   $11,434   9.98%
   $(2,763) (24.69)%
   $ 1,534   34.45%
   $(5,049)   (4.00)%
      –0–   –0–
   $(6,278)   (2.68)%
   $ 5,156   1.48%
         Liabilities
   $ 349   1.86%
   $ 303   22.41%
   $ 925   Infinite
   $ 45   22.17%
   $ 1,622   8.00%
   $(3,000) (71.43)%
   $(3,250)   (3.82)%
   $(6,250)   (7.01)%
   $(4,628)   (4.23)%
      Owner's Equity
   $ 6,522   4.09%
   $ 3,262   4.10%
   $ 9,784   4.10%
   $ 5,156   1.48%

6. 198X 45.81%
   198Y 42.15%
8. 198X 5.65:1
   198Y 5.75:1

10. $ 5,655   2.84%
    $ (307) (8.58)%
    $ 5,962   3.05%
    $20,286   34.69%
    $(14,750) (9.97)%
    $ 5,536   2.68%
    $ 4,784   6.07%
    $ 752   .59%
    $ 5,210   7.70%
    $ 880   3.63%
    $ 500   5.56%
       –0–   –0–
       –0–   –0–
    $ (173) (3.99)%
    $ 56   1.81%
    $ 1,263   2.96%
    $ 3,947   15.84%
    $ (205) (47.02%)
    $ 4,152   16.96%

CHAPTER 17

17.1 Statistical Measures

SKILL EXERCISES, page 477
2. 414.2 **4.** .59 **6.** 28 **8.** 840.5 **10.** .6665
12. 26 **14.** 165

APPLICATIONS, page 478
2. Mean 85.88889
Median 86
Mode 86
Mean most accurate and data is alike with small amount of variation
4. $1,292.75 more this year; 15.94% increase

17.2 Statistical Tables and Charts

SKILL EXERCISES, page 482
2. C **4.** B **6.** D **8.** B **10.** C

APPLICATIONS, page 483
1. Table, bar chart

17.3 Completion of Presentation

SKILL EXERCISES, page 485
2. A **4.** E

APPLICATIONS, page 486
2. Line chart with separate line for each age group using time as the horizontal axis.

17.4 Statistical Dispersion—The Standard Deviation

SKILL EXERCISES, page 489
2. 58.6 3,433.96 **4.** −11.2 125.44 **6.** 6 36
8. 18.6 345.96 **10.** 3.2 10.24 **12.** −19 361
14. 3 9 **16.** 3.3397 **18.** 2.8284 **20.** 6.2531

APPLICATIONS, page 491
2. Mean 77.43 Std. Dev. 12.62 **4.** Mean 1.23 Std. Dev. .29 **6.** Mean 14.53 Std. Dev. 3.54 **8.** Mean 483.33 Std. Dev. 81.43 **10.** Mean 3.8 Std. Dev. 2.4

Let's Review

2. 49.5 **4.** Footnote **6.** Median 15.9, large variation
8. Mean = 783 **10.** Source note

APPENDIX A

Loan Payment Schedule

2. $2,232.00 **4.** Yes, $208.71, $2,018.20

Descriptive Statistics

2. Mean 14.962 Std. Dev. 3.696472
4. Std. Dev. 11.47547

Open to Buy

2. $38,421 **4.** $791,962.50

Average Margin

2. 30.4% **4.** 32.58%

Breakeven Analysis

2. 762.074 **4.** 28.71% $196,635.30

Annuity Value

2. $49,998.74 **4.** Yes, $40,535.56

Inventory Turnover

2. 2.90 **4.** .56

Depreciation

2. $2,696.30 **4.** S/Yrs. $4,256

Determine Interest Rate

2. 13.5% **4. (a)** 12.66% **(b)** 12.33% Option b

Financial Ratios

2. Current ratio 1.73 Acid test .71 Debt/Equity .68
4. Current ratio 4.13 Acid test 1.50 Debt/Equity 2.23

APPENDIX B

Let's Review

2. 1,067 units **4.** 56% **6.** 8.36% **8.** 2,704 units
10. $187,593.10

APPENDIX C

U.S. Symbols

SKILL EXERCISES, page A–24
2. Package **4.** Number or pounds **6.** Box
8. Ream **10.** Each

APPLICATIONS, page A–25
2. $1,368.75   **4.** $263.25   **6.** $90.00   **8.** $460.80
10. $180.00

U.S. Weights and Measures

SKILL EXERCISES, page A–27
2. .11111 30   **4.** .0625 × .01 5   **6.** 160 .25
8. 17 36   **10.** 27 16   **12.** 2000 688,000
14. .037037 30   **16.** .125 2,690   **18.** .0005 150.4
20. .027778 77   **22.** .25 196.5   **24.** .0625 11

APPLICATIONS, page A–28
2. 69,184 cu. ft.   **4.** $2,350.08   **6.** 19,800 yd.
8. 356.9 loads   **10.** 56 bbl.

Metric Conversions

SKILL EXERCISES, page A–30
2. .62143 164.06   **4.** .035273 264.55   **6.** 1.8 +32 86°   **8.** 1.05697 52.85   **10.** 1.0936 8,530.08
12. .26420 12.68   **14.** .454 5.45   **16.** 3.782 × .001 0.57   **18.** .0929 332.58   **20.** 1.1025 540.23
22. .3048 299.92   **24.** .07645 265.43

APPLICATIONS, page A–31
2. 217.24 km   **4.** 12.68 gal.   **6.** 15,890 kg   **8.** 74.57 mph   **10.** 10.04 gal.

Photo Credits

Page	Source
1	Ken Robert Buck, The Picture Cube
14	Jeff Finneran, Chevrolet, General Motors
20	Alexander Lowry, Photo Researchers, Inc.
27	Left: Texas Instruments. Right: Texas Instruments
30	Owen Franken, Stock, Boston
39	Steve Potter, Stock, Boston
52	Wayne Wilson, Rapho/Photo Researchers, Inc.
62	Richard Pasley, Stock, Boston
68	Statistical Abstract of the U.S. and *The Boston Globe*, Boston, MA
79	Photographie Giraudon, Art Resource
91	John Maher, Stock, Boston
101	Bryce Flynn, Stock, Boston
106	Barbara Rios, Photo Researchers, Inc.
114	Gale Zucker, Stock, Boston
140	IBM
146	Barbara Alper, Stock, Boston
175	Gabor Demjen, Stock, Boston
185	Jeffry W. Myers, Freelance Photographers Guild
197	Michael Weisbrot, Stock, Boston
210	Ryder Truck
216	Jean-Claude Lejeune, Stock, Boston
232	Peter Menzel, Stock, Boston
252	Jean-Claude Lejeune, Stock, Boston
267	Townsend Dickinson, Photo Researchers, Inc.
288	AAA Insurance Agency, Inc., Rockland, MA
295	Christopher Morrow, Stock, Boston
302	Chester Higgins, Jr., Photo Researchers, Inc.
324	Christopher Morrow, Stock, Boston
353	Ellan Young, Photo Researchers, Inc.

Page	Source
368	A/P News Features and *The Boston Globe,* Boston, MA
373	The Photo Works, Photo Researchers, Inc.
384	Cory Wolinsky, Stock, Boston
387	Joseph Kugielsky
408	Peter Menzel, Stock, Boston
412	Blair Seitz, Photo Researchers, Inc.
423	Barbara Rios, Photo Researchers, Inc.
429	Christopher Morrow, Photo Researchers, Inc.
439	Renee Lynn, Photo Researchers, Inc.
449	Alltel Corporation
463	Tom Carroll, FPG
483	John Spragens, Jr., Photo Researchers, Inc.

Index

A
ABA numbers, 103, 108
Accidental death benefit (ADB), 273
Accumulated depreciation, 298
Acid-test ratio, 460
ACRS depreciation, 319–322
   schedule, 321, 324
Add-on interest, 237
Addend, 8
Addition
   addends, 8
   basic concept, 8
   fractions, 43
   sum, 8
Administrative salaries, as fixed cost, 418
Advertising, as cost of selling, 424
American Banking Assoc. numbers, 103, 108
Amortization
   home mortgage, 260
   loans, 244
Annual percentage rate (APR), 238
Annual periods, 341
Annuity
   definition of, 347
   ordinary, 347, 348
   present value, 354
Annuity due, 347–350
Annuity tables, A–48 – A–56
Approximation, 6
Approximation of APR, 238
Array, 474
Assessed rate, 268
Assessed value, 268
Assets, 442
Auto insurance
   BI/PD liability, 275
   collision, 275–277
   comprehensive, 275–277
   no fault injury, 275
   personal injury, 275
   types of coverage, 275–280
   uninsured motorist (UM), 275
Average daily balance, 232
Average inventory
   at cost, 399
   at retail, 399
   use in turnover, 399
Average margin
   category margins, 408
   concept of, 408
   percent of sales, 408
Averages
   mean, 472
   median, 472
   mode, 472

B
Balance sheet
   horizontal analysis, 451
   vertical analysis, 442
Bank discount, 219
Bank reconciliation
   nonsufficient funds check, 115
   outstanding checks, 116
   outstanding deposits, 116
   overdraft charge, 116
   service charge, 116
   tips, 117
Bank statement illustration, 115
Banker's method, 208
Bar charts, 479
Base, Rate, Part
   expressions, 81–83
   problem solving, 84–86
Bi-modal, 476
BI/PD liability insurance, 275
Bill of lading, 189
Billing period, 228
Billion, 5
Blank endorsement, 105
Bodily injury, 275
Bond discount, 365
Bond interest, 365
Bond market listing, 365
Bond premium, 365
Bonds
   buying, 366
   selling, 366
Book value, 298
Bookkeeping equation, 443
Borrowing, 11
Breakeven analysis
   breakeven point, A–15
   fixed costs, A–15
   formula method sales, A–19
   formula method units, A–18
   graph method sales, A–17
   graph method units, A–16
   total cost, A–15
   total revenue, A–15
   variable costs, A–15
Breakeven chart
   breakeven percent, A–17
   breakeven quantity, A–16
   concepts, A–15
   total cost line, A–15
   total revenue line, A–19
Breakeven formula
   revenue per unit, A–19
   total fixed costs, A–19–A–20
   total revenue, A–20

Breakeven formula *(continued)*
    total variable cost, A–20
    variable cost per unit, A–19
Buildings, as fixed cost, 418
Business symbols, A–23 – A–24

C

Calculator
    constant divide, 26
    constant multiply, 26
    memory, 26
    order of operations, 25
Calculator, use of, 24
Cancelled checks, 103, 115
Cash discount
    end of month, 185
    receipt of goods, 187
    regular dating, 182
Category breakdown, 484
Central tendency, 486
Change
    basic concept, 92–93
    change condition, 92–93
    new condition, 92–93
    original condition, 92–93
    rate of change, 92–93
    rate of new condition, 92–93
Chart components, 484
Check components, 108
Check register
    components, 111
    preparing, 111–112
Check writing, 108
Co-insurance, 283
Collision insurance, 275–277
Column heading, 284
Commissions
    bonds, buy and sell, 366
    stock, buy and sell, 357
Commissions, earnings, 137
Common stock
    buying, 357
    selling, 359
Communications, as fixed cost, 418
Competition profit, as a profit component, 424
Complement, 173, 176, 178
Compound interest tables, A–48 – A–56
Compound interest
    present value, 353
    using calculator, 342
    using table, 340
Compound periods, 340
Compound periods per quarter, 341
Compound rate per period, 340
Comprehensive insurance, 275–277
Converting
    decimals to fractions, 62
    fractions to decimals, 59
    fractions to percent, 64
    percent to decimals, 67
Cost
    Business expense, 418
    cost + markup = price, 376
    cost-based pricing, 376
    fixed cost, 418
    rate of cost, 376, 380
    of selling, 424
    total production cost, 420
    variable cost, 419
Cost of goods, 399
Cost of goods sold, 446, 454
Cost, 298
Credit card
    account statement, 232
    average daily balance, 232
    billing period, 228
    total daily balance, 232
    unpaid balance, 228
Credit card payment
    ADB and payment, 234
    average daily balance, 234
    new purchases, 234
Creditors, 443
Cubic measure, 16
Current assets, 459
Current liabilities, 459
Current ratio, 459

D

Daily periods, 340
Damaged goods, as cost of selling, 424
Debt-to-equity ratio, 460
Decimal
    positions, 58
    reading, 58
    rounding, 58
Decimal point, 4
Decimal system, 4
Decimal to fraction conversion, 62
Decimals, place names, 58
Declining balance depreciation, 312–313
Deductions
    federal income tax, 143
    FICA tax, 140
    mandatory, 140
    social security tax, 140
        maximum, 142
    voluntary, 140
Demand profit, as a profit component, 424
Deposit slip, 104–106
Deposits, 104–105
Depreciation, 298
Depreciation methods
    ACRS, 319–322
        partial year, 324
    declining balance, 312
        partial year, 318
    straight line, 298–299
    sum-of-the-years' digits, 303
    units of production, 307
Difference, 11
Discount period, 219
Discounting
    bank discount, 219
    discount period, 219
    interest bearing note, 221
    maturity date, 217
    maturity value, 218
    non-interest bearing note, 222
    proceeds, 220
Dispersion, 487
Distance, Rate, Time
    expressions, 80–81
    problem solving, 80–81
Dividend, 18
Division
    basic concepts, 18
    dividend, 18
    fractions, 50
    mixed numbers, 50
    partial quotients, 18
    quotient, 18
    remainder, 18
Double time, 133
Drawer, 108

E

Earnings
    commission, 137
    graduated commissions, 137
    hourly, 131
    incentive pay, 137
    overtime
        double time, 133
        time and a half, 132
    piece rate, 136
    salary, 130
Earnings per share, 362
Earnings record, 146, 148
Economic Recovery Tax Act of 1981, 298
Effective rate, 346
Electronic funds transfer, 116
Employee's earnings record, 146, 148
Employee's Withholding Allowance Certificate, 143, 147, 148
Employer's payroll tax, 147
Employer's quarterly federal tax return, 147, 149
End of month, 185
Endorsements
    blank, 105
    qualified, 105
    restrictive, 105
    special, 105
Endowment, 273
EOM, 185
Equation, definition of, 77
Escrow
    account, 264
    insurance, 264
    property tax, 264
Estimating
    concepts of, 21–22
    products, 21
    quotients, 21
Exact time table, 204
Expedite delivery charge, 164
Exponent key, use, 345
Extending invoices, 167

F

Face value, 223
Factors, 14
Federal income tax deduction, 143
Federal Reserve Table, 238
Federal Reserve APR Tables, A–40 – A–47
Federal Unemployment Tax, 147
FICA tax deduction, 140
Financial statements, 442
First-in, first-out (FIFO) method, 326
Fixed cost, 418
FOB, 163
Footnotes, 484
Fraction
    addition, 43
    decimal conversion, 64
    denominator, 35
    division, 50
    higher terms, 37
    improper, 35, 39
    multiplication, 48
    numerator, 35
    percent conversion, 64
    proper, 35
    reducing, 37
    subtraction, 44
Fraction to percent conversion, 64
Fundamental accounting equation, 443
FUTA tax, 147

G

Graduated commissions, 137
Gross margin, 449, 454
Gross profit, 429

H
Hand calculator, 24
Horizontal analysis
   balance sheet, 451
   income statement, 453
Hourly earnings, 131

I
Identification title, 484
Incentive pay, 137
Income statement
   horizontal analysis, 453
   vertical analysis, 446
Income Tax Tables, A–36 – A–39
Installment
   amortization, 245
   amortization table, 246
   loans, 236–239
Installment payment, 244
Installment period, 236
Insurance
   ADB, 273
   automobile, 275–280
   auto rate class, 279
   co-insurance, 283
   life insurance types, 273
   ordinary life, 273
   pay life, 273
   personal liability, 285
   premium, 275
   property, 264, 280
   term, 273
   unemployment, 284
   workmen's compensation, 284
Intangible property, 298
Interest
   bond, 366
   compound, 339
   simple, 200
Interest bearing note, 216
Interest per month, 228
Interest, Principal, Rate, Time
   expressions, 86–87
   problem solving, 86–92
Inventory turnover
   data at cost, 399
   data at retail, 399
   different unit types, 401
Inventory valuation
   FIFO, 326
   LIFO, 328
   specific identification, 325
   weighted average, 329
Inventory, 325, 399
Invoice, 162

L
Labor, as variable cost, 420
Land, as fixed cost, 418
Last-in, first-out (LIFO) method, 328
LCD, 42
Liabilities, 442
License, as fixed cost, 418
Life insurance, 273–275
Line charts, 480
Liquid, 460
List price, 172, 175
Loan payoff
   interest-per-payment, 251
   rule of 78 method, 252
Loans
   loan fee, 238
   service charge, 238
   total contract price, 239
Long-term assets, 459
Long-term liabilities, 459
Lowest common denominator, 42

M
Maintained margin, concepts, 409
Maintenance, as variable cost, 420
Maintenance profit, as profit component, 424
Management determined profit, as profit component, 424
Margin
   conversion table, 390
   conversion to markup, 392
   cost + margin = price, 381
   on price, 381
   pricing on retail, 380
Margin rate, 401
Margin to markup conversion, 392
Markdown, 385
Market value, 268
Markup
   conversion table, 390
   markup on cost, 376
   markup to margin, 388
   rate of markup, 376
Markup to margin conversion, 388
Maturity date, 218
Maturity value, 218
Mean, 473
Median, 473
Memory, hand calculator, 25
Merchandise allowances, 164
Merchandise returns, 164
Metric conversions, A–29 – A–30
Metric prefixes
   centi, A–29
   kilo, A–29
   deci, A–29
   deka, A–29
   hecto, A–29
   milli, A–29
MICROPAK
   key, A–1
   menu, A–2
   MS/DOS, A–2
   prompt, A–1
   readiness instruction, A–2
   return key, A–1
MICROPAK programs
   annuity value, A–8
   average margin, A–7
   breakeven analysis, A–7
   depreciation schedule, A–9
   descriptive statistics, A–2
   financial ratios, A–11
   interest rate, A–10
   inventory turnover, A–9
   loan pay schedule, A–2
   open to buy, A–4
Mid-month convention, 321, 324
Mid-year convention, 320
Mill levy, 269–270
Mill, 270
Million, 5
Minimum monthly payment, 228
Minuend, 11
Mixed number
   addition, 43
   division, 50
   multiplication, 48
   subtraction, 44
Mode, 475
Monthly periods, 340
Monthly statement, 167
Mortgage
   escrow account, 264
   fixed rate, 260
   interest allocation, 262
   interest rates, 260
   periods of, 259–260
   PITI payment, 264–265
   principal and interest, 261
Multiplicand, 14
Multiplication
   basic concept, 14
   factors, 14
   fractions, 48
   mixed numbers, 48
   multiplicand, 14
   multiplier, 14
   partial product, 15
   product, 14
Multiplier, 14

N
Negotiable instruments, 216
Net income, 446, 453
Net price, 178
Net profit, 430
Net-income-to-equity ratio, 461
No fault insurance, 275
Nominal rate, 346
Non-interest bearing note, 223
Nonsufficient funds (NSF) check, 115–116
Number progressions
   change patterns, 74–75
   concepts and methods, 73–76
   solution steps, 73
Numerator
   fraction, 35
   time fraction, 203, 204

O
Odd lot, 359
Open to buy (OTB)
   at cost, 405
   at retail, 405
   concepts, 404
   cost vs. retail, 405
   merchandise available, 404
   merchandise needed, 404
Operating expenses, 446, 453
Order of operations, 25
Ordinary annuity, 347–348
Ordinary annuity, periodic payment, 351
Ordinary life, 273
Outstanding checks, 116
Outstanding deposits, 116
Overdraft charge, 112
Overtime earnings, 132
Owner's equity, 442

P
P/E ratio, 362
Packaging charge, 164
Partial payment, 189
Partial product, 15
Partial quotient, 18
Partial year depreciation
   ACRS, 324
   declining balance, 318
   straight line, 299
   sum-of-the-years' digits, 317
Pay life, 273
Payee, 108
Payoff of loan, 250

Payroll check, 152
Payroll register, 146, 148
Percent to decimal conversion, 67
Percents, 64
Perpetual inventory, 325
Personal injury insurance, 275
Personal property, 319
Physical inventory, 325
PI (principal and interest), 260
PI payment, 262
Pie charts, 481
Piece rate earnings, 136
Planned markdown, 404
Plant and equipment, 459
Population, 487
Power of ten, 11
Pre-manufactured parts, as variable cost, 420
Preferred stock, 357
Prepaid shipping, 163
Present value
   annuity, 354
   compound interest, 353
Present value tables, A–48 – A–56
Price
   rate of price, 376, 380
   retail price, 385
   sale price, 385
   selling price, 385
   with cost as base, 376
   with price as base, 380
Price/earnings ratio, 362
Pricing elements, 381
Prime number, 42
Principal
   definition, 200
   solving for, 211
Problem solving
   for change, 92–98
   important steps, 73
   more than and less than, 92
   strategy for, 73
   techniques for, 83
   using $D = R \times T$, 80–83
   using $I = P \times R \times T$, 86–92
   using $P = B \times R$, 84–86
   with formulas, 84–91
   word problems, 83–84
Problem variables
   identifying, 80–83
   stating variables, 77–79
Proceeds, 220
Product, 14
Production price
   total price, 424
   unit price, 425
Profit
   component of markup, 424
   gross profit, 429
   net profit, 430
Promissory note, 116, 216
Property
   insurance, 264, 280–284
   real, 259
Property tax
   assessed rate, 268
   assessed value, 268
   market value, 268
   mill levy, 269–270
   tax rate, 269
Purchase order, 160
Purchase requisition, 159
Purchases
   no down payment, 240
   with down payment, 241

Qualified endorsement, 105
Quantity discounts
   dollar value, 172
   number of units, 172
Quotient, 18

R

Rate classification, 279
Rate of change, 92–93
Rate of new condition, 92–93
Rate, simple interest, solving for, 212
Ratios
   acid-test, 460
   current, 459
   debt-to-equity, 460
   definition of, 458
   net-to-owner's equity, 461
Raw materials, as variable cost, 420
Reading decimals, 58
Real property, 319, 321
Receipt of goods, 187
Recovery periods, ACRS, 320
Reducing fractions, 37
Regular dating, 182
Regulation Z, 236
Remainder, 18
Restrictive endorsement, 105
Retail price, 385
Revenue, 446, 453
ROG, 187
Round lot, 358
Rounding
   approximations, 6
   decimals, 58
   whole numbers, 6
Rule of 78, 252

S

Salary, 130
Sale price, 385
Sales force, as cost of selling, 424
Sales overhead, as cost of selling, 424
Sales tax, 164
Salvage value, 298, 312
Sample, 487
Scale caption, 484
Scrap value, 298, 307
Security, as fixed cost, 418
Selling cost, 424
Selling price, 385
Semi-annual periods, 340, 341
Series trade discount, 178
Service charge, 112, 116
Shipping-in, as variable cost, 420
Shipping-out, as cost of selling, 424
Sight draft, 217
Signature card, 103, 104
Signature line, 105
Simple interest, 200
Simple interest amortization, 244
Single equivalent discount
   discount rate, 180
   net rate, 180
Sinking fund, 351
Social security tax deduction, 140
Social Security Tax Tables, A–34 – A–35
Source notes, 484
Special endorsement, 105
Specific identification method, 325
Square measure, 16
Square root, 487

Standard deviation
   population, 487
   sample, 487
State unemployment tax, 147
Statement, 167
Statistical
   charts, 479
   tables, 481
Stock
   dividends, 361
   market listing, 358
   odd lot, 359
   round lot, 358
Straight line depreciation, 298–299
Subtraction
   basic concept, 11
   borrowing, 11
   difference, 11
   fractions, 44
   minuend, 11
   subtrahend, 11
Subtrahend, 11
Suggested retail price, 175
Sum, 8
Sum-of-the-years' digits depreciation, 303–305
Supplier, 159
Supplies, as variable cost, 420
SUTA, 147

T

Table components, 484
Table information, 481
Tables
   annuity, A–48
   compound interest, A–48
   Federal Reserve APR, A–40
   income tax, A–36
   present value, A–48
   social security, A–34
Tables and charts
   bar chart, 479
   line chart, 480
   pie chart, 481
   presentation of, 483
   tables, 481
Tangible property, 298
Term insurance, 273
Thousand, 5
Time
   definition of, 200
   solving for, 213
Time and a half, 132
Time fraction
   denominator
      exact interest, 203
      ordinary interest, 207
   numerator
      30-day month, 203
      exact time, 203
Title, identification, 484
Total contract price, 239
Total income, 429
Total markup, 424
Total revenue, 429
Trade acceptance, 217
Trade discounts, 175–176
   series, 178
Truth in lending, 236
Turnover, inventory, 399

U

U.S. weights and measures, A–25 – A–26
Ungrouped data, 472

Uninsured motorist (UM) insurance, 275
Units of production depreciation, 307–309
Units, 5
Unpaid balance, 228
Utilities, as fixed cost, 418

V
Variable
   definition of, 77
   how to identify, 80–83
   use in equation, 78–79
   use in problems, 73–76
   variable statements, 77
Variable cost, 419
Vendor, 159
Verifying invoice extensions, 167
Vertical analysis
   balance sheet, 442
   income statement, 446

W
W-2, 147, 149
W-4, 143, 147, 148
Wage and tax statement, 147, 149
Wage payments, 152
Weighted average method, 329
Whole number, 4
   place names, 4
   place values, 4
Word problems, 83–84

Y
Yield, 365